PRENTICE HALL
WORLD STUDIES
WESTERN HEMISPHERE

Geography • History • Culture

In association with

DK

Discovery
CHANNEL
SCHOOL

PEARSON
Prentice
Hall

Boston, Massachusetts
Upper Saddle River, New Jersey

Program Consultants

Heidi Hayes Jacobs

Heidi Hayes Jacobs, Ed.D., has served as an education consultant to more than 1,000 schools across the nation and abroad. Dr. Jacobs serves as an adjunct professor in the Department of Curriculum on Teaching at Teachers College, Columbia University. She has written two best-selling books and numerous articles on curriculum reform. She received an M.A. from the University of Massachusetts, Amherst, and completed her doctoral work at Columbia University's Teachers College in 1981. The core of Dr. Jacobs' experience comes from her years teaching high school, middle school, and elementary school students. As an educational consultant, she works with K–12 schools and districts on curriculum reform and strategic planning.

Michal L. LeVasseur

Michal LeVasseur is the Executive Director of the National Council for Geographic Education. She is an instructor in the College of Education at Jacksonville State University and works with the Alabama Geographic Alliance. Her undergraduate and graduate work were in the fields of anthropology (B.A.), geography (M.A.), and science education (Ph.D.). Dr. LeVasseur's specialization has moved increasingly into the area of geography education. Since 1996 she has served as the Director of the National Geographic Society's Summer Geography Workshops. As an educational consultant, she has worked with the National Geographic Society as well as with schools and organizations to develop programs and curricula for geography.

Senior Reading Consultants

Kate Kinsella

Kate Kinsella, Ed.D., is a faculty member in the Department of Secondary Education at San Francisco State University. A specialist in second-language acquisition and content area literacy, she consults nationally on school-wide practices that support adolescent English learners and striving readers to make academic gains. Dr. Kinsella earned her M.A. in TESOL from San Francisco State University, and her Ed.D. in Second Language Acquisition from the University of San Francisco.

Kevin Feldman

Kevin Feldman, Ed.D., is the Director of Reading and Early Intervention with the Sonoma County Office of Education (SCOE) and an independent educational consultant. At the SCOE, he develops, organizes, and monitors programs related to K–12 literacy. Dr. Feldman has an M.A. from the University of California, Riverside in Special Education, Learning Disabilities and Instructional Design. He earned his Ed.D. in Curriculum and Instruction from the University of San Francisco.

Acknowledgments appear on pages 605–608, which constitutes an extension of this copyright page.

ISBN 0-13-204151-0
2345678910   11 10 09 08 07

Cartography Consultant

DK Andrew Heritage

Andrew Heritage has been publishing atlases and maps for more than 25 years. In 1991, he joined the leading illustrated nonfiction publisher Dorling Kindersley (DK) with the task of building an international atlas list from scratch. The DK atlas list now includes some 10 titles, which are constantly updated and appear in new editions either annually or every other year.

Academic Reviewers

Africa
Barbara B. Brown, Ph.D.
African Studies Center
Boston University
Boston, Massachusetts

Ancient World
Evelyn DeLong Mangie, Ph.D.
Department of History
University of South Florida
Tampa, Florida

Central Asia and
the Middle East
Pamela G. Sayre
History Department,
Social Sciences Division
Henry Ford Community College
Dearborn, Michigan

East Asia
Huping Ling, Ph.D.
History Department
Truman State University
Kirksville, Missouri

Eastern Europe
Robert M. Jenkins, Ph.D.
Center for Slavic, Eurasian and
East European Studies
University of North Carolina
Chapel Hill, North Carolina

Latin America
Dan La Botz
Professor, History Department
Miami University
Oxford, Ohio

Medieval Times
James M. Murray
History Department
University of Cincinnati
Cincinnati, Ohio

North Africa
Barbara E. Petzen
Center for Middle Eastern Studies
Harvard University
Cambridge, Massachusetts

Religion
Charles H. Lippy, Ph.D.
Department of Philosophy
and Religion
University of Tennessee
at Chattanooga
Chattanooga, Tennessee

Russia
Janet Vaillant
Davis Center for Russian
and Eurasian Studies
Harvard University
Cambridge, Massachusetts

United States and Canada
Victoria Randlett
Geography Department
University of Nevada, Reno
Reno, Nevada

Western Europe
Ruth Mitchell-Pitts
Center for European Studies
University of North Carolina
at Chapel Hill
Chapel Hill, North Carolina

Reviewers

Sean Brennan
Brecksville-Broadview Heights
City School District
Broadview Heights, Ohio

Stephen Bullick
Mt. Lebanon School District
Pittsburgh, Pennsylvania

Louis P. De Angelo, Ed.D.
Archdiocese of Philadelphia
Philadelphia, Pennsylvania

Paul Francis Durietz
Social Studies
Curriculum Coordinator
Woodland District #50
Gurnee, Illinois

Gail Dwyer
Dickerson Middle School,
Cobb County
Marietta, Georgia

Michal Howden
Social Studies Consultant
Zionsville, Indiana

Rosemary Kalloch
Springfield Public Schools
Springfield, Massachusetts

Deborah J. Miller
Office of Social Studies,
Detroit Public Schools
Detroit, Michigan

Steven P. Missal
Plainfield Public Schools
Plainfield, New Jersey

Catherine Fish Petersen
Social Studies Consultant
Saint James, Long Island, New York

Joe Wieczorek
Social Studies Consultant
Baltimore, Maryland

WESTERN HEMISPHERE

Develop Skills

Use these pages to develop your reading, writing, and geography skills.

Reading and Writing Handbook **RW1**

MAP◆MASTER™ Skills Handbook **M1**

How to Read Social Studies:
   Target Reading Skills. **M18, 138, 328**

Focus on Geography

Learn the basic tools and concepts of geography.

Introduction to Foundations of Geography **1**

DK World Overview **2**

CHAPTER 1 The World of Geography **8**

1 The Five Themes of Geography 10
Video: *What Is Geography?*

2 The Geographer's Tools 16
Video: *Geography Tools and Map Skills*

Chapter 1 Review and Assessment 23

CHAPTER 2 Earth's Physical Geography **26**

1 Our Planet, Earth 28

2 Forces Shaping Earth 33
Video: *Ever-Changing Earth*

3 Climate and Weather 40

4 How Climate Affects Vegetation 50

Chapter 2 Review and Assessment 55

CHAPTER 3 Earth's Human Geography **58**

1 Population 60

2 Migration 67
Video: *Migration: People on the Move*

3 Economic Systems 74

4 Political Systems 80

Chapter 3 Review and Assessment 85

CHAPTER 4 Cultures of the World 90

Discovery CHANNEL SCHOOL

1 Understanding Culture. 92
Video: *What Is Culture?*

2 Culture and Society. 96

3 Cultural Change 104

Chapter 4 Review and Assessment. 109

CHAPTER 5 Interacting With Our Environment . . 112

Discovery CHANNEL SCHOOL

1 Natural Resources. 114
Video: *The Natural Resources of an Island Nation*

2 Land Use 120

3 People's Effect on the Environment 128

Chapter 5 Review and Assessment. 133

Projects 136

Build a Regional Background

Learn about the geography, history, and culture of the United States and Canada.

Introduction to the United States and Canada . . .139

📖 **Regional Overview 140**

**CHAPTER 6 The United States and Canada:
Physical Geography 146**

   1 Land and Water. 148
      **Video: *The Geography of the United States
          and Canada***
   2 Climate and Vegetation 156
   3 Resources and Land Use. 163
   Chapter 6 Review and Assessment 169

**CHAPTER 7 The United States and Canada:
Shaped by History 172**

   1 The Arrival of the Europeans 174
      Video: *Pueblo Bonito*
   2 Growth and Conflict in the United States 180
   3 The U.S. on the Brink of Change 187
   4 The History of Canada. 193
   5 The United States and Canada Today 202
   Chapter 7 Review and Assessment 209

**CHAPTER 8 Cultures of the United States
and Canada 212**

   1 A Heritage of Diversity and Exchange 214
   2 The United States: A Nation of Immigrants. 222
   3 The Canadian Mosaic. 227
      Video: *Quebec's French Culture*
   Chapter 8 Review and Assessment 231

Focus on Countries

Create an understanding of the United States and Canada by focusing on specific regions.

CHAPTER 9 The United States **234**
    Country Databank 236
        Video: *The Geography of the United States*
    1 The Northeast: An Urban Center 248
        Video: *Paul Revere and the Minutemen*
    2 The South: The Growth of Industry 255
        Video: *Miami's Little Havana*
    3 The Midwest: Leaving the Farm 264
        Video: *Taming the Mississippi*
    4 The West: Using and Preserving Resources 271
        Video: *The Gold Rush*
    Chapter 9 Review and Assessment 277

CHAPTER 10 Canada **284**
    Country Databank 286
        Video: *The Geography of Canada*
    1 Ontario and Quebec: Bridging Two Cultures 290
        Video: *Toronto: Canada's Financial Center*
    2 The Prairie Provinces: Canada's Breadbasket 298
        Video: *Canada's Prairie Provinces*
    3 British Columbia: Economic and Cultural Changes . . 304
        Video: *British Columbia: Canada's Gateway to the Pacific*
    4 The Atlantic Provinces: Relying on the Sea 311
        Video: *Cultures of the Atlantic Provinces*
    5 The Northern Territories: New Frontiers 318
        Video: *The Northern Territories: Challenge of the Cold*
    Chapter 10 Review and Assessment 323

Projects **326**

Build a Regional Background

Learn about the geography, history, and culture of Latin America.

Introduction to Latin America **329**

 **Regional Overview** **330**

CHAPTER 11 Latin America: Physical Geography. .336

    1 Land and Water. 338
    Video: *The Geography of Latin America*

    2 Climate and Vegetation 343

    3 Resources and Land Use. 352

    Chapter 11 Review and Assessment 359

CHAPTER 12 Latin America:
                Shaped by Its History **366**

    1 Early Civilizations of Middle America 368

    2 The Incas: People of the Sun 373

    3 European Conquest 378
    Video: *Pizarro and the Empire of Gold*

    4 Independence 385

    5 From Past to Present. 392

    Chapter 12 Review and Assessment 397

CHAPTER 13 Cultures of Latin America **400**

    1 Cultures of Mexico and Central America. 402

    2 The Cultures of the Caribbean 410
    Video: *Caribbean Music: It's All in the Mix*

    3 The Cultures of South America. 415

    Chapter 13 Review and Assessment 421

Focus on Countries

Create an understanding of Latin America by focusing on specific countries.

CHAPTER 14 Mexico and Central America 424

Country Databank 426

Video: *Mexico and Central America: Navigating the Highs and Lows*

1 Mexico: Moving to the City 430

Video: *Living in Mexico: Natural Hazards*

2 Guatemala: Descendants of an Ancient People 437

Video: *Guatemala's Coffee Economy*

3 Panama: An Important Crossroads 444

Video: *Panama: Deforestation*

Chapter 14 Review and Assessment 451

CHAPTER 15 The Caribbean 454

Country Databank 456

Video: *The Caribbean: Dynamic Lands and Cultures*

1 Cuba: Clinging to Communism 462

Video: *Baseball and Cuba Go Hand in Glove*

2 Haiti: A Struggle for Democracy 470

Video: *Haiti: A Striving Nation*

3 Puerto Rico: An American Commonwealth 476

Video: *Puerto Rico: Past and Present*

Chapter 15 Review and Assessment 483

CHAPTER 16 South America **486**

Country Databank 488

Video: *South America: Adapting to a Varied Landscape*

1 Brazil: Geography Shapes a Nation 494

Video: *Brazil's Carnival*

2 Peru: An Ancient Land Looks to the Future 501

Video: *Making a Living in Peru*

3 Chile: Land of Contrasts 507

Video: *Santiago, Chile: Between the Andes and the Sea*

4 Venezuela: Oil Powers the Economy 516

Video: *The Liberator: Simón Bolívar*

Chapter 16 Review and Assessment 523

Projects **526**

Reference Section **528**

Atlas 530

Country Databank 546

Glossary of Geographic Terms 554

Gazetteer 556

Glossary 562

Index 576

Acknowledgments 605

- Learn map skills with the MapMaster Skills Handbook.
- Practice your skills with every map in this book.
- Interact with every map online and on CD-ROM.

Maps and illustrations created by DK help build your understanding of the world. The DK World Desk Reference Online keeps you up to date.

Video/DVD

The World Studies Video Program takes you on field trips to study countries around the world.

Interactive Textbook

The *World Studies* Interactive Textbook online and on CD-ROM uses interactive maps and other activities to help you learn.

Special Features

COUNTRY DATABANK

Read about the states that make up the United States.

Alabama 236
Alaska 236
Arizona 237
Arkansas 237
California. 237
Colorado 237
Connecticut 238
Delaware 238
Florida 238
Georgia 238
Hawaii 239
Idaho 239
Illinois 239
Indiana 239
Iowa 239
Kansas 240
Kentucky 240
Louisiana 240
Maine 240
Maryland 240
Massachusetts. 240
Michigan 241
Minnesota 241
Mississippi. 241
Missouri. 241
Montana 242
Nebraska 242
Nevada 242
New Hampshire 242
New Jersey 243
New Mexico. 243
New York 243
North Carolina. 243
North Dakota. 244
Ohio. 244

Oklahoma 244
Oregon 244
Pennsylvania. 244
Rhode Island. 244
South Carolina 245
South Dakota 245
Tennessee 245
Texas. 245
Utah 246
Vermont 246
Virginia 246
Washington. 246
West Virginia. 247
Wisconsin 247
Wyoming 247

Read about the provinces and territories that make up Canada.

Alberta 286
British Columbia 286
Manitoba 287
New Brunswick 287
Newfoundland
  and Labrador 287
Northwest Territories. . .287
Nova Scotia. 287
Nunavut 288
Ontario 288
Prince Edward Island . .288
Quebec 289
Saskatchewan. 289
Yukon Territory 289

COUNTRY DATABANK

Read about the countries that make up Latin America.

Belize. 426
Costa Rica 427
El Salvador. 427
Guatemala 427
Honduras 428
Mexico. 428
Nicaragua 429
Panama 429
Antigua and Barbuda. 456
Bahamas 457
Barbados 457
Cuba 457
Dominica 458
Dominican Republic 458
Grenada. 458
Haiti 459
Jamaica 459
Puerto Rico. 459
Saint Kitts and Nevis 460
Saint Lucia 460
Saint Vincent and the Grenadines 460
Trinidad and Tobago. 461
Argentina. 488
Bolivia 489
Brazil 489
Chile. 489
Colombia 490
Ecuador 490
Guyana 491
Paraguay 491
Peru 491
Suriname 492
Uruguay 492
Venezuela 493

COUNTRY PROFILES

Theme-based maps and charts provide a closer look at countries, regions, and provinces.

The Northeast (Economics) 250
The South (Culture) 256
The Midwest (Economics) 265
The West (Geography) 272
Ontario (Government) 292
Quebec (History) 296
Prairie Provinces (Economics) .300
British Columbia (Geography) .306
The Atlantic Provinces (Economics) 313
The Northern Territories (Government) 320
Mexico (Economics) 432
Guatemala (Culture) 439
Panama (Geography) 446
Cuba (Government) 465
Haiti (History) 472
Puerto Rico (Government) 479
Brazil (Culture) 498
Peru (Geography) 502
Chile (Economics) 508
Venezuela (Economics) 518

Citizen Heroes

Meet people who have made a difference in their country.

Clara Barton 186
Louis Riel 195
José Martí 388
Mothers of the "Disappeared" 418
Justina Tzoc 440
Loune Viaud 473

Skills for Life

Learn skills that you will use throughout your life.

Using Reliable Information 14
Using Climate Graphs 48
Analyzing and Interpreting Population Density Maps . . 72
Making Valid Generalizations 102
Making Predictions 126
Identifying Frame of Reference 154
Interpreting Diagrams 200
Using Graphic Organizers 220
Understanding Circle Graphs 262
Writing a Summary 316
Analyzing and Interpreting Climate Maps 350
Making a Timeline 390
Distinguishing Fact and Opinion 408
Drawing Inferences and Conclusions 442
Comparing and Contrasting 468
Synthesizing Information 514

Links

See the fascinating links between social studies and other disciplines.

Links Across Time

    The Silk Road 78

    Living Underground 191

    Why "Latin" America? 340

Links Across the World

    Higher and Higher. 268

    The Baseball Connection. .466

Links to Language Arts

    V. S. Naipaul: Trinidad and Beyond 412

    The "Real" Robinson Crusoe. 511

Links to Math

    Time Zones and Longitude .29

    Acres and Timber Yields 129

    Using Your Fingers and Toes 216

    The Concept of Zero 369

Links to Science

    Plant Fossils 51

    The Next Hawaiian Island .150

    Sanctuary 301

    High Tide. 314

    What Is a Hurricane? 345

    Earthquake-Proof Buildings. 376

    The Photosynthesis "Factory" 495

Links to Technology

    Digital Tunes 107

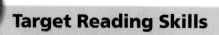

Target Reading Skills

Chapter-by-chapter reading skills help you read and understand social studies concepts.

Clarifying Meaning 8, 172, 366

Comparing and Contrasting. 58, 234, 486

Identifying the Main Idea 112, 212, 454

Using Cause and Effect 400

Using Context 26, 284, 424

Using the Reading Process. 146, 336

Using Sequence 90

Eyewitness Technology

Detailed drawings show how technology shapes places and societies.

Weather Forecasting 46

The Hybrid Car 130

Pueblo Village 176

The Skyscraper 252

Aztec Farming 371

The Panama Canal 449

DIAGRAPHICS

Investigate geographic concepts using diagrams, maps, and photographs.

The Hemispheres 11

The Global Grid 12

Maps of Different Scale 22

The Revolution of Earth 30

Earth's Layers. 34

How Continents Move 36

Plate Movements 38

The Water Cycle 41

Air Circulation and Wind 42

The World: Climate Regions 44

The World: Natural Vegetation 53

The World: Population Density 62

Migration in South Asia 69

How Does World Trade Work? 78

The Development of Agricultural Technology 94

The World: Major Language Groups. 98

The World: Major Religions 100

Stages of Economic Activity 122

Boston: A Changing Landscape 124

Video/DVD

Explore the geography, history, and cultures of the United States, Canada, and Latin America.

What Is Geography? 11
Geography Tools and Map Skills 18
Ever-Changing Earth 38
Migration: People on the Move...................70
What is a Culture?............................93
The Natural Resources of an Island Nation 115
The Geography of the United States and Canada 149
Pueblo Bonito 175
Quebec's French Culture 228
The Geography of the United States 236
Paul Revere and the Minutemen 251
Miami's Little Havana 260
Taming the Mississippi 269
The Gold Rush...............................273
The Geography of Canada......................286
Toronto: Canada's Financial Center 293
Canada's Prairie Provinces 299
British Columbia: Canada's Gateway to the Pacific 307
Cultures of the Atlantic Provinces 312
The Northern Territories: Challenge of the Cold......321
The Geography of Latin America 339
Pizarro and the Empire of Gold 383
Caribbean Music: It's All in the Mix...............413
Mexico and Central America:
    Navigating the Highs and Lows 426
Living in Mexico: Natural Hazards................434
Guatemala's Coffee Economy 439
Panama: Deforestation 447
The Caribbean: Dynamic Lands and Cultures........456
Baseball and Cuba Go Hand in Glove 465
Haiti: A Striving Nation 471
Puerto Rico: Past and Present 479
South America: Adapting to a Varied Landscape 488
Brazil's Carnival.............................496
Making a Living in Peru........................504
Santiago, Chile: Between the Andes and the Sea 512
The Liberator, Simón Bolívar 521

Literature

Selections by noted authors bring social studies to life.

My Side of the Mountain
    by Jean Craighead George 88
Childtimes by Eloise Greenfield, *et. al.* 280
The Surveyor by Alma Flor Ada 362

Same-Shape Maps M6
Equal-Area Maps M7
Robinson Maps M7
Western Europe M8
London M9
Political Africa M10
Physical Africa M11
India: Climate Regions M12
India: Official Languages M13
Migration to Latin America, 1500–1800 . . . . M14
World Land Use M16
The World: Political 2
The World: Physical 4
The World: Population Density 6
The Hemispheres 11
The Global Grid 12
Making a Mercator Map 18
Making an Equal-Area Map 19
The World: Robinson Projection 19
China: Physical 20
Georgia Highways 21
Greater London 22
Central London 22
The Globe: Place Location .24
The World: Time Zones 29
Zones of Latitude 32
Plates 250 Million Years Ago 38
Plates 150 Million Years Ago 38
Plates 75 Million Years Ago 38
Present-Day Plates 38
The World: Precipitation 43
The World: Climate Regions 44
The World: Natural Vegetation 53
Oceans and Seas: Place Location 56
The World: Early Farming and Modern Industry 61
The World: Population Density 62
Migration in South Asia 69
The World: Levels of Development 77
Continents: Place Location .86
The World: Major Language Groups 98
The World: Major Religions 100

The World: Natural Resources 115
Boston: A Changing Landscape 124
Natural Resources: Place Location 134
The United States and Canada: Relative Location 140
The United States and Canada: Relative Size 140
Political United States and Canada 141
Physical United States and Canada 142
Climates of the United States and Canada 143
Focus on Regions of the United States and Canada . . . 144
United States and Canada: Physical 147
Tornadoes in the United States 158
United States and Canada: Vegetation 160
United States and Canada: Natural Resources 164
The United States and Canada: Place Location 170
North America in 1753 173
North America in 1783 177
Growth of the United States From 1783 181
Indian Removal During the 1830s 182
A Nation Divided, 1861 184
Canada's Provinces and Territories 196
Wind Patterns and Air Pollution 204
Canada: Place Location 210
Migration to North America 213
Native Americans and Europeans, 1753 215
Native American Groups: Place Location 232
Regions of the United States 235
An Urban Megalopolis 249
The Northeast: Population Density 250
The South: Land Use 256
The Sun Belt States 260
The Midwest: Major Highways 265
Major Rail Routes of the Late 1800s 269
The West: Precipitation 272
The United States: Place Location 278
Canada: Political 285
Ontario: Population Density 292
Quebec: Population Density 296
Prairie Provinces: Land Use 300
British Columbia: Natural Resources 306
Major Trade Routes Across the Pacific Ocean 309
Atlantic Provinces: Natural Resources 313

European Land Claims, 1682 and 1763 314

The Northern Territories:
    Native North American Groups. 320

Canada: Place Location 324

Latin America: Relative Location 330

Latin America: Relative Size. .330

Political Latin America. 331

Physical Latin America. 332

Latin America: Major Hydroelectric Plants. 333

Focus on Countries in Latin America 334

Latin America: Physical 337

Regions of Latin America. 339

Latin America: Climate Regions. 344

Latin America: Vegetation Regions 348

Latin America: Natural Resources 353

Latin America: Place Location 360

Latin America: Early Civilizations. 367

European Conquest of Latin America 382

South American Independence 387

Latin America: Place Location 398

Latin America: Languages 401

Latin America: Place Location 422

Mexico and Central America: Political 425

Mexico: Resources and Manufacturing 432

The Growth of Mexico City 434

Guatemala: Languages 439

Shipping Routes and the Panama Canal 445

Panama: Vegetation 446

Mexico and Central America: Place Location 452

The Caribbean: Political 455

Cuba: Political 465

Haiti: Political. 472

Puerto Rico: Population Density. 479

The Caribbean: Place Location 484

South America: Political 487

Brazil: Population Density 498

Peru: Three Regions 502

Chile: Products and Resources 508

Venezuela: Products and Resources. 518

South America: Place Location. 524

MAP MASTER™

Atlas 530
The World: Political .530
The World: Physical .532
United States: Political. 534
North and South America: Political 536
North and South America: Physical 537
Europe: Political. 538
Europe: Physical 539
Africa: Political 540
Africa: Physical 541
Asia: Political. 542
Asia: Physical. 543
Oceania. 544
The Arctic. 545
Antarctica 545

Charts, Graphs, and Tables

World Population. 6
Climate Graph: São Paulo, Brazil 48
Charleston, South Carolina 49
Climate Graph: Helsinki. 56
Birth and Death Rates in Selected Countries, 2006 64
World Population Growth, 1200–2000 65
World Urban and Rural Populations, 1800–2000. 70
World Internet Users, 1996–2005 107
The World's Top Petroleum Producers and Consumers. 118
Average Temperatures for Miami and Toronto. 157
Electric Power 167
Timeline: Post-Civil War to the Present 190
The Great Lakes and the St. Lawrence Seaway 206
Origin of Immigrants to the United States, 2003 224
Canada: Ethnic Groups and Immigrants. 228
The Northeast: Types of Services 250
Northeast Population Density, 2000. 250
Economy of the Northeast 250
African American Migration by Region, 1990–2000 . . 256
Hispanic Population of the South, 2002. 256
The United States: Ethnic Groups. 263
Major Religions 263
Midwest Economy 265
Chicago, Major Transportation Hub 265

MAP MASTER™ Interactive

Go online to find an interactive version of every MapMaster™ map in this book. Use the Web Code provided to gain direct access to these maps.

How to Use Web Codes:

1. Go to **www.PHSchool.com**.

2. Enter the Web Code.

3. Click Go!

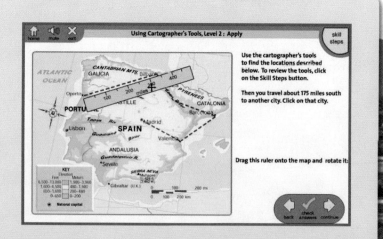

Number of United States Farm Workers, 1910–2000...266

California Cropland 272

Leading Hydroelectric Power-Producing States, 2006 ..272

Internet Company Shutdowns....................275

The Canadian Government 291

The House of Commons.........................292

The Structure of Government 292

Languages Spoken in Montreal..................296

Timeline: Early Canadian History.................296

Timeline: Recent Quebec History.................296

Number of Farms in Prairie Provinces 300

Average Size of Farms in Prairie Provinces 300

Percent of Canadian Grains Grown in
    Prairie Provinces............................300

Income From Mining in British Columbia, 2005......306

Canadian Wood and Paper Products Production 306

Cod Fishing in Newfoundland 313

Aquaculture in Newfoundland and Labrador........313

Economic Activities in the Atlantic Provinces........313

Population and Area of Northern Canada 320

Nunavut Legislature 320

Latin America: Sources of Energy.................333

Vertical Climate Zones..........................346

World Coffee Prices, 1965–2005 356

Timeline: Mayan, Aztec, and Incan Civilizations,
    A.D. 300–1600 374

The Columbian Exchange 383

Foreign Debt of Latin American Nations, 2005 394

The World's Five Largest Urban Areas, 2003 405

Mexico's Exports...............................432

Mexico's Trading Partners 432

Guatemala: Ethnic Groups 439

Mayan Towns 439

Panama Canal Facts 446

Land Use.....................................446

Cuba: Control of Productive Land, 1980 and 2002 465

Party Representation in Cuba and the
    United States, 2004 465

Timeline: Foreign Influence in Haiti Since
    Independence..............................472

About One in Seven Haitians Has Emigrated........472

Haiti Today 472

Puerto Ricans in the Mainland United States, 2000 ...477

Citizen Status in Iowa versus Puerto Rico 479

2004 Puerto Rico Election Results.................479

Two Cities, Two Climates........................496

Cultural Regions of Brazil 498

Brazil's Ethnic Groups 498

Peru: Characteristics of Three Regions.............502

Peru's Population 502

Chile: Average Annual Income per Citizen..........508

Chile's Exports.................................508

U.S. Petroleum Imports From Venezuela, 1980–2005 ..517

World Crude Oil Prices, 1970–2005................518

Leading World Oil Exporters, 2004 518

Venezuela: Earnings From Exports, 2005............518

Building Geographic Literacy

Learning about a country often starts with finding it on a map. The MapMaster™ system in *World Studies* helps you develop map skills you will use throughout your life. These three steps can help you become a MapMaster!

The MAP★MASTER™ System

1 Learn

You need to learn geography tools and concepts before you explore the world. Get started by using the MapMaster Skills Handbook to learn the skills you need for success.

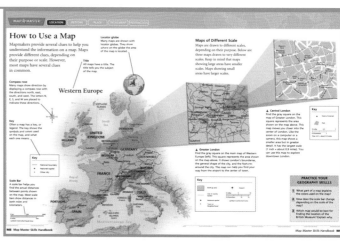

Location The Equator runs through parts of Latin America, but it is far from other parts of the region.

Locate Find the Equator on the map. Which climates are most common in Latin America, and how far is each climate region from the Equator?

Draw Conclusions How do climates change as you move away from the Equator?

Go Online
PHSchool.com Use Web Code **lfp-1142** for step-by-step **map skills practice.**

2 Practice

You need to practice and apply your geography skills frequently to be a MapMaster. The maps in *World Studies* give you the practice you need to develop geographic literacy.

3 Interact

Using maps is more than just finding places. Maps can teach you many things about a region, such as its climate, its vegetation, and the languages that the people who live there speak. Every MapMaster map is online at **PHSchool.com,** with interactive activities to help you learn the most from every map.

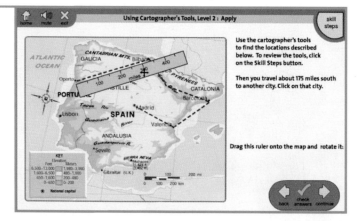

Learning With Technology

You will be making many exciting journeys across time and place in *World Studies*. Technology will help make what you learn come alive.

Go Online
PHSchool.com

For: An activity on Ellis Island
Visit: PHSchool.com
Web Code: lhd-4302

For a complete list of features for this book, use Web Code lek-1002.

Go Online at PHSchool.com

Use the Web Codes listed below and in each Go Online box to access exciting information or activities.

How to Use the Web Code:
1. Go to **www.PHSchool.com**.
2. Enter the Web Code.
3. Click Go!

Western Hemisphere Activities

Web Code	Activity
lep-3700	Composite Volcano Eruption
lep-3701	Water Cycle
lep-3702	The Seasons
lep-3707	Continental Drift
	History Interactive
lhp-4700	Explore the Lessons of Battle
lhp-4701	Inside Fort Sumter
lhp-4703	Discover a Steam Engine
lhp-4705	Explore the Sharecropping Cycle
lfd-1700	Tour a Maya City
lfp-1701	Learn more about Maya Achievements
lfp-1702	Tour the Panama Canal
lfp-1704	Travel Along the Inca Roads
	MapMaster
lfp-1703	Aztec Empire
lfd-1705	Maya Cities
lfp-1706	Inca Empire
lfp-1707	Geography of South America
lfp-1708	Geography of Mexico
lfp-1709	Geography of Mesoamerica
lhp-4702	The Western Front
lhp-4704	The American Revolution
lhp-4706	Growth of the United States to 1853
lhp-4707	States Take Sides
lhp-4708	Land Taken from Native Americans

For additional activities, please see PHSchool.com, webcode lek-1002

The Water Cycle

The water cycle is a continuous process in which water moves through the environment. The sun is the source of energy that drives the water cycle. Click the Water Cycle button below to explore the parts of the water cycle.

DK World Desk Reference Online

There are more than 190 countries in the world. To learn about them, you need the most up-to-date information and statistics. The **DK World Desk Reference Online** gives you instant access to the information you need to explore each country.

Reading Informational Texts

Reading a magazine, an Internet page, or a textbook is not the same as reading a novel. The purpose of reading nonfiction texts is to acquire new information. On pages, M18, 138, and 328 you'll read about some ⟳ **Target Reading Skills** that you'll have a chance to practice as you read this textbook. Here we'll focus on a few skills that will help you read nonfiction with a more critical eye.

Analyze the Author's Purpose

Different types of materials are written with different purposes in mind. For example, a textbook is written to teach students information about a subject. The purpose of a technical manual is to teach someone how to use something, such as a computer. A newspaper editorial might be written to persuade the reader to accept a particular point of view. A writer's purpose influences how the material is presented. Sometimes an author states his or her purpose directly. More often, the purpose is only suggested, and you must use clues to identify the author's purpose.

Distinguish Between Facts and Opinions

It's important when reading informational texts to read actively and to distinguish between fact and opinion. A fact can be proven or disproven. An opinion cannot—it is someone's personal viewpoint or evaluation.

For example, the editorial pages in a newspaper offer opinions on topics that are currently in the news. You need to read newspaper editorials with an eye for bias and faulty logic. For example, the newspaper editorial at the right shows factual statements in blue and opinion statements in red. The underlined words are examples of highly charged words. They reveal bias on the part of the writer.

More than 5,000 people voted last week in favor of building a new shopping center, but the opposition won out. The margin of victory is irrelevant. Those radical voters who opposed the center are obviously self-serving elitists who do not care about anyone but themselves.

This month's unemployment figure for our area is 10 percent, which represents an increase of about 5 percent over the figure for this time last year. These figures mean unemployment is getting worse. But the people who voted against the mall probably do not care about creating new jobs.

Identify Evidence

Before you accept an author's conclusion, you need to make sure that the author has based the conclusion on enough evidence and on the right kind of evidence. An author may present a series of facts to support a claim, but the facts may not tell the whole story. For example, what evidence does the author of the newspaper editorial on the previous page provide to support his claim that the new shopping center would create more jobs? Is it possible that the shopping center might have put many small local businesses out of business, thus increasing unemployment rather than decreasing it?

Evaluate Credibility

Whenever you read informational texts, you need to assess the credibility of the author. This is especially true of sites you may visit on the Internet. All Internet sources are not equally reliable. Here are some questions to ask yourself when evaluating the credibility of a Web site.

- ☐ Is the Web site created by a respected organization, a discussion group, or an individual?
- ☐ Does the Web site creator include his or her name as well as credentials and the sources he or she used to write the material?
- ☐ Is the information on the site balanced or biased?
- ☐ Can you verify the information using two other sources?
- ☐ Is there a date telling when the Web site was created or last updated?

Writing for Social Studies

Writing is one of the most powerful communication tools you will ever use. You will use it to share your thoughts and ideas with others. Research shows that writing about what you read actually helps you learn new information and ideas. A systematic approach to writing—including prewriting, drafting, revising, and proofing—can help you write better, whether you're writing an essay or a research report.

Narrative Essays

Writing that tells a story about a personal experience

1 Select and Narrow Your Topic

A narrative is a story. In social studies, it might be a narrative essay about how an event affected you or your family.

2 Gather Details

Brainstorm a list of details you'd like to include in your narrative.

3 Write a First Draft

Start by writing a simple opening sentence that conveys the main idea of your essay. Continue by writing a colorful story that has interesting details. Write a conclusion that sums up the significance of the event or situation described in your essay.

4 Revise and Proofread

Check to make sure you have not begun too many sentences with the word *I*. Replace general words with more colorful ones.

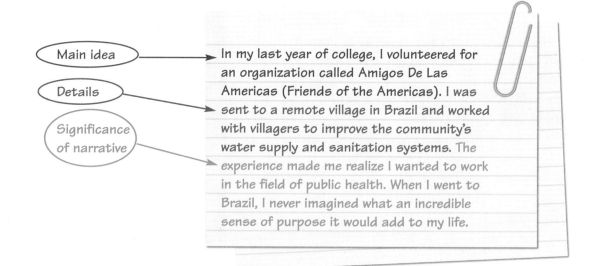

Main idea → In my last year of college, I volunteered for an organization called Amigos De Las Americas (Friends of the Americas). I was

Details → sent to a remote village in Brazil and worked with villagers to improve the community's water supply and sanitation systems. The

Significance of narrative → experience made me realize I wanted to work in the field of public health. When I went to Brazil, I never imagined what an incredible sense of purpose it would add to my life.

Persuasive Essays

Writing that supports an opinion or position

1 Select and Narrow Your Topic

Choose a topic that provokes an argument and has at least two sides. Choose a side. Decide which argument will appeal most to your audience and persuade them to understand your point of view.

2 Gather Evidence

Create a chart that states your position at the top and then lists the pros and cons for your position below, in two columns. Predict and address the strongest arguments against your stand.

3 Write a First Draft

Write a strong thesis statement that clearly states your position. Continue by presenting the strongest arguments in favor of your position and acknowledging and refuting opposing arguments.

4 Revise and Proofread

Check to make sure you have made a logical argument and that you have not oversimplified the argument.

Main Idea

Supporting (pro) argument

Opposing (con) argument

Transition words

It is vital to vote in elections. When people vote, they tell public officials how to run the government. Not every proposal is carried out; however, politicians do their best to listen to what the majority of people want. Therefore, every vote is important.

Expository Essays

Writing that explains a process, compares and contrasts, explains causes and effects, or explores solutions to a problem

1 Identify and Narrow Your Topic

Expository writing is writing that explains something in detail. It might explain the similarities and differences between two or more subjects (compare and contrast). It might explain how one event causes another (cause and effect). Or it might explain a problem and describe a solution.

2 Gather Evidence

Create a graphic organizer that identifies details to include in your essay.

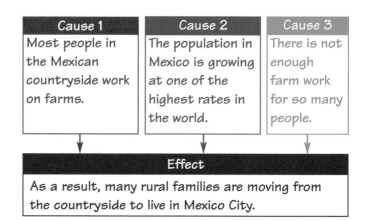

Cause 1	Cause 2	Cause 3
Most people in the Mexican countryside work on farms.	The population in Mexico is growing at one of the highest rates in the world.	There is not enough farm work for so many people.

Effect

As a result, many rural families are moving from the countryside to live in Mexico City.

3 Write Your First Draft

Write a topic sentence and then organize the essay around your similarities and differences, causes and effects, or problem and solutions. Be sure to include convincing details, facts, and examples.

4 Revise and Proofread

Research Papers

Writing that presents research about a topic

1 Narrow Your Topic

Choose a topic you're interested in and make sure that it is not too broad. For example, instead of writing a report on Panama, write about the construction of the Panama Canal.

2 Acquire Information

Locate several sources of information about the topic from the library or the Internet. For each resource, create a source index card like the one at the right. Then take notes using an index card for each detail or subtopic. On the card, note which source the information was taken from. Use quotation marks when you copy the exact words from a source.

> Source #1
> McCullough, David. *The Path Between the Seas: The Creation of the Panama Canal, 1870-1914.* N.Y., Simon and Schuster, 1977.

3 Make an Outline

Use an outline to decide how to organize your report. Sort your index cards into the same order.

> Outline
> I. Introduction
> II. Why the canal was built
> III. How the canal was built
>   A. Physical challenges
>   B. Medical challenges
> IV. Conclusion

Introduction

Building the Panama Canal

Ever since Christopher Columbus first explored the Isthmus of Panama, the Spanish had been looking for a water route through it. They wanted to be able to sail west from Spain to Asia without sailing around South America. However, it was not until 1914 that the dream became a reality.

Conclusion

It took eight years and more than 70,000 workers to build the Panama Canal. It remains one of the greatest engineering feats of modern times.

4 Write a First Draft

Write an introduction, a body, and a conclusion. Leave plenty of space between lines so you can go back and add details that you may have left out.

5 Revise and Proofread

Be sure to include transition words between sentences and paragraphs. Here are some examples:

To show a contrast—*however, although, despite.*

To point out a reason—*since, because, if.*

To signal a conclusion—*therefore, consequently, so, then.*

Evaluating Your Writing

Use this table to help you evaluate your writing.

	Excellent	Good	Acceptable	Unacceptable
Purpose	Achieves purpose—to inform, persuade, or provide historical interpretation—very well	Informs, persuades, or provides historical interpretation reasonably well	Reader cannot easily tell if the purpose is to inform, persuade, or provide historical interpretation	Purpose is not clear
Organization	Develops ideas in a very clear and logical way	Presents ideas in a reasonably well-organized way	Reader has difficulty following the organization	Lacks organization
Elaboration	Explains all ideas with facts and details	Explains most ideas with facts and details	Includes some supporting facts and details	Lacks supporting details
Use of Language	Uses excellent vocabulary and sentence structure with no errors in spelling, grammar, or punctuation	Uses good vocabulary and sentence structure with very few errors in spelling, grammar, or punctuation	Includes some errors in grammar, punctuation, and spelling	Includes many errors in grammar, punctuation, and spelling

CONTENTS

Five Themes of Geography	M1	How to Use a Map	M8
Understanding Movements of Earth	M2	Political and Physical Maps	M10
		Special-Purpose Maps	M12
Understanding Globes	M4	Human Migration	M14
Map Projections	M6	World Land Use	M16

Go Online PHSchool.com Use Web Code **lap-0000** for all of the maps in this handbook.

Five Themes of Geography

Studying the geography of the entire world is a huge task. You can make that task easier by using the five themes of geography: location, regions, place, movement, and human-environment interaction. The themes are tools you can use to organize information and to answer the where, why, and how of geography.

▲ **Location**
This museum in England has a line running through it. The line marks its location at 0° longitude.

LOCATION

1 Location answers the question, "Where is it?" You can think of the location of a continent or a country as its address. You might give an absolute location such as 40° N and 80° W. You might also use a relative address, telling where one place is by referring to another place. *Between school and the mall* and *eight miles east of Pleasant City* are examples of relative locations.

REGIONS

2 Regions are areas that share at least one common feature. Geographers divide the world into many types of regions. For example, countries, states, and cities are political regions. The people in any one of these places live under the same government. Other features, such as climate and culture, can be used to define regions. Therefore the same place can be found in more than one region. For example, the state of Hawaii is in the political region of the United States. Because it has a tropical climate, Hawaii is also part of a tropical climate region.

MOVEMENT

4 Movement answers the question, "How do people, goods, and ideas move from place to place?" Remember that what happens in one place often affects what happens in another. Use the theme of movement to help you trace the spread of goods, people, and ideas from one location to another.

PLACE

3 Place identifies the natural and human features that make one place different from every other place. You can identify a specific place by its landforms, climate, plants, animals, people, language, or culture. You might even think of place as a geographic signature. Use the signature to help you understand the natural and human features that make one place different from every other place.

INTERACTION

5 Human-environment interaction focuses on the relationship between people and the environment. As people live in an area, they often begin to make changes to it, usually to make their lives easier. For example, they might build a dam to control flooding during rainy seasons. Also, the environment can affect how people live, work, dress, travel, and communicate.

◄ **Interaction**
These Congolese women interact with their environment by gathering wood for cooking.

PRACTICE YOUR GEOGRAPHY SKILLS

1 Describe your town or city, using each of the five themes of geography.

2 Name at least one thing that comes into your town or city and one that goes out. How is each moved? Where does it come from? Where does it go?

Understanding Movements of Earth

The planet Earth is part of our solar system. Earth revolves around the sun in a nearly circular path called an orbit. A revolution, or one complete orbit around the sun, takes 365¼ days, or one year. As Earth orbits the sun, it also spins on its axis, an invisible line through the center of Earth from the North Pole to the South Pole. This movement is called a rotation.

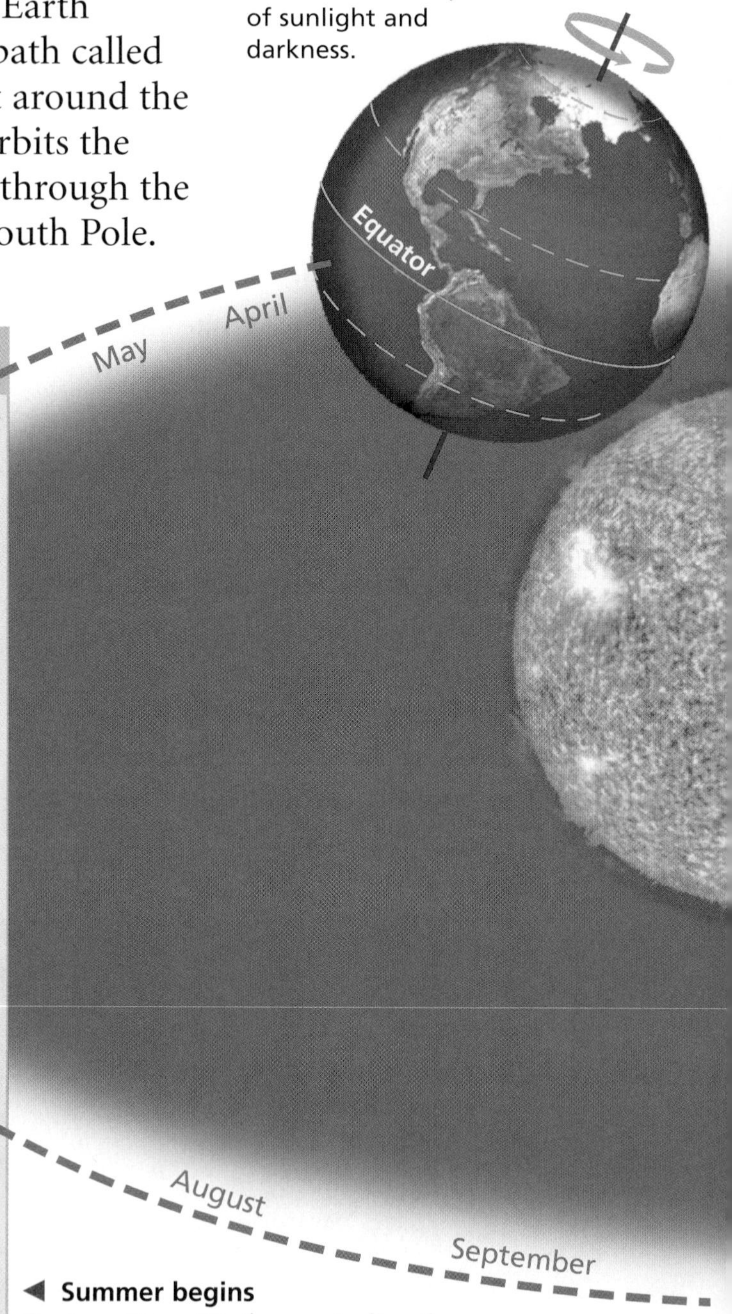

How Night Changes Into Day

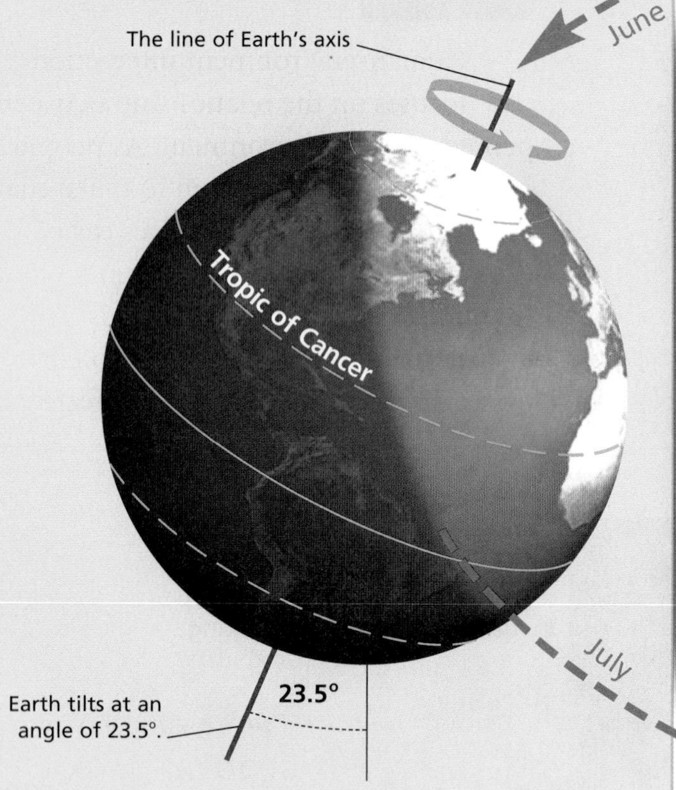

The line of Earth's axis

Tropic of Cancer

Earth tilts at an angle of 23.5°.

23.5°

Earth takes about 24 hours to make one full rotation on its axis. As Earth rotates, it is daytime on the side facing the sun. It is night on the side away from the sun.

▼ **Spring begins**
On March 20 or 21, the sun is directly overhead at the Equator. The Northern and Southern Hemispheres receive almost equal hours of sunlight and darkness.

Equator

June
May
April

July

August

September

◄ **Summer begins**
On June 21 or 22, the sun is directly overhead at the Tropic of Cancer. The Northern Hemisphere receives the greatest number of sunlight hours.

The Seasons

Earth's axis is tilted at an angle. Because of this tilt, sunlight strikes different parts of Earth at different times in the year, creating seasons. The illustration below shows how the seasons are created in the Northern Hemisphere. In the Southern Hemisphere, the seasons are reversed.

PRACTICE YOUR GEOGRAPHY SKILLS

1 What causes the seasons in the Northern Hemisphere to be the opposite of those in the Southern Hemisphere?

2 During which two days of the year do the Northern Hemisphere and Southern Hemisphere have equal hours of daylight and darkness?

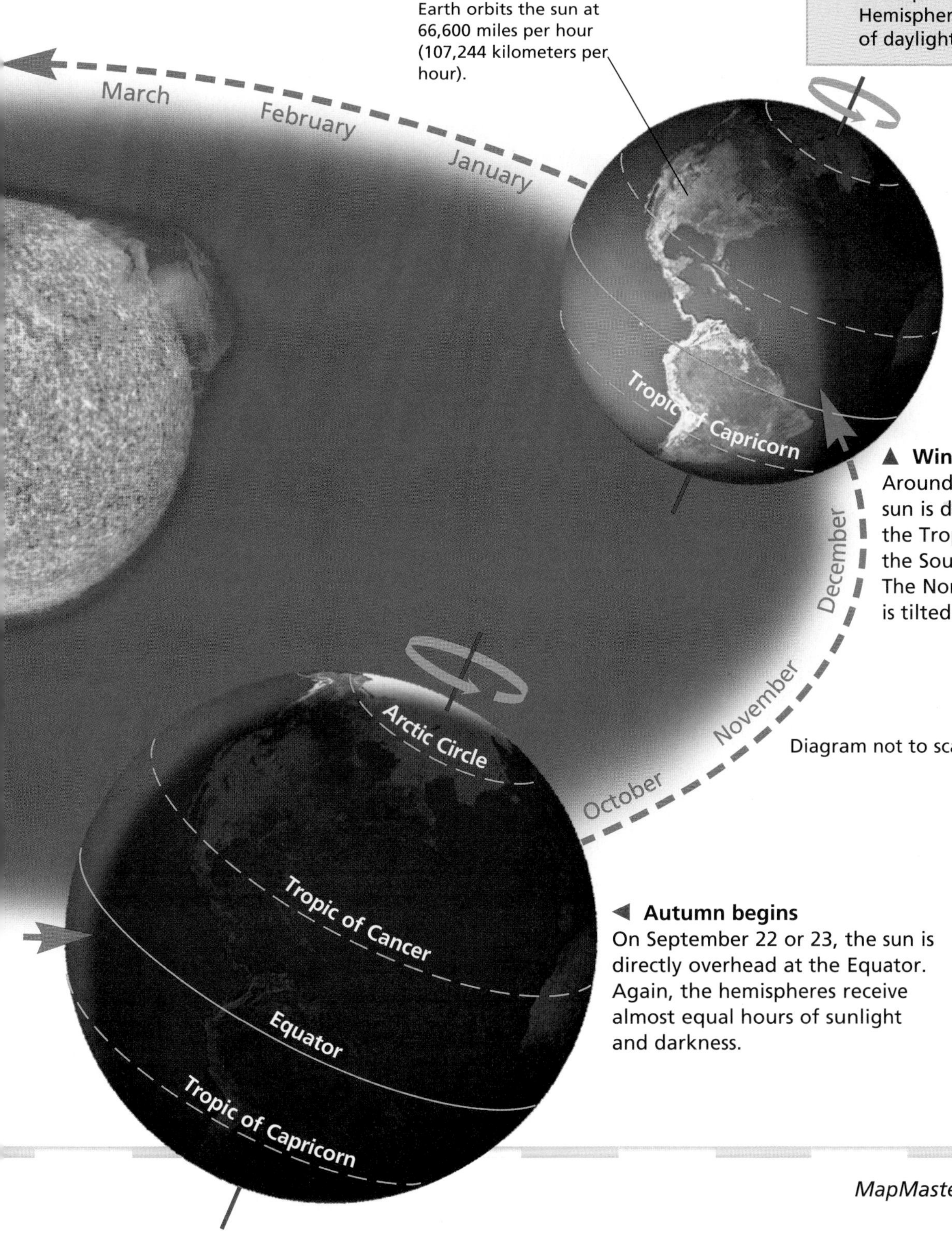

Earth orbits the sun at 66,600 miles per hour (107,244 kilometers per hour).

March
February
January

Tropic of Capricorn

▲ **Winter begins**
Around December 21, the sun is directly overhead at the Tropic of Capricorn in the Southern Hemisphere. The Northern Hemisphere is tilted away from the sun.

December

November

October

Diagram not to scale

Arctic Circle

Tropic of Cancer

Equator

Tropic of Capricorn

◀ **Autumn begins**
On September 22 or 23, the sun is directly overhead at the Equator. Again, the hemispheres receive almost equal hours of sunlight and darkness.

Understanding Globes

A globe is a scale model of Earth. It shows the actual shapes, sizes, and locations of all Earth's landmasses and bodies of water. Features on the surface of Earth are drawn to scale on a globe. This means that a small unit of measure on the globe stands for a large unit of measure on Earth.

Parallels of Latitude

Geographers divide the globe along imaginary horizontal lines called parallels of latitude. One of these latitude lines is the Equator, located halfway between the North and South Poles. Parallels of latitude are measured in degrees (°). One degree of latitude represents a distance of about 69 miles (111 kilometers).

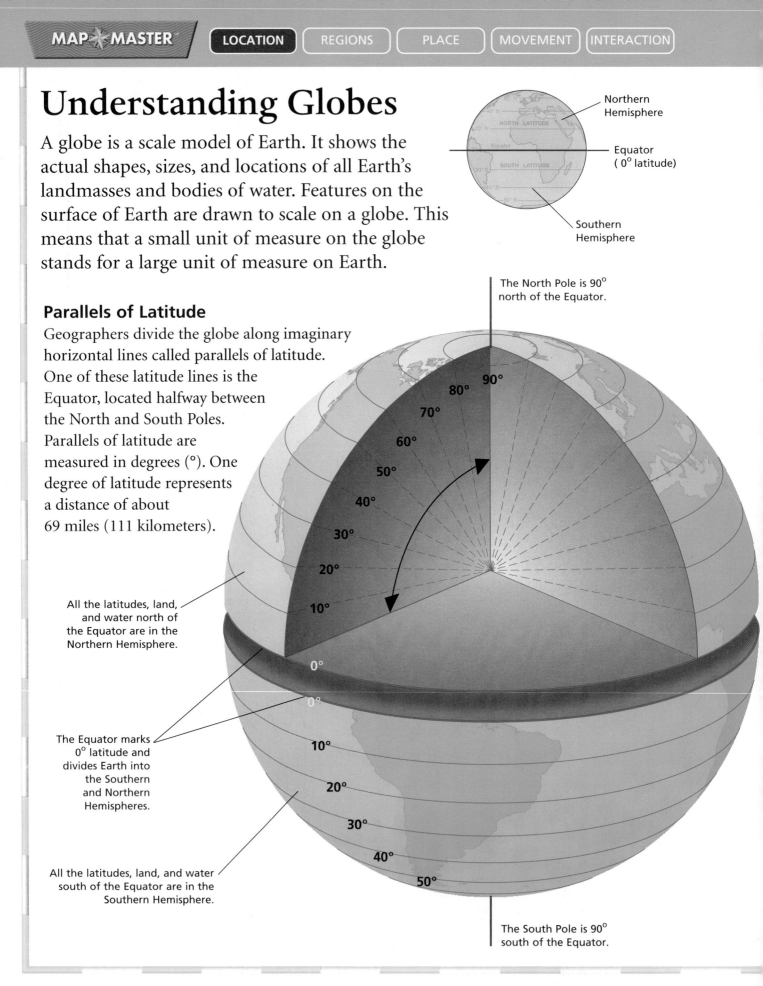

Northern Hemisphere

Equator (0° latitude)

Southern Hemisphere

The North Pole is 90° north of the Equator.

All the latitudes, land, and water north of the Equator are in the Northern Hemisphere.

The Equator marks 0° latitude and divides Earth into the Southern and Northern Hemispheres.

All the latitudes, land, and water south of the Equator are in the Southern Hemisphere.

The South Pole is 90° south of the Equator.

Meridians of Longitude

Geographers also divide the globe along imaginary vertical lines called meridians of longitude, which are measured in degrees (°). The longitude line called the Prime Meridian runs from pole to pole through Greenwich, England. All meridians of longitude come together at the North and South Poles.

PRACTICE YOUR GEOGRAPHY SKILLS

1 Which continents lie completely in the Northern Hemisphere? In the Western Hemisphere?

2 Is there land or water at 20° S latitude and the Prime Meridian? At the Equator and 60° W longitude?

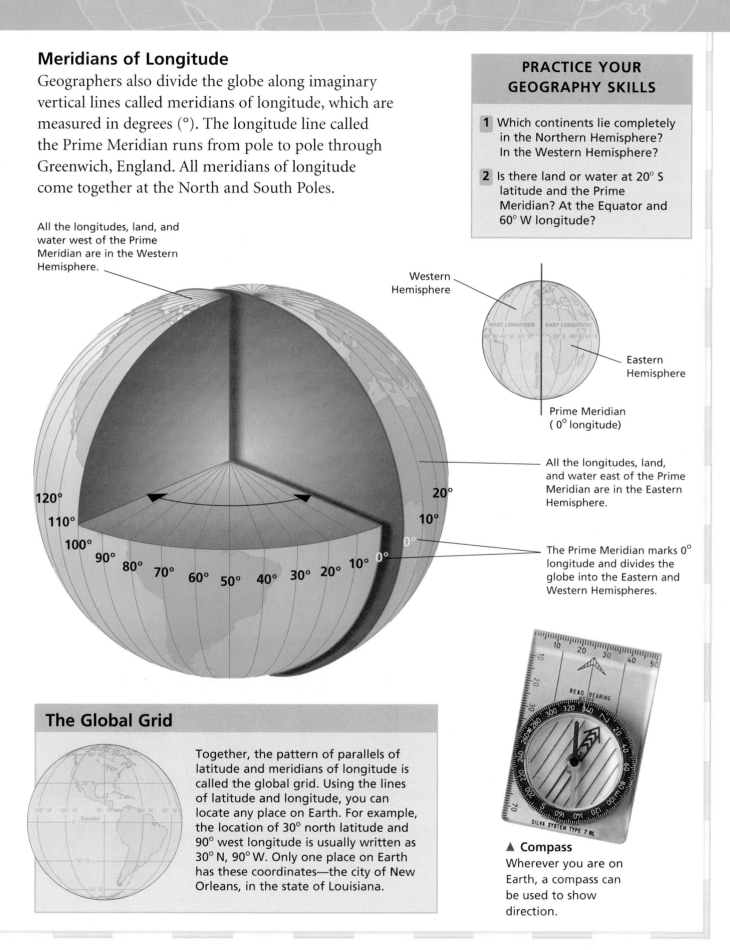

All the longitudes, land, and water west of the Prime Meridian are in the Western Hemisphere.

Western Hemisphere

Eastern Hemisphere

Prime Meridian (0° longitude)

All the longitudes, land, and water east of the Prime Meridian are in the Eastern Hemisphere.

The Prime Meridian marks 0° longitude and divides the globe into the Eastern and Western Hemispheres.

The Global Grid

Together, the pattern of parallels of latitude and meridians of longitude is called the global grid. Using the lines of latitude and longitude, you can locate any place on Earth. For example, the location of 30° north latitude and 90° west longitude is usually written as 30° N, 90° W. Only one place on Earth has these coordinates—the city of New Orleans, in the state of Louisiana.

▲ **Compass**
Wherever you are on Earth, a compass can be used to show direction.

Map Projections

Maps are drawings that show regions on flat surfaces. Maps are easier to use and carry than globes, but they cannot show the correct size and shape of every feature on Earth's curved surface. They must shrink some places and stretch others. To make up for this distortion, mapmakers use different map projections. No one projection can accurately show the correct area, shape, distance, and direction for all of Earth's surface. Mapmakers use the projection that has the least distortion for the information they are presenting.

▲ **Global gores**
Flattening a globe creates a string of shapes called gores.

Same-Shape Maps

Map projections that accurately show the shapes of landmasses are called same-shape maps. However, these projections often greatly distort, or make less accurate, the size of landmasses as well as the distance between them. In the projection below, the northern and southern areas of the globe appear more stretched than the areas near the Equator.

To turn Earth into a same-shape map, mapmakers must stretch the gores into rectangles.

Equator

Stretching the gores makes parts of Earth larger. This enlargement becomes greater toward the North and South Poles.

Equator

Mercator projection ▶
One of the most common same-shape maps is the Mercator projection, named for the mapmaker who invented it. The Mercator projection accurately shows shape and direction, but it distorts distance and size. Because the projection shows true directions, ships' navigators use it to chart a straight-line course between two ports.

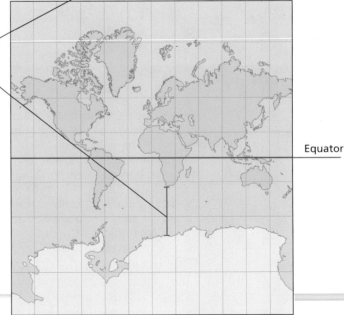

Equal-Area Maps

Map projections that show the correct size of landmasses are called equal-area maps. In order to show the correct size of landmasses, these maps usually distort shapes. The distortion is usually greater at the edges of the map and less at the center.

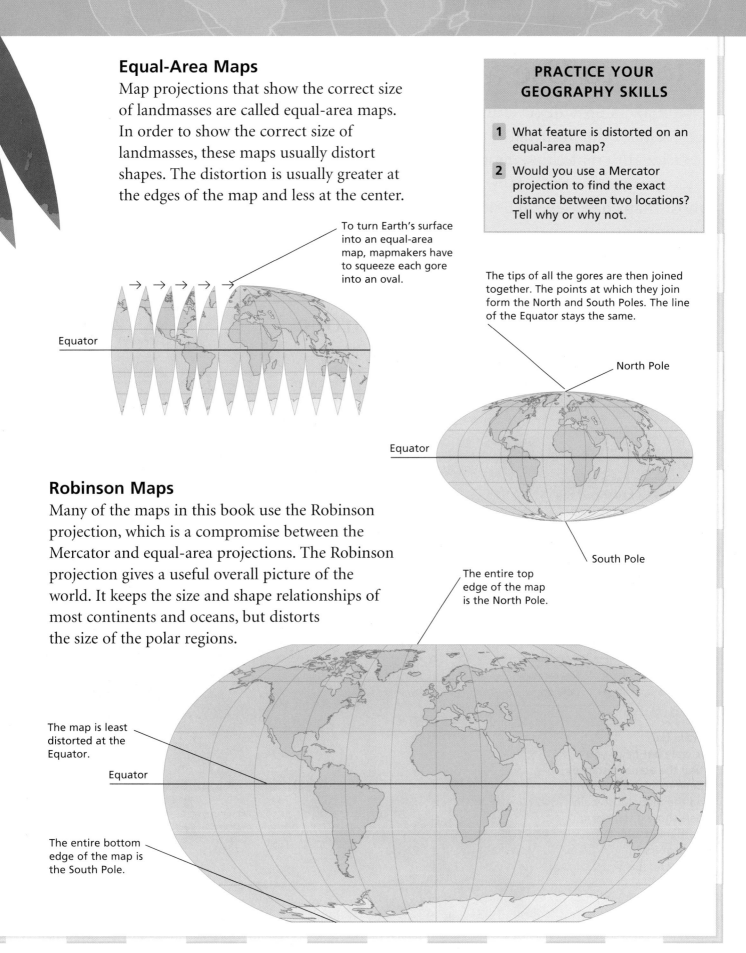

To turn Earth's surface into an equal-area map, mapmakers have to squeeze each gore into an oval.

Equator

The tips of all the gores are then joined together. The points at which they join form the North and South Poles. The line of the Equator stays the same.

North Pole

Equator

South Pole

Robinson Maps

Many of the maps in this book use the Robinson projection, which is a compromise between the Mercator and equal-area projections. The Robinson projection gives a useful overall picture of the world. It keeps the size and shape relationships of most continents and oceans, but distorts the size of the polar regions.

The entire top edge of the map is the North Pole.

The map is least distorted at the Equator.

Equator

The entire bottom edge of the map is the South Pole.

How to Use a Map

Mapmakers provide several clues to help you understand the information on a map. Maps provide different clues, depending on their purpose or scale. However, most maps have several clues in common.

Locator globe
Many maps are shown with locator globes. They show where on the globe the area of the map is located.

Title
All maps have a title. The title tells you the subject of the map.

Compass rose
Many maps show direction by displaying a compass rose with the directions north, east, south, and west. The letters N, E, S, and W are placed to indicate these directions.

Key
Often a map has a key, or legend. The key shows the symbols and colors used on the map, and what each one means.

Scale bar
A scale bar helps you find the actual distances between points shown on the map. Most scale bars show distances in both miles and kilometers.

Western Europe

Key

——	National border
⊛	National capital
•	Other city

0 miles 300
0 kilometers 300
Lambert Azimuthal Equal Area

Map labels: SHETLAND ISLANDS (U.K.), North Sea, Glasgow, Copenhagen, DENMARK, Hamburg, Berlin, UNITED KINGDOM, Dublin, IRELAND, NETHERLANDS, Amsterdam, The Hague, GERMANY, London, Brussels, BELGIUM, Frankfurt, Prague, CZECH REPUBLIC, LUXEMBOURG, Luxembourg, Paris, Munich, Vienna, AUSTRIA, English Channel, FRANCE, Bern, LIECHTENSTEIN, SWITZERLAND, Lyon, Milan, SAN MARINO, Bay of Biscay, Toulouse, MONACO, ITALY, Adriatic Sea, Marseille, Marseille, ANDORRA, CORSICA (France), VATICAN CITY, Rome, PORTUGAL, Madrid, Barcelona, SARDINIA (Italy), Tyrrhenian Sea, Lisbon, SPAIN, BALEARIC ISLANDS (Spain), Seville, Mediterranean Sea, SICILY (Italy)

Maps of Different Scales

Maps are drawn to different scales, depending on their purpose. Here are three maps drawn to very different scales. Keep in mind that maps showing large areas have smaller scales. Maps showing small areas have larger scales.

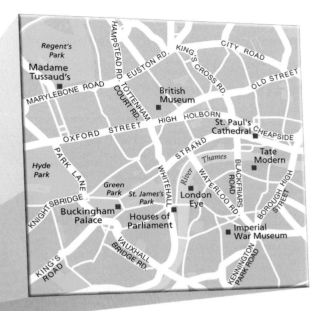

▲ Greater London
Find the gray square on the main map of Western Europe (left). This square represents the area shown on the map above. It shows London's boundaries, the general shape of the city, and the features around the city. This map can help you find your way from the airport to the center of town.

▲ Central London
Find the gray square on the map of Greater London. This square represents the area shown on the map above. This map moves you closer into the center of London. Like the zoom on a computer or a camera, this map shows a smaller area but in greater detail. It has the largest scale (1 inch represents about 0.9 mile). You can use this map to explore downtown London.

Key

■ Point of interest

Park

0 miles   0.5   1
0 kilometers   1

Key

Built-up area

Airport

City or county border

0 miles   10   20
0 kilometers   20
Lambert Conformal Conic

⊛ National capital

• Town or neighborhood

PRACTICE YOUR GEOGRAPHY SKILLS

1 What part of a map explains the colors used on the map?

2 How does the scale bar change depending on the scale of the map?

3 Which map would be best for finding the location of the British Museum? Explain why.

Political Maps

Political maps show political borders: continents, countries, and divisions within countries, such as states or provinces. The colors on political maps do not have any special meaning, but they make the map easier to read. Political maps also include symbols and labels for capitals, cities, and towns.

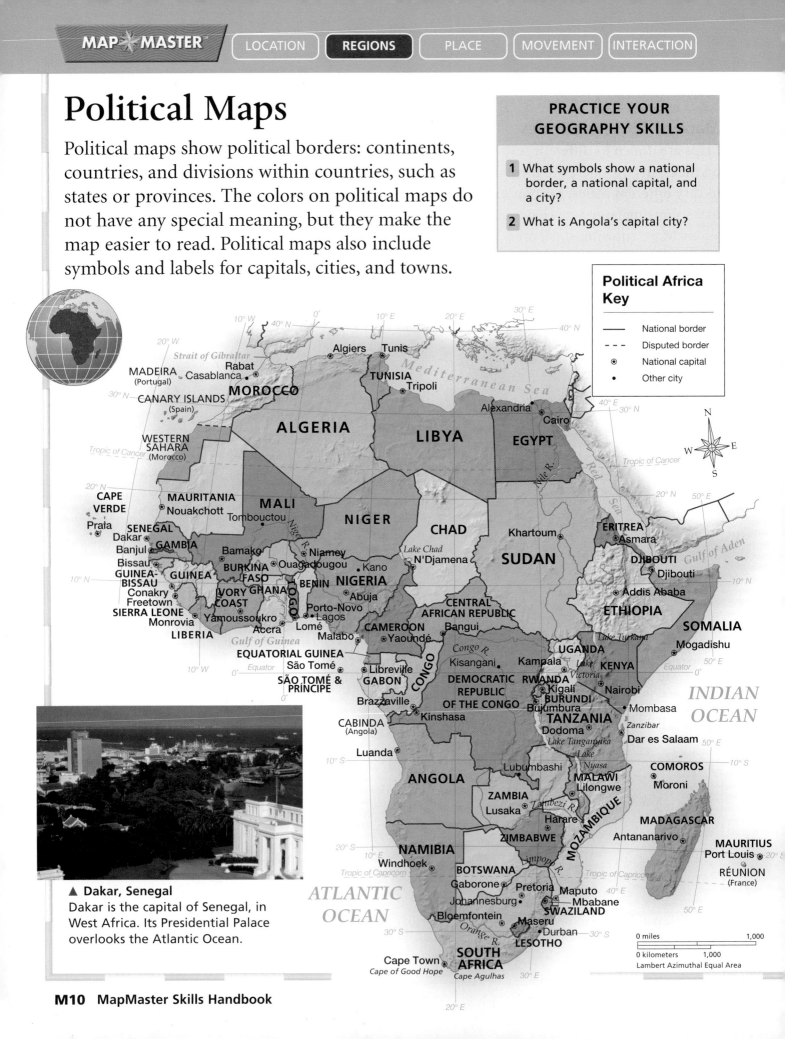

Political Africa Key

——	National border
- - -	Disputed border
⊛	National capital
•	Other city

▲ **Dakar, Senegal**
Dakar is the capital of Senegal, in West Africa. Its Presidential Palace overlooks the Atlantic Ocean.

0 miles 1,000
0 kilometers 1,000
Lambert Azimuthal Equal Area

Physical Maps

Physical maps represent what a region looks like by showing its major physical features, such as hills and plains. Physical maps also often show elevation and relief. Elevation, indicated by colors, is the height of the land above sea level. Relief, indicated by shading, shows how sharply the land rises or falls.

PRACTICE YOUR GEOGRAPHY SKILLS

1 Which areas of Africa have the highest elevation?

2 How can you use relief to plan a hiking trip?

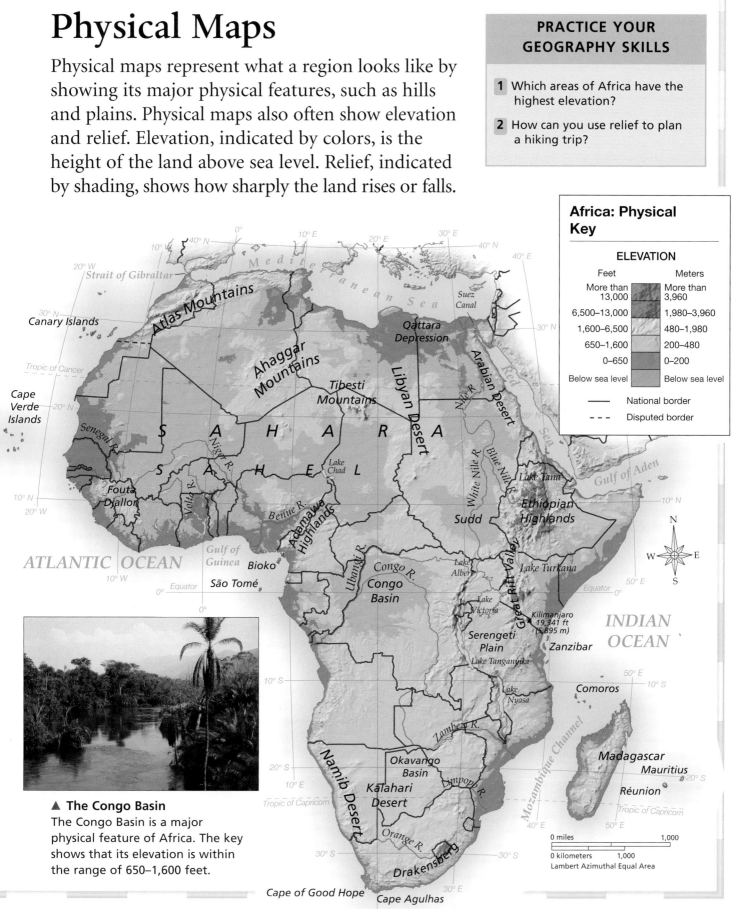

Africa: Physical Key

ELEVATION

Feet	Meters
More than 13,000	More than 3,960
6,500–13,000	1,980–3,960
1,600–6,500	480–1,980
650–1,600	200–480
0–650	0–200
Below sea level	Below sea level

—— National border

- - - Disputed border

▲ **The Congo Basin**
The Congo Basin is a major physical feature of Africa. The key shows that its elevation is within the range of 650–1,600 feet.

0 miles 1,000
0 kilometers 1,000
Lambert Azimuthal Equal Area

Special-Purpose Maps: Climate

Unlike the boundary lines on a political map, the boundary lines on climate maps do not separate the land into exact divisions. For example, in this climate map of India, a tropical wet climate gradually changes to a tropical wet and dry climate.

PRACTICE YOUR GEOGRAPHY SKILLS

1 What part of a special-purpose map tells you what the colors on the map mean?

2 Where are arid regions located in India? Are there major cities in those regions?

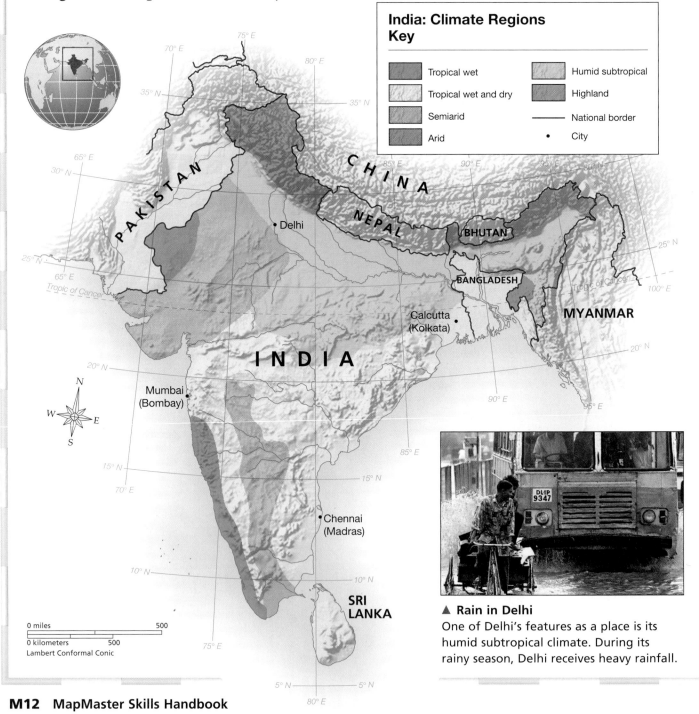

India: Climate Regions Key

- Tropical wet
- Tropical wet and dry
- Semiarid
- Arid
- Humid subtropical
- Highland
- National border
- City

▲ **Rain in Delhi**
One of Delhi's features as a place is its humid subtropical climate. During its rainy season, Delhi receives heavy rainfall.

0 miles 500
0 kilometers 500
Lambert Conformal Conic

Special-Purpose Maps: Language

This map shows the official languages of India. An official language is the language used by the government. Even though a region has an official language, the people there may speak other languages as well. As in other special-purpose maps, the key explains how the different languages appear on the map.

PRACTICE YOUR GEOGRAPHY SKILLS

1 What color represents the Malayalam language on this map?

2 Where in India is Tamil the official language?

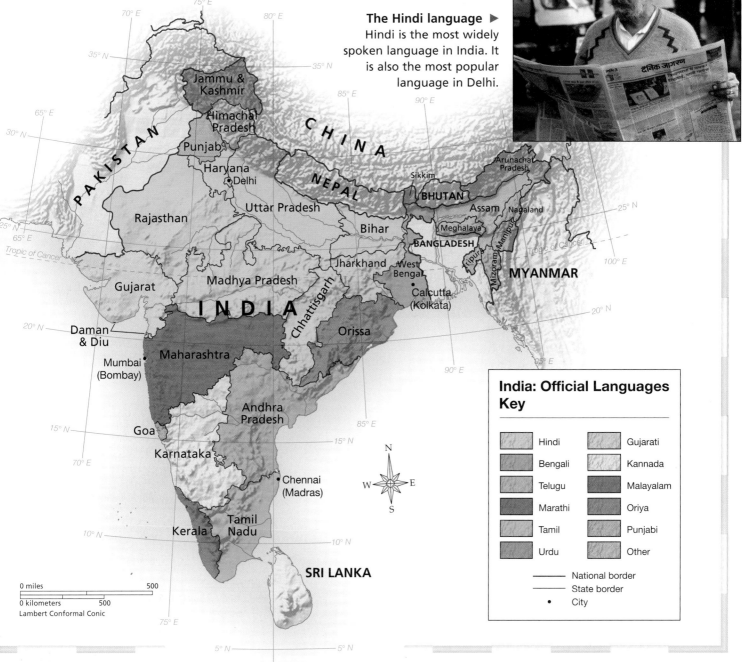

The Hindi language ▶
Hindi is the most widely spoken language in India. It is also the most popular language in Delhi.

India: Official Languages Key

Hindi	Gujarati
Bengali	Kannada
Telugu	Malayalam
Marathi	Oriya
Tamil	Punjabi
Urdu	Other

—— National border
—— State border
• City

0 miles 500
0 kilometers 500
Lambert Conformal Conic

Human Migration

Migration is an important part of the study of geography. Since the beginning of history, people have been on the move. As people move, they both shape and are shaped by their environments. Wherever people go, the culture they bring with them mixes with the cultures of the place in which they have settled.

Explorers arrive ▼

In 1492, Christopher Columbus set sail from Spain for the Americas with three ships. The ships shown here are replicas of those ships.

▲ **Native American pyramid**

When Europeans arrived in the Americas, the lands they found were not empty. Diverse groups of people with distinct cultures already lived there. The temple-topped pyramid shown above was built by Mayan Indians in Mexico, long before Columbus sailed.

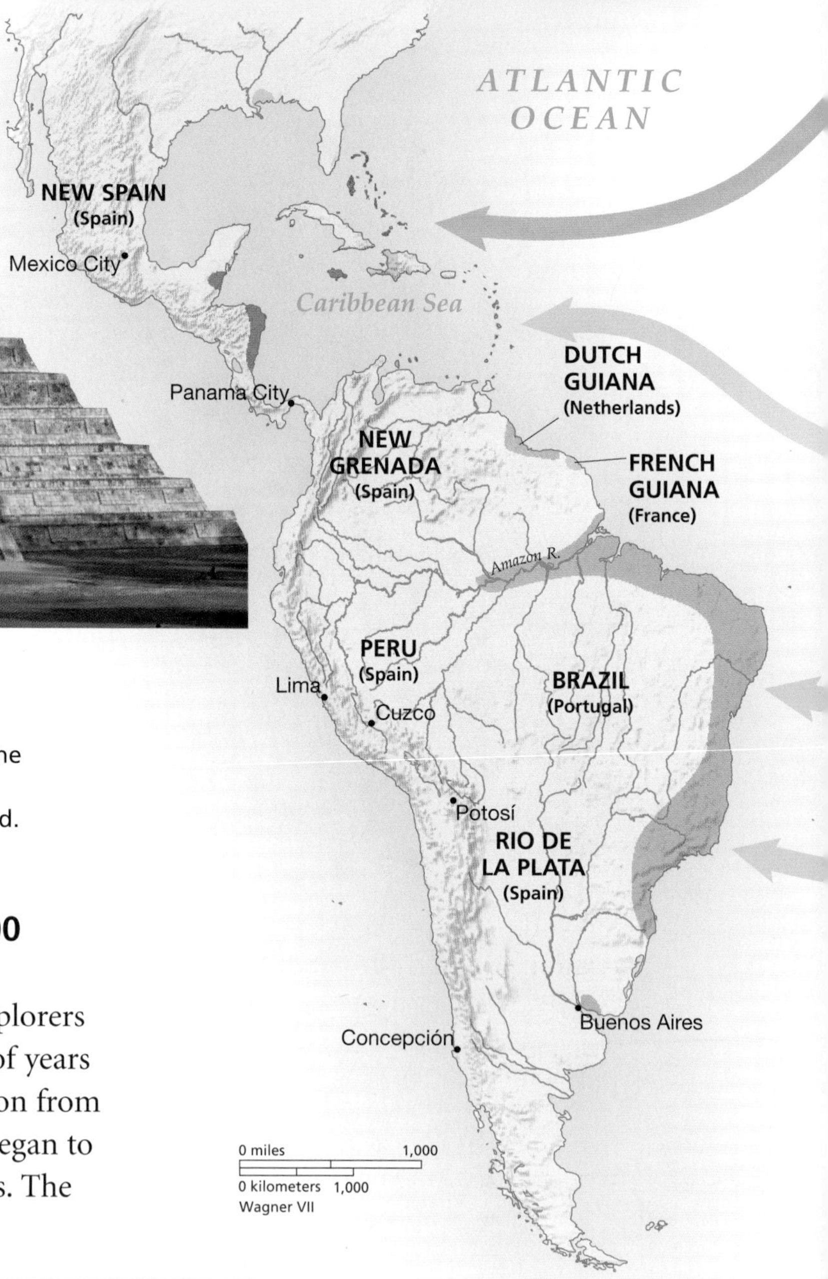

Migration to the Americas, 1500–1800

A huge wave of migration from the Eastern Hemisphere began in the 1500s. European explorers in the Americas paved the way for hundreds of years of European settlement there. Forced migration from Africa started soon afterward, as Europeans began to import African slaves to work in the Americas. The map at the right shows these migrations.

ATLANTIC OCEAN

NEW SPAIN
(Spain)

Mexico City

Caribbean Sea

Panama City

DUTCH GUIANA
(Netherlands)

NEW GRENADA
(Spain)

FRENCH GUIANA
(France)

Amazon R.

PERU
(Spain)

Lima

Cuzco

BRAZIL
(Portugal)

Potosí

RIO DE LA PLATA
(Spain)

Concepción

Buenos Aires

0 miles   1,000
0 kilometers 1,000
Wagner VII

SCOTLAND
IRELAND   ENGLAND
           NETHERLANDS
FRANCE
EUROPE
PORTUGAL SPAIN

MOROCCO

N
W — E
S

WALO   **A F R I C A**

Saint-Louis
Fort James
Cacheu

AKAN
STATES

Niger R.

Elmina   BENIN
Axim Accra

Congo R.

Congo
Basin

KONGO
Luanda

Benguela

*ATLANTIC
OCEAN*

Migration to Latin America, 1500–1800
Key

←	European migration	▨	Spain and possessions
←	African migration	▨	Portugal and possessions
——	National or colonial border	▨	Netherlands and possessions
····	Traditional African border	▨	France and possessions
▨	African State	▨	England and possessions

PRACTICE YOUR GEOGRAPHY SKILLS

1 Where did the Portuguese settle in the Americas?

2 Would you describe African migration at this time as a result of both push factors and pull factors? Explain why or why not.

"Push" and "Pull" Factors

Geographers describe a people's choice to migrate in terms of "push" factors and "pull" factors. Push factors are things in people's lives that push them to leave, such as poverty and political unrest. Pull factors are things in another country that pull people to move there, including better living conditions and hopes of better jobs.

▲ **Elmina, Ghana**
Elmina, in Ghana, is one of the many ports from which slaves were transported from Africa. Because slaves and gold were traded here, stretches of the western African coast were known as the Slave Coast and the Gold Coast.

World Land Use

People around the world have many different economic structures, or ways of making a living. Land-use maps are one way to learn about these structures. The ways that people use the land in each region tell us about the main ways that people in that region make a living.

World Land Use Key

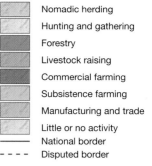

	Nomadic herding
	Hunting and gathering
	Forestry
	Livestock raising
	Commercial farming
	Subsistence farming
	Manufacturing and trade
	Little or no activity
——	National border
- - - -	Disputed border

▲ **Wheat farming in the United States**
Developed countries practice commercial farming rather than subsistence farming. Commercial farming is the production of food mainly for sale, either within the country or for export to other countries. Commercial farmers like these in Oregon often use heavy equipment to farm.

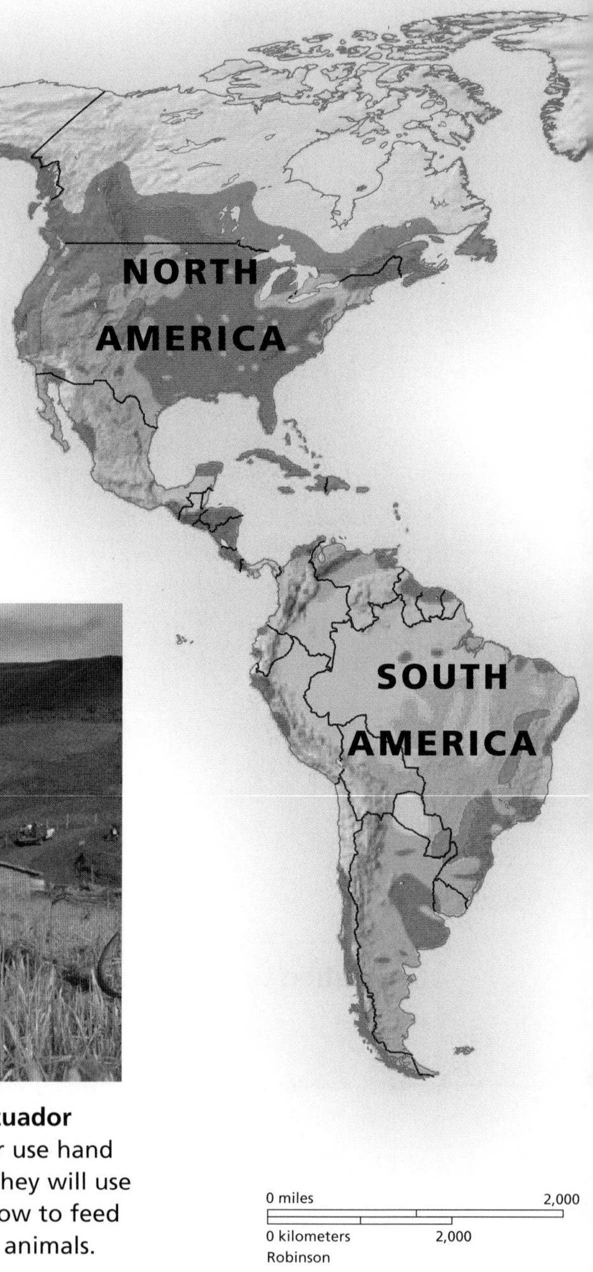

Levels of Development

Notice on the map key the term *subsistence farming*. This term means the production of food mainly for use by the farmer's own family. In less-developed countries, subsistence farming is often one of the main economic activities. In contrast, in developed countries there is little subsistence farming.

▲ **Growing barley in Ecuador**
These farmers in Ecuador use hand tools to harvest barley. They will use most of the crop they grow to feed themselves or their farm animals.

NORTH AMERICA

SOUTH AMERICA

0 miles   2,000
0 kilometers   2,000
Robinson

▲ Growing rice in Vietnam
Women in Vietnam plant rice in wet rice paddies, using the same planting methods their ancestors did.

PRACTICE YOUR GEOGRAPHY SKILLS

1 In what parts of the world is subsistence farming the main land use?

2 Locate where manufacturing and trade are the main land use. Are they found more often near areas of subsistence farming or areas of commercial farming? Why might this be so?

EUROPE

ASIA

AFRICA

N
W · E
S

AUSTRALIA

◄ Herding cattle in Kenya
Besides subsistence farming, nomadic herding is another economic activity in Africa. This man drives his cattle across the Kenyan grasslands.

How to Read Social Studies

Target Reading Skills

The Target Reading Skills introduced on this page will help you understand the words and ideas in this section on geography and in other social studies reading you do. Each chapter focuses on one of these reading skills. Good readers develop a bank of reading strategies, or skills. Then they draw on the particular strategies that will help them understand the text they are reading.

Chapter 1 Target Reading Skill

Clarifying Meaning If you do not understand something you are reading right away, you can use several skills to help clarify the meaning of the word or idea. In this chapter you will practice these strategies for clarifying meaning: rereading, reading ahead, and paraphrasing.

Chapter 2 Target Reading Skill

Using Context Using the context of an unfamiliar word can help you understand its meaning. Context includes the words, phrases, and sentences surrounding a word. In this chapter you will practice using these context clues: descriptions, definitions, comparisons, and examples.

Chapter 3 Target Reading Skill

Comparing and Contrasting You can use comparison and contrast to sort out and analyze information you are reading. Comparing means examining the similarities between things. Contrasting is looking at differences. In this chapter you will practice these skills: comparing and contrasting, identifying contrasts, making comparisons, and recognizing contrast signal words.

Chapter 4 Target Reading Skill

Using Sequence Noting the order in which significant events take place can help you understand and remember them. In this chapter you will practice these sequence skills: sequencing, or finding the order of events, sequencing important changes, and recognizing sequence signal words.

Chapter 5 Target Reading Skill

Identifying the Main Idea Since you cannot remember every detail of what you read, it is important that you identify the main ideas. The main idea of a section or paragraph is the most important point and the one you want to remember. In this chapter you will practice these skills: identifying stated and implied main ideas and identifying supporting details.

FOUNDATIONS of GEOGRAPHY

Are you curious about our world? Do you want to know why winters are cold and summers are hot? Have you wondered why some people live and work in cities and others work on farms in the countryside? If you answered yes to any of these questions, you want to know more about geography.

Guiding Questions

The text, photographs, maps, and charts in this book will help you discover answers to these Guiding Questions.

 Geography What are Earth's major physical features?

 History How have people's ways of life changed over time?

 Culture What is a culture?

 Government What types of government exist in the world today?

Economics How do people use the world's natural resources?

Project Preview

You can also discover answers to the Guiding Questions by working on projects. Project possibilities are listed on page 136 of this book.

Investigate the Political World

There are more than 190 independent countries in the world. Some of those countries have dependencies, or areas outside of those countries that belong to them. Every land area where people live belongs to some country. The blue areas on maps in this book show the world's oceans, seas, and lakes. The other colors on this map show the areas of the world's countries and dependencies.

Go Online
PHSchool.com Use Web Code nfp-3020 for the interactive maps on these pages.

▲ **Denmark**
Denmark is one of the oldest continuously existing states. Christiansborg Palace is the seat of the Danish Parliament.

◄ **Niagara Falls**
The border between the United States and Canada runs through the falls. Both countries share its tourist and power-generating benefits.

LOCATION

1 Examine Country Borders

Governments have drawn the borders between countries. Some borders follow mountains or rivers. Others are straight lines. On the map, look at the United States and Canada. These are the large yellow and pink countries in North America. Parts of their borders are straight, but others are crooked. Why might this be? What might explain the location of other borders on this map?

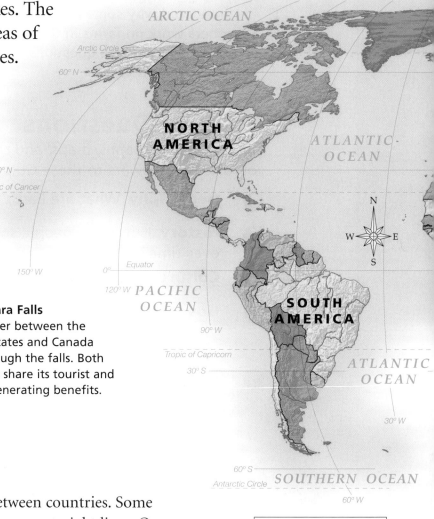

The World: Political Key

—— National border
- - - Disputed border

PLACE

2 Analyze the Continents

Notice the six black labels on the world map. These labels name continents. Which continent's name is also the name of a country? You can see that some continents have more countries than others. Which continent is made up mostly of small countries?

▲ **Russia**
St. Basil's Cathedral was built in the 1500s in Moscow, the Russian capital. At that time, the Russian church had great political power.

ARCTIC OCEAN

EUROPE

ASIA

AFRICA

PACIFIC OCEAN

INDIAN OCEAN

AUSTRALIA

Tropic of Cancer

Equator

Tropic of Capricorn

Arctic Circle

60° N

30° N

60° S

0°

30° E

60° E

90° E

120° E

150° E

180°

0 miles — 3,000
0 kilometers — 3,000
Robinson

▲ **East Timor**
These people are celebrating the independence of East Timor, which became a nation in 2002.

◄ **Ghana**
The traditional leader of the Asante people in Ghana is called the Asantehene. Otumfuo Opoku Ware II held this position for thirty years.

World Overview **3**

Investigate the Physical World

People's lives are constantly shaped by their physical environment. The physical features of a place often determine where and how people live. Yet the physical world is always changing, too. Some changes come very slowly. For example, it took millions of years for Earth's crust to lift and form mountains. Other changes are fast and dramatic, such as when a volcano erupts or an earthquake hits.

▲ **Alaska**
Glaciers like this one at Portage, Alaska, have shaped the land for thousands of years.

PLACE

3 Infer From a Map

Notice the bumpy texture and brownish colors on the map. These indicate a mountainous landscape. Now find the continent of South America. Look for the Amazon Basin. What does the key tell you about its elevation? Notice the photograph of the Tigre River as it weaves through the basin. Describe that landscape. Now find the Andes on the map, and describe what you would expect to see there.

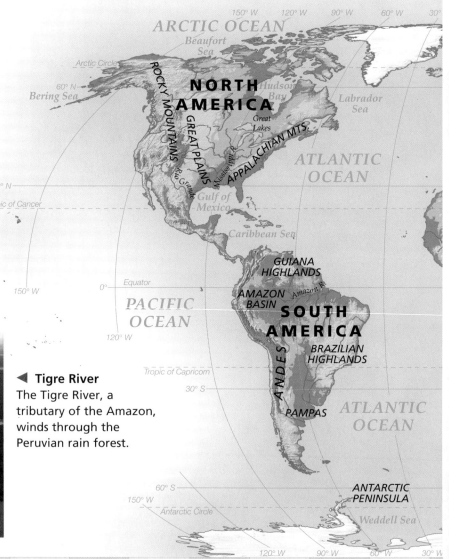

◄ **Tigre River**
The Tigre River, a tributary of the Amazon, winds through the Peruvian rain forest.

HUMAN-ENVIRONMENT INTERACTION
4 Examine Landforms as Barriers

Physical barriers can make movement between areas difficult. For example, take a look at the continents in the map below. Some of them are separated from one another by vast areas of water. Examine the elevation key. Look closely at the map's labels. What other physical landforms might have acted as barriers to movement?

▲ **Mount Fuji, Japan**
Volcanoes such as this one have created islands along the rim of the Pacific Ocean.

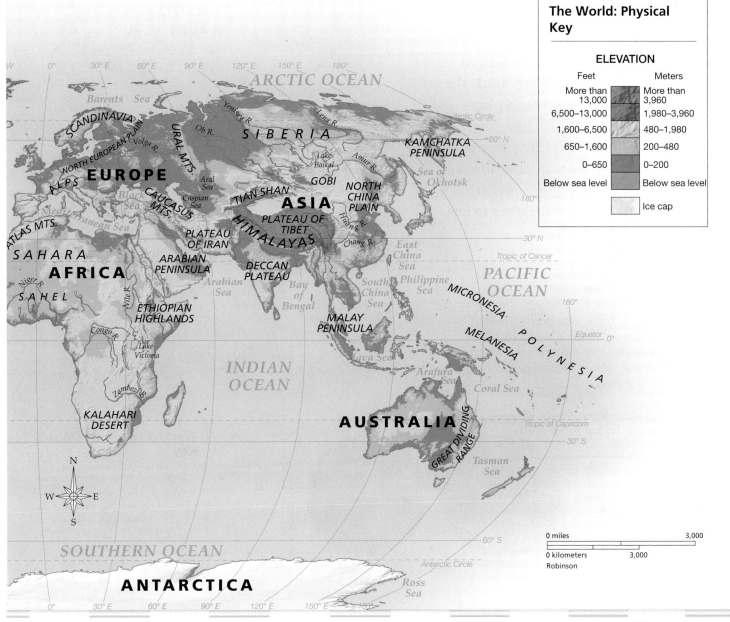

The World: Physical Key

ELEVATION

Feet		Meters
More than 13,000		More than 3,960
6,500–13,000		1,980–3,960
1,600–6,500		480–1,980
650–1,600		200–480
0–650		0–200
Below sea level		Below sea level
	Ice cap	

Investigate Population

For thousands of years, the world's population grew slowly. In the past 200 years, however, health care, living conditions, and food production have greatly improved. This has led to a huge population burst. In 1800, the world's population numbered less than 1 billion people. Today, it is more than 6 billion, and growing quickly.

▲ **China**
A crowd of people walk through a park in the capital city of Beijing. China has the largest population of any country in the world.

REGIONS

5 Analyze Population Density

A population density map shows you where the world's people live. Study the world population map. Which places have many people? Which have few? Why do you think people live where they do? As you study the map, refer to the world physical map on the previous page. It may give you some clues to help you answer these questions.

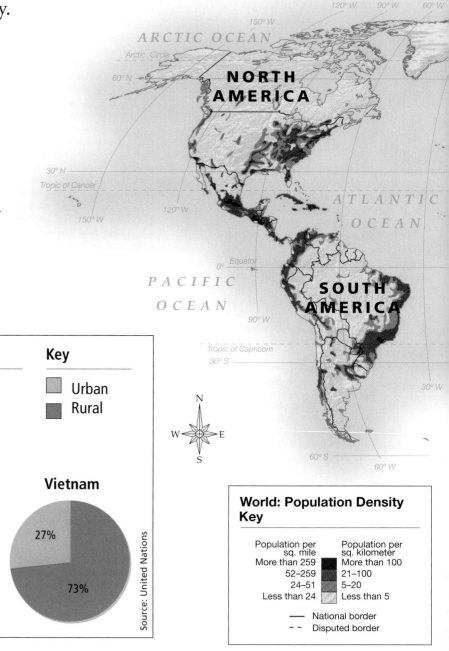

World Population

In the United Kingdom, most people live in cities. In Panama, the population is almost equally divided between urban and rural areas. In some Asian countries, such as Vietnam, people live mainly in rural areas.

Key

- Urban
- Rural

United Kingdom
- 11%
- 89%

Panama
- 58%
- 42%

Vietnam
- 27%
- 73%

Source: United Nations

World: Population Density Key

Population per sq. mile	Population per sq. kilometer
More than 259	More than 100
52–259	21–100
24–51	5–20
Less than 24	Less than 5

— National border
- - Disputed border

MOVEMENT

6 Compare Continents

When high population densities cover large areas, those areas have large populations. Look at the continents on the map. Which continent do you think has the largest population, based on the size of its areas of high population density? Which continent do you think has the lowest population? Compare North America and South America on the map. Which continent do you think has the larger population?

▲ **New Zealand**
The Whanganui River flows through a New Zealand national park. New Zealand has a low population density.

0 miles   3,000

0 kilometers   3,000
Robinson

PRACTICE YOUR GEOGRAPHY SKILLS

1. In Asia there is a ring of dense population next to an area with low population. Look at the physical map of the world on pages 4 and 5. What landform may explain this difference?

2. Look at Northern Africa. Find the area of heavy population that forms a curving line on the map. How does the physical map on pages 4 and 5 explain this?

Monaco is the most densely populated European nation. ▶

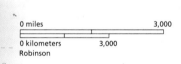

The World of Geography

Chapter Preview

This chapter will introduce you to the study of Earth, the planet where we live.

Section 1
The Five Themes of Geography

Section 2
The Geographer's Tools

Target Reading Skill

Clarifying Meaning In this chapter you will focus on clarifying meaning by learning how to read ahead and how to paraphrase.

▶ A satellite launched from the space shuttle *Discovery* orbits Earth.

The Five Themes of Geography

Prepare to Read

Objectives

In this section you will
1. Learn about the study of Earth.
2. Discover five ways to look at Earth.

Taking Notes

As you read the section, look for details about each of the five themes of geography. Copy the web diagram below and write down details related to each theme. Add ovals as needed for additional themes or details.

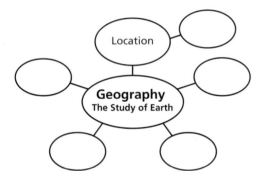

Target Reading Skill

Reread or Read Ahead If you do not understand a passage, reread it to look for connections among the words and sentences. Reading ahead can also help. Words and ideas may be clarified further on.

Key Terms

- **geography** (jee AHG ru fee) *n.* the study of Earth
- **cardinal directions** (KAHR duh nul duh REK shunz) *n.* the directions north, east, south, and west
- **latitude** (LAT uh tood) *n.* the distance north or south of Earth's Equator, in degrees
- **longitude** (LAHN juh tood) *n.* the distance east or west of the Prime Meridian, in degrees
- **hemisphere** (HEM ih sfeer) *n.* a half of Earth
- **parallel** (PA ruh lel) *n.* a line of latitude
- **meridian** (muh RID ee un) *n.* a line of longitude

Geographers use maps and other tools to understand Earth.

The Study of Earth

Geography is the study of Earth, our home planet. Geographers try to answer two basic questions: Where are things located? and, Why are they there? To find answers to these questions, geographers consider Earth from many points of view.

✔ **Reading Check** What questions do geographers try to answer?

Five Ways to Look at Earth

Five themes can help you organize information about Earth and its people. These themes are location, regions, place, movement, and human-environment interaction. They can help you understand where things are located, and why they are there.

Location Geographers begin to study a place by finding where it is, or its location. Geographers use both cardinal and intermediate directions to describe location. The **cardinal directions** are north, east, south, and west. Intermediate directions lie between the cardinal directions. For example, northwest is halfway between north and west.

Geographers also use two special measurements of Earth to describe location. **Latitude** is the distance north or south of the Equator, measured in units called degrees. Degrees are units that measure angles. **Longitude** is the distance east or west of the Prime Meridian, measured in degrees.

Lines of latitude are east-west circles around the globe. All points on the circle have the same latitude. The line of latitude around the middle of the globe, at 0 degrees (0°) of latitude, is the Equator. Lines of longitude run north and south. The Prime Meridian is the line of longitude that marks 0° of longitude.

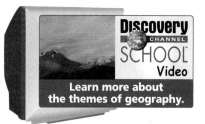

Learn more about the themes of geography.

The Hemispheres

The Equator and the Prime Meridian both divide Earth in two. Each half of Earth is called a **hemisphere.** The Equator divides Earth into Northern and Southern hemispheres. The Prime Meridian divides Earth into Eastern and Western hemispheres.

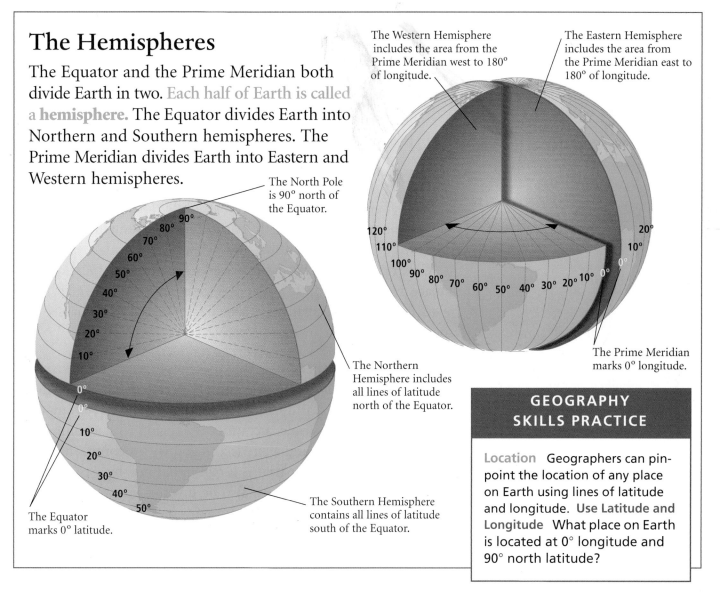

The Western Hemisphere includes the area from the Prime Meridian west to 180° of longitude.

The Eastern Hemisphere includes the area from the Prime Meridian east to 180° of longitude.

The North Pole is 90° north of the Equator.

The Prime Meridian marks 0° longitude.

The Northern Hemisphere includes all lines of latitude north of the Equator.

The Southern Hemisphere contains all lines of latitude south of the Equator.

The Equator marks 0° latitude.

GEOGRAPHY SKILLS PRACTICE

Location Geographers can pinpoint the location of any place on Earth using lines of latitude and longitude. **Use Latitude and Longitude** What place on Earth is located at 0° longitude and 90° north latitude?

The Global Grid

Lines of longitude and latitude form a global grid. Geographers can identify the absolute location of any point on Earth by finding the latitude and longitude lines that intersect at that point. Lines of latitude are also called **parallels,** because they run east and west and are parallel to one another. This means that they never cross. Lines of longitude are also called **meridians.** Meridians run north and south, from the North Pole to the South Pole.

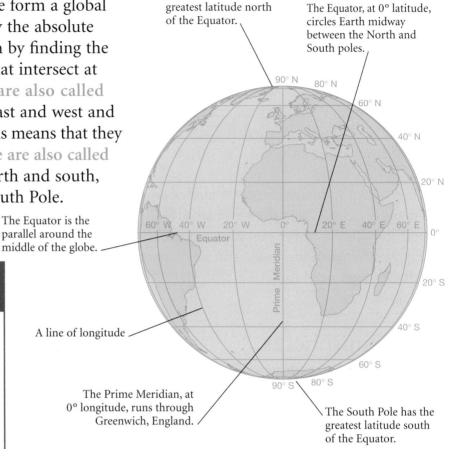

The North Pole has the greatest latitude north of the Equator.

The Equator, at 0° latitude, circles Earth midway between the North and South poles.

The Equator is the parallel around the middle of the globe.

A line of longitude

The Prime Meridian, at 0° longitude, runs through Greenwich, England.

The South Pole has the greatest latitude south of the Equator.

GEOGRAPHY SKILLS PRACTICE

Location Latitude and longitude are measured in degrees from imaginary lines on Earth's surface. **Compare and Contrast** From which line is latitude measured? Where do degrees of longitude start?

Read Ahead Read ahead to see how physical features may define regions.

Lines of longitude and latitude form a global grid. This grid allows geographers to state the absolute location, or exact address, of any place on Earth. For example, Savannah, Georgia, is located at 32° north latitude and 81° west longitude.

Geographers also discuss relative location, or the location of a place relative to another place. A geographer might give the relative location of Tallahassee, Florida, by saying, "Tallahassee is about 400 miles northwest of Miami."

Regions Geographers use the theme of regions to group places that have something in common. A region has a unifying human or physical feature such as population, history, climate, or landforms. For example, a country is a region with a common national government, and a city is a region with a common local government. A school district is a region defined by a common school system. Land areas can also be divided into regions that share physical features, such as mountains or a dry climate. Physical regions of the western United States include the Rocky Mountains and the Mojave (mo HAH vee) Desert.

Place Geographers also study place. Place includes the human and physical features at a specific location. To describe physical features, you might say the climate is hot or cold. Or you might say that the land is hilly. To discuss human features, you might talk about how many people live in a place and the kinds of work they do. You might also describe their religions or the languages they speak.

Movement The theme of movement helps explain how people, goods, and ideas get from one place to another. For example, when people from other countries came to the United States, they brought traditional foods that enriched the American way of life. The theme of movement helps you understand such cultural changes. Movement helps you understand many other facts about the world. For example, radios and computers have helped music from the United States to spread and become popular around the world.

Human-Environment Interaction This theme explores how people affect their environment, or their natural surroundings, and how their environment affects them. Perhaps they have cut trails into the mountainside. Or they may have learned how to survive with little water.

Farmers in India
These women are using the wind to separate grain for flour from chaff, or husks. Farming is an example of human-environment interaction. **Infer** *Do you think that these farmers use much modern machinery?*

✓ **Reading Check** **What is the purpose of the five themes of geography?**

Section 1 Assessment

Key Terms
Review the key terms at the beginning of this section. Use each term in a sentence that explains its meaning.

Target Reading Skill
What did you learn about physical features and regions by reading ahead?

Comprehension and Critical Thinking
1. (a) Recall What do geographers study?

(b) Explain What basic questions guide geographers?
2. (a) Explain How can the five themes help geographers?
(b) Predict How might a geographer use the theme of movement to describe the area where you live?
3. (a) Define What does the theme of location cover?
(b) Contrast How would a description of your home town as a place be different from a description of your home town's location?

Writing Activity
Read the passage above on human-environment interaction. Then write a paragraph describing ways that people in your area interact with their natural environment.

Go Online
PHSchool.com
For: An activity on the five themes of geography
Visit: PHSchool.com
Web Code: led-3101

Using Reliable Information

Would you seek medical advice from a plumber? Would you go to an encyclopedia to keep track of this season's basketball scores? Of course you wouldn't. Information is only as good as its source. To get reliable information, you have to go to an appropriate, trustworthy, and knowledgeable source.

Learn the Skill

Follow these steps to determine whether information is reliable.

1. **Find out the source of the information.** If it comes from a printed source, find out the name of the source, the author, and the date of publication. If it appeared on television, find out the name, date, and type of program (news, drama, or documentary). Do not accept information from Internet sites that do not give a date and an author.

2. **Find out if the information is recent enough for your purpose.** If you need current information, search for recent newspaper articles and up-to-date Web sites. Even if your topic is historic, researchers may have discovered new information about it. Seek the most current information.

3. **Find out if the information is accurate.** On certain topics, nearly all sources agree. For other topics, try to find information on which several respected sources agree. To be clear, you might say, "Several sources agree that" or "According to." If reliable sources disagree, you might note that disagreement in your writing.

4. **Look up the author's qualifications and methods.** When you check out an author's qualifications, always ask yourself whether he or she has a bias, or a one-sided view.

Is it Reliable?

To see if a source is reliable, ask
- What is the source?
- Is it recent enough?
- Is it accurate?
- Is the author qualified or biased?

Practice the Skill

Now use steps 1–4 to answer some questions about reliable information.

 Where might you go to find information on the location of the capital of Japan? On the population of North Carolina? On the major industries of Cuba? On presidential election results in Russia?

 Would a 20-year-old encyclopedia be a reliable source of information on active volcanoes in Hawaii? On the type of money used in Europe? On the longest river in the world? Explain your answers.

3 If you heard in a television documentary that most of the world's diamonds are mined in southern Africa, how could you check the accuracy of that statement?

4 Suppose you do an Internet search for information on the amount of beef produced in the United States last year. The search leads you to articles by three authors. Who would be the best source of information: an economist for the U.S. Department of Agriculture, the largest cattle rancher in Texas, or a leading university expert on beef production? Explain your answer.

Apply the Skill

If you had to research a report on the health of children in India, what kinds of sources would you search for reliable information? Name at least two sources, and explain why they would be reliable.

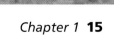

These boys are playing ball in front of the famed Taj Mahal, in India.

Prepare to Read

Objectives

In this section you will

1. Find out how maps and globes show information about Earth's surface.
2. See how mapmakers show Earth's round surface on flat maps.
3. Learn how to read maps.

Taking Notes

As you read this section, look for details about each of the following map topics: comparing maps with globes, map projections, and parts of a map. Copy the outline below and write each detail under the correct topic.

I. Maps and globes
 A. Globes
 B.
   1.
   2.
II. Projections
 A.

Target Reading Skill

Paraphrase When you paraphrase, you restate what you have read in your own words. For example, you could paraphrase the first paragraph after the heading Globes and Their Weaknesses this way:

"Mapmakers found that globes are the best way to show the shapes of continents, but at a different size."

As you read this section, paraphrase or restate the information after each red or blue heading.

Key Terms

- **scale** (skayl) *n.* relative size
- **distortion** (dih STAWR shun) *n.* loss of accuracy
- **geographic information systems** (jee uh GRAF ik in fur MAY shun SIS tumz) *n.* computer-based systems that provide information about locations
- **projection** (proh JEK shun) *n.* a way to map Earth on a flat surface
- **compass rose** (KUM pus rohz) *n.* a diagram of a compass showing direction
- **key** (kee) *n.* the section of a map that explains the symbols and colors on the map

A map can help you find directions.

Globes and Maps

As people explored Earth, they collected information about the shapes and sizes of islands, continents, and bodies of water. Map makers wanted to present this information accurately.

Globes and Their Weaknesses The best way was to put the information on a globe, or a model with the same round shape as Earth itself. By using an accurate shape for Earth, mapmakers could show the continents and oceans of Earth much as they really are. The only difference would be the scale, or relative size.

But there is a problem with globes. Try making a globe large enough to show the streets in your town. The globe might have to be larger than your school building. Imagine putting a globe that big in your pocket every morning! A globe just cannot be complete enough to be useful for finding directions and at the same time small enough to be convenient for everyday use.

Maps and Mapping People, therefore, use flat maps. Flat maps, however, present another problem. Earth is round. A map is flat. Can you flatten an orange peel without stretching or tearing it? There will be sections that are stretched or bent out of shape. The same thing happens when mapmakers create flat maps. It is impossible to show Earth on a flat surface without some distortion, or loss of accuracy. Something will look too large, too small, or out of place. Mapmakers have found ways to limit distortion of shape, size, distance, and direction.

Mapmakers rely on ground surveys, or measurements made on the ground, to make maps. They also use aerial photographs and satellite images.

Paraphrase
Target Skill Paraphrase the paragraph at the left in 25 words or fewer.

Aerial Photographs and Satellite Images

Aerial photographs are photographs of Earth's surface taken from the air. Satellite images are pictures of Earth's surface taken from a satellite in orbit. Both types of image are valuable sources of information for mapmakers because they provide current information about Earth's surface in great detail. But they are not useful for finding objects that are hidden, such as underground transit lines, or features such as streams that may be covered by vegetation. Also, like any map, flat aerial photographs and satellite images give a distorted view of Earth's surface.

Geographic Information Systems

A geographic information system, or GIS, is a computer-based system that links information to locations. A GIS is useful not only to geographers but also to governments and businesses. A GIS connects information with places. For example, if a business needs to decide where to open an office, it can use a GIS to choose a location where it will reach the most customers. Military planners may use a GIS to improve their knowledge of the places where troops will operate. A GIS also may be used to produce maps.

✓ **Reading Check** What are the advantages and disadvantages of each way of showing Earth's surface?

Satellite Image of North and South America
This satellite view shows parts of North and South America. A storm system covers part of the southeastern United States. **Analyze Images** *How might this image pose problems as a source for making maps?*

Getting It All on the Map

In 1569, a mapmaker named Gerardus Mercator (juh RAHR dus mur KAY tur) created a flat map to help sailors navigate, or plan journeys, around the globe. To make his map flat and to keep his grid rectangular, Mercator expanded the area between lines of longitude near the poles. Mercator's map was very useful to sailors because it showed directions accurately, even though sizes and distances were distorted. More than 400 years later, nearly all seagoing navigators still use the Mercator **projection,** or method of mapping Earth on a flat surface.

The Mercator Projection Mercator maps make areas near the poles look bigger than they are. This is because on a globe, the lines of longitude meet at the poles. To keep lines of longitude straight up and down, Mercator had to stretch the spaces between them north and south of the Equator. Land near the Equator was about the right size, but land areas near the poles became much larger. For example, on Mercator's map, Greenland looks bigger than South America. Greenland is actually only about one eighth as big as South America. Geographers call a Mercator projection a conformal map. It shows correct shapes but not true distances or sizes. What other areas, besides Greenland, do you think might look larger than they should?

Making a Mercator Map

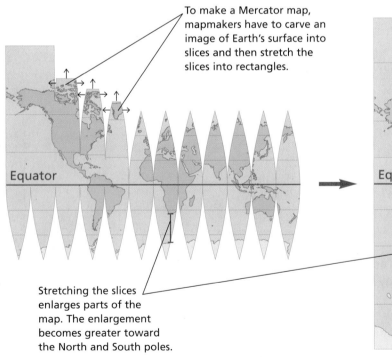

To make a Mercator map, mapmakers have to carve an image of Earth's surface into slices and then stretch the slices into rectangles.

Equator

Stretching the slices enlarges parts of the map. The enlargement becomes greater toward the North and South poles.

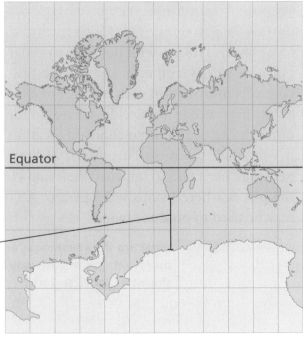

Equator

Equal-Area Projections An equal-area map shows the correct size of landmasses, but their shapes are altered. Lines that would be straight on Earth may be forced into curves to fit on the map's flat surface.

The Robinson Projection This projection is named for its designer, Arthur Robinson. Today, many geographers believe that the Robinson projection is the best world map available. It is used for most of the world maps in this book. This projection shows most distances, sizes, and shapes quite accurately. However, even a Robinson projection has distortions, especially in areas around the edges of the map.

Other Projections There are many other types of projections besides the ones shown here. Some are useful for showing small areas but not for showing the whole world. Others are good for specific purposes, such as planning a plane's flight route.

✓ **Reading Check** What are the strengths and weaknesses of the Mercator, equal-area, and Robinson projections?

Making an Equal-Area Map

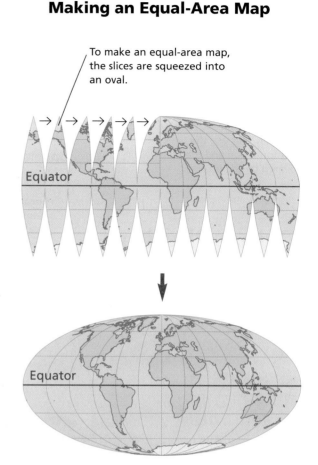

To make an equal-area map, the slices are squeezed into an oval.

Equator

Equator

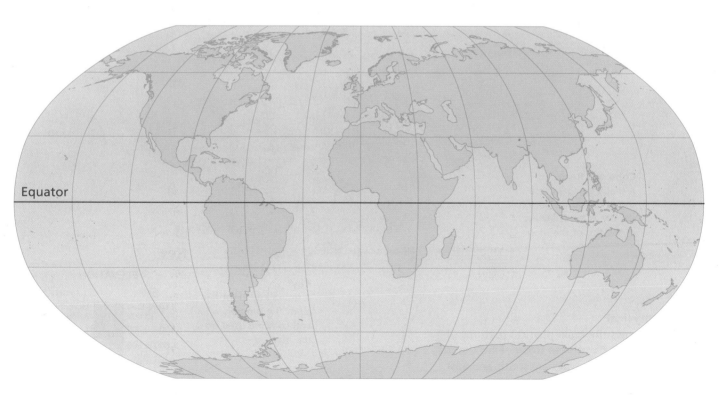

Equator

The World: Robinson Projection

Reading Maps

Look at the maps shown on these two pages. One is a physical map of the country of China. The other is a highway map of the state of Georgia. These maps cover completely different areas and show different kinds of information. Despite their differences, both maps have all of the basic parts that you will find on most maps. Knowing how to use these parts will help you to read and understand any kind of map.

Title
Most maps have a title near the top of the map. The title generally tells you the type of information and the area covered on the map.

Locator Globe
Maps may include a locator globe that shows on a globe the location of the area covered by the map.

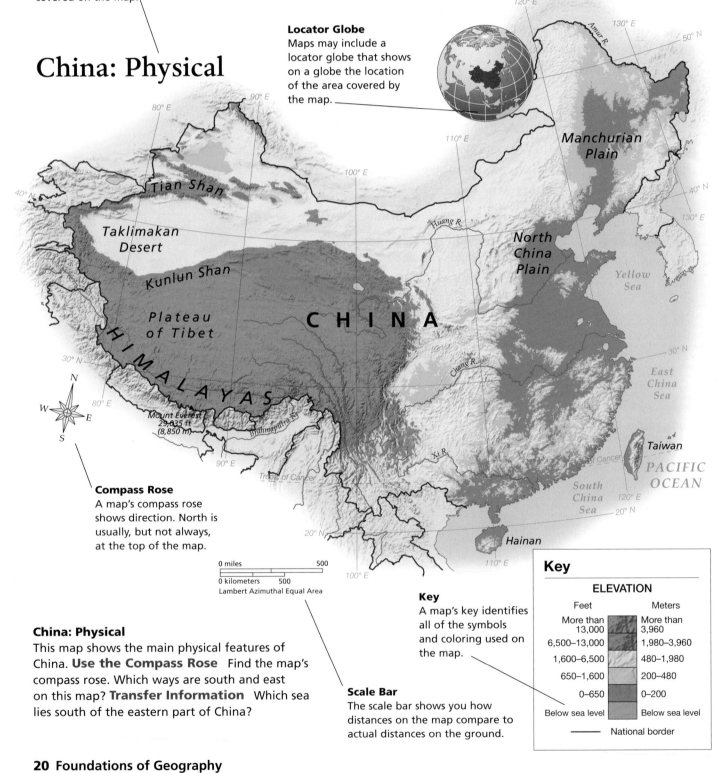

China: Physical

Compass Rose
A map's compass rose shows direction. North is usually, but not always, at the top of the map.

China: Physical
This map shows the main physical features of China. **Use the Compass Rose** Find the map's compass rose. Which ways are south and east on this map? **Transfer Information** Which sea lies south of the eastern part of China?

Scale Bar
The scale bar shows you how distances on the map compare to actual distances on the ground.

Key
A map's key identifies all of the symbols and coloring used on the map.

Key

ELEVATION

Feet		Meters
More than 13,000		More than 3,960
6,500–13,000		1,980–3,960
1,600–6,500		480–1,980
650–1,600		200–480
0–650		0–200
Below sea level		Below sea level
	— National border	

Georgia Highways

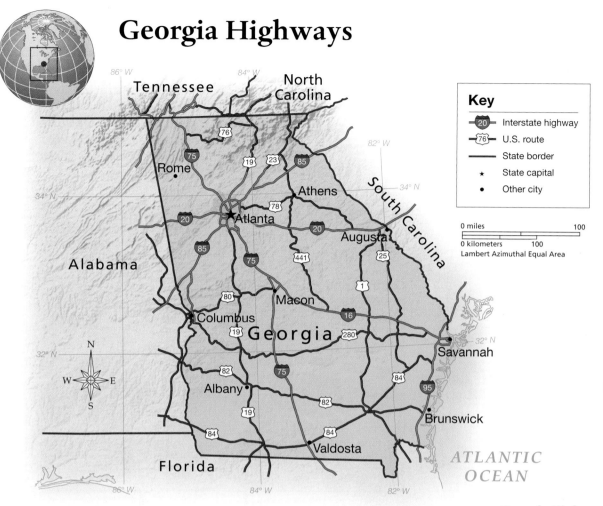

Key

—⟨20⟩—	Interstate highway
—⟨76⟩—	U.S. route
——	State border
★	State capital
•	Other city

0 miles — 100
0 kilometers — 100
Lambert Azimuthal Equal Area

The Parts of a Map Both maps on these pages have what geographers call a **compass rose,** a diagram of a compass showing direction. If you want to find directions such as north, south, east, or west, just look for the map's compass rose.

Both maps also have a scale bar. The scale bar shows how distances on the map compare to actual distances on the land. Scales vary, depending on the map. If you compare the scale bar on the map of China to the bar on the map of Georgia, you will see that the map of China covers much greater distances on the ground even though the map is not much bigger.

On any map, the **key,** or legend, is the part of the map that explains the symbols and shading on the map. For example, the key on the highway map of Georgia shows the colored lines that stand for different kinds of highways. While some maps use symbols, other maps, like the physical map of China, use coloring to present information. The key shows which colors stand for which elevations.

✔ **Reading Check** How do the different parts of a map help you to find information?

Georgia Highways
Notice that this map of Georgia has the same basic parts as the physical map of China: a title, a key, a locator globe, a compass rose, and a scale bar.
Use Scale *Using a ruler, measure the distance on the map between Atlanta and Macon. Then hold the ruler against the scale bar. How many miles is Atlanta from Macon?*

Maps of Different Scale

Maps with different scales have different uses. Maps with a large scale, such as the map of Greater London, give a general picture of a large area. Maps with a smaller scale, such as the map of Central London, show more detail and are useful for finding landmarks.

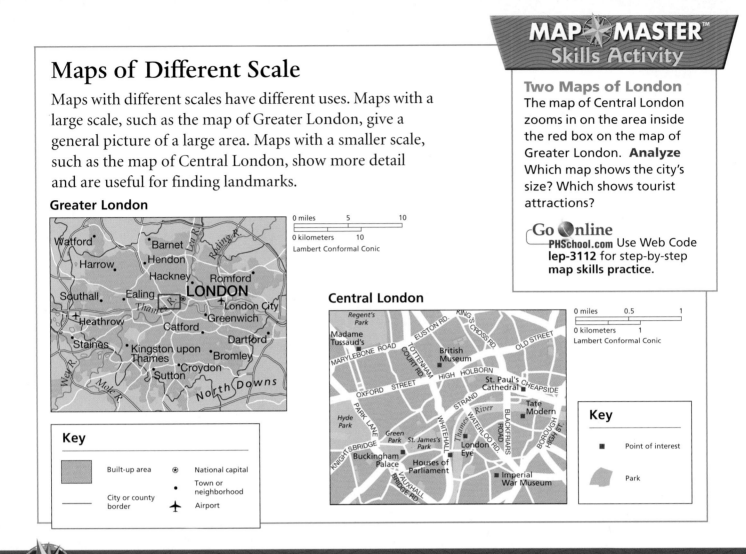

Greater London

0 miles 5 10
0 kilometers 10
Lambert Conformal Conic

Central London

0 miles 0.5 1
0 kilometers 1
Lambert Conformal Conic

Key

Built-up area
City or county border
⊛ National capital
• Town or neighborhood
✈ Airport

Key

■ Point of interest
Park

MAP MASTER™
Skills Activity

Two Maps of London
The map of Central London zooms in on the area inside the red box on the map of Greater London. **Analyze** Which map shows the city's size? Which shows tourist attractions?

Go Online
PHSchool.com Use Web Code **lep-3112** for step-by-step **map skills practice.**

Section 2 Assessment

Key Terms
Review the key terms at the beginning of this section. Use each term in a sentence that explains its meaning.

Target Reading Skill
Go back and find the paragraph under the heading The Mercator Projection. Paraphrase this paragraph, or rewrite it in your own words.

Comprehension and Critical Thinking
1. (a) Identify What information sources do mapmakers use?
(b) Evaluate What are the advantages and disadvantages of each information source?

(c) Predict To make a map of small streams in an area of thick vegetation, what source would a mapmaker most likely use?
2. (a) Recall What are the advantages and disadvantages of a Mercator projection and of an equal-area projection?
(b) Apply Information Which projection would you use to plan a voyage by ship in a straight line across an ocean?
3. (a) Define On a map, what are the key, title, compass rose, and scale bar?
(b) Synthesize Information If you made a map of places to shop in your area, what might you put in the map's key?

Writing Activity
Look at the physical map of China. Plan a route for a trip from its east coast to its western border. Using information from the map, describe the landscape that you will see along the way.

Go Online
PHSchool.com

For: An activity on maps
Visit: PHSchool.com
Web Code: led-3102

Review and Assessment

◆ Chapter Summary

Section 1: The Five Themes of Geography

- Geography is the study of Earth.
- Geographers can pinpoint any location on the surface of Earth using lines of latitude and longitude, which form an imaginary grid.
- There are five themes of geography—location, regions, place, movement, and human-environment interaction. They offer five ways to gather and understand information about places on Earth.

Section 2: The Geographer's Tools

- Maps can show more details of Earth's surface than globes, but showing Earth's round surface on flat maps causes distortion.
- Projections are different ways of showing Earth's round surface on a flat map.
- Parts of the map such as the key, compass rose, and scale bar can help you to find and understand information on any map.

Earth viewed from space

◆ Key Terms

Each of the statements below contains a key term from the chapter. If the statement is true, write *true*. If it is false, rewrite the statement to make it true.

1. The cardinal directions are north, east, south, and west.

2. Latitude is a measure of the distance north or south of Earth's Equator.

3. Longitude is a measure of the distance north or south of the Equator.

4. A hemisphere is a half of Earth.

5. A meridian is a line of latitude.

6. The scale is the part of the map that shows cardinal directions.

7. A projection is a way of mapping the flat surface of Earth onto a round globe.

8. The compass rose is the part of a map that shows symbols and their meanings.

9. The key is the part of the map that shows relative distances.

Review and Assessment (continued)

◆ Comprehension and Critical Thinking

10. (a) List What five themes can help you organize infomation about Earth?
(b) Categorize Under which theme would you discuss building a dam on a river in a desert?

11. (a) Recall How do geographers pinpoint the exact location of any place on Earth?
(b) Infer Why might it be useful to know the exact location of a place?

12. (a) Identify What unifying characteristics might be used to describe a region?
(b) Draw Conclusions Might a single place be part of more than one region? Explain.

13. (a) Recall What are the disadvantages of globes? What are the disadvantages of maps?
(b) Apply Information Which would be more helpful for studying the exact shapes of continents, a globe or a map?

14. (a) Describe What are the main features of the Mercator projection?
(b) Infer Why is the Mercator projection still used by navigators today?
(c) Generalize When might you want to use a projection other than the Mercator projection?

15. (a) List What are the basic parts that most maps have?
(b) Synthesize Information How can you use the parts of a new map to understand it?

◆ Skills Practice

Using Reliable Information In the Skills for Life activity in this chapter, you learned how to use reliable information. Review the steps for this skill. Then apply them to the text below. Suppose you found this text in a teen magazine. Decide whether you think the information is reliable. Write a sentence that explains why or why not.

"Japan is a very clean country. I spent a whole week in Japan. The buses and trains were very clean. I didn't go inside a Japanese home, but I bet they are very clean, too."

◆ Writing Activity: Geography

Write down the name of the place where you live. Below that name, list the five themes of geography. Next to each theme, describe how it applies to your city, town, or state.

MAP·MASTER™ Skills Activity

The Globe

Place Location For each place listed below, write the letter from the map that shows its location.

1. Prime Meridian
2. Equator
3. North Pole
4. South Pole
5. Europe
6. Africa
7. South America
8. North America

Go Online
PHSchool.com Use Web Code **lep-3113** for an interactive map.

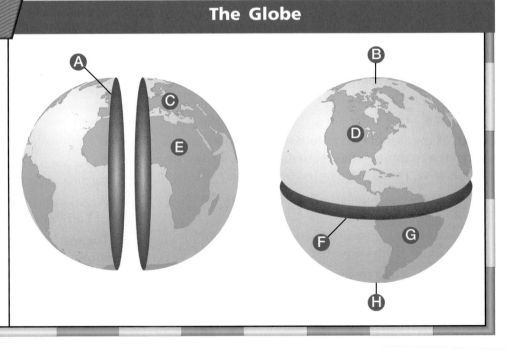

Standardized Test Prep

Test-Taking Tips

Some questions on standardized tests ask you to make mental maps. Do the exercise in the box below. Then follow the tips to answer the sample question.

> Draw a simple map of the world based on maps you have seen. Draw a rough shape for each landmass. Draw the Prime Meridian and the Equator across the map.

> **TIP** Find the continents on your map. How is the world divided into hemispheres?

Pick the letter that best answers the question.

Which continent lies completely in both the Northern Hemisphere and the Western Hemisphere?

A Europe

B Greenland

C North America

D Australia

> **TIP** Beware of careless errors. Read the question twice and think carefully about each answer choice.

Think It Through Australia is located completely in both the Southern Hemisphere and the Eastern Hemisphere. Europe is in the Northern Hemisphere but also mostly in the Eastern Hemisphere. Greenland is completely in both the Northern Hemisphere and the Western Hemisphere—as the question asks. But be careful! Greenland is not a continent. The answer is C.

Practice Questions

Use the tips above and other tips in this book to help you answer the following questions.

1. Which of the following is NOT a tool a geographer would use to study absolute location?

   A cardinal directions

   B climate

   C lines of latitude

   D degrees

2. What disadvantage do all flat maps share?

   A They have some sort of distortion.

   B They are hard to carry.

   C There are few sources to create them.

   D They can only show areas at a small scale.

3. A map with cities and colored lines marked with numbers is probably a type of

   A climate map.

   B road map.

   C physical map.

   D vegetation map.

Read the passage below and answer the question that follows.

This area is located in the United States, west of the Mississippi River. It is mainly hot and dry, with little rainfall, so people have built many dams there. Its landforms include rivers, canyons, and deserts.

4. Which of the five themes are used to describe this area?

   A location, movement, regions

   B movement, place, regions, human-environment interaction

   C regions, location, movement

   D location, place, human-environment interaction

Go Online
PHSchool.com

Use Web Code **lea-3103** for a **Chapter 1 self-test.**

Chapter Preview

This chapter will introduce you to the physical geography of Earth, including the planet's structure, climate, and vegetation.

Section 1
Our Planet, Earth

Section 2
Forces Shaping Earth

Section 3
Climate and Weather

Section 4
How Climate Affects Vegetation

Target Reading Skill

Context In this chapter you will focus on using context to help you understand unfamiliar words. Context includes the words, phrases, and sentences surrounding a word.

▶ Delicate Arch in Arches National Park, Utah

Our Planet, Earth

Prepare to Read

Objectives

In this section you will
1. Learn about Earth's movement in relation to the sun.
2. Explore seasons and latitude.

Taking Notes

Copy the table below. As you read this section, fill in the table with information about the movements of Earth relative to the sun, days and nights, seasons, and latitude. Add more lines as you need them.

Earth and the Sun

Rotation	Night and Day	Revolution and Seasons	Latitudes
•	•	•	•
•	•	•	•
•	•	•	•
•	•	•	•

Target Reading Skill

Use Context Clues You can sometimes find the meaning of a word by using context—the words and sentences around that word. In some cases the context will describe the word. In this example, the phrase in italics describes a planet:

A planet is a *large object that circles a star.*

As you read, look at the context for the word *galaxy* in the paragraph below. What do you think *galaxy* means?

Key Terms

- **orbit** (AWR bit) *n.* the path one body makes as it circles around another
- **revolution** (rev uh LOO shun) *n.* circular motion
- **axis** (AK sis) *n.* an imaginary line through Earth between the North and South poles, around which Earth turns
- **rotation** (roh TAY shun) *n.* a complete turn

The Milky Way Galaxy

Earth and the Sun

Earth, the sun, the planets, and the stars in the sky are all part of a galaxy, or family of stars. Our galaxy is just one of the billions of galaxies in the universe. We call our galaxy the Milky Way because, in a dark night sky, away from city lights, its billions of stars look like a trail of spilled milk. Our sun is one of those stars. The sun is just a tiny speck compared to the rest of the Milky Way, but it is the center of everything for Earth and the other planets in the solar system. The solar system includes Earth, the other planets, and other objects that orbit the sun.

Even though the sun is about 93 million miles (150 million kilometers) away, it provides Earth with heat and light. Earth travels around the sun in a nearly circular **orbit,** which is the path one body makes as it circles around another. Earth takes 365¼ days, or one year, to complete one **revolution,** or circular motion, in its orbit around the sun.

Understanding Days and Nights As Earth circles the sun, it also spins in space. Earth turns around its **axis**—an imaginary line running through Earth between the North and South poles. Each complete turn, or **rotation**, takes about 24 hours. As Earth rotates, it is night on the side away from the sun. As Earth turns toward the sun, the sun appears to rise. When a side of Earth faces the sun, it is daytime. Then, as that side of Earth turns away from the sun, the sun appears to set.

Time Zones Earth rotates toward the east, so the day starts earlier in the east. The time difference is just a few seconds per mile. If every town had its own local time, it would be very confusing. So, governments have divided the world into standard time zones. Times in neighboring zones are one hour apart. There are also a few nonstandard time zones with times less than a full hour away from their neighbors.

Links to
Math

Time Zones and Longitude Earth's surface is divided into 360 degrees of longitude: 180 degrees east and west of the Prime Meridian. Since Earth rotates at a steady rate in about 24 hours, its 24 standard time zones are centered the same number of degrees of longitude apart. Can you find this number? (*Hint:* The number is 360° ÷ 24.)

✓ **Reading Check** What is the connection between Earth's rotation and the change from day to night?

The World: Time Zones

MAP MASTER™
Skills Activity

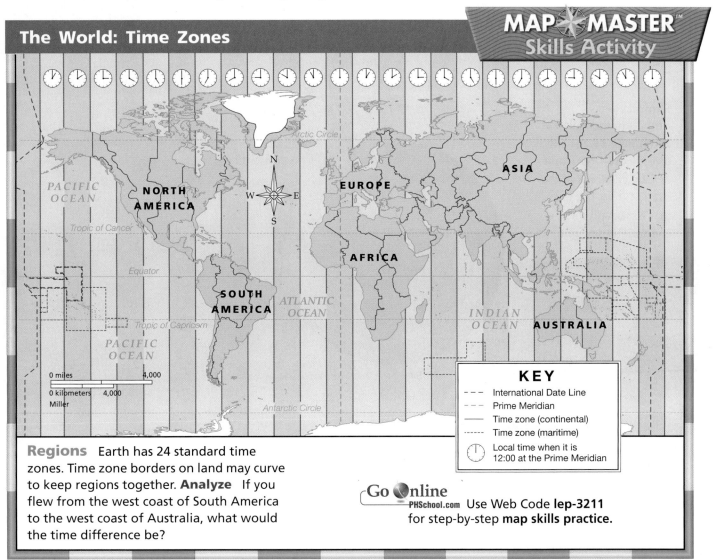

KEY
- - - International Date Line
- - - Prime Meridian
—— Time zone (continental)
-·-·- Time zone (maritime)
⊕ Local time when it is 12:00 at the Prime Meridian

Regions Earth has 24 standard time zones. Time zone borders on land may curve to keep regions together. **Analyze** If you flew from the west coast of South America to the west coast of Australia, what would the time difference be?

Go Online
PHSchool.com Use Web Code **lep-3211** for step-by-step **map skills practice.**

Seasons and Latitude

The axis of Earth is tilted relative to its orbit. At different points in Earth's orbit, the Northern Hemisphere may tilt toward or away from the sun. At other points in the orbit, neither hemisphere tilts toward or away from the sun. The revolution of the tilted planet Earth causes seasons.

At the summer solstice, the Northern Hemisphere is tilted farthest toward the sun. Places in this hemisphere have longer daylight and more direct sunlight at the solstice than at other times of the year. This direct sunlight causes the heat of summer.

Use Context Clues If you do not know what the summer solstice is, look at the words that follow this term in the text. They describe the summer solstice.

The Revolution of Earth

As Earth travels around the sun, the tilt of its axis causes our seasons. Each hemisphere shifts from the long days and direct sun of summer to the short days and indirect sun of winter, and then back again. This diagram shows seasons in the Northern Hemisphere.

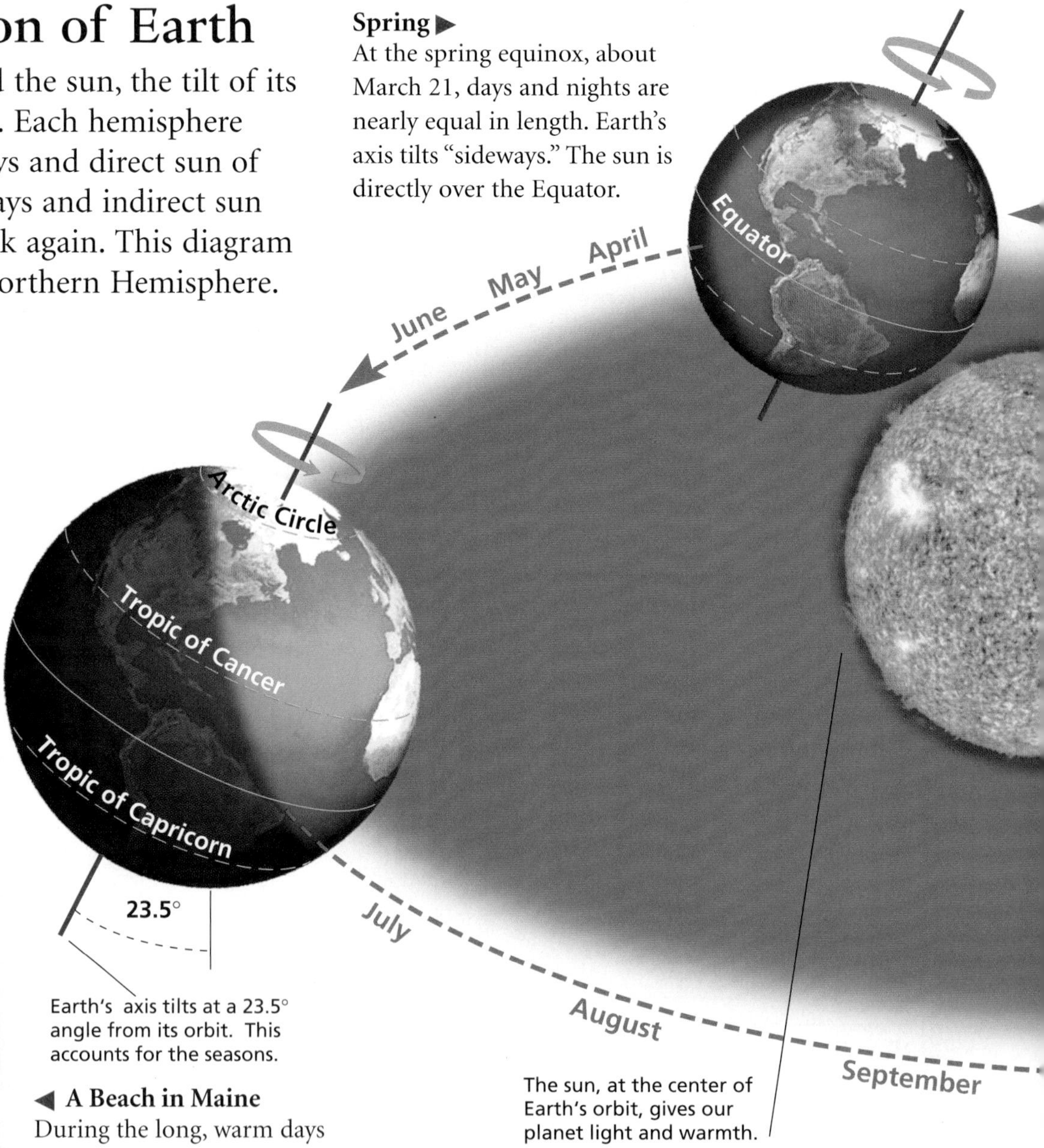

Summer ▶
At the summer solstice, about June 21, the sun is directly over the Tropic of Cancer. North of the Arctic Circle, the sun never sets, and there is continuous daylight.

Spring ▶
At the spring equinox, about March 21, days and nights are nearly equal in length. Earth's axis tilts "sideways." The sun is directly over the Equator.

June   May   April

Equator

Arctic Circle

Tropic of Cancer

Tropic of Capricorn

23.5°

Earth's axis tilts at a 23.5° angle from its orbit. This accounts for the seasons.

July

August

September

The sun, at the center of Earth's orbit, gives our planet light and warmth.

◀ A Beach in Maine
During the long, warm days of summer, green plants grow and people head for beaches.

Diagram not to scale

As Earth moves through its orbit, the Northern Hemisphere is tilted farther from the sun. Sunlight is less direct, and we have the chill of fall. When the Northern Hemisphere is tilted farthest from the sun at the winter solstice, days are short, the sun's rays reach us at a steep angle, and we have cold weather. Finally, Earth's revolution moves the Northern Hemisphere back toward the sun, and we have the warming trend of spring.

When the Northern Hemisphere is tilted toward the sun, the Southern Hemisphere is tilted away, and vice versa, so the seasons are reversed in the Southern Hemisphere.

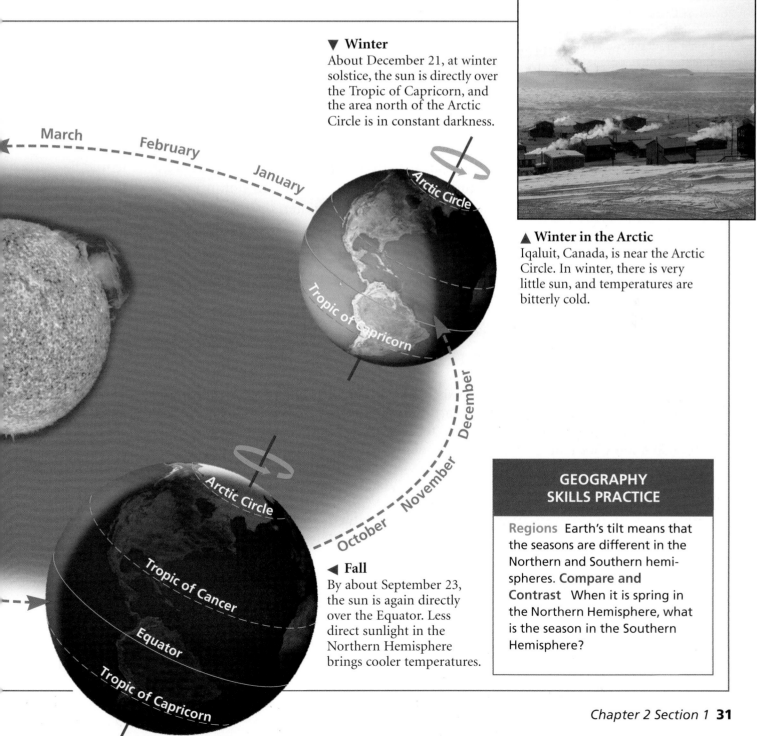

▼ Winter
About December 21, at winter solstice, the sun is directly over the Tropic of Capricorn, and the area north of the Arctic Circle is in constant darkness.

▲ Winter in the Arctic
Iqaluit, Canada, is near the Arctic Circle. In winter, there is very little sun, and temperatures are bitterly cold.

◄ Fall
By about September 23, the sun is again directly over the Equator. Less direct sunlight in the Northern Hemisphere brings cooler temperatures.

March
February
January
Arctic Circle
Tropic of Capricorn

Arctic Circle
Tropic of Cancer
Equator
Tropic of Capricorn

October November December

GEOGRAPHY SKILLS PRACTICE

Regions Earth's tilt means that the seasons are different in the Northern and Southern hemispheres. **Compare and Contrast** When it is spring in the Northern Hemisphere, what is the season in the Southern Hemisphere?

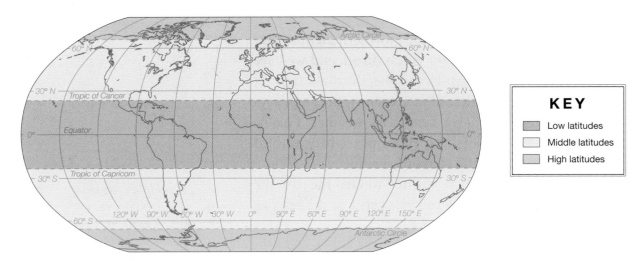

KEY

- Low latitudes
- Middle latitudes
- High latitudes

Zones of Latitude

The low latitudes, or tropics, are the single orange band around the Equator. The middle latitudes are the two yellow bands just to the north and south. The two green zones in the far north and south are the high latitudes, or polar zones.

Latitudes The areas between the Tropic of Cancer and the Tropic of Capricorn are called the low latitudes, or the tropics. The tropics have fairly direct sunlight and hot weather all year.

The areas above the Arctic Circle and below the Antarctic Circle are the high latitudes, or the polar zones. Though the polar zones may receive long hours of sunlight during the summer, the sun is never directly overhead. They are cool or very cold all year.

The areas between the high and low latitudes are the middle latitudes, or the temperate zones. In summer, these areas receive fairly direct sunlight. In winter, they get very indirect sunlight. So, the middle latitudes have marked seasons: a hot summer, a cold winter, and a moderate spring and fall.

✓ **Reading Check** What is the relation between seasons and latitude?

Section 1 Assessment

Key Terms

Review the key terms at the beginning of this section. Use each term in a sentence that explains its meaning.

Target Reading Skill

Find the phrase *winter solstice* on page 31. Use context to figure out its meaning. What do you think it means? What clues helped you find a meaning?

Comprehension and Critical Thinking

1. (a) Define What is the rotation of Earth?

(b) Synthesize Information How is Earth's rotation connected to the change from day to night?

2. (a) Identify On the time zone map on page 29, find the time zone where you live.

(b) Evaluate What is the time difference between your home and Greenwich, England?

(c) Analyze How is this time difference related to Earth's rotation?

3. (a) Recall What is Earth's tilt?

(b) Describe How does Earth's orbit affect its tilted hemispheres?

(c) Identify Cause and Effect How do Earth's tilt and orbit cause the seasons?

Writing Activity

Write a short passage for a younger child, explaining the movements of Earth.

For: An activity on our planet, Earth
Visit: PHSchool.com
Web Code: led-3201

Forces Shaping Earth

Prepare to Read

Objectives

In this section you will
1. Learn about the planet Earth.
2. Explore the forces inside Earth.
3. Explore the forces on Earth's surface.

Taking Notes

As you read this section, look for details about Earth's structure, Earth's landforms, forces inside Earth, how continents move, and forces on Earth's surface. Copy the web diagram below, add more branches and ovals as needed, and write each detail in the correct oval.

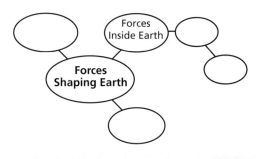

Forces
Inside Earth

Forces
Shaping Earth

Target Reading Skill

Use Context Clues You can sometimes find the meaning of a word or phrase by using context. Sometimes the context will define or restate the word. In this example, the phrase in italics defines *continent*:

> A continent, or *one of Earth's large land areas . . .*

As you read, look at the context for the phrase *Ring of Fire* in the paragraph below. What do you think the phrase *Ring of Fire* means?

Key Terms

- **core** (kawr) *n.* the sphere of very hot metal at the center of Earth
- **mantle** (MAN tul) *n.* the thick layer around Earth's core
- **crust** (krust) *n.* the thin, rocky layer on Earth's surface
- **magma** (MAG muh) *n.* soft, nearly molten rock
- **plate** (playt) *n.* a huge block of Earth's crust
- **weathering** (WETH ur ing) *n.* a process that breaks rocks down into small pieces
- **erosion** (ee ROH zhun) *n.* the removal of small pieces of rock by water, ice, or wind

Understanding Earth

Around the rim of the Pacific Ocean is a string of volcanoes and earthquake belts called the "Ring of Fire." About 80 percent of the world's earthquakes and many of the world's active volcanoes occur in that ring. Earthquakes and volcanoes are two forces that shape and reshape Earth. They are one reason why Earth's surface constantly changes. They also provide clues about Earth's structure.

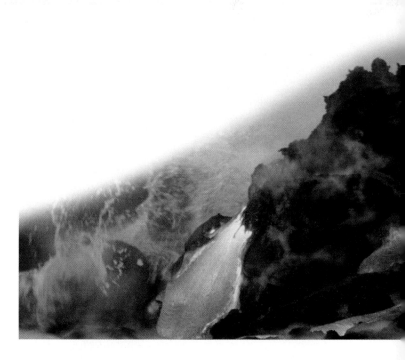

Hot rock from inside Earth flows into the Pacific Ocean to form new land in Hawaii.

What Is Earth Made Of? To understand the forces that shape Earth, you must study Earth's structure. A sphere of very hot metal at the center of Earth is called the **core.** The **mantle** is a thick, hot, rocky layer around the core. The thin layer of rocks and minerals that surrounds the mantle is called the **crust.** In effect, the crust floats on top of the mantle. The heat of the core and mantle helps shape Earth's crust. The surface of the crust includes Earth's land areas as well as the ocean floors.

Earth's Layers

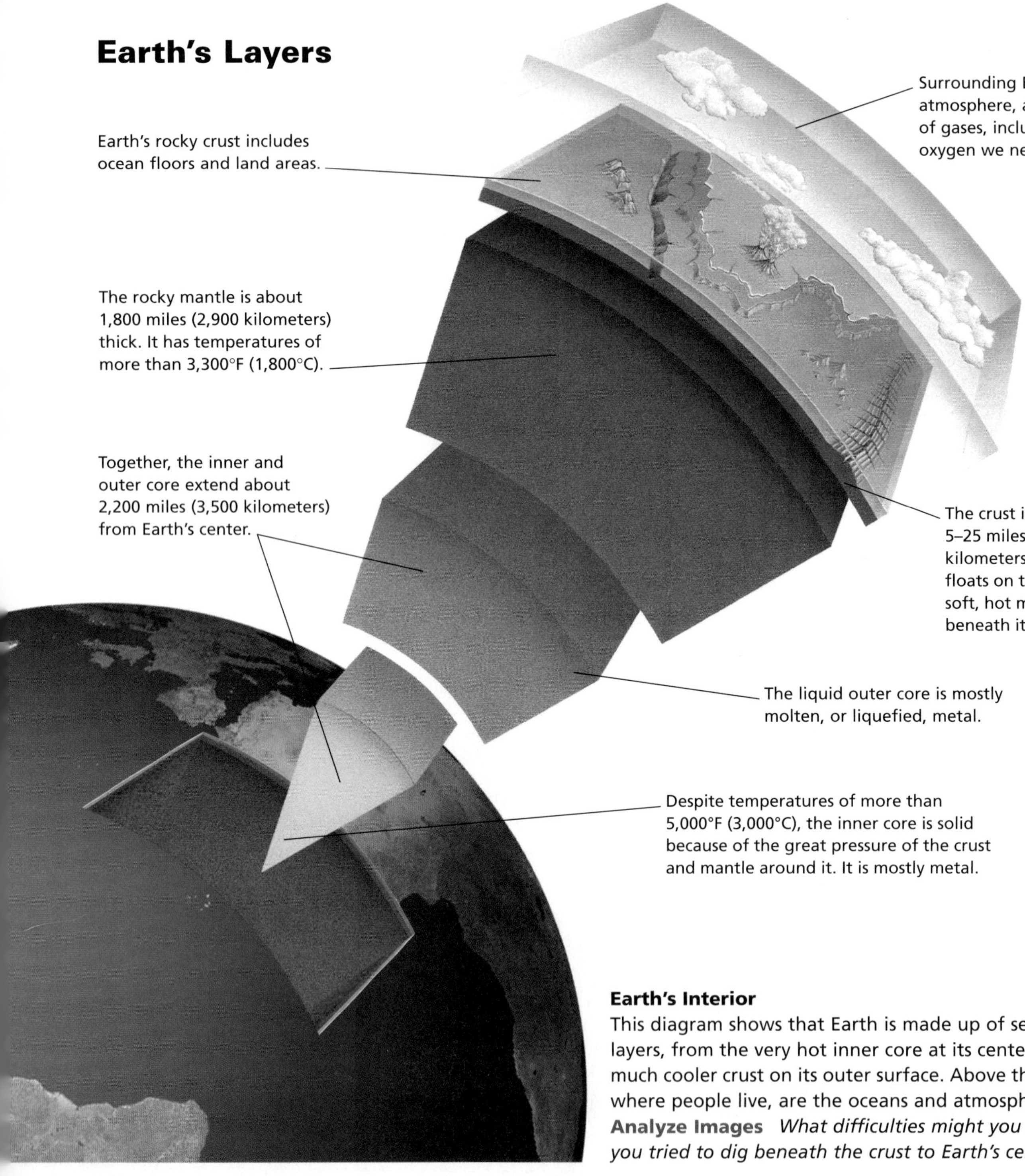

Earth's rocky crust includes ocean floors and land areas.

The rocky mantle is about 1,800 miles (2,900 kilometers) thick. It has temperatures of more than 3,300°F (1,800°C).

Together, the inner and outer core extend about 2,200 miles (3,500 kilometers) from Earth's center.

Surrounding Earth is the atmosphere, a layer of gases, including the oxygen we need to live.

The crust is only 5–25 miles (8–40 kilometers) thick. It floats on top of the soft, hot mantle beneath it.

The liquid outer core is mostly molten, or liquefied, metal.

Despite temperatures of more than 5,000°F (3,000°C), the inner core is solid because of the great pressure of the crust and mantle around it. It is mostly metal.

Earth's Interior
This diagram shows that Earth is made up of several layers, from the very hot inner core at its center to the much cooler crust on its outer surface. Above the crust, where people live, are the oceans and atmosphere.
Analyze Images *What difficulties might you have if you tried to dig beneath the crust to Earth's center?*

Water and Air Less than 30 percent of Earth's surface is land. Water covers more than 70 percent of Earth's surface in lakes, rivers, seas, and oceans. The oceans hold about 97 percent of Earth's water. This water is salty. Very little of Earth's water is fresh water, or water without salt. Most fresh water is frozen in ice sheets near the North and South poles. People can use only a small part of Earth's fresh water. This fresh water comes from lakes, rivers, and ground water, which are fed by rain.

Above Earth's surface is the atmosphere, a layer of gases a few miles thick. It provides life-giving oxygen to people and animals, and carbon dioxide to plants.

Landforms Many different landforms, or shapes and types of land, cover Earth's land surfaces. Mountains are landforms that rise more than 2,000 feet (610 meters) above sea level or the surrounding flatlands. They are wide at the bottom and rise steeply to a narrow peak or ridge. A volcano is a kind of mountain. Hills are landforms with rounded tops, which rise above the surrounding land but are lower and less steep than mountains. A plateau is a large, mostly flat area that rises above the surrounding land. At least one side of a plateau has a steep slope. Plains are large areas of flat or gently rolling land.

✓ **Reading Check** Which layer of Earth contains all of its landforms?

Use Context Clues If you do not know what the atmosphere is, notice that a definition follows the phrase. The definition tells you what the word means.

Land and Water
Ice floes float near Alexander Island, off the coast of Antarctica. Salt water covers most of Earth's surface. Most fresh water is ice, frozen in polar regions such as Antarctica. **Analyze Images** *What landforms can you see in this photograph?*

Forces Inside Earth

Heat deep inside Earth is constantly reshaping the planet's surface. The intense heat causes rock to rise toward the surface. Where streams of this soft, nearly molten rock called **magma** reach Earth's crust, they push up the crust to form volcanoes. Volcanoes spew molten rock, or lava, from inside Earth. Streams of magma may also push the crust apart along seams. Huge blocks of Earth's crust called **plates** are separated by these seams. Plates may include continents or parts of continents. Each plate also includes part of the ocean floor. Along seams, mainly beneath oceans, streams of magma rise from inside Earth. As the magma cools, it forms new crust and pushes the old crust away from the seams.

How Continents Move

Rising magma forms new crust along seams between Earth's plates. Beneath the surface, some scientists believe, magma moves like a conveyor belt. The belt drags the growing plates and the continents that they carry.

Where two plates push against each other, the pressure makes the crust bend and buckle to form steep mountains.

Plates move only an inch or two (a few centimeters) a year.

Crust

Mantle

Earthquakes occur when blocks of crust slide sideways against each other.

Some scientists think that sheets of mantle act like conveyor belts that move the plates of crust above them.

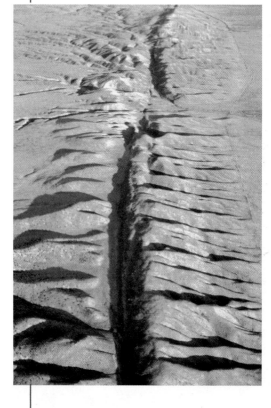

◀ **Two plates rub together along the San Andreas Fault in California.**

Sheets of magma rise to the surface from Earth's interior along a seam between plates of crust.

Volcanoes and Earthquakes Where a plate of ocean crust collides with a plate of continental crust, the ocean crust plunges underneath the continental plate and melts. Molten rock surges upward, exploding onto the surface through a volcano. The Ring of Fire surrounds the plates that make up the Pacific Ocean. Streams of magma also form volcanoes at places other than plate boundaries. Such volcanoes have shaped the Hawaiian Islands, which are far from a plate boundary.

When two plates push together, the crust cracks and splinters from the pressure. The cracks in Earth's crust are called faults. When blocks of crust rub against each other along faults, they release huge amounts of energy in the form of earthquakes.

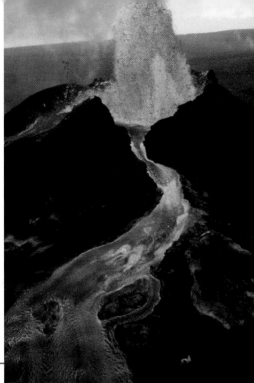

▲ **Molten rock pours from a volcano in Hawaii.**

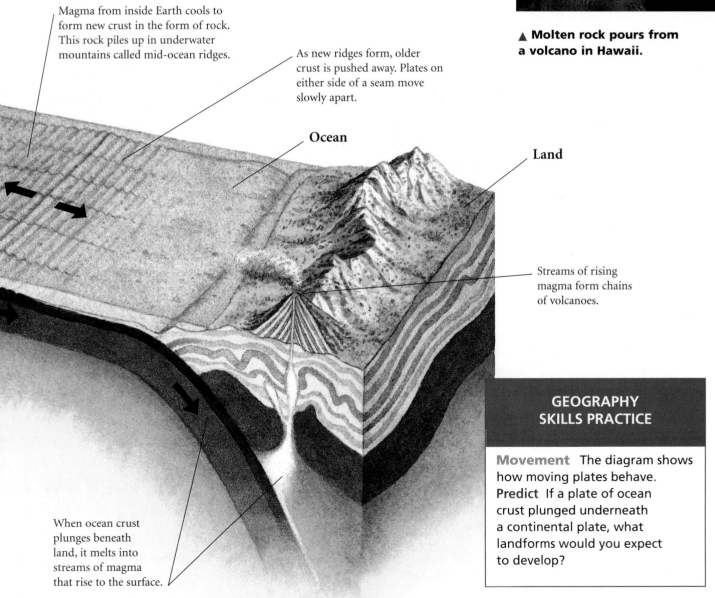

Magma from inside Earth cools to form new crust in the form of rock. This rock piles up in underwater mountains called mid-ocean ridges.

As new ridges form, older crust is pushed away. Plates on either side of a seam move slowly apart.

Ocean

Land

Streams of rising magma form chains of volcanoes.

When ocean crust plunges beneath land, it melts into streams of magma that rise to the surface.

GEOGRAPHY SKILLS PRACTICE

Movement The diagram shows how moving plates behave. **Predict** If a plate of ocean crust plunged underneath a continental plate, what landforms would you expect to develop?

Explore the movement of continental plates.

A World of Moving Plates For hundreds of years, geographers wondered how Earth's landmasses took their present shapes and positions. When they looked at the globe, they thought they saw matching shapes in continents that are very far apart. Now that they know how forces inside Earth move continents, they know that those continents were once close together.

✓ **Reading Check** How do continents move apart?

Plate Movements

Plates 250 million years ago

Plates Shifting Through Time

Most geographers believe that long ago Earth had only one huge continent. They call it Pangaea (pan JEE uh). About 200 million years ago, they conclude, plate movement began to split Pangaea apart. They think that these pieces came to form the continents that we know today. **Analyze** *According to these maps, which present-day continents were once joined together?*

Plates 150 million years ago

Plates 75 million years ago

Present-Day Plates

The map below shows Earth's modern plates and plate edges. It also shows how the plates are moving. Earthquakes and volcanoes cluster along plate edges. **Identify** *Which plate is colliding with the North American Plate?*

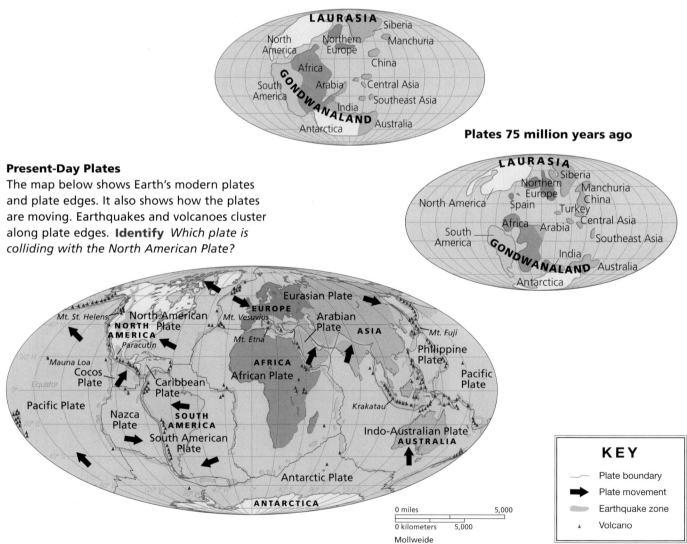

KEY

- ‿ Plate boundary
- ➤ Plate movement
- ▨ Earthquake zone
- ▲ Volcano

0 miles 5,000
0 kilometers 5,000
Mollweide

Forces on Earth's Surface

Forces inside Earth move plates apart, produce volcanoes, and slowly build up Earth's crust. Other forces slowly wear it down and reshape it. The forces that wear Earth down are not as dramatic as volcanoes, but over time they are just as effective.

Weathering is a process that breaks rocks down into tiny pieces. Water, ice, and living things like lichens on rocks all cause weathering. Weathering helps create soil, too. Tiny pieces of rock combine with decayed animal and plant material to form soil.

Once this breaking down has taken place, landforms are reshaped by **erosion,** or the removal of small pieces of rock by water, ice, or wind. Hundreds of millions of years ago, the Appalachian Mountains in the eastern United States were as high as the Rocky Mountains of the western United States now are. Rain, snow, and wind slowly wore them down into much lower peaks.

When water, ice, and wind remove material, they deposit it downstream or downwind to create new landforms. Plains are often made of material carried from upstream by rivers.

✔ **Reading Check** What landforms are products of weathering and erosion?

Weathering and erosion formed this natural sandstone bridge in Jordan.

![compass star] **Section 2 Assessment**

Key Terms
Review the key terms at the beginning of this section. Use each term in a sentence that explains its meaning.

Target Reading Skill
Find the word *landforms* in the last paragraph of page 35. Use the context to find its meaning. What does it mean? What clues did you use to find its meaning?

Comprehension and Critical Thinking
1. (a) List What are Earth's three main layers?

(b) Synthesize Information How do those layers interact?
2. (a) Recall What forces inside Earth shape Earth's surface?
(b) Explain How do these forces explain the movement of the continents?
(c) Predict How might a continent split in two?
3. (a) Identify What forces cause weathering and erosion?
(b) Compare and Contrast How is erosion different from weathering?

Writing Activity
Think about the region where you live. Does it have steep mountains or volcanoes, rounded hills, or plains? Write a paragraph describing some of the natural forces that are slowly reshaping your region.

For: An activity on Pangaea
Visit: PHSchool.com
Web Code: led-3202

Climate and Weather

Prepare to Read

Objectives

In this section you will
1. Learn about weather and climate.
2. Explore latitude, landforms, and precipitation.
3. Discover how oceans affect climate.

Taking Notes

As you read this section, look for topics related to climate and weather, such as landforms, precipitation, oceans, and storms. Copy the outline below and add headings as needed to show the relationships among these topics.

| I. Weather |
| II. Climate |
| A. Latitudes |
| B. |
| 1. |
| 2. |
| III. Storms |

Target Reading Skill

Use Context Clues You can sometimes learn the meaning of a word or phrase when the context gives a comparison. In this example, the word *cyclone* is compared to the phrase in italics.

> A cyclone is like *a huge spiral escalator moving air upward*.

Key Terms

- **weather** (WETH ur) *n.* the condition of the air and sky from day to day
- **precipitation** (pree sip uh TAY shun) *n.* water that falls to the ground as rain, sleet, hail, or snow
- **temperature** (TEM pur uh chur) *n.* how hot or cold the air is
- **climate** (KLY mut) *n.* the average weather over many years
- **tropical cyclone** (TRAHP ih kul SY klohn) *n.* an intense wind and rain storm that forms over oceans in the tropics.

This Inuit woman and child are dressed for their cold climate.

Weather or Climate?

Every morning, most people check the weather before they get dressed. But in some parts of India, people have very serious reasons for watching the **weather,** or the condition of the air and sky from day to day. In parts of India, it rains only during one time of year. No one living there wants the rainy days to end too soon. That rain must fill the wells with enough fresh water to last for the entire year.

In India, people are concerned about **precipitation,** or water that falls to the ground as rain, sleet, hail, or snow. When you get dressed in the morning, you may want to know the **temperature,** or how hot or cold the air is. Weather is mainly measured by temperature and precipitation.

The **climate** of a place is the average weather over many years. Climate is not the same as weather. Weather is what people see from day to day. Climate is what usually happens from year to year.

✓ **Reading Check** What is the difference between weather and climate?

Why Climates Vary

Earth has many climates. Some climates are so hot that people rarely need to wear a sweater. In some cold climates, snow stays on the ground most of the year. And there are places on Earth where more than 30 feet (9 meters) of rain falls in a single year.

Climate depends on location. Places in the low latitudes, or tropics, have hot climates, because they get direct sunlight. Places in the high latitudes, or polar regions, have cold climates, because their sunlight is indirect.

Air and water spread heat around the globe as they move. Without wind and water, places in the tropics would overheat. Oceans gain and lose heat slowly, so they keep temperatures mild near coasts. Mountains can also affect climates.

✓ **Reading Check** How does latitude affect temperature?

Cherrapunji, India, averages 37 feet (11 meters) of rain a year. The rain then flows into lakes, streams, and waterfalls.

The Water Cycle

Water evaporates from bodies of water or land areas where rain has fallen and rises into the sky.

The heated water vapor condenses to form clouds made up of little drops of water.

As moist air rises, it cools and drops its moisture. This can happen when air is forced up a mountain slope or when air rises in a storm system.

Water seeps into the ground or runs into streams. It then flows to the sea or evaporates again.

The Water Cycle
Water evaporates from the surface and then falls back as precipitation. **Predict** Which side of a mountain will get more rain, the side facing the wind, or the side facing away?

Air Circulation and Wind

Winds and air currents move heat and moisture between different parts of Earth. These currents follow regular patterns related to latitude. The diagram below shows these circular patterns of air movement, which form a series of belts, or cells, that circle Earth.

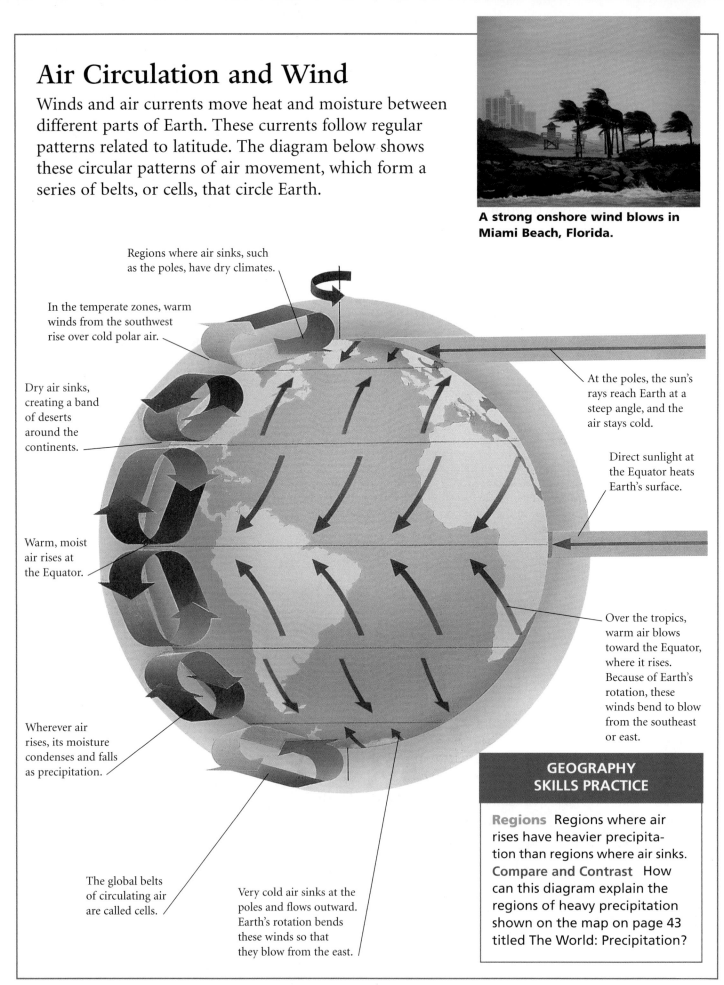

A strong onshore wind blows in Miami Beach, Florida.

Regions where air sinks, such as the poles, have dry climates.

In the temperate zones, warm winds from the southwest rise over cold polar air.

Dry air sinks, creating a band of deserts around the continents.

Warm, moist air rises at the Equator.

Wherever air rises, its moisture condenses and falls as precipitation.

The global belts of circulating air are called cells.

Very cold air sinks at the poles and flows outward. Earth's rotation bends these winds so that they blow from the east.

At the poles, the sun's rays reach Earth at a steep angle, and the air stays cold.

Direct sunlight at the Equator heats Earth's surface.

Over the tropics, warm air blows toward the Equator, where it rises. Because of Earth's rotation, these winds bend to blow from the southeast or east.

GEOGRAPHY SKILLS PRACTICE

Regions Regions where air rises have heavier precipitation than regions where air sinks. **Compare and Contrast** How can this diagram explain the regions of heavy precipitation shown on the map on page 43 titled The World: Precipitation?

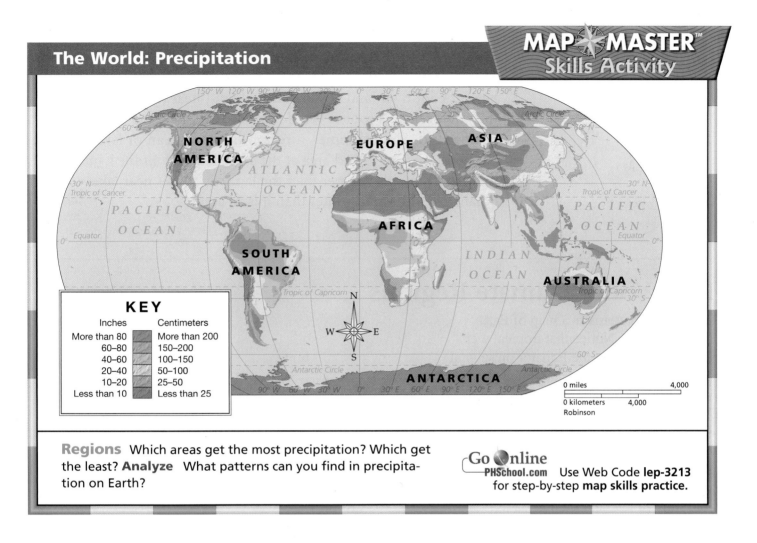

KEY

Inches		Centimeters
More than 80		More than 200
60–80		150–200
40–60		100–150
20–40		50–100
10–20		25–50
Less than 10		Less than 25

0 miles 4,000
0 kilometers 4,000
Robinson

Regions Which areas get the most precipitation? Which get the least? **Analyze** What patterns can you find in precipitation on Earth?

Go Online
PHSchool.com Use Web Code **lep-3213** for step-by-step **map skills practice.**

Oceans and Climates

The oceans help distribute Earth's heat and shape climates. Global wind patterns help create ocean currents, which are like vast rivers in the oceans. Ocean currents move across great distances. Generally, warm water flows away from the Equator, while cold water moves toward the Equator.

Oceans and Currents In the Atlantic Ocean, the Gulf Stream, a warm current, travels northeast from the tropics. The Gulf Stream and the North Atlantic Current carry warm water all the way to western Europe. That warm water gives western Europe a milder climate than other regions at the same latitude.

The cold Peru Current moves north from Antarctica along the coast of South America. The city of Antofagasta (ahn toh fah GAHS tah) lies along that coast, in Chile. Even though Antofagasta is closer than Miami, Florida, is to the Equator, the average temperature in Antofagasta during the hottest month of summer is just 68°F (20°C).

Use Context Clues
Target Skill If you do not know what ocean currents are, notice that they are compared to vast rivers in the ocean. How does the comparison help you find the meaning?

The Ocean's Cooling and Warming Effects Bodies of water affect climate in other ways, too. Water takes longer to heat or cool than land. As the air and land heat up in summer, the water remains cooler. Wind blowing over the water cools the nearby land. So in summer, a region near an ocean or lake will be cooler than an inland area at the same latitude. In the winter, the water remains warmer than the land. So places near lakes or oceans are warmer in winter than inland areas.

The World: Climate Regions

You can see patterns in a map of Earth's climate regions. Notice that tropical wet climate regions hug the Equator on several continents. Farther from the Equator are arid and semiarid climate regions. Elsewhere, regions where the wind blows off the ocean have wetter climates than regions farther inland. Each climate region on this map is described more fully in the next section.

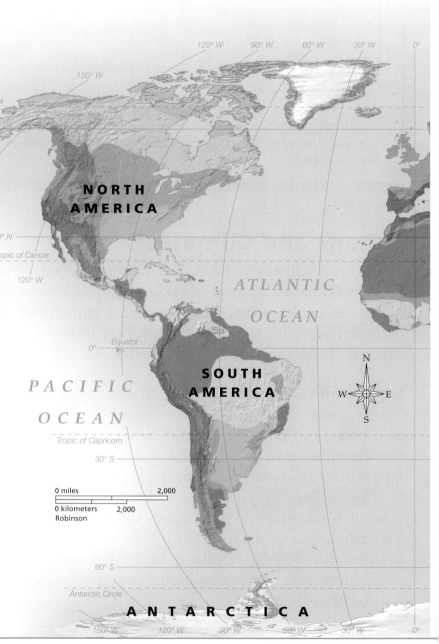

▲ **Arid** This view from the air shows the Colorado River winding through the Grand Canyon in Arizona.

Consider San Francisco, California, and St. Louis, Missouri. Both cities are near 38° north latitude. However, San Francisco borders the Pacific Ocean. In winter, the ocean is warmer than the air. The ocean keeps San Francisco much warmer than St. Louis in winter. In summer, the ocean is cooler than the air, so it keeps San Francisco cool.

✓ **Reading Check** **During the summer, are places near the ocean warmer or cooler than places inland?**

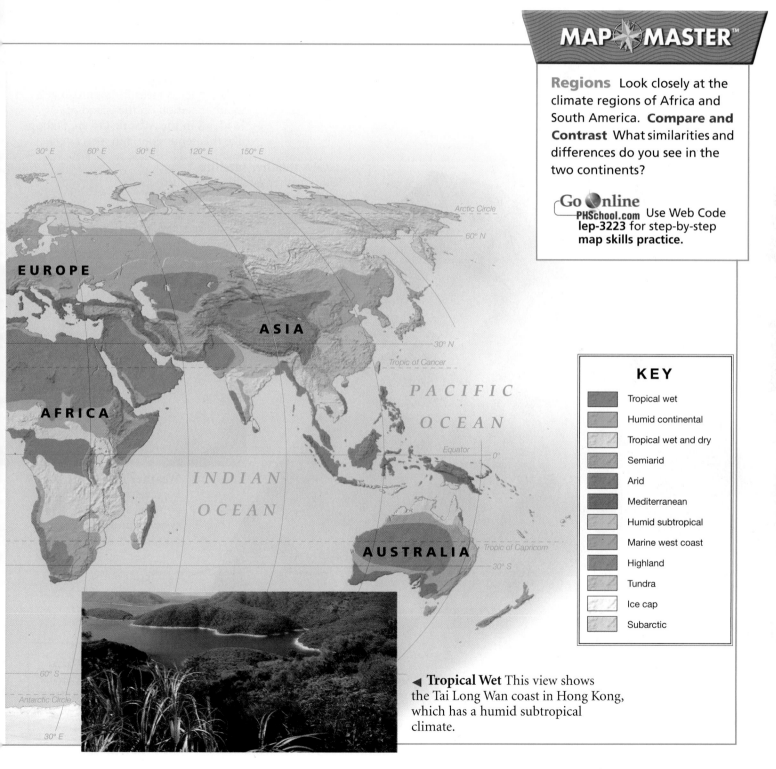

MAP★MASTER™

Regions Look closely at the climate regions of Africa and South America. **Compare and Contrast** What similarities and differences do you see in the two continents?

Go Online
PHSchool.com Use Web Code **lep-3223** for step-by-step **map skills practice.**

KEY

	Tropical wet
	Humid continental
	Tropical wet and dry
	Semiarid
	Arid
	Mediterranean
	Humid subtropical
	Marine west coast
	Highland
	Tundra
	Ice cap
	Subarctic

EUROPE

ASIA

AFRICA

PACIFIC OCEAN

INDIAN OCEAN

AUSTRALIA

◄ **Tropical Wet** This view shows the Tai Long Wan coast in Hong Kong, which has a humid subtropical climate.

Weather Forecasting

Television weather forecasters rely on scientists and equipment from all over the world. Weather stations record local conditions. Satellites orbit overhead to photograph large weather systems. Weather balloons and radar provide still more data. The results, displayed on weather maps or presented in forecasts, can warn citizens of an approaching hurricane or simply remind people to carry an umbrella.

Weather station
This ranger is measuring rainfall at a weather station on the island of Madeira in the Atlantic Ocean. Stations like this send reports to forecasters.

Weather satellites
Scientists use satellites in space to record everything from wind patterns to the height of waves.

Solar cell panels power the spacecraft.

GOES weather satellite
U.S. weather satellites are called GOES (Geostationary Operational Environmental Satellites). They circle Earth in time with Earth's rotation, so they always stay above the same spot.

A hurricane

Weather map
Forecasters track weather patterns and storm systems, and display data on weather maps.

A gathering storm

ANALYZING IMAGES
How might a satellite help forecasters predict the weather?

Raging Storms

Wind and water can make climates milder, but they also can create large and dangerous storms. **Tropical cyclones are intense wind and rain storms that form over oceans in the tropics.** Tropical cyclones that form over the Atlantic Ocean are called hurricanes. The winds near the center of a hurricane can reach speeds of more than 100 miles (160 kilometers) per hour. Hurricanes produce huge swells of water called storm surges, which flood over shorelines and can destroy buildings.

Tornadoes are like funnels of wind that can reach 200 miles (320 kilometers) per hour. The winds and the low air pressure they create in their centers can wreck almost anything in their path. They can be just as dangerous as hurricanes, but they affect much smaller areas.

Other storms are less dangerous. In winter, blizzards dump huge amounts of snow on parts of North America. And severe rainstorms and thunderstorms strike the continent most often in spring and summer.

Hurricane Katrina
In 2005 Hurricane Katrina caused massive destruction along the southeastern coast of the United States.
Synthesizing Information
Is a hurricane more likely on a tropical coast or in a polar region far from the ocean?

✓ **Reading Check** Which storms cover larger areas, hurrricanes or tornadoes?

Section 3 Assessment

Key Terms
Review the key terms at the beginning of this section. Use each term in a sentence that explains its meaning.

Target Reading Skill
Find the word *tornadoes* in the second paragraph on this page. Using the context, find out its meaning. What clues did you use to find its meaning?

Comprehension and Critical Thinking
1. (a) Identify What is climate?
(b) Explain How is climate different from weather?
(c) Analyze Are hurricanes an example of climate or of weather?
2. (a) Recall What kind of climate occurs in most places near the Equator?
(b) Contrast Why are climates near the poles different from climates near the Equator?
3. (a) Recall How do bodies of water affect temperatures?
(b) Predict A city in the interior of a continent has very cold winters. How would you expect winter temperatures to differ in a coastal city at the same latitude as the interior city?

Writing Activity
Write a paragraph describing your region's climate, or average weather. Are winters usually warm or cold? What can you say about summers? Do oceans affect your climate? How much precipitation does your region get? Is it mostly rain, or snow, or a mix?

Writing Tip Remember that every paragraph needs a main idea. Make a general statement about your climate in a topic sentence. Then add sentences with supporting details about your climate.

Using Climate Graphs

Menghai, China, receives about 40 to 60 inches (100 to 150 centimeters) of rainfall each year.

"Everybody talks about the weather, but nobody does anything about it," goes an old joke attributed to the humorist Mark Twain. It's still true, although today we track the weather so that we can predict and prepare for it. One way geographers track weather patterns is by making a climate graph. A climate graph usually presents information about average precipitation and average temperature. Often it shows a whole year of information, so you can see how conditions change with the seasons.

Learn the Skill

To read a climate graph, follow the steps below.

1 **Identify the elements of the graph.** A climate graph is actually two graphs in one: a line graph that shows temperature and a bar graph that shows rainfall. The scale on the left side goes with the line graph, and the scale on the right side goes with the bar graph. The scale along the bottom shows a time period.

2 **Study the line graph.** Notice changes in temperature from month to month and from season to season. Draw a conclusion about the temperature of the place.

Climate Graph: São Paulo, Brazil

°F scale (left): 90, 80, 70, 60, 50, 40, 30, 20, 10, 0, -10
In. scale (right): 20, 18, 16, 14, 12, 10, 8, 6, 4, 2, 0
Months: Jan Feb Mar Apr May Jun Jul Aug Sep Oct Nov Dec

Curved line shows average temperatures in degrees Fahrenheit. **Bars** show rainfall in inches.
SOURCE: World Climate (www.worldclimate.com)

3 **Study the bar graph.** Again, notice changes for months and for seasons. Draw a conclusion about rainfall.

4 **Use your conclusions about both graphs to draw an overall conclusion about the climate of the location.** Does the location appear to have hot seasons and cold seasons? Or does it have a rainy season and a dry season? State your conclusion.

Practice the Skill

Look at the graph of São Paulo, Brazil, on page 48.

1 Read the labels on the sides and bottom of the graph. What do the numbers on the left side measure? What do the numbers on the right side measure? Look at the green bars. Which do they measure, temperature or rainfall? How do you know? Look at the line graph. What does it show? Now, look at the scale along the bottom of the graph. What period of time does it show?

2 Describe the shape of the line graph—is it generally flat, or does it go up and down? What and when is São Paulo's highest average temperature? Its lowest temperature? Do you think São Paulo has a hot season and a cold season? Write a conclusion about temperatures in the city.

3 What do the bars in the bar graph show? Are they generally the same height, or do they differ from month to month? What and when are São Paulo's highest and lowest average rainfall? Do you think São Paulo has a wet season and a dry season? Write a conclusion about rainfall in the city.

4 Using your conclusions about São Paulo's climate, write a summary that includes answers to these questions: What kind of seasons does the city have? Does the weather change much during the year?

Apply the Skill

To make your own climate graph, draw a large square on graph paper. Divide the square into 10 horizontal rows and 12 vertical columns. Title your graph "Climate Graph of Charleston, South Carolina." Then label the left side of your graph using one colored pencil and the right side with a different colored pencil. Write the months of the year along the bottom. Using the temperature and precipitation information in the table above, plot your line graph. Draw the lines with the same colored pencils you used to make the labels for temperature and precipitation.

Charleston, South Carolina

Month	Temperature (°Fahrenheit)	Precipitation (inches)
Jan	48.4	2.9
Feb	50.9	3.0
Mar	57.7	3.6
Apr	65.3	2.4
May	72.7	3.2
Jun	78.8	4.7
Jul	81.7	6.8
Aug	81.0	6.4
Sept	76.6	5.1
Oct	67.8	2.9
Nov	59.5	2.1
Dec	52.2	2.7

How Climate Affects Vegetation

Prepare to Read

Objectives

In this section you will
1. Investigate the relationship between climate and vegetation.
2. Explore Earth's vegetation regions.
3. Study vertical climate zones.

Taking Notes

As you read, look for details about Earth's natural vegetation regions. Copy the chart below and list each type of climate in the first row of boxes. Add boxes as needed. In the box underneath each type of climate, list facts about each vegetation region that occurs in that type of climate.

```
                Climates and Vegetation
    ┌──────────────┬──────────────┬──────────────────┐
    Tropical Climates   Dry Climates   Moderate Climates
    • ____          • ____          • ____
    • ____          • ____          • ____
    • ____          • ____          • ____
    • ____          • ____          • ____
```

Target Reading Skill

Use Context Clues
You can sometimes learn the meaning of a word or phrase when the context gives examples. In the passage below, the meaning of the word *scrub* is given by the examples in italics.

> Scrub includes *bushes, small trees, and low, woody undergrowth.*

Key Terms

- **vegetation** (vej uh TAY shun) *n.* plants that grow in a region
- **tundra** (TUN druh) *n.* an area of cold climate and low-lying vegetation
- **canopy** (KAN uh pea) *n.* the layer formed by the uppermost branches of a rain forest
- **savanna** (suh VAN uh) *n.* a parklike combination of grasslands and scattered trees
- **desert scrub** (DEZ urt skrub) *n.* desert vegetation that needs little water
- **deciduous trees** (dee SIJ oo us treez) *n.* trees that lose their leaves seasonally
- **coniferous trees** (koh NIF ur us treez) *n.* trees that produce cones to carry seeds

Jackfruit, an Asian fruit, grows huge in the tropical wet climate of Hainan Island, China.

Climate and Vegetation

There are five broad types of climate: tropical, dry, temperate marine, temperate continental, and polar. Each climate has its own types of natural **vegetation,** or plants that grow in a region. This is because different plants require different amounts of water and sunlight and different temperatures to survive. The map titled The World: Natural Vegetation, on page 53, shows the location of Earth's vegetation regions. If you compare this map with the map on pages 44 and 45 titled The World: Climate Regions, you will see that climate regions and vegetation regions often cover similar areas.

Tropical Climates In the tropics, there are two main climates. Both are hot. A tropical wet climate has year-round rainfall. Its typical vegetation is tropical rain forest. A tropical wet and dry climate has two seasons: a rainy season and a dry season. This climate supports grasslands and scattered trees.

Dry Climates Arid and semiarid climates have very hot summers and generally mild winters. They get very little rain. The driest arid climate regions have little or no vegetation. Others have plants that need little water. Semiarid climates get a little more rain. They support shrubs and grasses.

Temperate Marine Climates Temperate marine climates are found in the middle latitudes, usually near coastlines. There are three types: Mediterranean, marine west coast, and humid subtropical. The marine west coast and humid subtropical climates get plenty of rain. In the humid subtropical climate, the rain falls mainly in summer. Mediterranean climates get less rain, and it falls mainly in winter. All of the climates have mild winters. Mediterranean and humid subtropical climates generally have hot summers. With their heavy rainfall, marine west coast and humid subtropical climates support a variety of forests. The drier Mediterranean climates have their own vegetation, known as Mediterranean vegetation.

Temperate Continental Climates In a humid continental climate, summer temperatures are moderate to hot, but winters can be very cold. This climate supports grasslands and forests. Regions with subarctic climates are drier, with cool summers and cold winters. Most subarctic climate regions are forested.

Polar Climates The polar climates are cold all year-round. The **tundra** is an area, near the Arctic Circle, of cold climate and low-lying vegetation. The word *tundra* refers both to the vegetation and the climate, which has short, cool summers and long, very cold winters. Ice cap climates are bitterly cold all year. These areas are covered with ice. No vegetation can grow there.

✓ **Reading Check** Why are climate and vegetation related?

Earth's Vegetation Regions

Geographers divide Earth into regions that share similar vegetation. A place's vegetation depends mainly on its climate, but also on other things, such as soil quality.

Plant Fossils In ancient rocks in Wyoming, scientists have found fossils of palm trees. Millions of years ago, sediments such as sand or ash buried the plants quickly. Over thousands of years, the sediment and plants within turned to rock. Scientists study fossils to learn about ancient climate and vegetation.

Polar bears crossing the tundra in Churchill, Manitoba, Canada

This tropical rain forest in Brazil supports dense vegetation.

Use Context Clues
Target Skill If you do not know what Mediterranean vegetation is, consider the examples and other information given by the context. What does the context tell you about this vegetation?

- **Tropical Rain Forest** Because there is so much sunlight, heat, and rain, thousands of kinds of plants grow in a rain forest. Some trees rise 130 feet (40 meters) into the air. The dense, leafy layer formed by the uppermost branches of the rainforest is called the **canopy**. Other plants grow to lower heights in the shade beneath the canopy.

- **Tropical Savanna** In tropical areas with winter dry seasons or more limited rainfall, there is a parklike landscape of grasslands with scattered trees known as **savanna**.

- **Desert** In the driest parts of deserts, there may be no vegetation at all. Elsewhere, plants grow far apart. Their roots absorb scarce water before it evaporates in the heat.

- **Desert Scrub** Semiarid areas and deserts with a little more rain support **desert scrub**, or low desert vegetation that needs little water. Some plants flower only when it rains, so that seeds have a better chance to survive.

- **Mediterranean Vegetation** Mediterranean vegetation includes grasses, shrubs, and low trees. These plants must hold water from the winter rains to survive warm, dry summers.

- **Temperate Grassland** Vast grasslands straddle regions with semiarid and humid continental climates. The wetter grasslands, in humid continental climates, have a mix of tall grasses and other plants that is sometimes called prairie.

- **Deciduous Forest** Marine west coast, humid subtropical, and humid continental climates all support forests of **deciduous trees**, or trees that lose their leaves in the fall.

- **Coniferous and Mixed Forest** These same climates also support areas of coniferous and mixed forest. **Coniferous trees** are trees that produce cones to carry seeds. They generally have needles, not leaves. These features protect trees in drier climates. Mixed forests combine both coniferous and deciduous trees.

- **Tundra** The tundra is an area of cold climate and low-lying vegetation. Tundra vegetation includes mosses, grasses, and low shrubs that bloom during the brief, cool summers.

- **Highland** In highland regions, vegetation depends on elevation, since temperatures drop as elevation rises. Tropical forests may grow at low elevations, with grasslands and coniferous forests farther up. Still higher, tundra vegetation may grow.

- **Ice Cap and Pack Ice** Around the poles, thick ice caps form on land. Masses of ice called pack ice cover the sea. No vegetation can grow there.

✓ **Reading Check** What types of vegetation grow in deserts?

The World: Natural Vegetation

This map shows the natural vegetation regions of the world. The locations of these regions depend mainly on climate. Like the climates that support them, vegetation regions vary according to their distance from the Equator and the amount of precipitation they receive.

The Sahara ▶
The world's largest desert has vast sand dunes with little or no vegetation. This picture also shows an oasis, or a place in the desert where underground water allows trees or crops to grow.

MAP★MASTER™ Skills Activity

Location In which parts of Earth do you find tropical rain forests? **Compare and Contrast** Find tropical wet climates on the map in the previous section titled The World: Climate Regions. How do those locations compare with the locations of tropical rain forests?

Go Online
PHSchool.com Use Web Code **lep-3214** for step-by-step **map skills practice.**

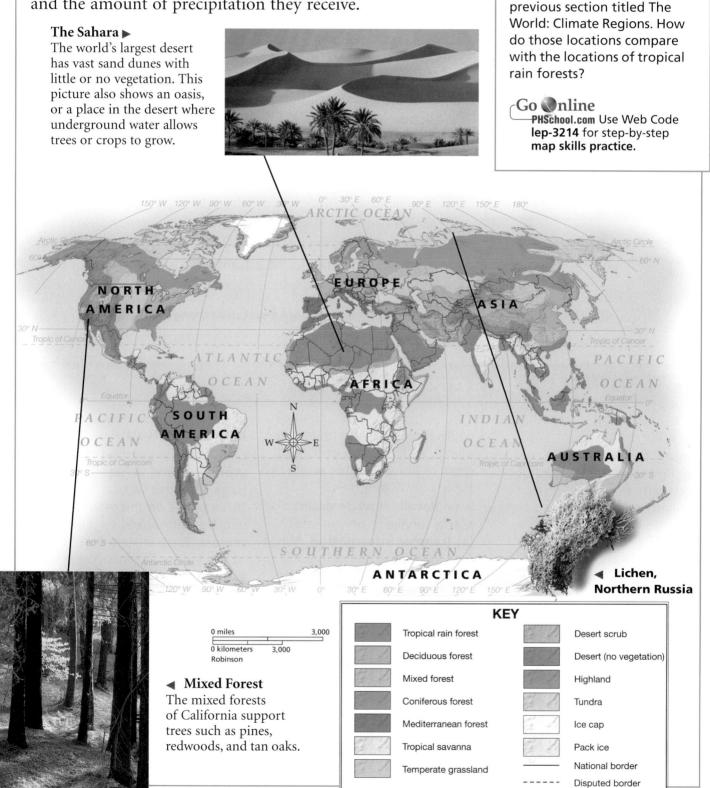

◀ Lichen, Northern Russia

◀ Mixed Forest
The mixed forests of California support trees such as pines, redwoods, and tan oaks.

0 miles 3,000
0 kilometers 3,000
Robinson

KEY

Tropical rain forest	Desert scrub
Deciduous forest	Desert (no vegetation)
Mixed forest	Highland
Coniferous forest	Tundra
Mediterranean forest	Ice cap
Tropical savanna	Pack ice
Temperate grassland	——— National border
	- - - - Disputed border

Vertical Climate Zones

The climate at the top of Mount Everest, in southern Asia, is like Antarctica's. But Mount Everest is near the Tropic of Cancer, far from the South Pole. It is so cold at the top of the mountain because the air becomes cooler as elevation increases. Mountains have vertical climate zones, where the climate and vegetation depend on elevation.

In a tropical region, vegetation that needs a tropical climate will grow only near the bottom of a mountain. Farther up is vegetation that can grow in a temperate climate. Near the top is vegetation that can grow in a polar climate.

Picture yourself on a hike up a mountain in a temperate climate. Grassland surrounds the base of the mountain, and temperatures are warm. You begin to climb and soon enter an area with more precipitation and lower temperatures than below. The grassland gives way to a coniferous forest.

As you continue to climb, you find only scattered, short trees. Finally, it is too cold even for them. There are only the low shrubs, short grasses, and mosses of a tundra. At the mountain's peak, you find permanent ice, where no vegetation grows.

Forested valley at the foot of Machapuchare, a mountain in Nepal

✓ **Reading Check** How does vegetation change with elevation?

Section 4 Assessment

Key Terms
Review the key terms at the beginning of this section. Use each term in a sentence that explains its meaning.

Target Reading Skill
Find the phrase *tundra vegetation* on page 52. Use context to figure out its meaning. What do you think it means? What clues helped you find the meaning?

Comprehension and Critical Thinking
1. (a) List What are the five main types of climate?
(b) Evaluate How do differences in climate affect plant life?

(c) Analyze Why do low-lying plants, such as scrub or tundra, grow in some climates, while rich forests grow in others?
2. (a) Recall How do desert plants survive in dry climates?
(b) Transfer Information What features of the plants in your region allow them to grow in your region's climate?
3. (a) Define What is a vertical climate zone?
(b) Explain How do vertical climate zones affect vegetation on a mountain?
(c) Compare and Contrast Why is vegetation at the top of a tall mountain different from vegetation at the bottom?

Writing Activity
Look at the map titled The World: Natural Vegetation on page 53 in this section. Choose three places on the map that are in different natural vegetation regions. Then write a description of the types of plants you would expect to see if you visited each place you have chosen.

> **Writing Tip** Since you are writing about three different types of natural vegetation, you may want to compare and contrast them. When you compare, you point out similarities. When you contrast, you focus on differences.

Review and Assessment

◆ Chapter Summary

Section 1: Our Planet, Earth
- Earth's rotation on its axis changes day to night and night to day.
- The tilt of Earth's axis causes our seasons.

Section 2: Forces Shaping Earth
- Earth's three main layers are the crust, the mantle, and the core.
- Forces inside Earth move plates of crust to form mountains and volcanoes.
- Wind, water, and ice wear down and reshape Earth's surface.

Section 3: Climate and Weather
- Climate is the average weather in a region over a long period of time.
- Climate depends on latitude, landforms, and nearness to an ocean.
- Winds and ocean currents help spread Earth's warmth. They can also cause dangerous storms.

Section 4: How Climate Affects Vegetation
- Vegetation depends mainly on climate.
- Earth can be divided into several natural vegetation regions.
- Climate and vegetation change with elevation.

Delicate Arch, Utah

◆ Key Terms

Each of the statements below contains a key term from the chapter. If the statement is true, write *true*. If it is false, rewrite the statement to make it true.

1. Earth's movement around the sun is called rotation.

2. The mantle is a thick, rocky layer around Earth's core.

3. Earth's crust is at the center of the planet.

4. Magma is hot, flowing rock beneath Earth's surface.

5. The Appalachian Mountains have been worn down over time by erosion.

6. If you want to know how hot it will be tomorrow, you can look at a climate report.

7. Temperature measures how hot or how cold something is.

8. Vegetation is a term for the plants that grow in a region.

9. Deciduous forests grow in polar climates.

◆ Comprehension and Critical Thinking

10. (a) Recall How many standard time zones is Earth divided into?
(b) Analyze How are time differences related to the rotation of Earth?

11. (a) Identify As Earth moves around the sun, what event happens about June 21?
(b) Explain How does Earth's movement make summers hot and winters cold?
(c) Apply Information Why is Antarctica cold even in summer?

12. (a) Recall How much of Earth's water is fresh?
(b) Predict If Earth's climate became colder, how might the fresh water supply be affected?

13. (a) Recall What causes winds?
(b) Contrast What are some negative and positive effects of wind and water in the tropics?

14. (a) Describe How do oceans shape climate?
(b) Synthesize Information Why do some coastal cities in the tropics stay cool?

15. (a) Describe How does climate affect vegetation?
(b) Evaluate A tropical climate has year-round rainfall. Can forests grow there? Explain why or why not.

◆ Skills Practice

Using Special Geography Graphs Review the steps you learned in the Skills For Life activity in this chapter. Then look at the climate graph for Helsinki, Finland, below. After you have analyzed the graph, write a paragraph that summarizes Helsinki's climate.

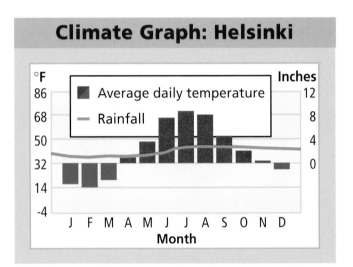

Climate Graph: Helsinki

Average daily temperature
Rainfall

◆ Writing Activity: Science

Reread the descriptions of dry climates and of desert vegetation regions. Then design a plant that could live in these regions. Describe how it would get light, water, and nutrients.

MAP MASTER™ Skills Activity

Oceans and Seas

Place Location For each place listed below, write the letter that marks its location on the map.

1. Atlantic Ocean
2. Arctic Ocean
3. Indian Ocean
4. Mediterranean Sea
5. Pacific Ocean
6. Southern Ocean

Go Online
PHSchool.com Use Web Code **lep-3215** for step-by-step **map skills practice.**

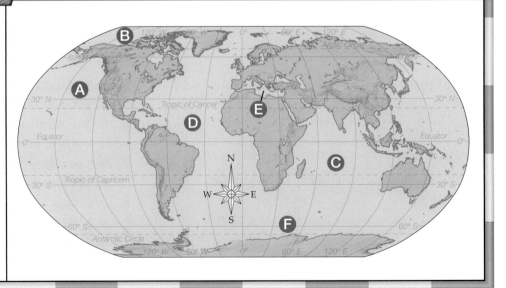

Standardized Test Prep

Test-Taking Tips

Some questions on standardized tests ask you to use map keys. Read the precipitation map key below. Then follow the tips to answer the sample question.

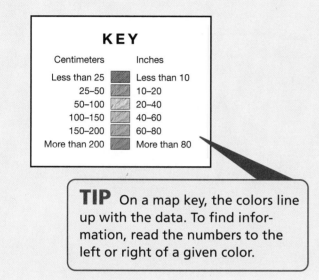

TIP On a map key, the colors line up with the data. To find information, read the numbers to the left or right of a given color.

Pick the letter that best answers the question.

On a precipitation map, the southern coastal states are colored dark green. According to the key at the left, how many inches of rain does this region get each year?

A 20–40
B 60–80
C 50–100
D 150–200

TIP To be sure you understand what the question is asking, restate it in your own words: *The color DARK GREEN on the map key stands for how many inches of rain each year?*

Think It Through The question asks about inches of rain, but the answers C and D show numbers from the centimeter column. The numbers 20–40 (answer A) are next to yellow, not dark green. The numbers 60–80 are next to dark green in the inches column. The answer is B.

Practice Questions

Use the tips above and other tips in this book to help you answer the following questions:

1. When the Northern Hemisphere has days and nights of equal length, it is
   A summer solstice.
   B spring equinox.
   C New Year's Day.
   D winter solstice.

2. Which of the following is NOT an example of a landform?
   A a mountain
   B a plateau
   C a plain
   D an atmosphere

3. In which vegetation region would you find a plant with shallow roots, meant to absorb water before it evaporates?
   A desert
   B deciduous forest
   C coniferous forest
   D tropical savanna

Study the following map key and answer the question that follows.

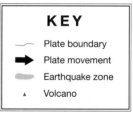

4. On a map with this key, you would find places where earthquakes happen by looking for
   A a brown area.
   B a red triangle.
   C a black arrow.
   D a black line.

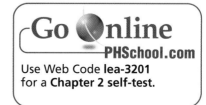

Use Web Code **lea-3201**
for a **Chapter 2 self-test**.

Chapter Preview

This chapter will introduce you to Earth's human geography, or the patterns of human activity on Earth.

Section 1
Population

Section 2
Migration

Section 3
Economic Systems

Section 4
Political Systems

Target Reading Skill

Comparison and Contrast In this chapter you will focus on the text structure by learning how to compare and contrast. Comparing and contrasting can help you to sort out and analyze information.

▶ Woman harvesting rice on a terrace built by people in southern China

Population

Objectives

In this section you will
1. Learn about population distribution.
2. Explore population density.
3. Investigate population growth.

Taking Notes

Copy the concept web below. As you read this section, fill in the web with information about the causes and effects of population density and of population growth. Add more ovals as needed.

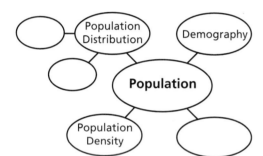

Target Reading Skill

Comparison and Contrast Comparing and contrasting can help you sort out information. When you compare, you examine the similarities between things. When you contrast, you look at the differences. As you read this section, compare and contrast population distribution and population density. Look for the similarities and differences between these two concepts.

Key Terms

- **population** (pahp yuh LAY shun) *n.* total number of people in an area
- **population distribution** (pahp yuh LAY shun dis trih BYOO shun) *n.* the way the population is spread out over an area
- **demography** (dih MAH gruh fee) *n.* the science that studies population distribution and change
- **population density** (pahp yuh LAY shun DEN suh tee) *n.* the average number of people per square mile or square kilometer
- **birthrate** (BURTH rayt) *n.* the number of live births each year per 1,000 people
- **death rate** (deth rayt) *n.* the number of deaths each year per 1,000 people

A crowded village on the Nile River near Aswan, Egypt

Population Distribution

The world's **population,** or total number of people, lives in uneven clusters on Earth's surface. Some places have many people. Other places are almost empty. **Population distribution** is the way the population is spread out over an area.

Demography is the science that tries to explain how populations change and why population distribution is uneven. Demographers study rates of birth, marriage, and death. And they ask why people move from one place to another.

Population and Places People usually don't move without a good reason. People may move because they can live better in a new place. Other times, people are forced to move, or they move because they cannot feed their families. However, as long as people can make a living where they are, they usually stay in that area. So, regions with large populations tend to keep them.

Population and History In the past, most people lived on farms where they grew their own food. They lived where the climate provided enough water and warm weather to support crops. Regions with a long history of farming, good soil, and plenty of water became crowded. These regions still have large populations. Most places too cold or too dry for farming still have small populations.

New Population Clusters However, after about 1800, improved transportation and new ways of making a living changed things. Railroads and steamships made it easier for people to move long distances, even across oceans. New jobs in factories and offices meant that more people were living in cities, where they could make a living without farming the land. Crowded cities grew in regions that once had few people, such as the United States, Australia, and northern Europe.

Villages in France have grown through centuries of farming.

✓ **Reading Check** Why are some parts of the world more crowded than others?

The World: Early Farming and Modern Industry

MAP MASTER™ Skills Activity

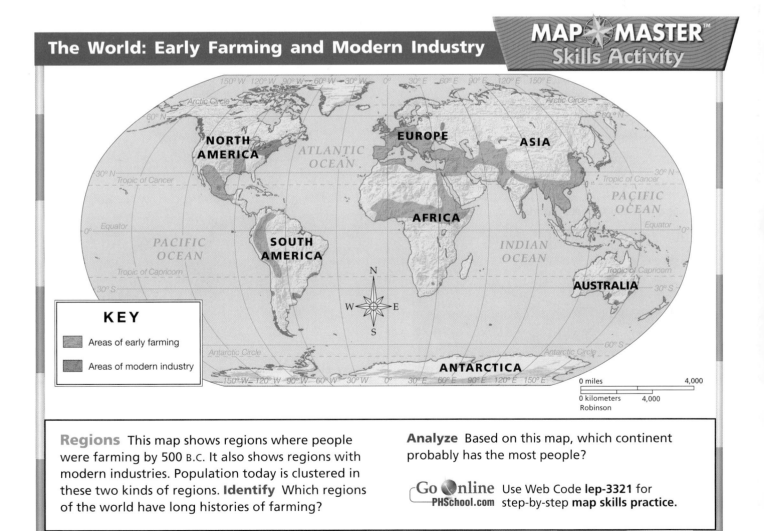

KEY

▨ Areas of early farming

▨ Areas of modern industry

0 miles 4,000
0 kilometers 4,000
Robinson

Regions This map shows regions where people were farming by 500 B.C. It also shows regions with modern industries. Population today is clustered in these two kinds of regions. **Identify** Which regions of the world have long histories of farming?

Analyze Based on this map, which continent probably has the most people?

Go Online
PHSchool.com Use Web Code lep-3321 for step-by-step **map skills practice**.

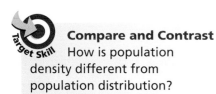

Target Skill

Compare and Contrast
How is population density different from population distribution?

Population Density

How many people live in your neighborhood? How big is that neighborhood? If you take the population of an area and divide it by the size of that area in square miles or square kilometers, you can get a sense of how crowded or empty that area is. The average number of people per square mile or square kilometer is called **population density.**

Population distribution and population density both describe where people live. Population density differs from population distribution, however, because it gives an average number of people for an area. Population distribution gives actual numbers of people for an area.

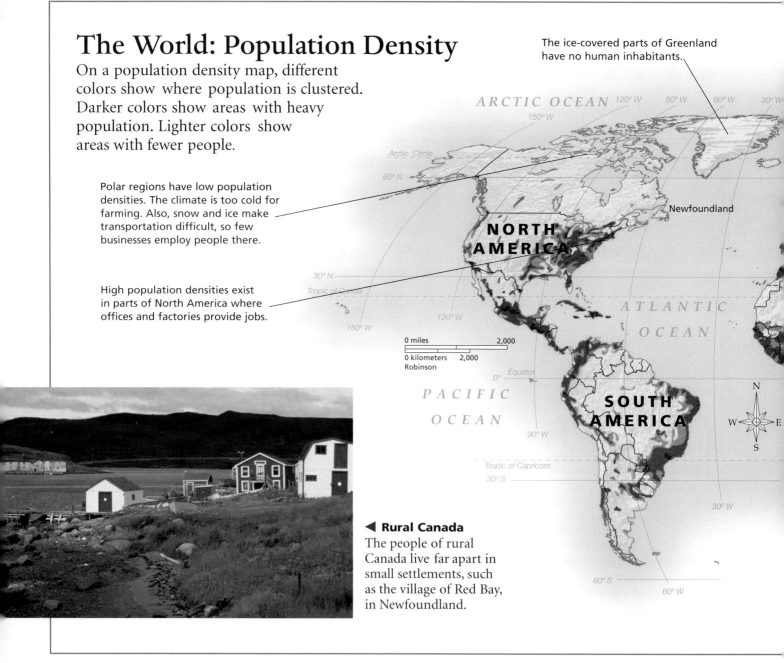

The World: Population Density

On a population density map, different colors show where population is clustered. Darker colors show areas with heavy population. Lighter colors show areas with fewer people.

The ice-covered parts of Greenland have no human inhabitants.

Polar regions have low population densities. The climate is too cold for farming. Also, snow and ice make transportation difficult, so few businesses employ people there.

High population densities exist in parts of North America where offices and factories provide jobs.

◀ **Rural Canada**
The people of rural Canada live far apart in small settlements, such as the village of Red Bay, in Newfoundland.

Population density varies from one area to another. In a country with a high density, such as Japan, people are crowded together. Almost half of Japan's 127 million people live on only 17 percent of the land, or an area the size of West Virginia. In Tokyo, there is a population density of more than 25,000 people per square mile (9,664 per square kilometer). In contrast, Canada has a low overall population density. It has about 9 people per square mile (3 per square kilometer). Canada is bigger than the United States, but has only about one ninth as many people.

✓ **Reading Check** **Which has a higher population density, a city or an area in the countryside?**

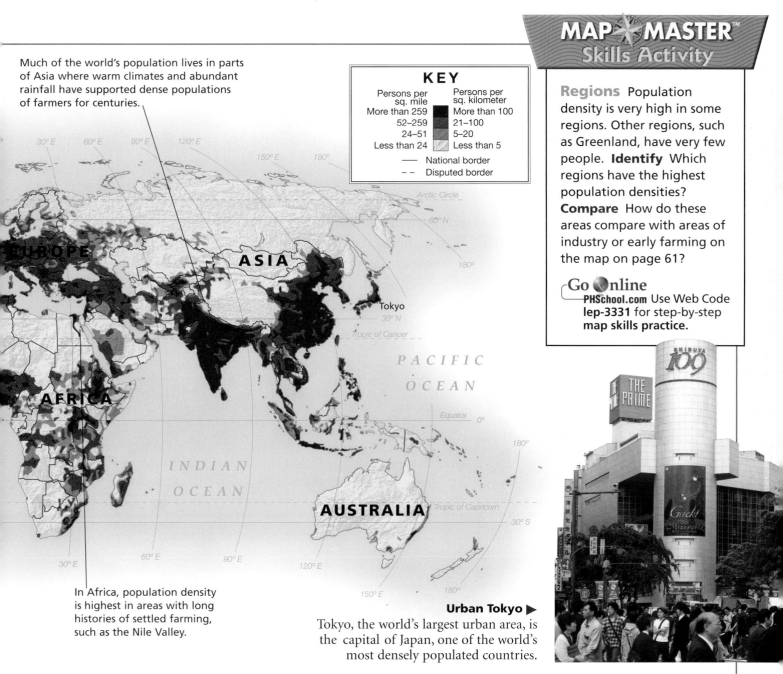

Much of the world's population lives in parts of Asia where warm climates and abundant rainfall have supported dense populations of farmers for centuries.

KEY

Persons per sq. mile		Persons per sq. kilometer
More than 259	■	More than 100
52–259		21–100
24–51		5–20
Less than 24		Less than 5
—— National border		
– – Disputed border		

EUROPE

ASIA

AFRICA

Tokyo

PACIFIC OCEAN

INDIAN OCEAN

AUSTRALIA

In Africa, population density is highest in areas with long histories of settled farming, such as the Nile Valley.

Urban Tokyo ▶
Tokyo, the world's largest urban area, is the capital of Japan, one of the world's most densely populated countries.

MAP MASTER™
Skills Activity

Regions Population density is very high in some regions. Other regions, such as Greenland, have very few people. **Identify** Which regions have the highest population densities? **Compare** How do these areas compare with areas of industry or early farming on the map on page 61?

Go Online
PHSchool.com Use Web Code lep-3331 for step-by-step map skills practice.

Population Growth

Suppose that all the years from A.D. 1 to A.D. 2000 took place in a single day. As the day began at midnight, there would be 300 million people in the world. Twelve hours later, at noon, there would be just 310 million people. By 8:24 P.M., the population would double to 600 million. It would double again by 10:05 P.M. to 1.2 billion. By 11:20, it would double again to 2.4 billion, and then double yet again by 11:48 to 4.8 billion, before reaching 6 billion as the day ended at midnight. As you can see, the world's population has grown very quickly in recent times. There are several reasons for this rapid growth.

Birthrates and Death Rates At different times in history, populations have grown at different rates. Demographers want to understand why. They know that population growth depends on the birthrate and the death rate. The **birthrate** is the number of live births each year per 1,000 people. The **death rate** is the number of deaths each year per 1,000 people.

For thousands of years, the world's population grew slowly. In those years, farmers worked without modern machinery. Food supplies often were scarce. People lived without clean water or waste removal. Many millions of people died of infectious diseases. As a result, although the birthrate was high, so was the death rate. The life expectancy, or the average number of years that people live, was short.

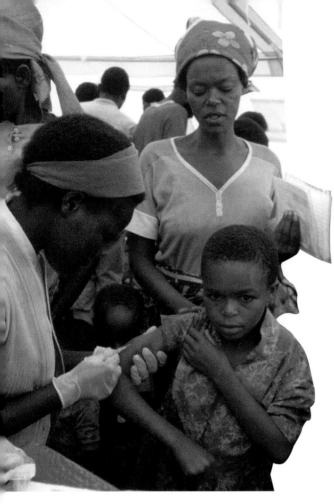

Modern Medicine
This Rwandan refugee is getting a measles vaccination in Tanzania. Modern medicine has lengthened lifespans worldwide.
Analyze *Does vaccination raise birth rates or lower death rates? Explain why.*

Graph Skills

If you subtract deaths from births, you get a country's rate of natural growth. When there are more deaths than births, the native-born population drops. **Identify** Which of the countries shown here has the highest birthrate? **Compare** Where is the population growing, Russia or the United States?

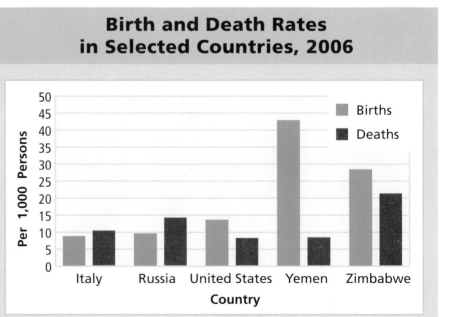

Birth and Death Rates in Selected Countries, 2006

Per 1,000 Persons — Births / Deaths

Countries: Italy, Russia, United States, Yemen, Zimbabwe

Reasons for Population Growth Today This all changed after the 1700s. Death rates dropped sharply. In some countries, birthrates increased. As a result, populations have grown very fast. In some countries, the population has doubled in less than 20 years. Meanwhile, people live longer than ever. In the United States, people born in 1900 could expect to live for 47 years. Today, they can expect to live for 77 years.

Scientific progress explains much of this change. First, new farming methods have increased the world's food supply. Scientists have improved important food crops and found new ways to protect crops against insects. Scientists have also found ways to raise crops with less water. These recent scientific improvements in agriculture are called the Green Revolution.

The second set of scientific advances has come in health and medicine. Scientists have convinced local governments to provide clean drinking water and sanitary waste removal. These measures sharply reduce disease. Researchers have also developed vaccines to prevent disease and antibiotics to fight infections. As a result, people live many more years.

Due to a high birthrate and a low death rate, Yemen's population is skyrocketing.

Graph Skills

In recent centuries, population growth has soared. There are now 18 times as many people as there were 600 years ago. **Identify** Around what year did the world's population begin to rise rapidly? **Analyze a Graph** Looking at this graph, how can you tell that the world's population rose more quickly in recent years than in earlier centuries?

World Population Growth, 1200–2000

(Graph: y-axis labeled "Billions of people" from 0 to 7; x-axis labeled "Year" from 1200 to 2000)

SOURCE: United States Census Bureau

Overcrowding in Bangladesh
These Bangladeshis are returning from a festival. Bangladesh's population has grown faster than its public services. This results in overcrowding, as seen on this train. **Infer** *What other aspects of life in Bangladesh might be affected by rapid population growth?*

The Challenges of Population Growth Today, food supplies have increased and people live longer. Even so, people in many countries still face serious problems. Some nations, such as those in Southwest Asia, do not have enough fresh water. In parts of Asia and Africa, the population is growing faster than the food supply. Often, these countries do not have enough money to buy food elsewhere.

Population growth puts pressure on all aspects of life. The populations of many countries are increasing so fast that not everyone can find jobs. There are not enough schools to educate the growing number of children. Decent housing is scarce. Public services such as transportation and sanitation are inadequate.

Rapid population growth also affects the environment. For instance, forests in many countries are disappearing. People in poorer countries cut down the trees for wood and fuel. Clearing forests causes other problems. In a forest, tree roots hold soil in place, and forest soils soak up rain. With the forest gone, heavy rainfall may wash away the soil and cause dangerous floods. Demand for wood and fuel in wealthier countries also uses up the world's scarce resources. All of Earth's people must work to meet this challenge.

✓ **Reading Check** **Why have populations risen rapidly in recent times?**

Section 1 Assessment

Key Terms
Review the key terms at the beginning of this section. Use each term in a sentence that explains its meaning.

Target Reading Skill
How are population density and population distribution similar? How are they different?

Comprehension and Critical Thinking
1. (a) Recall In what parts of the world did most people live before modern times?
(b) Explain How does history help explain population distribution today?

(c) Contrast How is population distribution today different from the days before modern science was developed?
2. (a) Define What is population density?
(b) Transfer Information To figure out the population density of an area, what two pieces of information do you need?
3. (a) Recall How has population growth changed in 100 years?
(b) Explain What accounts for this change?
(c) Identify Cause and Effect What are the effects of this change in population growth?

Writing Activity
Suppose that you are a demographer studying the area where you live. How does population density vary across your area? Where is population growth taking place? Write a short description of your area's demography.

For: An activity on population
Visit: PHSchool.com
Web Code: led-3301

Migration

Prepare to Read

Objectives

In this section you will
1. Learn about migration, or people's movement from one region to another.
2. Investigate urbanization, or people's movement to cities.

Taking Notes

Copy the chart below. As you read this section, fill in the chart with information about voluntary and involuntary migration and about urbanization.

```
                    Migration
        ┌───────────────┬───────────────┐
  Voluntary      Involuntary      Urbanization
  Migration      Migration
    •                •                •
    •                •                •
    •                •                •
    •                •                •
```

Target Reading Skill

Identify Contrasts
When you contrast two situations, you examine how they differ. Although both voluntary and involuntary migration involve the movement of people, the reasons for that movement differ. As you read, list the differences between voluntary and involuntary migration.

Key Terms

- **migration** (my GRAY shun) *n.* the movement of people from one place or region to another
- **immigrants** (IM uh grunts) *n.* people who move into one country from another
- **urbanization** (ur bun ih ZAY shun) *n.* the movement of people to cities, and the growth of cities
- **rural** (ROOR ul) *adj.* located in the countryside
- **urban** (UR bun) *adj.* located in cities and towns

Why People Migrate

For thousands of years, people have moved to new places. People's movement from one place or region to another is called **migration**. **Immigrants** are people who move into one country from another.

In the years from 1850 to 1930, more than 30 million Europeans moved to live in the United States. Since 1971, more than 4.5 million people have migrated here from Mexico, and more than 2.5 million have migrated from the Caribbean islands. Since 1971, Central America, the Philippines, China, and Vietnam have all lost more than 1 million immigrants to the United States. More than 800,000 immigrants have come from both South Korea and India.

During the late 1800s and early 1900s, millions of immigrants to the United States stopped at Ellis Island in New York Harbor.

Cubans in Little Havana
These men ordering food at a cafe are part of a large community of Cuban immigrants in Miami, Florida. **Analyze Images** *What aspects of their life in Cuba have these immigrants preserved in their new home?*

Identify Contrasts How is involuntary migration different from voluntary migration?

Voluntary Migration in the Past Voluntary migration is the movement of people by their own choice. Today, most people move by their own choice. The push-pull theory says that people migrate because difficulties "push" them to leave. At the same time, the hope for a better life "pulls" people to a new country.

The push-pull theory helps to explain the great Irish migration in the 1840s and 1850s. In those years, 1.5 million people left Ireland for the United States. What pushed so many Irish people to come to America? In the 1840s, disease destroyed Ireland's main crop—potatoes. Hunger pushed people to migrate. Job opportunities pulled Irish families to the United States.

Voluntary Migration Today The same theory explains most migration today. The main sources of migration are countries where many people are poor and jobs are few. In some countries, such as Vietnam and Central American countries, wars have made life dangerous and difficult.

In China, Vietnam, and Cuba, governments limit people's freedom. These problems push people to leave. Meanwhile, the possibility of good jobs and political freedom pulls people to the United States and other well-off, democratic countries.

Involuntary Migration Sometimes people are forced to move. Because these people do not choose to move, their movement is known as involuntary migration. During the early 1800s, the British sent prisoners to Australia to serve their sentences. When their sentences were done, many stayed. War also forces people to migrate to escape death or serious danger.

The Transatlantic Slave Trade Perhaps the biggest involuntary migration in history was the transatlantic slave trade. From the 1500s to the 1800s, millions of Africans were enslaved and taken against their will to European colonies in North and South America. These Africans traveled under inhumane conditions across the Atlantic Ocean, chained inside ships for more than a month.

At first, their descendants in the United States lived mainly on the east coast. As cotton farming spread west, many enslaved African Americans were forced to migrate again, this time to new plantations in the Mississippi Valley and Texas.

✓ **Reading Check** **Why do people migrate?**

Migration in South Asia

At the end of British colonial rule in 1947, most of South Asia was divided along religious lines into two countries. India had a Hindu majority. Pakistan was mainly Muslim. Fearing religious discrimination or violence, Muslims from India and Hindus from Pakistan fled across the new borders. Many died when violence broke out during these massive migrations.

Movement This map shows migrations by South Asians. **Identify** Which countries did South Asia's largest migrations involve? **Contrast** How do the reasons for movement out of South Asia differ from the reasons for migration within the region?

Go Online
PHSchool.com Use Web Code **lep-3312** for step-by-step map skills practice.

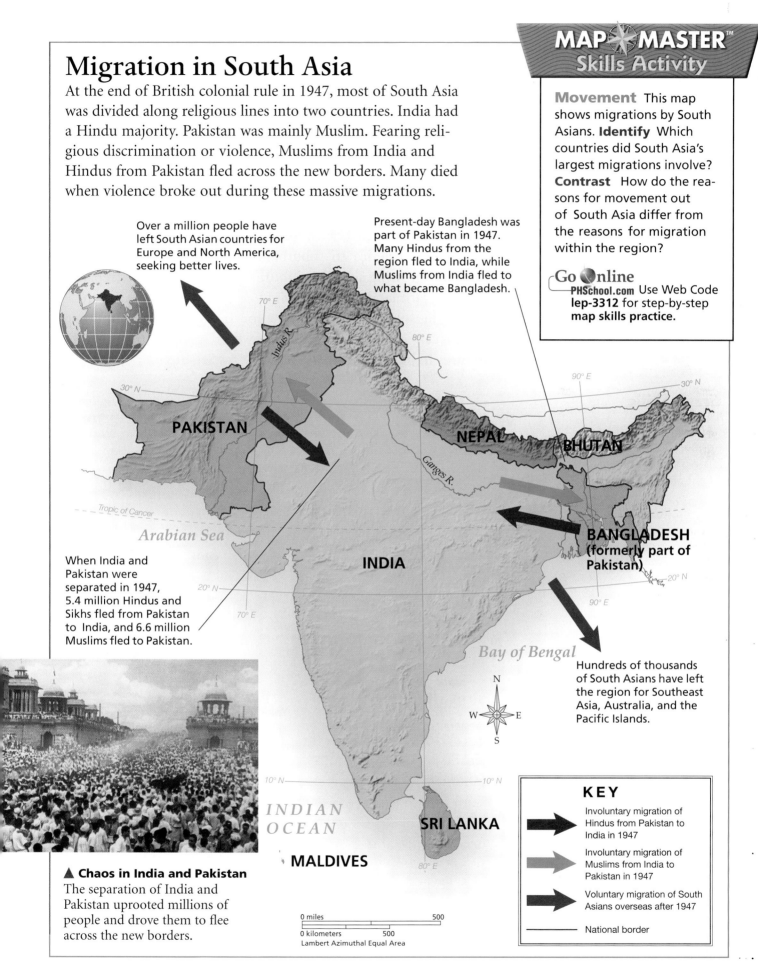

Over a million people have left South Asian countries for Europe and North America, seeking better lives.

Present-day Bangladesh was part of Pakistan in 1947. Many Hindus from the region fled to India, while Muslims from India fled to what became Bangladesh.

Indus R.

70° E

80° E

90° E

30° N

30° N

PAKISTAN

NEPAL

BHUTAN

Ganges R.

Tropic of Cancer

Arabian Sea

BANGLADESH (formerly part of Pakistan)

When India and Pakistan were separated in 1947, 5.4 million Hindus and Sikhs fled from Pakistan to India, and 6.6 million Muslims fled to Pakistan.

INDIA

20° N

20° N

70° E

90° E

Bay of Bengal

N
W E
S

Hundreds of thousands of South Asians have left the region for Southeast Asia, Australia, and the Pacific Islands.

10° N

10° N

INDIAN OCEAN

SRI LANKA

80° E

MALDIVES

▲ **Chaos in India and Pakistan**
The separation of India and Pakistan uprooted millions of people and drove them to flee across the new borders.

0 miles 500
0 kilometers 500
Lambert Azimuthal Equal Area

KEY

➡ Involuntary migration of Hindus from Pakistan to India in 1947

➡ Involuntary migration of Muslims from India to Pakistan in 1947

➡ Voluntary migration of South Asians overseas after 1947

— National border

Discovery CHANNEL SCHOOL Video
Learn more about migration.

Urbanization

Millions of people in many countries have migrated to cities from farms and small villages. In recent years, the population of some cities has grown tremendously. The movement of people to cities and the growth of cities is called **urbanization.**

Cities and Suburbs In Europe and North America, the growth of industry during the 1800s pulled people from the countryside to cities. They hoped for jobs in factories and offices. Since about 1950, urbanization has given way in Europe and North America to suburbanization, or the movement of people to growing suburbs. Suburbanization sometimes replaces valuable farmland with sprawling development. Because most people in suburbs rely on cars for transportation, suburban sprawl can increase pollution. However, people still move to suburbs to pursue the dream of home ownership.

▮ Graph Skills

All over the world, city populations have soared. The photographs of Cape Town, South Africa, below, show how that city has expanded.
Identify What percent of the world's people lived in cities in 1800?
Predict Based on information from the graph, how do you think the world's rural and urban populations will compare in 2050?

World Urban and Rural Populations, 1800-2000

Legend: ■ Urban ■ Rural

Y-axis: Percentage (0–100)
X-axis: Year (1800, 1960, 1980, 2000)

Cape Town, 1938   Modern Cape Town

Urbanization on Other Continents In Asia, Africa, and Latin America, people are still streaming from the countryside to growing cities. Indonesia is an example. In the past, most Indonesians lived in **rural** areas, or areas in the countryside. Recently, more and more Indonesians have moved to **urban** areas, or areas in cities and nearby towns. For example, in 1970, about 3.9 million people lived in Greater Jakarta, Indonesia's capital. By 2000, its population was about 11 million. Jakarta is not unique. Greater São Paulo, Brazil, grew from 8 million residents in 1970 to nearly 18 million residents in 2000.

The problem in cities like Jakarta and São Paulo is that too many people are moving to the city too fast. Cities cannot keep up. They cannot provide the housing, jobs, schools, hospitals, and other services that people need. Traffic jams and crowds often make getting around a struggle.

With so many daily problems, why do people flock to São Paulo and other big cities? As hard as life is in the cities, it can be even harder in the countryside, where there are few jobs and a shortage of land to farm. Most migrants to the city are seeking a better life for their families. They are looking for jobs, modern houses, and good schools. Above all, most want better lives for their children.

✔ **Reading Check** How is the population of urban areas changing in Africa, Asia, and Latin America?

São Paulo, Brazil
São Paulo is Brazil's largest city.
Analyze Images *Do you think that this city has a high or a low population density?*

 ## Section 2 Assessment

Key Terms
Review the key terms at the beginning of this section. Use each term in a sentence that explains its meaning.

⊙ Target Reading Skill
Contrast involuntary migration and voluntary migration. How are these two forms of migration different? List at least two differences between the two kinds of migration.

Comprehension and Critical Thinking
1. (a) Identify What are push factors and what are pull factors?
(b) Explain How do push factors and pull factors explain people's decision to migrate?
(c) Compare and Contrast Do push and pull factors account for involuntary migration? Explain why or why not.
2. (a) Recall What is urbanization?
(b) Identify Cause and Effect What are the causes and some of the effects of urbanization?

Writing Activity
Suppose that you are moving to the United States from one of the countries listed in the second paragraph on page 67. Write a paragraph describing your reasons for leaving that country and what attracts you to the United States.

For: An activity on migration
Visit: PHSchool.com
Web Code: led-3302

Analyzing and Interpreting Population Density Maps

Crowds gather in Amsterdam on Queen's Day, a national holiday in the Netherlands.

How dense is the population where you live? If you drew an imaginary five-mile square around your house and counted the number of people who lived within the square, would there be many residents, or few?

Population density is the average number of persons living within a certain area. You can find out how densely populated a place is by reading a population density map.

Learn the Skill

To read and interpret a population density map, follow these steps.

1 **Read the title and look at the map to get a general idea of what it shows.** The title and map key will show you that the topic of the map is population density.

2 **Read the key to understand how the map uses symbols and colors.** Each color represents a different population density range, as explained in the map key.

3 **Use the key to interpret the map.** Identify areas of various densities on the map. Some places average less than one person per square mile. In other places, thousands of people might be crammed into one square mile.

4 **Draw conclusions about what the map shows.** The history, geography, and cultural traditions of a place affect its population density. Draw on this information, plus what you read on the map, to make conclusions about why particular areas have a higher or a lower population density.

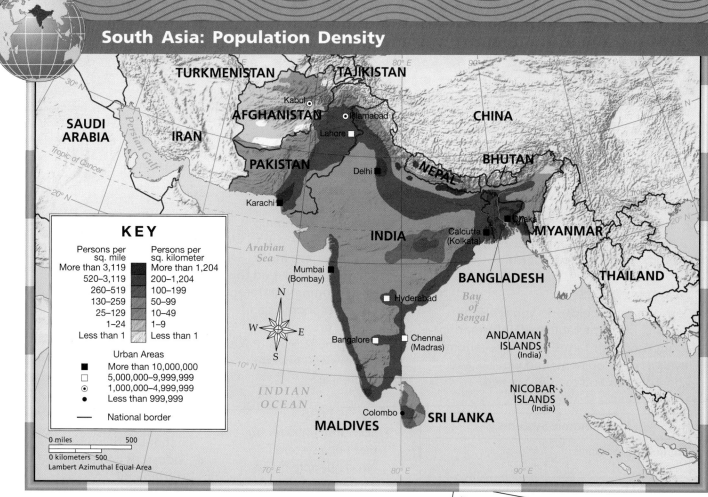

South Asia: Population Density

KEY

Persons per sq. mile	Persons per sq. kilometer
More than 3,119	More than 1,204
520–3,119	200–1,204
260–519	100–199
130–259	50–99
25–129	10–49
1–24	1–9
Less than 1	Less than 1

Urban Areas
- ■ More than 10,000,000
- ◻ 5,000,000–9,999,999
- ◉ 1,000,000–4,999,999
- • Less than 999,999
- — National border

0 miles 500
0 kilometers 500
Lambert Azimuthal Equal Area

Practice the Skill

Use steps 1–4 to read and interpret the population density map above.

1. What is the topic of this map? Notice that the map has relief—that is, markings that indicate hills and mountains. It also has labels for cities and nations of South Asia.

2. Study the map key carefully. How many different colors are in the key? What color is used for the lowest population density? What color is used for the highest density?

3. Using the key, identify the areas of highest and lowest population densities in South Asia. Write a sentence or two that describes where the most and the fewest people are located.

4. Write a conclusion that makes a general statement about South Asia's population density and suggests possible reasons for the patterns shown on the map.

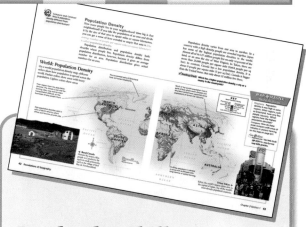

Apply the Skill

Now take a closer look at the map titled The World: Population Density on pages 62 and 63. Find the areas of greatest density. From what you already know and what you see on the map, what features do you think influence where people choose to live? Think about rivers and mountains as well as nearness to a coast or to the Equator.

Prepare to Read

Key Questions

In this section you will

1. Examine different kinds of economies.
2. Investigate levels of economic development.
3. Study global trade patterns.

Taking Notes

Copy the table below. As you read this section, fill in the table with information about economic terms, kinds of economies, levels of development, and world trade. Add columns and rows as needed.

Economic Systems	
Kinds of Economies	• •
Levels of Development	• •

Target Reading Skill

Make Comparisons
Comparing economic systems enables you to see what they have in common. As you read this section, compare different kinds of economies and levels of economic development. Who makes decisions and how do people live?

Key Terms

- **economy** (ih KAHN uh mee) *n.* a system in which people make, exchange, and use things that have value
- **producers** (pruh DOOS urz) *n.* owners and workers
- **consumers** (kun SOOM urz) *n.* people who buy and use products
- **capitalism** (KAP ut ul iz um) *n.* an economic system in which individuals own most businesses
- **communism** (KAHM yoo niz um) *n.* an economic system in which the central government owns factories, farms, and offices
- **developed nations** (dih VEL upt NAY shunz) *n.* nations with many industries and advanced technology
- **developing nations** (dih VEL up ing NAY shunz) *n.* nations with few industries and simple technology

Consumers choose produce at a market in Honolulu, Hawaii.

Different Kinds of Economies

An **economy** is a system in which people make, exchange, and use things that have value and that meet their wants or needs. Economies differ from one country to another. In any economy, owners and workers are **producers.** The things they sell are called products **Consumers** are people who buy and use products.

There are three basic economic questions: What will be produced? How will it be produced? And, for whom will it be produced? The answers to these questions depend on the economy.

Modern economies differ in who owns workplaces. The owners generally decide how products are produced. In some countries, most workplaces are privately owned. In others, the government owns most workplaces.

New York Stock Exchange
Stocks are bought and sold on the busy trading floor of the New York Stock Exchange. **Draw Conclusions** *Would you expect to find a busy stock exchange in a communist economy? Explain why or why not.*

Private Ownership Capitalism is an economic system in which private individuals own most businesses. Capitalism is also called a free-market economy because producers compete freely for consumers' business.

In capitalism, people may save money in banks. Banks lend money to people and businesses in return for interest, or a percentage fee for the use of money. Banks also pay interest to savers. Under capitalism, people may directly invest in, or commit money to, a business. Owners of a business are also investors in that business.

Government Ownership Communism is an economic system in which the central government owns farms, factories, and offices. It controls the prices of goods and services, how much is produced, and how much workers are paid. The government decides where to invest resources. Today, only a few of the world's nations practice communism.

Mixed Ownership Hardly any nation has a "pure" economic system. For example, the United States has a capitalist economy. However, governments build and maintain roads and provide other services. In communist countries, you may find a few small private businesses.

In some countries, the government may own some industries, while others belong to private owners. This system of mixed ownership is sometimes called a mixed economy.

✓ Reading Check **What are the differences between capitalism and communism?**

Levels of Economic Development

Three hundred years ago, most people made their own clothes. Then came a great change. People invented machines to make goods. They found new sources of power to run the machines. Power-driven machines were a new technology, or way of putting knowledge to practical use. This change in the way people made goods was called the Industrial Revolution.

The Industrial Revolution created a new economic pattern. Nations with more industries and more advanced technology are considered **developed nations.** Because they are still developing economically, nations with fewer industries and simpler technology are considered **developing nations.** People live differently in developed and developing nations.

Developed Nations Only about one fifth of the world's people live in developed nations. These nations include the United States, Canada, Japan, and most European nations. People in these nations use goods made in factories. Businesses use advanced technologies to produce goods and services.

In developed nations, most people live in towns and cities. They work in offices and factories. Machines do most of the work. Most people have enough food and water. Most citizens can get an education and healthcare.

In developed nations, most food is grown by commercial farmers. These are farmers who grow crops mainly for sale rather than for their own needs. Commercial farms use modern technologies, so they need fewer workers than traditional farms.

Developed nations can have some problems. Unemployment is a challenge. Not everyone can find a job. Industry and cars can cause air, land, and water pollution. Developed nations are working to solve these problems.

Target Skill

Make Comparisons What do developed nations have in common with developing nations?

Most of Thailand's subsistence farmers grow rice.

The World: Levels of Development

MAP MASTER™
Skills Activity

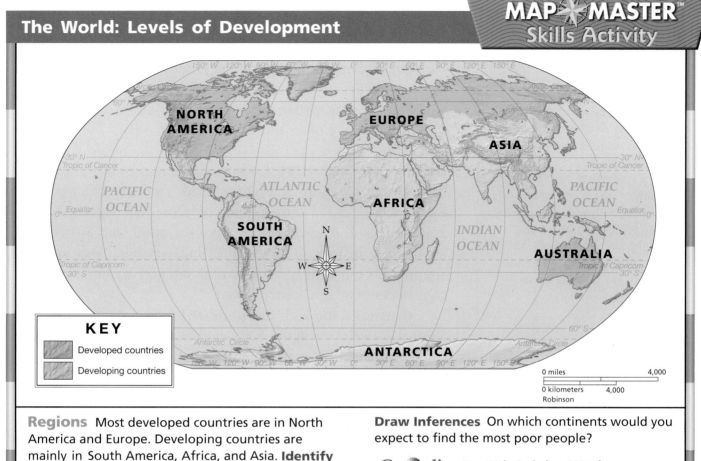

KEY
- Developed countries
- Developing countries

0 miles — 4,000
0 kilometers — 4,000
Robinson

Regions Most developed countries are in North America and Europe. Developing countries are mainly in South America, Africa, and Asia. **Identify** On which continents would you expect advanced industries, and farming that is mainly commercial?

Draw Inferences On which continents would you expect to find the most poor people?

Go Online Use Web Code **lep-3321** for PHSchool.com step-by-step **map skills practice.**

Developing Nations Not every economy is like that of the United States. Most of the people in the world live in developing nations, which are mainly in Africa, Asia, and Latin America.

Developing nations do not have great wealth. Many people are subsistence farmers, or farmers who raise food and animals mainly to feed their own families. Their farms have little or no machinery. People and animals do most of the work.

Many developing nations face great challenges. These include disease, food shortages, unsafe water, poor education and healthcare, and political unrest.

People in developing nations are confronting these challenges. Some nations, such as Saudi Arabia and South Africa, have grown richer by selling natural resources. Others, such as Thailand and China, have built successful industries. The more industrial developing nations are gradually becoming developed countries themselves.

Many people in developed nations work in offices.

✓ **Reading Check** How do developed nations differ from developing nations?

Chapter 3 Section 3 **77**

Links Across
Time

The Silk Road
Long-distance trade is nothing new. Hundreds of years ago, merchants brought silks and other luxuries from China to ancient Rome along the Silk Road across Asia. However, those merchants had to load goods on the backs of animals or carry the goods themselves. They could take only light-weight, valuable goods. Today, ships, trains, and trucks can carry heavy and inexpensive goods long distances.

World Trade Patterns

Different countries have different economic strengths. Developed nations have strong industries with advanced technology. Some developing nations have low-cost industries. Other developing nations may grow plantation cash crops, or they may produce oil or minerals.

Different Specialties Countries' economies differ not only because they are more or less developed. They also differ because each country has a different set of economic specialties. For example, Saudi Arabia has vast amounts of oil, and Switzerland has a long history of producing fine watches. Because each country has different specialties, each country has products that consumers in other countries want.

Countries trade with one another to take advantage of one another's special strengths. For example, the United States makes some of the world's best computers. But the United States needs oil. Saudi Arabia has plenty of oil, but it needs computers. So Saudi Arabia sells oil to the United States, and the United States sells computers to Saudi Arabia.

How Does World Trade Work?

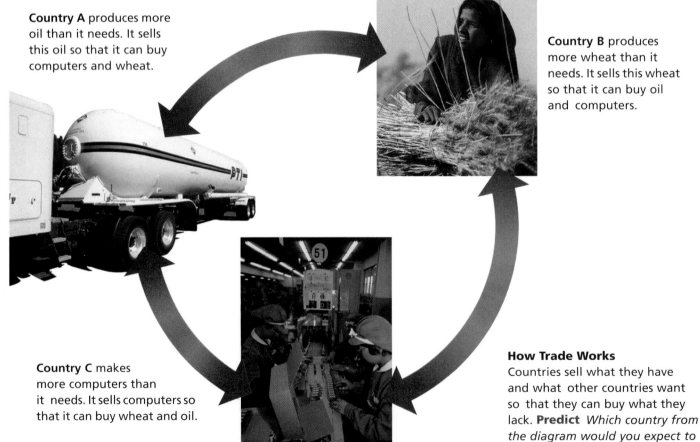

Country A produces more oil than it needs. It sells this oil so that it can buy computers and wheat.

Country B produces more wheat than it needs. It sells this wheat so that it can buy oil and computers.

Country C makes more computers than it needs. It sells computers so that it can buy wheat and oil.

How Trade Works
Countries sell what they have and what other countries want so that they can buy what they lack. **Predict** Which country from the diagram would you expect to sell oil so that it can buy tea?

Interdependence As world trade has grown, countries have grown interdependent, or dependent on one another. The United States depends on other countries for oil and inexpensive industrial goods. Meanwhile, other countries depend on the United States for computers and other products.

Developed nations tend to sell products made using advanced technologies. Developing nations tend to sell foods, natural resources such as oil, and simple industrial products. In return, they buy high-technology goods from developed countries.

Some countries have formed trade alliances to reduce the costs of trade. For example, the United States, Canada, and Mexico belong to the North American Free Trade Agreement, or NAFTA. Most European countries belong to the European Union. Businesses may face increased competition from foreign competitors within these alliances, and workers may lose their jobs. However, businesses may benefit from increased sales in other countries. Consumers benefit from these alliances because they pay less for products from other countries.

Moving Goods
Much of the world's trade travels on container ships, like this one in Dubai, United Arab Emirates. These ships can carry huge loads across oceans. **Draw Conclusions** *How does technology make world trade easier?*

✔ **Reading Check** **Why do countries trade with one another?**

Section 3 Assessment

Key Terms
Review the key terms at the beginning of this section. Use each term in a sentence that explains its meaning.

Target Reading Skill
What are two ways developed and developing countries are similar?

Comprehension and Critical Thinking
1. (a) Identify Who owns farms, factories, and offices in a communist economy?
(b) Compare and Contrast How is ownership different in a capitalist economy?

2. (a) Identify What is a country's level of development?
(b) Describe What are the main differences in level of development between countries?
(c) Predict What can we predict about a country's economy if we know its level of development?
3. (a) List What are two major trade alliances?
(b) Explain What is the main purpose of these alliances?
(c) Analyze What are some reasons why a country might want to join a trade alliance?

Writing Activity
Suppose you run a company, and you want to expand to another nation. Would you choose a capitalist or communist nation? A developed or developing nation? Would you choose a nation that belongs to a trade alliance? Write a letter to investors explaining your choice.

For: An activity on economic systems
Visit: PHSchool.com
Web Code: led-3303

Prepare to Read

Objectives
In this section you will
1. Examine different types of states.
2. Investigate types of government.
3. Learn about alliances and international organizations.

Taking Notes
Copy the table below. As you read, fill the table with information about types of states, types of governments, and international organizations.

Political Systems		
Types of State	Types of Government	Alliances and International Organizations
• • •	• • •	• • •

Target Reading Skill

Use Contrast Signal Words
Signal words point out relationships among ideas or events. Certain words, such as *like* or *unlike*, can signal a comparison or contrast. As you read this section, notice the comparisons and contrasts among different types of states and governments. What signal words indicate the comparisons and contrasts?

Key Terms
- **government** (GUV urn munt) *n.* a body that makes and enforces laws
- **state** (stayt) *n.* a region that shares a government
- **dependency** (dee PEN dun see) *n.* a region that belongs to another state
- **nation-state** (NAY shun stayt) *n.* a state that is independent of other states
- **city-state** (SIH tee stayt) *n.* a small city-centered state
- **empire** (EM pyr) *n.* a state containing several countries
- **constitution** (kahn stuh TOO shun) *n.* a set of laws that define and often limit a government's power

In 1994, Eritreans celebrated the first anniversary of their country's independence.

Types of States

Long ago, most people lived in small, traditional communities. All adults took part in group decisions. Some small communities still make decisions this way, but they are now part of larger units called nations. Nations are too large for everyone to take part in every decision. Still, nations have to protect people and resolve conflicts between individuals and social groups. In modern nations, these needs are met by **governments,** or organizations that set up and enforce laws.

You may remember that a region is an area united by a common feature. A **state** is a region that shares a government. You probably live in a state that is part of the United States. But the political units that we call "states" in the United States are just one kind of state. The entire United States can also be called a state. It is a region that shares a common government—the federal government.

Dependencies and Nation-States Some regions are **dependencies,** or regions that belong to another state. Others, like the United States, are **nation-states,** or states that are independent of other states. Each has a common body of laws. Nation-states are often simply called nations. Every place in the world where people live is part of a nation-state or dependency.

Most nation-states are large, but some are tiny. The smallest is Vatican City, which is surrounded by the city of Rome in Italy. Vatican City covers only about 109 acres (44 hectares)!

How States Developed The first real states formed in Southwest Asia more than 5,000 years ago when early cities set up governments. Small city-centered states are called **city-states.** Later, military leaders conquered large areas and ruled them as **empires,** or states containing several countries.

After about 1500, European rulers founded the first true nation-states. European nations established dependencies all over the world. When those dependencies became independent, they formed new nation-states.

✓ **Reading Check** **What is the difference between a government and a state?**

Use Contrast Signal Words

The first sentence in the paragraph at the left begins with the word *some.* The second sentence begins with *others.* These words signal that a contrast will be made. What contrast is being made?

Vatican City
St. Peter's Basilica, shown below, is the seat of the pope. He leads the Roman Catholic Church and rules Vatican City. **Infer** *What must be true about Vatican City for it to be a nation-state?*

Kim Jong II
Kim Jong II, the dictator of North Korea, making a rare public appearance.
Analyze Images *What group in North Korea might be a source of power for Kim Jong II?*

Types of Government

Each state has a government. There are many different kinds of government. Some governments are controlled by a single person or a small group of people. Others are controlled by all of the people.

Direct Democracy The earliest governments were simple. People lived in small groups. They practiced direct democracy, a form of government in which all adults take part in decisions. Many towns in New England today practice direct democracy. Decisions are made at town meetings where all adult residents can speak and vote.

Tribal Rule In time, communities banded together into larger tribal groups. Members of the tribe had a say in group decisions. But chiefs or elders usually made the final decision about what to do. Decisions were based upon the culture's customs and beliefs.

Absolute Monarchy Until about 200 years ago, one of the most common forms of government was absolute monarchy. In that system, a king or queen who inherits the throne by birth has complete control. Few absolute monarchies still exist today. Saudi Arabia is an example of a surviving absolute monarchy.

Dictatorship There are other countries today, however, where just one person rules. A leader who is not a king or queen but who has almost total power over an entire country is called a dictator. Dictatorship is rule by such a leader. Nations ruled by dictators include Cuba, Libya, and North Korea. Dictatorships differ from absolute monarchies because most dictators don't inherit power. Instead, they seize power. Dictators usually remain in power by using violence against their opponents. Dictators deny their people the right to make their own decisions.

Oligarchy Oligarchies are governments controlled by a small group of people. The group may be the leadership of a ruling political party. For example, China is an oligarchy controlled by the leadership of the Communist Party. There are other types of oligarchy. Myanmar, also called Burma, is run by a group of military officers. A group of religious leaders controls Iran. As in a dictatorship, ordinary people have little say in decisions.

Constitutional Monarchy Most monarchies today are constitutional monarchies, or governments in which the power of the king or queen is limited by law. The United Kingdom, the Netherlands, and Kuwait are examples. These nations have **constitutions,** or sets of laws that define and often limit the government's power. In a constitutional monarchy, the king or queen is often only a symbol of the country.

Representative Democracy Representative democracies are governments run by representatives that the people choose. Many constitutional monarchies are also representative democracies. In a representative democracy, the people indirectly hold power to govern and rule. They elect representatives who create laws. If the people do not like what a representative does, they can refuse to reelect that person. Citizens can also work to change laws they do not like. A constitution sets rules for elections, defines the rights of citizens, and limits the powers of the government. This system ensures that power is shared. The United States, Canada, and India are examples of representative democracies.

✓ **Reading Check** **What do absolute monarchies, dictatorships, and oligarchies have in common?**

Queen Beatrix of the Netherlands heads a constitutional monarchy.

Representative Democracy Members of the United States House of Representatives, shown below, are elected by the people of their districts. **Contrast** *How does a representative democracy differ from a direct democracy?*

International Organizations

Nations may make agreements to work together in an alliance. Members of an alliance are called allies. Alliances provide for nations to assist each other with defense. For example, members of the North Atlantic Treaty Organization (NATO) have agreed to defend any fellow member who is attacked.

Military bodies such as NATO are just one type of organization that is international, or involving more than one nation. Some international bodies are mainly economic in purpose. The European Union, for example, promotes economic unity among member nations in Europe.

The United Nations is an international organization meant to resolve disputes and promote peace. Almost all nations of the world belong to the United Nations. Every member has a vote in the General Assembly of the United Nations. But only the United Nations Security Council can make decisions over the use of force. The United States and four other permanent members have the power to prevent action in the Security Council.

The United Nations sponsors other international organizations with special purposes. For example, the Food and Agriculture Organization combats hunger worldwide. The United Nations Children's Fund (UNICEF) promotes the rights and well-being of children.

The United Nations headquarters in New York, New York

✓ **Reading Check** **What is the purpose of the United Nations?**

Section 4 Assessment

Key Terms
Review the key terms at the beginning of this section. Use each term in a sentence that explains its meaning.

Target Reading Skill
Reread the first paragraph on page 82. Which two main types of government are contrasted? Look for contrast signal words.

Comprehension and Critical Thinking
1. (a) Identify What were the earliest types of states?

(b) Compare and Contrast How did those early states differ from modern nation-states?

2. (a) List What are the main types of government?

(b) Categorize In which types of government do ordinary citizens take part in decisions?

3. (a) Define What is an alliance?

(b) Compare and Contrast What are the differences and similarities between alliances and other international organizations?

Writing Activity
Which type of government described in this section appeals most to you? Write a paragraph explaining your preference, and why it appeals to you.

Writing Tip When you write a paragraph, state the main idea in a topic sentence. In this case, the topic sentence will tell the type of government that you prefer. Other sentences should support the main idea with arguments.

Review and Assessment

◆ Chapter Summary

Section 1: Population
- Where people live depends on factors such as climate, soil, and history.
- Population density measures the average number of people living in an area.
- Scientific progress has spurred population growth, which is straining Earth's resources.

Section 2: Migration
- People migrate to seek a better life, or, in some cases, because they have no other choice.
- Cities are growing rapidly in some regions.

Section 3: Economic Systems
- Economic systems may have private ownership of businesses, government ownership, or a mixture of both.
- Developed countries have more industry and technology than developing countries.
- Trade connects countries as buyers and sellers.

Section 4: Political Systems
- The world is divided into nation-states.
- States have governments that differ in the amount of power that citizens have.
- Nation-states may join together in alliances and international organizations.

Harvesting rice in China

◆ Key Terms

Each of the statements below contains a key term from the chapter. If the statement is true, write *true*. If it is false, rewrite the statement to make it true.

1. A country's population is the number of people who live there.

2. Population density measures the size of cities.

3. The movement of people from one region to another is migration.

4. Urbanization is the movement of people to cities.

5. An economy is a system of government.

6. Consumers are people who sell products.

7. Developing nations have few industries and simple technologies.

8. A government is a body that makes and enforces laws and resolves conflicts among its people.

9. A state is a system of government.

◆ Comprehension and Critical Thinking

10. (a) Define What is population distribution?
(b) Explain What factors affect population distribution in a region?
(c) Compare and Contrast How are those factors different today than they were when most people were farmers?

11. (a) Identify How has the size of world populations changed in recent years?
(b) Identify Cause and Effect What difficulties have resulted from the change in the size of world populations?

12. (a) Define What is voluntary migration?
(b) Make Generalizations Why do people choose to migrate?

13. (a) Define What is capitalism?
(b) Contrast How does capitalism differ from communism?

14. (a) List What are some challenges faced by developing countries?
(b) Infer Why do developing countries face these challenges?

15. (a) Identify What are two types of democracy?
(b) Contrast How do democracies differ from other forms of government?

◆ Skills Practice

Using Population Density Maps In the Skills for Life activity in this chapter, you learned how to read a population density map using the map key.

Review the steps you followed to learn this skill. Then review the map on pages 62 and 63, titled The World: Population Density. Using the map key, describe what each color on the map represents and then list the most sparsely populated areas shown. Finally, draw conclusions about why these areas have such small populations.

◆ Writing Activity: Math

Suppose you are a demographer projecting population growth for three countries. Use the following information to create a population bar graph for each country:

	Birthrate	Death Rate
Country A	14.2	8.7
Country B	9.8	9.7
Country C	9.4	13.9

Then, write a brief paragraph explaining your graph. For each country, is the population increasing, decreasing, or stable? Explain why.

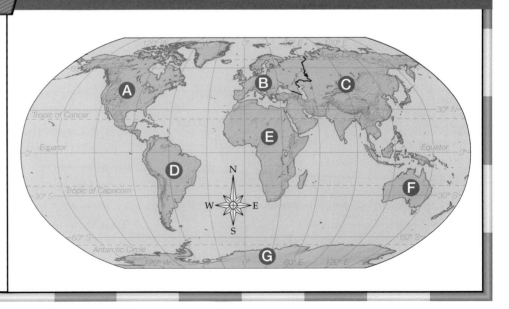

MAP MASTER™
Skills Activity

Continents

Place Location For each place listed below, write the letter from the map that shows its location.

1. Asia
2. Antarctica
3. Africa
4. South America
5. North America
6. Europe
7. Australia

Go Online
PHSchool.com Use Web Code **lep-3215** for an **interactive map.**

Standardized Test Prep

Test-Taking Tips

Some questions on standardized tests ask you to analyze a reading selection for a main idea. Read the passage in the box below. Then follow the tips to answer the sample question.

This region has one of the highest population densities in the world. As many as 5,000 people per square mile live in parts of the region. There are good reasons for this heavy population density. The land is fertile. Though the desert is not far away, the river contains plenty of water for the people who live there.

TIP As you read each sentence, think about what main idea it supports.

Pick the letter that best answers the question.

Which sentence states this passage's main idea?

A Demographers study human populations.

B Egypt's Nile River valley supports a large population.

C People find ways to adapt to their environment.

D Many people live near the Mississippi River.

TIP Cross out answer choices that don't make sense. Then pick from the remaining choices the one that BEST answers the question.

Think It Through The passage does not mention demographers. So you can cross out answer A. You can also rule out C, because the passage does not discuss people adapting to their environment. Answers B and D both mention specific regions. Which region does the paragraph describe? The paragraph mentions a desert. There is no desert near the Mississippi River. So the answer is B.

Practice Questions

Use the tips above and other tips in this book to help you answer the following questions.

1. The number of people per square mile is a region's
   A population distribution.
   B population.
   C elevation.
   D population density.

2. People moving to a different region to seek better farming opportunities is an example of
   A trade.
   B voluntary migration.
   C involuntary migration.
   D urbanization.

3. In which of the following does the government own most workplaces?
   A capitalism
   B developing country
   C communism
   D developed country

Read the following passage, and answer the question that follows.

A constitutional monarch has little power. Under some constitutions, elected representatives have the law-making power instead of the monarch. In such cases, the government works much like other representative democracies.

4. What is the main idea of this passage?
   A An absolute monarch has great power.
   B Constitutions are always democratic.
   C A constitutional monarchy may also be a representative democracy.
   D A constitutional monarch cannot interfere with representative democracy.

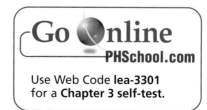

Go Online
PHSchool.com

Use Web Code **lea-3301** for a **Chapter 3 self-test.**

My Side of the Mountain
By Jean Craighead George

Prepare to Read

Background Information

Have you ever camped out overnight? Have you ever built a fire in order to keep warm? Suppose you had no electricity or your home had no heating system. How would you cope with the natural world without modern technology? Do you think that living closer to the natural world would change you in any significant way?

Sam Gribley is the fictional hero of the novel *My Side of the Mountain*. When he decided to live close to nature, he built a tree house in the Catskill Mountains of New York and then moved in with his only companion, Frightful, a falcon. This excerpt describes their first winter in the mountains.

Objectives

As you read this selection, you will

- Identify the skills Sam needed to survive alone in the wilderness.
- Discover how Sam came to understand the natural world.

Fog-shrouded woodland in the Catskill Mountains, New York

I lived close to the weather. It is surprising how you watch it when you live in it. Not a cloud passed unnoticed, not a wind blew untested. I knew the moods of the storms, where they came from, their shapes and colors. When the sun shone, I took Frightful to the meadow and we slid down the mountain on my snapping-turtle-shell sled. She really didn't care much for this.

When the winds changed and the air smelled like snow, I would stay in my tree, because I had gotten lost in a blizzard one afternoon and had to hole up in a rock ledge until I could see where I was going. That day the winds were so strong I could not push against them, so I crawled under the ledge; for hours I wondered if I would be able to dig out when the storm blew on. Fortunately I only had to push through a foot of snow. However, that taught me to stay home when the air said "snow." Not that I was afraid of being caught far from home in a storm, for I could find food and shelter and make a fire anywhere, but I had become as attached to my <u>hemlock</u> house as a brooding bird to her nest. Caught out in the storms and weather, I had an urgent desire to return to my tree, even as The Baron Weasel returned to his den, and the deer to their <u>copse</u>. We all had our little "patch" in the wilderness. We all fought to return there.

I usually came home at night with the nuthatch that roosted in a nearby sapling. I knew I was late if I tapped the tree and he came out. Sometimes when the weather was icy and miserable, I would hear him high in the trees near the edge of the meadow, <u>yanking</u> and yanking and flicking his tail, and then I would see him wing to bed early. I considered him a pretty good <u>barometer</u>, and if he went to his tree early, I went to mine early too. When you don't have a newspaper or radio to give you weather bulletins, watch the birds and animals. They can tell when a storm is coming. I called the nuthatch "Barometer," and when he holed up, I holed up, lit my light, and sat by my fire <u>whittling</u> or learning new tunes on my reed whistle. I was now really into the <u>teeth of winter</u>, and quite fascinated by its activity. There is no such thing as a "still winter night." Not only are many animals running around in the breaking cold, but the trees cry out and limbs snap and fall, and the wind gets caught in a ravine and screams until it dies.

✓ **Reading Check** **What did Sam name the nuthatch? Explain why.**

hemlock (HEM lahk) *n.* an evergreen tree with drooping branches and short needles
copse (kahps) *n.* a thicket of small trees or shrubs
yank (yangk) *v.* to give the call made by a nuthatch
barometer (buh RAHM uh tur) *n.* an instrument for forecasting changes in the weather; anything that indicates a change
whittle (WHIT ul) *v.* to cut or pare thin shavings from wood with a knife
teeth of winter (teeth uv WIN tur) *n.* the coldest, harshest time of winter

About the Selection

My Side of the Mountain, by Jean Craighead George (New York: E. P. Dutton, 1959), includes sketches of Sam Gribley's adventures.

Review and Assessment

Comprehension and Critical Thinking

1. (a) Identify When the weather is bad, what is Sam's "urgent desire"?
(b) Compare To what does Sam compare this desire?
(c) Interpret What does Sam tell us about himself when he makes a comparison?
2. (a) Recall What are some of the clues Sam has about what the weather will be like?
(b) Describe What parts of the natural world does Sam seem to notice most?
(c) Evaluate Sometimes Sam talks about the wind and trees as if they were alive. Think about your relationship with nature. How is it like Sam's? How is it different?

Writing Activity

Make a list of sounds you hear only in winter. What are the tastes and smells that make you think of winter? List them. What are the sights of winter? Add them to your list. Then write an essay describing the place you most like to be in winter and explain why.

About the Author

Jean Craighead George (b. 1919) often went camping, climbed trees, and studied living things as she grew up. Ms. George has been writing about nature and its lessons since she was eight years old, and has written more than 80 books for young readers.

Chapter
4 Cultures of the World

Chapter Preview

This chapter will introduce you to the concept of culture, the things that make up culture, and the ways in which cultures change.

Section 1
Understanding Culture

Section 2
Culture and Society

Section 3
Cultural Change

Target Reading Skill

Sequence In this chapter, you will focus on the text structure by identifying the order, or sequence, of events. Noting the sequence of events can help you understand and remember the events.

▶ Young women in traditional dress at a festival in Pushkar, India

Understanding Culture

Prepare to Read

Objectives
In this section you will
1. Learn about culture.
2. Explore how culture has developed.

Taking Notes
Copy the concept web below. As you read this section, fill in the web with information about culture, its relation to the environment, and how it has developed. Add ovals as needed for concepts in the section.

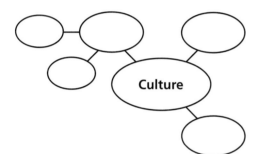

Culture

Target Reading Skill

Understand Sequence
A sequence is the order in which a series of events occurs. Noting the sequence of important events can help you understand and remember the events. You can show the order of events by making a sequence chart. Write the first event, or thing that sets the other events in motion, in the first box. Then write each additional event in a box. Use arrows to show how one event leads to the next.

Key Terms
- **culture** (KUL chur) *n.* the way of life of a people, including their beliefs and practices
- **cultural landscape** (KUL chur ul LAND skayp) *n.* the parts of a people's environment that they have shaped and the technology they have used to shape it
- **civilization** (sih vuh luh ZAY shun) *n.* an advanced culture with cities and a system of writing
- **institution** (in stuh TOO shun) *n.* a custom or organization with social, educational, or religious purposes

A grandfather in Japan teaching his grandson to use chopsticks

What Is Culture?

Culture is the way of life of a people, including their beliefs, customs, and practices. The language people speak and the way they dress are both parts of their culture. So are the work people do, what they do after work or school, and the ideas that influence them.

Elements of Culture Parents pass culture on to their children, generation after generation. Ideas and ways of doing things are called cultural traits. Over time, cultural traits may change.

Some elements of a culture are easy to see. They include material things, such as houses, television sets, food, and clothing. Sports and literature are visible elements of culture as well. Things you cannot see or touch are also part of culture. They include spiritual beliefs, government, and ideas about right and wrong. Finally, language is a very important part of culture.

People and Their Land Geographers study themes of culture, especially human activities related to the environment. The theme of human-environment interaction deals with these activities. Geographers want to know how the environment affects culture. For example, Japan is a nation of mountainous islands, with limited farmland. So the Japanese have turned to the sea. Fish and seaweed are popular foods in Japan.

However, environment does not dictate culture. Like Japan, Greece is a nation of mountainous islands and peninsulas surrounded by the sea. The Greeks eat some fish, but they have cleared mountainsides as well for use as pasture. Goats and sheep graze on the mountainsides and provide food for the Greeks.

Geographers are also interested in the effect people have on their environment. Often the effect is tied to a culture's technology, even if that technology is simple. For example, the Greeks have cleared their rugged land for pasture. The Japanese harvest seaweed.

A **cultural landscape** is the parts of a people's environment that they have shaped and the technology they have used to shape it. This varies from place to place. On hilly Bali (BAH lee), in Indonesia, farmers have carved terraces into hillsides. On the plains of northern India, farmers have laid out broad, flat fields.

✔ **Reading Check** **How are culture and environment related?**

Balinese Terraces
A farmer on the island of Bali, in Indonesia, crosses terraced rice fields.
Analyze *How has Bali's environment affected its culture? How has Bali's culture affected its environment?*

Learn more about culture.

The Development of Culture

Scientists think that early cultures had four major advances in technology. First was the invention of tools millions of years ago. Second and third were the control of fire and the beginning of agriculture. Fourth was the development of **civilizations,** or advanced cultures with cities and the use of writing.

Technology and Civilization For most of human existence, people were hunters and gatherers. While traveling from place to place, they collected wild plants, hunted game, and fished.

Later, people discovered how to grow crops. They tamed wild animals to help them with work or to raise for food. Over time, more and more people relied on farming for most of their food. Historians call this great change the Agricultural Revolution.

Agriculture provided a steady food supply. Agriculture let farmers grow more food than they needed. In parts of Asia and Africa, some people worked full time on crafts such as metal-working. They traded their products for food. People began to develop laws and government. To store information, they developed writing. These advances in culture produced the first true civilizations about 5,000 years ago.

Early civilizations developed new technologies, such as irrigation, that let people grow more crops. Over time, farming and civilization spread throughout the world.

The Development of Agricultural Technology

Sickle
The first farmers used hand-held sickles to harvest grain. The first sickles had stone blades. Later sickles, like the one shown here, had metal blades.

Horse-drawn reaper
By the late 1800s, farmers were using animal-powered machinery, such as this sail reaper, to harvest grain.

Combine harvester
Today, farmers harvest grain with large-scale, motorized machinery, such as this combine.

Tools for Harvesting When the Agricultural Revolution began, people used simple hand-powered tools. The Industrial Revolution later brought industrial tools to the fields.
Draw Conclusions *How do you think the development of tools for harvesting affected the amount that each farmer could harvest?*

Then, about 200 years ago, people began to invent new technologies that used power-driven machinery. This change marked the beginning of the Industrial Revolution. It led to the growth of cities, science, and even more advanced technologies, such as computers and space flight.

Understand Sequence What important events led to the Industrial Revolution?

Development of Institutions Before the Agricultural Revolution, people had simple institutions, customs and organizations with social, educational, or religious purposes. These included extended families and simple political institutions, such as councils of elders.

As people gathered in larger groups and formed cities, they needed more complex institutions. People developed organized religions, with priests, ceremonies, and temples. Armies and governments appeared with states. Teachers started schools.

In the modern world, we have many different kinds of institutions, including museums, sports clubs, corporations, political parties, and universities. These institutions are important parts of our culture.

✔ **Reading Check** What allowed civilizations to develop?

Oxford University, in Oxford, England, is more than 800 years old.

Section 1 Assessment

Key Terms
Review the key terms at the beginning of this section. Use each term in a sentence that explains its meaning.

Target Reading Skill
Place the following events in the order in which they occurred: the development of civilization; the invention of tools; the development of industry; and the beginnings of agriculture.

Comprehension and Critical Thinking
1. (a) Define What is a cultural landscape?
(b) Explain What are the most important cultural traits that shape a people's cultural landscape?
(c) Identify Cause and Effect If two cultures occupy similar environments, why might their cultural landscapes still differ?
2. (a) Identify What was the Agricultural Revolution?
(b) Sequence What cultural advances followed the Agricultural Revolution?

Writing Activity
Think of all the ways that the culture of your region has shaped its landscape. Write a short paragraph describing your cultural landscape and the cultural traits that shaped it.

For: An activity on culture
Visit: PHSchool.com
Web Code: led-3401

Culture and Society

Prepare to Read

Objectives

In this section you will
1. Learn how people are organized into groups.
2. Investigate language.
3. Explore the role of religion.

Taking Notes

Copy the outline below. As you read this section, fill in the outline with information about how society is organized, about language, and about religion. Add letters and numbers as needed.

> I. How society is organized
>   A. Social classes
>   B.
>   1.
>   2.
> II. Language
>   A.

 **Target Reading Skill**

Understand Sequence
Noting the sequence of important changes can help you understand and remember the changes. You can show a sequence of changes by simply listing the changes in the order in which they occurred. As you read this section, list the sequence of the changes in people's ability to improve their status.

Key Terms

- **society** (suh SY uh tee) *n.* a group of people sharing a culture
- **social structure** (SOH shul STRUK chur) *n.* a pattern of organized relationships among groups of people within a society
- **social class** (SOH shul klas) *n.* a grouping of people based on rank or status
- **nuclear family** (NOO klee ur FAM uh lee) *n.* a mother, a father, and their children
- **extended family** (ek STEN did FAM uh lee) *n.* a family that includes several generations

A nuclear family in the United Kingdom

How Society Is Organized

Think about the people you see every day. Do you spend each day meeting random strangers? Or do you see the same family members, classmates, and teachers every day? Chances are, there is a pattern to your interactions.

A group of people sharing a culture is known as a **society.** Every society has a **social structure,** or a pattern of organized relationships among groups of people within the society. A society may be as small as a single community or as large as a nation or even a group of similar nations. Smaller groups within a society work together on particular tasks. Some groups work together to get food. Others protect the community. Still others educate children. Social structure helps people work together to meet one another's basic needs.

The family is the basic, most important social unit of any society. Families teach the customs and traditions of the culture to their children. Through their families, children learn how to dress, to be polite, to eat, and to play.

Social Classes Cultures also have another kind of social organization—social classes, or groupings of people based on rank or status. A person's status or position may come from his or her wealth, land, ancestors, or education. In some cultures in the past, it was often hard—or impossible—for people to move from one social class to another. Today, people in many societies can improve their status. They can obtain a good education, make more money, or marry someone of a higher class.

Understand Sequence
How has people's ability to improve their status changed over time?

Kinds of Families Not all cultures define family in the same way. In some cultures, the basic unit is a nuclear family, or a mother, a father, and their children. This pattern is common in developed nations such as the United States, Australia, and Germany. The nuclear family gets its name from the word *nucleus*, which means "center."

Other cultures have extended families, or families that include several generations. In addition to a central nuclear family of parents and their sons or daughters, there are the wives or husbands of those sons or daughters. The family also includes grandchildren, or the children of those sons or daughters. In extended families, older people often help care for the children. They are respected for their knowledge and experience. Older family members pass on traditions. Extended families are less common than they used to be. As rural people move to cities, nuclear families are becoming more common.

✓ **Reading Check** What is the basic social unit of societies?

A Salvadoran-American Family
This family includes grandparents and more than one set of parents. **Infer** *Is this a nuclear family or an extended family?*

A teacher using sign language with hearing-impaired students

Language

All cultures have language. In fact, language provides a basis for culture. People learn their cultures mainly through language. Most communication with others depends on language. Think how hard it would be if you had no way to say, "Meet me by the gate after school." How could you learn if you could not ask questions?

A culture's language reflects the things that are important in that culture. For example, English has words for Christian and Jewish concepts, such as *baptism* and *sabbath.* Some languages lack words for these concepts because their speakers are not Jewish or Christian. But those languages have words for concepts in their people's religions that have no English translation.

The World: Major Language Groups

This map shows the locations of the world's major language groups. Languages in each of these groups share a common ancestor, a language spoken long ago that gradually changed to become several related languages. For example, English and German are both Indo-European languages that share a common ancestor. Can you recognize the German words *Land, Mann,* and *Wagen?*

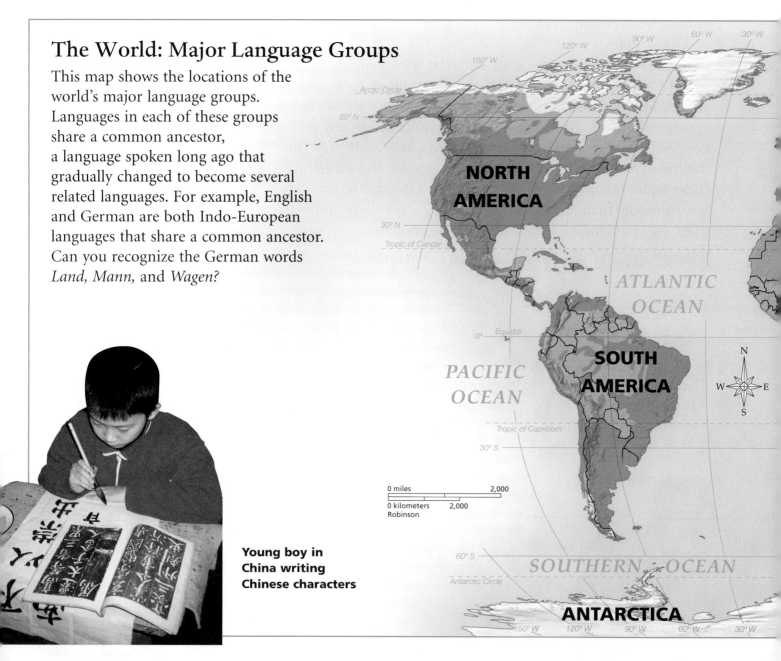

Young boy in China writing Chinese characters

In some countries, people speak more than one language. For example, Canada has two official languages, French and English. In the United States, you may usually hear English, but you can also hear Spanish, Chinese, Haitian Creole, and many other languages. India has 16 official languages, but people there speak more than 800 languages!

People who speak each language are culturally different in some ways from other people in their country who speak other languages. They may celebrate different festivals or have different customs for such things as dating or education. That is because each language preserves shared ideas and traditions.

✓ **Reading Check** **What is the relation between language and culture?**

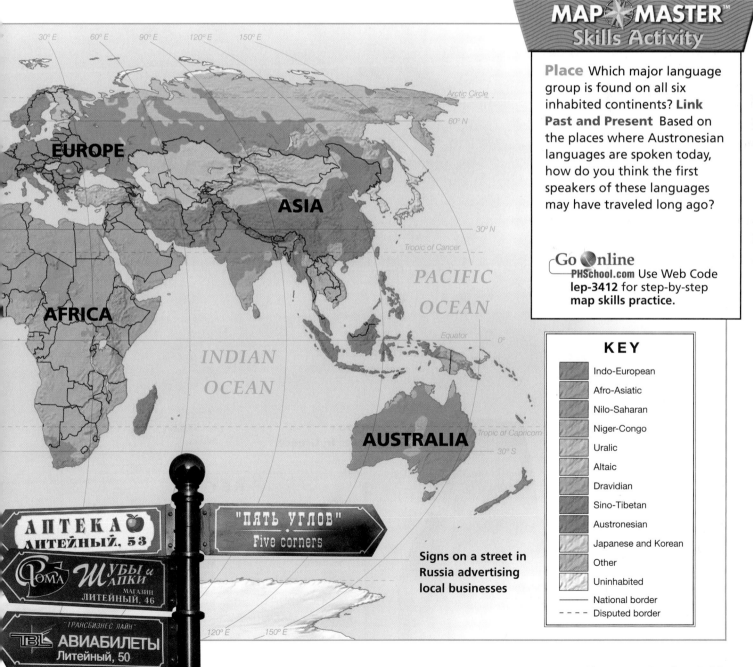

MAP MASTER™
Skills Activity

Place Which major language group is found on all six inhabited continents? **Link Past and Present** Based on the places where Austronesian languages are spoken today, how do you think the first speakers of these languages may have traveled long ago?

Go Online
PHSchool.com Use Web Code **lep-3412** for step-by-step map skills practice.

KEY

- Indo-European
- Afro-Asiatic
- Nilo-Saharan
- Niger-Congo
- Uralic
- Altaic
- Dravidian
- Sino-Tibetan
- Austronesian
- Japanese and Korean
- Other
- Uninhabited
- ——— National border
- - - - - Disputed border

Signs on a street in Russia advertising local businesses

The World: Major Religions

The major religions of the world all began in Asia. India was the birthplace of Sikhism, Hinduism, and Buddhism, all of which later spread to other countries. The other great world religions had their start in Southwest Asia: first Judaism, then Christianity, and finally Islam. These religions also later spread to other parts of the world.

Young Buddhist monks in Thailand

MAP MASTER™ Skills Activity

Place Which of the continents has the greatest variety of religions?

Draw Inferences Why do you think this is so?

Go Online
PHSchool.com Use Web Code **lep-3422** for step-by-step **map skills practice.**

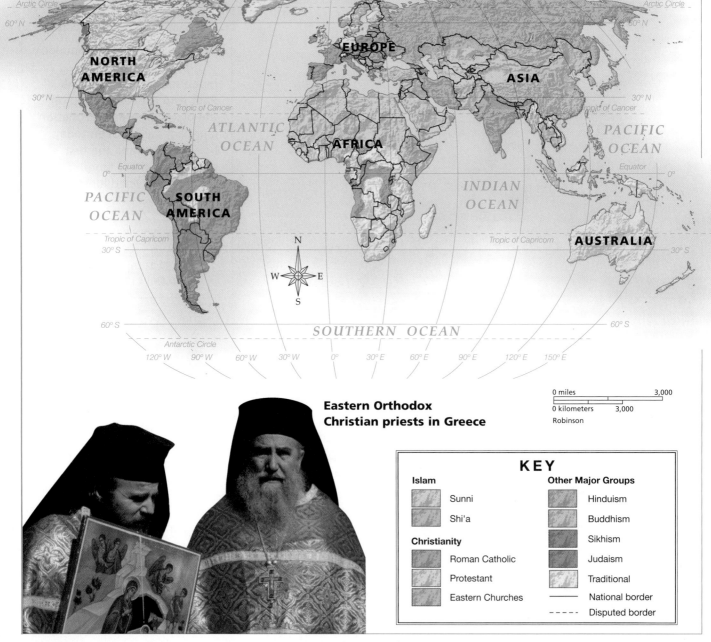

Eastern Orthodox Christian priests in Greece

0 miles 3,000
0 kilometers 3,000
Robinson

KEY

Islam
- Sunni
- Shi'a

Christianity
- Roman Catholic
- Protestant
- Eastern Churches

Other Major Groups
- Hinduism
- Buddhism
- Sikhism
- Judaism
- Traditional
- —— National border
- ----- Disputed border

100 Foundations of Geography

Religion

Religion is an important part of every culture. For example, most of the people of Saudi Arabia are Muslim. In some countries, such as the United States, people follow more than one religion. Beliefs and practices may differ among religions. However, religion remains important to many people.

Religion can help people make sense of the world. Religion can provide comfort and hope for people facing difficult times. And religion can help answer questions about the meaning and purpose of life. Religion also guides people in ethics, or standards of accepted behavior.

Religious beliefs vary. Members of some religions, such as Islam, Judaism, and Christianity, believe in one God. Members of other religions, such as Hinduism and traditional religions, believe in more than one god. But all religions have prayers and rituals. Every religion celebrates important places and times. And all religions expect people to treat one another well and to behave properly.

✓ **Reading Check** Why is religion important to people?

This temple, in Amritsar, India, is a holy place of Sikhism.

Section 2 Assessment

Key Terms
Review the key terms at the beginning of this section. Use each term in a sentence that explains its meaning.

Target Reading Skill
Place the following events in young people's lives in the correct sequence: learning their culture's language and learning their culture's beliefs.

Comprehension and Critical Thinking
1. (a) Identify What is the role of social structure in society?
(b) Explain What is the place of families in a social structure?
(c) Predict Would you expect the members of one family to fall within one social class or more than one?
2. (a) Recall How is language related to culture?
(b) Identify Cause and Effect Why do you think people who speak different languages tend to have different cultures?
3. (a) Identify What values do all religions share?
(b) Draw Conclusions How might those values help people of different religions overcome conflicts?

Writing Activity
In a journal entry, explore the ways in which family and language connect you to other people in your society.

Writing Tip When you write a journal entry, write about experiences from your own life. You may also express your own opinions and perspectives. For this exercise, think about which of your activities and interests involve family or the use of language.

A generalization is a broad conclusion. Some generalizations are valid—that is, they have value or worth—because they can be drawn reasonably from specific facts. Other generalizations are not valid, because they draw unreasonably broad conclusions and are not based on fact.

Many statements have clues that tell you they should be evaluated for validity. For example, statements with words such as *everybody* or *everyone* are very broad. They should always be evaluated. Is the statement "Everybody needs salt" a valid generalization? It is, because it is based on the scientifically proven fact that humans cannot survive without salt in our diet. However, generalizations such as "Everybody loves chocolate" are not valid. They draw unreasonably broad conclusions and cannot be proved.

You need to know how to evaluate a generalization to see if it is valid. You also have to know how to make a valid generalization yourself.

Learn the Skill

To make a valid generalization, follow these steps:

1 **Identify specific facts contained within a source of information.** Make sure you understand the topic that the facts support.

2 **State what the facts have in common, and look for patterns.** Do any of the facts fit together in a way that makes a point about a broad subject? Do data in a table or graph point toward a general statement?

3 **Make a generalization, or broad conclusion, about the facts.** Write your generalization as a complete sentence or a paragraph.

4 **Test the generalization and revise it if necessary.** You can test the validity of a generalization by using the guidelines in the box at the left.

Testing for Validity

To find whether a generalization is valid, ask
- Are there enough facts—at least three in a short passage—to support the generalization?
- Do I know any other facts that support the generalization?
- Does the statement overgeneralize or stereotype a group of people? Words such as *all*, *always*, or *every* signal overgeneralization. Words such as *some*, *many*, *most*, and *often* help prevent a statement from being overgeneralized.

Practice the Skill

Read the passage at the right describing three cultures, and then make a generalization about these cultures.

 What is the topic of the text? List at least three specific facts that relate to that topic.

 What do the facts you listed have in common? Do they suggest a general idea about the topic?

3 Make a generalization about the topic. Write it in a complete sentence. List three facts that support it.

4 Test your generalization to see if it is valid. If it is not valid, try rewriting it so that it is more limited. Be careful of exaggerated wording.

Apply the Skill

Turn to page 97 and read the paragraph under the heading Kinds of Families. Make as many generalizations as you can, and test them for their validity. Explain why each generalization is or is not valid.

The Maya thrived in present-day Mexico and Central America from about A.D. 300 to 900. Corn was their principal crop. They developed a sophisticated civilization, but they had abandoned their great cities by about A.D. 900. At about that time, the Hohokam people were growing corn and beans in what is now Arizona. The Hohokam left their settlements during the 1400s, possibly because of drought. Meanwhile, between about A.D. 900 and 1300, the Anasazi people lived to the northeast. They also grew corn. The Anasazi built multistory dwellings up against high cliff walls. Many families lived in these homes. During a drought in the late 1200s, the Anasazi abandoned some of their villages.

An extended Islamic family, spanning three generations, from the rural east coast of Malaysia

Objectives

In this section you will
1. Explore how cultures change.
2. Learn how ideas spread from one culture to another.

Taking Notes

Copy the concept web below. As you read this section, fill in the web with information about cultural change. Add ovals as needed for the concepts in the section.

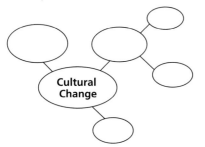

Cultural Change

Target Reading Skill

Recognize Words That Signal Sequence

Signal words point out relationships among ideas or events. To help keep the order of events clear, look for words such as *first, later,* or *at that time* that signal the order in which the events took place.

Key Terms

- **cultural diffusion** (KUL chur ul dih FYOO zhun) *n.* the movement of customs and ideas
- **acculturation** (uh kul chur AY shun) *n.* the process of accepting new ideas and fitting them into a culture

Blue jeans and denim shirts have changed with the times.

How Cultures Change

All cultures change over time. The history of blue jeans is an example of cultural change. Some people think that blue jeans are typical American clothes. But many cultures contributed to them. Blue jeans were invented in the United States in the 1800s. They were marketed by Levi Strauss. Strauss was a German-born merchant who moved to California. He made the jeans with a cloth called denim. This may be a shortened form of *serge de Nîmes,* the name of a similar cloth from France.

At first, only Americans wore blue jeans, but they later became popular in other countries. In the 1980s, the Japanese and the French developed stonewashing. It made brand-new denim jeans look worn. Since then, designers from Asia, Europe, and America have promoted new styles, such as ripped and "dirty" denim. Today, jeans are popular all over the world. And the word *jeans* comes from an old French name for Genoa, an Italian city where a cloth similar to denim was first made. What could be more American than jeans?

Why Cultures Change Just as jeans have changed over time, so, too, has American culture. Cultures change all the time. Because culture is an entire way of life, a change in one part changes other parts. Changes in the natural environment, technology, and ideas all affect culture.

New Technologies New technologies also change a culture. During the 1800s and early 1900s, the growth of industry and the spread of factories drew large numbers of Americans from the countryside to the nation's cities. Factories offered jobs to thousands of men, women, and children. Limited transportation meant that people had to live close to the factories. Cities grew larger as a result.

This all changed after the invention of the car in the late 1800s. Within a few years, advances in technology made cars more affordable. By 1920, many Americans had cars. People could live farther from their jobs and drive to work. Soon after, the idea of owning a house with a yard became more popular. The result has been the growth of sprawling suburbs since the mid-1900s and a new culture based on car travel.

A teenager using a cell phone

A "bullet train" in Japan
Japanese engineers have developed new technologies that allow these trains to travel at speeds of more than 180 miles (300 kilometers) per hour. **Infer** *How might such high speeds affect how far away people can live from their work?*

How One Change Can Lead to Others Think of other ways technology has changed the culture of the United States. Radio and television brought entertainment and news into homes. Today instant information is part of our culture. Computers change how and where people work. Computers even help people live longer since doctors use computers to diagnose and treat patients. Radio, television, and computers add new words to our language, such as *broadcast, channel surfing,* and *hacker.* What other new words can you think of?

Cultural Change Over Time Cultural change has been going on for a long time. Controlling fire helped early people survive in colder climates. When people started raising animals and growing crops, ways of life also changed. People began to work in the same fields year after year. Before that, they had roamed over a wider area looking for wild plant and animal foods.

✓ Reading Check **How did the invention of cars change culture?**

How Ideas Spread

Advances in transportation technology, such as the airplane, make it easier for people to move all over the world. When they move, people bring new kinds of clothing and tools with them. They also bring ideas about such things as ways to prepare food, teach children, practice their religion, or govern themselves.

Ideas can travel to new places in other ways. People may obtain goods from another culture by trade and then learn to make those goods themselves. People may also learn from other cultures through written material. The movement of customs and ideas is called **cultural diffusion.**

How Cultures Adopt New Ideas One example of cultural diffusion is the game of baseball. Baseball began as an American sport, but today it is played in countries all around the world. That is an example of cultural diffusion. The Japanese love baseball. However, they have changed the game to fit their culture. These changes are an example of **acculturation,** or the process of accepting new ideas and fitting them into a culture. Americans value competition. They focus on winning. A game of baseball does not end until one team wins. But in Japan, a game can end in a tie. The Japanese do not mind a tie game. In Japan, how well you play is more important than winning.

A woman practicing yoga, a form of meditation that spread from Asia to Europe and North America

Communication Technology and the Speed of Change

What's the fastest way to get from your house to Japan? Would you use a jet plane? A phone call? The Internet? A fax? All these answers can be correct. The answer depends on whether you want to transport your body, your voice, a picture, or just words on a sheet of paper.

For thousands of years, cultures changed slowly. People and goods moved by foot or wagon or sailing ship, so ideas and technology also moved slowly. Recently, communication technology has increased the speed of change. Faxes and computers transport information almost instantly. Magazines and television shows can bring ideas and information from all over the world to any home. This rapid exchange of ideas speeds up cultural change.

Technology has brought many benefits. Computers let scientists share information about how to cure diseases. Telephones let us instantly talk to relatives thousands of miles away. In the Australian Outback, students your age use closed-circuit television and two-way radios to take part in class from their own homes.

Links to
Technology

Digital Tunes Until recent years, music lovers had to lug around tapes or CDs. The invention of MP3s and MP3 players changed that. Fans can now download and store thousands of songs in MP3 format from the Internet. They no longer need bulky tapes and CDs.

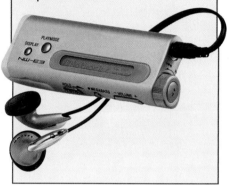

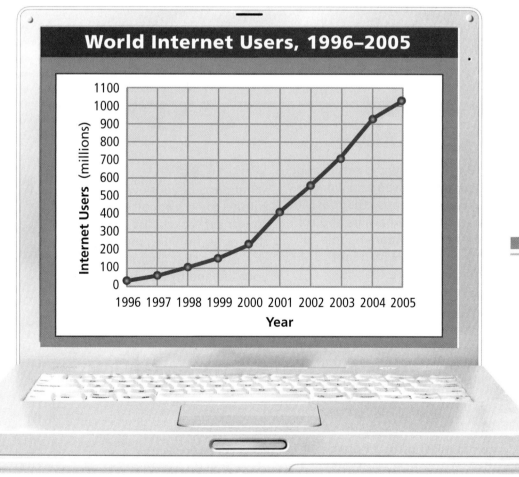

World Internet Users, 1996–2005

Graph: Internet Users (millions) vs. Year

■ Graph Skills

Internet use grew rapidly after 1996. **Identify** What was the number of Internet users in 2005?

Predict Based on the trend shown in the graph, how do you think the number of Internet users has changed since 2005?

Defending Their Heritage
In 1988 Aborigines, descendants of Australia's original inhabitants, protested the 200th anniversary of the arrival of Europeans. **Analyze Images** *What evidence do you see that the Aborigines' culture has changed over the past 200 years?*

Defending Traditions Change can help, but it can also hurt. If things change too fast, people may feel that their culture is threatened. Valuable traditions can disappear. Once traditional knowledge has been lost, it can never be regained. In many parts of the world, people are working to preserve, or save, their own cultures before it is too late. They do not want to lose what is valuable in their culture. They want to save the artistic traditions, the religious beliefs, and the wisdom that enriched the lives of past generations for the sake of future generations.

✓ **Reading Check** **How has technology affected the speed of cultural change?**

Section 3 Assessment

Key Terms
Review the key terms at the beginning of this section. Use each term in a sentence that explains its meaning.

Target Reading Skill
Review the second paragraph on page 107. Find the words that signal a sequence of events related to communication technologies.

Comprehension and Critical Thinking
1. (a) Describe What cultural changes in America followed the invention of cars?

(b) Explain How did cars change where people lived and worked?
(c) Predict Suppose that gasoline became more expensive and computers allowed more people to work at home. How might American culture change?
2. (a) List What are two main ways in which ideas travel from one culture to another?
(b) Describe Give an example of an idea that has passed from one culture to another.
(c) Compare and Contrast How has the spread of ideas changed with modern communication technologies?

Writing Activity
What parts of your own culture come from other countries? Make a list detailing the foods, fashions, music, or customs that are part of your life and that come from other countries.

For: An activity on cultural change
Visit: PHSchool.com
Web Code: led-3403

◆ Chapter Summary

Section 1: Understanding Culture

- Culture is an entire way of life that is shaped by people's environment and that also shapes people's environment.
- Culture developed over time from simple technologies and institutions to more advanced technologies and institutions.

Section 2: Culture and Society

- A society is a group of people sharing a culture and held together by a social structure.
- Language expresses the basic concepts of a culture and transmits those concepts to young people.
- Religions help people make sense of the world. They are an important source of values for cultures and teach people to treat one another fairly.

Section 3: Cultural Change

- Changes in the environment or in technology lead to changes in culture.
- Ideas move among cultures through the movement of people, through trade, and through communication technologies.

Traditional dress in India

◆ Key Terms

Each of the statements below contains a key term from the chapter. If the statement is true, write *true*. If it is false, rewrite the statement to make it true.

1. The culture of a people is their way of life, including their beliefs and customs.

2. A civilization is an organization with social, educational, or religious purposes.

3. An institution is an advanced culture with cities and the use of writing.

4. A society is a group of people sharing a culture.

5. A pattern of organized relationships among groups of people is a social structure.

6. An extended family consists of two parents and their children.

7. A nuclear family includes two grandparents, their children, and their grandchildren.

8. Cultural diffusion is the movement of customs or ideas from one culture to another.

9. Acculturation is an accumulation of several cultures in a single place.

◆ Comprehension and Critical Thinking

10. **(a) Describe** What elements make up a culture?
(b) Apply Information Which of these elements might influence a people's environment, and how?

11. **(a) Describe** What was the Agricultural Revolution?
(b) Explain How did it affect population?
(c) Draw Conclusions How did it allow the growth of cities?

12. **(a) Describe** How does social class affect a person's status in society?
(b) Link Past and Present How has people's ability to improve their status changed?

13. **(a) Recall** Which major religions started in Asia?
(b) Infer What might explain their spread?

14. **(a) Describe** How did the development of industry and factories change culture?
(b) Compare and Contrast How do those changes compare with the ways technology has changed culture in your lifetime?

15. **(a) List** What technologies contribute to cultural change today?
(b) Draw Conclusions How have new technologies affected the rate of cultural change?

◆ Skills Practice

Making Valid Generalizations In the Skills for Life activity in this chapter, you learned to make generalizations. You also learned how to make sure that generalizations are valid, or justified, based on facts. You learned not to overgeneralize, or make claims that go beyond the facts.

Review the steps that you followed to learn this skill. Then reread the paragraphs on pages 94 and 95 under the heading Development of Culture. List several facts about the changes described there. Finally, use these facts to make a valid generalization about those changes.

◆ Writing Activity: Math

Look at the graph titled World Internet Users 1996–2005 on page 107. Find the number of Internet users in 1996 and the number of Internet users nine years later in 2005. How many more users were there in 2005 than in 1996? Based on this information, predict how many Internet users there will be in 2014, nine years after the latest date shown on this graph. Write a short paragraph describing your results and your prediction.

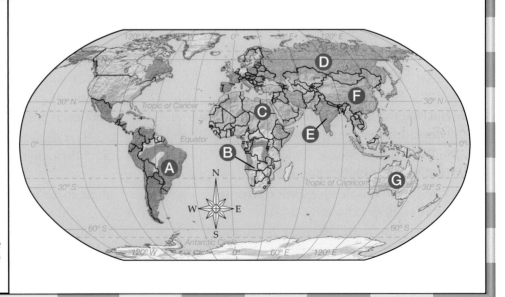

MAP MASTER™
Skills Activity

World Religions

Place Location For each religion listed below, write the letter that marks its location on the map.
1. Buddhism
2. Eastern Christianity
3. Hinduism
4. Islam
5. Protestant Christianity
6. Roman Catholic Christianity
7. Traditional religions

Go Online
PHSchool.com Use Web Code **lep-3414** for an **interactive map.**

Standardized Test Prep

Test-Taking Tips

Some questions on standardized tests ask you to supply information using prior knowledge. Analyze the web diagram below. Then follow the tips to answer the sample question.

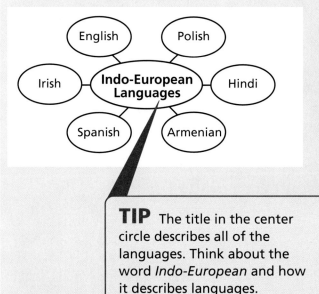

TIP The title in the center circle describes all of the languages. Think about the word *Indo-European* and how it describes languages.

Pick the letter that best answers the question.

Another language that belongs on this web is

A ~~Mandarin Chinese.~~

B Swahili.

C ~~Japanese.~~

D Greek.

TIP Use your prior knowledge—what you know about history, geography, or government—to help you rule out choices.

Think It Through The word *Indo-European* describes languages of India and Europe. Therefore, you can rule out answers A and C because these languages do not come from India or Europe. That leaves Swahili and Greek. You may not be sure about where Swahili is spoken, but you probably know from prior reading that Greece (where people speak Greek) is in Europe. The correct answer is D.

Practice Questions

Use the tips above and other tips in this book to help you answer the following questions:

1. The Agricultural Revolution led

   A to a rebellion by farmers against taxes.

   B to widespread hunger.

   C to an increase in population.

   D people to begin using tools.

2. How does family structure change when countries become more developed?

   A People lose interest in their families.

   B Nuclear families become more common.

   C People move in with their grandparents, aunts, and uncles.

   D Extended families become more common.

3. Which of the following does NOT contribute to cultural change?

   A technological change

   B migration

   C tradition

   D television

Read the following passage, and answer the question that follows.

This country is the birthplace of three major religions. It is located on Earth's largest continent. Its neighbors include Bangladesh and Sri Lanka. The country has more than a billion inhabitants. Its people speak hundreds of different languages. Many people from this country have migrated overseas.

4. What country does the passage describe?

   A Israel

   B Mexico

   C India

   D China

Use Web Code **lea-3401** for a **Chapter 4 self-test.**

Interacting With Our Environment

Chapter Preview

This chapter will introduce you to the ways in which people interact with their natural surroundings.

Section 1
Natural Resources

Section 2
Land Use

Section 3
People's Effect on the Environment

Target Reading Skill

Main Idea In this chapter you will construct meaning by identifying the main idea in a paragraph and the details that support it. Identifying a paragraph's main idea can help you remember what you have read.

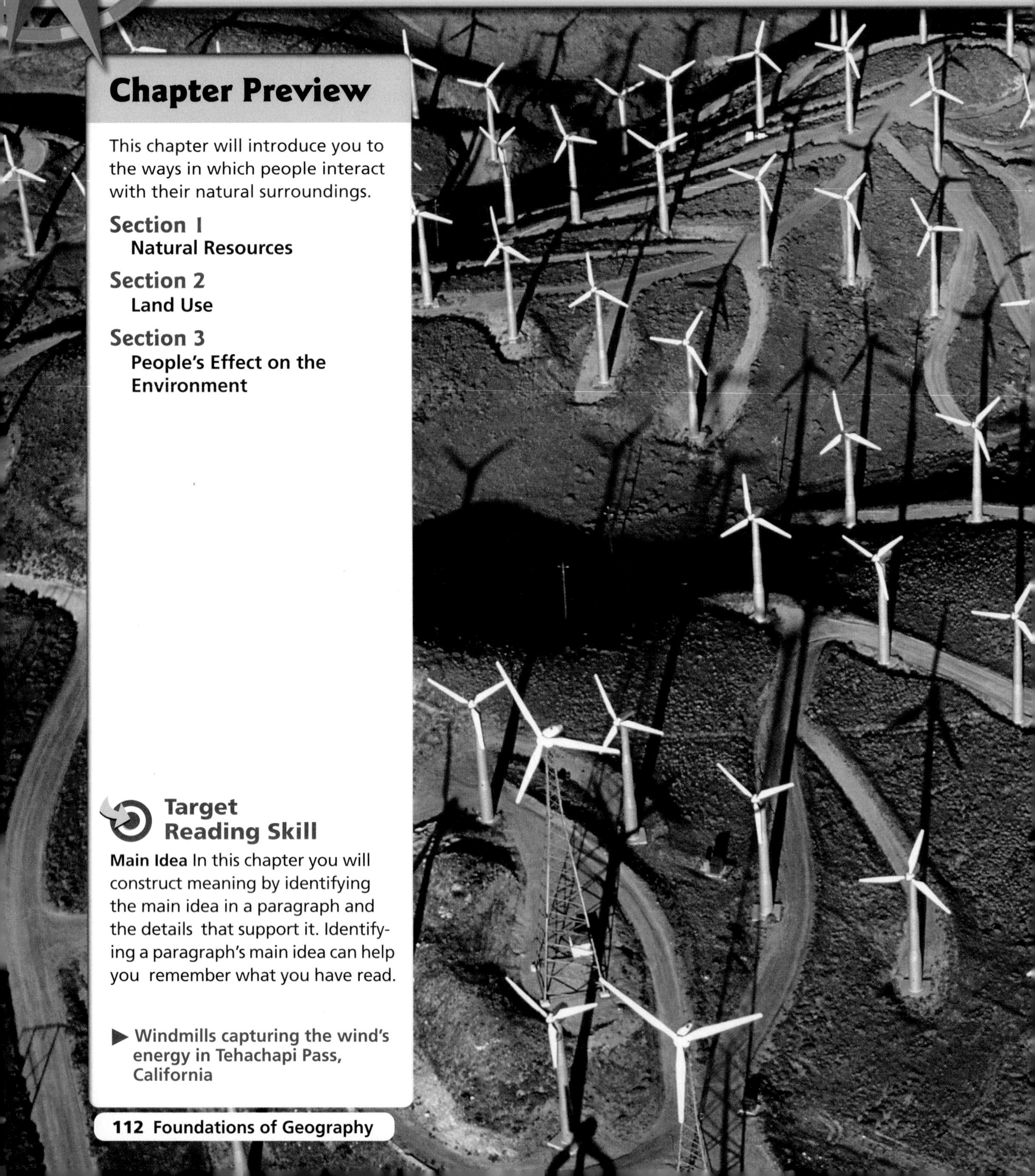

▶ Windmills capturing the wind's energy in Tehachapi Pass, California

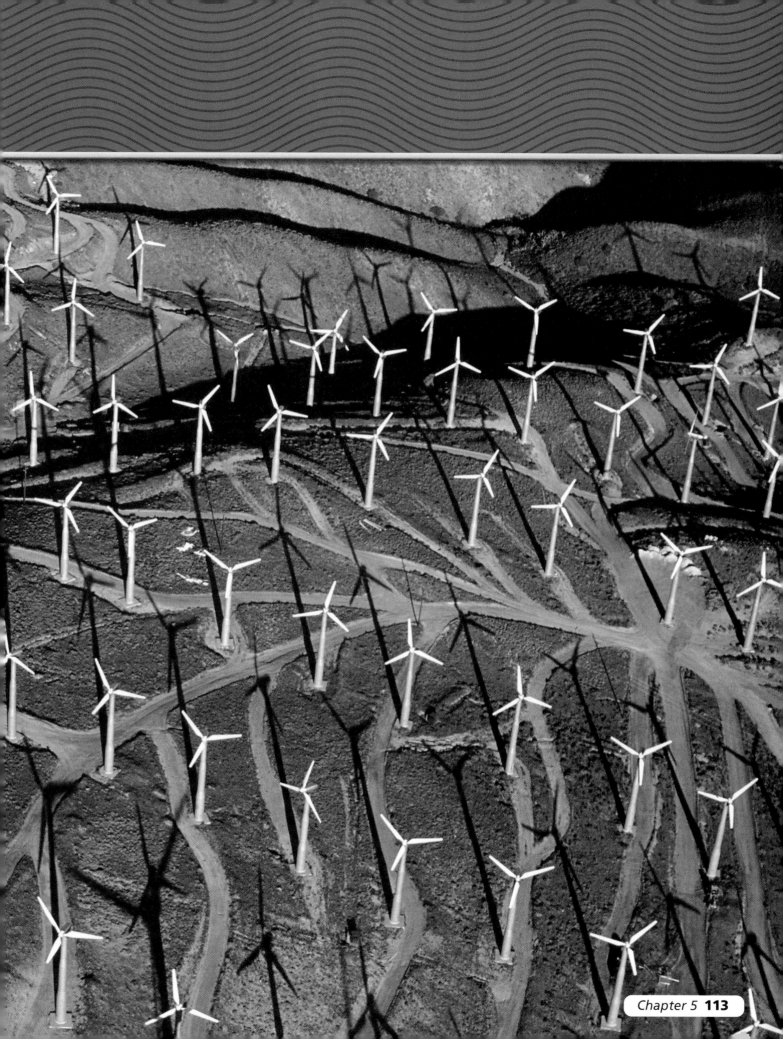

Prepare to Read

Objectives

In this section you will
1. Learn about natural resources.
2. Investigate energy.

Taking Notes

Copy the outline below. Add letters, numbers, and headings as needed. As you read this section, fill in the outline with information about natural resources and energy.

I. Natural resources
  A. Renewable resources
  B.
    1.
    2.
II. Energy
  A.

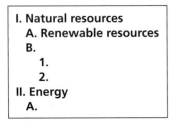

Target Reading Skill

Identify Main Ideas
Good readers identify the main idea in every written paragraph. The main idea is the most important point—the one that includes all of the other points. Sometimes this idea is stated directly. For example, in the first paragraph below, the first sentence states the paragraph's main idea. As you read, note the main idea of each paragraph.

Key Terms

- **natural resources** (NACH ur ul REE sawr siz) *n.* useful materials found in the environment
- **raw materials** (raw muh TIHR ee ulz) *n.* natural resources that must be worked to be useful
- **renewable resources** (rih NOO uh bul REE sawr siz) *n.* natural resources that can be replaced
- **nonrenewable resources** (nahn rih NOO uh bul REE sawr siz) *n.* natural resources that cannot be replaced

Men constructing a wooden hut in Kenya

What Are Natural Resources?

Everything that people use or consume is made with **natural resources,** or useful materials found in the environment. When people talk about natural resources, they usually mean such things as water, minerals, and vegetation.

All people need water, food, clothing, and shelter to survive. People drink water. People eat food that the soil produces. So do the animals that provide eggs, cheese, meat, and wool. Homes are made from wood, clay, and steel.

People can use some resources just as they are found in nature. Fresh water is one of these. But most resources must be changed before people can use them. Natural resources that must be worked to be useful are called **raw materials.** For example, people cannot just go out and cut down a tree if they want paper. Trees are the raw materials for paper and wood. To make paper, the wood must be soaked and broken up to create pulp. (Pulp is a kind of soup of wood fibers.) Machines collect the wet fibers on screens to form sheets of paper.

Renewable Resources The environment is filled with natural resources, but not all resources are alike. Geographers divide them into two main groups.

The first group is renewable resources, or resources that can be replaced. Some resources are replaced naturally because of the way Earth works. In the water cycle, water evaporates into the air and falls as rain, snow, hail, or sleet. This happens over and over again. Therefore, Earth has an unchanging amount of water. Other materials that go through natural cycles include nitrogen and carbon.

Some types of energy are also renewable resources. Using wind to make electricity will not use the wind up. Wind results from differences in the way the sun heats Earth. As long as the sun shines, there will always be more wind. Solar energy, or energy from the sun, is a renewable resource. No matter how much people use, there will always be more. Geothermal energy uses differences in heat between Earth's surface and its interior. This heat difference will not disappear in the foreseeable future.

Discovery CHANNEL SCHOOL Video
Explore the environment of an island nation.

Identify Main Ideas Which sentence states the main idea of the paragraph at the left?

The World: Natural Resources

MAP MASTER Skills Activity

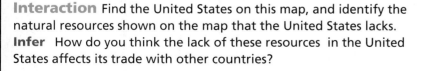

KEY

- Gold
- Silver
- Copper
- Lead
- △ Tin
- Nickel
- Tungsten
- Uranium
- Bauxite
- Phosphate
- Diamond
- — National border
- - - - Disputed border

0 miles 4,000
0 kilometers 4,000
Robinson

Interaction Find the United States on this map, and identify the natural resources shown on the map that the United States lacks.
Infer How do you think the lack of these resources in the United States affects its trade with other countries?

Go Online
PHSchool.com Use Web Code lep-3213 for step-by-step **map skills practice**.

Solar cells on the roof of a house in Felsberg, Germany

Living Resources Living things that provide natural resources, such as plants and animals, are also renewable resources. Like other resources, they must be properly managed so that people do not overuse them.

For example, a timber company may cut down all the trees in an area for use as wood. But the company may then plant new trees to replace the ones they cut. Even if they do not, seeds left in the ground will probably produce new trees. Every day, the people of the world eat many chickens and ears of corn. But farmers always make sure to grow more corn and chickens to replace what people eat. If people are careful, they can have a steady supply of these renewable living resources.

Nonrenewable Resources The second major group of resources is called **nonrenewable resources, or resources that cannot be replaced.** Most nonliving things, such as metal ores, most minerals, natural gas, and petroleum—or crude oil—are nonrenewable resources. If people keep mining minerals and burning fuels such as coal and oil, they will eventually run out. Therefore, people need to use these resources carefully. If they do run out, people will need to find substitutes for them.

Although they are nonrenewable, many metals, minerals, and materials such as plastics can be recycled. Recycling does not return these materials to their natural state. Still, they can be recovered and processed for reuse. Recycling these materials helps to conserve nonrenewable resources.

Fossil Fuels Most scientists think that coal, natural gas, and petroleum are fossil fuels, or fuels created over millions of years from the remains of prehistoric living things. If people continue using coal at today's rate, known supplies may run out in several hundred years. At current rates of use, known supplies of oil and natural gas may run out in less than 100 years.

If oil and natural gas are fossil fuels, they are renewable, since living things today will become fossil fuels in millions of years. But if these fuels take so long to develop, they are nonrenewable for our purposes.

✓ **Reading Check** **What is the difference between renewable and nonrenewable resources?**

A Special Resource: Energy

Many natural resources are sources of energy. People use energy not only from fossil fuels, but also from the wind and the sun. Dams produce hydroelectric power by harnessing the power of falling water.

Energy is itself a resource that is needed to make use of other natural resources. Consider cotton. It takes energy to harvest cotton from a field, to spin the cotton into thread, and to weave it into fabric. Workers use energy to travel to a garment factory. It takes energy to sew a shirt with a sewing machine. It also takes energy to transport the shirt by ship and truck to a retail store. Finally, the consumer uses energy to bring the shirt home.

Located on the border between Oregon and Washington, the Bonneville Dam produces hydroelectric power.

Strip Mining Coal
The machine below extracts coal from this exposed deposit in Banwen Pyrddin, Wales, United Kingdom.
Apply Information *Do you think that coal is a recyclable, renewable, or nonrenewable resource?*

Pipes running across an oil field in Meyal, Pakistan

Energy "Have's" and "Have Not's" People in every country need energy. But energy resources are not evenly spread around the world. Certain areas are rich in energy resources. Others have very few.

Countries with many rivers, such as Canada and Norway, can use water energy to create electricity. Countries like Saudi Arabia and Mexico have huge amounts of oil that they sell to other countries. Countries like Japan and the United States do not produce as much energy as they use. These countries have to buy energy from other countries.

Meeting Energy Needs in the Future Over time, energy use worldwide has grown rapidly. Yet our supplies of fossil fuels may be limited. It seems likely that the world's people will need to find other sources of energy. Many possibilities exist.

Already, some countries, such as Denmark and Germany, are developing renewable energy sources such as wind and solar energy. Other sources of energy that will not run out are tidal energy, from the rise and fall of Earth's oceans, and geothermal energy, or energy from the heat of Earth's interior. Biomass, or plant material, is a renewable source of energy. These energy sources can reduce a country's need for imported oil.

Atomic energy uses radioactive materials, which are non-renewable but plentiful. Some people oppose atomic energy because radioactive materials can be dangerous. Others support it as a plentiful energy source that does not pollute the air.

Graph Skills

Some countries produce more oil than they use. These countries can sell their extra oil to other countries. Others consume more oil than they produce and have to buy it from other countries. **Identify** Which of the countries on this graph have to buy almost all of their oil? **Compare and Contrast** Which country buys the most oil?

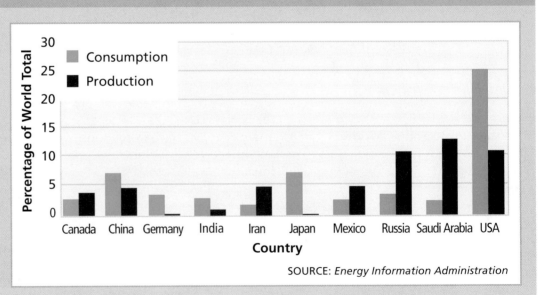

The World's Top Petroleum Producers and Consumers

SOURCE: *Energy Information Administration*

Fossil fuels will last longer if people use less energy. New technologies, such as hybrid cars, can reduce a country's need for imported oil by burning less gas per mile. Other technologies offer energy savings in heating and lighting buildings and in making new products. If people manage to use less energy, they will not need to buy as much from foreign countries. They will also have an easier time meeting their energy needs in the future.

Geothermal power
In addition to producing energy, the geothermal power plant at Svartsengi, Iceland, heats the mineral-rich water of the Blue Lagoon. **Infer** *Are fossil fuels used to heat this pool?*

✓ **Reading Check** **Why do some countries have to import energy?**

Section 1 Assessment

Key Terms
Review the key terms at the beginning of this section. Use each term in a sentence that explains its meaning.

Target Reading Skill
State the main idea of the paragraph on this page.

Comprehension and Critical Thinking
1. (a) Identify Why is wood considered a renewable resource?

(b) Apply Information What needs to happen after trees are cut in order for wood to remain a renewable resource?
2. (a) List Name some sources of energy other than fossil fuels.
(b) Categorize What do these energy sources have in common, and how do they differ from fossil fuels?
(c) Draw Conclusions Why might we need to use more of these energy sources in the future?

Writing Activity
Think about what you did this morning before you came to school. Write a journal entry describing the natural resources that you used and all of the ways that you used energy at home and on your way to school.

For: An activity on natural resources
Visit: PHSchool.com
Web Code: led-3501

Prepare to Read

Objectives

In this section you will
1. Study the relation between land use and culture.
2. Investigate the relation between land use and economic activity.
3. Explore changes in land use.

Taking Notes

Copy the concept web below. As you read the section, fill in the ovals with information about land use. Add ovals as needed.

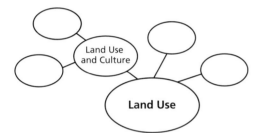

Target Reading Skill

Identify Supporting Details Sentences in a paragraph may provide details that support the main idea. These details may give examples or explanations. In the second paragraph on this page, this sentence states the main idea: "Even in similar environments, people may use land differently because they have different cultural traits." Note three details in the paragraph that explain this main idea.

Key Terms

- **environment** (en VY run munt) *n.* natural surroundings
- **manufacturing** (man yoo FAK chur ing) *n.* the large-scale production of goods by hand or by machine
- **colonization** (kayl uh nih ZAY shun) *n.* the movement of settlers and their culture to a new country
- **industrialization** (in dus tree ul ih ZAY shun) *n.* the growth of machine-powered production in an economy

A peanut farmer in Georgia inspecting his crop

Land Use and Culture

How people use the land depends on their culture. People may use their land differently because their cultures have developed in different **environments**, or natural surroundings. For example, the Inuit live in a cold, arctic climate. It is too cold to grow crops, so the Inuit use their land mainly for hunting wild animals, and they rely heavily on fishing. The Japanese live in a warmer, moister climate. Although much of Japan is too steep to farm, the Japanese use much of the remaining land for crops. Their main crop is rice, which grows well in the warm, moist climate of Japan.

Even in similar environments, however, people may use land differently because they have different cultural traits. For example, Georgia has a warm, moist climate like that of southern Japan. But Georgia does not produce much rice. Instead, Georgians raise chickens and grow crops such as peanuts. While the Japanese eat rice at nearly every meal, Americans eat more meat and peanut butter.

Cultures and Landscapes The examples of the Inuit and the Japanese show how people's environments help to shape their cultures. People's cultures, in turn, help shape the landscapes where they live. For example, in some parts of the Philippines, a culture of rice farming and a shortage of level land has led people to carve terraces into hillsides. Thousands of years ago, Western Europe was covered with forests. As farming cultures spread across that region, people cleared forests to use the land for farming. Today, most of Western Europe is open fields and pastures. Few forests remain.

Land Use and Cultural Differences As the examples of Japan and Georgia show, however, similar environments do not necessarily produce similar cultures. People may respond differently to those environments, depending on their culture. For example, much of the western United States has a dry climate. Many crops need irrigation, or an artificial water supply. The Middle East also has climates too dry for most crops to grow without irrigation. However, the two regions have different cultures and different responses to this challenge. In the western United States, farmers use modern irrigation systems. For example, drip irrigation provides water to each plant through little pipes or tubes. Some Middle Eastern farmers use qanats, or brick irrigation channels, to bring water to their crops. Both cultures face similar environments, but they interact with those environments differently.

✔ **Reading Check** How is land use related to culture?

Drip irrigation of grape vines in eastern Washington State

Irrigation in Yemen
This man is walking along a qanat, or brick irrigation channel, in Jiblah, Yemen. **Analyze Images** *What clues do you see in this landscape that suggest a need for irrigation?*

Land Use and Economic Activity

In some places, people use the land and its resources to make a living by farming, fishing, or mining. In other places, people work in factories, where they turn natural resources into finished products. In still other places, people sell or distribute products and make a living by providing services. These three ways of making a living correspond to three stages of economic activity. Geographers use stages of economic activity as a way to understand land use.

Identify Supporting Details

Which details in the paragraph at the right give examples of first-level activities?

First-Level Activities In the first stage, people use land and resources directly to make products. They may hunt, cut wood, mine, or fish. They also may herd animals or raise crops. This is the first stage of activities. At this stage, people interact directly with the land or the sea. Most of the world's land is used for first-level activities. However, in developed countries such as the United States, only a small percentage of the people make a living at first-level activities.

Stages of Economic Activity

A series of economic activities connect a flock of sheep in a pasture to a wool sweater in a store. Sheep-raising, a first-level activity, makes it possible to manufacture woolen goods such as sweaters, a second-level activity. Manufacturing makes it possible to deliver sweaters to stores. Stores can then sell the sweaters. Delivery and sales are both third-level activities.

A flock of sheep being driven to a pasture in New Zealand

▲ **Farming, a first-level activity**
This farmer is shearing a sheep, or trimming away its wool. Raising and shearing sheep are first-level activities, or direct uses of natural resources.

Second-Level Activities At the second stage, people process the products of first-level activities. Most second-level activity is **manufacturing**, or the large-scale production of goods by hand or by machine. Manufacturing may turn a farmer's corn crop into cornflakes for your breakfast. Manufacturing, especially in urban areas, is an important land use in developed countries.

Third-Level Activities At the third stage, a person delivers boxes of cornflakes to your local grocery store. Third-level activities are also known as services. These activities do not produce goods. They may help sell goods. They often involve working directly for customers or for businesses. Many businesses offering services—doctors' offices, banks, automobile repair shops, shopping malls, and fast-food restaurants—are part of everyday living. Services are also clustered in urban areas, especially in developed countries.

✓ **Reading Check** How is most of the world's land used?

GEOGRAPHY SKILLS PRACTICE

Human-Environment Interaction Each activity shown here occurs in a different part of New Zealand.
Apply Information Which activities occur in rural areas, and which activities are likely to occur in urban areas?

▲ **Manufacturing, a second-level activity**
Second-level activities process natural resources to make goods, such as the wool this worker is processing at a New Zealand mill.

Retail sales, a third-level activity ▶
Selling manufactured goods, such as this sweater, in a store is a third-level activity. This woolen-goods store is in New Zealand.

Boston: A Changing Landscape

English colonists founded Boston, Massachusetts, on a narrow peninsula surrounded by water, marshes, and forest. The colonists cleared most of the forest for farmland. The colonists also built dams, piers, and retaining walls along the waterfront. By the 1800s, Boston's growing industries and growing population of workers faced a land shortage. Boston's solution was to drain marshes and to create new land by filling in areas of water. At first, Boston's people filled in around existing piers. Then, they filled in tidal ponds behind dams. Finally, they filled in whole bodies of open water.

MAP★MASTER™
Skills Activity

Human-Environment Interaction Colonization and industrialization transformed Boston's landscape. **Identify** How much of the forest around Boston remained after colonization? **Compare and Contrast** How did Boston's land area change between colonial times and today?

Go Online
PHSchool.com Use Web Code **lep-3312** for step-by-step **map skills practice.**

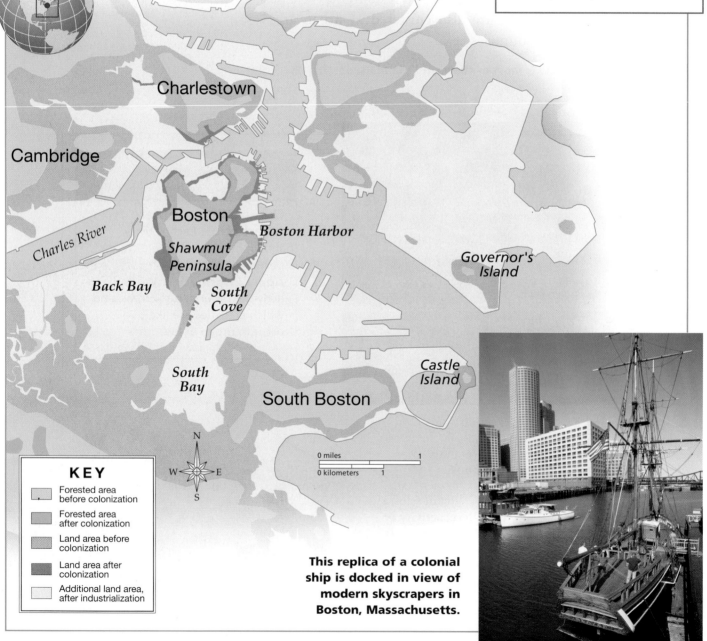

Charlestown

Cambridge

Boston

Charles River

Boston Harbor

Shawmut Peninsula

Back Bay

South Cove

Governor's Island

South Bay

Castle Island

South Boston

N W E S

0 miles 1
0 kilometers 1

KEY

Forested area before colonization

Forested area after colonization

Land area before colonization

Land area after colonization

Additional land area, after industrialization

This replica of a colonial ship is docked in view of modern skyscrapers in Boston, Massachusetts.

Changes in Land Use

When a region undergoes **colonization,** or a movement of new settlers and their culture to a country, the newcomers may change that region's landscape to fit their cultural practices. For example, if farmers move to a region without farms, they will create farms. Similarly, as people find new ways of making a living, they start using the land in new ways, too.

Colonization Before European colonists came to Australia, there was no farming and no livestock raising. In North and South America before colonization, European crops such as wheat and grapes were unknown. So were livestock such as cows and chickens. When Europeans settled these continents, they cleared large areas for use as farmland and livestock pasture.

Industrialization and Sprawl Since the 1800s, the growth of machine-powered production, or **industrialization,** has changed landscapes in many countries. Cities have grown around industrial facilities worldwide. Since 1900, suburbs have spread out from cities in the United States and other developed countries to cover more and more land. The spread of cities and suburbs is known as sprawl.

✔ Reading Check How did European colonization change landscapes in North and South America?

Vineyards in Australia
Grapes did not grow in Australia before European colonists arrived. Now grapes thrive in Australia's Hunter Valley. **Infer** *What would have been different about this landscape before European colonization?*

Section 2 Assessment

Key Terms
Review the key terms at the beginning of this section. Use each term in a sentence that explains its meaning.

Target Reading Skill
State three details that explain the main idea of the second paragraph on page 120.

Comprehension and Critical Thinking
1. (a) Describe How have rice farmers in the Philippines transformed the landscape?

(b) Infer Why is the Philippines' farm landscape different from Western Europe's?
2. (a) Recall What are second-level activities?
(b) Categorize Name some examples of second-level activities.
(c) Compare and Contrast How do second-level activities differ from third-level activities?
3. (a) Recall What is industrialization?
(b) Identify Causes How is industrialization related to sprawl?

Writing Activity
Write a short encyclopedia article on land use around your hometown. Describe how culture has affected land use. Mention the different levels of economic activity around your town. Finally, give an example of a change in land use in or near your hometown.

Writing Tip Encyclopedia articles contain descriptions and statements of facts. Be careful not to express personal thoughts or opinions.

Making Predictions

The Oval Office, where leaders make predictions, is at the center of this photo of the White House.

When you watch an adventure movie, half the fun is in predicting what happens next. Decision makers, such as American presidents, make predictions, too, and their predictions guide their decisions. Good decision makers take actions that they predict will have good results. When you predict, you make an educated guess about the effects of a certain cause. The key word here is *educated*. Without knowledge, you can't predict—you just guess.

Learn the Skill

Follow these steps to make a good prediction.

1. **Identify a situation that has not been resolved.** As you read information, ask yourself questions, such as, "What will happen next? What effects will this situation produce?"

2. **Make a list of probable outcomes, or effects.** If possible, analyze examples of similar causes that have known effects.

3. **Make an educated guess about which outcome is most likely.** In order to make an *educated* guess, use information that you know or that you research.

4. **State your prediction.** In your prediction, explain why you think the cause will produce a particular effect, or outcome.

Practice the Skill

Read the text in the box at the right. Then predict the consequences of global struggles for water.

1 From what you have read about water supplies in Southwest Asia, identify a major issue that has not been resolved. State the problem as a question.

2 This chapter discusses problems in global oil supply. How are oil and water issues similar? What effects have resulted from world oil shortages? Study the graphic organizer below. It shows results that might occur when one country controls other countries' water.

3 Of the possible outcomes in the graphic organizer, which seems the most likely? Make an educated guess, using what you know about the oil issue.

4 Here's how your prediction might begin: "As the world's need for water grows, water-rich countries will probably _____."

During the 1900s, oil-rich nations became wealthy and powerful by controlling world oil supplies. In the present century, water supplies may determine who is rich or poor. Much of the world's usable fresh water comes from rivers that flow through many countries. Nearly half the people in the world live in international river basins. Yet many of the countries that share rivers have no water treaties. Countries along these rivers build dams to store water for themselves. Nations downstream worry that they might run out of water. In Southwest Asia, Turkey controls sources of water flowing south into Syria and Iraq. A proposed system of 22 dams could allow Turkey to withhold water from its neighbors. Syria and Iraq have plentiful oil but not enough water.

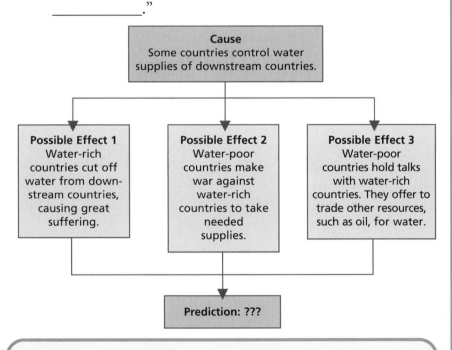

Cause
Some countries control water supplies of downstream countries.

Possible Effect 1
Water-rich countries cut off water from downstream countries, causing great suffering.

Possible Effect 2
Water-poor countries make war against water-rich countries to take needed supplies.

Possible Effect 3
Water-poor countries hold talks with water-rich countries. They offer to trade other resources, such as oil, for water.

Prediction: ???

Apply the Skill

Study the graph on page 118. Note how much oil the United States consumes and produces. What do you learn from these facts? Make a prediction about what America might do when world oil supplies run low. Create a graphic organizer like the one on this page to help you make a prediction.

People's Effect on the Environment

Prepare to Read

Objectives

In this section you will
1. Investigate how first-level activities affect the environment.
2. Explore how second- and third-level activities affect the environment.

Taking Notes

Copy the table below. As you read this section, fill in the table with information about people's effect on the environment. Add rows to the table as needed.

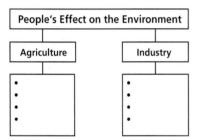

```
People's Effect on the Environment
   ┌──────────────┴──────────────┐
  Agriculture                  Industry
  ┌──────────┐               ┌──────────┐
  │ •        │               │ •        │
  │ •        │               │ •        │
  │ •        │               │ •        │
  │ •        │               │ •        │
  └──────────┘               └──────────┘
```

Target Reading Skill

Identify Implied

Main Ideas Identifying main ideas can help you remember what you read. The details in a paragraph can add up to the main idea, even if it is not stated directly. For example, the details in the first paragraph below add up to this main idea: "While first-level activities are necessary for human survival, they also reshape the environment."

Key Terms

- **deforestation** (dee fawr uh STAY shun) *n.* a loss of forest cover in a region
- **biodiversity** (by oh duh VUR suh tee) *n.* a richness of different kinds of living things in a region
- **civil engineering** (SIV ul en juh NIHR ing) *n.* technology for building structures that alter the landscape, such as dams, roads, and bridges
- **pollution** (puh LOO shun) *n.* waste, usually man-made, that makes the air, water, or soil less clean

First-Level Activities

First-level activities, or direct interaction with raw materials, provide the food and resources that people need to live. They also transform the physical environment. For example, agriculture replaces wild plants and animals with the domesticated plants and animals that people need for food and other products.

Creating Farmland As countries have grown, they have met the challenge of feeding their people in different ways. The Great Plains of North America once supported wild grasses and buffalo. Today, farmers in that region grow corn and wheat and raise cattle. In the Netherlands, the people have drained lakes, bays, and marshes to create dry farmland. While creating new farmland destroyed wild grasslands and wetlands, the new land has fed millions.

A rancher driving cattle in Manitoba, Canada

Environmental Challenges Agriculture, forestry, and fishing provide food and resources that people need to live. At the same time, they sometimes have harmful effects on the environment. For example, wood is needed to build houses. But cutting down too many trees can result in **deforestation,** or the loss of forest cover in a region. Cutting forests may result in the loss of more than trees and other plants. Animals that depend on the forest for survival may also suffer. Deforestation can lead to a loss of **biodiversity**, which is a richness of different kinds of living things. So timber companies face the challenge of harvesting needed wood while limiting damage to the environment.

Farmers often use fertilizers and other chemicals to grow more crops. This makes it possible to feed more people. But when rain washes these chemicals into streams, they sometimes harm fish and other water-dwelling creatures. Fish are a tasty and healthy food source. But if fishers catch too many, they may threaten the fishes' survival. Farmers and fishers face the challenge of feeding the world's people without harming important resources.

Finding a Balance The key is to find a balance. Around the world, governments, scientists, and business people are working to find ways of meeting our need for food and resources without harming the environment. One solution is planting tree farms for timber. When the trees are mature, they can be cut and new trees can be replanted without harming ancient forests. Farmers can grow crops using natural methods or use chemicals that will not damage waterways. Fishers can limit their catch of endangered fish and harvest fish that are more plentiful.

✔ **Reading Check** How do people benefit when new farmland is created?

Deforestation
Timber companies and farmers have cut down rain forests in Indonesia.
Apply Information *What are some of the advantages and disadvantages of cutting down forests?*

Links to
Math

Acres and Timber Yields
Tree farms, like the one below, in Newbury, England, are one way to fight deforestation. If these oak trees grow to yield 80,000 board feet of timber per acre (466 cubic meters per hectare), and the farm covers 300 acres (121 hectares), how much timber will the farm produce?

The Hybrid Car

Cars with gasoline engines are fast and can go long distances, but they pollute. Electric cars don't emit dangerous chemicals, but they can be driven only for a short distance before their batteries need to be recharged. The hybrid car combines the best features of gasoline and electric cars. It is fast and can go long distances, but it uses less gasoline and pollutes less. The hybrid car gets about 46 miles per gallon, while the conventional car of the same size gets about 33.

Traffic Jam
Today, traffic jams are common as drivers commute daily in and out of cities. Waiting in traffic jams wastes a lot of fuel and adds to air pollution.

Hybrid cars are made of lightweight materials. It takes less fuel to move a lighter car.

The electric motor draws energy from the battery to accelerate the car. When the car's brakes are applied, the motor recharges, or sends energy back to, the battery.

The small gasoline engine has the same power as a motorcycle, but it uses less fuel. It pollutes less than an ordinary car engine.

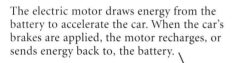

Fuel tank

The battery drives an electric motor, which assists the engine during acceleration.

The tires are inflated to a higher pressure than in an ordinary car. The higher pressure reduces energy loss.

ANALYZING IMAGES
How do hybrid cars save fuel?

Second- and Third-Level Activities

Over the years, industry, or second-level activities, and services, or third-level activities, have transformed deserts, prairies, woodlands, and marshes. They have created our familiar urban landscapes of housing developments, offices, factories, railroads, and highways.

Providing Jobs, Reshaping the Environment Industrial and service activities provide most of the jobs in developed countries such as the United States. Those activities are the basis for the developed countries' prosperity. They are also the main land use in urban areas.

The main purpose of some of these activities is to change the environment. **Civil engineering** is technology for building structures that alter the landscape, such as dams, canals, roads, and bridges. Dams create reservoirs that cover large areas with water. They also provide water for farms and cities and protect areas downstream from flooding.

Other industrial and service activities have side effects on the environment. For example, shopping malls require large areas to be paved for parking. Industries use large amounts of resources and release industrial wastes into the environment. Service activities require the construction of roads, telephone lines, and power lines.

Identify Implied Main Ideas
In one sentence, state what all the details in the paragraph at the left are about.

A Landscape Shaped by Industry
The waterfront in Rotterdam, Netherlands, has been shaped to meet the needs of industry. **Analyze Images** *How might this landscape have been different before it was shaped by industry?*

Recycling
These seventh-grade students in Syracuse, New York, are sorting materials for recycling. **Apply Information** *What environmental problems does recycling help to solve?*

Environmental Challenges Industry is not the only source of **pollution**, waste that makes the air, soil, or water less clean. The trash that we throw away may pollute the soil, water, or air. Exhaust from cars and trucks is another source of air pollution. Many scientists believe that air pollution may cause higher temperatures or other changes in our climate.

Finding Solutions Working together, scientists, governments, businesses, and ordinary people can find solutions to these problems. One solution is to use more fuel-efficient vehicles, such as hybrid cars. Vehicles that burn less fuel create less air pollution. Renewable energy sources, such as solar power and wind power, can also reduce the need to burn fuels that pollute the air. In addition, reducing pollution may reduce the risk of harmful climate changes.

Many cities and counties in the United States have introduced waste recycling. Recycling reduces the amount of waste that local governments must burn or dump. It also saves natural resources. For example, when paper is recycled, fewer trees must be cut down to make new paper.

Finding solutions to environmental problems is one of the greatest challenges of our time. If we all work together, we can meet this challenge.

✓ **Reading Check** How do industrial activities affect the environment?

Section 3 Assessment

Key Terms
Review the key terms at the beginning of this section. Use each term in a sentence that explains its meaning.

Target Reading Skill
State the main idea of each paragraph on this page.

Comprehension and Critical Thinking
1. (a) **Recall** What are the causes of deforestation?

(b) **Identify Cause and Effect** How does deforestation threaten the environment?
2. (a) **List** List ways in which industrial and service activities transform landscapes.
(b) **Categorize** Which of these ways are common to both industrial and service activities?
(c) **Analyze** How are industrial activities different from service activities in their impact on the environment?

Writing Activity
Write a journal entry in which you discuss how your own activities today may have affected the environment.

For: An activity on the environment
Visit: PHSchool.com
Web Code: led-3503

Review and Assessment

◆ Chapter Summary

Section 1: Natural Resources

- Almost everything that people use or consume is made with natural resources, which are either renewable or nonrenewable.
- Energy is a special resource needed for most economic activities, but some sources of energy are in limited supply, and some nations need to buy energy resources from others.

Section 2: Land Use

- How people use the land depends on their culture.
- Three levels of economic activity account for most land use.
- Land use changes when newcomers settle a region and as cultures change over time.

Section 3: People's Effect on the Environment

- First-level activities provide needed food and resources, but they reduce the land available for wild plants and animals.
- Second- and third-level activities provide jobs, but they can also pollute the environment.

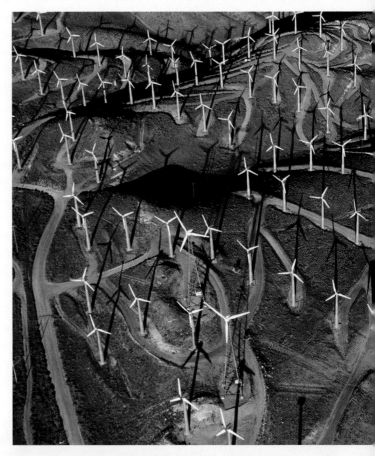

Windmills in California

◆ Key Terms

Each of the statements below contains a key term from the chapter. If the statement is true, write *true*. If it is false, rewrite the statement to make it true.

1. Raw materials are natural resources that can be used without reworking.

2. Renewable resources are natural resources that can be replaced.

3. Natural resources that cannot be replaced are called nonrenewable resources.

4. Our environment is our natural surroundings.

5. Manufacturing does not produce goods but involves working directly for customers.

6. Industrialization is the growth of manufacturing in an economy.

7. Deforestation is the planting of trees to replace forests cut down for timber.

8. Biodiversity is the loss of plant and animal life due to deforestation.

9. Pollution is waste, usually made by people, that makes air, soil, or water less clean.

◆ Comprehension and Critical Thinking

10. (a) List List at least three renewable resources.
(b) Explain Why is each of these resources renewable?
(c) Compare and Contrast How do renewable resources differ from nonrenewable resources?

11. (a) Recall Do all countries have adequate energy supplies?
(b) Analyze What energy sources are available to all countries?

12. (a) Recall Does culture affect land use?
(b) Predict What might happen to land use in a region if people with a different culture colonized it?

13. (a) List List three first-level activities.
(b) Compare and Contrast How do those activities differ from second- and third-level activities?

14. (a) Describe How can people obtain wood without cutting down wild forests?
(b) Predict How would leaving forests in place affect biodiversity?

15. (a) Describe What causes pollution?
(b) Infer How might companies and individuals reduce pollution?

◆ Skills Practice

Making Predictions In the Skills for Life activity on pages 126 and 127, you learned to make predictions. You also learned how to make sure that a prediction is an educated guess. That is, predictions should be based on information about the situation or about similar situations.

Review the steps that you followed to learn this skill. Then reread the paragraphs on pages 118 and 119 under the heading Meeting Energy Needs in the Future. List several facts about the issues described there. Finally, use these facts to make a prediction about how those issues might be resolved in the future.

◆ Writing Activity: Language Arts

Identify an environmental problem that interests you. Write a story about people solving the environmental problem. For your story, create characters with different roles in creating or solving the environmental problem. You should also create a plot for your story that describes how people come up with a solution to the problem and carry out that solution.

MAP ✦ MASTER™
Skills Activity

Natural Resources

Place Location Refer to the map titled The World: Natural Resources on page 115. For each natural resource listed below, write the letter from the map at the right that shows its location.

1. Bauxite
2. Diamond
3. Nickel
4. Phosphates
5. Tungsten

Go Online
PHSchool.com Use Web Code **lep-3514** for an **interactive map.**

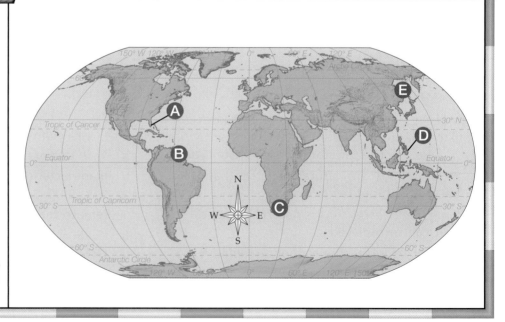

Standardized Test Prep

Test-Taking Tips

Some questions on standardized tests ask you to find a main idea by analyzing a reading selection. Read the passage below. Then follow the tips to answer the sample question.

> Saudi Arabia, Mexico, Iraq, Venezuela, and Russia have large oil reserves. The United States and China are rich in coal and natural gas. Many Northern European countries have rivers with water energy to create electricity. By contrast, Japan has few energy sources.

TIP As you read the paragraph, try to identify its main idea, or most important point. Every sentence in a paragraph supports this main idea.

Pick the letter that best answers the question.

This paragraph describes which kind of resources?

A capital resources

B human resources

C natural resources

D entrepreneurial resources

TIP Look for key words in the question and in the answer choices that connect to the paragraph. In this case, the key word is *resources*.

Think It Through Start with the main idea of the paragraph: Different countries have different energy sources. What kind of resources are these energy sources: oil, coal, gas, and water? Energy is not a human resource. You may not know the words *entrepreneurial* or *capital*. But you probably recognize *natural resources* as useful materials found in the environment—such as oil, coal, gas, and water. The correct answer is C.

Practice Questions

Use the tips above and other tips in this book to help you answer the following questions:

1. Wind energy is a
   A fossil fuel.
   B raw material.
   C renewable resource.
   D nonrenewable resource.

2. When colonists settle in a new environment,
   A they will use land just as they did in their old environment.
   B the environment will not change.
   C they will adjust their previous land uses to the new environment.
   D they will give up all familiar land uses.

3. Which of the following environmental problems does paper recycling help solve?
   A deforestation
   B pollution
   C deforestation and pollution
   D neither deforestation nor pollution

Read the following passage and answer the question that follows.

Sierra Leone's economy produces raw materials and cash crops. The country's people mine diamonds, iron ore, and aluminum ore. People on the coast catch fish. Its farmers produce coffee, cocoa, rice, and palm oil. They also raise poultry and other livestock.

4. The passage's main idea refers to which type of activities?
   A first-level activities
   B second-level activities
   C third-level activities
   D financial activities

Use Web Code **lea-3501** for a **Chapter 5 self-test.**

Projects

Create your own projects to learn more about geography. At the beginning of this book, you were introduced to the **Guiding Questions** for studying the chapters and the special features. But you can also find answers to these questions by doing projects on your own or with a group. Use the questions to find topics you want to explore further. Then try the projects described on this page or create your own.

1 **Geography** What are Earth's major physical features?

2 **History** How have people's ways of life changed over time?

3 **Culture** What is a culture?

4 **Government** What types of government exist in the world today?

5 **Economics** How do people use the world's natural resources?

Project

RESEARCH A COUNTRY'S CULTURE

Desktop Countries
What countries did your ancestors come from? Select one country and do some research on it. Interview someone, perhaps a relative from that country, or read about it. Find a recipe you can prepare to share with the class. Then make a desktop display about the country you have chosen. Write the name of the country on a card and put it on your desk. Add a drawing of the country's flag or map, or display a souvenir. On place cards, write several sentences about each object. Take turns visiting everyone's "desktop countries."

Project

CREATE A PHYSICAL MAP

Focus on Part of the Whole
The world and its population are extremely varied. Choose a particular region or country. If you are working with a group, have each person choose a different country on a continent. Learn everything you can about the country's physical geography, the population, and the lifestyles of the people there. Use encyclopedias, almanacs, or other books.

Set up a display based on your research. Prepare a large map that includes important physical features of the land. Add captions that explain how the land's physical geography affects people's lives.

How to Read Social Studies

Target Reading Skills

The Target Reading Skills introduced on this page will help you understand the words and ideas in this section on the United States and Canada and in other social studies reading you do. Each chapter focuses on one of these reading skills. Good readers develop a bank of reading strategies, or skills. Then they draw on the particular strategies that will help them understand the text they are reading.

Chapter 6 Target Reading Skills

Reading Process Previewing can help you understand and remember what you read. In this chapter you will practice using these previewing skills: setting a purpose for reading, predicting what the text will be about, and asking questions before you read.

Chapter 7 Target Reading Skills

Clarifying Meaning If you do not understand something you are reading right away, you can use several skills to clarify the meaning of the word or idea. In this chapter you will practice these strategies for clarifying meaning: rereading, reading ahead, paraphrasing, and summarizing.

Chapter 8 Target Reading Skills

Main Idea Since you cannot remember every detail of what you read, it is important to identify the main ideas. The main idea of a section or paragraph is the most important point and the one you want to remember. In this chapter you will practice these skills: identifying both stated and implied main ideas and identifying supporting details.

Chapter 9 Target Reading Skills

Comparison and Contrast You can use comparison and contrast to sort out and analyze information you are reading. Comparing means examining the similarities between things. Contrasting is looking at differences. In this chapter you will practice these skills: comparing and contrasting, using signal words, identifying contrasts, and making comparisons.

Chapter 10 Target Reading Skills

Using Context Using the context of an unfamiliar word can help you understand its meaning. Context includes the words, phrases, and sentences surrounding a word. In this chapter you will practice using these context clues: definitions, interpreting nonliteral meanings, your own general knowledge, and cause and effect.

The UNITED STATES and CANADA

Spreading "from sea to shining sea," the United States and Canada take up nearly seven eighths of North America. In this book, you'll see how the United States and Canada are working to create a good life for every citizen in these vast countries.

Guiding Questions

The text, photographs, maps, and charts in this book will help you discover answers to these Guiding Questions.

1. **Geography** How has physical geography affected the cultures of the United States and Canada?

2. **History** How have historical events affected the cultures of the United States and Canada?

3. **Culture** How has the variety of people in the United States and Canada benefited and challenged the two nations?

4. **Government** How do the governments of the United States and Canada differ? How are they alike?

5. **Economics** How did the United States and Canada become two of the wealthiest nations in the world?

Project Preview

You can also discover answers to the Guiding Questions by working on projects. Several project possibilities are listed on page 326 of this book.

Investigate the United States and Canada

Stretching from the Pacific Ocean to the Atlantic Ocean, the United States is the world's fourth largest country. Canada is slightly larger and stretches across five time zones. Though roughly the same size, the United States has far more people—nearly 10 times the population of Canada.

▲ **The Northern Territories, Canada**
Snowmobiles and dogsleds make travel possible in the far north.

CANADA

UNITED STATES

LOCATION
1 Locate the United States and Canada

How would you describe Canada's location? One way would be to compare its location to that of the United States. Which country extends farther north? Which country is closer to Russia? Which country has more of its land touching the Arctic Ocean? Based on the relative locations of these two countries, estimate which has a colder climate.

REGIONS
2 Estimate the Length of the United States and Canada

How does Canada's length from north to south compare to the length of the continental United States? With a ruler, measure the United States from its southernmost border to its border with Canada. Now measure the length of Canada. Which is longer? Now measure both countries from east to west. Which is wider?

Political United States and Canada

Key

— National border

⊛ National capital

0 miles — 1,000
0 kilometers — 1,000
Lambert Azimuthal Equal Area

PLACE

3 Find States, Provinces, and Territories

Which two of the 50 United States do not share a border with any other state? Which Canadian territory reaches the farthest north? Which states border Canada? Which provinces border the United States? Name the cities that are the national capitals of the United States and Canada. Notice that the United States and Canada together make up most of the continent of North America. What other country is on the same continent?

▲ **Niagara Falls**
The Niagara Falls lie on the border between Canada and the United States.

Physical United States and Canada

INTERACTION

4 Find Important Bodies of Water

What three oceans surround the United States and Canada? What bodies of water lie on the border between the United States and Canada? The largest bay in the world is located in Canada. What is its name? Would you enter the bay from the Pacific Ocean or from the Atlantic Ocean?

▲ **Lake Superior**
One of the five Great Lakes, Superior is the farthest north. It lies along the border of the United States and Canada.

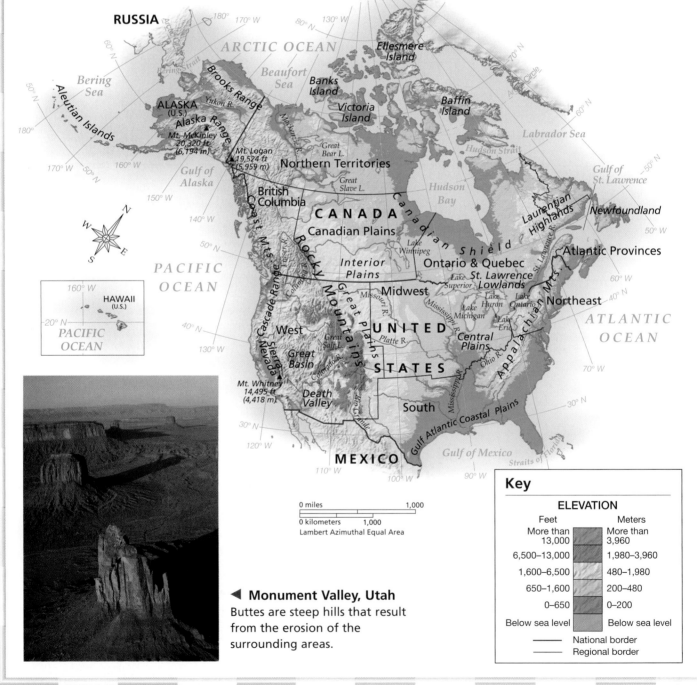

0 miles 1,000
0 kilometers 1,000
Lambert Azimuthal Equal Area

◀ **Monument Valley, Utah**
Buttes are steep hills that result from the erosion of the surrounding areas.

Key

ELEVATION

Feet		Meters
More than 13,000		More than 3,960
6,500–13,000		1,980–3,960
1,600–6,500		480–1,980
650–1,600		200–480
0–650		0–200
Below sea level		Below sea level

———— National border
———— Regional border

Climates of the United States and Canada

The climates of the United States and Canada range widely. Average annual temperatures vary from 71° F in Florida to 27° F in Alaska. Because of its greater distance from the Equator, Canada has much cooler temperatures than the United States. In both countries it is hotter in the interior in the summer and colder and windier in the winter.

Key

——	National border
▓	Tropical wet
░	Tropical wet and dry
▒	Semiarid
▓	Arid
▓	Mediterranean
▒	Humid continental
▒	Marine west coast
░	Humid subtropical
▒	Subarctic
░	Tundra
▓	Highland

0 miles 1,000
0 kilometers 1,000
Lambert Azimuthal Equal Area

REGIONS
5 Explore Influences on Climate

Compare the physical map of the United States and Canada on the previous page with the climate map above. How might landforms affect weather and rainfall? Notice that from Miami, Florida to Yellowknife, Canada the climate changes from tropical wet and dry to subarctic. Give reasons for this great shift in climates.

PRACTICE YOUR GEOGRAPHY SKILLS

1 On your hike in the western mountains you camped at the foot of Mount Rainier. Then you crossed an international border. What country are you in now?

2 You just flew over the mouth of the Mackenzie River and are headed for Victoria Island in Canada. Are you north or south of the Arctic Circle?

3 You are traveling through the Gulf of St. Lawrence toward the Great Lakes. What river will you take?

▲ **Mount Rainier National Park, Washington**

Focus on Regions of the United States and Canada

Now that you've investigated the geography of the United States and Canada, take a closer look at some of the regions that make up these two countries.

Use Web Code **Ihp-4000** for the **interactive maps** on these pages.

RUSSIA

ARCTIC OCEAN

Bering Sea

Beaufort Sea

Yukon R.

ALASKA (U.S.)

Mackenzie R.

Great Bear L.

Northern

C A

British Columbia

Prairie

PACIFIC OCEAN

West

Great Salt L.

HAWAII (U.S.)

PACIFIC OCEAN

▲ British Columbia

British Columbia has important ties to the Pacific Rim nations across the ocean. Its largest city, Vancouver, is one of North America's great cities. Almost all trade between Canada and the Pacific Rim passes through its harbor, which never freezes.

◄ The West

The West has an abundance of natural and human resources. Although the West produces 85 percent of America's gold, water is one of the most precious natural resources in the region.

The South ▶

The South is a warm region with a climate perfect for growing crops. Its booming industries have drawn many people from within the country and overseas. The Mardi Gras festival is one example of the region's cultural diversity.

Atlantic Provinces ▶

The four Canadian provinces that make up the Atlantic Provinces all border the Atlantic Ocean. Fishing and other maritime industries have always supported the economy and way of life of this region.

Key

— National border
— Regional border
⊛ Capital city

0 miles   1,000
0 kilometers   1,000
Lambert Azimuthal Equal Area

▲ **Ontario and Quebec**

These two provinces are Canada's most populous provinces. Ontario contains Ottawa, the national capital, shown above. French speakers make up a majority of the population of Quebec.

◀ **The Midwest**

Though the Midwest is still "America's Breadbasket," most family farms there have given way to larger corporate farms. The region is also an important transportation center.

The U.S. and Canada: Physical Geography

Chapter Preview

This chapter will introduce you to the geography of the United States and Canada and show how geography affects the people who live in the region.

Section 1
Land and Water

Section 2
Climate and Vegetation

Section 3
Resources and Land Use

Target Reading Skill

Reading Process In this chapter you will use previewing to help you understand and remember what you read.

► Talbot Lake, Canada

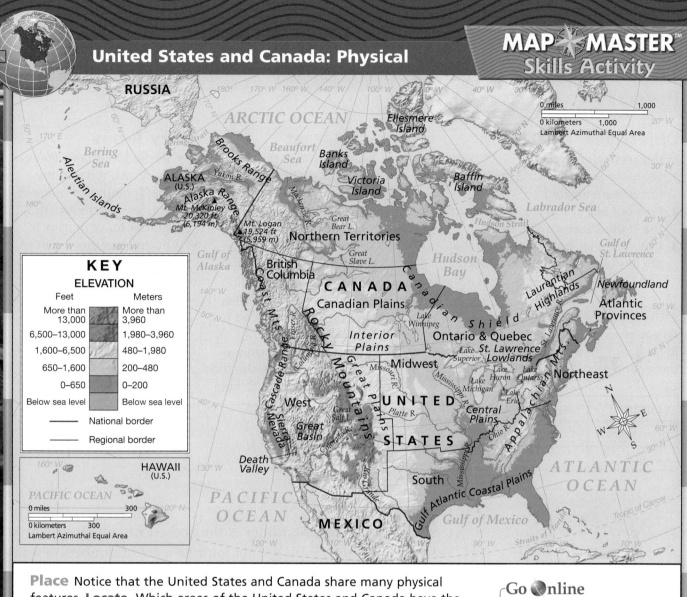

RUSSIA

ARCTIC OCEAN

Bering Sea

Aleutian Islands

Brooks Range

ALASKA (U.S.)

Yukon R.

Alaska Range

Mt. McKinley 20,320 ft (6,194 m)

Mt. Logan 19,524 ft (5,959 m)

Beaufort Sea

Banks Island

Victoria Island

Mackenzie R.

Great Bear L.

Northern Territories

Great Slave L.

Ellesmere Island

Baffin Island

Hudson Strait

Labrador Sea

Gulf of St. Lawrence

Newfoundland

Gulf of Alaska

British Columbia

CANADA

Canadian Plains

Canadian Shield

Hudson Bay

Lake Winnipeg

Laurentian Highlands

Atlantic Provinces

KEY

ELEVATION

Feet		Meters
More than 13,000		More than 3,960
6,500–13,000		1,980–3,960
1,600–6,500		480–1,980
650–1,600		200–480
0–650		0–200
Below sea level		Below sea level

National border

Regional border

Coast Mts.

Fraser R.

Rocky Mountains

Columbia R.

Cascade Range

Sierra Nevada

Interior Plains

Great Plains

Midwest

Missouri R.

Lake Superior

Ontario & Quebec

St. Lawrence Lowlands

St. Lawrence R.

Lake Michigan

Lake Huron

Lake Ontario

Lake Erie

Appalachian Mts.

Northeast

West

Great Salt L.

Great Basin

UNITED

Platte R.

Mississippi R.

Central Plains

Ohio R.

N

W E

S

Death Valley

Colorado R.

STATES

Rio Grande

South

Gulf Atlantic Coastal Plains

ATLANTIC OCEAN

HAWAII (U.S.)

PACIFIC OCEAN

| 0 miles | 300 |
| 0 kilometers | 300 |

Lambert Azimuthal Equal Area

PACIFIC OCEAN

MEXICO

Gulf of Mexico

Tropic of Cancer

Straits of Florida

| 0 miles | 1,000 |
| 0 kilometers | 1,000 |

Lambert Azimuthal Equal Area

Place Notice that the United States and Canada share many physical features. **Locate** Which areas of the United States and Canada have the highest elevation? **Predict** How might people use the land in these mountainous regions?

Go Online
PHSchool.com Use Web Code
lhp-4110 for step-by-step
map skills practice.

Prepare to Read

Objectives

In this section you will

1. Learn where the United States and Canada are located.
2. Find out about the major landforms of the United States and Canada.
3. Explore major bodies of water that are important to the United States and Canada.

Taking Notes

As you read the section, look for the main ideas about land and water. Copy the table below and record your findings in it.

Country	Landforms	Bodies of Water
United States		
Canada		

Target Reading Skill

Set a Purpose for Reading
Before you read this section, look at the headings, maps, and photographs to see what the section is about. Then set a purpose for reading this section. For example, your purpose might be to find out about the geography of the United States and Canada. Use the Taking Notes table to help you meet your purpose.

Key Terms

- **Rocky Mountains** (RAHK ee MOWN tunz) *n.* the major mountain range in western North America
- **glacier** (GLAY shur) *n.* a huge, slow-moving mass of snow and ice
- **Great Lakes** (grayt layks) *n.* the world's largest group of freshwater lakes
- **tributary** (TRIB yoo tehr ee) *n.* a river or stream that flows into a larger river

Alaska's Mount McKinley is the highest mountain in North America. In 1992, Ruth Kocour joined a team of climbers to scale the 20,320-foot (6,194-meter) peak. After the team had set up camp at 9,500 feet (2,896 meters), the first storm arrived. The team quickly built walls of packed snow to shield their tents from the wind. They dug a snow cave to house their kitchen and waited for the storm to end. Kocour recalls, "Someone on another team went outside for a few minutes, came back, and had a hot drink. His teeth cracked."

Maybe camping in the mountains is not for you. Perhaps you would prefer the sunny beaches of Florida, the giant forests of the Northwest, or the rugged coastline of Nova Scotia. Maybe you would like to see the Arizona desert or the plains of central Canada. The landscape of the United States and Canada varies greatly.

Climbers on Mount McKinley

A Global Perspective

The United States and Canada are located in North America. To the east is the Atlantic Ocean, and to the west is the Pacific Ocean. To the north, Canada borders the Arctic Ocean, while to the south, the United States borders Mexico and the Gulf of Mexico. The United States also includes Alaska, a huge state bordering northwest Canada, and Hawaii, a group of Pacific islands more than 2,000 miles (3,220 kilometers) west of California.

✔ **Reading Check** **Which bodies of water border the United States and Canada?**

A Scenic Landscape
This view of the Pioneer Valley along the Connecticut River in Massachusetts was taken from Mount Sugarloaf. **Draw Conclusions** *What can you conclude about the northeastern region of the United States from this photo?*

Landforms

From outer space, the United States and Canada appear as one landmass, with mountain ranges or systems, and vast plains running from north to south. Locate these mountains and plains on the United States and Canada: Physical map on page 147.

Extending about 3,000 miles (4,830 kilometers) along the western section of the continent, the Rocky Mountains are the largest mountain system in North America. In the east, the Appalachian (ap uh LAY chun) Mountains are the United States' second-largest mountain system. They stretch about 1,500 miles (2,415 kilometers). In Canada, the Appalachian Mountains meet the Laurentian (law REN shun) Highlands.

Between the Rockies and the Appalachians lies a huge plains area. In Canada, these lowlands are called the Interior Plains. In the United States, they are called the Great Plains and the Central Plains. Much of this region has rich soil. In the wetter, eastern area, farmers grow crops like corn and soybeans. In the drier, western area, farmers grow wheat and ranchers raise livestock.

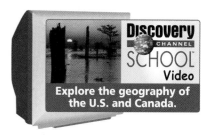

DISCOVERY CHANNEL
SCHOOL Video
Explore the geography of the U.S. and Canada.

The Next Hawaiian Island
Volcanic eruptions in the Pacific Ocean, like the one shown above in Volcano National Park, created the islands of Hawaii. Loihi (loh EE hee), off the southern tip of Hawaii, is the world's most active volcano. But no one has seen it erupt. Its peak is 3,000 feet (914 meters) below the ocean's surface. Years of continuous eruption have produced layer after layer of molten lava. Scientists predict that in 100,000 years or less, Loihi will rise above the surface of the ocean and become the next Hawaiian island.

Special Features of the United States The United States has several unique features. The Gulf-Atlantic Coastal Plain runs along its eastern and southern coasts. In the Northeast, this plain is narrow; it broadens as it spreads south and west. Flat, fertile land and access to the sea attracted many settlers to this area.

A region of plateaus and basins lies west of the Rockies. Perhaps the most notable feature of this area is the Great Basin. In the northeast section of this bowl-shaped region is the Great Salt Lake. Death Valley is in the southwest section. Much of Death Valley lies below sea level. It is also the hottest place in North America. Summer temperatures there exceed 125°F (52°C).

Volcanoes To the west of this region lie three more mountain ranges. They are the Coast Ranges along the Pacific, the Sierra Nevada in California, and the Cascades in Washington and Oregon. Volcanoes produced the Cascades. Volcanoes form when magma, or molten rock, breaks through Earth's crust. Once it comes up to the surface, the molten rock is called lava. One of the volcanoes in the Cascades—Mount St. Helens—erupted in 1980. The eruption was so powerful that people as far away as Montana had to sweep volcanic ash off of their cars.

Glaciers Far to the north, snow and ice cover Alaska's many mountains. Glaciers, huge, slow-moving sheets of ice, fill many of the valleys among these mountains. Glaciers form over many years when layers of snow press together, thaw a little, and then turn to ice. Valley glaciers are found in high mountain valleys where the climate is too cold for the ice to melt. In North America, these valley glaciers move through the Rocky and Cascade mountains, the Sierra Nevada, and the Alaskan ranges.

Special Features of Canada Canada, too, has a number of unique features. East of Alaska lies the Yukon (YOO kahn) Territory. Mount Logan, Canada's highest peak, is located there in a range called the Coast Mountains. The Coast Mountains, which stretch south along the Pacific Ocean, are located only in Canada. They are not part of the United States Coast Ranges.

Farther east, beyond the Interior Plains, lies the Canadian Shield. This huge region of ancient rock covers about half of Canada. The land on the shield is rugged, so few people live there.

Southeast of the shield along the St. Lawrence River are the St. Lawrence Lowlands. These lowlands are Canada's smallest land region. However, they are home to more than half of the country's population. The region is also Canada's manufacturing center. And because the lowlands have fertile soil, farmers in this region produce about one third of the country's crops.

✓ **Reading Check** **Describe two physical features of the United States and Canada.**

Set a Purpose for Reading
If your purpose is to learn about the geography of Canada, how do the three paragraphs at the left help you meet your goal?

Major Bodies of Water

Both the United States and Canada have important lakes and rivers. People use these bodies of water for transportation, recreation, and industry. Many American and Canadian cities developed near these bodies of water. Find these waterways on the United States and Canada: Physical map on page 147.

The Great Lakes Lakes Superior, Michigan, Huron, Erie, and Ontario make up the **Great Lakes,** the world's largest group of freshwater lakes. Lake Superior is the deepest lake, with a mean depth of 487 feet (148 meters). Lake Erie is the shallowest lake at only 62 feet (19 meters) deep. Only Lake Michigan lies entirely in the United States. The other four lie on the border between the United States and Canada.

Glaciers formed the Great Lakes during an ice age long ago. As the glaciers moved, they dug deep trenches in the land. Water from the melting glaciers filled these trenches to produce the Great Lakes. Today, the Great Lakes are important waterways in both the United States and Canada. Shipping on the Great Lakes has helped to develop the industries of both countries.

A satellite image of the Great Lakes, which create a natural border between the United States and Canada

The Continental Divide
The Rocky Mountains form the continental divide and are the site of several national parks, including Grand Teton National Park in Wyoming (large photo).
White-water rafters paddle along Flathead River in Montana, west of the Rockies (small photo).
Explain *In what direction does the Flathead River flow?*

Major Rivers of the United States The largest river in the United States is the Mississippi River. Its source, or starting point, is in Minnesota. From there, the river flows through the Central Plains to the Gulf of Mexico. Two other major rivers, the Ohio and the Missouri, are tributaries of the Mississippi. A **tributary** (TRIB yoo tehr ee) is a stream or river that flows into a larger river. The Mississippi River system includes hundreds of tributaries and branches. Together they form about 12,000 miles (19,000 kilometers) of navigable water.

The Mighty Mississippi Water levels tend to rise in the spring when heavy rain combines with melting snow from the mountains. If the soil cannot soak up the excess water, flooding can occur. In 1993, the Upper Mississippi Valley experienced a disastrous flood. It caused nearly 50 deaths and damages totaling more than 15 billion dollars.

People have used the Mississippi River as an important transportation route for hundreds of years. Today, it is one of the busiest waterways in the world. Cargo ships transport many products, including iron, steel, chemicals, and even space rockets.

Look at the United States and Canada: Physical map on page 147 and find the Rocky Mountains. Notice that the Fraser, Columbia, and Colorado rivers form in the Rockies and flow west. Now find the Platte and Missouri rivers. They flow east from the Rockies. This is because the Rockies form the Continental Divide, the boundary that separates rivers flowing to the Pacific Ocean from those flowing to the Atlantic Ocean.

Major Rivers of Canada The Mackenzie River, Canada's longest, forms in the Rocky Mountains and flows north to the Arctic Ocean. It runs for more than 2,600 miles (4,197 kilometers). Although for most of its course the Mackenzie winds through sparsely populated, dense forest area, it is an important transportation route.

In the 1880s, steamboats on the Mackenzie took supplies to local trading posts. Today, ships carry energy and mineral resources from the oil and natural gas fields in the region.

Canada's second major river is the St. Lawrence River. It is one of North America's most important transportation routes, flowing from the Great Lakes to the Atlantic Ocean. A system of locks and canals enables large ships to navigate it. From the St. Lawrence, ships can reach the Great Lakes ports that serve the farmland and industries of the region. Thus, the St. Lawrence is an important trade route between the United States and Canada. Millions of tons of cargo move along the St. Lawrence River each year.

✓ **Reading Check** Name the five Great Lakes.

Section 1 Assessment

Key Terms
Review the key terms at the beginning of this section. Use each term in a sentence that explains its meaning.

Target Reading Skill
How did having a purpose for reading help you to understand important ideas in this section?

Comprehension and Critical Thinking
1. (a) Recall Describe the borders of the United States and Canada.
(b) Predict How do you think the climates of Hawaii and Alaska differ?

2. (a) Describe What is the largest mountain system in North America?
(b) Identify Effects How have the physical features of the United States and Canada affected the lives of the people there?
3. (a) Locate Which bodies of water lie on the border between the United States and Canada?
(b) Explain Why are these bodies of water important?
(c) Draw Conclusions Why did many people coming to the United States and Canada hundreds of years ago settle along coastal plains and rivers?

Writing Activity
Suppose that you are on vacation in the United States or Canada. Write a postcard to a friend describing the physical features that you have seen. Before you begin, review the information you recorded in your Taking Notes table.

For: An activity on Mt. McKinley
Visit: PHSchool.com
Web Code: lhd-4101

"It's a freak storm," Ian e-mailed excitedly to his friends. "Four inches of snow already, and we might get six inches total. It's awful!"

"Awful?" Janet replied. "It's just a few inches. What's the big deal?"

"JUST a few inches?" Ian typed. "This city is paralyzed. Cars are stuck everywhere. Our camping trip this weekend is cancelled. It's a disaster."

Luann responded to both of her friends. "Of course it's a disaster to Ian. He lives in Georgia. No way is the South prepared to deal with a snowstorm in April."

"Well, up here in Quebec, we're not afraid of a little snow!" Janet wrote back.

"Okay, calm down," wrote Luann. "Your opinion depends on what you're used to."

In other words, your opinion depends on your frame of reference.

Learn the Skill

Follow the steps below to understand frame of reference.

1 **Identify the topic being discussed.** Look for evidence that an opinion is being expressed. When people state their opinions, they often reveal information about their frame of reference.

2 **Identify the author's opinion on the issue.** An opinion is what someone believes. It is not a fact, which is something that can be proved.

3 **Identify what you know about the author's background.** Some background factors are age, personality, family, culture, nationality, concerns, and historical era.

4 **Ask how the author's background might have influenced his or her beliefs.** Think about whether the person's opinions would be different if he or she came from a different place, culture, family, or time in history.

Practice the Skill

The text in the box on the right comes from Inuit students in Nunavut. The Inuit, a Native American culture group, persuaded the Canadian government to create the territory of Nunavut in 1999. Read what the students wrote just before the creation of their new homeland.

1 This text has no title, but you can give it a title that reflects the main topic. What title would you give it?

2 The students give both description and opinion. Which parts of the text are description, and which are opinion?

3 You already know some facts about the students' background: They are Canadian, and they are Inuit. What else can you discover about the students' background?

4 The students' opinions are shaped by their frame of reference. Explain how your own frame of reference might make you feel differently about Nunavut.

"There are not very many people, but all of us are friends. We share the same culture and language, Inuktitut. You can learn from elders. We help each other. . . .

"[W]e go to school, church, cadets, the hall, and the gym. We play [games], watch T.V., listen to music, play and watch sports (especially hockey), . . . dance, and sleep. We also stay home, visit with our parents, clean, look after children, and try to finish our homework. . . . We eat seal meat, caribou, arctic char, walrus, . . . and also we eat various types of birds. . . .

"Nunavut is independence. The creation of Nunavut means that we, the Inuit, are going to have our own land. . . . It means a lot to us, the Inuit youth. It means making choices for ourselves. We are proud of Nunavut."
—*Grade 10 students at Ataguttaaluk High in Igloolik, a town in central Nunavut, above the Arctic Circle*

Inuit sculptor

Apply the Skill

Think of an issue that you feel strongly about. Describe your own frame of reference, and show how it has influenced your opinion.

Climate and Vegetation

Prepare to Read

Objectives

In this section you will
1. Learn what climate zones the United States and Canada have.
2. Identify the natural vegetation zones of the United States and Canada.

Taking Notes

As you read the section, look for details about climate and vegetation. Copy the chart below and write each detail under the correct heading.

```
            Climate and Vegetation
    ┌──────────┬──────────┬──────────┬──────────┐
    Tundra    Grassland   Desert     Forest
                          Scrub
    •          •          •          •
    •          •          •          •
    •          •          •          •
```

Target Reading Skill

Predict Making predictions about your text helps you set a purpose for reading and remember what you read. Before you begin, preview the section by looking at the headings, photographs, and maps. Then predict what the text might discuss about climate and vegetation. As you read the section, connect what you read to your prediction. If what you learn doesn't support your prediction, change it.

Key Terms

- **tundra** (TUN druh) *n.* a cold, dry region covered with snow for more than half the year
- **permafrost** (PUR muh frawst) *n.* a permanently frozen layer of ground below the top layer of soil
- **prairie** (PREHR ee) *n.* a region of flat or rolling land covered with grasses
- **province** (PRAH vins) *n.* a political division of land in Canada

On a hot and sunny February morning, a reporter left his home in Miami Beach, Florida, and headed for the airport. Wearing lightweight pants and a short-sleeved shirt, he boarded a plane to snowy Toronto. Was he forgetting something? Surely he knew that the temperature would be below freezing in Canada.

He did, indeed, know all about the bitter cold that would greet him when he got off the plane. But he was going to research an article on Toronto's tunnels and underground malls. He wanted to find out whether people could really visit hotels, restaurants, and shops without having to go outside and brave the harsh Canadian winter.

A climate-controlled shopping center in Toronto, Ontario

Climate Zones

Climate is weather patterns that an area experiences over a long period of time. Climate zones in the United States and Canada range from a desert climate to a polar climate. Factors such as latitude, or a location's distance north or south of the Equator, mountains, and oceans all affect the climates found in different regions.

Climates of Canada   Generally, the farther a location is from the Equator, the colder its climate. Look at the climate regions map on page 143 of the Regional Overview. Notice that much of Canada lies well north of the 40° N line of latitude, a long way from the Equator. Therefore, much of Canada is very cold!

Ocean Effects   The ocean affects Canada's climates, too. Water heats up and cools down more slowly than land. Winds blowing across water on to land tend to warm the land in winter and cool the land in summer. Therefore, areas that are near an ocean generally have milder climates. Also, winds blowing across the ocean pick up moisture. When these winds blow over land, they drop the moisture in the form of rain or snow.

Being a great distance from the ocean also affects climate. Inland areas often have climate extremes. Find Winnipeg, in Canada's Interior Plains, on the climate map. Winter temperatures here are very cold, averaging around 0°F (−18°C). Yet summer temperatures run between 70°F and 90°F (20°C and 32°C).

Mountain Effects   Mountains are another factor that influence climate. Winds blowing from the Pacific Ocean rise as they meet mountain ranges in the west. As they rise, the winds cool and drop their moisture. The air is dry by the time it reaches the other side of the mountains, and it warms up as it returns to lower altitudes. This is called the Chinook effect. The area on the side of the mountains away from the wind is in a rain shadow. A rain shadow is an area on the dry, sheltered side of a mountain, which receives little rainfall.

■ Graph Skills

Located in different climate regions, Miami, Florida, and Toronto, Canada, experience very different average temperatures. **Identify** In which month does Miami experience the coolest temperatures? Which month is the coolest in Toronto?
Compare Which month has the least difference between the average temperature in Miami and Toronto?

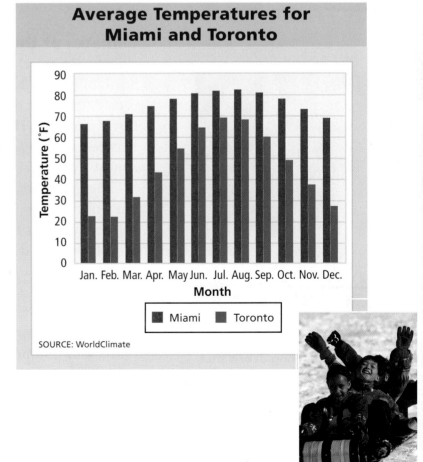

Average Temperatures for Miami and Toronto

SOURCE: WorldClimate

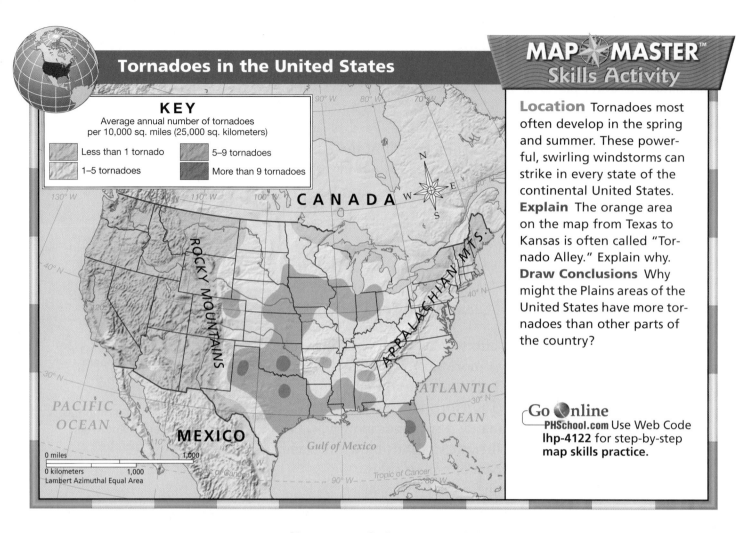

Tornadoes in the United States

KEY

Average annual number of tornadoes
per 10,000 sq. miles (25,000 sq. kilometers)

Less than 1 tornado

1–5 tornadoes

5–9 tornadoes

More than 9 tornadoes

CANADA

ROCKY MOUNTAINS

APPALACHIAN MTS.

PACIFIC OCEAN

MEXICO

Gulf of Mexico

ATLANTIC OCEAN

0 miles 1,000

0 kilometers 1,000

Lambert Azimuthal Equal Area

Tropic of Cancer

Location Tornadoes most often develop in the spring and summer. These powerful, swirling windstorms can strike in every state of the continental United States. **Explain** The orange area on the map from Texas to Kansas is often called "Tornado Alley." Explain why. **Draw Conclusions** Why might the Plains areas of the United States have more tornadoes than other parts of the country?

Go Online
PHSchool.com Use Web Code **lhp-4122** for step-by-step map skills practice.

A tornado produces high winds and flying debris that can cause heavy damage to structures in its path.

Climates of the United States Location also influences climate. On the climate map on page 143, notice that Alaska lies north of the 60° N line of latitude. Far from the Equator, Alaska is cold for much of the year. Now find Hawaii and the southern tip of Florida. They lie near or within the tropics, the area between the 23½° N and 23½° S lines of latitude. There, it is almost always warm.

The Pacific Ocean and mountains affect climate in the western United States. Wet winds from the ocean drop their moisture before they cross the mountains. As a result, the eastern sections of California and Arizona are semiarid or desert. Death Valley, which is located there, has the lowest average rainfall in the country—about 2 inches (5 centimeters) a year.

East of the Great Plains, the country has continental climates. In the north, summers are warm and winters are cold and snowy. In the south, summers tend to be long and hot, while winters are mild. The coastal regions of these areas sometimes experience violent weather. In summer and fall, hurricanes and tropical storms develop in the Atlantic Ocean.

✓ **Reading Check** What factors affect climate?

Natural Vegetation Zones

Climate in the United States and Canada helps produce four major kinds of natural vegetation, or plant life. As you can see on the United States and Canada: Vegetation map on page 160, these are tundra, grassland, desert scrub, and forest.

Predict Based on what you've read so far, is your prediction on target? If not, revise or change your prediction now.

Northern Tundras The tundra, found in the far north, is a cold, dry region that is covered with snow for more than half the year. The Arctic tundra contains permafrost, a layer of permanently frozen soil. During the short, cool summer, the soil above the permafrost thaws. Mosses, grasses, and bright wildflowers grow there. Life is hard in the tundra. However, some Inuits (IN oo its), a native people of Canada and Alaska, once called Eskimos, live there. They make a living by fishing and hunting.

Grasslands Grasslands are regions of flat or rolling land covered with grasses. They are located in areas where there is enough rain to support grasses but not enough to support forests. In North America, grasslands are called prairies. The world's largest prairie lies in the Central and Great Plains of North America. It stretches from the American central states into the Canadian provinces of Alberta, Saskatchewan (sas KACH uh wahn), and Manitoba. These three provinces are sometimes called the Prairie Provinces. A province is a political division of Canada, much like one of our states. Look at the temperate grasslands region of the United States and Canada: Vegetation map on page 160 to locate the prairies, or plains areas, of the United States and Canada.

Two Vegetation Zones
The natural vegetation of the northern tundra (large photo) differs greatly from the natural vegetation of the grasslands (smaller photo). **Draw Conclusions** *How does climate affect the vegetation that grows in the tundra and grasslands?*

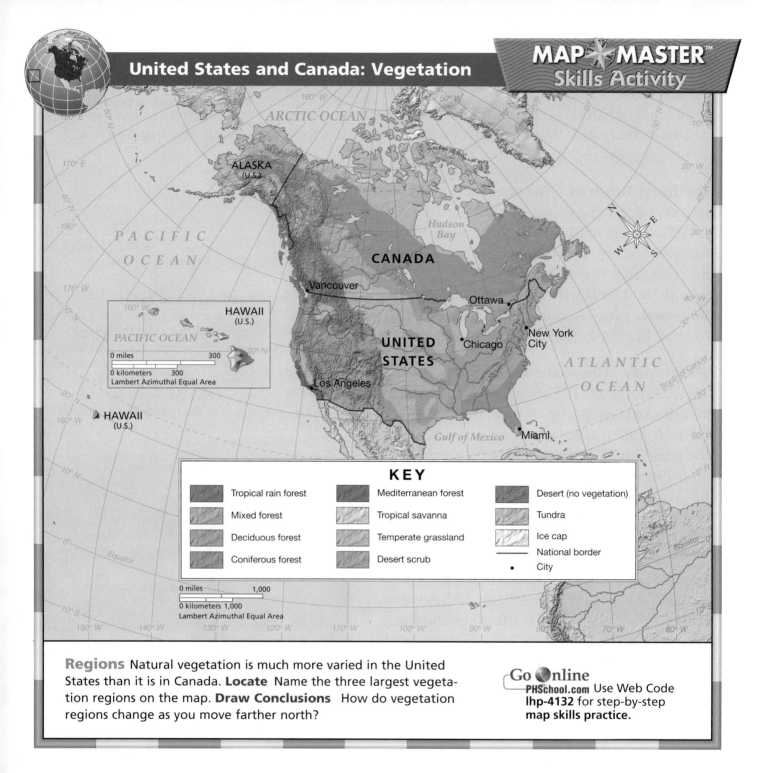

United States and Canada: Vegetation

MAP★MASTER™
Skills Activity

ALASKA (U.S.)

ARCTIC OCEAN

PACIFIC OCEAN

CANADA

Hudson Bay

Vancouver

Ottawa

New York City

Chicago

UNITED STATES

ATLANTIC OCEAN

Los Angeles

HAWAII (U.S.)

PACIFIC OCEAN

0 miles 300
0 kilometers 300
Lambert Azimuthal Equal Area

HAWAII (U.S.)

Gulf of Mexico Miami

KEY

Tropical rain forest	Mediterranean forest
Mixed forest	Tropical savanna
Deciduous forest	Temperate grassland
Coniferous forest	Desert scrub

Desert (no vegetation)
Tundra
Ice cap
—— National border
• City

0 miles 1,000
0 kilometers 1,000
Lambert Azimuthal Equal Area

Regions Natural vegetation is much more varied in the United States than it is in Canada. **Locate** Name the three largest vegetation regions on the map. **Draw Conclusions** How do vegetation regions change as you move farther north?

Go Online
PHSchool.com Use Web Code **lhp-4132** for step-by-step **map skills practice.**

When pioneers first encountered the prairies in what is now the Midwest, they described it as "a sea of grass." Today, farmers grow fields of corn and soybeans there. Farther west, the Great Plains receive less rainfall. Therefore, only short grasses will grow. These grasses are ideal for grazing cattle. The land is also suitable for growing wheat. The Prairie Provinces, too, have many wheat farms and cattle ranches.

Desert Scrub With little rainfall, desert and semiarid regions have limited vegetation. What plants there are have adapted to drought conditions or survive through their deep root systems. The Great Basin, a large, dry region between the Rocky Mountains and the Sierra Nevada in the United States, is one example of a desert region. It covers about 190,000 square miles (492,000 square kilometers) of the West and includes Death Valley. The majority of Nevada and western Utah lie within the Great Basin.

The Sierras block the Great Basin from moisture-bearing winds that come off the Pacific Ocean. Thus, the entire region is in a rain shadow. With annual rainfall of only six to twelve inches (15 to 30 centimeters), the basin cannot support large numbers of people. But, many sheep graze on the area's shrubs.

For many years, the Great Basin was an obstacle that delayed the development of the West, because conditions made it difficult for explorers to cross it. Many people sought alternate routes around the Great Basin as they headed west during the California Gold Rush in 1849.

Life in the Desert
Despite little rain and scorching heat, hundreds of plants and animals, such as the scorpion below, live in the desert. **Draw Conclusions** *How might these plants and animals have adapted to the harsh desert environment?*

An autumn landscape in the Charlevoix region of Quebec, Canada

Forests Forests cover nearly one third of the United States and almost one half of Canada. The mild climate of the northern Pacific Coast encourages great forests of coniferous (koh NIF ur us) trees, such as pine, fir, and spruce. Coniferous trees have cones that carry and protect their seeds. The Rockies are blanketed with coniferous forests. From the Great Lakes across southeastern Canada and New England, and down to the southeastern United States, you will find mixed forests. These are forests of coniferous trees mixed with deciduous (dee SIJ oo us) trees. Deciduous trees shed their leaves in the fall.

One of Canada's best-known symbols is the deciduous sugar maple tree. The sugar maple leaf appears on Canada's flag. In addition, sugar maples produce a sweet sap that can be made into maple syrup and maple sugar—two Canadian specialties.

✓ **Reading Check** **Name the four major kinds of natural vegetation in the United States and Canada.**

Section 2 Assessment

Key Terms
Review the key terms at the beginning of this section. Use each term in a sentence that explains its meaning.

Target Reading Skill
What did you predict about this section? How did your prediction guide your reading?

Comprehension and Critical Thinking
1. (a) Recall Describe the major climate zones of the United States and Canada.

(b) Summarize How do oceans influence climate?
(c) Generalize What geographic features might lead someone to settle in Vancouver rather than in Winnipeg?
2. (a) Locate Where is the largest prairie in the world?
(b) Infer Why do more people live in the prairies than in the tundra?
(c) Identify Effects How does the vegetation of the prairies affect economic activity there?

Writing Activity
Describe the climate zones you would pass through if you traveled from northwestern Canada to the southeastern United States.

Go Online
PHSchool.com

For: An activity on Florida's Everglades
Visit: PHSchool.com
Web Code: lhd-4102

Resources and Land Use

Prepare to Read

Objectives

In this section you will

1. Learn about the major resources of the United States.
2. Find out about the major resources of Canada.

Taking Notes

As you read the section, look for details about the resources of the United States and Canada. Copy the table below and write each detail under the correct subject heading.

Resource	United States	Canada
Farmland		
Water		
Energy and minerals		
Forests		

Target Reading Skill

Preview and Ask Questions Before you read this section, preview the headings and photographs to see what the section is about. Write one or two questions that will help you understand or remember something important in the section. Then read to answer your questions.

Key Terms

- **alluvial soil** (uh LOO vee ul soyl) *n.* fertile topsoil left by a river, especially after a flood
- **agribusiness** (AG ruh biz niz) *n.* a large company that runs huge farms
- **hydroelectricity** (hy droh ee lek TRIH suh tee) *n.* electric power produced by moving water
- **fossil fuel** (FAHS ul FYOO ul) *n.* a fuel formed over millions of years from animal and plant remains

Surrounded by majestic redwood forests, Carlotta, California, has little more than a gas station and a general store. Yet on one day in September 1996, police arrested more than 1,000 people there. Was Carlotta filled with outlaws like some old Wild West town? No, but it was the scene of a showdown. A logging company wanted to cut down some of the oldest redwood trees in the world. Protesters wanted to preserve the forest and the animals that live there. Both sides believed in the importance of natural resources. But they disagreed strongly about how to use them. As in Carlotta, people all over North America use their natural resources for recreation, industry, and energy.

Redwood National Park, California

Resources of the United States

Native Americans, pioneers, and explorers in North America knew centuries ago that it was a land of plenty. Abundant resources helped to build two of the world's leading economies.

Farmland Both the Midwest and the South have rich, dark soils that are suitable for farming. Along the Mississippi and other river valleys are **alluvial** (uh LOO vee ul) **soils**, the fertile topsoil left by a river after a flood. Until the 1900s, most American farms were owned by families. Since then, large companies have bought many family farms. Southern California's Imperial Valley has vast vegetable fields operated by agribusinesses. An **agribusiness** is a large company that runs huge farms.

U.S. and Canada: Natural Resources

MAP MASTER™
Skills Activity

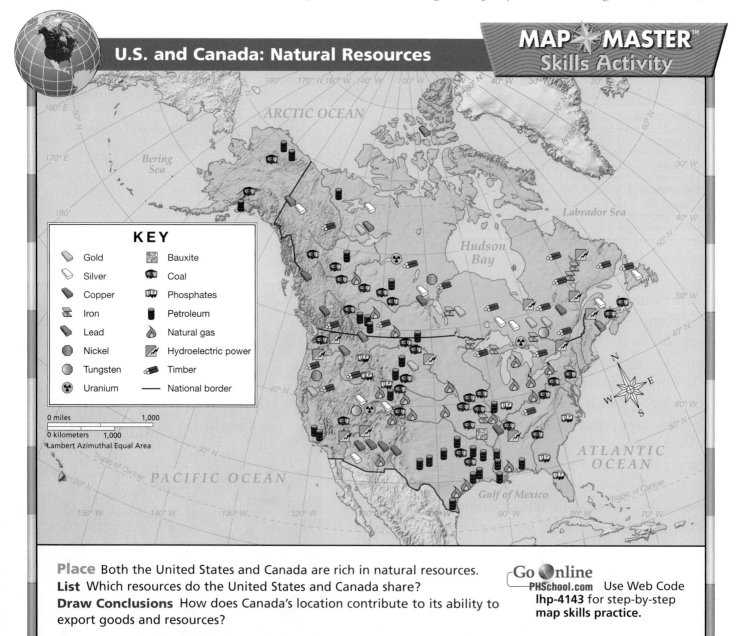

KEY

Gold		Bauxite	
Silver		Coal	
Copper		Phosphates	
Iron		Petroleum	
Lead		Natural gas	
Nickel		Hydroelectric power	
Tungsten		Timber	
Uranium		— National border	

0 miles 1,000
0 kilometers 1,000
Lambert Azimuthal Equal Area

Place Both the United States and Canada are rich in natural resources.
List Which resources do the United States and Canada share?
Draw Conclusions How does Canada's location contribute to its ability to export goods and resources?

Go Online
PHSchool.com Use Web Code
lhp-4143 for step-by-step
map skills practice.

Water Water is a vital resource. People need water to drink and to grow crops. Factories rely on water for many industrial processes, including cooling machinery. Both industry and farmers use rivers to transport goods. The Mississippi, Ohio, and Missouri rivers are important shipping routes.

Water is used for other purposes, too. Dams along many rivers produce **hydroelectricity** (hy droh ee lek TRIH suh tee), or electric power generated by moving water. The Grand Coulee (KOO lee) Dam on the Columbia River in the state of Washington produces more hydroelectricity than any other dam in the United States.

An irrigation system watering several fields on a California farm

Forests People have claimed that before Europeans arrived, a squirrel could leap from one tree to another all the way from the Atlantic Coast to the Mississippi River. That is no longer true, but America's forests are still an important resource. Large forests extend across the Pacific Northwest, the South, the Appalachians, and areas around the Great Lakes. They produce lumber, wood pulp for paper, and fine wood for furniture.

Energy and Mineral Resources The United States produces and consumes more fossil fuels than any other country. **Fossil fuels** are sources of energy that formed from animal and plant remains. Petroleum, natural gas, and coal are all fossil fuels. Although the United States imports most of its oil from other countries, the biggest oil reserves in North America are along the northern coast of Alaska. A pipeline carries oil from the wells in Prudhoe Bay to the port of Valdez in the south. From here, giant tankers carry the oil away to be refined.

The Trans-Alaska Pipeline Workers prepare a section of the 800-mile (1,280-kilometer) pipeline for welding. **Identify Effects** How did the construction of the Trans-Alaska Pipeline produce growth for both the population and the economy of Alaska?

Natural Gas Natural gas is a mixture of gases found beneath Earth's surface. To be usable, natural gas must be processed after it is removed from the ground. Its major use is as a fuel. Natural gas heats many homes in the United States. Large gas fields can be found in the Texas Panhandle, Louisiana, and Alaska. Natural gas can be transported by pipeline or in specially designed tanker ships.

Coal Coal is another important fossil fuel. Many power plants burn coal to produce electricity. It is also used to produce steel, as well as to heat and power industrial facilities. The United States has about 2,500 coal mines, totaling nearly 25 percent of the world's coal reserves. Over the past 30 years, modern mining equipment has nearly tripled the productivity of these mines. Wyoming, Kentucky, West Virginia, and Pennsylvania are the main coal-producing states in the country.

Mining In addition, the United States has valuable deposits of copper, gold, iron ore, and lead. Mining accounts for a small percentage of the country's economy and employs less than one percent of its workers. But these minerals are very important to other industries and have fueled industrial expansion.

✓ **Reading Check** Why is water an important natural resource?

Preview and Ask Questions

Ask yourself a question about the paragraph at the right.

Mining Machinery
A coal miner uses a mining machine to dig into the face of a coal deposit. **Analyze** *Why is coal such an important resource in the United States?*

Electric Power

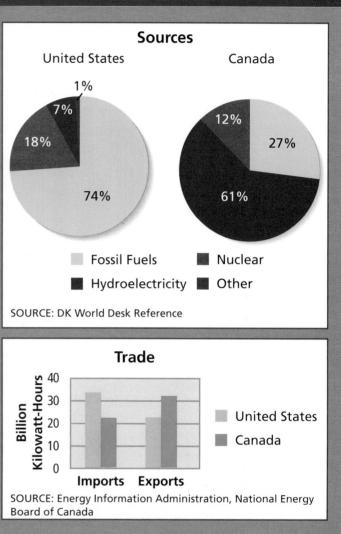

Sources

United States

- 1%
- 7%
- 18%
- 74%

Canada

- 12%
- 27%
- 61%

☐ Fossil Fuels   ■ Nuclear

■ Hydroelectricity   ■ Other

SOURCE: DK World Desk Reference

Trade

Billion Kilowatt-Hours (y-axis: 0, 10, 20, 30, 40)

Imports   Exports

☐ United States   ■ Canada

SOURCE: Energy Information Administration, National Energy Board of Canada

Resources of Canada

Canada's first European settlers earned their living as fur trappers, loggers, fishers, and farmers. Today, the economic picture has changed. Less than five percent of Canada's workers earn their living in these ways.

Farmland Less than 10 percent of Canada's land is suitable for farming. Most is located in the Prairie Provinces. This region produces most of Canada's wheat and beef. The St. Lawrence Lowlands are another major agricultural region. This area produces grains, milk, vegetables, and fruits.

Water Canada has more lakes than any other country in the world. About nine percent of the world's fresh water is in Canada. Before the first railroads were built in the 1800s, the only way to reach some parts of the country was by water. Today, the St. Lawrence and Mackenzie rivers serve as important shipping routes.

Minerals and Energy Resources The Canadian Shield contains much of Canada's mineral wealth. Most of the nation's iron ore comes from mines near the Quebec-Newfoundland border. The region also has large deposits of gold, silver, zinc, copper, and uranium. The Prairie Provinces, particularly Alberta, have large oil and natural gas deposits.

Canada harnesses the rivers of Quebec Province to make hydroelectricity. These rivers generate enough hydroelectric power that some of it can be sold to the northeastern United States.

■ Chart Skills

Both the United States and Canada use fossil fuels to produce electricity. Fossil fuels are nonrenewable resources, meaning that once used they are not easily replaced. The United States and Canada also make use of renewable resources such as the hydroelectricity produced by the dam above. **Name** What energy source produces the largest percentage of Canada's electricity? **Analyze** Which nation is more dependent on the other for its energy? Explain.

Tugboats tow huge booms, or lines of connected floating logs, harvested from Canada's forests.

Forests With almost half its land covered in forests, Canada is a leading producer and exporter of timber products. These products include lumber, paper, plywood, and wood pulp. The climate in British Columbia produces Canada's densest tall-timber forests. Large amounts of rain and a long growing season contribute to the growth of large evergreens with hard wood ideal for construction lumber. The provinces of Ontario and Quebec also produce large amounts of timber.

✓ **Reading Check** **What resources are found in the Canadian Shield?**

Section 3 Assessment

Key Terms
Review the key terms at the beginning of this section. Use each term in a sentence that explains its meaning.

Target Reading Skill
What questions did you ask that helped you to learn and remember something from this section?

Comprehension and Critical Thinking
1. (a) List Describe the major natural resources of the United States.

(b) Explain How have energy resources shaped the economy and the standard of living of the United States?
(c) Infer What economic challenges might a country with few natural resources face?
2. (a) Note How much of Canada's land can be used for farming?
(b) Summarize How is water used as a resource in Canada?
(c) Compare Based on what you know about the physical geography of the two countries, in what ways do you think the resources are similar?

Writing Activity
What do you think is the most important resource in the United States and Canada? Write a paragraph explaining your choice.

Writing Tip Be sure to include examples, details, facts, and reasons that support the main idea of your paragraph.

Review and Assessment

◆ Chapter Summary

Section 1: Land and Water
- Both the United States and Canada are located in North America.
- The United States and Canada have many mountain ranges and plains areas.
- Bodies of water such as the Great Lakes provide transportation and support industry.

Section 2: Climate and Vegetation
- Climate zones in the United States and Canada range from a desert climate to a polar climate.
- Varied climates in the United States and Canada help to produce varied vegetation.

Section 3: Resources and Land Use
- Farmland, forests, water, and minerals are all important resources for the United States and Canada.
- Natural resources affect the economies of the United States and Canada.

Montana

Scorpion in a desert in California

◆ Key Terms

Use each key term below in a sentence that shows the meaning of the term.

1. agribusiness
2. alluvial soil
3. glacier
4. Great Lakes
5. hydroelectricity
6. Rocky Mountains
7. tributary
8. tundra
9. permafrost
10. prairie
11. province
12. fossil fuel

◆ Comprehension and Critical Thinking

13. (a) Identify What landform lies between the Rocky and Appalachian mountains?
(b) Draw Conclusions How does climate affect the crops grown there?

14. (a) Define What is the Canadian Shield?
(b) Compare and Contrast Why do more people live in the St. Lawrence Lowlands than on the Canadian Shield?

15. (a) Explain How does the Pacific Ocean help to keep Canada's west coast climate mild?
(b) Contrast How does the west coast climate differ from the climate that Canada's Interior Plains experiences? Explain.

16. (a) Explain How does latitude affect climate?
(b) Apply Information How might geography and climate affect the way people live in the Canadian territory of Nunavut?

17. (a) Recall Tundra, grassland, desert scrub, and forests are major types of what?
(b) Identify Cause and Effect How do the climate and vegetation of the tundra affect how Inuits live?

18. (a) Identify Until the 1900s, who owned and ran most American farms?
(b) Explore the Main Idea How are most American farms run today?
(c) Draw Conclusions How has this change in ownership affected American farmers?

◆ Skills Practice

Identifying Frame of Reference Review the steps you followed in the Skills for Life activity in this chapter. Then reread the first two paragraphs of Section 3. First, identify the topic being discussed. Then, list some reasons why the logging company and the protesters might have different opinions on how to use natural resources. Finally, identify the frames of reference for people on both sides of the issue.

◆ Writing Activity: Science

Suppose that you are a meteorologist, or a scientist who studies Earth's weather patterns. Create two possible weather maps for the United States and Canada. One map should show a typical winter day and the other a typical summer day. The weather maps should show changes in the weather across the two countries.

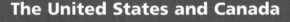

MAP MASTER™
Skills Activity

Place Location Write the letter from the map that shows its location.
1. Canadian Shield
2. Great Basin
3. Great Plains
4. Rocky Mountains
5. Appalachian Mountains
6. Pacific Ocean
7. Atlantic Ocean
8. Great Lakes

Go Online
PHSchool.com Use Web Code lhp-4153 for an interactive map.

The United States and Canada

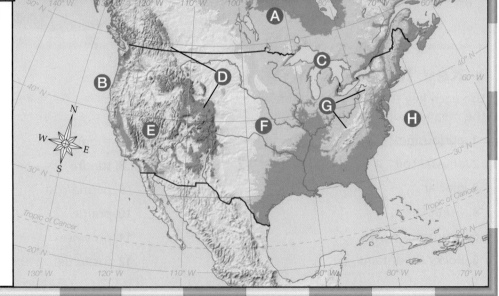

Standardized Test Prep

Test-Taking Tips

Some questions on standardized tests ask you to make mental maps. Read the paragraph below. Then follow the tips to answer the sample question about Canada.

> Jessie is working on a crossword puzzle. She studies the following clue and knows the correct answer: Which large Canadian city is located on one of the Great Lakes?
>
> What is her answer?

TIP Try to picture a map of the United States and Canada. Then try to place each of the cities on this mental map—from east to west.

Make a mental map of the United States and Canada. Then pick the letter that best answers the question.

A Ottawa
B Toronto
C ~~Chicago~~
D ~~Vancouver~~

TIP Rule out choices that do not make sense. Then choose the best answer from the remaining choices.

Think It Through You can rule out Vancouver because it is on the west coast of Canada. Chicago is on Lake Michigan, but it is in the United States. That leaves Ottawa and Toronto. Ottawa is farther north than Toronto. It is on a waterway, the Ottawa River, but not on one of the Great Lakes. The answer is B, Toronto, which is on Lake Ontario.

Practice Questions

Use the tips above and other tips in this book to help you answer the following questions.

1. Because of its location near the Pacific Ocean and the Coast Mountains, Canada's northwestern coast is
   A hot and dry.
   B bitterly cold.
   C wet and snowy.
   D wet and mild.

2. Which vegetation region shared by the United States and Canada is the largest in the world of its kind?
   A prairie
   B tundra
   C desert
   D savanna

3. The United States is the world's second-largest producer of
   A coal, petroleum, and natural gas.
   B iron ore.
   C hydroelectricity.
   D wood and wood products.

Make a mental map of Canada. Then answer the question below.

4. This region of Canada lies east of the Interior Plains. It covers about half of Canada. Few people live in this region.
   A the St. Lawrence Lowlands
   B the Canadian Shield
   C the Laurentian Highlands
   D the St. Lawrence Seaway

Go Online
PHSchool.com
Use Web Code lha-4103
for a **Chapter 6 self-test.**

Chapter

7

The U.S. and Canada: Shaped by History

Chapter Preview

This chapter presents the history of the United States and Canada and shows how that history affects the region to this day.

Section 1
The Arrival of the Europeans

Section 2
Growth and Conflict in the United States

Section 3
The United States on the Brink of Change

Section 4
The History of Canada

Section 5
The United States and Canada Today

Target Reading Skill

Clarifying Meaning In this chapter you will focus on skills you can use to clarify meaning as you read.

▶ The Washington Monument as seen from the Lincoln Memorial in Washington, D.C.

MAP✦MASTER™
Skills Activity

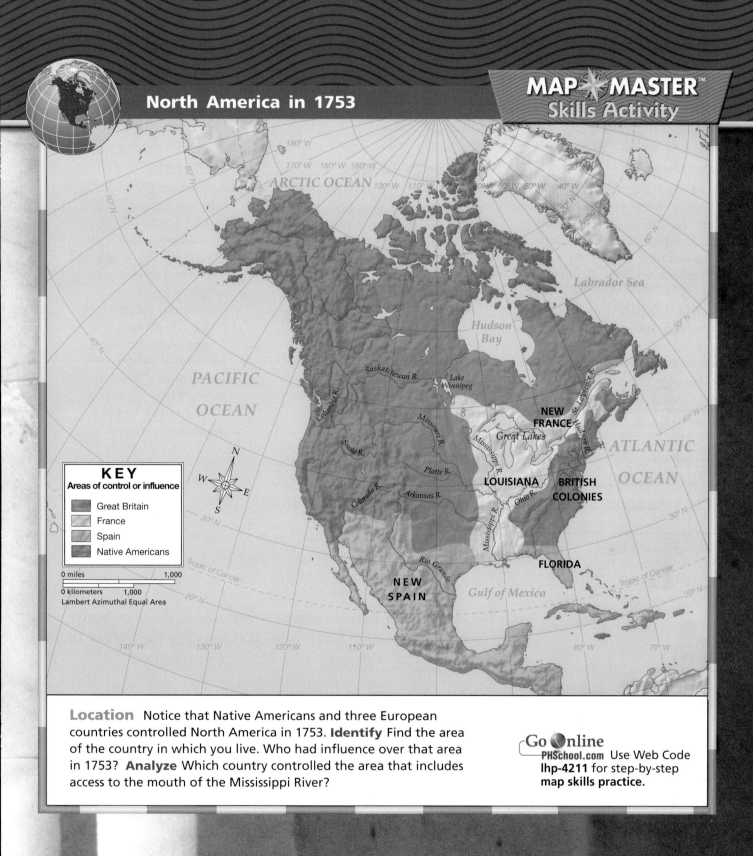

KEY
Areas of control or influence

- Great Britain
- France
- Spain
- Native Americans

0 miles   1,000
0 kilometers   1,000
Lambert Azimuthal Equal Area

ARCTIC OCEAN

PACIFIC OCEAN

Labrador Sea

Hudson Bay

Saskatchewan R.

Lake Winnipeg

Columbia R.

Snake R.

Missouri R.

Great Lakes

NEW FRANCE

St. Lawrence R.

Hudson R.

ATLANTIC OCEAN

Platte R.

Mississippi R.

Ohio R.

LOUISIANA

BRITISH COLONIES

Colorado R.

Arkansas R.

Rio Grande

NEW SPAIN

Mississippi R.

FLORIDA

Gulf of Mexico

Tropic of Cancer

Location Notice that Native Americans and three European countries controlled North America in 1753. **Identify** Find the area of the country in which you live. Who had influence over that area in 1753? **Analyze** Which country controlled the area that includes access to the mouth of the Mississippi River?

Go Online
PHSchool.com Use Web Code
lhp-4211 for step-by-step
map skills practice.

Prepare to Read

Objectives

In this section you will
1. Learn who the first Americans were.
2. Discover the effects the arrival of Europeans had on Native Americans.
3. Find out how the United States won its independence from Great Britain.

Taking Notes

As you read the section, look for important events that have taken place in North America. Copy the table below and write each event in the correct time period.

Events in North American History	
1400s	
1500s	
1600s	
1700s	

Target Reading Skill

Reread Rereading is a strategy that can help you understand words and ideas in the text. If you do not understand a certain passage, reread it to look for connections among the words and sentences.

Key Terms

- **indigenous** (in DIJ uh nus) *adj.* belonging to a certain place
- **missionary** (MISH un ehr ee) *n.* a person who tries to convert others to his or her religion
- **indentured servant** (in DEN churd SUR vunt) *n.* a person who must work for a period of years to gain freedom
- **boycott** (BOY kaht) *n.* a refusal to buy or use goods and services

Native American artifacts

Louise Erdrich is an American writer. She is also part Native American. In one of her novels, she describes the variety of Native American cultures before the Europeans arrived:

> **❝[They] had hundreds of societies . . . whose experience had told them that the world was a pretty diverse place. Walk for a day in any direction and what do you find: A tribe with a whole new set of gods, a language as distinct from your own as Tibetan is from Dutch. . . .❞**
>
> —*Louise Erdrich,* The Crown of Columbus

The First Americans

Many scientists think that Native Americans migrated from Asia. Perhaps as early as 30,000 years ago, they theorize, small groups of hunters and gatherers reached North America from Asia.

This migration from Asia to North America took place during the last ice age. At that time, so much water froze into thick ice sheets that the sea level dropped. As a result, a land bridge was exposed between Siberia and Alaska. Hunters followed herds of bison and mammoths across this land bridge. Other migrating people may have paddled small boats and fished along the coasts.

Over time, the first Americans spread throughout North and South America. They developed different ways of life to suit the environment of the places where they settled.

Many Native Americans disagree with this theory, believing they have always lived in the Americas. In any case, all people consider Native Americans **indigenous** (in DIJ uh nus) people, meaning they belong to and are native to this place.

✓ **Reading Check** **How did migrating people reach North America?**

The Europeans Arrive

Life for the millions of indigenous people in the Americas began to change after 1492. That year, Christopher Columbus, a sea captain sailing from Spain, explored islands in the Caribbean Sea. His voyage opened the way for European colonization.

Spanish Claims to the Americas The Spanish settlers who followed Columbus spread out across the Americas. Some went to the present-day southwestern United States and Mexico. Others went to Florida, the Caribbean islands, and South America. Spain gained great wealth from its American colonies.

Learn about early Native American houses.

Taos, New Mexico
Although Native Americans had inhabited the area for centuries, Spanish explorers arrived in present-day Taos (TAH ohs), New Mexico in 1540. They built the church below in 1617. **Predict** *How might life have changed for Native Americans after Spanish explorers arrived?*

Pueblo Village

When the Pueblo Indians of the Southwest learned how to grow corn and other crops, they no longer had to move about to hunt and gather food. As they became more settled and grew larger harvests, they built stone corn cribs. Over time, these storerooms became larger, and the Pueblos began to build their houses and villages around them.

Acoma Pueblo, New Mexico
The Acoma Pueblo sits high on a 357-foot (109-meter) sandstone rock. It is also known as "Sky City."

The village walls were made of adobe bricks, cemented together with mud. A coating of mud plaster, lime plaster, or stucco covered the bricks and protected the wall.

The Pueblos planted and tended crops of squash, beans, and corn close to the village.

After mud and straw were mixed together, people poured the mixture into molds where they dried into bricks.

Light reached the inside of the pueblo through doors and windows, allowing people inside to weave and cook.

Making adobe bricks
A present-day craftsman in Rancho de Taos, New Mexico, uses ancient methods to create bricks out of mud.

ANALYZING IMAGES
Why were the tops of the village rooms flat, instead of roofed?

The colonists often enslaved Native Americans. They forced Native Americans to work in mines or on farms. Working conditions were so harsh that thousands died. Spanish missionaries tried to make Native Americans more like Europeans, often by force. **Missionaries** (MISH un ehr ees) are religious people who want to convert others to their religion.

French Claims to the Americas   Seeing Spain's success, other countries also wanted colonies in the Americas. French explorers claimed land along the St. Lawrence and Mississippi rivers. Unlike the Spanish, who were interested in gold, the French were interested in fur. French traders and missionaries often lived among the Native Americans and learned their ways. However, both the French and the Spanish brought disease along with them. Millions of Native Americans died from diseases that they had never been exposed to before, such as smallpox and measles.

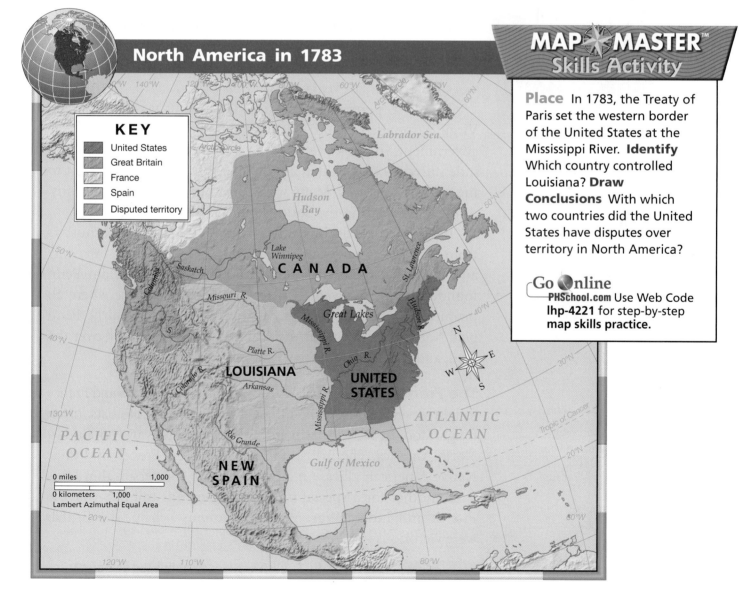

North America in 1783

KEY
- United States
- Great Britain
- France
- Spain
- Disputed territory

MAP MASTER™
Skills Activity

Place In 1783, the Treaty of Paris set the western border of the United States at the Mississippi River. **Identify** Which country controlled Louisiana? **Draw Conclusions** With which two countries did the United States have disputes over territory in North America?

Go Online
PHSchool.com Use Web Code **lhp-4221** for step-by-step **map skills practice.**

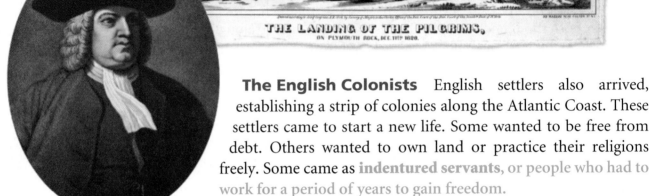

THE LANDING OF THE PILGRIMS,
ON PLYMOUTH ROCK, DEC. 11TH 1620.

In 1620, a group of about 100 Pilgrims sailed to New England on the *Mayflower* (right). In 1682, William Penn (left) arrived in the colony of Pennsylvania, which means "Penn's woods."

Reread
Target Skill Reread to see why the French and Indian War was fought.

The English Colonists English settlers also arrived, establishing a strip of colonies along the Atlantic Coast. These settlers came to start a new life. Some wanted to be free from debt. Others wanted to own land or practice their religions freely. Some came as **indentured servants,** or people who had to work for a period of years to gain freedom.

The first permanent English settlement was Jamestown, Virginia, founded in 1607. By 1619, it had the beginnings of self-government. In the same year, the first Africans arrived there as indentured servants. Later, about 1640, Africans were brought to the colonies as slaves. Many were forced to work on plantations, or the large farms in the South where cash crops were grown.

In 1620, the Pilgrims arrived in Plymouth, Massachusetts from England. They wanted to worship God in their own way and to govern themselves. About 60 years later, William Penn founded the Pennsylvania Colony. He wanted a place where all people, regardless of race or religion, were treated fairly. Penn paid Native Americans for their land. Later, settlers took over the land, and then fought Native Americans to control it.

The French and Indian War In the 1700s, Britain and France fought several wars. When they fought, their colonists often fought, too. In 1754, Britain and France went to war over land in North America. The British fought against the French and their Native American allies. An ally is a country or person that joins with another for a special purpose. Americans call this war the French and Indian War. With the colonists' help, the British were victorious in 1763.

✓ **Reading Check** Why did English settlers establish the colonies?

The Break With Britain

Despite their victory, the British wanted an army in North America to protect the colonists. The British thought the colonists should help pay for the war and for their defense. They put taxes on many British goods the colonists bought. Because no one represented the colonists in the British Parliament, they could not protest these taxes. Many of them began to demand "no taxation without representation." They also **boycotted**, or refused to buy, British goods.

Resentment grew against British rule, causing the Revolutionary War to break out in 1775. Thomas Jefferson summarized the colonists' views in the Declaration of Independence. His words inspired many colonists to fight. In 1781, George Washington led the American forces to victory. The Treaty of Paris, signed in 1783, made American independence official.

Before they won independence, the 13 colonies worked on a plan of government called the Articles of Confederation. But Congress was not given the power to tax. After the war, the 13 new states agreed to form a stronger central government. They wrote the Constitution, which set up the framework for our federal government. Approved in 1788, it is still the highest law of the United States.

✓ **Reading Check** What was the problem with the Articles of Confederation?

This statue commemorates the Minutemen of the American Revolution who stood their ground against British troops on April 19, 1775.

Section 1 Assessment

Key Terms
Review the key terms at the beginning of this section. Use each term in a sentence that explains its meaning.

Target Reading Skill
What word or idea were you able to clarify by rereading?

Comprehension and Critical Thinking
1. (a) Recall Where do many scientists think the first Americans came from?

(b) Identify Point of View Why might Native Americans today disagree with the theory of migration?
2. (a) Explain Describe how different European groups settled in the Americas.
(b) Summarize How did Europeans affect Native American life?
3. (a) Name What document is the framework for the United States government?
(b) Identify Cause and Effect Why did the colonists object to the taxes placed on them by the British?

Writing Activity
Write a paragraph discussing how life in the Americas might have been different if Columbus's voyage had not taken place.

> **Writing Tip** Begin your paragraph with a topic sentence that states your main idea. Give at least two examples of how life might have been different.

Growth and Conflict in the United States

Prepare to Read

Objectives

In this section you will

1. Explore the effects of westward expansion in the United States.
2. Discover the causes and effects of the Civil War.

Taking Notes

As you read the section, look for details about the causes and effects of westward expansion and the Civil War. Copy the flow-chart below and write each detail under the correct heading.

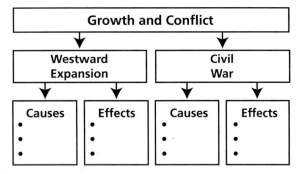

Target Reading Skill

Read Ahead Reading ahead is a strategy that can help you understand words and ideas in the text. If you do not understand a certain passage, it might help to read ahead. A word or an idea may be clarified further on.

Key Terms

- **Louisiana Purchase** (loo ee zee AN uh PUR chus) *n.* the sale of land in North America in 1803 by France to the United States

- **immigrant** (IM uh grunt) *n.* a person who moves to a new country in order to settle there
- **Industrial Revolution** (in DUS tree ul rev uh LOO shun) *n.* the change from making goods by hand to making them by machine
- **abolitionist** (ab uh LISH un ist) *n.* a person who believed that enslaving people was wrong and who wanted to end the practice
- **segregate** (SEG ruh gayt) *v.* to set apart, typically because of race or religion

Meriwether Lewis and William Clark with their Native American translator Sacajawea

In 1804, President Thomas Jefferson sent Meriwether Lewis and William Clark with a company of men to explore the land west of the Mississippi River. They would eventually travel all the way to the Pacific Coast and back—about 8,000 miles (13,000 kilometers).

As they journeyed up the Missouri River, Lewis and Clark found plants and animals completely new to them. They also created accurate, highly valuable maps of the region. As they traveled with their Native American translator, a Shoshone (shoh SHOH nee) woman named Sacajawea, Lewis and Clark met many Native American groups. Sacajawea helped Lewis and Clark communicate with the various groups. During these meetings, the two men tried to learn about the region and set up trading alliances. Few of the Native Americans they met had any idea how the visit would change their way of life.

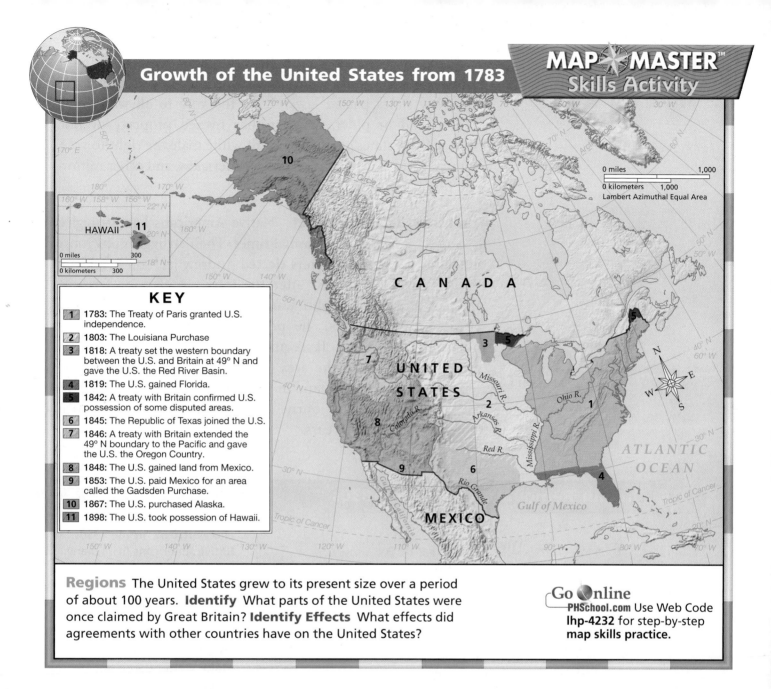

Growth of the United States from 1783

MAP MASTER™
Skills Activity

KEY

1 **1783:** The Treaty of Paris granted U.S. independence.

2 **1803:** The Louisiana Purchase

3 **1818:** A treaty set the western boundary between the U.S. and Britain at 49° N and gave the U.S. the Red River Basin.

4 **1819:** The U.S. gained Florida.

5 **1842:** A treaty with Britain confirmed U.S. possession of some disputed areas.

6 **1845:** The Republic of Texas joined the U.S.

7 **1846:** A treaty with Britain extended the 49° N boundary to the Pacific and gave the U.S. the Oregon Country.

8 **1848:** The U.S. gained land from Mexico.

9 **1853:** The U.S. paid Mexico for an area called the Gadsden Purchase.

10 **1867:** The U.S. purchased Alaska.

11 **1898:** The U.S. took possession of Hawaii.

Regions The United States grew to its present size over a period of about 100 years. **Identify** What parts of the United States were once claimed by Great Britain? **Identify Effects** What effects did agreements with other countries have on the United States?

Go Online
PHSchool.com Use Web Code
lhp-4232 for step-by-step
map skills practice.

A Nation Grows

The United States had not always owned the land that Lewis and Clark explored, called the Louisiana Territory. But, the purchase of this land set the country on a new course of westward expansion.

The Louisiana Purchase   First France, and then Spain, owned the Louisiana Territory. In 1800, war in Europe forced Spain to give it back to France. In 1803, France offered to sell all the land between the Mississippi River and the eastern slopes of the Rocky Mountains to the United States—for only $15 million. This sale of land, called the **Louisiana Purchase,** doubled the size of the United States. The land would later be split into more than a dozen states.

As the country grew, so did the meaning of democracy. In the 13 original states, only white males who owned property could vote. New states passed laws giving the vote to all white men 21 years old or older, whether they owned property or not. Eventually, all states gave every adult white male the right to vote. Women, African Americans, Native Americans, and other minorities, however, could not vote.

The Indian Removal Act Native Americans had struggled to keep their land since colonial times. Their struggle grew more difficult in 1828, when voters elected Andrew Jackson President. President Jackson looked after the interests of poor farmers, laborers, and settlers who wanted Native American lands in the Southeast. In 1830, he persuaded Congress to pass the Indian Removal Act. It required the Cherokees and other Native Americans in the area to leave their homelands. They were sent to live on new land in present-day Oklahoma. So many Cherokees died on the journey that the route they followed is known as the Trail of Tears.

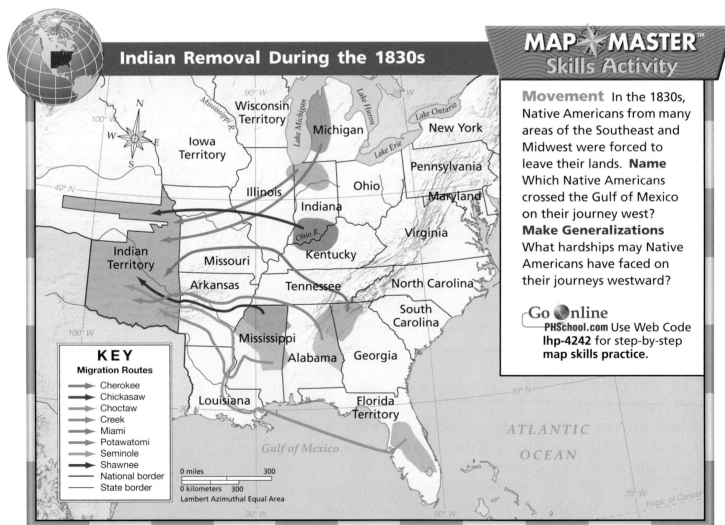

Indian Removal During the 1830s

KEY
Migration Routes
→ Cherokee
→ Chickasaw
→ Choctaw
→ Creek
→ Miami
→ Potawatomi
→ Seminole
→ Shawnee
— National border
— State border

0 miles 300
0 kilometers 300
Lambert Azimuthal Equal Area

MAP MASTER™ Skills Activity

Movement In the 1830s, Native Americans from many areas of the Southeast and Midwest were forced to leave their lands. **Name** Which Native Americans crossed the Gulf of Mexico on their journey west? **Make Generalizations** What hardships may Native Americans have faced on their journeys westward?

Go Online
PHSchool.com Use Web Code **lhp-4242** for step-by-step map skills practice.

Manifest Destiny Many Americans believed that the United States had a right to own all the land from the Atlantic to the Pacific. This belief, called Manifest Destiny, was used to justify further westward expansion. In the 1840s, American wagon trains began to cross the continent heading for the West.

The United States also looked to the Southwest. In 1836, American settlers in the Mexican territory of Texas had rebelled against Mexican rule. The Texans had then set up the Lone Star Republic. In 1845, Texas became part of the United States. Only a year later, the United States went to war with Mexico. The United States won the war and gained from Mexico much of what is now the Southwest region.

The Industrial Revolution At the same time, thousands of people were pouring into cities in the Northeast. Some had left farms to work in factories. Others were **immigrants,** or people who move to one country from another. These people came from Europe in search of jobs in the United States. They were spurred by the **Industrial Revolution,** or the change from making goods by hand to making them by machine.

The first industry to change was textiles, or cloth-making. New spinning machines and power looms enabled people to make cloth more quickly than they could by hand. Other inventions, such as the steam engine, made travel easier and faster. Steamboats and steam locomotives moved people and goods rapidly. By 1860, railroads linked most major northeastern and southeastern cities.

✓ Reading Check **What did the Indian Removal Act do?**

The Clermont, 1807
Robert Fulton demonstrates his steam-powered paddle-wheel boat, the *Clermont,* which used a steam engine improved by James Watt.
Draw Conclusions *How did the inventions of the Industrial Revolution change people's lives?*

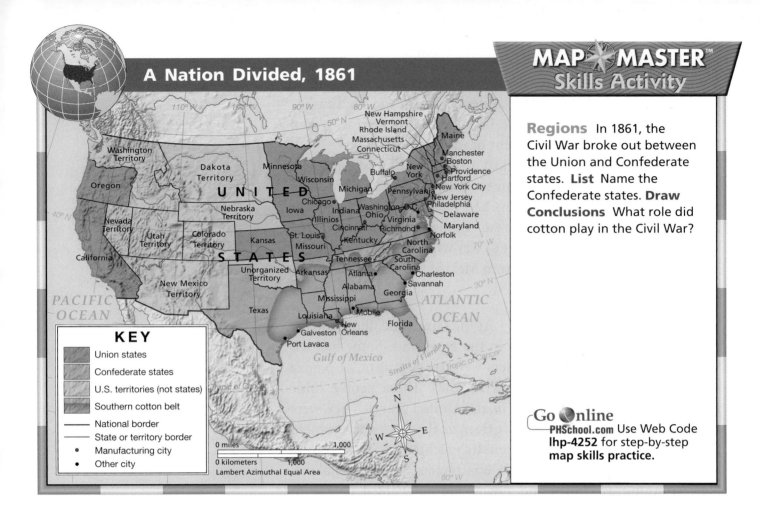

A Nation Divided, 1861

Washington Territory
Oregon
Nevada Territory
California
Utah Territory
New Mexico Territory

Dakota Territory
Minnesota
Wisconsin
Nebraska Territory
Iowa
Colorado Territory
Kansas
Unorganized Territory
Arkansas
Texas

UNITED
Michigan
Chicago
Indiana
Illinois
St. Louis
Missouri
Cincinnati
Kentucky
Tennessee
Mississippi
Alabama
Georgia
Louisiana
New Orleans
Galveston
Port Lavaca

STATES
Ohio
Washington, D.C.
Virginia
Richmond
North Carolina
South Carolina
Atlanta
Charleston
Savannah
Mobile
Florida

New Hampshire
Vermont
Rhode Island
Massachusetts
Connecticut
Maine
Manchester
Boston
New York
Buffalo
Hartford
Providence
Pennsylvania
New York City
New Jersey
Philadelphia
Delaware
Maryland
Norfolk

PACIFIC OCEAN
ATLANTIC OCEAN
Gulf of Mexico
Straits of Florida
Tropic of Cancer

KEY
- Union states
- Confederate states
- U.S. territories (not states)
- Southern cotton belt
- National border
- State or territory border
- Manufacturing city
- Other city

0 miles 1,000
0 kilometers 1,000
Lambert Azimuthal Equal Area

Regions In 1861, the Civil War broke out between the Union and Confederate states. **List** Name the Confederate states. **Draw Conclusions** What role did cotton play in the Civil War?

Go Online
PHSchool.com Use Web Code lhp-4252 for step-by-step map skills practice.

Read Ahead
Keep reading to see how harvesting cotton affected the nation's history.

The Civil War and Reconstruction

With the textile industry growing as a result of the Industrial Revolution, the demand for cotton grew as well. Cotton required many laborers for planting and harvesting. This is one reason why slaves were an important part of plantation life.

In 1793, Eli Whitney invented the cotton gin, which quickly removed seeds from cotton. The cotton gin made cotton easier to process after it was picked. Cotton farming boomed. However, growing cotton quickly wore out the soil. To keep up production, farmers wanted to expand into western lands. But that meant that slavery would spread into the new territories. Some people did not want this. The debate began. Should the states or the federal government decide about the issue of slavery in the new territories?

Causes of Conflict Before California asked to be admitted to the union as a free state in 1850, there were equal numbers of slave and free states. After a heated debate, Congress granted California's request. The Southern states were not pleased. To gain their support, Congress also passed the Fugitive Slave Act. It required that runaway slaves must be returned to their owners. This action only intensified the argument over slavery.

The South Breaks Away In 1852, Harriet Beecher Stowe published *Uncle Tom's Cabin,* a novel about the evils of slavery. After reading this book, thousands of Northerners became abolitionists (ab uh LISH un ists). **Abolitionists** were people who believed that slavery was wrong and wanted to end, or abolish, its practice. Many helped enslaved people escape to Canada. There, slavery was illegal. Most Southerners, however, felt that abolitionists were robbing them of their property.

The debate over slavery raged. When Abraham Lincoln, a Northerner, was elected President in 1860, many Southerners feared they would have little say in the government. As a result, some Southern states seceded, or withdrew, from the United States. They founded a new country—the Confederate States of America, or the Confederacy.

The Civil War In 1861, the Civil War between the Northern states and the Confederacy erupted. It lasted four years. The North, known as the Union, had more industry, wealth, and soldiers. The Confederacy had experienced military officers. It also had cotton. Many foreign countries bought southern cotton. Southerners hoped that these countries would help support the Confederacy in its struggle.

Despite the North's advantages, the war dragged on. In 1863, Lincoln issued the Emancipation Proclamation. This declared that enslaved people in areas loyal to the Confederacy were free, and it gave the North a new battle cry—freedom! Thousands of African Americans joined the fight against the South.

Fighting for Their Cause
These African American soldiers are outside of their barracks at Fort Lincoln, Washington, D.C. Twenty-three African Americans received the Congressional Medal of Honor (below right), the country's highest military honor. **Draw Conclusions** *Why do you think African Americans were willing to fight for the Union?*

Clara Barton

When the Civil War began, Clara Barton learned that many soldiers were suffering because of the lack of supplies on the front lines. She decided to help by setting up an organization to deliver supplies to men wounded in battle. She also worked as a nurse in hospitals located near battlefields. Because of her gentle and helpful ways, Barton earned the name Angel of the Battlefield. Years later, she founded the American branch of the Red Cross.

Reconstruction The Civil War ended in 1865 when the Confederates surrendered. Lincoln wanted the Southern states to return willingly to the Union. This was the first step in his plan for the Reconstruction, or rebuilding, of the nation. Less than a week after the end of the war, Lincoln was assassinated, or murdered. Vice President Andrew Johnson tried to carry out Lincoln's plan. But Congress resisted his efforts. Finally, Congress took complete control of Reconstruction. The Union Army governed the South until new state officials were elected.

In 1877, the Union Army withdrew. But Southern lawmakers soon voted to **segregate,** or separate, black people from white people. Segregation affected all aspects of life. Southern states passed laws, called Jim Crow laws, that separated blacks and whites in schools, restaurants, theaters, trains, streetcars, playgrounds, hospitals, and even cemeteries. Some African Americans brought lawsuits to challenge segregation. The laws passed during Reconstruction would become the basis of the civil rights movement in later years. The difficult struggle to preserve the United States had succeeded. But the long struggle to guarantee equality to all Americans still lay ahead.

✓ **Reading Check** Why did some Southern states secede from the United States?

Section 2 Assessment

Key Terms
Review the key terms at the beginning of this section. Use each term in a sentence that explains its meaning.

🎯 Target Reading Skill
What word or idea were you able to clarify by reading ahead?

Comprehension and Critical Thinking
1. (a) List In what ways did the United States increase the area of its land?

(b) Identify Effects How did the growing nation affect Native Americans?

(c) Identify Causes What factors led to a population boom in northeastern cities?

2. (a) Identify Why did the Southern states withdraw from the Union?

(b) Explore the Main Idea How did the issue of slavery become a cause of the Civil War?

(c) Analyze How did segregation affect African Americans?

Writing Activity
Write an entry on a plan for Reconstruction that President Lincoln might have made in his diary.

For: An activity on the Civil War
Visit: PHSchool.com
Web Code: lhd-4202

The U.S. on the Brink of Change

Prepare to Read

Objectives

In this section you will
1. Explore what happened in the United States from 1865 to 1914.
2. Find out what happened during the World Wars.
3. Explore the challenges the United States faces at home and abroad.

Taking Notes

As you read the section, look for details about the United States becoming a world power. Copy the outline below and fill in each main idea and detail.

> I. The United States from 1865 to 1914
> A. Moving to the Midwest
>   1.
>   2.
> B.
> II.

🎯 Target Reading Skill

Paraphrase Paraphrasing can help you understand what you read. When you paraphrase, you restate in your own words what you have read. As you read this section, paraphrase, or "say back," the information following each red or blue heading.

Key Terms

- **labor force** (LAY bur fawrs) *n.* the supply of workers
- **Holocaust** (HAHL uh kawst) *n.* the murder of six million Jews during World War II
- **Cold War** (kohld wawr) *n.* a period of great tension between the United States and the Soviet Union
- **civil rights** (SIV ul ryts) *n.* the basic rights due to all citizens
- **terrorist** (TEHR ur ist) *n.* a person who uses violence and fear to achieve goals

---

Jacob Riis was an angry man. In one of his books, he introduced his readers to slum life in the late 1800s. He wanted other people to be angry, too—angry enough to change things.

> **Come over here. Step carefully over this baby—it is a baby, in spite of its rags and dirt—under these iron bridges called fire escapes, but loaded down . . . with broken household goods, with washtubs and barrels, over which no man could climb from a fire. . . . That baby's parents live in the rear tenement [apartment] here. . . . There are plenty of houses with half a hundred such in [them].**
>
> —*Jacob Riis,* How the Other Half Lives

An 1886 photo of a slum by Jacob Riis

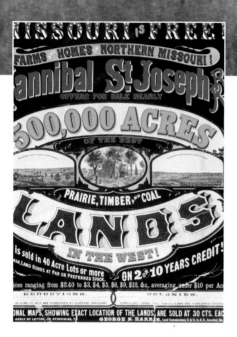

Settling the Plains
A wagon train travels in the Oklahoma Territory around 1900 (above). Railroads such as the Hannibal and St. Joseph recruited farmers to buy and settle land, as advertised in the poster above. **Draw Conclusions** *How did the Homestead Act and the railroads help to speed up settlement of the Midwest?*

Paraphrase
Paraphrase this paragraph in 25 words or less.

From 1865 to 1914

By the late 1800s, a handful of rich people had made millions of dollars in industry. The Industrial Revolution had also made life easier for the middle class—the group of people that included skilled workers and successful farmers. But life did not improve for the poor. City slums were crowded with immigrants. These newcomers were a huge **labor force, or supply of workers.** Many couldn't speak English. Employers paid them little. Even small children worked so that families could make ends meet.

Reformers like Jacob Riis began to protest such poverty. In Chicago, Jane Addams set up a settlement house, or community center, for poor immigrants. Mary Harris Jones helped miners organize for better wages. Because of her work to end child labor, people called her Mother Jones.

Moving to the Midwest   To leave poverty behind, many people moved to the open plains and prairies of the Midwest. The United States government attracted settlers to this region with the Homestead Act of 1862. This act gave free land to settlers. Settlers faced a difficult life on the plains. Still, thousands came west, helped by the development of railroads that connected the East Coast with the West.

New Territories   The United States also expanded beyond its continental borders. In 1867, the United States bought the territory of Alaska from Russia. In 1898, the United States took control of Hawaii. In that same year, the United States fought and won the Spanish-American War. The victory gave the United States control of the Spanish lands of Puerto Rico, Guam, and the Philippines. By the 1900s, America had a strong economy, military might, and overseas territory.

✓ **Reading Check**   **How did the United States get Alaska?**

The World at War

Now the United States had a major role in world affairs. As a result, the country was drawn into international conflicts. In 1914, World War I broke out in Europe. President Woodrow Wilson did not want America to take part, but when Germany began sinking American ships, Wilson had no choice. He declared war. The United States joined the Allied Powers of Great Britain and France. In 1917, thousands of American soldiers sailed to Europe. They fought against the Central Powers, which included Germany, Austria-Hungary, and Turkey. With this added strength, the Allies won the war in 1918. The terms of peace in the Treaty of Versailles punished Germany severely. Its harshness led to another worldwide conflict 20 years later.

The Economy Collapses Following World War I, the United States' economy boomed. Women enjoyed new freedoms and the hard-won right to vote. More and more people bought cars, refrigerators, radios, and other modern conveniences.

In 1929, however, the world was overcome by an economic disaster called the Great Depression. In America, factories closed, people lost their jobs, and farmers lost their farms. Many banks closed, and people lost their life's savings. In 1933, President Franklin D. Roosevelt took office. He created a plan called the New Deal. This was a series of government programs to help people get jobs and to restore the economy. Some of these programs, like Social Security, are still in place today. Social Security provides income to people who are retired or disabled.

Americans at War
Nurses place a wounded soldier on a stretcher during World War I (below). Recruitment posters such as the one below called on Americans to join the military. **Draw Inferences** *Why do you think this poster was effective in getting Americans to volunteer for military duty?*

This Rosie the Riveter poster from World War II encouraged women to join the workforce.

A Second World War The Great Depression affected people around the world. In Germany, Adolf Hitler rose to power, promising to restore Germany's wealth and power. He began World War II. In 1941, Germany's ally, Japan, attacked the United States naval base at Pearl Harbor, Hawaii. The United States declared war on Japan. Germany then declared war on the United States.

The United States sent armed forces to fight in Europe and in the Pacific. President Roosevelt, who led the nation in war, did not live to see peace. He died in April 1945, and Vice President Harry S Truman became President.

In May of 1945, the Allies defeated the Germans. During the summer of 1945, President Truman decided to drop two atomic bombs on Japan. That convinced Japan to surrender. Finally, World War II was over.

By the end of the war in 1945, Europe was in ruins. People around the world learned that Hitler had forced Jews, Gypsies, Slavs, and others into brutal prison camps. Millions of people, including some six million Jews, were murdered. This horrible mass murder is called the **Holocaust** (HAHL uh kawst).

✓ **Reading Check** What led the United States to take part in World War II?

Timeline Skills

The United States has been involved in both domestic and international conflicts since the Civil War ended. **Identify** Which of the wars shown did not involve open warfare? **Compare** How long was this war, compared to the others shown on the timeline?

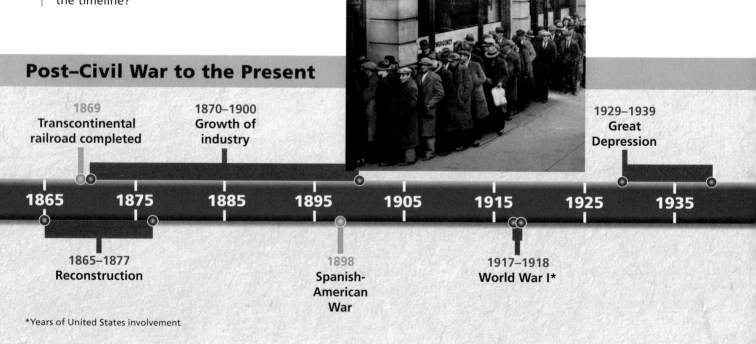

Post–Civil War to the Present

1869
Transcontinental railroad completed

1870–1900
Growth of industry

1929–1939
Great Depression

1865 — 1875 — 1885 — 1895 — 1905 — 1915 — 1925 — 1935

1865–1877
Reconstruction

1898
Spanish-American War

1917–1918
World War I*

*Years of United States involvement

The U.S. at Home and Abroad

Following World War II, the United States was a world super-power. It faced new challenges and responsibilities both at home and abroad.

Tension with the Soviets In 1922, the Soviet Union had been created. It adopted a form of government called communism. Under this system, the state owns all property, such as farms and factories, on behalf of its citizens.

After World War II, the Soviet Union took control of many Eastern European countries. The United States feared the Soviets were trying to spread communism throughout the world. As a result, the United States and the Soviet Union entered the **Cold War**, a period of great tension. The Cold War lasted about four decades. Although the two countries never faced each other in an actual war, two wars grew out of this tension—the Korean War and the Vietnam War.

The Fight for Civil Rights The economy boomed in the post-war years, but not all citizens shared in the benefits. In the South, racial segregation was a way of life. Many African Americans began to unite to win their **civil rights**, or the rights belonging to all citizens. The movement had many leaders, including Martin Luther King, Jr. He led peaceful marches and organized boycotts against companies that practiced discrimination, or unfair treatment of a group or person. The movement's success inspired others who felt they were treated unfairly, including women and Mexican Americans.

Links Across Time

Living Underground During the Cold War, many Americans became concerned about the possibility of a nuclear war with the Soviet Union. The United States government encouraged families to build fallout, or bomb, shelters as shown below. A fallout shelter is a concrete and steel structure designed to protect people from nuclear radiation. Many of these shelters were underground. A typical bomb shelter would have canned food, bottled water, first-aid supplies, and other necessities.

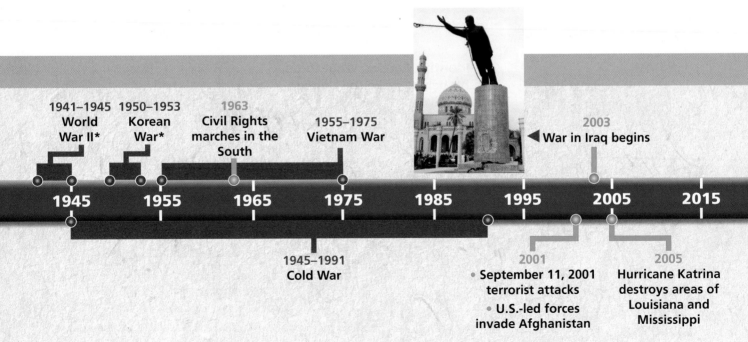

1941–1945
World War II*

1950–1953
Korean War*

1963
Civil Rights marches in the South

1955–1975
Vietnam War

2003
◀ **War in Iraq begins**

1945   1955   1965   1975   1985   1995   2005   2015

1945–1991
Cold War

2001
• **September 11, 2001 terrorist attacks**
• **U.S.-led forces invade Afghanistan**

2005
Hurricane Katrina destroys areas of Louisiana and Mississippi

Firefighters walk away from the rubble of the World Trade Center towers in New York City.

America in the World Today At the beginning of the twenty-first century, Americans continued to look for solutions to long-term problems, such as homelessness, low wages, and pollution.

The economy reached new heights in the 1990s, powered by the Internet business revolution. The Internet is a network of interconnected computers that allows users to access computerized information. After a downturn in the early 2000s, the economy continued to grow. At the same time, it faced challenges such as high oil prices and rising federal debt.

The United States also faced a new challenge at home and abroad—on September 11, 2001, terrorists attacked the World Trade Center in New York City and the Pentagon in Washington, D.C. Terrorists use violence to frighten people or governments or to express their views. In response to these and possible future attacks, the United States took military action in both Afghanistan and Iraq. Saddam Hussein (sah DAHM hoo SAYN), Iraq's brutal dictator, was captured by coalition troops in December 2003. However, the United States continues to maintain a military presence in Iraq. The United States works with its allies around the world, especially Great Britain, to fight terrorism.

✓ **Reading Check** What countries were involved in the Cold War?

Section 3 Assessment

Key Terms
Review the key terms at the beginning of this section. Use each term in a sentence that explains its meaning.

Target Reading Skill
Paraphrase the paragraph on page 189 under the red heading The World at War.

Comprehension and Critical Thinking
1. (a) Recall How did the Industrial Revolution affect poor immigrants in the late 1800s?

(b) Identify Causes What three events helped make the United States a world power?

2. (a) List What countries made up the Central Powers in World War I?

(b) Sequence Describe the events that led to World War II.

3. (a) Explain What gains in equality did African Americans make after World War II?

(b) Identify Cause and Effect How might African American gains in civil rights affect other groups?

Writing Activity
Write a paragraph about what it means for a country to be a world power. What challenges would a world power face? What special responsibilities might it have?

For: An activity on the Homestead Act
Visit: PHSchool.com
Web Code: lhp-4203

4
The History of Canada

Prepare to Read

Objectives

In this section you will

1. Learn about why France and Britain were rivals in Canada.
2. Discover how Canada became an independent nation.
3. Explore how Canada became a world power in the 1900s.

Taking Notes

As you read the section, look for events that happened before and after the British North America Act in 1867. Copy the table below and write each event in the correct column.

British North America Act (1867)	
Before	**After**
•	•
•	•
•	•

Target Reading Skill

Summarize When you summarize, you review and state, in the correct order, the main points you have read. Summarizing what you read is a good technique to help you comprehend and study. As you read, pause occasionally to summarize what you have read.

Key Terms

- **dominion** (duh MIN yun) *n.* a self-governing area subject to Great Britain
- **bilingual** (by LIN gwul) *adj.* able to speak two languages

Haida portrait mask

The Haida people of British Columbia tell this tale. As in many Native American tales, nature plays an important role.

> ❝While he was crying and singing his dirge [sad song], a figure emerged from the lake. It was a strange animal, in its mouth a stick that it was gnawing. On each side of the animal were two smaller ones also gnawing sticks. Then the largest figure . . . spoke, 'Don't be so sad! It is I, your wife, and your two children. We have returned to our home in the water. . . . Call me the Beaver woman.'❞
>
> —*Haida tale*

To the Haida and other native peoples in Canada, beavers were especially important. Imagine how they felt when European trappers killed almost all of the beavers to make fur hats.

The Battle of Quebec, 1759
The Battle of Quebec was a turning point in the Seven Years' War. This painting illustrates how British troops found a passage through the cliffs that protected Quebec. **Analyze Images** *Do you think that Quebec would have fallen to the British if troops had not found a passage in? Explain why or why not.*

The French and the British

The profitable fur trade in Canada was a source of conflict for France and Great Britain. They had fought wars all over the world, but had signed a peace treaty in 1713. The treaty gave Great Britain the Hudson Bay region, Newfoundland, and part of Acadia, which later became the southeastern corner of Canada.

The peace was uneasy. Against their will, French Catholics in Acadia came under the rule of British Protestants. The French controlled the lowlands south of Hudson Bay and lands around the St. Lawrence River. Both countries wanted to control the Ohio River valley, farther to the south. The French wanted the beavers for furs. The British wanted the land for settlement.

Great Britain Gains Control The contest for this region erupted into the Seven Years' War in 1756. The British won the decisive Battle of Quebec in 1759. The Treaty of Paris, signed in 1763, gave Great Britain complete control over Canada. Some French settlers returned to France. Those who stayed resisted English culture. The first two British governors of Canada were sympathetic to the French and passed the Quebec Act. It gave the French people in Quebec the right to speak their own language, practice their own religion, and follow their own customs.

Two Colonies Emerge During the American Revolution, some Americans did not want independence from Britain. They were called Loyalists. After the war, many Loyalists moved to Canada. But most did not want to live in a French culture. To avoid problems, Great Britain divided the land into two colonies, Upper Canada and Lower Canada. Most Loyalists moved into Upper Canada, which is now called Ontario. French Canadians remained in Lower Canada, which is now Quebec.

✓ **Reading Check** Why was Canada divided into two colonies?

Canada Seeks Independence

The people of Upper and Lower Canada worked together during the War of 1812. They fought to protect Canada from invasion by the United States. Once the War of 1812 ended, however, Canadians with different backgrounds stopped cooperating with one another. Both French Canadians and British Canadians hated British rule. Many felt Britain was too far away to understand their needs. But the two groups did not join in rebellion. In 1837, a French Canadian named Louis Papineau (LOO ee pah pea NOH) organized a revolt in Lower Canada. His goal was to establish the region as a separate country. The British easily defeated the rebels. The same thing happened in Upper Canada. William Mackenzie led the people against British rule. Again, the British put down the separatist rebellion.

A Peaceful Revolution   Still, British leaders were afraid more trouble was coming. They sent the Earl of Durham to learn what was wrong. When Durham returned, he had many suggestions. First, he suggested that the Canadians be given more control of their government. He also thought all of the colonies should be united. But the British government united only Upper and Lower Canada to form the Province of Canada. Nova Scotia, Newfoundland, Prince Edward Island, and New Brunswick were not included in this union. If Canada were completely united, the British feared the Canadians might make a successful rebellion.

Citizen Heroes

Louis Riel

A Voice of Protest
In 1869, the Canadian government wanted to finish the cross-country railroad across the flat plains region. Louis Riel, leader of the Métis (may TEEZ)—mixed European and Native American people—objected to the plan. The Métis said that the railroad would bring new settlers, who would take away their land. The government refused to stop, so Riel led an armed revolt. It failed, and Riel was later executed for treason, but the government did set aside land for the Métis. Today, the Métis consider Riel a hero.

The Canadian Pacific Railway
On November 7, 1885, Canada's far-flung provinces were tied together as the last spike was driven in, completing the Canadian Pacific Railway. **Draw Conclusions** *Why was a railroad connecting all of Canada important to Canadians?*

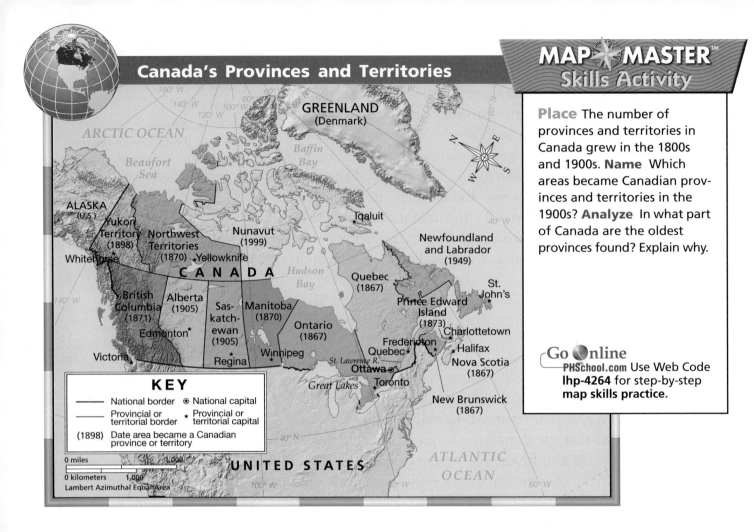

Canada's Provinces and Territories

MAP MASTER™
Skills Activity

Place The number of provinces and territories in Canada grew in the 1800s and 1900s. **Name** Which areas became Canadian provinces and territories in the 1900s? **Analyze** In what part of Canada are the oldest provinces found? Explain why.

Go Online
PHSchool.com Use Web Code **lhp-4264** for step-by-step map skills practice.

KEY

— National border ⊛ National capital

— Provincial or territorial border ★ Provincial or territorial capital

(1898) Date area became a Canadian province or territory

0 miles 1,000
0 kilometers 1,000
Lambert Azimuthal Equal Area

Summarize
Summarize this page. Be sure to include two factors that led Canada to become a world power.

Canadians believed that all provinces should be represented in their government. In 1864, leaders met to work out a plan to form a union. On July 1, 1867, the British Parliament accepted the British North America Act. This made Canada "one Dominion under the name of Canada." A **dominion** is a self-governing area. Canada was not completely independent from Great Britain, but now a central government would run the country. Canadians would elect their own leaders. Without a war, Canadians had won the right to control their own government.

After its "peaceful revolution," Canada saw years of growth and change. Skilled European farmers settled in Canada's western plains. Gold and other valuable minerals were discovered in the Yukon Territory in the 1890s. That brought miners to the far northwest. Canada was becoming rich and important.

Canada Becomes a World Power When Britain entered World War I, Canadians were still British subjects. Canada, therefore, entered the war, too. Canada willingly sent soldiers and resources overseas. Canada contributed so much to the Allied victory that the young country became a world power.

✓ **Reading Check** Why didn't the British want Canada to be united?

Canada: Postwar to the Present

During World War II, Canadians built factories. They made war supplies and goods such as clothes and shoes. Because of the war, people could not get such products from Europe. After the war, Canadian goods found a ready market in the United States and Europe.

Also, during the postwar years, immigrants poured into Canada. They came from Asia, Europe, Africa, and the Caribbean. The newcomers filled jobs in factories and businesses. Soon, Canada became one of the world's most important industrial nations.

The Growth of Industry   Industrialization strengthened the economy but brought back old arguments. British Canadians built new factories in Quebec. That alarmed French Canadians. In 1969, the government passed new laws that made Canada a **bilingual** country. That is, Canada had two official languages— English and French. However, by 1976 some French Canadians did not want to be part of Canada. Quebec, they argued, should be independent. Many people in Quebec still feel that way today.

Canadian Industry
Canadians, such as this factory worker tending to spools of nylon (above), made important supplies during World War II. One year after the war, plans for the first Canadian-designed and built jet fighter (left) began. Nearly 700 planes were built to defend North America in case of a future attack and to participate in overseas operations. **Draw Conclusions** *What were the effects of WWII on Canadian industries?*

A New Constitution Although the British North America Act in 1867 gave Canadians the right to control their own government, it was still necessary for Great Britain to approve amendments to the Canadian constitution. That changed in 1982 when the Canadians adopted a new constitution. It gave Canadians the power to change their constitution without Great Britain's permission. Canada was now completely independent.

A Parliamentary System Canada's government is modeled on the British parliamentary system. Canada has a constitutional monarchy. A set of laws states what the monarch—the king or queen—can or cannot do. Because the monarch lives in Great Britain, he or she must appoint someone in Canada to act as a representative. This position is called the governor-general. Since World War II, the governor-general has been a Canadian citizen. Although the monarch is the head of state, he or she does not make any political decisions. That is the job of the prime minister, who is the head of government.

Canada is also called a parliamentary democracy. The group of representatives that makes its laws is modeled on the British parliament. Canada's Parliament, like Great Britain's, has two chambers: the House of Commons and the Senate. The House of Commons is made up of elected representatives. The governor-general appoints the members of the Senate. Senators are allowed to hold office until they are 75 years old.

Canada's Parliament Buildings
The Parliament Buildings are an example of the Gothic style of architecture, which is from medieval times. This type of architecture developed in Western Europe between the 1100s and 1500s.
Draw Conclusions *How do the Parliament Buildings reflect Canada's heritage?*

The Commonwealth of Nations Another tie between Canada and Great Britain is its membership in the Commonwealth of Nations. It is a voluntary organization, whose member countries are former British colonies. The purpose of the Commonwealth of Nations is to consult and cooperate with one another, particularly in matters of trade and economics. In addition, Great Britain gives members financial aid and advice. At one time, the Commonwealth of Nations was the only worldwide political organization besides the United Nations.

Supporters greet Queen Elizabeth in Iqaluit, Nunavut, at the start of her twelve-day tour of Canada.

Although Great Britain's Queen Elizabeth II is the head of the Commonwealth of Nations, her role is symbolic. In 2002, for the celebration of her fiftieth year as monarch, she traveled from one end of the Commonwealth to the other, from Nunavut to Australia.

Canada in the World Today Today, Canada works both on its own and closely with international agencies to carry out foreign policy. It provides humanitarian aid to nations struck by natural disasters, such as Indonesia after a 2006 earthquake. Canada is involved in diplomatic and humanitarian missions to troubled countries from Haiti to Sudan. It has contributed to rebuilding both Afghanistan and Iraq. In addition, Canada maintains close trade and diplomatic ties with the United States.

✓ **Reading Check** Why did Canadians write a new constitution?

Section 4 Assessment

Key Terms
Review the key terms at the beginning of this section. Use each term in a sentence that explains its meaning.

Target Reading Skill
Write a summary of the paragraph on page 196 called Canada Becomes a World Power.

Comprehension and Critical Thinking
1. (a) List What two countries came into conflict in Canada in the 1700s?

(b) Sequence How did the fur trade lead to war in Canada?

2. (a) Explain Why did Canadians object to British rule?

(b) Summarize How did Canadians win control of their government without going to war?

3. (a) Recall How did Canada become an industrial power after World War II?

(b) Link Past and Present How is Canada still tied to Britain today?

Writing Activity
Compare and contrast the ways in which Canada and the United States became independent nations.

Writing Tip One way to organize your comparison is subject by subject, or by first explaining how the United States became independent and then how Canada did.

Suppose that your pen pal in Canada wants to know what your school looks like. Which should you do: write her a letter describing your school or send her a photograph?

A photo would show her in an instant what your school looks like. But a letter could describe details a photograph might not show. Perhaps you would send both.

There is another way to show what something looks like *and* describe it in words: You could draw a diagram. A diagram is a picture that shows how something works or is made. It usually includes labels that tell about certain parts of the picture. It is a combination of the letter and the photograph you would send to your pen pal.

A diagram is like a game of show-and-tell—the picture shows and the labels tell.

Learn the Skill

To understand how to interpret information in a diagram, follow the steps below.

1 **Study the picture.** Notice the various parts of the picture. Get visual information from it.

2 **Read the labels.** Sometimes the labels will be numbered or will appear in a certain order to explain a step-by-step process.

3 **Summarize the information in the diagram.** From the information you gather by studying the picture and the labels, write a summary describing what the diagram shows you.

Practice the Skill

Look at How a Locomotive Works, below, as you practice interpreting a diagram.

1 From the title, you can tell what the diagram shows. As you look at the picture, what information can you learn—even before you read the labels?

2 The labels in this diagram are meant to be read in a particular order. Do you know why? Notice that this diagram has both labels and arrows. What do the arrows show?

3 Write a paragraph describing how a locomotive works. Write as if the reader did not have the picture to look at. Don't simply repeat the text in the labels, but summarize the information in the labels and picture.

How a Locomotive Works

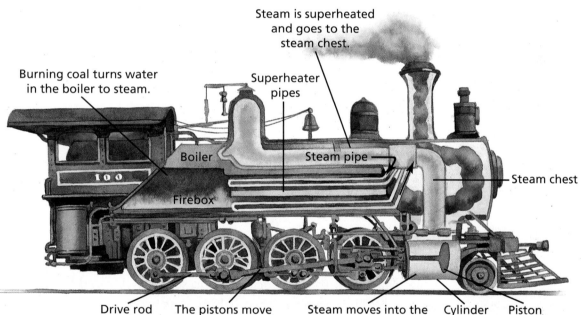

Steam is superheated and goes to the steam chest.

Burning coal turns water in the boiler to steam.

Superheater pipes

Boiler

Steam pipe

Steam chest

Firebox

Drive rod

The pistons move the drive rods, which turn the wheels.

Steam moves into the cylinders, where it pushes the pistons back and forth.

Cylinder

Piston

Apply the Skill

Find a photograph of a bicycle in a catalog or a magazine. Then, write a paragraph describing what the bicycle looks like, what parts it has, and how the parts work.

Now draw a diagram of a bicycle. Make labels showing how it works.

Compare the picture, the paragraph, and the diagram. Which one does the best job of showing and explaining how a bicycle works?

The United States and Canada Today

Prepare to Read

Objectives
In this section you will
1. Identify the environmental concerns the United States and Canada share today.
2. Find out about the economic ties the United States and Canada have to each other and to the world.

Taking Notes
As you read the section, look for details about the environmental concerns and economic ties that the United States and Canada share. Copy the concept web below and fill in the details.

Concerns Shared by the United States and Canada

Target Reading Skill
Reread or Read Ahead Rereading and reading ahead are strategies that can help you understand words and ideas in the text. If you do not understand a certain passage, reread it to look for connections among the words and sentences. It might also help to read ahead, because a word or an idea may be clarified further on.

Key Terms
- **acid rain** (as id rayn) *n.* rain containing acids that are harmful to plants and trees
- **tariff** (tar if) *n.* a fee charged on imported goods
- **free trade** (free trayd) *n.* trade without taxes on imported goods

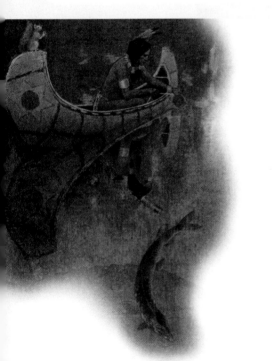

A painting of an Iroquois fishing from a canoe

The birch-bark canoes paddled into the village of Sault Sainte Marie, on the border of the present-day United States and Canada. The canoes carried fishing nets made from strands of willow bark and baskets full of lake trout. The Native American fishermen unloaded their baskets at the shore. Any fish they did not eat that day would be dried on racks and saved for later or ground up and used as fertilizer for crops.

For centuries, the lake trout of the Great Lakes provided food for both Native Americans and European settlers. By the mid-1950s, lake trout were the most valuable fish in the Upper Great Lakes. Lake trout were soon overharvested. In some of the Great Lakes, the lake trout almost disappeared.

In 1955, Canada and the United States joined to create the Great Lakes Fishery Commission. Members of the commission worked together to find ways of protecting lake trout and many other species of fish in the Great Lakes. This is just one of the ways the United States and Canada have become cooperative neighbors.

Environmental Issues

The United States and Canada share many geographic features—the coasts of the Atlantic and Pacific oceans, the Great Lakes, and the Rocky Mountains, for example. Both countries use natural resources in similar ways. And both have used technology to meet their needs. But technology has left its mark on their water, air, forests, and futures.

Solving Water Problems Can you picture a river on fire? Impossible, you say? In 1969, a fire started on the Cuyahoga River (ky uh HOH guh RIV er). That river flows past Cleveland, Ohio, and then empties into Lake Erie. For many years, Cleveland had poured waste, garbage, and oil into the river. The layer of pollutants was so thick that it caught on fire.

The Cuyahoga was typical of the rivers that empty into Lake Erie. So much pollution had been dumped into the lake that most of the fish had died. Swimming in the river was unthinkable. The fire on the Cuyahoga was a wake-up call. The United States and Canada signed an agreement promising to cooperate in cleaning up the lake. Agreements such as this have greatly reduced freshwater pollution in the United States. Today, people again enjoy fishing and boating on the Cuyahoga.

The Cuyahoga River
In June 1969, firefighters hosed down flames from the Cuyahoga River fire (below). **Analyze Images** *Looking at the river today (inset), what positive effects came out of the cleanup effort?*

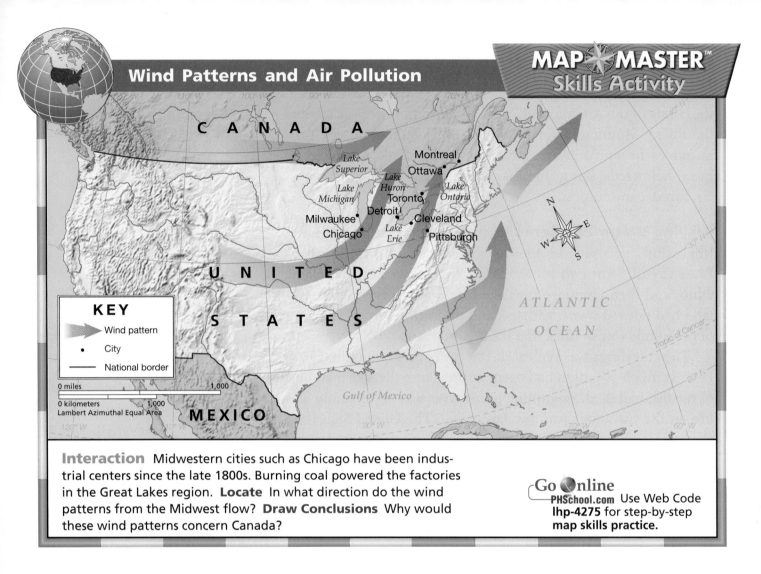

CANADA

Lake Superior

Montreal
Ottawa

Lake Huron
Lake Michigan
Toronto
Lake Ontario

Milwaukee
Detroit
Cleveland

Chicago
Lake Erie
Pittsburgh

UNITED

STATES

ATLANTIC OCEAN

KEY

→ Wind pattern

• City

— National border

0 miles 1,000
0 kilometers 1,000
Lambert Azimuthal Equal Area

MEXICO

Gulf of Mexico

Tropic of Cancer

Interaction Midwestern cities such as Chicago have been industrial centers since the late 1800s. Burning coal powered the factories in the Great Lakes region. **Locate** In what direction do the wind patterns from the Midwest flow? **Draw Conclusions** Why would these wind patterns concern Canada?

Go Online
PHSchool.com Use Web Code
lhp-4275 for step-by-step
map skills practice.

Improving Air Quality

On many days, you can look around most big cities and see that the air is filled with a brown haze. This pollution is caused by cars and factories burning fossil fuels. Not only is this air unhealthy to breathe, but it can also create other serious problems hundreds of miles away. Pollutants in the air combine with moisture to form acid. **Acid rain** is rain that dissolves these acids and carries them to Earth. This acid kills plants, trees, and fish. Coal-burning power plants in the West and Midwest United States create acid rain problems in the Northeast and in the Great Lakes area. Winds carry these acids long distances.

Acid rain caused by United States power plants has affected forests and lakes in Canada. The two countries signed agreements to control air quality in the 1980s. A 2002 government progress report showed that rain acidity was reduced in Canada by 45 percent and in the United States by 35 percent.

Aerial view of Toronto's hazy skyline and harbor, Ontario, Canada

Renewing Forests "I'm like a tree—you'll have to cut me down," cried Kim McElroy in 1993. The other demonstrators with her agreed. They were blocking the path of logging trucks trying to enter the forest of Clayoquot Sound on Vancouver Island, British Columbia. The protesters believed that cutting down the trees would damage the environment. In similar forests throughout the United States and Canada, logging companies practiced clear-cutting, or cutting down all the trees in an area. Without trees, soil washes away, other plants die, and animals lose their homes.

On the other hand, people need lumber for building. Paper companies need wood pulp to make their products. People who work for logging companies need their jobs.

The Canadian and American governments want to maintain both the forests and the timber industry. They are working to develop ways of doing that. For example, British Columbia passed a law that sets aside parts of the Clayoquot Sound's forests for logging. The law also imposes new rules on loggers to prevent damage in the areas where cutting is allowed.

✓ **Reading Check** **Why is there disagreement about logging in some forests?**

The Old and the New
A hill in the Queen Charlotte Islands of British Columbia, Canada (below), shows clear-cut forest growth. The man in the inset photo plants new trees. **Draw Conclusions** *How does planting new trees help to keep soil from washing away? Why is that important?*

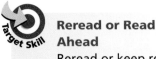

Reread or Read Ahead

Reread or keep reading to see the economic links between the United States and Canada.

"Economics Has Made Us Partners"

Not all next-door neighbors get along as well as the United States and Canada. President John F. Kennedy once described the relationship this way: "Geography has made us neighbors. History has made us friends. Economics has made us partners." With 5,527 miles (8,895 kilometers) of border between the two countries, economic cooperation has benefited both. Part of this cooperation has been in transportation between the countries, particularly around the Great Lakes.

The St. Lawrence Seaway   Have you ever heard of someone going over Niagara Falls in a barrel? The barrel would drop about 190 feet (58 meters)—a crazy stunt! Suppose you have a cargo of manufactured goods in Cleveland to send to Montreal. You would like to ship by water, because it is the cheapest and most direct means of transportation. But Niagara Falls lies between Cleveland and Montreal. And after passing the falls, your cargo would have to travel down another 250 feet (76 meters) in the St. Lawrence River before it reached Montreal. What do you do?

The Great Lakes and the St. Lawrence Seaway

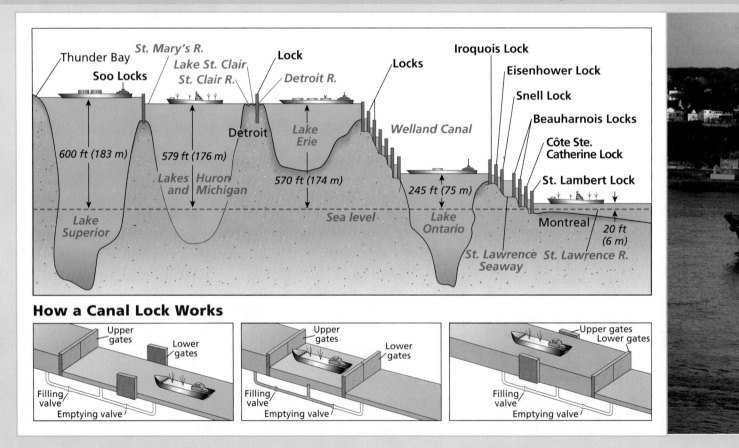

How a Canal Lock Works

To solve this problem, the United States and Canada built the St. Lawrence Seaway. Completed in 1959, it is a system of locks, canals, and dams that allows ships to move from one water level to another. A lock is an enclosed area on a canal that raises or lowers ships from one water level to another. Now, ships can travel from Duluth, Minnesota, on Lake Superior, all the way to the Atlantic Ocean. The St. Lawrence Seaway makes it much easier for the United States and Canada to trade with each other and with Europe. The St. Lawrence Seaway has been called Canada's highway to the sea because of the volume of goods that travels its length.

Trade   What country is the biggest trading partner of the United States? It is Canada. And, the United States is Canada's largest trading partner, too. About three fourths of all of Canada's foreign trade—both exports and imports—is with the United States. Our economies are interdependent. That means that in order to be successful, each country needs to do business with the other.

Diagram Skills

Ships traveling from the Atlantic Ocean to Lake Superior must go through a series of locks along the St. Lawrence Seaway. **Describe** How do the locks allow ships to make the great change in elevation between the Atlantic and the Great Lakes? **Identify Effects** How did building the St. Lawrence Seaway affect the economies of the United States and Canada?

The emblem of the Organization of American States shows the furled flags of its member nations.

Since 1988, the United States and Canada have signed two important trade agreements. The Free Trade Agreement (FTA) put an end to **tariffs**, or fees charged on imported goods. Tariffs raise the cost of goods, so the amount of trade can be limited. By eliminating tariffs, Canada and the United States agreed to have **free trade**, trade without taxes on imported goods. In 1994, this agreement was expanded to include Mexico. The goal of the North American Free Trade Agreement (NAFTA) is to encourage trade and economic growth in all three countries. The agreement affects many major industries, including agriculture, trucking, and manufacturing. Since these agreements were made, trade among the three countries has increased. Although some jobs in the United States have been created because of increased imports, other jobs have been lost because American companies have moved to Mexico.

Interdependent Countries   The United States and Canada are interdependent politically as well as economically. Both Canada and the United States belong to the Organization of American States, or OAS. This international organization was formed to promote cooperation among countries in the Western Hemisphere. The member countries work with one another to promote political, economic, military, and cultural cooperation. The main goals of OAS are to maintain peace in the Western Hemisphere and to prevent other countries from interfering within the region.

✓ **Reading Check**   What are the main goals of the member countries in the Organization of American States?

Section 5 Assessment

Key Terms
Review the key terms at the beginning of this section. Use each term in a sentence that explains its meaning.

Target Reading Skill
What word or idea were you able to clarify by rereading or reading ahead?

Comprehension and Critical Thinking
1. (a) Explain What are some environmental problems the United States and Canada share?

(b) Summarize How have these two countries worked together to solve these problems?
(c) Identify Effects How can one nation's problems affect another?
2. (a) Note What country is the largest trading partner of the United States?
(b) Make Generalizations How has the St. Lawrence Seaway made trade easier for the United States and Canada?
(c) Identify the Main Idea What is the goal of NAFTA?

Writing Activity
Write a paragraph that explains the main reasons that Canada and the United States are important to each other.

Writing Tip Begin your paragraph with a topic sentence that states your main idea. Be sure to include examples, details, and facts that support your main idea.

Review and Assessment

◆ Chapter Summary

Native American artifact

Section 1: The Arrival of the Europeans

- The first Americans are called Native Americans.
- The lives of Native Americans changed after Europeans arrived.
- The 13 colonies won independence after the Revolutionary War.

Section 2: Growth and Conflict in the United States

- The United States doubled its size in 1803 with the Louisiana Purchase.
- The Industrial Revolution changed the way people in America lived.
- The Civil War pitted the North against the South.

Section 3: The United States on the Brink of Change

- The Industrial Revolution helped the rich but not the poor.
- The United States fought two world wars and became a superpower.
- After years of fighting various wars, Americans faced new terrorist threats.

Section 4: The History of Canada

- Britain fought France to gain control of Canada.
- Canadians won the right to control their own government.
- Today, Canada is completely independent of Great Britain.

Section 5: The United States and Canada Today

- The United States and Canada work together to solve environmental issues.
- The United States and Canada are each other's largest trading partners.

Civil War soldiers

◆ Key Terms

Each of the statements below contains a key term from the chapter. If the statement is true, write *true*. If it is false, rewrite the statement to make it correct.

1. A **missionary** is a person who must work for a period of years to gain freedom.
2. A **tariff** is a fee charged on imported goods.
3. **Acid rain** forms over millions of years from plant and animal remains.
4. The **Industrial Revolution** was a period of great tension between the United States and the Soviet Union.
5. A **dominion** is a self-governing area that is subject to the United States.
6. Canada is a **bilingual** country, meaning that it has two official languages.
7. A **boycott** is a refusal to buy or use goods and services.
8. An **abolitionist** is a person who moves to a new country in order to settle there.

◆ Comprehension and Critical Thinking

9. (a) Compare Why were Spanish and French explorers interested in the Americas?
(b) Identify Cause and Effect How did the treatment of Native Americans reflect the different interests of the Spanish and the French explorers?

10. (a) Explain How did the Industrial Revolution change the textile industry?
(b) Draw Conclusions How might this change have affected workers?

11. (a) Identify What was the Homestead Act?
(b) Draw Inferences How did railroads help settle the American West more quickly?

12. (a) Name Where did some Loyalists move after the American Revolution?
(b) Identify Frame of Reference Why would Loyalists have opposed independence from Britain?

13. (a) Define What kind of government does Canada have?
(b) Name What system is the Canadian government modeled on?
(c) Draw Conclusions What duties might a monarch have, since he or she is not the head of the government?

14. (a) Describe How has geography contributed to the trade partnership between Canada and the United States?
(b) Draw Inferences What other factors might explain this strong trade relationship?

◆ Skills Practice

Interpreting Diagrams In the Skills for Life activity in this chapter, you learned how to interpret information in a diagram. You also learned that labels on a diagram often should be read in a certain order.

Review the steps you followed to learn this skill. Then reread the part of Section 5 called Improving Air Quality. Create a diagram showing the cycle of acid rain. Remember to label your diagram clearly.

◆ Writing Activity: Language Arts

Compare and contrast the histories of the United States and of Canada. Write a paragraph describing the ways in which the growth, settlement, and independence of the United States and Canada were similar and ways in which they were different.

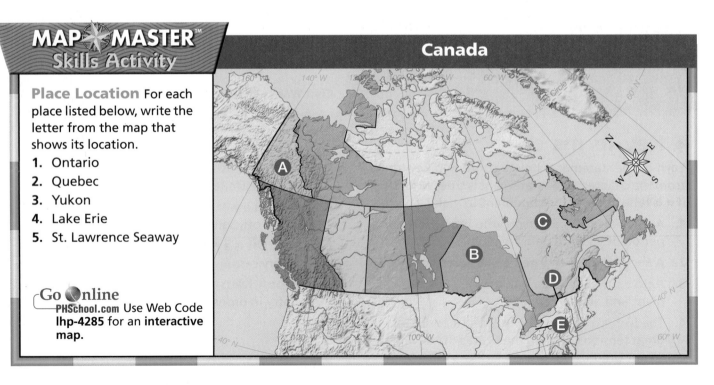

MAP MASTER™
Skills Activity

Canada

Place Location For each place listed below, write the letter from the map that shows its location.

1. Ontario
2. Quebec
3. Yukon
4. Lake Erie
5. St. Lawrence Seaway

Go Online
PHSchool.com Use Web Code **lhp-4285** for an **interactive map.**

Standardized Test Prep

Test-Taking Tips

Some questions on standardized tests ask you to analyze primary sources. Read the excerpt below from a famous United States document. Then follow the tips to answer the sample question.

> "All legislative Powers herein granted shall be vested in a Congress of the United States, which shall consist of a Senate and House of Representatives. . . . The House of Representatives shall be composed of Members chosen every second Year by the People of the several states. . . . The Senate of the United States shall be composed of two Senators from each State for six Years; and each Senator shall have one Vote."

TIP Try to identify the main idea, or most important point, of the passage.

Pick the letter that best answers the question.

Which document does this extract come from?

A ~~Declaration of Independence~~

B United States Constitution

C Federalist Papers

D ~~Pledge of Allegiance~~

TIP Use what you already know about United States history and government to help you find the *best* answer.

Think It Through Start with the main idea of the extract: *The Congress is supposed to make laws.* Which document explains the powers of each branch of government? You can rule out A and D. The Pledge is a statement of loyalty. The Declaration of Independence explains why colonists cut their ties to England. That leaves B and C. Maybe you aren't sure about the Federalist Papers, but you probably know that the Constitution is the plan for our government—including Congress. The correct answer is B.

Practice Questions

Use the tips above and other tips in this book to help you answer the following questions.

1. Which event encouraged immigrants and farmworkers to look for jobs in cities?
   - **A** the Civil War
   - **B** the Industrial Revolution
   - **C** the Louisiana Purchase
   - **D** the Indian Removal Act

2. What was the result of the Seven Years' War?
   - **A** Canada became independent.
   - **B** France lost, but kept control over Quebec.
   - **C** Great Britain gained control over all of Canada.
   - **D** Canada became a dominion of Great Britain.

Read the excerpt on Article 102, and then answer the question that follows.

> *Article 102: Objectives*
> a) eliminate barriers to trade in, and facilitate the cross-border movement of, goods and services between the territories of the Parties;
> b) promote conditions of fair competition in the free-trade area.

3. Which document does this excerpt most likely come from?
   - **A** the British North America Act
   - **B** the Treaty of Paris
   - **C** NAFTA
   - **D** the Quebec Act

Go Online PHSchool.com
Use Web Code lha-4205 for a **Chapter 7 self-test.**

8 Cultures of the United States and Canada

Chapter Preview

This chapter will introduce you to the cultures of the United States and Canada.

Section 1
A Heritage of Diversity and Exchange

Section 2
The United States: A Nation of Immigrants

Section 3
The Canadian Mosaic

🎯 Target Reading Skill

Main Idea In this chapter you will focus on skills you can use to identify the main ideas as you read.

▶ Young people enjoy an amusement park ride in Orlando, Florida.

Migration to North America

MAP MASTER™
Skills Activity

ASIA

NORTH AMERICA

EUROPE

ASIA

ARCTIC OCEAN

Caribbean Islands

AFRICA

PACIFIC OCEAN

SOUTH AMERICA

ATLANTIC OCEAN

INDIAN OCEAN

AUSTRALIA

Equator

N
W E
S

0 miles 5,000
0 kilometers 5,000
Robinson

KEY

United States and Canada

Route of Migration

Movement Both the United States and Canada have long histories of welcoming immigrants from around the world. **Locate** Where are most of the arrows pointing to on the map? **Predict** What factors in people's lives might cause them to immigrate to the United States or Canada?

Go Online
PHSchool.com Use Web Code **lhp-4311** for step-by-step **map skills practice.**

A Heritage of Diversity and Exchange

Prepare to Read

Objectives

In this section you will
1. Explain how cultural patterns developed in the United States and Canada.
2. Discuss the cultural patterns that exist today in the United States and Canada.

Taking Notes

As you read this section, add facts and details to the outline. Use Roman numerals to indicate the major headings of the section, capital letters for the subheadings, and numbers for the supporting details.

> **A Heritage of Diversity and Exchange**
> I. Patterns of culture develop
>   A.
>   B.
> II.

Target Reading Skill

Identify Main Ideas It is not possible to remember every detail that you read. Good readers therefore identify the main idea in every paragraph or section. The main idea is the most important or the biggest point—the one that includes all the other points in the section. As you read, write the main idea that is stated in each section.

Key Terms

- **cultural diversity** (KUL chur ul duh VUR suh tee) *n.* a variety of cultures
- **cultural exchange** (KUL chur ul eks CHAYNJ) *n.* the process by which different cultures share ideas and ways of doing things
- **ethnic group** (ETH nik groop) *n.* a group of people who share a common language, history, and culture

Fur traders at Fort Garry, present-day Winnipeg, in Manitoba, Canada

By 1763, Canada and the eastern half of the present-day United States were one land, governed by Great Britain. When the Revolutionary War ended in 1783, new political boundaries were created. A new country, the United States, was born.

New political borders, however, did not divide cultural regions that already existed. The same patterns of **cultural diversity,** or a wide variety of cultures, continued.

> **❝By 1810, many . . . merchants were . . . immigrants, as were almost all the millers, mechanics, store-keepers, . . . and the majority of the farmers. . . . [They] had been lured by economic opportunities. . . . ❞**
>
> —*D. W. Meinig, The Shaping of America*

This passage describes American immigrants to Canada. At that time, Americans in the northeastern United States were more comfortable with the culture of southern Canada than with some of the cultures within their own country.

Patterns of Culture Develop

The United States and Canada have always been culturally diverse. Both countries are geographically diverse, too—that is, they have a variety of landforms, climates, and vegetation. The cultures of the first Americans reflected their environments. Native Americans near the ocean ate a great deal of fish and told stories about the sea. Native Americans in forests learned how to trap and hunt forest animals. They also traded with each other. When groups trade, they receive more than just goods. They also get involved in **cultural exchange**, or the process by which different cultures share ideas and ways of doing things.

Cultural Exchange When Europeans arrived in North America, they changed Native American life. Some changes came from things that Europeans brought with them. For example, there were no horses in the Americas before the Spanish explorers arrived. Once horses were introduced, they became an important part of Native American culture.

Native American in the Badlands of South Dakota

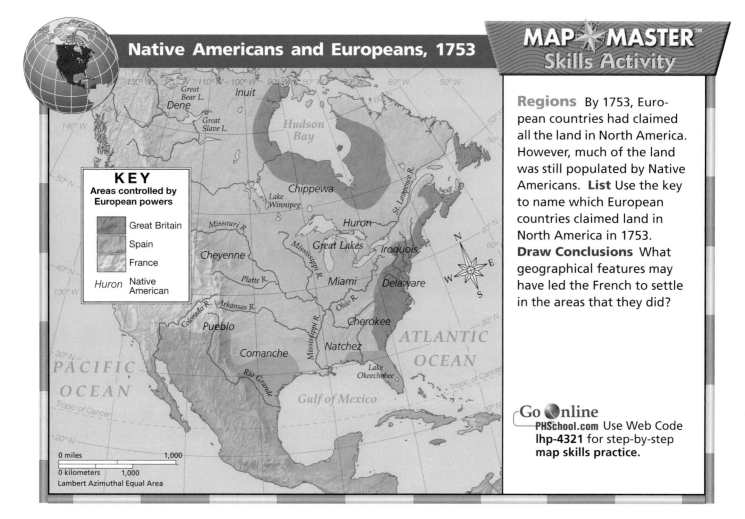

Native Americans and Europeans, 1753

KEY
Areas controlled by European powers

- Great Britain
- Spain
- France
- *Huron* Native American

Inuit
Dene
Great Bear L.
Great Slave L.
Hudson Bay
Chippewa
Lake Winnipeg
Missouri R.
Huron
St. Lawrence R.
Great Lakes
Iroquois
Cheyenne
Mississippi R.
Miami
Delaware
Platte R.
Colorado R.
Arkansas R.
Ohio R.
Pueblo
Cherokee
Comanche
Natchez
Lake Okeechobee
PACIFIC OCEAN
Rio Grande
ATLANTIC OCEAN
Tropic of Cancer
Gulf of Mexico

0 miles 1,000
0 kilometers 1,000
Lambert Azimuthal Equal Area

MAP MASTER™
Skills Activity

Regions By 1753, European countries had claimed all the land in North America. However, much of the land was still populated by Native Americans. **List** Use the key to name which European countries claimed land in North America in 1753.

Draw Conclusions What geographical features may have led the French to settle in the areas that they did?

Go Online
PHSchool.com Use Web Code **lhp-4321** for step-by-step map skills practice.

Harvesting Wheat
These farmers in Manitoba, Canada, are harvesting wheat with a horse-drawn reaper, which cuts grain.
Identify Causes *Why did farming attract many immigrants to the United States and Canada?*

Links to

Math

Using Your Fingers and Toes Native American groups developed number systems to help when conducting trade with others. The Chukchee, who hunted reindeer along the Bering Strait, used their fingers to count. The question *How many?* is translated "How many fingers?" Their word for *five* is "hand," for *ten*, "both hands," and for *twenty,* "man"—meaning both hands and both feet.

Native Americans also contributed to European culture. The French learned how to trap and to survive in the forest. English families learned to grow local foods such as corn. Cultural exchange also took place between enslaved Africans and their owners. The Africans learned English and used European tools. African music and foods entered the daily lives of slave owners.

Immigrant Contributions This give-and-take happens every time immigrants come to a country. When Russian and Ukrainian settlers came to Canada's Prairie Provinces, they brought a kind of hardy wheat from their home country. Farmers soon learned that it grew well in Canada's climate. These immigrants helped the region become the leading wheat-growing area in Canada today. Members of other ethnic groups have made important contributions to American and Canadian cultures, too. An **ethnic group** is a group of people who share a common language, history, and culture.

✓ **Reading Check** What are two examples of cultural exchange?

Cultural Patterns Today

The United States and Canada share similar cultural patterns and histories because both of them were once British colonies. Both of their cultures have also been shaped by immigration. With huge amounts of land to be cultivated, or worked on in order to raise crops, the governments of the United States and Canada first encouraged immigration to increase the work force. With the Industrial Revolution, the end of slavery, and the rise of cities, the demand for workers was great.

Today, the United States and Canada continue to attract immigrants because they are wealthy nations with stable governments. Many immigrants come seeking political asylum, religious freedom, or economic opportunities. Others come to escape famine, disease, or overcrowding in their homelands. They all come looking to improve their lives.

Fitting In When immigrants move from their homeland to another country, they often have to make difficult decisions. As immigrants build a life in a new country, they must learn different laws and customs. Often they need to learn a new language, too. Some immigrants work hard to keep up the customs of their home culture as they settle in. Many feel torn between their cultural heritage and their new life.

For instance, when he was 14 years old, Herman immigrated to the United States from Guyana, a country in South America. Five years later, someone asked him if he felt Guyanese or American. He said, "I'm in between. Deep down inside, where I was born, that's what I am. You can't change a tiger['s] stripe."

Others, however, try to put as much of their old life behind them as they can. When Louisa and her husband immigrated to Saskatchewan, Canada, from Hong Kong, they were eager to start their new lives:

> **"It takes time to adapt to a new environment. It is sometimes difficult for one to change one's life abruptly. However, it is the reality that we must fit in. We are determined to succeed in overcoming the difficulties and to live a Canadian way of life."**
>
> —*Louisa, a Chinese immigrant*

Identify Main Ideas
Target Skill Which sentence states the main idea under the heading Cultural Patterns Today?

Celebrating Cultures
The dancers below march in a parade during Carnival Miami in Florida. The photo on the left is a busy street in Chinatown in Vancouver, British Columbia. **Analyze Images** *In what ways do the photographs below show how immigrants have blended their traditional cultures with their new cultures?*

Play Ball!
Baseball is widely considered to be the "national pastime" of the United States. It is also a popular sport in Canada. One professional baseball team in Canada competes against American teams in the major leagues. **Conclusions** *How does professional baseball link the United States and Canada both culturally and economically?*

Maintaining Traditions Almost all immigrants cling to some of the things that remind them of their former homes. Many large cities in the United States and Canada have areas where certain ethnic groups live or conduct business, such as Chinatown in Vancouver and Little Havana in Miami.

Of course, people maintain traditions in their own homes as well. Think about your family or your friends' families. Do they use special phrases from the language they learned from their parents or grandparents? Do they eat special foods? Customs give people a sense of identity. They also enrich life in both the United States and Canada.

Cultural Ties The United States and Canada are historically and economically linked. They share a border, a continent, and have felt Britain's influence on their history and language. Although the population of the United States is nearly ten times larger than that of Canada, the people are very much alike.

At least three fourths of people in both countries live in urban areas. Most Canadians live within 200 miles (320 kilometers) of the United States' border. Canadians and Americans dress alike and eat similar foods. The majority of both Canadians and Americans are either Roman Catholic or Protestant. Both nations have long life expectancies and high rates of literacy, or the ability to read and write. Canadians and Americans often read the same books and magazines, listen to the same music, and watch many of the same movies and television shows.

Economic Ties With vast resources and strong economies, both the United States and Canada have a high standard of living. A standard of living is a measure of the amount of goods, services, and leisure time people have. Their economies are linked, too. The total amount of trade that takes place each year between the United States and Canada is larger than it is between any other two countries. Changes in business trends in the United States are quickly reflected in the Canadian business sector. The two nations trade in manufactured goods, forestry products, and food items. They also trade heavily in energy, such as oil, coal, and electricity.

In addition, millions of Canadians travel to the United States each year. Nearly two million Canadians visit Florida alone, spending more than a billion dollars there. Most of these tourists, known as Snowbirds, come to escape Canada's long, cold winters. Likewise, most of Canada's tourists are American. Americans can travel to Canada almost as easily as they would to a different state.

✓ **Reading Check** What cultural characteristics do the United States and Canada have in common?

Tourists visit the Grand Canyon (upper photo) and Quebec City (lower photo).

Section 1 Assessment

Key Terms
Review the key terms at the beginning of this section. Use each term in a sentence that explains its meaning.

Target Reading Skill
State the main ideas in Section 1.

Comprehension and Critical Thinking
1. (a) Recall Describe how Native American cultures reflected their environments.

(b) Analyze How did the arrival of Europeans affect Native American cultures?

2. (a) List Note the similarities between the United States and Canada.

(b) Explore the Main Idea How are the economies of the United States and Canada linked?

(c) Draw Conclusions The economy of which country—the United States or Canada—is more dependent on the other's?

Writing Activity
Write a poem about a custom that is important to your family or the family of a friend. Start by listing words or phrases that describe the details of the family custom.

> **Writing Tip** After you write a first draft of the poem, read it aloud. Circle words that do not offer a clear picture of the custom. Replace them with more lively words.

"Today we're going to brainstorm," Ms. King told her social studies class. She drew a large circle at the center of the chalkboard, and inside it she wrote *Cultures of the United States.* "This is our topic. Now, give me the names of some important culture groups in our country."

The ideas flew fast. "European settlers!" "Before them, Native Americans." "Hispanics!" "African Americans!" "Asians!" Ms. King put each group in its own circle and connected it with a line to the center circle.

"Great start! Now give me details about each of these groups," she urged her students. "What ideas did Europeans bring here?"

She made several small circles and connected them to the large circle, saying, *"European settlers."* She filled in the circles as the students brainstormed the topic: *democracy . . . architecture . . . English language . . . banking . . . measurements . . . medicine. . . .*

By the time she finished, the chalkboard looked like a spider web. In fact, the connected circles made what is sometimes called a *web diagram.* It is also known as a *concept web.*

A concept web is a type of *graphic organizer,* a diagram that puts information into a graphic, or visual, form to make it easier to understand.

Learn the Skill

Like an outline, a concept web begins with a main topic and adds subtopics and details. Follow the steps below to learn about concept webs.

1. **Identify a main topic.** A main topic generally has at least two subtopics. Identify the subtopics.

2. **Draw a circle at the center of the concept map.** Label it with the main topic.

3. **For each subtopic, draw a circle.** Label the circles. Attach them to the main circle with lines to show that the subtopics are related to the main topic.

4. **If necessary, divide the subtopics even further.** Some subtopics have subtopics of their own. To show this, draw more circles, label them, and attach them to the circle with the subtopics.

Practice the Skill

Suppose you want to write a paper about your culture. Refer to the steps on the previous page and the concept web below to see how you might organize your thoughts.

1 Your topic is My Culture. You know that many factors affect a person's culture. Those factors will be your subtopics.

2 The concept web below shows My Culture in an oval at the center.

3 The ovals connected to the center show that religion, family history, languages, and the celebration of special occasions are parts of a person's culture.

4 Add supporting details that relate to family history and the other subtopics. These details go in the empty ovals shown below.

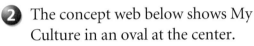

Today, many people can trace their family's history through photographs. This family has photographs of their grandfather (from top to bottom) as a baby, as a young man, with his wife and children, and with his grandson.

Apply the Skill

Choose a part of the text in Section 1. Using the steps for this skill, make a concept web that shows the main idea, subtopics, and details.

The United States: A Nation of Immigrants

Prepare to Read

Objectives

In this section you will
1. Learn about the people of the United States.
2. Find out about the culture of the United States.

Taking Notes

As you read this section, look for details about the cultural diversity of the United States. Copy the chart below and record your findings in it.

Causes	Event	Effects
• • •	The U.S. is culturally diverse	• • •

Target Reading Skill

Identify Supporting Details The main idea of a paragraph or section is supported by details that give further information about it. These details may explain the main idea or give examples or reasons. As you read, note the details that explain the main idea in this section: "The United States is a diverse nation."

Key Terms

- **reservation** (rez ur VAY shun) *n.* an area of land set aside for a special purpose
- **treaty** (TREE tee) *n.* a formal agreement, usually between two or more nations

This view of life in the United States comes from an immigrant arriving in Ellis Island in 1920:

> **I feel like I had two lives. You plant something in the ground, it has its roots, and then you transplant it where it stays permanently. That's what happened to me. . . . All of a sudden, I started life new, amongst people whose language I didn't understand. . . . [E]verything was different . . . but I never despaired, I was optimistic. . . . [T]his is the only country where you're not a stranger, because we are all strangers. It's only a matter of time who got here first.**
>
> —*Lazarus Salamon, a Hungarian immigrant*

The People of the United States

The population of the United States has been growing steadily since the first national census was taken in 1790. About 4 million people lived in the nation then. Today, more than 280 million people live in the United States.

The Statue of Liberty

Despite the vast size of the United States, its people share many common attitudes and traditions. These experiences help bring Americans together. At the same time, Americans are a diverse mix of races, ethnicities, and religions.

The First People Today's Native Americans are descendents of the first people to live in the Americas. Most experts believe that the first Americans migrated from Asia across the Bering Strait thousands of years ago. Gradually, the human population spread south across North America.

When European settlers arrived in North America, they often came into conflict with the Native Americans who were living there. As Europeans moved west, they forced the local Indians to move to land already occupied by other Native American groups.

The United States government pursued a general policy of supporting white settlement. They established **reservations, or federal lands set aside for Native Americans,** and forced Native Americans to relocate.

Conflict With Settlers From 1778 to 1871, the United States government wrote and signed hundreds of **treaties, or formal agreements,** with American Indian groups. In these treaties, Native Americans agreed to interact peacefully with settlers. They also agreed to give up much of their land. In return, the federal government promised to pay for that land and to protect them.

Most of these treaties were broken, often because settlers wanted to expand onto reservation lands. When settlers violated these treaties, Native Americans fought back. They were fighting not only for their land but for their resources and way of life. Native Americans fought more than 1,000 battles throughout the West between 1861 and 1891.

Native Americans Today In the 1960s, Native Americans began to seek economic and political equality. Several groups, including the American Indian Movement (AIM), formed to work for better living conditions and equal rights. They called on the government to address their concerns. The United States has since passed a series of reforms, giving money and land to Native American groups. Today, about 2.5 million people in the United States are Native American.

Fighting For Civil Rights
Dennis Banks, a leader in the American Indian Movement (AIM), leads a protest in South Dakota. **Draw Inferences** *Why do you think Banks chose Mount Rushmore as the site for the protest?*

Identify Supporting Details

Which details in the paragraph at the right tell about diversity?

Immigrants The United States has always been a nation of immigrants. However, the first major wave of immigration took place from 1830 to 1890. These immigrants were mainly Protestants from England, Scotland, Scandinavia, and Germany who came to farm the land. They adapted fairly easily to the American ways of life because of their similar backgrounds. These ethnic groups would continue to come to the United States in large numbers until World War I.

The first large influx of Chinese immigrants came in 1849, during the California Gold Rush. More Chinese arrived in the 1860s to lay track for the transcontinental railroad. They had a more difficult time than Europeans adjusting to life in the United States. Widespread unemployment and fierce competition for gold led to violence and discrimination against many Asian immigrants.

A Second Wave of Immigrants The second major wave of immigration took place from 1880 to 1920. Unlike the first wave, these immigrants went to work in factories, mills, and mines. Immigrants from southern and eastern Europe dominated the second wave: Jews from Russia and Poland, Roman Catholics from Poland and Italy, and some of the Greek Orthodox faith. Like the Asian immigrants before them, they dressed differently, ate different foods, and spoke different languages. They often worked in poor conditions for low wages.

Graph Skills

Thousands of people attend the annual Ninth Avenue International Food Festival in New York City. The festival features food from nearly 30 countries along the mile-long celebration. **Identify** Where do most immigrants to the United States come from? **Draw Conclusions** What languages might the immigrants from those regions speak?

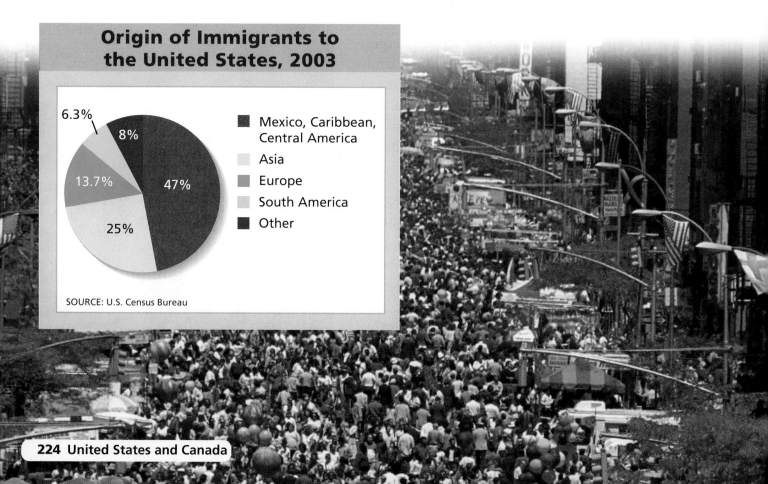

Origin of Immigrants to the United States, 2003

6.3%
8%
13.7%
47%
25%

- Mexico, Caribbean, Central America
- Asia
- Europe
- South America
- Other

SOURCE: U.S. Census Bureau

The writings of Zora Neale Hurston, Ralph Waldo Emerson, and Sandra Cisneros (from far left) reflect the diversity of the books that Americans read.

Immigrants Today Non-Europeans form the largest immigrant groups coming to the United States today. Most immigrants arrive from Asia and Latin America. The hard work of these immigrants, and of those before them, have helped develop the United States agriculturally, industrially, and economically. They also helped create a culturally diverse nation.

✓ **Reading Check** Where do most immigrants arrive from today?

United States Culture

Have you ever eaten bagels, tacos, dim sum, or spaghetti? Have you listened to music at a Caribbean carnival or watched a dragon parade on Chinese New Year? Diverse foods, books, music, and pastimes all enrich the lives of Americans.

Literature A distinctly American literature emerged in the nineteenth century, as Ralph Waldo Emerson and others wrote about politics and nature. By the twentieth century, America's diversity had begun to influence its literature. Playwright Eugene O'Neill had an Irish background, while Zora Neale Hurston wrote novels about what it was like to be African American. Traditions such as Native American folk tales and slave narratives also gained importance. American literature is now more varied than ever before, reflecting the diversity in today's culture.

Musical Traditions In addition to diverse literature, Americans listen to and create many different kinds of music, from classical to popular. Popular music includes country, rap, rock, reggae, and jazz. Although it has its roots in African rhythms, jazz developed in the South, in places like New Orleans, Louisiana. African American singers and musicians, such as Louis Armstrong and Duke Ellington, made jazz popular around the world.

Pianist and composer Duke Ellington and trumpeter Louis Armstrong rehearse their first recording together in a New York City recording studio in 1946.

Probably the most popular style of music to originate in the United States is rock-and-roll. A combination of rhythm and blues, gospel, and country music, rock music first became popular in the 1950s. It created a sensation all over the country and quickly spread from the United States to Europe and Asia. It remains one of the most popular musical styles throughout the world today.

Sports Many Americans watch and participate in sports activities. Sports in North America go all the way back to Native American groups who played a form of lacrosse. In the late 1800s, sports such as tennis, hiking, and golf grew in popularity. Organized team sports also began to develop a following near the end of the 1800s.

Three major sports were invented in the United States: baseball, basketball, and football. Baseball soon became the national pastime, producing sports heroes like Babe Ruth in the early 1900s. Today, baseball's popularity has spread to Japan, the Caribbean, Russia, Mexico, and Central America.

Basketball was invented in 1891 and quickly gained popularity in schools and colleges throughout the country.

✓ **Reading Check** Which major sports were invented in the United States?

Section 2 Assessment

Key Terms

Review the key terms at the beginning of this section. Use each term in a sentence that explains its meaning.

Target Reading Skill

State the details that support the main idea on page 225 that the United States is diverse.

Comprehension and Critical Thinking

1. (a) Explain How did the United States government support white settlement in the West?

(b) Draw Inferences Why did the government send Native Americans to live on land that was not considered valuable?

(c) Analyze Information How were Native Americans at a disadvantage in their conflict with white settlers?

2. (a) Note When did American literature begin to have a distinct voice?

(b) Identify Causes When and how did American literature become more diverse?

(c) Synthesize Information How has the immigrant experience influenced American culture?

Writing Activity

Write an entry in your journal explaining how the literature and music of the United States reflect diverse cultures. When you write a journal entry, you can let your ideas flow without stopping to edit what you write.

For: An activity on Ellis Island
Visit: PHSchool.com
Web Code: lhd-4302

Section 3

The Canadian Mosaic

Prepare to Read

Objectives

In this section you will
1. Find out about the people of Canada.
2. Learn about Canadian culture.

Taking Notes

As you read this section, look for details that show why Canadians consider their society to be a mosaic. Copy the concept web below and record your findings in it.

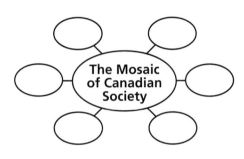

Target Reading Skill

Identify Main Ideas
Identifying main ideas can help you remember the most important ideas that you read. Sometimes, the main ideas are not stated directly. All the details in a section add up to a main idea, but you must state the main idea yourself. Carefully read the details in the two paragraphs below. Then, state the main idea of these paragraphs.

Key Terms

• **melting pot** (MELT ing paht) *n.* a country in which many cultures blend together to form a single culture
• **reserve** (rih ZURV) *n.* an area of land set aside by the government

A crowd celebrates Canada Day.

Over the years, Canada has been as welcoming to immigrants as the United States. However, one important difference between the countries is the way in which they view immigration. The United States considers itself to be a **melting pot, or a country in which all cultures blend together to form a single culture.** In this view, immigrants are encouraged to adopt American ways. Canadians view immigration in a slightly different way, as one Canadian journalist explains:

"Canadians believe . . . in a mosaic of separate pieces, with each chunk becoming part of the whole physically but retaining its own separate identity, color, and tastes. This certainly makes for an interesting mix. Importantly, it provides Canadians with an identity peg, one major way to see themselves as different from Americans, as they must. And as they are. "

—*Andrew H. Malcolm*

The People of Canada

Today, Canada has a population of more than 31 million people. Many of them are immigrants. At first, Canada's leaders preferred Christian European settlers. At times, laws set limits on immigrants who were Jews, Asians, or Africans. But that has changed. Today, people of all ethnic groups move to Canada.

French Canadians Sometimes, the ties among Canadians are not as strong as those among Americans. People in the United States rarely talk about forming independent states or countries. Some Canadian groups do. French Canadians in Quebec are concerned about preserving their heritage. Special laws promote French culture and language. Street and advertising signs are written in both French and English. But many French Canadians want Quebec to become a separate country. To show their determination, they have license plates that read *Je me souviens,* or "I remember." This phrase refers to remembering their French heritage.

First Nations Canada's indigenous peoples, called First Nations, also want to preserve their culture. They are trying to fix past problems by working with existing governments.

In Canada, as in the United States, early European settlers took over the native peoples' lands. Many indigenous peoples were sent to **reserves,** or areas that the government set aside for them, similar to reservations in the United States. Others were denied equal rights. Recently, laws have been passed allowing First Nations to use their own languages in their schools.

■ Graph Skills

Canada is an ethnically diverse country. **Identify** Where do most immigrants to Canada come from? **Compare and Contrast** Compare the Origin of Immigrants to Canada chart here with the similar chart on page 224. How are they similar? How do they differ?

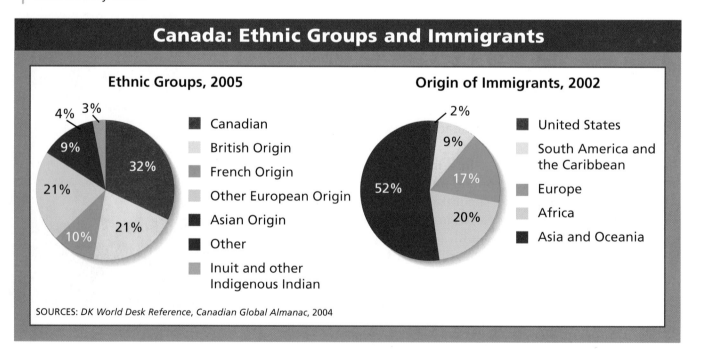

Canada: Ethnic Groups and Immigrants

Ethnic Groups, 2005

- 32% Canadian
- 21% British Origin
- 21% French Origin
- 10% Other European Origin
- 9% Asian Origin
- 4% Other
- 3% Inuit and other Indigenous Indian

Origin of Immigrants, 2002

- 52% United States
- 20% South America and the Caribbean
- 17% Europe
- 9% Africa
- 2% Asia and Oceania

SOURCES: *DK World Desk Reference, Canadian Global Almanac,* 2004

Inuits Canada's Inuits (IN oo its) lived in the Arctic for centuries as nomadic hunters and gatherers. They had excellent survival skills and were fine craftworkers. They made everything they needed using available materials, such as snow, stone, animal bones, and driftwood. Modern technology, however, allows them to buy the clothes and tools they used to make. Many Inuits have lost their traditional skills. As a result, some feel they are losing their identity.

Immigrants Because Britain and France were the first countries to colonize Canada, most Canadians were of British or French descent by the late 1800s. By the 1920s, many immigrants came from central and eastern Europe to farm the prairies in the west. But when the Depression hit in 1929, there was no longer a need for as many workers. The government restricted immigration.

After World War II, the economy began to grow again. With the need for more workers, millions of immigrants came to Canada. Many of them were from Africa, Asia, and Latin America and settled mainly in large urban areas. For example, many Asian immigrants settled in Vancouver and Toronto. Since World War II, Canada's population has more than doubled. Much of that growth is because of immigrants and their children.

✓ **Reading Check** How has technology changed the way that Inuits live?

Remembering Canada's History
The community of Chemainus, British Columbia, is famous for its collection of 35 larger-than-life historical murals. **Analyze Images** *How does this mural honor the role that the country's indigenous peoples have played in Canada's history?*

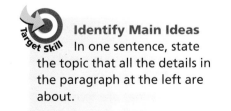

Identify Main Ideas In one sentence, state the topic that all the details in the paragraph at the left are about.

Playing hockey on an outdoor ice rink

Canadian Culture

Canada has made a special effort to encourage people to be Canadian and to express their ethnic heritage at the same time. One cultural issue does unite most Canadians: They feel that the United States has too much influence on their culture. Even today, Canadians search for ways to express their unique culture.

Canadian writers have long been famous for their work. From Lucy Maud Montgomery's *Anne of Green Gables* to writers of today, such as Margaret Atwood and Alice Munro, Canadian literature is popular throughout the world.

Canadian singers have made contributions to cultural life as well. Popular Canadian singers include Shania Twain and Céline Dion. Many singers maintain their ties to Canada even though their jobs often require them to be elsewhere. Since the 1960s, the Canadian recording industry has become a billion-dollar business.

Another billion-dollar industry in Canada is sports. Ice hockey is Canada's national sport. Every year, hockey teams from the United States and Canada compete for the Stanley Cup, a Canadian prize. Hockey serves not only as a national pastime but also as an important symbol of national identity.

✓ **Reading Check** Which industries bring billions of dollars into the Canadian economy?

Section 3 Assessment

Key Terms
Review the key terms at the beginning of this section. Use each term in a sentence that explains its meaning.

Target Reading Skill
State the main ideas in Section 3.

Comprehension and Critical Thinking
1. (a) List What are two languages spoken in Canada?

(b) Identify the Main Idea In what ways do French Canadians try to preserve their culture and language?
(c) Draw Conclusions Why do many French Canadians want Quebec to be an independent country?
2. (a) Explain How do Canadians try to express their culture?
(b) Make Generalizations Why do Canadians worry about the influence of the United States on their culture?

Writing Activity
Write a brief paragraph explaining why you think ice hockey developed in Canada.

For: An activity on immigrants
Visit: PHSchool.com
Web Code: lhd-4303

Review and Assessment

◆ Chapter Summary

Section 1: A Heritage of Diversity and Exchange

- Both the United States and Canada contain a wide variety of cultures.
- Immigrants have shaped the histories and cultures of the United States and Canada.
- The United States and Canada are important to each other for many reasons, including the cultural and economic ties that they share.

Section 2: The United States: A Nation of Immigrants

- The United States government fought many battles with Native Americans, pushing them westward.
- Millions of immigrants came to the United States to work on farms and railroads and in factories, mills, and mines.
- Diverse foods, literature, music, and sports help enrich life in the United States.

Section 3: The Canadian Mosaic

- Many immigrants come to Canada in search of a better life.
- First Nations, Inuits, and immigrants all add to the diversity of Canadian life.
- Canadians have made many contributions to the worlds of literature, music, and sports.

Quebec City

◆ Key Terms

Copy the lists of vocabulary words and definitions side by side on a sheet of paper. Then, draw a line from each term to its correct definition.

1. cultural diversity
2. cultural exchange
3. reservation
4. melting pot
5. ethnic group
6. treaty
7. reserve

A an area of land set aside for a special purpose

B an area of land set aside by the Canadian government

C a variety of cultures

D people who share a language, history, and culture

E a formal agreement

F the process in which different cultures share ideas and ways of doing things

G a country in which all cultures blend together to form a single culture

◆ Comprehension and Critical Thinking

8. (a) Explain Why did the United States and Canada first encourage immigration?
(b) Identify Causes Why do the United States and Canada continue to attract immigrants today?
(c) Identify Frame of Reference Why do some immigrants find it challenging to balance their cultural heritage with their new environment?

9. (a) Recall How do Canadians contribute to Florida's economy?
(b) Predict In what ways would Florida's economy be affected if these tourists vacationed somewhere else?

10. (a) Recall Why did most of the first wave of immigrants adapt fairly easily to life in the United States?
(b) Draw Conclusions Why was the second wave of immigrants discriminated against when the first wave of immigrants largely was not?

11. (a) Explain How does American society influence American music?
(b) Analyze What is it about jazz or rock-and-roll music that makes them uniquely American?

12. (a) Explain How are First Nations preserving their culture?
(b) Compare and Contrast Why is Canada characterized as a mosaic rather than as a melting pot?
(c) Identify Point of View Why is it important for Canadians to see themselves as different from Americans?

◆ Skills Practice

Using Graphic Organizers In the Skills for Life activity in this chapter, you learned how to use graphic organizers. You also learned that graphic organizers put information into a visual form.

Review the steps you followed to learn this skill. Then reread Cultural Patterns Today, beginning on page 216. Create a concept web about people's reasons for choosing to immigrate to the United States and Canada.

◆ Writing Activity: Math

In pairs or teams, research the different ethnic or cultural groups that are represented in your state. Calculate the results in percentage form. Then display the information as a circle graph. Write a brief summary of your findings.

MAP★MASTER™
Skills Activity

Native American Groups

Place Location For each Native American group listed below, write the letter from the map that shows its location.

1. Miami
2. Chippewa
3. Cherokee
4. Iroquois
5. Pueblo
6. Cheyenne
7. Comanche
8. Huron

Go Online
PHSchool.com Use Web Code **lhp-4333** for an **interactive map**.

Standardized Test Prep

Test-Taking Tips

Some questions on standardized tests ask you to analyze a passage to find a main idea. Read the passage below. Then follow the tips to answer the sample question.

> One Toronto radio station broadcasts in thirty languages. . . . In many Vancouver neighborhoods the street signs are in . . . English and Chinese. Toronto's city government routinely prepares its annual property tax notices in six languages: English, French, Chinese, Italian, Greek, and Portuguese.

TIP Before reading the answer choices, think of a main idea that would cover each sentence in the passage. Then match your idea to one of the answer choices.

Pick the letter that best answers the question.

What is the main idea of this passage?

A Toronto's city government prepares tax notices in many languages.

B The Chinese are an important ethnic group in Toronto.

C Many people in Toronto are bilingual, or speak two languages.

D Toronto has a diverse mix of people and ethnic groups.

TIP Read all of the answer choices before making a final choice. You can't be sure you have the right answer until you have read each one.

Think It Through You can rule out answer A, because it applies only to one of the sentences in the passage. You can rule out answer B because though it may be true, the Chinese are only one of the ethnic groups mentioned in the passage. Both answers C and D sound like they might be correct. Read answer C carefully. It isn't right because though the passage describes many languages, it does not say that most people in Toronto are bilingual. The correct answer is D.

Practice Questions

Use the tips above and other tips in this book to help you answer the following questions.

1. When two groups of people share ideas and ways of doing things, they are practicing
   A trade.   **B** cultural exchange.
   C cultural diversity.   **D** immigration.

2. What kind of standard of living do the United States and Canada have?
   A Both countries have low standards of living.
   B Both countries have high standards of living.
   C The United States has a high standard of living, while Canada's is low.
   D Canada has a high standard of living, while that of the United States is low.

3. Which group in Canada often talks about forming an independent country?
   A the Chippewa   **B** the British
   C the French Canadians **D** the Inuit

Read the passage below, and then answer the question that follows.

> Culture here has been shaped by a history of British colonization. It has also been shaped by immigrants who have come here from all over the world, bringing their cultures with them. Music, literature, and sports are important parts of the culture.

4. Based on what you have read, which country could this passage be describing?
   A either the United States or Canada
   B the United States
   C Canada
   D neither the United States nor Canada

Use Web Code lha-4303 for a **Chapter 8** self-test.

The United States

Chapter Preview

This chapter will introduce you to the four regions of the United States.

Country Databank
The Country Databank provides data on each of the fifty states.

Section 1
The Northeast
An Urban Center

Section 2
The South
The Growth of Industry

Section 3
The Midwest
Leaving the Farm

Section 4
The West
Using and Preserving Resources

 Target Reading Skill

Comparison and Contrast In this chapter you will focus on using comparison and contrast to help you sort out and analyze information.

▶ Members of the California National Guard display an American flag.

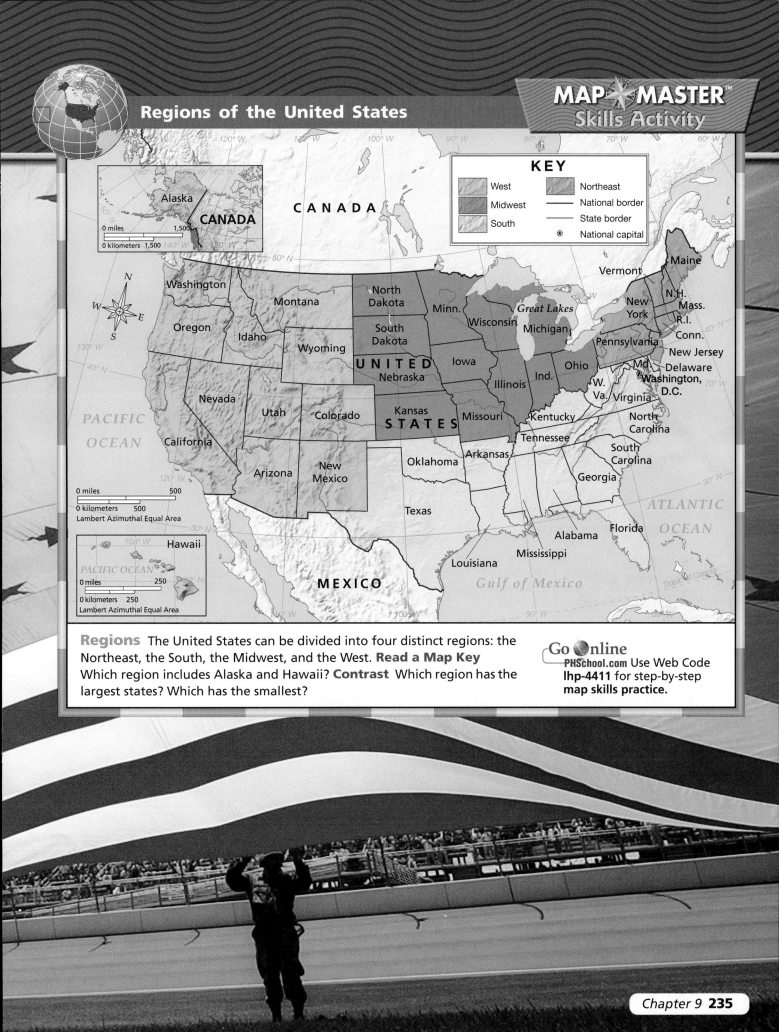

KEY

West	Northeast
Midwest	National border
South	State border
	⊛ National capital

Regions The United States can be divided into four distinct regions: the Northeast, the South, the Midwest, and the West. **Read a Map Key** Which region includes Alaska and Hawaii? **Contrast** Which region has the largest states? Which has the smallest?

Go Online
PHSchool.com Use Web Code
lhp-4411 for step-by-step
map skills practice.

Guide for Reading

This section provides an introduction to the fifty states that make up the United States.

- Look at the map on the previous page, and then read the information below to learn about each state.
- Analyze the data to compare the states.
- What are the characteristics that most of the states share?
- What are some of the key differences among the states?

Viewing the Video Overview

View the World Studies Video Overview to learn more about each of the states. As you watch, answer this question:

- What are the four major regions of the United States, and what natural resources does each region contribute to the economy of the country?

Discovery CHANNEL SCHOOL Video
Explore the geography of the United States.

Alabama

Year of Statehood	1819
Capital	Montgomery
Land Area	50,744 sq mi; 131,427 sq km
Population	4,447,100
Ethnic Group(s)	71.1% white; 26.0% African American; 1.7% Hispanic; 0.7% Asian; 0.5% Native American; 0.7% other
Agriculture	cotton, greenhouse products, peanuts
Industry	pulp, paper, chemicals, electronics

Alaska

Year of Statehood	1959
Capital	Juneau
Land Area	571,951 sq mi; 1,481,353 sq km
Population	626,932
Ethnic Group(s)	69.3% white; 15.6% Native American; 4.1% Hispanic; 4.0% Asian; 3.5% African American; 2.1% other
Agriculture	greenhouse products, barley, oats
Industry	petroleum, tourism, fishing

Geological formations of limestone, called tufa, in Mono Lake, California

Arizona

Year of Statehood	1912
Capital	Phoenix
Land Area	113,635 sq mi; 294,315 sq km
Population	5,130,632
Ethnic Group(s)	75.5% white; 25.3% Hispanic; 5.0% Native American; 3.1% African American; 1.8% Asian; 11.7% other
Agriculture	cotton, lettuce, cauliflower
Industry	manufacturing, construction, tourism

Arkansas

Year of Statehood	1836
Capital	Little Rock
Land Area	52,068 sq mi; 134,856 sq km
Population	2,673,400
Ethnic Group(s)	80.0% white; 15.7% African American; 3.2% Hispanic; 0.8% Asian; 0.8% Native American; 1.6% other
Agriculture	poultry, cattle, rice, soybeans
Industry	manufacturing, agriculture, tourism, forestry

California

Year of Statehood	1850
Capital	Sacramento
Land Area	155,959 sq mi; 403,934 sq km
Population	33,871,648
Ethnic Group(s)	59.5% white; 32.4% Hispanic; 10.9% Asian; 6.7% African American; 1.0% Native American; 17.1% other
Agriculture	poultry, cattle, milk
Industry	agriculture, tourism, apparel

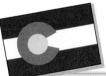

Colorado

Year of Statehood	1876
Capital	Denver
Land Area	103,718 sq mi; 268,630 sq km
Population	4,301,261
Ethnic Group(s)	82.8% white; 17.1% Hispanic; 3.8% African American; 2.2% Asian; 1.0% Native American; 7.3% other
Agriculture	poultry, cattle, corn, wheat
Industry	manufacturing, construction

Introducing The United States

Connecticut

Year of Statehood	1788
Capital	Hartford
Land Area	4,845 sq mi; 12,549 sq km
Population	3,405,565
Ethnic Group(s)	81.6% white; 9.1% African American; 9.4% Hispanic; 2.4% Asian; 0.3% Native American; 4.3% other
Agriculture	nursery stock, mushrooms, vegetables, sweet corn
Industry	manufacturing, retail trade, government

Delaware

Year of Statehood	1787
Capital	Dover
Land Area	1,954 sq mi; 5,061 sq km
Population	783,600
Ethnic Group(s)	74.6% white; 19.2% African American; 4.8% Hispanic; 2.1% Asian; 0.3% Native American
Agriculture	poultry, soybeans, potatoes, corn
Industry	chemicals, agriculture, finance

An alligator at Everglades National Park, Florida

Florida

Year of Statehood	1845
Capital	Tallahassee
Land Area	53,927 sq mi; 139,671 sq km
Population	15,982,378
Ethnic Group(s)	78.0% white; 16.8% Hispanic; 14.6% African American; 1.7% Asian; 0.3% Native American; 3.1% other
Agriculture	poultry, cattle, citrus fruits
Industry	tourism, agriculture, manufacturing

Georgia

Year of Statehood	1788
Capital	Atlanta
Land Area	57,906 sq mi; 149,977 sq km
Population	8,186,453
Ethnic Group(s)	65.1% white; 28.7% African American; 5.3% Hispanic; 2.1% Asian; 0.3% Native American; 2.5% other
Agriculture	poultry, cattle, peanuts, cotton
Industry	services, manufacturing, retail trade

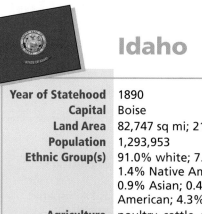

Hawaii

Year of Statehood	1959
Capital	Honolulu
Land Area	6,423 sq mi; 16,636 sq km
Population	1,211,537
Ethnic Group(s)	41.6% Asian; 24.3% white; 9.4% Native Hawaiian or Pacific Islander; 7.2% Hispanic; 1.8% African American; 0.3% Native American; 1.3% other
Agriculture	sugar, pineapples
Industry	tourism, defense, sugar

Idaho

Year of Statehood	1890
Capital	Boise
Land Area	82,747 sq mi; 214,315 sq km
Population	1,293,953
Ethnic Group(s)	91.0% white; 7.9% Hispanic; 1.4% Native American; 0.9% Asian; 0.4% African American; 4.3% other
Agriculture	poultry, cattle, potatoes
Industry	manufacturing, agriculture, tourism

Illinois

Year of Statehood	1818
Capital	Springfield
Land Area	55,584 sq mi; 143,963 sq km
Population	12,419,293
Ethnic Group(s)	73.5% white; 15.1% African American; 12.3% Hispanic; 3.4% Asian; 0.2% Native American; 5.8% other
Agriculture	livestock, corn, soybeans, wheat
Industry	services, manufacturing, travel

Indiana

Year of Statehood	1816
Capital	Indianapolis
Land Area	35,867 sq mi; 92,896 sq km
Population	6,080,485
Ethnic Group(s)	87.5% white; 8.4% African American; 3.5% Hispanic; 1.0% Asian; 0.3% Native American; 1.6% other
Agriculture	livestock, corn, soybeans, wheat
Industry	manufacturing, services, agriculture

Iowa

Year of Statehood	1846
Capital	Des Moines
Land Area	55,869 sq mi; 144,701 sq km
Population	2,926,324
Ethnic Group(s)	93.9% white; 2.8% Hispanic; 2.1% African American; 1.3% Asian; 0.3% Native American; 1.3% other
Agriculture	livestock, poultry, grain, corn
Industry	agriculture, communications, construction

Winner of the Indianapolis 500 race in Indiana

Introducing **The United States**

Kansas

Year of Statehood	1861
Capital	Topeka
Land Area	81,815 sq mi; 211,901 sq km
Population	2,688,418
Ethnic Group(s)	86.1% white; 7.0% Hispanic; 5.7% African American; 1.7% Asian; 0.9% Native American; 3.4% other
Agriculture	livestock, poultry, wheat, sorghum
Industry	manufacturing, finance, insurance

Kentucky

Year of Statehood	1792
Capital	Frankfort
Land Area	39,728 sq mi; 10,896 sq km
Population	4,041,769
Ethnic Group(s)	90.1% white; 7.3% African American; 1.5% Hispanic; 0.7% Asian; 0.2% Native American; 0.6% other
Agriculture	poultry, cattle, tobacco, corn
Industry	manufacturing, services, finance

Louisiana

Year of Statehood	1812
Capital	Baton Rouge
Land Area	43,562 sq mi; 112,826 sq km
Population	4,468,976
Ethnic Group(s)	63.9% white; 32.5% African American; 2.4% Hispanic; 1.2% Asian; 0.6% Native American; 0.7% other
Agriculture	poultry, soybeans, sugar cane
Industry	wholesale and retail trade, tourism

Maine

Year of Statehood	1820
Capital	Augusta
Land Area	30,862 sq mi; 76,933 sq km
Population	1,274,923
Ethnic Group(s)	96.9% white; 0.7% Asian; 0.7% Hispanic; 0.6% Native American; 0.5% African American; 0.2% other
Agriculture	poultry, potatoes, aquaculture
Industry	manufacturing, agriculture, fishing

Maryland

Year of Statehood	1788
Capital	Annapolis
Land Area	9,774 sq mi; 25,315 sq km
Population	5,296,486
Ethnic Group(s)	64.0% white; 27.9% African American; 4.3% Hispanic; 4.0% Asian; 0.3% Native American; 1.8% other
Agriculture	poultry, greenhouse and nursery products
Industry	manufacturing, biotechnology

Massachusetts

Year of Statehood	1788
Capital	Boston
Land Area	7,840 sq mi; 20,306 sq km
Population	6,349,097
Ethnic Group(s)	84.5% white; 6.8% Hispanic; 5.4% African American; 3.8% Asian; 0.2% Native American; 3.7% other
Agriculture	cranberries, greenhouse products, vegetables
Industry	services, trade, manufacturing

Michigan

Year of Statehood	1837
Capital	Lansing
Land Area	56,804 sq mi; 147,122 sq km
Population	9,938,444
Ethnic Group(s)	80.2% white; 14.2% African American; 3.3% Hispanic; 1.8% Asian; 0.6% Native American; 1.3% other
Agriculture	poultry, corn, wheat, soybeans
Industry	manufacturing, services, tourism, agriculture

Minnesota

Year of Statehood	1858
Capital	St. Paul
Land Area	79,610 sq mi; 206,190 sq km
Population	4,919,479
Ethnic Group(s)	89.4% white; 3.5% African American; 2.9% Asian; 2.9% Hispanic; 1.1% Native American; 1.3% other
Agriculture	livestock, poultry, corn, soybeans
Industry	agribusiness, forest products, mining

Mississippi

Year of Statehood	1817
Capital	Jackson
Land Area	46,907 sq mi; 121,489 sq km
Population	2,844,658
Ethnic Group(s)	61.4% white; 36.3% African American; 1.4% Hispanic; 0.7% Asian; 0.4% Native American; 0.5% other
Agriculture	cattle, poultry, cotton, rice
Industry	warehousing/distribution, services

Missouri

Year of Statehood	1821
Capital	Jefferson City
Land Area	68,886 sq mi; 178,415 sq km
Population	5,595,211
Ethnic Group(s)	84.9% white; 11.2% African American; 2.1% Hispanic; 1.1% Asian; 0.4% Native American; 0.9% other
Agriculture	livestock, poultry, soybeans, corn
Industry	agriculture, manufacturing, aerospace

Detroit, Michigan

Introducing The United States

Horses grazing in Montana

Montana

Year of Statehood	1889
Capital	Helena
Land Area	145,552 sq mi; 376,980 sq km
Population	902,195
Ethnic Group(s)	90.6% white; 6.2% Native American; 2.0% Hispanic; 0.5% Asian; 0.3% African American; 0.7% other
Agriculture	cattle, wheat, barley, sugar beets
Industry	agriculture, timber, mining, tourism

Nebraska

Year of Statehood	1867
Capital	Lincoln
Land Area	76,872 sq mi; 199,098 sq km
Population	1,711,263
Ethnic Group(s)	89.6% white; 5.5% Hispanic; 4.0% African American; 1.3% Asian; 0.9% Native American; 2.8% other
Agriculture	livestock, poultry, corn, sorghum
Industry	agriculture, manufacturing

Nevada

Year of Statehood	1864
Capital	Carson City
Land Area	109,826 sq mi; 284,449 sq km
Population	1,998,257
Ethnic Group(s)	75.2% white; 19.7% Hispanic; 6.8% African American; 4.5% Asian; 1.3% Native American; 8.4% other
Agriculture	hay, alfalfa seed, potatoes
Industry	tourism, mining, manufacturing

New Hampshire

Year of Statehood	1788
Capital	Concord
Land Area	8,968 sq mi; 23,227 sq km
Population	1,235,786
Ethnic Group(s)	96.0% white; 1.7% Hispanic; 1.3% Asian; 0.7% African American; 0.2% Native American; 0.6% other
Agriculture	dairy products, nursery and greenhouse products
Industry	tourism, manufacturing

New Jersey

Year of Statehood	1787
Capital	Trenton
Land Area	7,417 sq mi; 19,210 sq km
Population	8,414,350
Ethnic Group(s)	72.6% white; 13.6% African American; 13.3% Hispanic; 5.7% Asian; 0.2% Native American; 5.4% other
Agriculture	poultry, nursery and greenhouse products, tomatoes
Industry	pharmaceuticals, telecommunications

New Mexico

Year of Statehood	1912
Capital	Santa Fe
Land Area	121,356 sq mi; 314,312 sq km
Population	1,819,046
Ethnic Group(s)	66.8% white; 42.1% Hispanic; 9.5% Native American; 1.9% African American; 1.1% Asian; 17.1% other
Agriculture	cattle, hay, onions, chilies
Industry	government, services, trade

New York

Year of Statehood	1788
Capital	Albany
Land Area	47,214 sq mi; 122,284 sq km
Population	18,976,457
Ethnic Group(s)	67.9% white; 15.9% African American; 15.1% Hispanic; 5.5% Asian; 0.4% Native American; 7.1% other
Agriculture	cattle, poultry, apples, grapes
Industry	manufacturing, finance, communications

North Carolina

Year of Statehood	1789
Capital	Raleigh
Land Area	48,711 sq mi; 126,161 sq km
Population	8,049,313
Ethnic Group(s)	72.1% white; 21.6% African American; 4.7% Hispanic; 1.2% Native American; 2.3% other
Agriculture	livestock, poultry, tobacco, cotton
Industry	manufacturing, agriculture, tourism

The Exploris museum in Raleigh, North Carolina

Introducing **The United States**

North Dakota

Year of Statehood	1889
Capital	Bismarck
Land Area	68,976 sq mi; 178,648 sq km
Population	642,200
Ethnic Group(s)	92.5% white; 4.9% Native American; 1.2% Hispanic; 0.6% African American; 0.6% Asian; 0.4% other
Agriculture	cattle, spring wheat, durum, barley
Industry	agriculture, mining, tourism

Ohio

Year of Statehood	1803
Capital	Columbus
Land Area	40,948 sq mi; 106,055 sq km
Population	11,353,140
Ethnic Group(s)	85.0% white; 11.5% African American; 1.9% Hispanic; 1.2% Asian; 0.2% Native American; 0.8% other
Agriculture	livestock, poultry, corn, hay
Industry	manufacturing, trade, services

Oklahoma

Year of Statehood	1907
Capital	Oklahoma City
Land Area	68,667 sq mi; 177,848 sq km
Population	3,450,654
Ethnic Group(s)	76.2% white; 7.9% Native American; 7.6% African American; 5.2% Hispanic; 1.4% Asian; 4.6% other
Agriculture	livestock, poultry, wheat, cotton
Industry	manufacturing, mineral and energy exploration

Oregon

Year of Statehood	1859
Capital	Salem
Land Area	95,997 sq mi; 248,632 sq km
Population	3,421,399
Ethnic Group(s)	86.6% white; 8.0% Hispanic; 1.6% African American; 3.0% Asian; 1.3% Native American; 4.4% other
Agriculture	cattle, poultry, greenhouse products
Industry	manufacturing, services, trade, finance

Pennsylvania

Year of Statehood	1787
Capital	Harrisburg
Land Area	44,817 sq mi; 116,076 sq km
Population	12,281,054
Ethnic Group(s)	85.4% white; 10.0% African American; 3.2% Hispanic; 1.8% Asian; 0.1% Native American; 1.5% other
Agriculture	livestock, poultry, corn, hay
Industry	agribusiness, manufacturing, health care

Rhode Island

Year of Statehood	1790
Capital	Providence
Land Area	1,045 sq mi; 2,707 sq km
Population	1,048,319
Ethnic Group(s)	85.0% white; 8.7% Hispanic; 4.5% African American; 2.3% Asian; 0.5% Native American; 5.1% other
Agriculture	nursery products, turf, vegetables
Industry	services, manufacturing

South Carolina

Year of Statehood	1788
Capital	Columbia
Land Area	30,109 sq mi; 77,982 sq km
Population	4,012,012
Ethnic Group(s)	67.2% white; 29.5% African American; 2.4% Hispanic; 0.9% Asian; 0.3% Native American; 1.0% other
Agriculture	poultry, tobacco, cotton, soybeans
Industry	tourism, agriculture, manufacturing

South Dakota

Year of Statehood	1889
Capital	Pierre
Land Area	75,885 sq mi; 196,542 sq km
Population	754,844
Ethnic Group(s)	88.7% white; 8.3% Native American; 1.4% Hispanic; 0.6% African American; 0.6% Asian; 0.5% other
Agriculture	livestock, poultry, corn, soybeans
Industry	agriculture, services, manufacturing

Congaree Swamp National Monument, South Carolina

Tennessee

Year of Statehood	1796
Capital	Nashville
Land Area	41,217 sq mi; 106,752 sq km
Population	5,689,283
Ethnic Group(s)	80.2% white; 16.4% African American; 2.2% Hispanic; 1.0% Asian; 0.3% Native American; 1.0% other
Agriculture	cattle, poultry, tobacco, cotton
Industry	manufacturing, trade, services

Texas

Year of Statehood	1845
Capital	Austin
Land Area	261,797 sq mi; 678,054 sq km
Population	20,851,820
Ethnic Group(s)	71.0% white; 32.0% Hispanic; 11.5% African American; 2.7% Asian; 0.6% Native American; 11.8% other
Agriculture	livestock, poultry, cotton
Industry	manufacturing, trade, oil and gas extraction

Introducing The United States

Utah

Year of Statehood	1896
Capital	Salt Lake City
Land Area	82,144 sq mi; 212,753 sq km
Population	2,233,169
Ethnic Group(s)	89.2% white; 9.0% Hispanic; 1.7% Asian; 1.3% Native American; 0.8% African American; 4.9% other
Agriculture	poultry, hay, corn, wheat, barley
Industry	services, trade, manufacturing

Vermont

Year of Statehood	1791
Capital	Montpelier
Land Area	9,250 sq mi; 23,958 sq km
Population	608,827
Ethnic Group(s)	96.8% white; 0.9% Asian; 0.5% African American; 0.4% Native American; 1.2% other
Agriculture	dairy products, apples, maple syrup
Industry	manufacturing, tourism, agriculture

Rower in Seattle, Washington

Virginia

Year of Statehood	1788
Capital	Richmond
Land Area	39,594 sq mi; 102,548 sq km
Population	7,078,515
Ethnic Group(s)	72.3% white; 19.6% African American; 0.7% Hispanic; 3.7% Asian; 0.3% Native American; 0.1% Native Hawaiian or Pacific Islander; 2.0% other
Agriculture	cattle, poultry, tobacco
Industry	services, trade, government

Washington

Year of Statehood	1889
Capital	Olympia
Land Area	66,544 sq mi; 172,349 sq km
Population	5,894,121
Ethnic Group(s)	81.8% white; 7.5% Hispanic; 5.5% Asian; 3.2% African American; 1.6% Native American; 4.3% other
Agriculture	cattle, poultry, apples, potatoes
Industry	technology, aerospace, biotechnology

West Virginia

Year of Statehood	1863
Capital	Charleston
Land Area	24,078 sq mi; 62,362 sq km
Population	1,808,344
Ethnic Group(s)	95.0% white; 3.2% African American; 0.7% Hispanic; 0.5% Asian; 0.2% Native American; 0.2% other
Agriculture	apples, peaches, hay, tobacco
Industry	manufacturing, services, mining

Wisconsin

Year of Statehood	1848
Capital	Madison
Land Area	54,310 sq mi; 140,663 sq km
Population	5,363,675
Ethnic Group(s)	88.9% white; 5.7% African American; 3.6% Hispanic; 1.7% Asian; 0.9% Native American; 1.6% other
Agriculture	cattle, poultry, corn, hay
Industry	services, manufacturing, trade

Wyoming

Year of Statehood	1890
Capital	Cheyenne
Land Area	97,100 sq mi; 251,489 sq km
Population	493,782
Ethnic Group(s)	92.1% white; 6.4% Hispanic; 2.3% Native American; 0.8% African American; 0.6% Asian; 2.6% other
Agriculture	cattle, wheat, beans, barley
Industry	mineral extraction, oil, natural gas, tourism and recreation

SOURCE: U.S. Census; *World Almanac,* 2003
Note: Percentages may not total 100% due to rounding. The Hispanic population may be any race and is dispersed among racial categories.

Wisconsin dairy farm

Assessment

Comprehension and Critical Thinking

1. Compare and Contrast Compare the physical sizes and the population sizes of California and Rhode Island.

2. Draw Conclusions Are there characteristics that most of the states share? Explain.

3. Compare and Contrast What are some key differences among the states?

4. Categorize What are the major products of the South and the Midwest?

5. Make Generalizations Based on the data, make a generalization about industry in the United States.

6. Make a Timeline Create a timeline showing the year of statehood for 15 states.

Keeping Current

Access the **DK World Desk Reference Online** at **PHSchool.com** for up-to-date information about the United States.

Web Code: lhe-4401

The Northeast
An Urban Center

Prepare to Read

Objectives

In this section, you will
1. Learn how the large cities of the Northeast contribute to the economy of the United States.
2. Find out how the Northeast has been a port of entry for many immigrants.

Taking Notes

As you read this section, look for details about Boston, Philadelphia, and New York City. Copy the chart below, and record your findings in it.

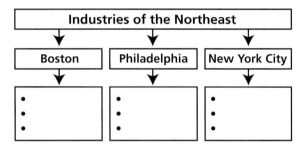

Industries of the Northeast

Boston	Philadelphia	New York City
• • •	• • •	• • •

Target Reading Skill

Compare and Contrast
Comparing and contrasting can help you sort out and analyze information. When you compare, you examine the similarities between things. When you contrast, you look at the differences between things. As you read this section, compare and contrast the large cities of the Northeast.

Key Terms

- **commute** (kuh MYOOT) *v.* to travel to work
- **megalopolis** (meg uh LAHP uh lis) *n.* a number of cities and suburbs that blend into one very large urban area
- **population density** (pahp yuh LAY shun DEN suh tee) *n.* the average number of people per square mile or square kilometer

Rush hour in a New York City subway station

For more than a century, life in New York City has been crowded. One hundred years ago, horse-drawn carriages caused traffic jams. Today, more than 3 million riders squeeze into New York's subway cars every day. Others travel the many miles of bus lines or catch one of the city's 12,000 taxis. And many people drive their own cars through the city's busy streets.

New York City is not unique. Washington, D.C., Boston, Massachusetts, and Philadelphia, Pennsylvania, are also crowded. In these big cities, thousands of people **commute,** or travel to work, each day. Many drive to work from suburbs that are far from the city's center. Even people who live in the city must travel from one area to another to work.

A Region of Cities

A nearly unbroken chain of cities runs from Boston to New York to Washington, D.C. This coastal region of the Northeast is a megalopolis (meg uh LAHP uh lis). A **megalopolis** is a region where the cities and suburbs have grown so close together that they form one big urban area. Find this area on the map below.

The Northeast is the most densely populated region of the United States. **Population density** is the average number of people per square mile (or square kilometer). The population density of New Jersey is 10 times greater than the density of Kentucky.

The Northeast's economy is based on its cities. Many were founded in colonial times, along rivers or near the Atlantic Ocean. These cities began as transportation and trade centers. Today, manufacturing, finance, communications, and government employ millions of urban northeasterners.

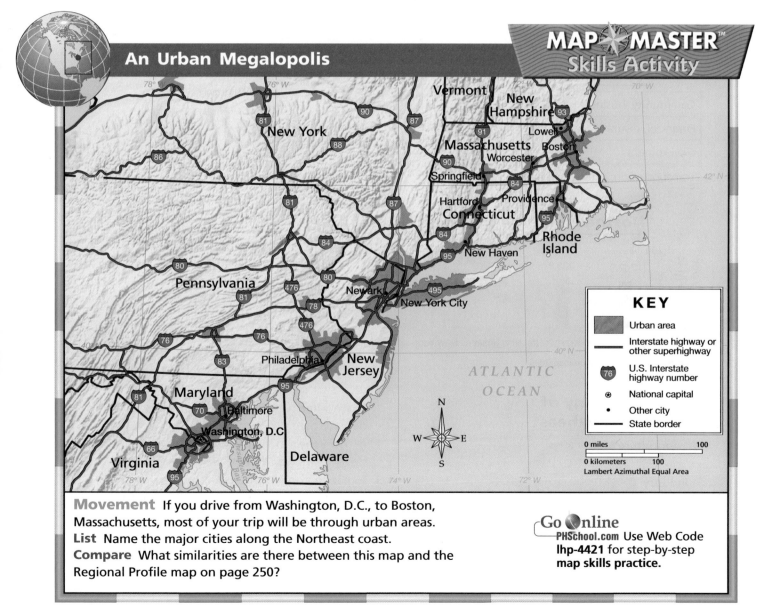

An Urban Megalopolis

MAP MASTER™
Skills Activity

KEY

- Urban area
- Interstate highway or other superhighway
- U.S. Interstate highway number
- National capital
- Other city
- State border

0 miles 100
0 kilometers 100
Lambert Azimuthal Equal Area

Movement If you drive from Washington, D.C., to Boston, Massachusetts, most of your trip will be through urban areas.
List Name the major cities along the Northeast coast.
Compare What similarities are there between this map and the Regional Profile map on page 250?

Go Online
PHSchool.com Use Web Code
lhp-4421 for step-by-step
map skills practice.

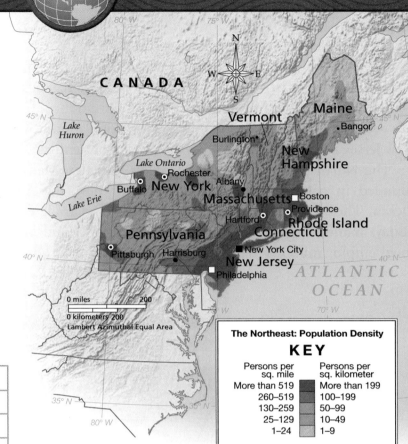

The Northeast

Although it is the nation's smallest region, the Northeast is the most heavily populated region in the United States. It has many large and old cities. New York is the center of international trade and finance, while Philadelphia was the birthplace of the Declaration of Independence and the United States Constitution. With so many people living in such a small area, services are an important part of the Northeast's economy. As you study the graphs and map, think about how population density affects an area's economy.

Types of Services

Community, business, personal
Financial, insurance, real estate
Government
Transportation, utilities, communication

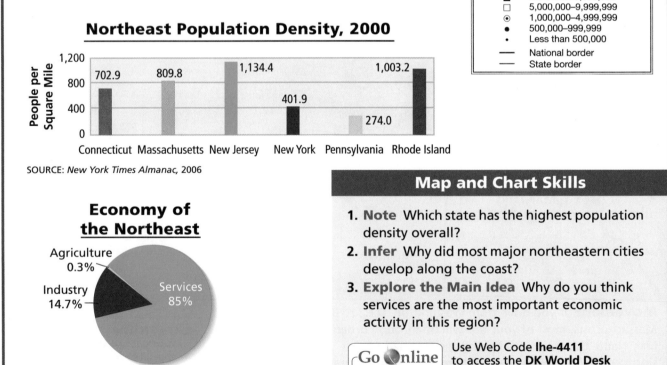

Northeast Population Density, 2000

People per Square Mile

- Connecticut: 702.9
- Massachusetts: 809.8
- New Jersey: 1,134.4
- New York: 401.9
- Pennsylvania: 274.0
- Rhode Island: 1,003.2

SOURCE: *New York Times Almanac*, 2006

Economy of the Northeast

- Agriculture 0.3%
- Industry 14.7%
- Services 85%

SOURCE: Bureau of Economic Analysis

The Northeast: Population Density

KEY

Persons per sq. mile	Persons per sq. kilometer
More than 519	More than 199
260–519	100–199
130–259	50–99
25–129	10–49
1–24	1–9

Urban Areas

- ■ More than 9,999,999
- ☐ 5,000,000–9,999,999
- ◉ 1,000,000–4,999,999
- • 500,000–999,999
- · Less than 500,000
- — National border
- — State border

Map and Chart Skills

1. **Note** Which state has the highest population density overall?
2. **Infer** Why did most major northeastern cities develop along the coast?
3. **Explore the Main Idea** Why do you think services are the most important economic activity in this region?

Go Online PHSchool.com

Use Web Code **lhe-4411** to access the **DK World Desk Reference Online.**

Boston In colonial times, the city of Boston was called the "hub of the universe." Boston remains an important city in the Northeast. It is a city filled with history. The American Revolution began when British troops marched from Boston to Concord in 1775. You can still visit buildings that date from before the American Revolution, including Paul Revere's house, which is the oldest building in the downtown area. Yet you will find that Boston is a very modern city, too.

The Boston area is known worldwide for its leading research centers, including dozens of colleges and universities. Cambridge (KAYM brij) is the home of Harvard, which was founded in 1636 and is the oldest university in the United States. Cambridge is also home to the Massachusetts Institute of Technology (MIT).

Boston is noted for its medical, science, and technology centers as well. Some of the best medical schools and hospitals in the country are located in Boston. Many medical firsts took place here, including the use of anesthesia (an es THEE zhuh) during surgery. Boston's universities and scientific companies often work together to carry out research and to design new products.

Boston's outdoor market, Haymarket, is one of the city's most famous attractions.

Philadelphia Many people consider Philadelphia to be the "cradle of the nation" because, like Boston, it was an important city in our nation's early history. It was once the capital of the country. It was in Philadelphia that America's founders wrote the Declaration of Independence and the Constitution. By the late 1700s, Philadelphia had become the political, financial, and commercial center of the nation. Home to the country's leading seaport until it was surpassed by New York's in the 1820s, Philadelphia quickly became a major shipbuilding center as well.

Today, Philadelphia is an industrial center. It is located on the Delaware River. Important land and water transportation routes pass through there. Ships, trucks, and trains bring in raw materials from other parts of Pennsylvania and from all over the world. Many factories process food, produce medical supplies, and manufacture chemicals. Hundreds of products are then shipped out for sale. In addition, Philadelphia has become a center of the health care industry, due to its several medical, dental, and pharmacology schools.

DISCOVERY CHANNEL SCHOOL Video
Learn about the Minutemen in the American Revolution.

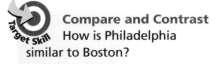
Compare and Contrast
How is Philadelphia similar to Boston?

The Skyscraper

After the Civil War, the United States grew rapidly. People streamed into the cities to fill jobs in new factories and offices. To create more office and living space, architects used new technology to build taller and taller structures. By the 1930s, the skylines of all major American cities were dominated by tall skyscrapers. The Empire State Building, shown at right, was built in 1931. At 1,252 feet (382 meters), it is the tallest skyscraper in New York City.

Rockefeller Center, New York City
Most modern skyscrapers wear a glass skin of windows.

High-speed elevators travel as fast as 1,400 feet (426 meters) a minute.

The outside of the building is covered with ten million bricks.

60,000 tons of steel were used to make the skeleton that supports the building.

About ten minutes is all it takes for the fittest runners to race up the 1,576 steps from the lobby to the 86th floor, in the Fleet Empire State Run-Up.

More than 200 steel and concrete piles support the 365,000-ton building.

Construction workers
Workers rest during the construction of New York City's Chrysler Building. Built in 1930, the building's owner hoped it would be the tallest in the world—but even taller buildings were soon built.

ANALYZING IMAGES
How does the structure of this building allow more offices in less space?

View From the Top
More than 30 million tourists visit New York City each year. Among the city's biggest tourist attractions are the theaters on 42nd Street (lower photo) and Central Park, which lies in the midst of a maze of skyscrapers (upper photo).
Identify Effects *What effect does tourism have on New York's economy?*

New York City The largest, wealthiest, and most influential city in the United States is New York City. More than 8 million people live there, making it one of the 10 largest cities in the world. The city covers an area of about 300 square miles (800 square kilometers) on islands and the mainland around the mouth of the Hudson River. Tunnels and bridges connect the various parts of the city.

New York is the center of fashion, publishing, advertising, and the arts in the United States. New York's Broadway is known for its plays and musicals, Fifth Avenue for its shopping, and Wall Street for its finance.

New York City is our nation's "money capital." About 350,000 New Yorkers work for banks and other financial institutions. The headquarters of many of the country's wealthiest corporations are in New York. The New York Stock Exchange is on Wall Street. Noted for its skyscrapers, New York City's skyline is recognized by people around the world.

On September 11, 2001, the city became a target of terrorists, who crashed two planes into the towers of the World Trade Center. The World Trade Center held government agencies and businesses that were involved in international trade. Nearly 3,000 people were killed as a result of the attack.

✓ **Reading Check** **Which city is considered the financial capital of the United States?**

Ports of Entry

Louis Waldman came to the United States in 1909, when he was seventeen years old. He landed at the Ellis Island immigration station in New York harbor:

Immigrants arrive at Ellis Island in 1920.

> **"Behind me was the bustling harbor with its innumerable boats, the sight of which made me seasick all over again. Facing me were the tall buildings of lower Manhattan, buildings which were more magnificent and higher than any I had ever imagined, even in my wildest dreams. ..."**
>
> —*Russian immigrant Louis Waldman*

From 1892 to 1954, millions of immigrants came to the United States through Ellis Island. Today, Ellis Island is a national monument.

Although New York was the main port of entry, Boston and Philadelphia were also important gateways for immigrants. In the 1700s, more German immigrants entered the country through Philadelphia than through any other port. In the 1800s, many Irish immigrants entered through both Philadelphia and Boston.

After arriving in these port cities, many immigrants stayed and built new lives. Today, all three cities are rich in ethnic diversity. To get a real sense of this ethnic diversity, just look at the names in the phonebooks of these big cities.

✓ **Reading Check** Where is Ellis Island located?

Section 1 Assessment

Key Terms

Review the key terms at the beginning of this section. Use each term in a sentence that explains its meaning.

Target Reading Skill

What are two ways that the cities of the Northeast are similar? What are two ways that they are different?

Comprehension and Critical Thinking

1. (a) Recall How many people live in New York City?

(b) Compare How does the population density of the Northeast compare with densities of other regions of the country?

(c) Cause and Effect How does population density affect the ways people live and work?

2. (a) Recall What city was the main port of entry for European immigrants in the 1800s?

(b) Identify the Main Idea Why might immigrants have chosen to live in the Northeast?

(c) Cause and Effect How have immigrants affected the culture of the Northeast?

Writing Activity

Which city described in this section are you most interested in learning more about? Make a list of things you would like to learn about this city. Then write a brief paragraph explaining why you want to learn these things.

Go Online
PHSchool.com

For: An activity on mass transit systems
Visit: PHSchool.com
Web Code: lhd-4401

Section 2
The South
The Growth of Industry

Prepare to Read

Objectives

In this section, you will
1. Learn how the South's land is important to its economy.
2. Read about how the growth of industry is changing the South.

Taking Notes

As you read this section, look for details about the growth of industry and how it has affected the economy. Copy the table below, and record your findings in it.

Industry	Products	Effects on Economy

Target Reading Skill

Use Signal Words Signal words point out relationships among ideas or events. Certain words, such as *however* or *like,* can signal a comparison or contrast. As you read this section, notice the contrast between what the South's economy was based on 50 years ago and what it is based on today. What signal words indicate the contrast?

Key Terms

- **petrochemical** (pet roh KEM ih kul) *n.* a substance such as plastic or paint that is made from petroleum
- **industrialization** (in dus tree ul ih ZAY shun) *n.* the process of building new industries in an area dominated by farming
- **Sun Belt** (sun belt) *n.* an area of the United States stretching from the southern Atlantic coast to the California coast

In 1895, at the age of fifteen, Catherine Evans Whitener had no idea that she was about to make history. Her friends and family liked the cotton bedspreads she made so much that she began to display them on her front porch in Dalton, Georgia. Her first sale earned her $2.50. After a large store placed an order for 24 bedspreads, an industry was born.

As interest in her work grew, Whitener began to train other girls to help produce the bedspreads. In 1917, she and her brother formed the Evans Manufacturing Company. Their company and others like it employed some 10,000 workers during the Great Depression. So many bedspreads were sold to travelers in the Dalton area that the highway through the town became known as "Bedspread Alley."

Catherine Evans Whitener

The Land of the South

There are many different ways that people in the South can make a living. The South's particular geography and climate make many of these jobs possible.

The region has a warm climate, and most parts of it receive plenty of rain. The wide coastal plains along the Atlantic Ocean and the Gulf of Mexico have rich soil. In addition, the South has a long growing season. There are between 200 and 290 frost-free days every year. Together, these features make much of the South an excellent place for growing crops such as cotton, rice, tobacco, and sugar cane and raising animals.

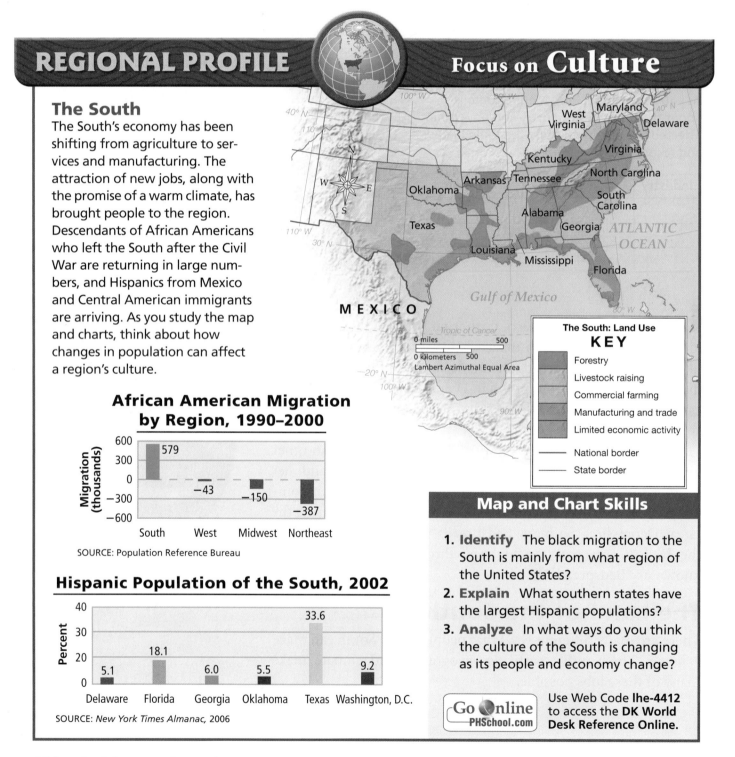

REGIONAL PROFILE

Focus on Culture

The South

The South's economy has been shifting from agriculture to services and manufacturing. The attraction of new jobs, along with the promise of a warm climate, has brought people to the region. Descendants of African Americans who left the South after the Civil War are returning in large numbers, and Hispanics from Mexico and Central American immigrants are arriving. As you study the map and charts, think about how changes in population can affect a region's culture.

The South: Land Use
KEY
- Forestry
- Livestock raising
- Commercial farming
- Manufacturing and trade
- Limited economic activity
- National border
- State border

0 miles 500
0 kilometers 500
Lambert Azimuthal Equal Area

African American Migration by Region, 1990–2000

Migration (thousands)

South	West	Midwest	Northeast
579	−43	−150	−387

SOURCE: Population Reference Bureau

Hispanic Population of the South, 2002

Percent

Delaware	Florida	Georgia	Oklahoma	Texas	Washington, D.C.
5.1	18.1	6.0	5.5	33.6	9.2

SOURCE: *New York Times Almanac,* 2006

Map and Chart Skills

1. **Identify** The black migration to the South is mainly from what region of the United States?
2. **Explain** What southern states have the largest Hispanic populations?
3. **Analyze** In what ways do you think the culture of the South is changing as its people and economy change?

Go Online
PHSchool.com

Use Web Code lhe-4412 to access the **DK World Desk Reference Online.**

Farming One of the most important parts of the South's economy is farming. For years, the South's major crop was cotton. By the 1950s, bedspread factories in Georgia alone consumed 500,000 bales of cotton every year. Many southern farmers once depended on cotton as their only source of income. Today, cotton still brings much money to the South, especially to Alabama, Mississippi, and Texas, but King Cotton no longer rules this region. In the 1890s, the boll weevil (bohl WEE vul), a kind of beetle, began to attack cotton plants in the South. Over the next 30 years, it destroyed cotton crops across the region. Without money from cotton, many farmers went bankrupt. Today, most southern farmers raise more than one crop.

Growing Conditions Some of these crops need special growing conditions. Citrus fruits require year-round warmth and sunshine. Florida has plenty of both. More oranges, tangerines, grapefruits, and limes are grown here than in any other state. Rice needs warm, moist growing conditions. Farmers in Arkansas, Louisiana, and Mississippi take advantage of their climate by growing rice along the coast of the Gulf of Mexico and in the Mississippi River valley.

Agricultural Products Some areas of the South have become famous for their agricultural products. Georgia has taken one of its products as its nickname—the Peach State. Georgia is also known for its peanut and pecan crops. Texans raise more cattle than do farmers in any other state. All of these items are just a sample of the diversity of southern agriculture.

The Cotton Crop
Although cotton (below) is no longer the South's major crop, it is still important to the region's economy. **Identify Effects** *How did boll weevils (above) affect the South's economy and way of farming?*

Offshore Drilling
The rig provides a platform for oil drilling in the Gulf of Mexico. **Draw Conclusions** *Why is drilling for oil an important industry in the South?*

Drilling and Mining In some parts of the South, what is under the soil is as important as what grows in it. In Louisiana, Oklahoma, and Texas, companies drill for oil and natural gas. These can be used as fuel and made into **petrochemicals,** which are substances, such as plastics, paint, nylon, and asphalt, that come from petroleum. In Alabama, Kentucky, West Virginia, and Tennessee, miners dig for coal. Southern states are leading producers of minerals such as salt, sulfur, and zinc. The South also produces many important building materials, including crushed stone, construction sand and gravel, and cement.

Fishing and Forestry Many people in the South make a living in fishing and forestry. The Chesapeake Bay area of Maryland and Virginia is famous for its shellfish, including clams, crabs, and scallops. Mississippi leads the nation in catfish farming. However, the South's fishing industry is strongest in Louisiana, Texas, and Florida. The timber industry is active in most of the southern states. Softwood trees like southern pine are turned into lumber or paper. People use hardwood trees to make furniture. North Carolina has the nation's largest hardwood furniture industry.

✓ **Reading Check** **Name two kinds of crops that need special growing conditions.**

Southern Cities and Industries

Some people still think of the South as it was in the early 1900s—a slow-moving, mostly rural region. But over the past 50 years, this region has gone through many changes. Although the South's rural areas are still important to its economy, most people in the South today live in cities. Some work in factories or in high-technology firms. Others work in tourism or in one of the other service industries in this region's growing economy. This change from an agriculture-based economy to an industry-based economy is called **industrialization.**

Textiles One of the most important industries in the South is the textile industry. Textile mills make cloth. They were originally built in this region to use the South's cotton. Today, many mills still make cotton cloth. Others now make cloth from synthetic, or human-made, materials. The textile industry is strongest in Georgia, the Carolinas, and Virginia.

Technology One expanding set of industries is in the field of high technology, or very specialized, complex technology. For example, workers develop computers and other electronics and figure out better ways to use them. Some centers of high technology are Raleigh-Durham, North Carolina, and Austin, Texas.

Another high-technology industry is the aerospace business. In Cape Canaveral, Florida, Houston, Texas, and Huntsville, Alabama, people work for the National Aeronautics and Space Administration (NASA). Some people train as astronauts, while others run the space shuttle program. Atlanta, Georgia, is now a center for the cable television industry.

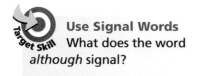
Use Signal Words
Target Skill What does the word *although* signal?

Space Camp
Every year, people attend United States Space Camp in Huntsville, Alabama. As one student (left) sits in the cockpit of a space shuttle, other students (right) experiment with the feeling of being in outer space. **Analyze Images** *How do these photographs reflect the high-technology industry?*

Transportation and Tourism A big part of the South's economy depends on moving goods and people into and out of the region. Most of the South's largest cities play important roles in this transportation industry. Miami, Florida, and New Orleans, Louisiana, are major ports. Miami is a center for goods and people going to and from Central and South America. New Orleans is a gateway between the Gulf of Mexico and the Mississippi River system. It is also an important port for oil tankers.

Some of the people the transportation industry brings to the South come to stay. Thousands come to work in the South's new industries. Thousands more choose to move to the South because of its climate. The South is part of the Sun Belt. The **Sun Belt** is the broad area of the United States that stretches from the southern Atlantic coast to the coast of California. It is known for its warm weather. The population of the Sun Belt has been rising for the past few decades. Some arrivals are older adults who want to retire to places without cold, snowy winters. Others come to take advantage of both the weather and the work that the Sun Belt offers.

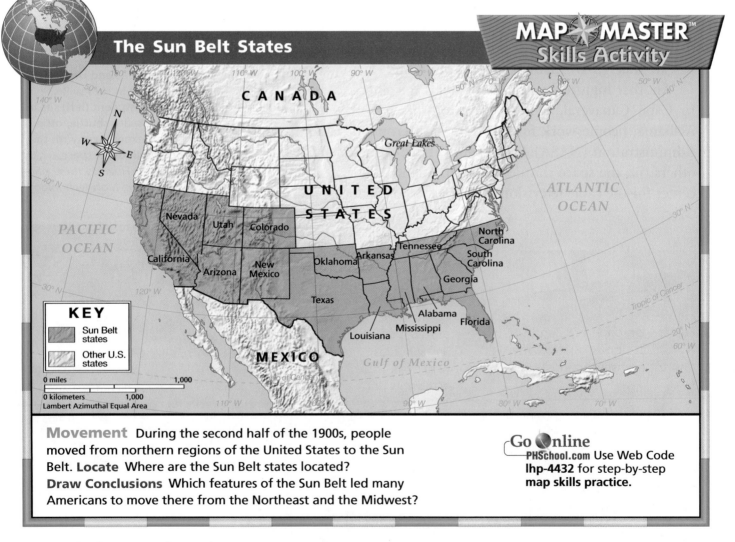

The Sun Belt States

MAP MASTER Skills Activity

KEY
Sun Belt states
Other U.S. states

0 miles 1,000
0 kilometers 1,000
Lambert Azimuthal Equal Area

Movement During the second half of the 1900s, people moved from northern regions of the United States to the Sun Belt. **Locate** Where are the Sun Belt states located?
Draw Conclusions Which features of the Sun Belt led many Americans to move there from the Northeast and the Midwest?

Go Online
PHSchool.com Use Web Code
lhp-4432 for step-by-step map skills practice.

Warm weather also brings to the South people who only plan to visit. These people fuel the region's tourist industry. In winter, tourists flock to the sunny beaches of Florida and the Gulf Coast. In the summer, they hike in the mountains of the Appalachians and Ozarks. Southern historic cities such as Charleston, South Carolina, or New Orleans, Louisiana, draw tourists at any time of the year. In states throughout the South, there are always fun and exciting things to see and to do.

The Nation's Capital The city of Washington is not in a state. Instead, it is in the District of Columbia, which lies between the states of Maryland and Virginia. This area of land was chosen in 1790 as the site for the nation's capital. Located on the shore of the Potomac River, Washington, D.C., is a planned city. Many people consider Washington to be one of the most beautiful cities in the world. It has wide avenues, grand public buildings, and dramatic monuments, including the Supreme Court, the Library of Congress, the Washington Monument, and the Lincoln Memorial. The city's major avenues are named after the states. As the nation's capital, Washington is home to the nation's leaders and to hundreds of foreign diplomats.

Tourists on a paddleboat near the Jefferson Memorial in Washington, D.C.

✓ **Reading Check** **Where is the city of Washington located?**

Section 2 Assessment

Key Terms
Review the key terms at the beginning of this section. Use each term in a sentence that explains its meaning.

Target Reading Skill
Review the section Fishing and Forestry on page 258. Find the word that signals contrast in relation to the fishing industry.

Comprehension and Critical Thinking
1. (a) List Name five of the southern states.
(b) Draw Conclusions How have the geography and climate of the South shaped its economy?

(c) Summarize In what ways has the South's economy changed since the 1800s?
2. (a) Recall Why has the population of the Sun Belt been increasing?
(b) Explain Why have many people in the South moved from rural to urban areas?
(c) Identify Cause and Effect How has the South's economy affected this population growth?

Writing Activity
Suppose that you work in an advertising firm in Atlanta, Georgia; Houston, Texas; or Miami, Florida. Create an advertisement persuading people to move to your city or state. It can be designed for a newspaper or a magazine. It can also be for radio, television, or the Internet.

Go Online
PHSchool.com

For: An activity on oil
Visit: PHSchool.com
Web Code: lhd-4402

Chris walked across the playground with his new friend Kyung, who had just moved to Florida from Korea. Kyung looked up at the sun.

"It's really hot here. Does the entire United States get weather like this?"

"Let me think," said Chris. "In the Northwest it rains a lot, and I don't think it gets quite as hot as here. Arizona and New Mexico do, for sure. The Midwest has some really hot summers but freezing-cold winters. And then there's arctic Alaska—the summers don't get too hot there, even though the sun shines all night long. The United States gets a lot of different weather."

Boston meteorologist Mish Michaels

Meteorologists collect an amazing variety of weather information from all over the country. One way they present data on temperatures, rainfall, and other weather information is to put it into graphs.

Learn the Skill

Follow the steps below to learn how to read and interpret a circle graph.

1 **Study the elements of the circle graph.** Read the title of the graph and all the labels. Make sure that you understand the purpose of the graph.

2 **Study the information shown in the graph.** The full circle represents 100 percent, or all, of something. Identify what the circle represents.

3 **Compare the portions within the graph.** Each division of the circle represents a certain percentage, or portion, of the whole. The portions should always add up to 100 percent. Notice which piece is the biggest—that is, the highest percentage. Which piece is the smallest?

4 **Draw conclusions from the graph.** Draw conclusions about the topic of the graph. Your conclusion should attempt to explain any differences or similarities in the sizes of the pieces of the circle.

Practice the Skill

Refer to the circle graph on the right and follow the steps for interpreting it.

 After reading the title and labels of the graph, what do you think is its purpose?

 What does the full circle represent—the circle is 100 percent of what?

3 What does each colored portion of the graph represent? Which is the largest portion? Which is the smallest portion?

4 Write a conclusion statement about the graph. Explain the meaning of the differences in the sizes of the portions.

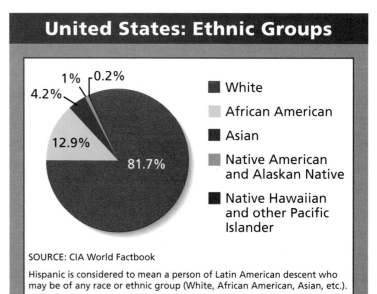

United States: Ethnic Groups

1% 0.2%
4.2%
12.9%
81.7%

■ White
■ African American
■ Asian
■ Native American and Alaskan Native
■ Native Hawaiian and other Pacific Islander

SOURCE: CIA World Factbook

Hispanic is considered to mean a person of Latin American descent who may be of any race or ethnic group (White, African American, Asian, etc.).

Major Religions

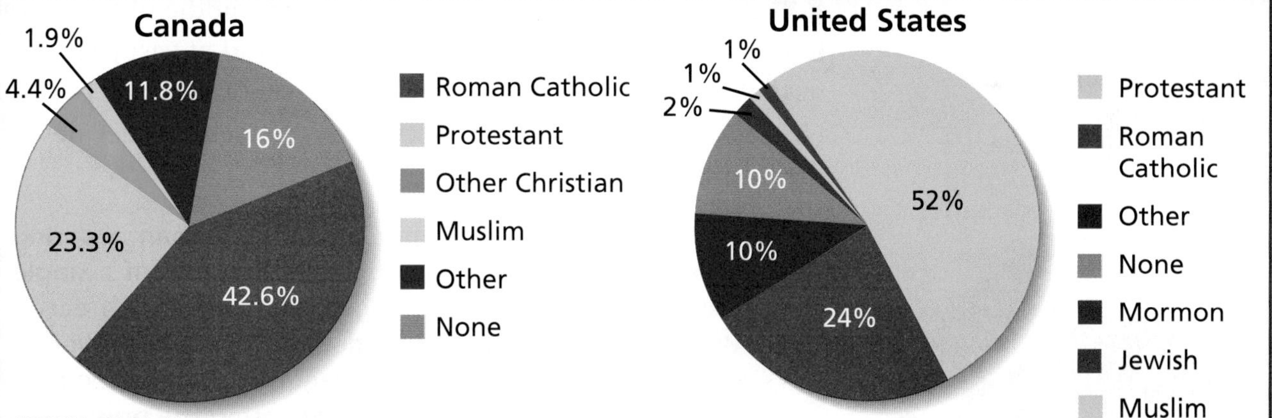

Canada

1.9%
4.4% 11.8%
16%
23.3%
42.6%

■ Roman Catholic
■ Protestant
■ Other Christian
■ Muslim
■ Other
■ None

United States

1%
1%
2%
10%
10%
52%
24%

■ Protestant
■ Roman Catholic
■ Other
■ None
■ Mormon
■ Jewish
■ Muslim

SOURCE: CIA World Factbook

Apply the Skill

Study the two circle graphs above. Following the steps in this skill, write a conclusion statement about each graph. Then compare the graphs and write a conclusion about their similarities and differences.

The Midwest
Leaving the Farm

Prepare to Read

Objectives

In this section, you will

1. Read about how technology is changing life on farms.
2. Learn how changes in farming are affecting the development of cities.

Taking Notes

As you read this section, look for details that show how changes in agriculture have caused cities to grow. Copy the chart below, and record your findings in it.

CAUSES	EVENT	EFFECTS
•	Changes in agriculture	•
•		•
•		•

Target Reading Skill

Identify Contrasts When you contrast two or more situations, you examine how they differ. In this section you will read about family farms and corporate farms. Although they both rely on technology, they differ in how they use it. As you read, list all of the differences between family farms and corporate farms.

Key Terms

- **mixed-crop farm** (mikst krahp fahrm) *n.* a farm that grows several different kinds of crops
- **recession** (rih SESH un) *n.* a decline in business activity and economic prosperity
- **corporate farm** (KAWR puh rit fahrm) *n.* a large farm that is run by a corporation, or an agricultural company

Present-day harvesting machines (below) work the land much faster than horse-driven plows once did (bottom).

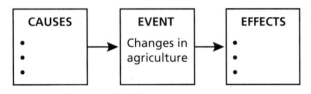

Nebraska is one of several states in the middle of the country that make up the Midwest. Nebraska is a land of vast prairies and fertile farmland. Willa Cather's 1913 novel *O Pioneers!* is set on a Nebraska farm. A daughter of pioneers herself, Cather describes the farmland in great detail:

> **There are few scenes more gratifying than a spring plowing in that country, where the furrows of a single field often lie a mile in length, and the brown earth, with such a strong, clean smell, and such a power of growth . . . in it, yields itself eagerly to the plow; rolls away from the shear, not even dimming the brightness of the metal, with a soft, deep sigh of happiness. . . . The grain is so heavy that it bends toward the blade and cuts like velvet.**
>
> —*Willa Cather,* O Pioneers!

Farming in the Midwest has changed since Cather's time. Tractors have replaced horse-drawn farm equipment. Electricity and roads have been brought out to rural farms. Today, technology continues to change the way people farm the land.

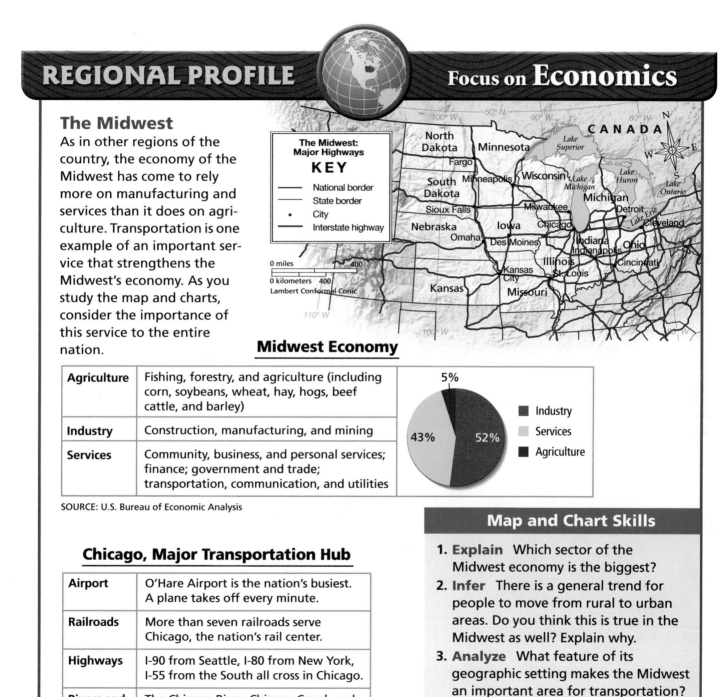

REGIONAL PROFILE   Focus on **Economics**

The Midwest

As in other regions of the country, the economy of the Midwest has come to rely more on manufacturing and services than it does on agriculture. Transportation is one example of an important service that strengthens the Midwest's economy. As you study the map and charts, consider the importance of this service to the entire nation.

The Midwest: Major Highways

KEY

— National border
— State border
• City
— Interstate highway

0 miles 400
0 kilometers 400
Lambert Conformal Conic

Midwest Economy

Agriculture	Fishing, forestry, and agriculture (including corn, soybeans, wheat, hay, hogs, beef cattle, and barley)
Industry	Construction, manufacturing, and mining
Services	Community, business, and personal services; finance; government and trade; transportation, communication, and utilities

SOURCE: U.S. Bureau of Economic Analysis

5%
43% 52%

■ Industry
■ Services
■ Agriculture

Chicago, Major Transportation Hub

Airport	O'Hare Airport is the nation's busiest. A plane takes off every minute.
Railroads	More than seven railroads serve Chicago, the nation's rail center.
Highways	I-90 from Seattle, I-80 from New York, I-55 from the South all cross in Chicago.
Rivers and waterways	The Chicago River, Chicago Canal, and Lake Michigan carry commercial shipping traffic.

SOURCE: Chicago Department of Aviation

Map and Chart Skills

1. **Explain** Which sector of the Midwest economy is the biggest?
2. **Infer** There is a general trend for people to move from rural to urban areas. Do you think this is true in the Midwest as well? Explain why.
3. **Analyze** What feature of its geographic setting makes the Midwest an important area for transportation?

Go Online
PHSchool.com
Use Web Code
Ihe-4413 for
DK World Desk
Reference Online.

Technology Changes Farm Life

The Midwest is often called the heartland because it is the agricultural center of our nation. The soil is rich, and the climate is suitable for producing corn, wheat, soybeans, and livestock. Inventions such as the steel plow, the windmill, and barbed wire helped settlers carve out farms on the plains. Drilling equipment helped to make wells deep enough to reach water. These tools also helped make farms productive. Technological advances continue to improve farming techniques today.

Family Farms Decline   Until the 1980s, small family farms were common in the Midwest. Many of these farms were mixed-crop farms. On a **mixed-crop farm,** several different kinds of crops are grown. This was a sensible way for farmers to work. If one crop failed, the farm had others to fall back on.

In the 1960s and 1970s, family farms prospered. The world population was rising, and demand for American farm products was high. Farmers felt that they could increase their business if they enlarged their farms. To build bigger farms, farmers bought more land and equipment. But all of this cost money. Many farmers borrowed money from local banks.

In the early 1980s, there was a countrywide **recession** (rih SESH un), or a downturn in business activity. The demand for farm products decreased. Then, interest rates on bank loans increased. As a result, many farmers were not able to make enough money to pay their loans. Some families sold their farms. More than one million American farmers have left the land since 1980.

Graph Skills

In the early 1900s, about one third of the workers in the United States worked on farms, such as the Illinois farm shown below. **Describe** What is the pattern of the number of farm workers shown in the graph? **Analyze Information** What does the information on the graph tell you about farming today?

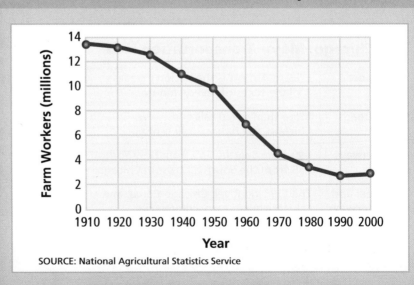

Number of U.S. Farm Workers, 1910–2000

SOURCE: National Agricultural Statistics Service

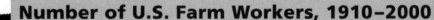

Corporate Farms Rise A small number of agricultural companies bought many of these family farms. When these agricultural companies combine several small family farms into one large farm, it is called a **corporate farm.** Large corporations can afford to buy the expensive land and equipment that modern farming requires. These large farms are run efficiently and make a profit.

Corporate farmers rely on machines and computers to do much of the work. This means that corporate farms employ fewer workers. Kansas offers a good example of corporate farming, since it has fewer workers and larger farms. In Kansas, 90 percent of the land is farmland, but fewer than 1 percent of the people are farmers. Most of the people in Kansas live and work in cities such as Wichita.

Small family farms do still exist in the Midwest. But most of them struggle to earn enough money for supporting a family. Family farmers usually need to have another job as well. Many people look to the cities for more job opportunities.

✓ **Reading Check** Why did so many families sell or leave their farms?

Identify Contrasts
How are corporate farms different from family farms?

Cities Develop in the Midwest

Many Midwestern cities began as centers of transportation and processing. Farmers from the surrounding area would send their harvests and livestock to nearby cities to be processed and shipped east. The largest processing city was Chicago, Illinois.

Chicago Located on Lake Michigan, Chicago was surrounded by prairies and farms in the mid-1800s. Farmers sent corn, wheat, cattle, and hogs to the mills and meat-packing plants in the city. Here the raw materials were turned into foods and shipped east by way of the Great Lakes. When railroads were built, Chicago really boomed. By the late 1800s, it had become a steel-making and manufacturing center. What was one of the most important manufactured products made in Chicago? You probably guessed it: farm equipment.

Today, Chicago is the biggest city in the heartland. It is known for its ethnic diversity and lively culture. It is the hub of major transportation routes including highways, railroads, airlines, and shipping routes. Chicago is also the home of the first steel skyscraper—the Home Insurance Company Building—and many other architectural wonders. For a bird's-eye view of Chicago, go to the top of the Sears Tower, one of the tallest buildings in the world.

Links Across The World

Higher and Higher Until 1996, Chicago's Sears Tower, at 1,454 feet (443 meters), was the world's tallest building. The photo below shows the view from the Sears Tower. The twin Petronas Towers in Malaysia then held the title. In 2004, the Taipei 101 building in Taipei, Taiwan, gained the title of world's tallest building, topping out at 1,671 feet (509 meters). Today, even taller skyscrapers are being planned in cities around the world.

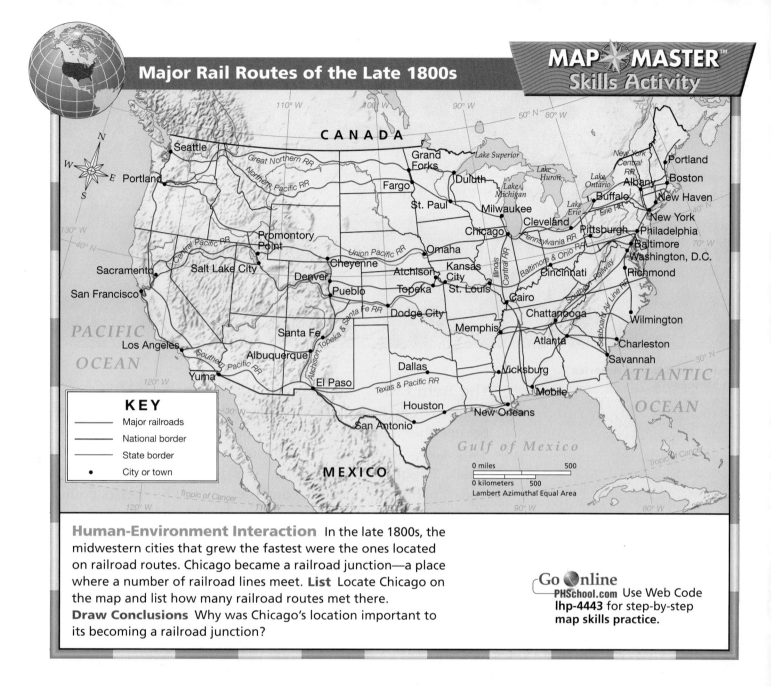

KEY

— Major railroads
— National border
— State border
• City or town

0 miles 500
0 kilometers 500
Lambert Azimuthal Equal Area

Human-Environment Interaction In the late 1800s, the midwestern cities that grew the fastest were the ones located on railroad routes. Chicago became a railroad junction—a place where a number of railroad lines meet. **List** Locate Chicago on the map and list how many railroad routes met there.
Draw Conclusions Why was Chicago's location important to its becoming a railroad junction?

Go Online
PHSchool.com Use Web Code
lhp-4443 for step-by-step map skills practice.

Detroit and St. Louis Two other large cities in the Midwest are Detroit, Michigan, and St. Louis, Missouri. They have both played an important role in the country's history. Why do you think Detroit is called the Motor City? You will find the headquarters of America's automobile manufacturers here. General Motors, Ford, and Daimler Chrysler have their main offices and factories in the city.

Covered wagons, not cars, used to roll through St. Louis. Located on the Mississippi River, this city was the starting point for pioneers heading west. Its location on the banks of the Mississippi River made it an important city in the days before railroads. Today, a huge stainless steel arch beside the river marks St. Louis as the Gateway to the West. St. Louis is also a banking and commercial center.

DISCOVERY
CHANNEL
SCHOOL Video
Find out about the powerful Mississippi River.

Inside the Mall of America in Minnesota

The Twin Cities Minneapolis is the largest city in Minnesota, followed by St. Paul. Together, they are known as the Twin Cities because they are next to each other on the Mississippi River. The Twin Cities were once the flour-milling center of the United States. Pillsbury and Company was founded there in 1872. Today, publishing, medical, computer, and art businesses flourish there. The city's suburbs have replaced hundreds of square miles of fertile land once used for farming.

✓ **Reading Check** Where was the world's first skyscraper located?

Section 3 Assessment

Key Terms
Review the key terms at the beginning of this section. Use each term in a sentence that explains its meaning.

Target Reading Skill
What are two ways that farming in the 1960s and 1970s was different from farming since the 1980s?

Comprehension and Critical Thinking
1. (a) Explain Why is the Midwest called the nation's heartland?

(b) Explore the Main Idea Why did family farmers face hard times in the 1980s?

(c) Predict What do you think the future holds for family farmers?

2. (a) Recall How did some midwestern cities get their starts?

(b) Identify Effects How did railroads affect the growth of midwestern cities?

(c) Draw Inferences How might Chicago's location affect its growth today?

Writing Activity
Suppose that you are a farmer and you have decided to sell your farm and move to a city. Write a letter to a friend explaining your decision.

For: An activity on the automobile industry
Visit: PHSchool.com
Web Code: lhd-4403

Prepare to Read

Objectives

In this section you will
1. Learn about the natural resources of the West.
2. Read about the challenges facing the urban West.

Taking Notes

As you read this section, look for ways that natural resources are used and conserved in the West. Copy the table below, and record your findings in it.

Resources of the West	
Using Resources	**Conserving Resources**
•	•
•	•
•	•

Target Reading Skill

Make Comparisons
Comparing two or more situations enables you to see how they are alike. As you read this section, compare how different parts of the West use and manage resources. Write the information in your Taking Notes table.

Key Terms

- **forty-niner** (FAWRT ee NY nur) *n.* the nickname for a miner who took part in the California Gold Rush of 1849
- **responsible development** (rih SPAHN suh bul dih VEL up munt) *n.* balancing the needs of the environment, community, and economy
- **mass transit** (mas TRAN sit) *n.* a system of subways, buses, and commuter trains used to transport large numbers of people

From colonial days to the present, Americans have been drawn westward. Over time, explorers and settlers have pushed out the farthest boundaries of the western frontier. In the 1780s, the frontier was considered to be the land as far west as the Mississippi River. Twenty years later, it included all of the land to the Rocky Mountains. By the 1850s, the frontier was the region that we now think of as the West—the land from the Rocky Mountains to the Pacific Ocean. By the 1900s, it also included Alaska and Hawaii.

Although the boundaries of the West have changed dramatically over the years, one factor has remained the same: People are attracted westward by the promise of the land.

Rocky Mountains, Colorado

Natural Resources of the West

For well over 400 years, people have been drawn to the West by its wealth of natural resources. The Spanish had already settled in the Southwest when the Pilgrims arrived in New England in the 1620s. After Lewis and Clark's exploration of the Louisiana Territory in the early 1800s, more people moved westward.

REGIONAL PROFILE   Focus on Geography

The West

Water is an important resource of the West—more important even than gold. Farmers have always needed large quantities of water to irrigate their lands. Today, as large cities and their populations grow, people are demanding more and more water for every-day use. Study the map and charts, and think about how water availability and use are shaping this region.

California Cropland

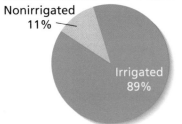

Nonirrigated 11%

Irrigated 89%

SOURCE: National Agriculture Statistics Service

Leading Hydroelectric Power-Producing States, 2006

States	Thousands of Megawatt Hours
Washington	14,650
Oregon	7,854
California	8,088
New York*	4,173
Alabama*	1,913
Idaho	1,736
Tennessee*	1,557

SOURCE: Energy Information Administration, US Department of Energy
*not a western state

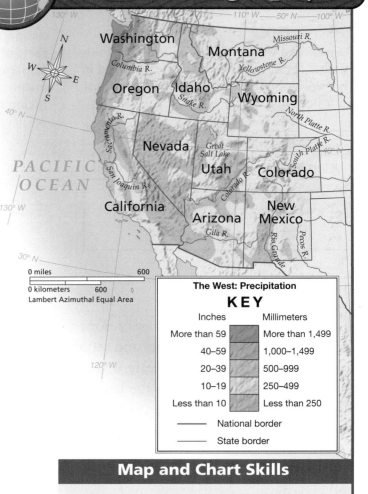

The West: Precipitation
KEY

Inches		Millimeters
More than 59		More than 1,499
40–59		1,000–1,499
20–39		500–999
10–19		250–499
Less than 10		Less than 250

——— National border
——— State border

Map and Chart Skills

1. **Locate** Which areas of the West receive the most rain?
2. **Identify** What state produces the most hydroelectric power?
3. **Analyze** There is a category of law devoted to water use. What issues might be addressed by lawyers who specialize in water use?

Use Web Code lhe-4414 to access the **DK World Desk Reference Online.**

Mineral Resources Before gold was discovered in California, Native Americans and Spanish settlers lived in the region. With the California Gold Rush, the population exploded. The sleepy port of San Francisco boomed into a prosperous city. Its population grew from 800 people in 1848 to 25,000 just two years later. The first miners and prospectors of the Gold Rush were called **forty-niners** because they arrived in 1849. They arrived, bought supplies, and headed off to the Sierra Nevada expecting to strike it rich. Few of them succeeded, but many remained in the West.

A gold strike in 1858 in Colorado led to the founding of the city of Denver. Similar events took place in Nevada, Idaho, and Montana in the 1860s. Further discoveries of valuable minerals, including silver and copper, drew more and more people to the West. A mining town formed around each new discovery.

All of these new settlers needed homes, and the timber to build them with was in large supply in the the Pacific Northwest. After the Civil War, logging camps, sawmills, and paper mills sprang up in Washington, Oregon, and northern California. At first, the resources of the West seemed unlimited. The use of these resources created wealth and many jobs. However, it also brought with it new challenges.

Learn more about the
California Gold Rush.

The Cost of Mining
Merchants and traders supplied miners with food, clothing, and tools. Supplies were hauled from the river ports to the mining camps by wagons and mules. This caused increased prices. With the population boom and the difficulty of getting supplies up to the camps, the cost of living for miners was high. **Conclude** *Was trying to strike it rich worth the amount of time, effort, and money needed? Explain your answer.*

The Cost of Mining

Hoe
1850s cost = $12.00
In today's $ = $273.00

Pickaxe
1850s cost = $8.00
In today's $ = $183.00

Tin pan
1850s cost = $4.00
In today's $ = $92.00

Ounce of gold
1850s cost = $16.00
In today's $ = $366.00

Old Faithful is the best-known geyser in Yellowstone National Park, Wyoming.

Managing Resources California's population continued to grow after the Gold Rush. To meet the demand for new houses, loggers leveled many forests. Engineers built dams to pipe water through the mountains to coastal cities. Next to the dams, they built hydroelectric plants. Cities like San Francisco got water and power this way, but the dams flooded whole valleys of the Sierras.

To save parts of the West as natural wilderness, Congress created several national parks and forests. Yet these parks are not trouble-free. California's Yosemite (yoh SEM uh tee) National Park now gets so many visitors that it suffers from traffic jams and air pollution in the summer. Some of the scenic views in Montana's Glacier National Park are also reduced by hazy skies.

Some westerners are working on **responsible development,** or balancing the needs of the environment, the community, and the economy. For example, Yosemite now limits the number of campers in the park. Dam building has stopped. In addition, some logging companies are working to preserve the environment by planting new trees to replace the ones that have been cut down. Advanced technology, such as power plants with better pollution-control devices, can help meet energy and environmental needs.

✓ **Reading Check** What caused California's population to grow in the 1800s?

The Urban West

Most westerners today are not miners, farmers, or loggers. Rather, they live and work in cities. Their challenge is to figure out how to use natural resources wisely.

Portland, Oregon "Your town or mine?" two land developers asked each other in 1845. They were at the same site and predicted the development of a major port city. Located near the junction of the Willamette and Columbia rivers, how could they fail? Francis W. Pettygrove of Portland, Maine, won the coin toss. He named the site after his hometown in the East.

Portland became a trade center for lumber, fur, grain, salmon, and wool. In the 1930s, new dams produced cheap electricity. Portland attracted many manufacturing industries.

Seattle, Washington The port city of Seattle was founded in the early 1850s. It was named after a Native American leader who helped the area's first settlers. Seattle has grown into a bustling city of more than half a million people.

Years of unchecked growth eventually led to problems. In the 1960s, a group of local citizens started a campaign to revitalize the local economy. A bridge was built across Lake Washington to help residents commute. Sewage was cleaned up from Lake Washington, and many neighborhood parks were created. The group also kept Pike Place Market from being destroyed. It is the oldest continuously run market in the country. Farmers have sold their crops and produce there since 1907.

San Jose, California Urban sprawl is a local challenge in San Jose. The area around San Jose was once known for its beautiful orchards and farms. Now it is called Silicon Valley because it is a part of the computer industry.

San Jose's most valuable resource is now its people. They come from all parts of the world. The greater population density has created crowded freeways and air pollution. To counter these problems, San Jose has built a light-rail mass transit system. A **mass transit** system replaces individual cars with energy-saving buses or trains.

Make Comparisons
What do Portland and Seattle have in common?

■ Graph Skills

The Internet boom of the 1990s saw between 7,000 and 10,000 Internet companies start up. It began to decline dramatically by the beginning of 2000.
Describe In what year did the most Internet companies shut down?
Predict If the number of company shutdowns continues, what would be the effect on urban sprawl?

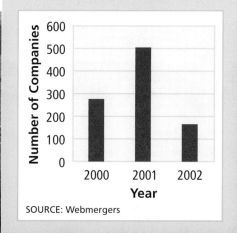

Internet Company Shutdowns

SOURCE: Webmergers

The Hollywood sign hovers over Los Angeles, California, and is a reminder that the city is home to the entertainment industry. Cameramen (lower photo) shoot a movie on a local set.

Los Angeles, California Los Angeles is another California city whose people are its greatest resource. It has grown from a small Mexican village in the 1780s to the second-most-populated city in the United States. The Gold Rush and the building of the transcontinental railroad helped the city grow.

By the 1920s, the movie, petroleum, and manufacturing industries all brought more people to the city. Today, Los Angeles is a center for banking and aircraft manufacturing. But, it is most noted for its entertainment industry. In addition to the Hollywood movie industry, the headquarters of many of the country's recording companies and radio and television networks are located here. Many broadcasts are in foreign languages, especially Spanish. Hispanics are the largest ethnic group in the city, followed by Asians.

✓ **Reading Check** Why did San Jose need a mass transit system?

Section 4 Assessment

Key Terms
Review the key terms at the beginning of this section. Use each term in a sentence that explains its meaning.

Target Reading Skill
Compare Los Angeles today to what it was like in the 1780s.

Comprehension and Critical Thinking
1. (a) Recall What event took place in California in 1849?
(b) Identify Cause and Effect How did that event lead to the formation of towns and cities?

(c) Infer How did the population explosion affect the West's natural resources?
2. (a) Explain How did Portland, Oregon, get its name?
(b) Summarize What natural resources made Portland a good location for a city?
(c) Predict How might these resources be protected today?

Writing Activity
What natural resources are there in your community? In what ways do people use these natural resources? Write a paragraph describing the natural resources in your area and how they are used.

Go Online
PHSchool.com

For: An activity on Denver
Visit: PHSchool.com
Web Code: lhd-4404

Review and Assessment

◆ Chapter Summary

Section 1: The Northeast

- A chain of cities runs from Boston, Massachusetts, to Washington, D.C.
- The Northeast is the most densely populated region of the United States.
- Many immigrants entered the United States through one of the ports in the Northeast.

Section 2: The South

- The South's warm climate and abundant rainfall make it suitable for growing many crops.
- Drilling, mining, fishing, and forestry are important industries in the South.
- Many people have moved from rural towns to the cities for better job opportunities.

Section 3: The Midwest

- Technology has changed the way that American farms operate.
- Many small family farms have closed because they are unprofitable.
- Many Midwestern cities got their start as places that processed and shipped farm products.

Section 4: The West

- The West has a wide array of natural resources.
- Managing these natural resources is an important task for people in the West.
- People are some of the urban West's most valuable resources.

Haymarket in Boston, Massachusetts

◆ Key Terms

Use each key term below in a sentence that shows the meaning of the term.

1. commute
2. megalopolis
3. population density
4. petrochemical
5. industrialization
6. Sun Belt
7. mixed-crop farm
8. recession
9. corporate farm
10. forty-niner
11. mass transit

◆ Comprehension and Critical Thinking

12. (a) List What are some of the large cities in the Northeast?
(b) Compare and Contrast Choose two of the Northeast's cities. How are they similar? How have they developed differently?

13. (a) Locate Which city in the Northeast was attacked by terrorists in 2001?
(b) Draw Conclusions Why might terrorists have targeted that city in particular?

14. (a) Explain What features make the South a good place for farming?
(b) Identify What was the South's most important crop until the 1900s?
(c) Predict How might farming in the South have been different without the boll weevil?

15. (a) Recall How do people in the South make a living other than by farming?
(b) Draw Conclusions How is Georgia important to the textile industry?

16. (a) Summarize How did the recession in the 1980s affect farmers?
(b) Compare and Contrast How are mixed-crop farming and corporate farming different?

17. (a) Name What are the main natural resources of the West?
(b) Summarize How have people used these natural resources?
(c) Compare and Contrast How has the way people manage natural resources in the West changed since the 1800s?

◆ Skills Practice

Understanding Circle Graphs In the Skills for Life activity in this chapter, you learned that information can be given in the form of circle graphs.

Review the steps you followed to learn this skill. Then reread the Regional Profile of the Midwest on page 265. Study the Midwest Economy circle graph on that page. Identify what percentage of the graph each part represents. Use the information in the circle graph to draw conclusions about the economy of the Midwest.

◆ Writing Activity: Science

Suppose that you are the science reporter for a newspaper covering the history of farming on the plains. Write a brief report about how advances in science and technology have contributed to successfully farming the land.

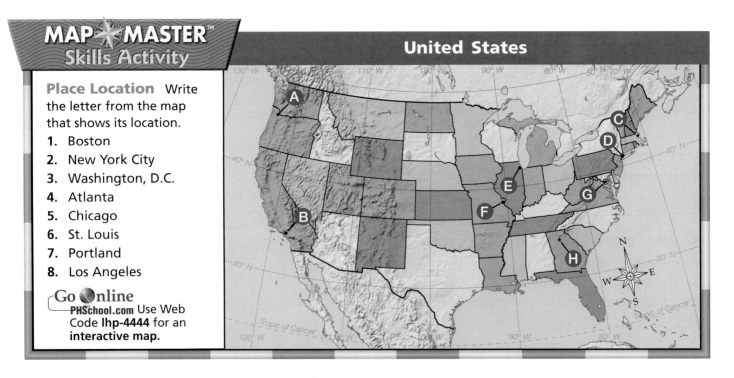

MAP MASTER™
Skills Activity

Place Location Write the letter from the map that shows its location.
1. Boston
2. New York City
3. Washington, D.C.
4. Atlanta
5. Chicago
6. St. Louis
7. Portland
8. Los Angeles

Go Online
PHSchool.com Use Web Code lhp-4444 for an interactive map.

United States

Standardized Test Prep

Test-Taking Tips

Some questions on standardized tests ask you to analyze graphs. Study the graph below. Then follow the tips to answer the sample question.

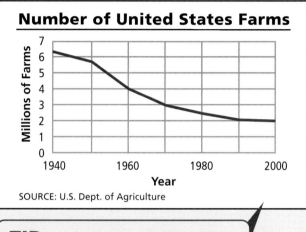

Number of United States Farms

SOURCE: U.S. Dept. of Agriculture

TIP When you study a graph, read the title to understand its subject. Then study information on the left side and bottom of the graph.

Based on this graph, it is clear that the

A size of farms has decreased since the 1940s.

B size of farms increased during the last half of the 1900s.

C number of farms steadily decreased during the last half of the 1900s.

D number of farms probably will increase during the first twenty years of the present century.

TIP Restate the question to make sure you understand what it is asking. "Based on the graph, what conclusion can you draw about United States farms?"

Think It Through Read the title of the graph. You can eliminate A and B because they are about the *size* of American farms. What does the graph show about the *number* of farms? The number line goes down after 1940, but there is no indication that the number of farms will increase in the 2000s. The correct answer is C.

Practice Questions

Use the tips above and other tips in this book to help you answer the following questions.

1. The most densely populated region of the United States is the
   A South.　　　　　B Midwest.
   C Northeast.　　　D West.

2. What caused San Francisco to grow into a large city?
   A the Gold Rush
   B hydroelectricity
   C the logging industry
   D Lewis and Clark's expedition

3. The Midwest's largest city is
   A Detroit, Michigan.　　B St. Louis, Missouri.
   C Minneapolis, Minnesota.　　D Chicago, Illinois.

Study the graph below, and then answer the question that follows.

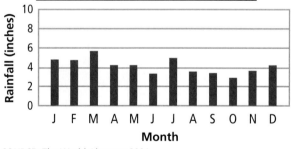

Atlanta, Georgia: Rainfall

SOURCE: *The World Almanac*, 2001

4. In which month is the average temperature highest in Atlanta? How much rain falls in that month?
   A March; 5.5 inches　　B May; 6 inches
   C July; 6 inches　　　　D September; 3 inches

Go Online PHSchool.com
Use Web Code lha-4404 for a **Chapter 9 self-test**

From **Childtimes**

By Eloise Greenfield and Lessie Jones Little, with material by Pattie Ridley Jones

Prepare to Read

Background Information

How much do people know about the lives of their grandparents or their parents as children? Suppose someone wanted to write a history of his or her family. How could he or she find information?

You can learn a great deal from seeing how a single family lives through several generations. Every family history reflects the history of the place where that family lives. The following excerpts come from a memoir, or a story of personal experience, written by a mother, a daughter, and a grandmother. The book tells the story of their family, as well as the growth of their hometown, Parmele, North Carolina.

Objectives

In this section you will

1. Learn how and why the town of Parmele changed over three generations.
2. Identify elements that the memoirs of the three generations have in common.

About the Selection

Childtimes: A Three-Generation Memoir was published in 1979 by Thomas Y. Crowell.

✓ **Reading Check**

How did the town of Parmele get its name?

Pattie Frances Ridley Jones—born in Bertie County, North Carolina, December 15, 1884

Parmele, North Carolina

Towns build up around work, you know. People go and live where they can find jobs. And that's how Parmele got started.

At first, it was just a junction, a place where two railroads crossed. Two Atlantic Coast Line railroads, one running between Rocky Mount and Plymouth, and one running between Kinston and Weldon. Didn't too many people live around there then, and those that did were pretty much spread out.

Well, around 1888, a Yankee named Mr. Parmele came down from New York and looked the place over, and he saw all those big trees and decided to start a lumber company. Everybody knew what that meant. There were going to be jobs! People came from everywhere to get work. I was right little at that time, too little to know what was going on, but everybody says it was something to see how fast that town grew. All those people moving in and houses going up. They named the town after the man who made the jobs, and they called it *Pomma-lee.*

The lumber company hired a whole lot of people. They hired workers to lay track for those little railroads they call tram roads that they were going to run back and forth between the town and the woods. They hired lumberjacks to chop the trees down and cut them up into logs, and load them on the tram cars. They hired men to build the mill and put the machinery in, and millworkers to run the machines that would cut the logs into different sizes and dry them and make them nice and smooth. . . .

Lessie Blanche Jones Little—born in Parmele, North Carolina, October 1, 1906

Parmele

I used to hear Papa and Mama and their friends talking about the lumber mill that had been the center of life in Parmele before I was born, but there wasn't any mill when I was growing up. The only thing left of it was the sawdust from all the wood they had sawed there. The sawdust was about a foot thick on the land where the mill had been. I used to love to walk on it. It was spongy, and it made me feel like I was made of rubber. I'd take my shoes off and kind of bounce along on top of it. But that was all that was left of the mill.

My Parmele was a train town. The life of my town moved around the trains that came in and out all day long. About three hundred people lived in Parmele, most of them black. There were three black churches, a Baptist, a Methodist, and a Holiness, and one white church. Two black schools, one white. There wasn't even one doctor, and not many people would have had the money to pay one, if there had been. If somebody got down real bad sick, a member of the family would go by horse and buggy to a nearby town and bring the doctor back, or sometimes the doctor would ride on his own horse.

Most of the men and women in Parmele earned their living by farming. Some did other things like working at the tobacco factory in Robersonville, but most worked on the farms that were all around in the area, white people's farms usually. When I was a little girl, they earned fifty cents a day, a farm day, sunup to sundown, plus meals. After they got home, they had all their own work to do, cooking and cleaning, laundry, chopping wood for the woodstove, and shopping. . . .

A steam engine pulls a train through the countryside.

Parmele had trains coming in and going out all day long. Passenger trains and freight trains. There was always so much going on at the station that I wouldn't know what to watch. People were changing trains and going in and out of the cafe and the restaurant. They came from big cities like New York and Chicago and Boston, and they were all wearing the latest styles. Things were being unloaded, like furniture and trunks and plows and cases of fruit and crates of clucking chickens, or a puppy, or the body of somebody who had died and was being brought back home. And every year around the last two weeks in May, a special train would come through. It had two white flags flying on the locomotive, and it was carrying one hundred carloads of white potatoes that had been grown down near <u>Pamlico Sound</u>, where everybody said the soil was so rich they didn't even have to fertilize it.

The train station was a gathering place, too. A lot of people went there to relax after they had finished their work for the day. They'd come downtown to pick up their mail, or buy a newspaper, and then they'd just stand around laughing and talking to their friends. And on Sundays fellas and their girls would come all the way from other towns, just to spend the afternoon at the Parmele train station. . . .

It was hard for Papa to find work. Not long after Sis Clara died, we moved to Mount Herman, a black section of Portsmouth, Virginia. Papa worked on the docks there, and even though he didn't make much money, the work was steady. But when we moved back to Parmele, it was hard for him to find any work at all. . . .

Eloise Glynn Little Greenfield—born in Parmele, North Carolina, May 17, 1929

Daddy Makes a Way

When I was three months old, Daddy left home to make a way for us. He went North, as thousands of black people had done, during slavery and since. They went North looking for safety, for justice, for freedom, for work, looking for a good life. Often one member of a family would go ahead of the others to make a way—to find a job and a place to live. And that's what my father did.

In the spring of 1926, Daddy had graduated from high school, Parmele Training School. He had been offered a scholarship by Knoxville College in Tennessee, but he hadn't taken it. He and Mama had gotten married that fall, and now they had Wilbur and me to take care of. Mama had been teaching school since her graduation from Higgs, but she had decided to stop.

Pamlico Sound (PAM lih koh sownd) *n.* a long body of water off the coast of North Carolina that separates the Hatteras Islands from the mainland

✓ **Reading Check**

What kind of work did Eloise's father do before he went to Washington, D.C.?

Sharecroppers in the South

Nineteen twenty-nine was a bad time for Daddy to go away, but a worse time for him not to go. The <u>Great Depression</u> was about to begin, had already begun for many people. All over the United States, thousands of people were already jobless and homeless.

In Parmele, there were few permanent jobs. Some seasons of the year, Daddy could get farm work, harvesting potatoes and working in the tobacco fields. Every year, from August to around Thanksgiving, he worked ten hours a day for twenty-five cents an hour at a tobacco warehouse in a nearby town, packing tobacco in huge barrels and loading them on the train for shipping. And he and his father were house movers. Whenever somebody wanted a house moved from one place to another, Daddy and Pa would jack it up and attach it to a windlass, the machine that the horse would turn to move the house. But it was only once in a while that they were called on to do that.

So, one morning in August 1929, Mama went with Daddy to the train station and tried to hold back her tears as the Atlantic Coast Line train pulled out, taking him toward Washington, D.C. Then she went home, sat in the porch swing, and cried.

In Washington, friends helped Daddy find a room for himself and his family to live in, and took him job hunting. He found a job as a dishwasher in a restaurant, and in a few weeks, he had saved enough money for our train fare.

Great Depression (grayt dee PRESH un) *n.* an economic collapse that began in 1929 and lasted throughout the 1930s, causing many people to lose their jobs

Review and Assessment

Thinking About the Selection

1. (a) Recall Why was the town located where it was? What caused the town to first begin to grow?
(b) Identify Why did building a sawmill attract more people to Parmele? How did they earn a living after the mill closed?
(c) Evaluate How did the life of a young person in Parmele compare with your own?
2. (a) Respond What do these memoirs tell you about how hard life in Parmele was at different time periods?

(b) Infer What aspect of their parents' lives most shaped the lives of these women when they were young girls?
(c) Compare and Contrast What do the three narrators have in common? How are they different?

Writing Activity

Write a Memoir Write a memoir of your own childhood. Use the point of view of yourself as an older person. Talk about the forces that have most shaped your life.

About the Author

Eloise Greenfield (b. 1929) was born in Parmele, North Carolina. She has received dozens of awards and honors for her more than thirty books of poetry, biography, and fiction. Greenfield's fiction often depicts strong, loving African American families and contains positive messages for all of her readers. She currently lives in Washington, D.C.

Chapter Preview

This chapter will introduce you to the provinces and territories of Canada.

Country Databank

The Country Databank provides data of each of the provinces and territories in Canada.

Section 1
Ontario and Quebec
Bridging Two Cultures

Section 2
The Prairie Provinces
Canada's Breadbasket

Section 3
British Columbia
Economic and Cultural Changes

Section 4
The Atlantic Provinces
Relying on the Sea

Section 5
The Northern Territories
New Frontiers

Target Reading Skill

Context In this chapter, you will focus on using context to help you understand unfamiliar words. Context includes the words, phrases, and sentences surrounding the word.

▶ Lighthouse in Peggy's Cove, Nova Scotia, Canada

MAP★MASTER™
Skills Activity

KEY

— National border

— Provincial or
territorial border

⊛ National capital

★ Provincial or
territorial capital

• Other city

0 miles   1,000

0 kilometers   1,000

Lambert Azimuthal Equal Area

Regions Canada is politically divided into ten provinces and three territories. **Locate** Describe the relative locations of Quebec, Saskatchewan, and British Columbia. **Draw Conclusions** Which of the three provinces do you think Europeans settled first? Explain your answer.

Go Online
PHSchool.com Use Web Code
lhp-4511 for step-by-step
map skills practice.

Introducing
Canada

COUNTRY DATABANK

Guide for Reading

This section provides an introduction to the ten provinces and three territories that make up Canada.

- Look at the map on the previous page, and then read the information below to learn about each province and territory.
- Analyze the data to compare the provinces and territories.
- What are the characteristics that most of the provinces and territories share?
- What are some of the key differences among the provinces and territories?

Viewing the Video Overview

View the World Studies Video Program Overview to learn more about each of the provinces and territories. As you watch, answer these questions:

- Why do most Canadians live in the southern part of the country?
- What factors influenced where the big cities of Canada developed?

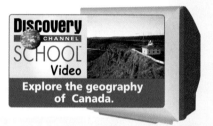

Discovery CHANNEL **SCHOOL** Video
Explore the geography of Canada.

Alberta

Capital	Edmonton
Land Area	247,999 sq mi; 642,317 sq km
Population	3,101,561
Language(s)	English, Chinese, German, French
Agriculture	livestock, wheat, canola, dairy products, barley, poultry, potatoes, nurseries, vegetables, eggs, sugar beets, honey
Industry	manufacturing, construction, oil production and refinery

British Columbia

Capital	Victoria
Land Area	357,214 sq mi; 925,186 sq km
Population	4,118,141
Language(s)	English, Chinese, Punjabi, German, French
Agriculture	nurseries, livestock, dairy products, vegetables, poultry, fruit, potatoes, ginseng, canola, wheat
Industry	forestry, wood and paper, mining, tourism, agriculture, fishing, manufacturing

Odyssium is Edmonton, Alberta's space and science center.

Manitoba

Capital	Winnipeg
Land Area	213,728 sq mi; 553,556 sq km
Population	1,150,038
Language(s)	English, German, French
Agriculture	wheat, livestock, canola, dairy products, potatoes, barley, poultry, eggs, nurseries, vegetables, corn, honey
Industry	manufacturing, agriculture, food industry, mining, construction

New Brunswick

Capital	Fredericton
Land Area	27,587 sq mi; 71,450 sq km
Population	756,939
Language(s)	English, French
Agriculture	potatoes, dairy products, poultry, nurseries, livestock, eggs, fruit
Industry	manufacturing, fishing, mining, forestry, pulp and paper, agriculture

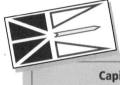

Newfoundland and Labrador

Capital	St. John's
Land Area	144,362 sq mi; 373,872 sq km
Population	531,820
Language(s)	English, French
Agriculture	dairy products, eggs, nurseries, vegetables, potatoes, hogs
Industry	mining, manufacturing, fishing, logging and forestry, electricity production, tourism

Northwest Territories

Capital	Yellowknife
Land Area	456,789 sq mi; 1,183,085 sq km
Population	40,071
Language(s)	English, French, Inuktitut
Agriculture	potatoes, hay, nurseries, livestock
Industry	construction, mining, utilities, services, tourism

Nova Scotia

Capital	Halifax
Land Area	20,594 sq mi; 53,338 sq km
Population	943,497
Language(s)	English, French
Agriculture	dairy products, poultry, livestock, nurseries, fruit, eggs, vegetables
Industry	manufacturing, fishing and trapping, mining, agriculture, pulp and paper

Snowy owl

Introducing Canada

Nunavut

Capital	Iqaluit
Land Area	747,533 sq mi; 1,936,113 sq km
Population	29,016
Language(s)	Inuktitut, English
Industry	mining, tourism, shrimp and scallop fishing, hunting and trapping, arts and crafts production

Ontario

Capital	Toronto
Land Area	354,340 sq mi; 917,741 sq km
Population	11,977,360
Language(s)	English, French, Chinese, Italian, German, Portuguese, Polish, Spanish, Punjabi
Agriculture	livestock, dairy products, nurseries, vegetables, poultry, soybeans, corn, tobacco, eggs, fruit, wheat, ginseng, maple products
Industry	manufacturing, construction, agriculture, forestry, mining

Prince Edward Island

Capital	Charlottetown
Land Area	2,185 sq mi; 5,660 sq km
Population	135,294
Language(s)	English, French
Agriculture	potatoes, dairy products, livestock, vegetables
Industry	agriculture, tourism, fishing, manufacturing

Cape Tryon on Prince Edward Island

Quebec

Capital	Quebec
Land Area	594,860 sq mi; 1,365,128 sq km
Population	7,432,005
Language(s)	French, English, Italian
Agriculture	dairy products, livestock, poultry, vegetables, corn, nurseries, maple products, fruit, potatoes, soybeans, barley, tobacco, wheat
Industry	manufacturing, electric power, mining, pulp and paper, transportation equipment

Saskatchewan

Capital	Regina
Land Area	251,866 sq mi; 591,670 sq km
Population	1,001,224
Language(s)	English, German, Cree, Ukrainian, French
Agriculture	wheat, livestock, canola, barley, lentils, dairy products, poultry, potatoes, nurseries, eggs, honey
Industry	agriculture, mining, manufacturing, electric power, construction, chemical production

Musicians in Montreal, Quebec

Yukon Territory

Capital	Whitehorse
Land Area	186,661 sq mi; 474,391 sq km
Population	29,552
Language(s)	English, German, French
Agriculture	nurseries, vegetables, poultry
Industry	mining, tourism

SOURCES: *CIA World Factbook*, 2002; *World Almanac*, 2003; *Canadian Global Almanac*, 2003, Canada Census, 2001

Assessment

Comprehension and Critical Thinking

1. Compare and Contrast Compare Nunavut and Ontario based on physical size and population size.

2. Draw Conclusions What characteristics do the three territories share?

3. Contrast How has geographic location affected the populations

and industries of Canada's provinces and territories?

4. Categorize What are the major products in Canada?

5. Infer What can you infer about Nunavut if there are no agricultural products listed?

6. Make a Bar Graph Create a bar graph showing the population of the provinces and territories of Canada.

Keeping Current

Access the **DK World Desk Reference Online** at **PHSchool.com** for up-to-date information about Canada.

Go Online
PHSchool.com

Web Code: lhe-4501

Ontario and Quebec
Bridging Two Cultures

Prepare to Read

Objectives

In this section you will
1. Read about the seat of the Canadian government in Ontario.
2. Learn about the French cultural influence in Quebec.

Taking Notes

As you read this section, look for ways that people in Quebec are preserving and celebrating their culture. Copy the concept web below, and record your findings in it.

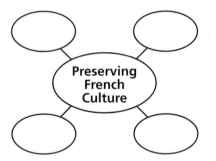

Preserving French Culture

 **Target Reading Skill**

Use Context Clues When you come across an unfamiliar word, you can often figure out its meaning from clues in the context. The context refers to the surrounding words, phrases, and sentences. Sometimes the context will define the word. In this example, the phrase in italics explains what a tariff is: Both countries charged tariffs, or *fees,* on imported goods.

Key Terms

- **federation** (fed ur AY shun) *n.* a union of states, groups, provinces, or nations
- **Francophone** (FRANG koh fohn) *n.* a person who speaks French as his or her first language
- **Quiet Revolution** (KWY ut rev uh LOO shun) *n.* a peaceful change in the government of Quebec
- **separatist** (SEP ur uh tist) *n.* a person who wants Quebec to become an independent country

The Macdonald-Cartier Bridge

Much of the border between Ontario and Quebec is formed by the Ottawa River. The Macdonald-Cartier Bridge stretches across the river, connecting the two provinces. The bridge is named for two Canadian political leaders, one an English speaker and one a French speaker. While the bridge links the two provinces, its very name characterizes the differences between the provinces—people in Ontario speak English primarily, while people in Quebec mostly speak French.

In spite of this significant distinction, Ontario and Quebec have much in common. They are home to Canada's two largest cities—Toronto, Ontario, and Montreal, Quebec. They are the two most populous provinces in Canada. Canada's capital, Ottawa, is located in Ontario. But government functions spill over into the city of Hull, Quebec, located on the other end of the Macdonald-Cartier Bridge. Hull is considered Ottawa's "sister city" because a number of federal government office buildings dot its landscape.

Ontario

The province of Ontario is perhaps Canada's most diverse province geographically. Located on the United States border, it reaches from Hudson Bay in the north to the Great Lakes in the south. Ontario's northern region is part of the Canadian Shield, the region of ancient rock that covers about half of Canada. The Canadian Shield has rocky terrain, rugged winters, and is sparsely populated. Ontario's southern lowlands have milder winters and warm summers. About one third of Canada's entire population lives in this southern area.

Canada's Federal Government

Canada is a federation, or union, of 10 provinces and 3 territories. In the Canadian federation, each province has its own government. Each of these governments shares power with Canada's central government, located in Ottawa.

Although Canada's formal head of state is the monarch of Britain, Canada has complete power over its own government. The head of state, represented by the governor general, performs mainly ceremonial duties, such as hosting politicians from other countries, supporting charitable causes, and honoring the achievements of Canadians. Unlike the United States, in which the president is head of state as well as head of government, Canada has a separate head of government, called the prime minister. The prime minister leads the government and is part of Canada's central legislature—the Canadian Parliament.

Ottawa

Ottawa has been a capital city since the middle of the nineteenth century, when Upper and Lower Canada—present-day Ontario and Quebec—formed the Province of Canada. Ottawa was selected as the capital because it was located on the border of the two territories. In 1867, Nova Scotia and New Brunswick joined Ontario and Quebec to become the Dominion of Canada, an autonomous, or self-governing, member of the British Empire.

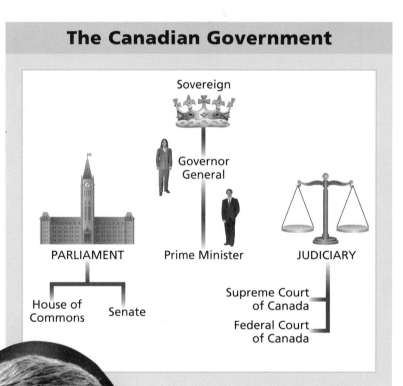

The Canadian Government

Sovereign

Governor General

Prime Minister

PARLIAMENT

House of Commons   Senate

JUDICIARY

Supreme Court of Canada

Federal Court of Canada

■ Diagram Skills

In the Canadian government structure, the executive, or prime minister, proposes laws; the legislature, Parliament, adopts laws; and the judiciary interprets laws. Stephen Harper, shown at left, was elected as Canadian prime minister in 2006. **Identify** Name the two houses of Parliament. **Contrast** How does Canada's head of state differ from the President of the United States?

Ontario

Canada separated from England very gradually. It went from a dependent colony of England, to a dominion, and finally to an independent nation with ties to Great Britain through the British Commonwealth of Nations. As you study the map and charts, compare and contrast Canada's government with that of the United States.

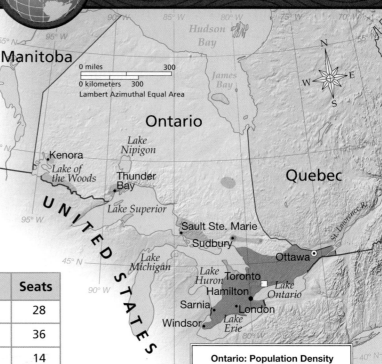

Ontario: Population Density

KEY

Persons per sq. mile	Persons per sq. kilometer
More than 129	More than 49
25–129	10–49
1–24	1–9
Less than 1	Less than 1

Urban Areas
- □ More than 4,999,999
- ⊙ 1,000,000–4,999,999
- ● 500,000–999,999
- • Less than 500,000
- — National border
- — Provincial or territorial border

The House of Commons

Province or Territory	Seats
Alberta	28
British Columbia	36
Manitoba, Saskatchewan	14
New Brunswick	10
Newfoundland and Labrador	7
Northwest Territories, Nunavut, Yukon Territory	1
Nova Scotia	11
Ontario	106
Prince Edward Island	4
Quebec	75

SOURCE: *Canadian Global Almanac, 2003*

Structure of Government

	Canada	United States
Head of State (ceremonial)	Queen of England / Governor General (the Queen's representative)	President (elected by the voters)
Head of Government (political)	Prime Minister (PM, the leader of the majority party in the House of Commons)	President
Legislature	Parliament • House of Commons (elected by the voters) • Senate (appointed by PM)	Congress • House of Representatives (elected) • Senate (elected)
Districts	Provinces and territories	States

Map and Chart Skills

1. **Note** Where is most of Ontario's population located?
2. **Explain** How does population affect the number of seats a province or territory has in the House of Commons?
3. **Analyze** What is the difference in the roles of the voters in Canada and in the United States?

Go Online
PHSchool.com

Use Web Code **lhe-4511** for **DK World Desk Reference Online.**

Toronto Each of Canada's provinces has a capital. Toronto is the capital of Ontario. It is also Canada's largest city and its commercial and financial center. Founded in 1793, Toronto was first known as York. Its location on Lake Ontario made it a major trade and transportation center. Toronto has come to be identified by its Canadian National (CN) Tower, which, at 1,815 feet (553 meters), is the world's tallest freestanding structure.

Toronto has matured into a cultural mosaic with a very diverse population—nearly half of its residents are foreign-born. After World War II, a large number of Europeans immigrated to Canada, with many settling in Toronto.

The most recent wave of immigrants included a large number of Asians. About 10 percent of Toronto's residents are of Chinese ethnicity. British, Italian, First Nations, Portuguese, East Indian, Greek, German, Ukrainian, Polish, and French are among the other ethnic groups that make up Toronto's population.

✓ **Reading Check** **Where is Canada's federal government located?**

Toronto Cityscape
The CN Tower (right) dominates Toronto's skyline. The large aerial photo taken from the tower shows Rogers Centre (formerly the SkyDome), home of the Toronto Blue Jays baseball team. It was the first domed stadium built with a roof that opens and closes.
Draw Conclusions *Why would a domed stadium be needed in Toronto?*

Discovery CHANNEL SCHOOL Video
Learn about Toronto: Canada's largest city

French Culture in Quebec

French culture first reached Quebec in the 1500s, when Jacques Cartier (zhahk kahr tee AY), a French explorer, sailed along the St. Lawrence River and landed in a village called Stadacona (stad uh KOH nuh). The Iroquois, the native people of the area, inhabited the village. Today, the site of that village is the city of Quebec, capital of the province of Quebec.

Cartier claimed the region we now know as Quebec for France and named it Canada. Great Britain, however, was also interested in the region. French and British forces fought for the land in four separate wars over a period of nearly 80 years. The last of the battles were part of the French and Indian War. In 1759, the British captured the city of Quebec. Within four years, France surrendered all of its North American land east of the Mississippi River to the British.

Despite Great Britain's victory, tens of thousands of French colonists remained in the region, and their descendants make up the majority of Quebec's population today. They are called **Francophones** (FRANG koh fohnz), or people who speak French as their first language. In Quebec's largest city, Montreal, and its surrounding areas, more than 65 percent of the population are Francophones.

French Influence in Quebec
French culture reached Quebec hundreds of years ago, and it still exists in the capital city today. **Analyze Images** *How can the influence of French culture be seen in this street in Quebec City?*

Francophones Seek Rights

In the 1960s, many Francophones began to express concern that their language and culture might die, because English was spoken in the schools and at work. They also believed that opportunities for Francophones in Quebec were not equal to those for English speakers. For the most part, Francophones got jobs with lower pay. So they set out to create change, in a movement that was similar to the civil rights movement in the United States in the 1960s. In 1960, the Liberal party, which supported Francophones, came to power in Quebec. Prime Minister Jean Lesage led the government in creating better job opportunities for Francophones and in modernizing education and health care in Quebec. This change in the government became known as the **Quiet Revolution** because great changes were brought about peacefully.

Disagreement on Separation
A Quebec resident (left) displays her opposition to separation. Other people carrying signs calling for independence and sovereignty rally to support the split from Canada (above). **Analyze Images** *What evidence is there that the woman at the left is against the Separatist Movement?*

The Separatist Movement During the Quiet Revolution, the separatist movement began to grow. **Separatists** are people who want to see Quebec break away from the rest of Canada and become an independent country. French-Canadian separatists saw important victories in the 1970s as French became the official language of Quebec and the children of immigrants to the province were required to learn French. But still, Quebec remained a province of Canada.

Not everyone in Quebec supported the idea of separation from Canada. In 1980, the provincial government held a referendum. In a referendum, voters cast ballots for or against an issue. This referendum asked voters whether Quebec should become a separate nation. A majority voted no.

In 1995, Quebec held another referendum. Again, Quebec's people voted to remain part of Canada. But this time the margin was very slim—50.6 percent voted against separation while 49.4 percent voted for it. Since then, separatists have lost power and positions in government, but they vow that they will continue to fight for Quebec's independence.

Use Context Clues If you do not know what a referendum is, look for a context clue. Here, the sentence following *referendum* is a definition of the term. What is a referendum?

Quebec

Like much of Canada, Quebec's early history was shaped by two countries—Great Britain and France. Unlike the rest of the nation, however, French influence has remained particularly strong in Quebec. The province's recent history reflects the importance of the French legacy in the region. As you study the map, chart, and timelines, think about how history and culture have interacted in Quebec throughout its history.

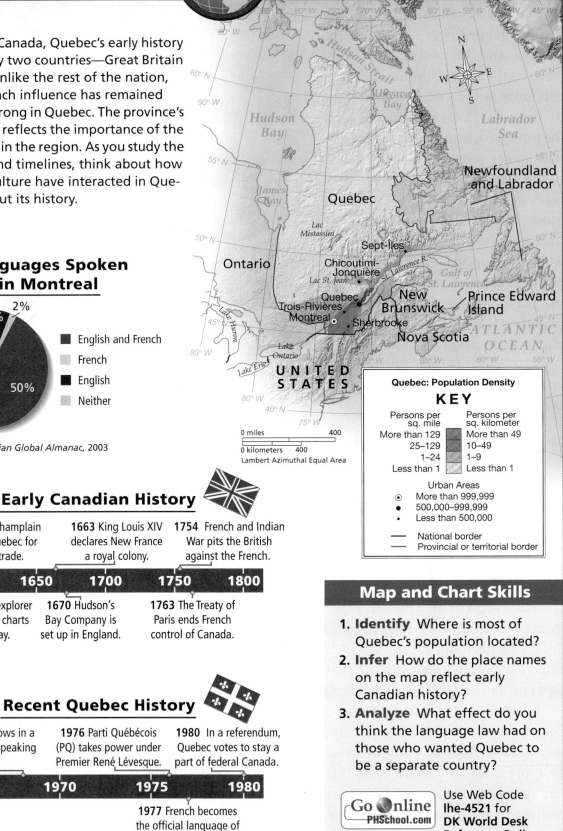

Languages Spoken in Montreal

- 2%
- 8%
- 40%
- 50%

- English and French
- French
- English
- Neither

SOURCE: *Canadian Global Almanac*, 2003

Quebec: Population Density

KEY

Persons per sq. mile	Persons per sq. kilometer
More than 129	More than 49
25–129	10–49
1–24	1–9
Less than 1	Less than 1

Urban Areas
- ⊙ More than 999,999
- ● 500,000–999,999
- · Less than 500,000

— National border
— Provincial or territorial border

0 miles 400
0 kilometers 400
Lambert Azimuthal Equal Area

Early Canadian History

1608 Samuel de Champlain builds a fort at Quebec for the French fur trade.

1663 King Louis XIV declares New France a royal colony.

1754 French and Indian War pits the British against the French.

| 1600 | 1650 | 1700 | 1750 | 1800 |

1610 English explorer Henry Hudson charts Hudson Bay.

1670 Hudson's Bay Company is set up in England.

1763 The Treaty of Paris ends French control of Canada.

Recent Quebec History

1968 Interest grows in a separate French-speaking province.

1976 Parti Québécois (PQ) takes power under Premier René Lévesque.

1980 In a referendum, Quebec votes to stay a part of federal Canada.

| 1965 | 1970 | 1975 | 1980 |

1977 French becomes the official language of Quebec.

Map and Chart Skills

1. **Identify** Where is most of Quebec's population located?

2. **Infer** How do the place names on the map reflect early Canadian history?

3. **Analyze** What effect do you think the language law had on those who wanted Quebec to be a separate country?

Go Online
PHSchool.com

Use Web Code **lhe-4521** for **DK World Desk Reference Online.**

Celebrating Quebec's Culture One of the ways in which Quebec's people celebrate their culture is through festivals. The Quebec Winter Carnival lasts 17 days. Fantastic ice sculptures adorn Quebec City, and canoe races take place among the ice floes in the St. Lawrence River.

Another Quebec festival honors St. Jean-Baptiste (zhahn bah TEEST), or John the Baptist, the patron saint, or special guardian, of French Canadians. This festival is held June 24. All over the province, people celebrate with bonfires, firecrackers, and street dances.

French style and cooking flourish in Quebec—with Quebec variations. Sugar pie, for example, uses maple sugar from the province's forests. Quebec also has French architecture. The people of Quebec take pride in preserving their lively culture.

✔ **Reading Check** **What is the official language of Quebec?**

An ice slide sculpture at Quebec City's Winter Carnival

Section 1 Assessment

Key Terms
Review the key terms at the beginning of this section. Use each key term in a sentence that explains its meaning.

Target Reading Skill
Find the word *autonomous* on page 291. Use context to figure out its meaning. What clue helped you figure out its meaning?

Comprehension and Critical Thinking
1. (a) Identify Who is the head of state in Canada?

(b) Contrast How does the head of state differ from the head of government?
(c) Analyze What are the possible benefits of this kind of system?
2. (a) Recall How many people in and around Montreal are Francophones?
(b) Make Generalizations Why are French-Canadians concerned with preserving their heritage?
(c) Summarize What has the Canadian government done to meet the demands of French-Canadians?

Writing Activity
You have read that some people in Quebec want to remain a part of Canada while others want Quebec to become a separate country. Write a paragraph giving your opinion on the subject. Be sure to give reasons for your point of view.

For: An activity on Quebec
Visit: PHSchool.com
Web Code: lhd-4501

Section 2

The Prairie Provinces
Canada's Breadbasket

Prepare to Read

Objectives

In this section you will

1. Learn why many immigrants came to the Prairie Provinces in the 1800s.
2. Read about how Canadians celebrate their cultural traditions.

Taking Notes

As you read this section, looks for details about European immigration to the Prairie Provinces. Copy the chart below, and record your findings in it.

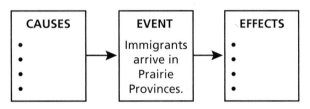

```
┌──────────┐     ┌──────────┐     ┌──────────┐
│  CAUSES  │     │  EVENT   │     │ EFFECTS  │
│  •       │ ──▶ │Immigrants│ ──▶ │  •       │
│  •       │     │ arrive in│     │  •       │
│  •       │     │ Prairie  │     │  •       │
│  •       │     │Provinces.│     │  •       │
└──────────┘     └──────────┘     └──────────┘
```

Target Reading Skill

Interpret Nonliteral Meanings Literal language means exactly what it says. Nonliteral language uses images to communicate an idea. Sometimes nonliteral language communicates a point more vividly than literal language. In this section, you will read about "Canada's Breadbasket." When you see these words, ask yourself: How does nonliteral language make a point about the Prairie Provinces region?

Key Terms

- **descent** (dee SENT) *n.* a person's ancestry
- **immunity** (ih MYOO nuh tee) *n.* a natural resistance to disease

Sheets of floating ice in Hudson Bay

One day in 1821, after a difficult journey, about 200 Swiss immigrants reached Hudson Bay in northern Canada. They wanted to become farmers in the region that now includes Saskatchewan (sas KACH uh wahn), Alberta, and Manitoba. Stories of good land and an excellent climate attracted the settlers to the vast plains. But no shelter, food, or supplies awaited them. The settlers survived only because the native people of the region, the Saulteaux (sawl TOH), helped them.

The winters were harsh. In summer they had to put up with drought, floods, and swarms of grasshoppers. With few trees on the plains, people built homes out of prairie sod—strips of grass with thick roots and soil attached. They cut it into blocks, which they piled up to make walls in the same way that American settlers did in the Midwest. "Soddies" were cheap, but if it rained, the roofs leaked. Few settlers had farming experience, and they did not anticipate such hardships.

The Prairie Provinces

Manitoba, Saskatchewan, and Alberta are located on the largest prairie in the world, stretching across the three provinces and down into the central United States. As a result, they are often called the Prairie Provinces. These provinces occupy lands where indigenous peoples have lived for thousands of years.

A Way of Life Ends The Cree and Saulteaux were among the indigenous peoples who lived on the plains in present-day Manitoba. The Cree, Blackfoot, and Assiniboine (uh SIN uh boyn) lived in present-day Alberta. The Chipewyan (chip uh WY un) and Sioux, also called Dakota, are native to Saskatchewan.

These native peoples were deeply connected to the plants and animals of their lands. Buffalo, in particular, were the foundation of their daily lives. Buffalo meat provided food, and buffalo hides were made into clothing. Regina, now the capital of Saskatchewan, was once a place the Cree called *Wascana,* which means "pile of bones." Here people made buffalo bones into tools. Despite their dependence on the buffalo, however, native peoples only used what they needed. Huge numbers of buffalo remained.

In the late 1870s, however, that changed. People of European **descent,** or ancestry, moved into the region and began killing off the buffalo herds that blanketed the region. People killed the buffalo both for sport and for their hides. In a few years, nearly all the buffalo were gone. At the same time, the government of Canada began to take over the indigenous peoples' land. Most agreed to give up their land and live on reserves. The ways of life of many indigenous peoples in the Plains region of North America had come to an end.

A Buffalo Hunt
By the 1730s, Plains Indians were able to trade for horses. **Analyze Images** *How did horses help the Plains Indians to hunt buffalo more effectively?*

Explore the Canadian Plains region.

Prairie Provinces

Canada is the world's second-largest exporter of wheat, after the United States. Although the size of farms in Canada is growing larger, there are fewer of them. Farmers take advantage of science and new technology to increase their crop production. But the new methods are expensive, so corporate farms are replacing small family farms. As you study the map and charts, think about where the food you eat comes from.

Number of Farms in Prairie Provinces

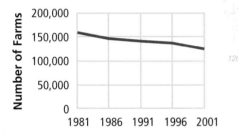

SOURCE: Statistics Canada

Average Size of Farms in Prairie Provinces

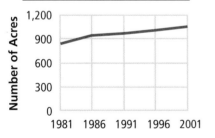

SOURCE: Statistics Canada

Percent of Canadian Grains Grown in Prairie Provinces

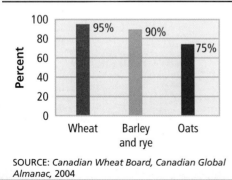

SOURCE: *Canadian Wheat Board, Canadian Global Almanac,* 2004

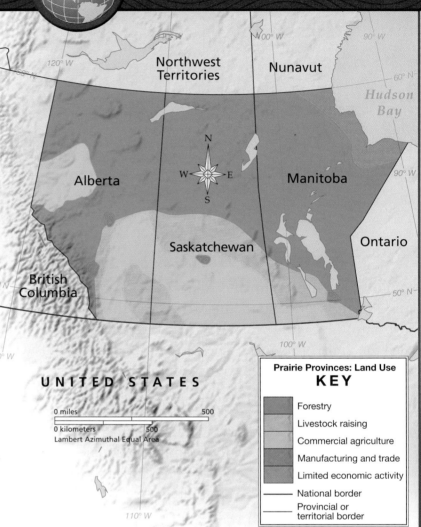

Prairie Provinces: Land Use
KEY

- Forestry
- Livestock raising
- Commercial agriculture
- Manufacturing and trade
- Limited economic activity
- National border
- Provincial or territorial border

0 miles — 500
0 kilometers — 500
Lambert Azimuthal Equal Area

Map and Chart Skills

1. **Identify** What important crops are grown in the Prairie Provinces?

2. **Note** How much larger was a Prairie Province farm in 2001 than in 1981?

3. **Draw Conclusions** How is it possible that the number of farms has decreased but the Prairie Provinces produce most of Canada's wheat, barley, rye, and oats?

Go Online
PHSchool.com

Use Web Code
lhe-4511 for **DK World Desk Reference Online.**

Increasing Immigration The population of the indigenous peoples also began to shrink. This happened, in part, because European immigrants brought diseases to which the Plains Indians did not have immunity, or natural resistance. At the same time, the European population swelled. The settlers were eager to farm the prairie. The Canadian government encouraged people to settle on the Plains. Newcomers would help the economy grow. In the late 1800s and early 1900s, Canada advertised free land in European newspapers. The advertisements worked, and immigration increased. From 1900 to 1910, the population of Alberta alone increased by more than 500 percent.

Until the early 1900s, nearly all Canadians were indigenous peoples or people of French or British descent. That quickly changed. German, French, Belgian, Ukrainian, Hungarian, and Scandinavian immigrants all came to the Prairie Provinces. These immigrants farmed, mined, ranched, and participated in the fur trade.

Links to
Science

Sanctuary Visitors to Saskatchewan's Grasslands National Park see some of North America's last untouched prairies. Ancient grasses called wheat grass, spear grass, and sage blow in the wind. The park is also home to 12 endangered and threatened species. They include hawks, burrowing owls, and short-horned lizards (below).

Prairie wheat grows in Saskatchewan, Canada.

Harvesting Wheat
This farmer harvests wheat near Saskatoon, Saskatchewan. Saskatchewan has more farmland than any other Canadian province. It is also Canada's largest producer of wheat. **Compare** *What part of the United States is similar to this part of Canada? Explain why.*

Farming the Land Many of the European immigrants who arrived became wheat farmers. In 1886, the completion of the Canadian Pacific Railway allowed settlers to reach the Prairie Provinces more easily. Better transportation also meant that wheat could be carried more quickly from farms to Canadian ports and then to the rest of the world. The wheat economy of Canada boomed.

Today, more than three fourths of Canada's farmland is in the Prairie Provinces. Wheat is still the major crop. Every year since the mid-1930s, Saskatchewan has produced more than half of Canada's wheat crop. This has helped Canada to become one of the world's leading exporters of wheat. It is no wonder then, that the region is known as Canada's Breadbasket. Although corporate farming is increasing, there are still more family-run farms in Canada than there are in the United States.

✓ **Reading Check** **Why is this region known as Canada's Breadbasket?**

Celebrating Traditions

Each year, cities of the Prairie Provinces celebrate their ethnic or cultural heritage. In Calgary, Alberta, the Calgary Stampede commemorates the area's ranching legacy. This ten-day rodeo event has been held in Calgary since 1912. It offers a large variety of events such as chuck-wagon races, cow-milking contests, and bull riding. For ten days every July, the city of Edmonton, Alberta, celebrates the gold rush with its Klondike Days. Popular events include the raft race and the sourdough pancake breakfast. (During the gold rush many prospectors ate sourdough bread and biscuits).

Festival du Voyageur is held each February in Winnipeg, the capital of Manitoba. It honors the French Canadian fur-trading heritage of the area and features traditional food, arts and crafts, and exhibits. And in Weyburn, Saskatchewan, residents pay tribute to wheat as the area's most important crop with the Weyburn Wheat Festival. A great deal of fun at this festival comes from harvesting competitions and plant shows. The smell of fresh-baked bread from outdoor ovens adds to the atmosphere.

Rodeo events take place during the Calgary Stampede in Calgary, Alberta.

✔ **Reading Check** Which Canadian festival celebrates ranching?

Section 2 Assessment

Key Terms
Review the key terms at the beginning of this section. Use each key term in a sentence that explains its meaning.

Target Reading Skill
Find the phrase "buffalo herds that blanketed the region" on page 299. Explain in your own words what it means.

Comprehension and Critical Thinking
1. (a) List Which three provinces make up the Prairie Provinces?
(b) Explain What attracted thousands of European immigrants to the Canadian Prairie Provinces?

(c) Identify Effects How did the lives of indigenous people in the Canadian plains change after Europeans arrived?
2. (a) Recall Name two ways that Canadians celebrate their cultural heritage.
(b) Identify Effects How have European immigrants influenced the life and culture of the Prairie Provinces?
(c) Draw Conclusions What do you think were the advantages and disadvantages of moving to the Canadian plains in the 1800s?

Writing Activity
Suppose that it is the year 1900, and you work for Canada's government. The government will give 160 acres of land to people willing to come to the Prairie Provinces to start farms. Make a poster advertising free land. Describe conditions that would make settlers want to come.

For: An activity on Saskatchewan
Visit: PHSchool.com
Web Code: lhd-4502

British Columbia
Economic and Cultural Changes

Prepare to Read

Objectives

In this section you will

1. Find out about the people and cultures of the Canadian West.
2. Learn what the economy and culture of British Columbia are like.

Taking Notes

As you read this section, look for details about the history of British Columbia. Copy the table below, and record your findings in it.

Events in British Columbian History	
10,000 years ago	
1700s	
1800s	
Today	

Target Reading Skill

Use Context Clues When you come across an unfamiliar word, you can sometimes figure out its meaning by using context—the surrounding words, phrases, and sentences. Sometimes the meaning of a word may not be clear until you have read an entire passage. However, you can infer the meaning of the unfamiliar word using general context clues and evaluating the information in the reading passage.

Key Terms

- **totem pole** (TOHT um pohl) *n.* a tall, carved pole containing the symbols of a particular Native American group, clan, or family
- **boomtown** (boom town) *n.* a settlement that springs up quickly to serve the needs of miners

Dancers at Chinese New Year in Vancouver, British Columbia

A visitor starts her day at a tiny coffee shop. All around her, people are speaking Dutch, Japanese, Spanish, German, and English. After having breakfast, the visitor gets into her car. On the radio, she hears country music—sung in French. Driving downtown, she passes street signs in Chinese, Indian men wearing turbans, a Korean travel agency, and a Thai restaurant. Where in the world is she? It may seem like the United Nations. But it is Vancouver (van KOO vur), British Columbia—a truly international city. As the largest city in British Columbia, Vancouver is the province's major center of industry, transportation, commerce, and culture.

The People of the Canadian West

The first people came to present-day British Columbia at least 10,000 years ago. They belonged to several ethnic groups and spoke many different languages. Each group had its own customs and a complex society. The people along the coast caught fish, whales, and shellfish. They also carved giant **totem poles,** or tall, carved poles containing the symbols of a particular group, clan, or family. Other groups lived and hunted game in the dense inland forests. Some people traded with one another and got along well. Others fought.

New Arrivals In the late 1700s, Spanish, British, and Russian explorers arrived in the area to trade. In 1778, James Cook, a British explorer, sailed to Vancouver Island, off the coast of British Columbia. A group of Nootka (NOOT kuh) people met the British and agreed to trade. These coastal people wanted iron tools, while the British wanted furs. When the British built a fur-trading post on the island, trade between the two groups began to flourish.

Trade changed the indigenous peoples' lives a great deal. Although fur traders did not permanently settle the area, they introduced tools, European-style clothing, and ideas. In 1858, everything changed. Gold was discovered along the Fraser River.

Indigenous Carvings
The Haida sculptor (below) works on a small totem pole. Large totem poles (right) are sometimes used to tell the history of a family or tribe. **Analyze Images** *What does this totem pole tell you about the lives of the indigenous people who carved it?*

British Columbia

More than 90 percent of British Columbia is owned by the government, which manages the land and its resources. The government sets certain rules about where and how forests can be cut, and then leases the land to private companies and loggers. More than 260,000 British Columbians depend on forestry for their jobs. British Columbia is the largest single exporter of softwood lumber in the world. As you study the map and charts, think about the importance of the provinces' natural resources.

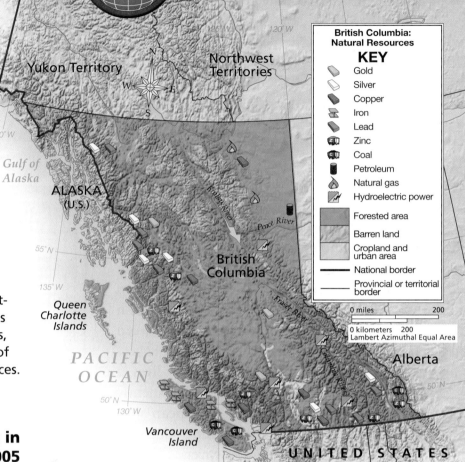

British Columbia: Natural Resources

KEY

- Gold
- Silver
- Copper
- Iron
- Lead
- Zinc
- Coal
- Petroleum
- Natural gas
- Hydroelectric power
- Forested area
- Barren land
- Cropland and urban area
- National border
- Provincial or territorial border

0 miles 200
0 kilometers 200
Lambert Azimuthal Equal Area

Income From Mining in British Columbia, 2005

Mineral	Dollars (millions)
Copper	$1,130
Zinc	$528
Gold	$255
Lead	$87

SOURCE: *Price Waterhouse Coopers, Canada*

Canadian Wood and Paper Products Production

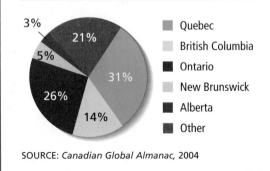

- Quebec — 21%
- British Columbia — 31%
- Ontario — 26%
- New Brunswick — 14%
- Alberta — 5%
- Other — 3%

SOURCE: *Canadian Global Almanac, 2004*

Map and Chart Skills

1. **Identify** Look at the map to describe the location of British Columbia's forests.
2. **Analyze Information** What is the total income British Columbia received in 2005 from mining copper, gold, zinc, and lead?
3. **Draw Conclusions** What do the charts tell you about the importance of forest products to the economy of British Columbia?

Go Online
PHSchool.com

Use Web Code lhe-4513 for **DK World Desk Reference Online.**

The Gold Rush A few years earlier, the British had established Victoria, a trading village on Vancouver Island. It was a small town of traders and farmers. Then, one Sunday morning in April 1858, an American paddlewheeler entered Victoria's harbor. It dropped off more than 400 men. They carried packs, blankets, spades, pickaxes, knives, and pistols. These rugged-looking characters had come to mine gold in the area. In a single morning, Victoria's population more than doubled.

Within weeks, tens of thousands more miners had arrived. Victoria quickly became a "stumptown"—all of its great trees had been chopped down to build shacks and boats. The town served as a supply center for the miners who were looking for gold on the Fraser River.

Two years later, miners also struck gold in the Cariboo Mountains in eastern British Columbia. Another wave of miners came from China, Europe, and the United States. The region was far from the coast and hard to reach, so the government built a 400-mile (644-kilometer) highway to it. Almost overnight, **boomtowns,** or settlements that were built to serve the needs of the miners, sprang up along the road. When the gold rush was over, many boomtowns died out.

Changes for Indigenous Peoples The thousands of settlers who arrived were taking gold from indigenous people's land—even taking over the land itself. In 1888, the British government took steps to confine some indigenous peoples to a small reserve. The indigenous peoples protested. The reserve was located on land that they had always lived on. How, they asked, could the government now "give" it to them?

Mining for Gold
This photograph, taken in 1900, shows a group of people looking for gold at Pine Creek, British Columbia.
Analyze Information *Why would most people choose to mine gold from creeks and streams rather than by digging deep into the ground?*

Use Context Clues If you do not know what a *paddlewheeler* is, consider these context clues. It was able to enter a harbor. It was carrying more than 400 passengers. Therefore, a paddlewheeler is _____.

Explore Vancouver, British Columbia's largest city.

An indigenous man uses a gaff, an iron hook with a long handle, to catch salmon on the Moricetown Indian Reserve in British Columbia.

Like indigenous peoples throughout Canada, they had little choice. In a few short years, native people had gone from being the great majority to being the smallest minority of the population. They were pushed onto small reserves. The government passed laws banning many of their customs, religions, and languages. Authorities took children from their parents and placed them in government-run schools.

Recently, the indigenous peoples of British Columbia have found new pride in their history and culture. Their art is thriving. They are also demanding political rights and land. As a result, tension has developed between indigenous peoples and other British Columbians. For example, in 1999 the Sechelt Indians were awarded thousands of acres of land northwest of Vancouver and more than $40 million Canadian dollars. Many people felt that these terms were too generous. In July 2002, residents of British Columbia voted to place limits on native land claims.

The Canadian Pacific Railway British Columbia officially joined Canada in 1871. One of the conditions of joining was that a transcontinental railroad would be built within 10 years. Construction began in 1875, but little progress was made until 1881. That spring, Canadians began work on the enormous project of building a railroad that would stretch from Montreal to Vancouver. The goal of the project was to unite Canada. Look at the physical map of Canada on page 142 and you can see what a huge task this was. There were countless obstacles—soaring mountains, steep valleys, and glaciers. Workers built bridges and blasted long tunnels through the mountains.

The railroad project brought more change to Canada. There were not enough workers available to complete the railway on schedule. Thousands of immigrants, particularly from Ireland and China, came to work on the railroad. Towns grew up along the railroad, and more newcomers moved in. In a few short years, British Columbia changed from a sparsely inhabited region to a settled one, complete with cities.

✔ **Reading Check** Why was the Canadian Pacific Railway built?

Economics and Culture

Although the Canadian Pacific Railroad connects all of Canada, the mountains are a barrier between British Columbia and the rest of the country. Today, most British Columbians live along the coast, west of the mountains. Many of them feel that their economic future lies with other countries more than with the rest of Canada.

The Pacific Rim Many British Columbians feel a link between their province and the Pacific Rim countries—nations that border the Pacific Ocean. One link is British Columbia's diverse people. More than 15 percent have Asian ancestors.

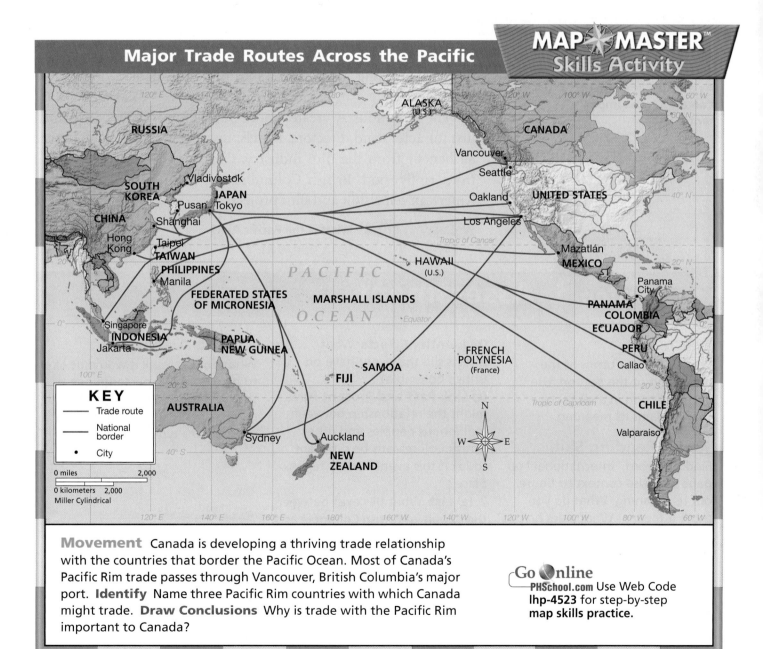

Major Trade Routes Across the Pacific

MAP☀MASTER™ Skills Activity

KEY
— Trade route
— National border
• City

0 miles 2,000
0 kilometers 2,000
Miller Cylindrical

Movement Canada is developing a thriving trade relationship with the countries that border the Pacific Ocean. Most of Canada's Pacific Rim trade passes through Vancouver, British Columbia's major port. **Identify** Name three Pacific Rim countries with which Canada might trade. **Draw Conclusions** Why is trade with the Pacific Rim important to Canada?

Go Online
PHSchool.com Use Web Code lhp-4523 for step-by-step map skills practice.

The water in Vancouver's harbor does not freeze. As a result, it's one of Canada's most important ports.

Trade is still another link between British Columbia and the Pacific Rim. Forty percent of the province's trade is with Asian countries. British Columbia wants good relationships with them. As a result, in British Columbian schools, students learn Asian languages. They learn Japanese, Cantonese Chinese, or Mandarin Chinese. Some even learn Punjabi (pun JAH bee), a language of India and Pakistan.

The Film Industry The television and film industry is another example of British Columbia's strong link to other countries. British Columbia is the third-largest film production center in North America—after New York and Los Angeles. More than 200 productions were filmed in the province in 2002, bringing more than $800 million Canadian dollars to the region.

The film industry creates about 50,000 jobs. The jobs are not just for actors and directors. Hotels, restaurants, and gas stations all benefit from the film industry. Only a two-hour plane ride from Hollywood, British Columbia is a good option for many American television and film projects.

✓ **Reading Check** What is the Pacific Rim?

Section 3 Assessment

Key Terms
Review the key terms at the beginning of this section. Use each key term in a sentence that explains its meaning.

Target Reading Skill
Find the word "international" on page 304. Use context to figure out its meaning. What do you think it means? What clues helped you arrive at a meaning?

Comprehension and Critical Thinking
1. (a) Recall What brought people to British Columbia in the late 1800s?

(b) Identify Effects What effects did this event have on British Columbia?
(c) Link Past and Present How might the relationship between indigenous peoples and other British Columbians be different today if this event hadn't taken place?
2. (a) List What ties exist between the people of British Columbia and the Pacific Rim?
(b) Analyze How does British Columbia's geography contribute to its economic and cultural ties with the Pacific Rim?

Writing Activity
What do you think it would be like to be a gold prospector in one of the gold rushes in Canada? Write a journal entry describing a gold prospector's typical workday.

Go Online
PHSchool.com

For: An activity on totem poles
Visit: PHSchool.com
Web Code: lhd-4503

The Atlantic Provinces
Relying on the Sea

Prepare to Read

Objectives

In this section you will
1. Learn what life is like on the Atlantic coast.
2. Discover how maritime industries affect the provinces.

Taking Notes

As you read this section, look for the causes and effects of overfishing. Copy the chart below, and record your findings in it.

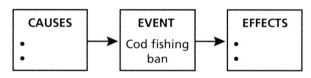

CAUSES	EVENT	EFFECTS
• •	Cod fishing ban	• •

Target Reading Skill

Use Context Clues Context, the words and phrases surrounding a word, can help you understand a word you may not know. One context clue to look for is cause and effect. The context clues show how the unfamiliar word is related to the cause or is the result of an action or idea. Clues to look for include *because, since, therefore,* and *so.*

Key Terms

- **exile** (EK syl) *v.* to force someone to leave his or her native land or home
- **maritime** (MA rih tym) *adj.* having to do with navigation or shipping on the sea
- **aquaculture** (AHK wuh kul chur) *n.* the cultivation of fish or water plants

Modern-day Norwegian explorer Helge Ingstad was aboard a ship in 1960 that stopped at a rocky peninsula in Newfoundland. The land formation was similar to what he had seen on ancient maps, and the scenery reminded him of the descriptions in Viking legends. After spotting what appeared to be the outlines of old building foundations, Ingstad believed he might be at the site of the first known Viking settlement in North America. Eight years of archaeological digs proved that Ingstad had unearthed a Viking settlement—possibly the very one that Leif Ericsson reached and named Vinland around the year 1000. Many artifacts were found at the site, including fireplaces, and a pit where iron may have been heated and formed into tools. The Viking settlement is now called L'Anse aux Meadows (lahns oh meh DOH). Viking buildings and artifacts have been reconstructed, and the historic site has become a popular tourist attraction.

From the time of the Vikings until today, the location of the Atlantic Provinces has had a huge influence on the region.

Some historians believe that Leif Ericsson may have landed here at L'Anse aux Meadows about 1,000 years ago.

Living on the Coast

Today, Newfoundland and Labrador, along with Prince Edward Island, New Brunswick, and Nova Scotia, make up the Atlantic Provinces. These provinces are located in eastern Canada, where they all share at least part of their border with the Atlantic Ocean. Many of the people in these provinces live on the coast. One exception is Prince Edward Island, where the population is evenly spread across the island. The people in the Atlantic Provinces are mainly of English, Irish, Scottish, and French descent.

Newfoundland and Labrador Five hundred years after the Vikings left their colony in Vinland, John Cabot rediscovered the island in 1497. He called it the *New Found Land*. About 100 years later, the island became England's first overseas colony. It was used mainly as a fishing station until settlers moved there permanently in the early 1600s. In 2001, the province's name officially changed from Newfoundland to Newfoundland and Labrador.

The province of Newfoundland and Labrador is the easternmost part of North America. Because of its location, the province is an important transatlantic transportation and communications center. It was here in 1901 that Guglielmo Marconi (goo lee EL moh mahr KOH nee) received the first wireless telegraph signals from across the Atlantic Ocean. More importantly, the province is located next to the Grand Banks, which at one time were the best fishing grounds in the world.

Use Context Clues
If you do not know what *transatlantic* means, look for a context clue. Use the cause and effect context clue and the surrounding sentences to figure out its meaning. What does *transatlantic* mean?

Northern gannets fly around Avalon Peninsula, Newfoundland and Labrador.

The Atlantic Provinces

Long before the Atlantic Provinces were settled, European fishermen had been coming to the Grand Banks to fish. The abundance and variety of fish astonished them. Since that time, fishing, especially cod fishing, has been a vital part of the region's economy. Because of overfishing, cod fishing was banned in 2003. People in the Atlantic Provinces are beginning to concentrate on other economic activities. As you study the map and charts, think about how a natural resource can affect a region's people and economy.

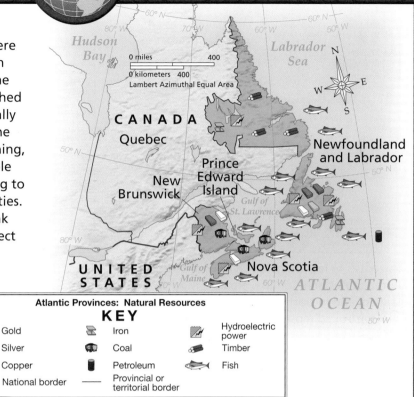

Atlantic Provinces: Natural Resources
KEY

Gold	Iron
Silver	Coal
Copper	Petroleum
— National border	— Provincial or territorial border
Hydroelectric power	Timber	Fish

Cod Fishing in Newfoundland

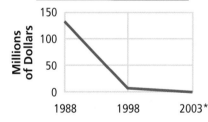

* Cod fishing banned throughout Canada
SOURCES: *The World Today Series: Canada, 2003; Boston Globe,* 2003

Aquaculture in Newfoundland and Labrador

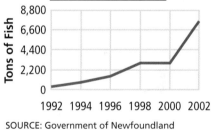

SOURCE: Government of Newfoundland

Economic Activities in the Atlantic Provinces

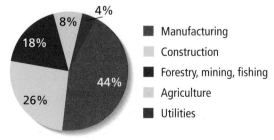

4%, 8%, 18%, 26%, 44%

- Manufacturing
- Construction
- Forestry, mining, fishing
- Agriculture
- Utilities

SOURCE: *Canadian Global Almanac,* 2003

Map and Chart Skills

1. **List** What are the Atlantic Provinces' major natural resources?
2. **Analyze** How has aquaculture changed in the past decade?
3. **Predict** How do you think the cod fishing ban will affect the region? How might it help the development of other economic activities?

Go Online PHSchool.com
Use Web Code **lhe-4514** for **DK World Desk Reference Online.**

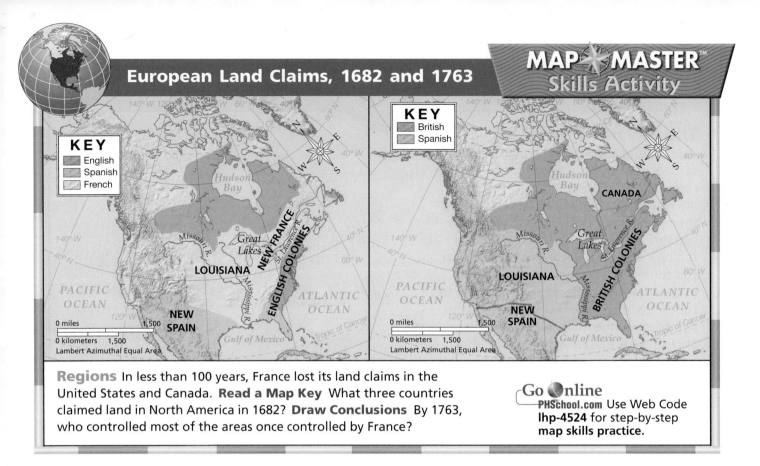

KEY
English
Spanish
French

KEY
British
Spanish

Regions In less than 100 years, France lost its land claims in the United States and Canada. **Read a Map Key** What three countries claimed land in North America in 1682? **Draw Conclusions** By 1763, who controlled most of the areas once controlled by France?

Go Online
PHSchool.com Use Web Code **lhp-4524** for step-by-step map skills practice.

Acadia Eastern Canada was once almost entirely populated by people of French descent. Nova Scotia, New Brunswick, and Prince Edward Island were part of Acadia. Here, in the early 1600s, the French established their first permanent North American settlement. French control of the area, however, did not last long. The English wanted this land, and the two countries fought over it many times. The area shifted from one country's control to the other's more than once. During the fighting, Acadians remained neutral.

In 1755, a time when Britain controlled the area, Britain feared that the French inhabitants of Acadia might secretly be loyal to France. As a result, Acadians were **exiled,** or forced to leave the area. Some exiled Acadians settled in Quebec or New Brunswick, while others moved to France, the West Indies, and other French colonies. Still others moved to present-day Louisiana, then a French settlement, where their descendants today are known as Cajuns. Britain gained permanent control over Acadia in 1763 at the end of the Seven Years' War. Many Acadians returned to the area only to find that the British had taken control of the fertile lands they had once farmed. So they took up fishing and lumbering instead to support themselves.

✓ **Reading Check** **When did Britain gain permanent control over Acadia?**

Links to
Science

High Tide The Bay of Fundy lies between New Brunswick and Nova Scotia. Its unique funnel shape—narrow with shallow water at the north end of the bay and wide with deep water where the bay opens into the ocean—causes some of the highest tides in the world. Water in the bay can rise as much as 60 feet at high tide. These exceptional tides carry about 100 billion tons of water in and out of the bay each day.

A Maritime Economy

Maritime means related to navigation or commerce on the sea. No term better sums up the focus of life in the Atlantic Provinces. The Atlantic Provinces are often called the Maritime Provinces. Much of the economy there depends on fishing.

In the 1800s, the demand for fishing vessels brought about the growth of the shipbuilding industry. The region led Canada in ship construction through most of the 1800s. The forestry industry in the area kept shipbuilders well supplied. Both industries helped the region's economy boom. Shipbuilding is still a major employer in the region, particularly in Nova Scotia.

Fishing is another major industry. However, the fishing industry has changed. In Newfoundland and Labrador, cod had been the primary catch until cod fishing was partially banned in 1992 and completely banned in 2003. The government banned cod fishing because the waters had been overfished. Tens of thousands of fishing jobs have been lost as a result of the ban.

Today, the province has turned its attention toward other types of fish to make up for loss of revenue from cod. Fish farming, or **aquaculture,** is a growing industry. Mussels are grown on Canada's eastern coast, and salmon farms are operating off the shores of New Brunswick.

Fishing village on Cape Breton Island, Nova Scotia

✓ **Reading Check** **Which Atlantic Province is a leader in the shipbuilding industry?**

Section 4 Assessment

Key Terms

Review the key terms at the beginning of this section. Use each key term in a sentence that explains its meaning.

Target Reading Skill

Find the word *overfished* on page 315. Use context to figure out its meaning. What clue helped you?

Comprehension and Critical Thinking

1. (a) List Name the provinces that make up the Atlantic Provinces.

(b) Explain Where are the Atlantic Provinces located?

(c) Analyze How has the location of Newfoundland and Labrador made it an important communications center?

2. (a) Recall What industries did fishing help to grow in the 1800s?

(b) Summarize How has the fishing industry in the Atlantic Provinces changed in recent years?

(c) Predict What role might the fishing industry play in the Atlantic Provinces' economy in the future?

Writing Activity

Suppose that you are a French farmer living in Acadia in 1755. The British have told you that you must move to Louisiana. Write a paragraph describing how you feel about the move.

Go Online
PHSchool.com

For: An activity on Nova Scotia
Visit: PHSchool.com
Web Code: lhd-4504

"Hey, how was your weekend?"

If your friend asked you this question, would you tell him everything that happened over the weekend? Of course you wouldn't. You would pick a few major events and state them as a conclusion. For instance, "I went to the ball game on Saturday afternoon and the movies on Saturday night. I was really busy."

When you're asked to summarize information, you find the main ideas and weave them into a conclusion. Being able to summarize information is a school survival skill. You need it to take tests, write essays, have debates, and understand what you read.

Learn the Skill

You can summarize many types of information: a novel, a news report, a movie—even a museum exhibit. These steps show you how to sum up information.

1 **Find and state the main idea of each paragraph or section of information you want to summarize.** You can often find a main idea in the topic sentence of a paragraph. If you are summarizing a large piece of information, you might want to jot down the main ideas.

2 **Identify what the main ideas have in common.** Look for the logic in how the ideas are presented. You might find events in chronological order. You might find causes and effects or comparisons. You can also look for main ideas that describe parts of a whole topic.

3 **Write a summary paragraph beginning with a topic sentence.** The topic sentence should draw together the main ideas you are summarizing. The main ideas on your list will become the supporting details of your summary.

Practice the Skill

Reread pages 294–295. Follow the steps on the previous page in order to summarize the text.

1 Read the heading and subheadings of this passage. List the main idea of each paragraph. For example, in the first paragraph, the first half of the topic sentence provides a strong main idea: "French culture first reached Quebec in the 1500s. . . ." If no one sentence states the whole main idea, you should form a statement in your own words. Now write down the main idea for the other paragraphs in this passage.

2 The main ideas in this passage are mostly in chronological order. In what other ways are they related?

3 One possible topic sentence for your summary might be this: "The province of Quebec has struggled to preserve its French heritage in a country dominated by English culture." Use this topic sentence, or write your own, and then complete the summary paragraph by adding explanations and details. The details will come from the main ideas on your list.

A welcome-to-Quebec sign in English and French.

Apply the Skill

Reread page 305. Follow the steps to summarize the information. Keep in mind that *change* is a major part of this passage.

The Northern Territories
New Frontiers

Prepare to Read

Objectives

In this section you will

1. Discover what life is like for people in Canada's far north.
2. Find out about the remote region of the Yukon Territory.
3. Understand how the new territory of Nunavut was formed.

Taking Notes

As you read the section, look for details about the government of the Northern Territories. Copy the concept web below, and record your findings in it.

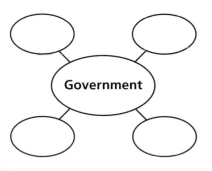

Government

 Target Reading Skill

Use Context Clues Words and phrases can take on different meanings in different situations. For example, if you are watching a play, and someone says that the *cast* is very talented, you would know that *cast* means the group of actors. But *cast* can also mean "to throw a fishing line" or "something you put on a broken arm." The information surrounding a word—whether it is a few other words, or phrases and sentences—is the context of that word.

Key Terms

- **aurora borealis** (aw RAWR uh bawr ee AL us) *n.* the colorful bands of light that can be seen in the skies of the Northern Hemisphere
- **Inuktitut** (ih NOOK tih toot) *n.* the native language of the Inuit

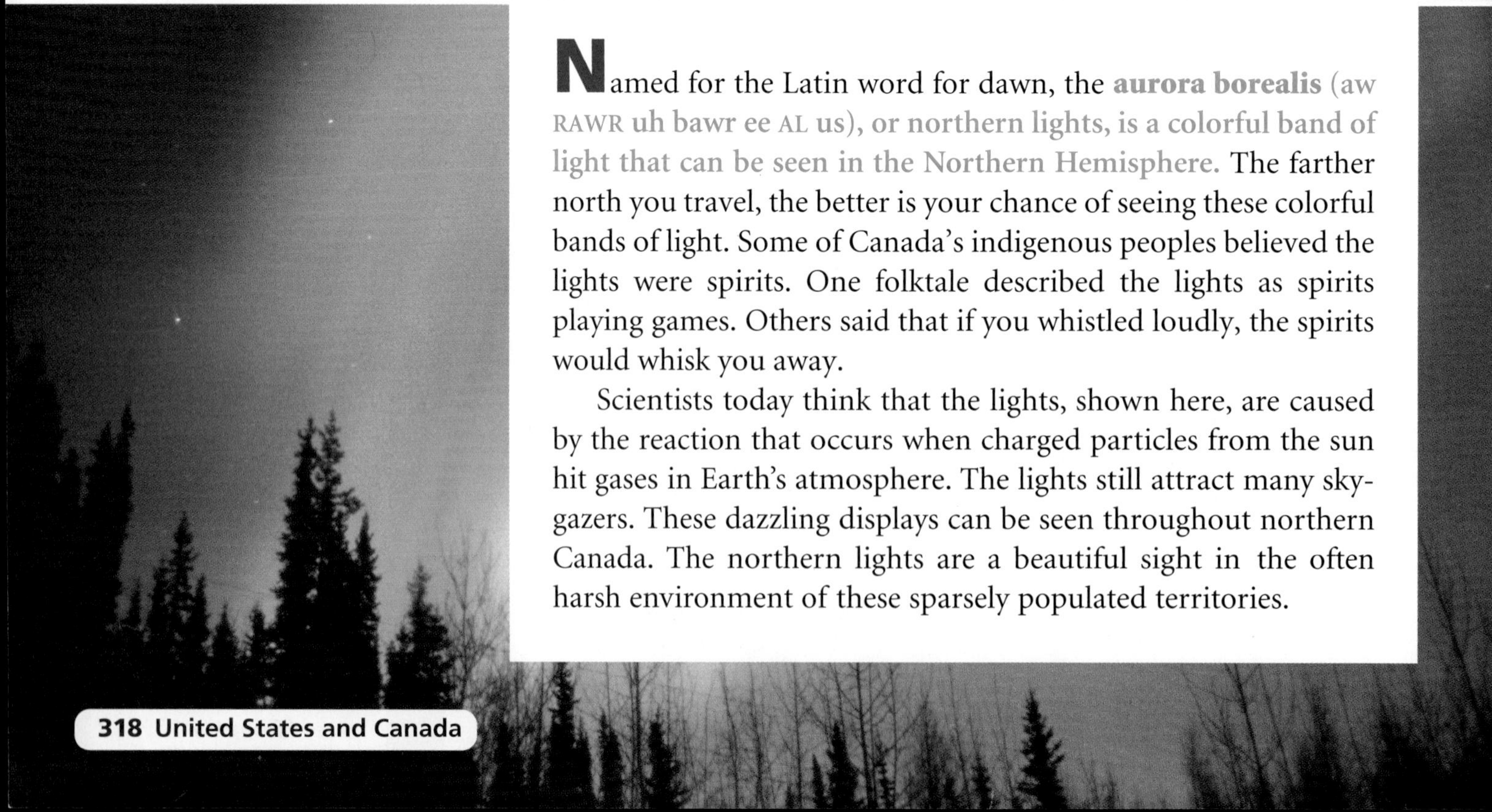

Named for the Latin word for dawn, the **aurora borealis** (aw RAWR uh bawr ee AL us), or northern lights, is a colorful band of light that can be seen in the Northern Hemisphere. The farther north you travel, the better is your chance of seeing these colorful bands of light. Some of Canada's indigenous peoples believed the lights were spirits. One folktale described the lights as spirits playing games. Others said that if you whistled loudly, the spirits would whisk you away.

Scientists today think that the lights, shown here, are caused by the reaction that occurs when charged particles from the sun hit gases in Earth's atmosphere. The lights still attract many sky-gazers. These dazzling displays can be seen throughout northern Canada. The northern lights are a beautiful sight in the often harsh environment of these sparsely populated territories.

The Far North

In addition to its provinces, Canada has three territories—the Northwest Territories, Yukon Territory, and Nunavut (NOO nuh voot). The territories make up more than one third of Canada's total land area and stretch far north into the Arctic Ocean. Despite the region's size, the people there comprise less than one percent of the nation's population. The main reason for the low population is the region's rugged terrain and harsh climate. The area is made up of tundra with little vegetation, icy waters, and subarctic forests.

Modern Inuits
This modern Inuit family travels on a snowmobile on Ellesmere Island.
Draw Conclusions *How does technology influence Inuit life?*

People of the Far North Another characteristic unique to this region is the large number of indigenous people who live there. In the Northwest Territories, almost 50 percent of the population is made up of indigenous peoples such as the Dene, Métis, and Inuit. In Nunavut, about 85 percent of the population are Inuit. In contrast, only about 14 percent of the Yukon population is made up of native people. The rest of the population is of European or other ancestry.

Contact with Europeans has changed many of the ways in which indigenous peoples live. Technology has played a major role. For example, seal hunting is an important part of Inuit life. Today, Inuit hunters use snowmobiles instead of dogsleds to cross the frozen land.

A Different Form of Government Members of the House of Commons, a part of the Canadian Parliament, represent both territories and provinces in the federal government. Each territory has its own legislative, or law-making, body similar to those of the provinces.

But, the federal government exercises more authority over the territories. While territories do have control over many of the same local concerns as provinces, such as education, the federal government controls other areas, such as some natural resources. Territories also have less power to tax than the provinces do.

 Reading Check **What percentage of Nunavut's population is Inuit?**

Target Skill **Use Context Clues** You know that *exercise* often refers to physical activity or putting something in action. Use part of that definition to help you understand *exercises authority*. What does *exercise* mean in this context? What is the meaning of the phrase *exercises authority*?

Northern Territories

Three territories—Nunavut, the Northwest Territories, and Yukon—make up this region. As territories, they have a different status from Canada's provinces. All three territories have legislatures, but there are no political parties. Decisions are made by agreement rather than by majority vote. Most of the territories' public land is controlled by the government in Ottawa. As you study the map and graphs, think about why and how Canada's territories are different from the nation's provinces.

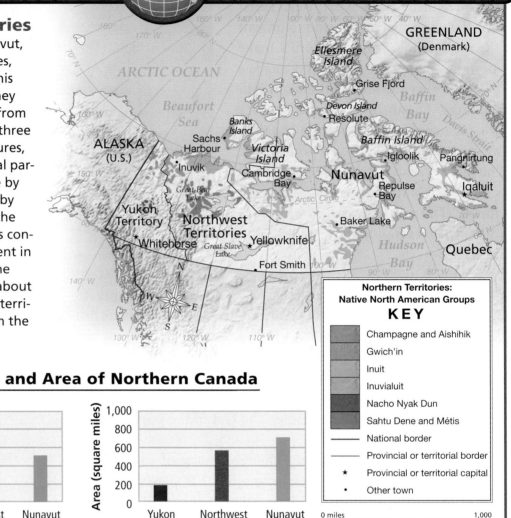

Northern Territories: Native North American Groups

KEY

- Champagne and Aishihik
- Gwich'in
- Inuit
- Inuvialuit
- Nacho Nyak Dun
- Sahtu Dene and Métis
- —— National border
- —— Provincial or territorial border
- ★ Provincial or territorial capital
- • Other town

0 miles 1,000
0 kilometers 1,000
Lambert Azimuthal Equal Area

Population and Area of Northern Canada

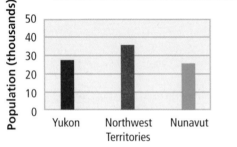

Population (thousands) — Yukon, Northwest Territories, Nunavut

SOURCE: Statistics Canada

Area (square miles) — Yukon, Northwest Territories, Nunavut

SOURCE: *Encyclopaedia Britannica*

Nunavut Legislature

Most provincial legislatures meet in a divided chamber. The party in power sits on one side, and the opposition sits on the other. The Nunavut legislature sits in a circle.

Map and Chart Skills

1. **Identify** What is the main ethnic group in Nunavut?
2. **Infer** How does the circular seating of the legislature serve the Nunavut decision-making process?
3. **Analyze** Would the organization of Nunavut's legislature work for the Canadian federal government in Ottawa? Explain why or why not.

Go Online
PHSchool.com

Use Web Code lhe-4515 for **DK World Desk Reference Online.**

Forming New Territories

All of Canada's northern land used to be one giant territory—the Northwest Territories. Over time, this vast land was split up into three separate territories.

Yukon Territory The Yukon Territory was once a district of the Northwest Territories. In 1898, an act of Parliament made it a separate territory. Many people are familiar with the Yukon Territory because of the Klondike Gold Rush. After gold was discovered in a branch of the Klondike River in 1896, thousands of prospectors swarmed to the area. Within two years, the population of the town of Dawson swelled to about 30,000. Saloons, banks, theaters, and dance halls sprang up there.

It was amazing that so many people were able to get to the area, because one of the main routes was the treacherous Chilkoot Pass, known as "the meanest 32 miles in the world." The end of the pass narrowed to less than three feet wide and became very steep. But the Yukon's era of prosperity was short-lived. By the end of 1898, the rush began to slow, and the population of the settlement declined quickly. Today, fewer than 1,300 people live in Dawson.

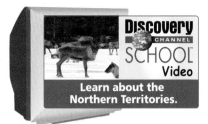

Discovery CHANNEL SCHOOL Video
Learn about the Northern Territories.

Building a New Capital
A new building was constructed in Iqaluit to house Nunavut's legislature. **Draw Conclusions** *How might the construction of a new capital have helped Nunavut's economy?*

Nunavut In 1993, the area now known as Nunavut was carved out of the eastern portion of the Northwest Territories. A constitutional act officially made Nunavut the third Canadian territory on April 1, 1999. A decades-long dream of the Inuit people to have their own self-governing territory became reality.

The Inuit, who make up most of Nunavut's population, proposed the formation of Nunavut in the 1970s. Nunavut means "our land" in **Inuktitut** (ih NOOK tih toot), the native language of the Inuit. When the matter came to a vote in 1982, residents overwhelmingly favored the creation of their own territory.

The construction of Nunavut's new capital, Iqaluit (ee KAH loo eet), provided many jobs for people. But Nunavut still faces several challenges. Leaders in the territory must work to keep its economy strong in spite of its remote location and harsh climate. The modernization of the area, which now has an Internet provider, a television broadcaster, and cellular phone service, may be a step in the right direction.

✓ **Reading Check** **Present-day Nunavut was once a part of which territory?**

This stop sign is in Inuktitut and English.

Section 5 Assessment

Key Terms
Review the key terms at the beginning of this section. Use each key term in a sentence that explains its meaning.

Target Reading Skill
Find the word *bands* on page 318. Use your own knowledge and the surrounding words and phrases to explain what *bands* means in this context.

Comprehension and Critical Thinking
1. (a) List Which three territories make up the Northern Territories?

(b) Compare and Contrast How do the governments of provinces and territories differ? How are they the same?

2. (a) Recall What event made the Yukon Territory famous?

(b) Identify Effects How did that event cause the town of Dawson to grow?

3. (a) Recall What is the newest territory in Canada?

(b) Identify Point of View Why might Inuits have wanted to create a self-governing territory?

Writing Activity
Suppose that you are Inuit, and you have always been a part of a minority in a larger territory. Describe what it might be like living for the first time in a territory where you are part of the majority.

For: An activity on Nunavut
Visit: PHSchool.com
Web Code: lhd-4505

Review and Assessment

◆ Chapter Summary

Section 1: Ontario and Quebec

- Canada's central government is located in Ottawa, Ontario.
- Toronto is Canada's financial center and largest city.
- French Canadians are concerned about preserving their cultural heritage, and some think that Quebec should become an independent country.

Section 2: The Prairie Provinces

- Manitoba, Saskatchewan, and Alberta are called the Prairie Provinces.
- Many European immigrants settled the Canadian plains in the late 1800s.
- Disease and the destruction of the buffalo in the late 1800s led to the end of many indigenous peoples' way of life.

Section 3: British Columbia

- Following the discovery of gold in 1858, the population of British Columbia grew rapidly.
- Indigenous peoples were pushed onto small reserves and were not allowed to practice many of their customs.
- British Columbia has geographic, economic, and cultural ties to foreign countries, especially those of the Pacific Rim.

Section 4: The Atlantic Provinces

- Newfoundland and Labrador, Prince Edward Island, New Brunswick, and Nova Scotia make up the Atlantic Provinces.
- The location of the Atlantic Provinces has shaped the history, culture, and economy of the people there.
- The economy of the Atlantic Provinces is dependent on the fishing industry.

Section 5: The Northern Territories

- The Northern Territories—made up of the Northwest Territories, Yukon Territories, and Nunavut—are the least-populated regions in Canada.
- The Northern Territories have a different form of government from that of Canada's provinces.
- Nunavut is the homeland of the Inuit, and Canada's newest territory.

Totem pole

◆ Key Terms

Each of the statements below contains a key term from the chapter. If the statement is true, write *true*. If it is false, rewrite the statement to make it true.

1. A separatist is a person who speaks French as his or her first language.

2. A boomtown is a settlement that springs up to serve the needs of miners.

3. Colorful bands of light that can be seen in the Northern Hemisphere are the aurora borealis.

4. Descent is a natural resistance to disease.

5. Aquaculture has to do with navigation or shipping on the sea.

6. After the Quiet Revolution, Nunavut became a separate territory.

7. An exile is someone who is forced to leave his or her homeland.

8. A federation is a union of states, groups, provinces, or nations.

Review and Assessment (continued)

◆ Comprehension and Critical Thinking

9. (a) Explain What is the role of the British monarch in Canadian government?
(b) Compare and Contrast How does the Canadian government differ from that of the United States?

10. (a) Recall What were the results of the 1980 and 1995 referendums on Quebec's independence?
(b) Analyze Why do so many people in Quebec want to separate from Canada?

11. (a) List In what ways was the buffalo important to indigenous peoples on the Plains?
(b) Identify Effects How might the destruction of the buffalo have affected the native people who lived there?

12. (a) List In the late 1700s, which countries sent explorers to present-day British Columbia?
(b) Summarize What was the relationship between the early explorers and the indigenous people of the region?
(c) Compare and Contrast How and why did the miners' relationship with native peoples differ from that of the early explorers?

13. (a) Locate Where was the first French settlement in North America?

(b) Summarize How did the lives of Acadians change after the British gained control over the region in 1763?

14. (a) Explain Why are the Northern Territories not heavily populated?
(b) Predict How does climate affect culture in the Northern Territories?

◆ Skills Practice

Writing a Summary Review the steps you followed in the Skills for Life activity in this chapter. Then reread the part of Section 3 under the heading Economics and Culture. Find and state the main idea of each paragraph. Then, identify what the main ideas have in common. Finally, write a summary paragraph that begins with a topic sentence.

◆ Writing Activity: Language Arts

Suppose that you have been asked to develop a proposal for a film to be set in British Columbia. You may choose to make a documentary or a historical film. Outline the events or the plot of the film on a storyboard—a series of sketches that show the sequence of major scenes in the film.

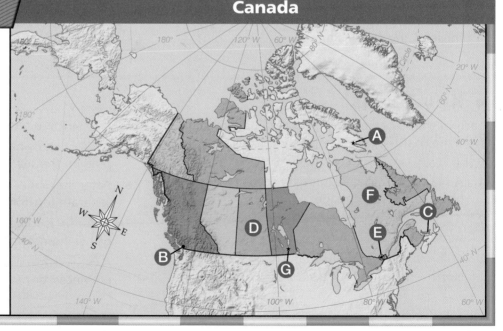

MAP★MASTER™ Skills Activity

Canada

Place Location For each place listed below, write the letter from the map that shows its location.

1. Quebec
2. Ottawa
3. Saskatchewan
4. Winnipeg
5. Vancouver
6. Prince Edward Island
7. Iqaluit

Go Online
PHSchool.com Use Web Code **lhp-4555** for an interactive map.

Standardized Test Prep

Test-Taking Tips

Some questions on standardized tests ask you to analyze a reading selection. Read the passage below. Then, follow the tips to answer the sample question.

TIP Read for key words that may help you answer the question. In this case, the key word is *Nunavut.*

In 1982, citizens of Canada's Northwest Territories were about to vote on whether to allow the creation of a self-governing homeland. It would be known as Nunavut and would be carved out of the territories. Someone argued, "We're asking for a share in the resources. We don't want to appear as beggars dependent on government handouts, but we are now being denied the resources that we so willingly gave up to support this nation."

TIP Try to answer the question before you look at the answer choices. Doing so may help you find the BEST answer.

Who might have made this argument?

  A a descendant of a French fur trader

  B a descendant of an English farmer

  C a descendant of an Inuit hunter

  D a descendant of a German logger

Think It Through The key word *Nunavut* will help you answer the question. What does the passage have to do with Nunavut? The speaker says the government owes his people resources that had been taken away. Which group wants a separate homeland that would give them control over their own resources? You can eliminate B and D. That leaves A and C. Some French in Quebec do want their own homeland. But, their resources and land were not taken away. The answer is C.

Practice Questions

Use the tips above and other tips in this book to help you answer the following questions.

1. Who is Canada's head of state?
   A the monarch of Britain
   B the prime minister
   C the governor of Ontario
   D the president

Read the passage below, and then answer the question that follows.

In the late 1800s, life changed for a group of people who lived on Canada's plains. They could not hunt the way they always had, and their lands were taken away by new settlers. They also began to get sick in large numbers from new diseases.

2. Who does this passage describe?
   A French Canadians
   B Scandinavian immigrants
   C Native Americans
   D German immigrants

3. British Columbia has special economic and cultural ties to
   A Russia.
   B the rest of Canada.
   C the northeastern United States.
   D the Pacific Rim.

4. Who first settled Canada's Atlantic Provinces in large numbers?
   A the French
   B the British
   C the Vikings
   D Americans

Go Online
PHSchool.com
Use Web Code lha-4505
for a **Chapter 10 self-test.**

Projects

Create your own projects to learn more about the United States and Canada. At the beginning of this section, you were introduced to the **Guiding Questions** for studying the chapters and special features. But you can also find answers to these questions by doing projects on your own or with a group.

 Geography How has physical geography affected the cultures of the United States and Canada?

 History How have historical events affected the cultures of the United States and Canada?

Culture How has the variety of people in the United States and Canada benefited and challenged the two nations?

 Government How do the governments of the United States and Canada differ? How are they alike?

 Economics How did the United States and Canada become two of the wealthiest nations in the world?

Project

SET UP A WEATHER STATION

Create a Weather Log
Set up a weather station to measure and record your local weather as you read this book. Measure the temperature each day at the same time. Also record the amount of precipitation and the wind direction. Record all of your findings in a weather log.

Each day, compare your local weather with the weather in other parts of the country. You can get this information from television, radio, the newspaper, or the Internet. When you have finished your measurements and recordings, create graphs to display your local readings. Then, compare your findings with the climate map in the Regional Overview.

Project

RESEARCH YOUR LOCAL HISTORY

Make a Timeline
Read about the history of your community at the local public library. Write down dates and descriptions of between 10 and 20 important events. Then, make a timeline large enough to hang on the wall of your classroom. Draw a picture of each event and place it next to its description on the timeline. Add several major events of United States history.

How to Read Social Studies

Target Reading Skills

The Target Reading Skills introduced on this page will help you understand the words and ideas in this section on Latin America and in other social studies reading you do. Each chapter focuses on one of these reading skills. Good readers develop a bank of reading strategies, or skills. Then they draw on the particular strategies that will help them understand the text they are reading.

Chapter 11 Target Reading Skill

Using the Reading Process Previewing can help you understand and remember what you read. In this chapter you will practice using these previewing skills: setting a purpose for reading, predicting what the text will be about, and asking questions before you read.

Chapter 12 Target Reading Skill

Clarifying Meaning If you do not understand something you are reading right away, you can use several skills to clarify the meaning of the word or idea. In this chapter you will practice these strategies for clarifying meaning: rereading, reading ahead, paraphrasing, and summarizing.

Chapter 13 Target Reading Skill

Using Cause and Effect Recognizing cause and effect will help you understand relationships among the situations and events you are reading about. In this chapter you will practice these skills: identifying cause and effect, recognizing multiple causes, and understanding effects.

Chapter 14 Target Reading Skill

Using Context Using the context of an unfamiliar word can help you understand its meaning. Context includes the words, phrases, and sentences surrounding a word. In this chapter you will practice using these context clues: definitions, contrast, and your own general knowledge.

Chapter 15 Target Reading Skill

Identifying the Main Idea Since you cannot remember every detail of what you read, it is important to identify the main ideas. The main idea of a section or paragraph is the most important point, the one you want to remember. In this chapter you will practice these skills: identifying both stated and implied main ideas, and identifying supporting details.

Chapter 16 Target Reading Skill

Comparing and Contrasting You can use comparison and contrast to sort out and analyze the information you are reading. Comparing means examining the similarities between things. Contrasting is looking at differences. In this chapter you will practice these skills: comparing and contrasting, identifying contrasts, and making comparisons.

LATIN AMERICA

The early peoples of Latin America created great civilizations from the riches of their land and their own ideas and skills. Their descendants have mixed with newcomers from around the world to create modern societies that blend the old and the new into vibrant and distinctive cultures.

Guiding Questions

The text, photographs, maps, and charts in this book will help you discover answers to these Guiding Questions.

1 **Geography** What are the main physical features of Latin America?

2 **History** How has Latin America been shaped by its history?

3 **Culture** What factors have affected cultures in Latin America?

4 **Government** What types of government have existed in Latin America?

5 **Economics** How has geography influenced the ways in which Latin Americans make a living?

Project Preview

You can also discover answers to the Guiding Questions by working on projects. Several project possibilities are listed on page 526 of this book.

Investigate Latin America

Latin America is a vibrant region in the midst of change. The region's northern edge is marked by the boundary between the United States and Mexico. To the south, it extends to the tip of South America. Latin America covers about 14 percent of Earth's surface.

▲ San Cristóbal de las Casas, Mexico

LOCATION

1 Explore Latin America's Location

Recall from the MapMaster Skills Handbook that when it's winter north of the Equator it's summer south of the Equator, and vice versa. Trace the line of the Equator on the map above with your finger. Next, break into small groups. Tell each other in what season your birthdays fall. Work together to figure out in what season your birthdays would be if you all lived in Santiago, Chile. What would the seasons be if you lived in Brasília, Brazil? If you lived in Mexico City, Mexico?

REGIONS

2 Compare the Size of Latin America and the United States

How does Latin America's length compare to the length of the continental United States? Take a piece of string and curve it along the west coast of the United States from the border with Canada to the border with Mexico. Cut the string the same length as the coast. Now see how many string lengths fit along the west coast of Latin America. Start at northern Mexico. Finish at the southern tip of South America. How many times longer is Latin America's Pacific Coast than the coast of the United States?

Political Latin America

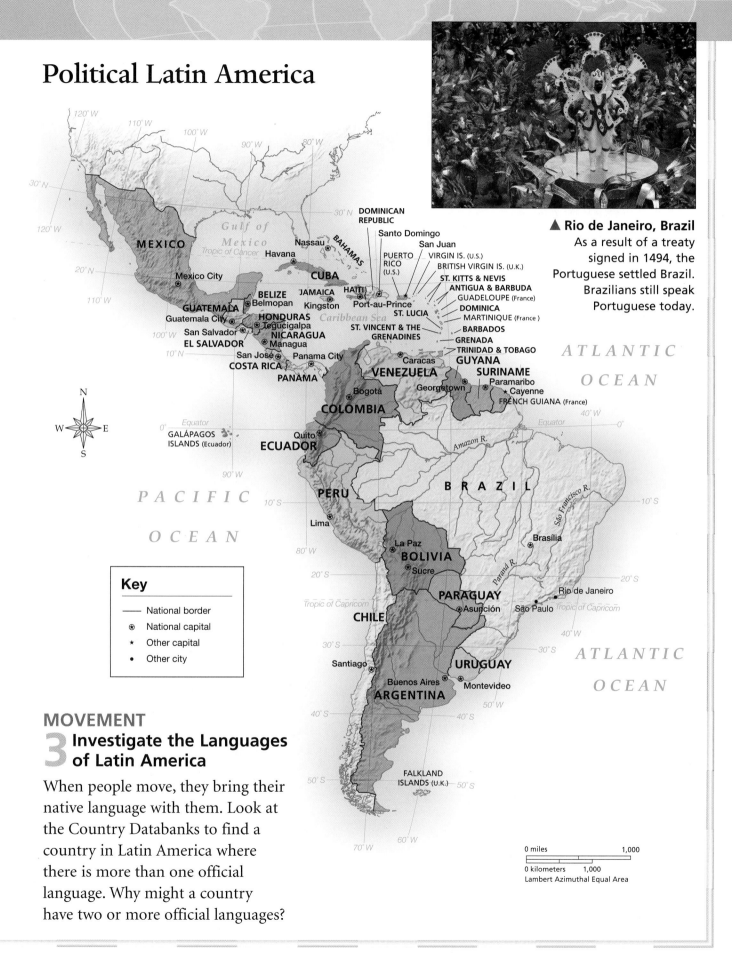

▲ Rio de Janeiro, Brazil
As a result of a treaty signed in 1494, the Portuguese settled Brazil. Brazilians still speak Portuguese today.

Key

— National border
⊛ National capital
★ Other capital
• Other city

0 miles 1,000
0 kilometers 1,000
Lambert Azimuthal Equal Area

MOVEMENT

3 Investigate the Languages of Latin America

When people move, they bring their native language with them. Look at the Country Databanks to find a country in Latin America where there is more than one official language. Why might a country have two or more official languages?

Physical Latin America

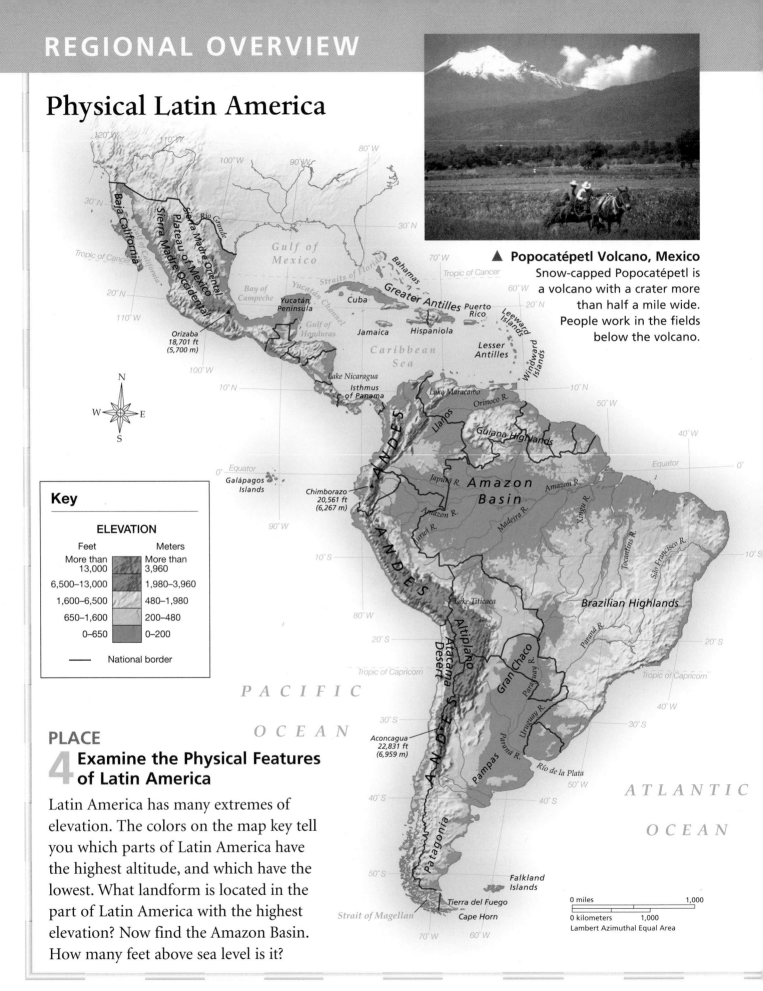

▲ **Popocatépetl Volcano, Mexico**
Snow-capped Popocatépetl is a volcano with a crater more than half a mile wide. People work in the fields below the volcano.

Key

ELEVATION

Feet		Meters
More than 13,000		More than 3,960
6,500–13,000		1,980–3,960
1,600–6,500		480–1,980
650–1,600		200–480
0–650		0–200
——	National border	

PLACE

4 Examine the Physical Features of Latin America

Latin America has many extremes of elevation. The colors on the map key tell you which parts of Latin America have the highest altitude, and which have the lowest. What landform is located in the part of Latin America with the highest elevation? Now find the Amazon Basin. How many feet above sea level is it?

0 miles 1,000
0 kilometers 1,000
Lambert Azimuthal Equal Area

Major Hydroelectric Plants

Electricity generated from water power is called hydroelectricity. One way to build a hydroelectric plant is to dam a river. The dam creates a large lake. When the dam gates open, water gushes from the lake to the river, turning huge paddles that create electricity. If you live in a region near a large river, your electricity may be generated in this way.

▲ **Itaipú Dam, Brazil/Paraguay**
Water surges through the gate at the Itaipú Dam. This dam supplies electricity to large areas of Brazil and Paraguay.

LOCATION

5 Investigate Latin America's Use of Hydroelectricity

The world's largest hydroelectric plant is located on the border of Brazil and Paraguay. Look at the circle graph below. How much of its power does Latin America get from hydroelectricity? From what energy source does Latin America get most of its power?

Latin America: Sources of Energy

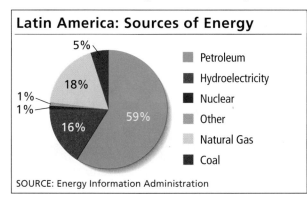

- 59%
- 18%
- 16%
- 1%
- 1%
- 5%

■ Petroleum
■ Hydroelectricity
■ Nuclear
■ Other
■ Natural Gas
■ Coal

SOURCE: Energy Information Administration

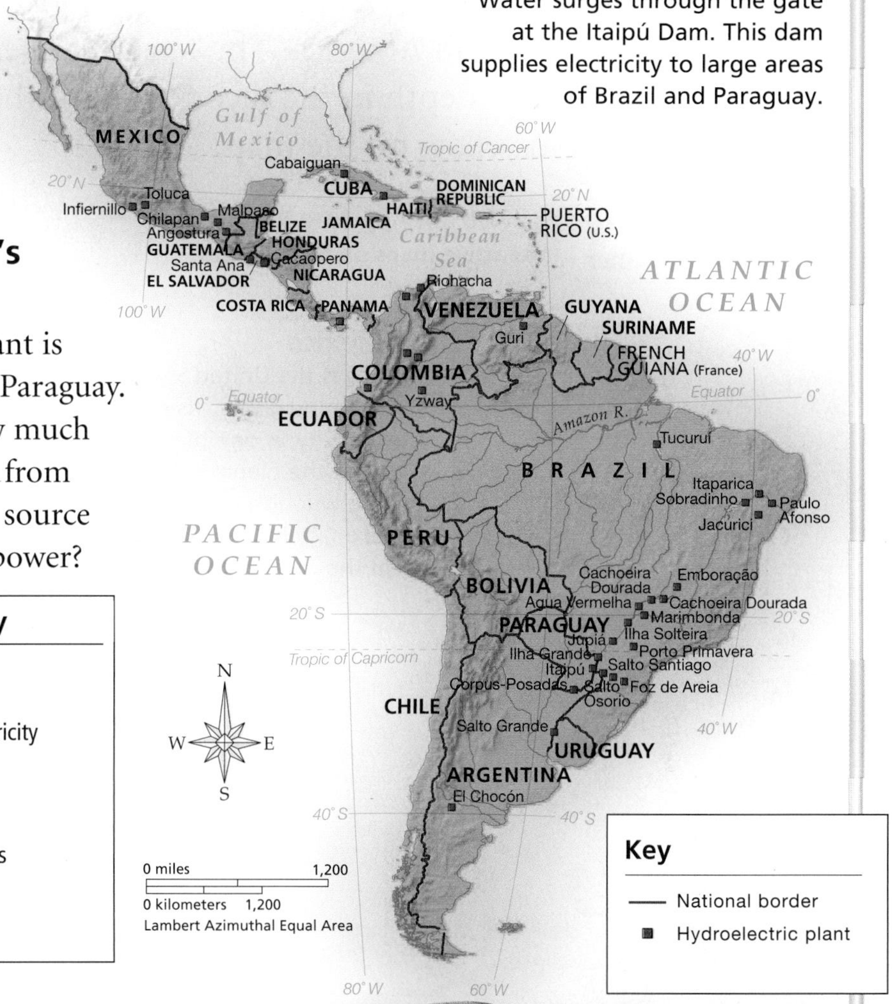

Key

— National border
■ Hydroelectric plant

0 miles 1,200
0 kilometers 1,200
Lambert Azimuthal Equal Area

PRACTICE YOUR GEOGRAPHY SKILLS

1 You are taking a trip through Latin America. You board your ship in Puerto Rico. You want to reach Panama. In which direction should you sail?

2 You are traveling through the Andes in Peru, looking for a large lake. What is it called?

3 You have traveled north again. You are looking for a hydroelectric plant in the far north of Brazil, near the coast. What is the plant called?

▲ **Lake Titicaca, Peru**

Focus on Countries in Latin America

Now that you've investigated the geography of Latin America, take a closer look at some of the countries that make up this region. The map shows all the countries of Latin America. The ten countries that you will study in depth in the second half of this book are shown in yellow on the map.

 Go Online
PHSchool.com
Use Web Code **lfp-1010** for the **interactive maps** on these pages.

120°W

30°N

Tropic of Cancer

MEXICO

Gulf of

20°N

110°W

N

W — E

S

100°W

GUATEMALA

EL SALVADOR

10°N

0° Equator

90°W

◀ **Mexico**
Mexico is the United States's southern neighbor. Its capital, Mexico City, is one of the largest cities on the planet. Many of the people who live and work in Mexico City have moved there from the countryside.

▲ **Haiti**
Haiti lies on the western third of the island of Hispaniola. It is the only nation in the Americas formed as a result of a successful revolt by enslaved Africans.

◀ **Peru**
Peru is a mountainous country that is home to many species of animals, including the llama. Llamas thrive in the mountains and their wool is used for clothing.

ATLANTIC
OCEAN

Mexico

30° N

70° W

BAHAMAS

Tropic of Cancer

CUBA

DOMINICAN
REPUBLIC

HAITI

BELIZE

JAMAICA

HONDURAS

Caribbean Sea

PUERTO
RICO
(U.S.)

20° N

ST. KITTS & NEVIS
ANTIGUA & BARBUDA
DOMINICA
ST. LUCIA
ST. VINCENT & THE GRENADINES
BARBADOS
GRENADA
TRINIDAD & TOBAGO

NICARAGUA

COSTA RICA

PANAMA

VENEZUELA

GUYANA

SURINAME

FRENCH GUIANA
(France)

COLOMBIA

ECUADOR

B R A Z I L

PERU

10° S

BOLIVIA

20° S

PARAGUAY

PACIFIC
OCEAN

CHILE

Tropic of Capricorn

URUGUAY

ARGENTINA

40° S

50° S

50° W

10° N

40° W

Equator 0°

10° S

20° S

Tropic of Capricorn

30° S

50° W

40° S

70° W   60° W

▲ Brazil

Brazil is the largest country in Latin America and is the home of São Paulo, the fastest-growing city in the world. Yet more than half of the country is made up of the Amazon rain forest, home to many diverse Native American groups who have lived there for thousands of years.

Key

— National border

☐ Countries with in-depth coverage

▨ Non-feature countries

0 miles   1,000

0 kilometers   1,000

Lambert Azimuthal Equal Area

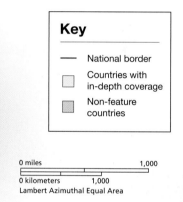

Chile ▶

Chile is a long, narrow country with a dramatic, mountainous landscape. In some parts of Chile, people still live much as their ancestors did.

Chapter 11

Latin America: Physical Geography

Chapter Preview

This chapter will introduce you to the geography of Latin America and show how geography affects the people who live there.

Section 1
Land and Water

Section 2
Climate and Vegetation

Section 3
Resources and Land Use

Target Reading Skill

Reading Process In this chapter you will focus on the reading process by using previewing to help you understand and remember what you read.

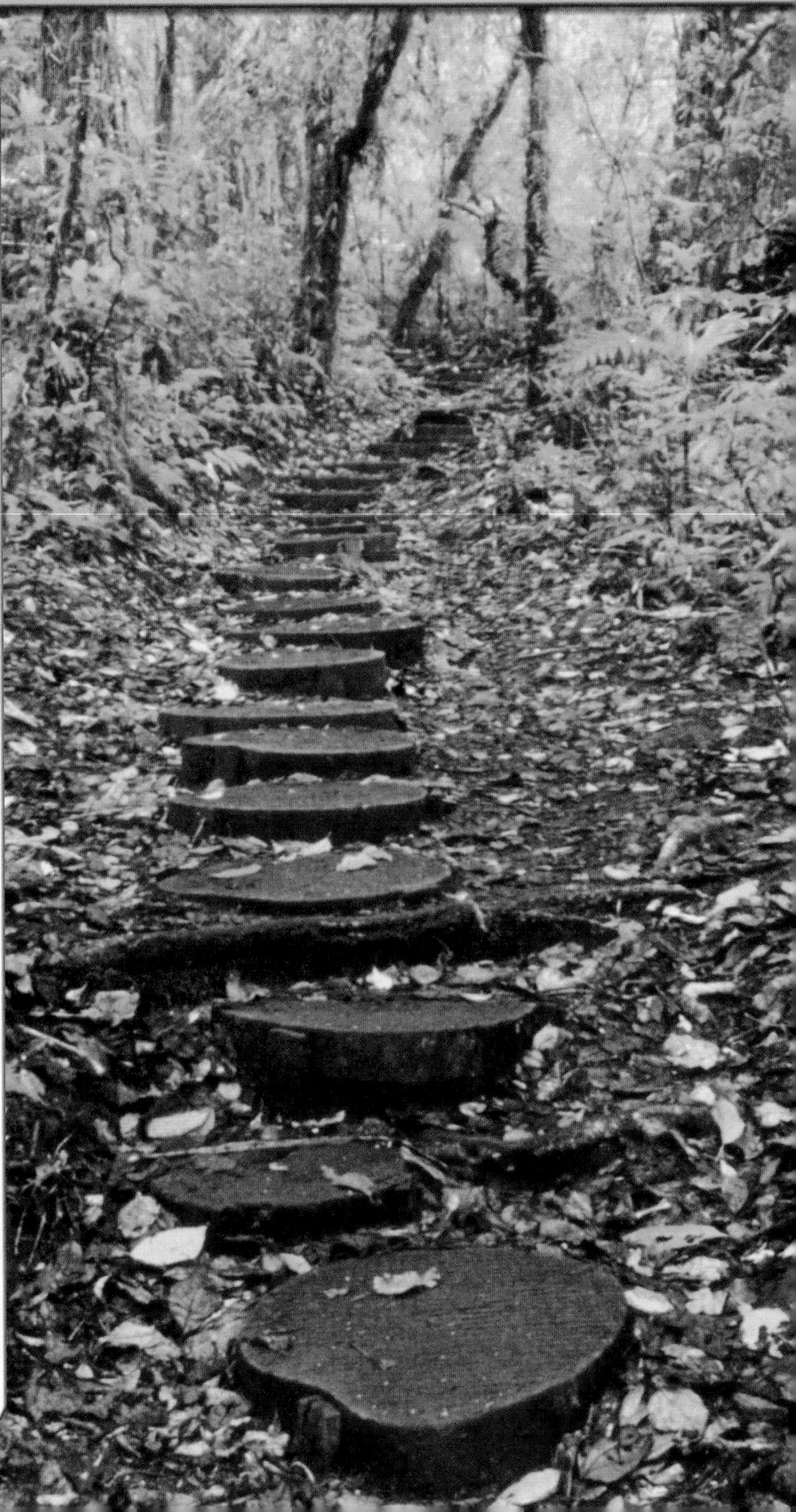

▶ **Stepping stones through a rain forest in Costa Rica**

Latin America: Physical

MAP MASTER™
Skills Activity

Place Latin America's geography is varied, but some landforms are found throughout the region. **Locate** Find the main mountain ranges in Latin America. Where are they located? **Compare and Contrast** How does the eastern part of South America compare to the western coastal region?

Go Online
PHSchool.com Use Web Code **lfp-1121** for step-by-step **map skills practice**.

ATLANTIC OCEAN

Sierra Madre Occidental
Central Plateau of Mexico
Sierra Madre Oriental
Río Grande

Gulf of Mexico

Tropic of Cancer

Greater Antilles
Cuba
Jamaica   Hispaniola
Puerto Rico
Lesser Antilles

Caribbean Sea

PACIFIC OCEAN

Isthmus of Panama

Orinoco R.
Guiana Highlands

ANDES

Amazon R.   Amazon R.

Amazon Basin

Galápagos Islands

Equator

Brazilian Highlands

Lake Titicaca

Atacama Desert

Paraguay R.
Paraná R.

Uruguay R.

Río de la Plata

ATLANTIC OCEAN

Tropic of Capricorn

Falkland Islands

Cape Horn

KEY
ELEVATION

Feet		Meters
More than 13,000		More than 3,960
6,500–13,000		1,980–3,960
1,600–6,500		480–1,980
650–1,600		200–480
0–650		0–200

— National border

0 miles   1,500
0 kilometers   1,500
Lambert Azimuthal Equal Area

Prepare to Read

Objectives

In this section you will
1. Learn where Latin America is located.
2. Discover the important landforms of Latin America.
3. Find out how Latin America's waterways have affected the region.

Taking Notes

As you read this section, look for the main ideas about the geography of Latin America. Copy the table below and record your findings in it.

Geography of Latin America		
Region	Landforms	Waterways
Middle America		
Caribbean		
South America		

Target Reading Skill

Preview and Set a Purpose When you set a purpose for reading, you give yourself a focus. Before you read this section, look at the headings, photos, and maps to see what the section is about. Then set a purpose for reading, such as learning about Latin America's geography. Now read to meet your purpose.

Key Terms

- **Middle America** (MID ul uh MEHR ih kuh) *n.* Mexico and Central America
- **plateau** (pla TOH) *n.* a large raised area of mostly level land
- **isthmus** (IS mus) *n.* a strip of land with water on both sides that joins two larger bodies of land
- **pampas** (PAM puz) *n.* flat grasslands in South America
- **rain forest** (rayn FAWR ist) *n.* a dense evergreen forest that has abundant rainfall year-round
- **Amazon River** (AM uh zahn RIV ur) *n.* a long river in northern South America
- **tributary** (TRIB yoo tehr ee) *n.* a river or stream that flows into a larger river

La Paz, Bolivia

What would it be like to land at the highest major airport in the world? Many visitors to La Paz, Bolivia, do just that. They land at El Alto airport. *El Alto* (el AL toh) means "the high one" in Spanish. It is a good name for this airport, which is located more than 13,000 feet (3,962 meters) up in the Andes Mountains.

Shortly after leaving the plane, some visitors may get mountain sickness. The "thin" air of the Andes contains less oxygen than most people are used to. Oxygen starvation makes visitors' hearts beat faster and leaves them short of breath. Later on in the day, the visitors may get terrible headaches. It takes a few days for newcomers' bodies to get used to the mountain air. But the people who live in the Andes do not have these problems. Their bodies are used to the mountain environment.

Where Is Latin America?

When visitors land in La Paz, Bolivia, they have arrived in South America, one of the regions of Latin America. Find Bolivia on the map titled Political Latin America on page 331. As you can see, Latin America is located in the Western Hemisphere, south of the United States. Notice that Latin America includes all the nations from Mexico to the tip of South America. It also includes the islands that dot the Caribbean (ka ruh BEE un) Sea.

Geographic features divide Latin America into three smaller regions, as you can see in the map below. They are Mexico and Central America, which is also called **Middle America;** the Caribbean; and South America. South America is so large that geographers classify it as a continent.

Learn about the geography of Latin America.

✓ **Reading Check** **What three regions make up Latin America?**

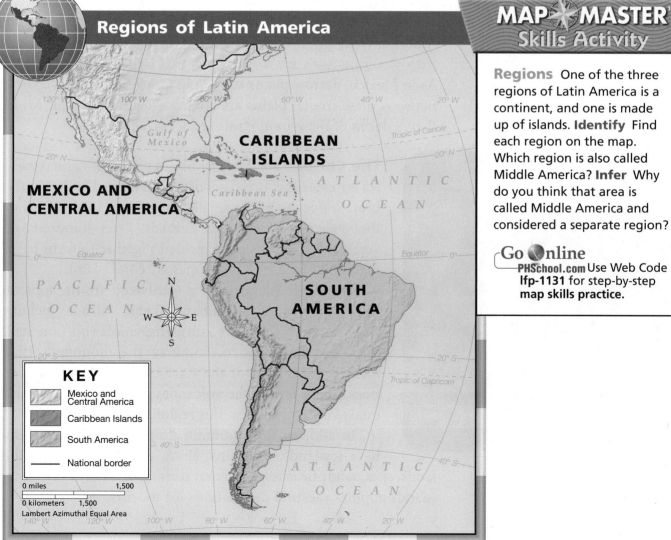

Regions of Latin America

MAP MASTER™
Skills Activity

Regions One of the three regions of Latin America is a continent, and one is made up of islands. **Identify** Find each region on the map. Which region is also called Middle America? **Infer** Why do you think that area is called Middle America and considered a separate region?

Go Online
PHSchool.com Use Web Code lfp-1131 for step-by-step map skills practice.

Why "Latin" America?
Why are three distinct regions called by one name, Latin America? About 500 years ago, Europeans sailed to the Americas. Most of those who settled in what is now called Latin America came from Spain and Portugal. These European colonists brought their own languages and ways of life with them. Today, most Latin Americans speak Spanish, Portuguese, or French. These languages have their roots in the ancient European language of Latin. As a result, the entire region is known as Latin America.

Landforms of Latin America

Picture mountains that pierce the clouds, and grassy plains that never seem to end. Imagine wet, dense forests and sun-baked deserts. This is Latin America, a region of variety and contrast.

Mexico and Central America Mexico and Central America stretch 2,500 miles (4,023 kilometers) from the United States border to South America. This distance is almost equal to the width of the United States from Los Angeles to New York City. Mountains dominate Middle America. These mountains are part of a long system of mountain ranges that extends from Canada through the United States all the way to the tip of South America.

Mexico's central plateau lies between two mountain ranges. A **plateau** (pla TOH) is a large raised area of mostly level land. Most of Mexico's people live there. However, the surrounding mountains make it difficult for people to travel to and from the central plateau. Along the east and west coasts of Mexico are narrow coastal plains.

Central America, located south of Mexico and north of South America, is an isthmus. An **isthmus** (IS mus) is a strip of land with water on both sides that joins two larger bodies of land. As in Mexico, narrow plains run along Central America's coasts. Between these coastal plains are steep, rugged mountains. More than a dozen of these mountains are active volcanoes.

A parrotfish swims by a coral reef in the Caribbean Sea.

The Caribbean The Caribbean region of Latin America is made up of two types of islands located in the Caribbean Sea. Some of the smaller islands are made of coral, the skeletons of tiny sea animals. Over hundreds of years, the skeletons have melded together to form large reefs and islands. The Bahamas are coral islands.

The larger islands of the Caribbean are the tops of huge underwater mountains. These islands include Cuba, Jamaica (juh MAY kuh), Hispaniola (his pun YOH luh), and Puerto Rico. Some of the mountains that formed the islands of the Caribbean were once volcanoes, and a few of the volcanoes are still active. Earthquakes are common in this region.

In addition to mountain ranges, these islands also have lowlands, or plains, along their coasts. Beautiful landscapes, sandy beaches, and coral reefs make many Caribbean islands popular vacation destinations for tourists.

South America The continent of South America has many types of landforms, but the Andes Mountains are probably the most impressive. The Andes run some 5,500 miles (8,900 kilometers) along the western coast of South America. In some places, the Andes rise to heights of more than 20,000 feet (6,100 meters). That's about as high as twenty 100-story buildings stacked one on top of another. Except for the Himalayan Mountains in Asia, the Andes are the highest mountains in the world.

The Andes are steep and difficult to cross. Even so, many people farm in this region. East of the Andes are rolling highlands. These highlands spread across parts of Brazil, Venezuela (ven uh ZWAY luh), Guyana (gy AN uh), and other South American countries. Farther south are the **pampas** (PAM puz), a large region of flat grasslands that stretches through Argentina (ahr jun TEE nuh) and Uruguay (YOOR uh gway). The pampas are similar to the Great Plains of the United States.

The eastern highlands and the Andes surround the Amazon River Basin. The Amazon River Basin contains the largest tropical rain forest in the world. A **rain forest** is a dense evergreen forest that has abundant rainfall throughout the year. This rain forest covers more than a third of the continent.

✓ **Reading Check** **Describe the Andes mountain range.**

Preview and Set a Purpose
If your purpose is to learn about the geography of Latin America, how does the paragraph at the left help you meet your goal?

Latin American Cowboys
These cowboys are herding cattle in the Patagonia region of Argentina.
Analyze Images *What details in the photo suggest that this scene is not taking place in the United States?*

Fishing the Rivers of Brazil
The families of these Brazilian fishers could not survive without their catch. **Infer** *Do you think these fishers sell their catch locally or send it to other countries? Use details from the photo to explain your answer.*

Latin America's Waterways

Latin America has some of the longest and largest bodies of water in the world. These waterways are important to the people of the region. Rivers serve as natural highways in places where it is hard to build roads. Fish from the rivers provide food. Rushing water from large rivers provides power to generate electricity.

Latin America's **Amazon** (AM uh zahn) **River** is the second-longest river in the world. Only the Nile in Africa is longer. The Amazon flows 4,000 miles (6,437 kilometers) from Peru across Brazil into the Atlantic Ocean. It carries more water than any other river in the world—about 20 percent of all the fresh river water on Earth! The Amazon gathers power from more than 1,000 tributaries that spill into it. **Tributaries** are the rivers and streams that flow into a larger river. With its tributaries, the Amazon drains an area of more than two million square miles.

The Paraná (pah rah NAH), Paraguay, and Uruguay rivers form the Río de la Plata system, which separates Argentina and Uruguay. In Venezuela, people travel on the Orinoco River and Lake Maracaibo (mar uh KY boh). Up in the Andes Mountains, Lake Titicaca is the highest lake in the world on which ships can travel. It lies 12,500 feet (3,810 kilometers) above sea level.

✓ **Reading Check** **What rivers form the Río de la Plata system?**

Section 1 Assessment

Key Terms
Review the key terms at the beginning of this section. Use each term in a sentence that explains its meaning.

Target Reading Skill
What was your purpose for reading this section? Did you accomplish it? If not, what might have been a better purpose?

Comprehension and Critical Thinking
1. (a) Name What are the three regions of Latin America?

(b) Synthesize Where are the regions located in relation to one another?
2. (a) Recall What are the main landforms of Latin America?
(b) Identify Cause and Effect How do mountain ranges affect life in Latin America?
3. (a) Identify Which is the largest river in Latin America?
(b) Analyze Information What are three important characteristics of that river?
(c) Generalize How do countries benefit from their waterways?

Writing Activity
If your family were planning to move to Latin America, which of its three regions would you prefer to live in? Write a paragraph explaining your choice.

Writing Tip Begin your paragraph with a topic sentence that states your main idea—your choice of region. Give at least two reasons for your choice. Support each reason with a specific detail.

Climate and Vegetation

Prepare to Read

Objectives

In this section you will
1. Find out what kinds of climate Latin America has.
2. Learn what factors influence climate in Latin America.
3. Understand how climate and vegetation influence the ways people live.

Taking Notes

As you read this section, look for the ways different factors affect climate and vegetation. Copy the table below and record your findings in it.

Factor	Effect on Climate	Effect on Vegetation

Target Reading Skill

Preview and Predict
Making predictions about your text helps you set a purpose for reading and remember what you read. Before you begin, look at the headings, photos, and anything else that stands out. Then predict what the text might be about. For example, you might predict that this section will tell about Latin America's climate and plants. As you read, if what you learn doesn't support your prediction, revise your prediction.

Key Terms

- **El Niño** (el NEEN yoh) *n.* a warming of the ocean water along the western coast of South America
- **elevation** (el uh VAY shun) *n.* the height of land above sea level
- **economy** (ih KAHN uh mee) *n.* the ways that goods and services are produced and made available to people

Every few years, something strange happens off the western coast of South America. Fish that usually thrive in the cold waters of the Pacific Ocean are driven away. At the same time, other changes occur on land. Areas that usually have dry weather get heavy rains, and low-lying regions are flooded. In other parts of Latin America, drought plagues the land and the people.

What brings this disaster to Latin America? It is **El Niño** (el NEEN yoh), a warming of the ocean water along the western coast of South America. It occurs every few years and influences global weather patterns. El Niño is Spanish for "the little boy." Peruvian fishermen gave it this name, which refers to the baby Jesus, because the warm water currents usually reach Peru around Christmas time. El Niño is one of many factors that affect climate in Latin America.

The warm water current of El Niño appears red in this view from space.

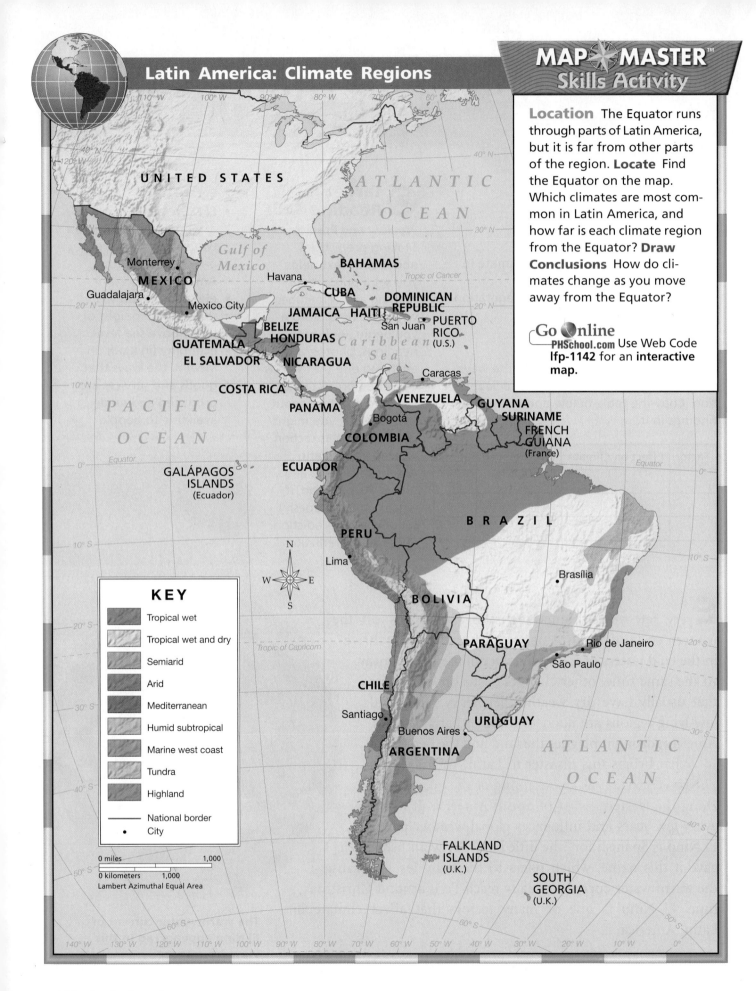

Latin America: Climate Regions

Location The Equator runs through parts of Latin America, but it is far from other parts of the region. **Locate** Find the Equator on the map. Which climates are most common in Latin America, and how far is each climate region from the Equator? **Draw Conclusions** How do climates change as you move away from the Equator?

Go Online
PHSchool.com Use Web Code **lfp-1142** for an **interactive map.**

UNITED STATES

ATLANTIC OCEAN

Gulf of Mexico

Monterrey
MEXICO
Guadalajara
Mexico City

BAHAMAS
Havana
CUBA
JAMAICA HAITI
DOMINICAN REPUBLIC
San Juan PUERTO RICO (U.S.)

BELIZE
HONDURAS
GUATEMALA
EL SALVADOR NICARAGUA
COSTA RICA
PANAMA

Caribbean Sea

Caracas
VENEZUELA GUYANA
SURINAME
FRENCH GUIANA (France)
Bogotá
COLOMBIA

PACIFIC OCEAN

GALÁPAGOS ISLANDS (Ecuador)

ECUADOR

PERU
Lima

BOLIVIA

BRAZIL

Brasília

PARAGUAY
Rio de Janeiro
São Paulo

CHILE
Santiago
Buenos Aires
URUGUAY
ARGENTINA

ATLANTIC OCEAN

FALKLAND ISLANDS (U.K.)

SOUTH GEORGIA (U.K.)

KEY

- Tropical wet
- Tropical wet and dry
- Semiarid
- Arid
- Mediterranean
- Humid subtropical
- Marine west coast
- Tundra
- Highland
- —— National border
- • City

0 miles 1,000
0 kilometers 1,000
Lambert Azimuthal Equal Area

The Climates of Latin America

What is the climate like where you live? Is it hot? Cold? Rainy? Dry? If you lived in Latin America, the climate might be any of these. Climate in Latin America can vary greatly even within the same country.

Hot, Cold, Wild, and Mild In parts of the Andes, below-zero temperatures can set your teeth chattering. Travel to the Amazon Basin, and you may be sweating in 90°F (32°C) heat. And don't forget your umbrella! This part of Latin America receives more than 80 inches (203 centimeters) of rain each year. If you prefer dry weather, visit the Atacama (ah tah KAH mah) Desert in Chile or the Sonoran Desert in Mexico. These areas are two of the driest places on Earth.

The weather in the Caribbean is usually sunny and warm. From June to November, however, the region is often hit with fierce hurricanes. In 2005, Hurricane Wilma shattered the sunny Caribbean weather with a wild blast. Winds howled at more than 185 miles per hour (300 kilometers per hour). Waves nearly 20 feet (6 meters) high smashed into the coast. The storm tore roofs off houses, shattered windows, and yanked huge trees from the ground. Wilma turned out to be the most intense hurricane ever recorded in the region.

Hurricanes are a part of life for people living in the Caribbean. But people in other parts of Latin America have to deal with other climates. For example, people who live in the mountains need to protect themselves against the cold. That's because the higher up the mountains you go, the cooler it gets.

Climate Regions of Latin America Look at the map titled Latin America: Climate Regions. You will notice that many parts of Latin America have a tropical wet climate. A tropical wet climate means hot, humid, and rainy weather all year round.

Other parts of Latin America have a tropical wet and dry climate. These areas are equally hot, but the rainy season does not last all year long. Parts of Mexico and Brazil and most of the Caribbean have a tropical wet and dry climate.

Much of Argentina, Uruguay, and Paraguay has a humid sub-tropical climate. Here, the summers are hot and wet while the winters are cool and damp. Farther south, the climate turns arid, or dry. This colder, drier area is called Patagonia (pat uh GOH nee uh).

✓ **Reading Check** Describe a tropical wet and dry climate.

Links to Science

What is a Hurricane?
A hurricane is a strong tropical storm with winds of 73 miles per hour (117 kilometers per hour) or more. Hurricanes get their energy from warm, humid air at the ocean's surface. As the warm air rises and forms clouds, more air is pulled into the developing storm. The winds spiral inward. As the storm grows, it creates very high winds and heavy rains. At the center of the hurricane is the "eye," an area of calm. After the eye passes over an area, the hurricane resumes. It can still cause serious damage, as Hurricane Mitch did in 1998 in countries such as Honduras and Nicaragua (photo below).

What Factors Affect Climate?

Have you ever hiked in the mountains? If so, you've probably noticed that as you climbed higher the temperature dropped.

One key factor affecting the climate of mountainous Latin America is **elevation**, the height of land above sea level. Look at the diagram titled Vertical Climate Zones. It shows how elevation affects climate. As you can see, the higher the elevation, the colder the temperature. Near the Equator, it may be a warm 80°F (27°C) at sea level. But above 10,000 feet (3,048 meters), the temperature may remain below freezing—too cold for people to live.

Location also affects Latin America's climate. Regions close to the Equator are generally warmer than those farther away. Look at the map titled Latin America: Climate Regions on page 344. Find the Equator. Which parts of Latin America are closest to the Equator? These regions are likely to have the warmest weather.

Wind patterns affect climate too. Winds move cold air from the North and South poles toward the Equator. They also move warm air from the Equator toward the poles. In the Caribbean, sea breezes help to keep temperatures moderate. Winds also affect rainfall in the Caribbean. More rain falls on the sides of islands facing the wind than on the sides facing away.

✓ **Reading Check** **How does nearness to the Equator affect climate?**

Diagram Skills

Even near the Equator, temperature varies with elevation. Notice the tree line. Above the tree line, it is too cold and windy for trees to grow. **Identify** What is the elevation of the tree line? Above what elevation is there snow year-round? **Draw Conclusions** Why is land between the tree line and the snow line used for grazing?

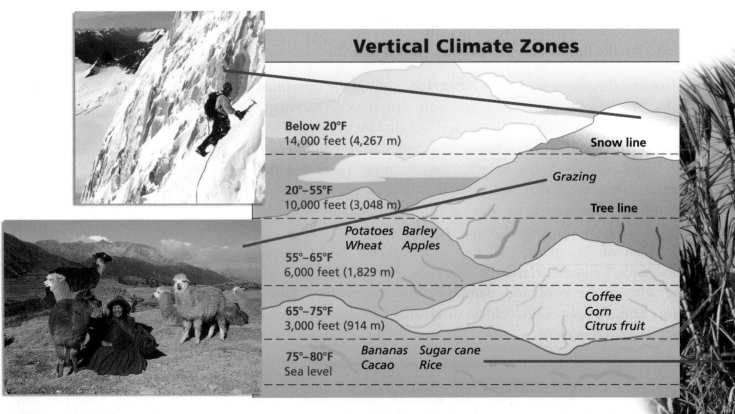

Vertical Climate Zones

Below 20°F 14,000 feet (4,267 m)	**Snow line**
	Grazing
20°–55°F 10,000 feet (3,048 m)	**Tree line**
Potatoes Barley Wheat Apples	
55°–65°F 6,000 feet (1,829 m)	
65°–75°F 3,000 feet (914 m)	Coffee Corn Citrus fruit
75°–80°F Sea level Bananas Sugar cane Cacao Rice	

Climate, Plants, and People

Imagine a forest so dense and lush that almost no sunlight reaches the ground. Broad green leaves, tangled vines, and thousands of species of trees and plants surround you. The air is hot and heavy with moisture. Welcome to the Amazon rain forest.

Now, suppose you have traveled to the coast of northern Chile. You're in the Atacama Desert. Winds carry no moisture to this barren land, and there are few signs of life. The Andes shield this parched region from rain. Parts of the desert have not felt a single raindrop in hundreds of years.

Vegetation Regions Latin America's varied climate and physical features make such extremes possible. Look at the map titled Latin America: Vegetation Regions on the next page. Notice which countries in Latin America have areas of tropical rain forest. Now, find these countries on the climate map. How do the tropical climate and heavy rainfall in these countries influence the vegetation that grows there?

Of course, not all of Latin America is either rain forest or desert. Many regions of Latin America with less extreme climates have different kinds of vegetation. For example, the pampas of Argentina and Uruguay are grassy plains where cattle are raised. Herding is also a way of life on grasslands high in the Andes Mountains, where Native Americans have raised llamas for centuries. Llamas are used mostly as pack animals. Their relatives, alpacas and vicuñas, provide fine wool.

Preview and Predict
Based on what you've read so far, is your prediction on target? If not, revise or change your prediction now.

Life in the Climate Zones
A mountain climber ascends above the snow line in Argentina (facing page, top), and llamas graze above the tree line (facing page, bottom). In the photo on this page, a woman harvests sugar cane in Barbados. **Generalize** *At what elevations would you expect to find most farms? Explain why.*

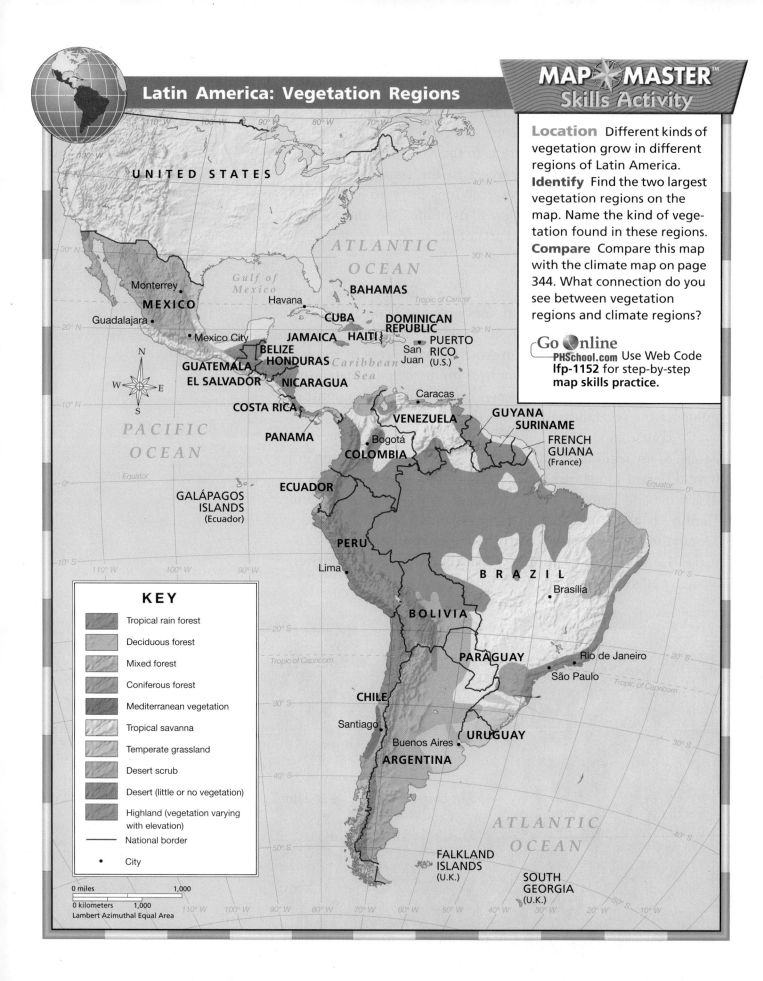

Latin America: Vegetation Regions

Location Different kinds of vegetation grow in different regions of Latin America.
Identify Find the two largest vegetation regions on the map. Name the kind of vegetation found in these regions.
Compare Compare this map with the climate map on page 344. What connection do you see between vegetation regions and climate regions?

Go Online
PHSchool.com Use Web Code
lfp-1152 for step-by-step
map skills practice.

UNITED STATES

ATLANTIC OCEAN

Gulf of Mexico

Monterrey
MEXICO
Havana
BAHAMAS
Tropic of Cancer
Guadalajara
CUBA
DOMINICAN
REPUBLIC
Mexico City
JAMAICA HAITI
BELIZE
San
PUERTO
RICO
GUATEMALA
HONDURAS
Juan
(U.S.)
Caribbean
Sea
EL SALVADOR NICARAGUA

COSTA RICA
Caracas

PACIFIC
OCEAN
VENEZUELA
GUYANA
SURINAME

PANAMA
Bogotá
FRENCH
GUIANA
COLOMBIA
(France)

ECUADOR
Equator

GALÁPAGOS
ISLANDS
(Ecuador)

PERU
B R A Z I L
Brasília

Lima

BOLIVIA

Tropic of Capricorn
PARAGUAY
Rio de Janeiro
São Paulo

CHILE

Santiago
URUGUAY
Buenos Aires

ARGENTINA

ATLANTIC
OCEAN

FALKLAND
ISLANDS
(U.K.)

SOUTH
GEORGIA
(U.K.)

KEY

- Tropical rain forest
- Deciduous forest
- Mixed forest
- Coniferous forest
- Mediterranean vegetation
- Tropical savanna
- Temperate grassland
- Desert scrub
- Desert (little or no vegetation)
- Highland (vegetation varying with elevation)
- ── National border
- • City

0 miles 1,000
0 kilometers 1,000
Lambert Azimuthal Equal Area

Crops and Climate Temperature and rainfall affect not only what plants grow naturally in a region, but also what crops people can grow there. Sugar cane, coffee, and bananas require warm weather and abundant rainfall. These crops are important to the economies of many countries around the Caribbean Sea. The **economy** is the ways that goods and services are produced and made available to people. Look again at the climate map on page 344. Why do you think the area around the Caribbean is well suited to growing these crops?

Elevation and Vegetation Elevation also affects vegetation. For example, palm trees and fruit trees that grow well in the coastal plains of Mexico and Central America would not survive high in the Andes. To grow at higher elevations, plants must be able to withstand cooler temperatures, strong winds, and irregular rainfall.

Look again at the diagram on page 346 titled Vertical Climate Zones. Notice the tree line and the snow line. It is too cold and windy for trees to grow above the tree line, but plants that grow low to the ground, such as grasses, are found in this area. Birds, bats, mice, foxes, and llamas also live here. Above the snow line, snow does not melt, and there is almost no wildlife.

Harvesting bananas in Honduras

✓ **Reading Check** **Describe how elevation affects the vegetation of a region.**

Section 2 Assessment

Key Terms
Review the key terms at the beginning of this section. Use each term in a sentence that explains its meaning.

Target Reading Skill
What did you predict about this section? How did your prediction guide your reading?

Comprehension and Critical Thinking
1. (a) Recall Describe Latin America's climate regions.

(b) Synthesize How does climate affect the ways that Latin Americans live?
2. (a) Identify Name three factors that affect climate.
(b) Apply Information Why might two areas near the Equator have very different climates?
3. (a) Name What two factors affect the kinds of vegetation that grow in a region?
(b) Infer Why do some farmers in Argentina raise apples while farmers in other parts of the country raise sheep?

Writing Activity
Would you pack differently for trips to the Atacama Desert and the Andes Mountains? Write a paragraph describing what you would take to each place and why.

For: An activity on the rain forest
Visit: PHSchool.com
Web Code: lfd-1102

Travel agent: Thanks for calling South America Travel Service. May I help you?

Customer: I'd like to visit South America, but I can't decide where to go. Could you send me brochures of places you recommend?

Travel agent: Certainly. And you might want to visit our Web site, which features a climate map of South America. You'll see that the region has many climates, offering activities from water skiing to snow skiing.

A special purpose map shows information about a particular topic. The climate map on the next page is a type of special purpose map. The travel agent knows that for most people, climate is an important factor in deciding where to vacation.

Learn the Skill

Use these steps to analyze and interpret a climate map.

1 **Read the map title and look at the map to get a general idea of what it shows.** Notice the area for which climate is being shown.

2 **Read the key to understand how the map uses symbols, colors, and patterns.** A climate map usually uses colors to represent different climates.

3 **Use the key to interpret the map.** Look for the different colors on the map. Notice where different climates are located, and what landforms and waterways are also in those locations.

4 **Draw conclusions about what the map shows.** Facts you discover when you analyze a climate map can help you draw conclusions about a place: what kinds of plants and animals live there or how the people make a living.

Practice the Skill

If you were the caller on page 350, where would you want to go on your vacation? List your favorite vacation activities, and then use the map on this page to identify several places you would like to visit.

1 Jot down the purpose of the map. What does it show?

2 Look at the key to see the different climates in South America. Identify the climates in which you could probably do the vacation activities on your list.

3 On the map, find the places that have the climates you have identified.

4 Use the climate map to draw conclusions about each place you found. Might the place have ocean views? Rock walls to climb? Forests with fascinating wildlife? Write your conclusions for each place, and choose a vacation destination.

Apply the Skill

Now take the role of the travel agent. You get an e-mail from an author. "I am writing a book that takes place in a desert region of South America that is also near the ocean. Where should I go to do my research?"

Turn to your map. **(a)** In what climate are you likely to find a desert? **(b)** What places in South America have that type of climate? **(c)** Among those places, which is closest to the ocean? Write a reply to the author. Suggest a location and explain why it will suit her needs.

Prepare to Read

Objectives
In this section you will
1. Find out what Latin America's most important natural resources are.
2. Learn why depending on a one-resource economy has been a problem for Latin American nations.

Taking Notes
As you read this section, look for the major resources of each region of Latin America. Copy the chart below and record your findings in it.

```
                Major Resources
  ┌──────────┬──────────┬──────────┐
  │  Middle  │ Caribbean│  South   │
  │ America  │          │ America  │
  ├──────────┼──────────┼──────────┤
  │    •     │    •     │    •     │
  │    •     │    •     │    •     │
  └──────────┴──────────┴──────────┘
```

Target Reading Skill

Preview and Ask Questions Before you read this section, preview the headings and illustrations to see what the section is about. Then write two questions that will help you understand or remember something important in the section. For example, you might ask, "What are the resources of Middle America?" Then read to answer your questions.

Key Terms
- **natural resources** (NACH ur ul REE sawrs uz) *n.* things found in nature that people can use to meet their needs
- **hydroelectricity** (hy droh ee lek TRIS ih tee) *n.* electric power produced by rushing water
- **one-resource economy** (wun REE sawrs ih KAHN uh mee) *n.* a country's economy based largely on one resource or crop
- **diversify** (duh VUR suh fy) *v.* to add variety

Quechua Indian women sort ore at a Bolivian tin mine.

Bolivia has long depended on its mineral resources for wealth. At first, silver helped to bring money into Bolivia's treasury. Soon, however, tin became even more important. For many years, Bolivia enjoyed the wealth that tin brought to the economy. Then, in the 1920s and 1930s, a worldwide economic crisis hit. Industries stopped buying tin, as well as other natural resources. Bolivia suffered as its main resource failed to bring in money. This economic crisis hit all of Latin America hard. It brought home a problem that many Latin American nations have: They rely too much on one resource.

Latin America's Resources

What do the following things have in common: fish, petroleum, water, silver, and forests? They are all natural resources of Latin America. **Natural resources** are things found in nature that people can use to meet their needs. Latin America's resources are as varied as its physical features and climate.

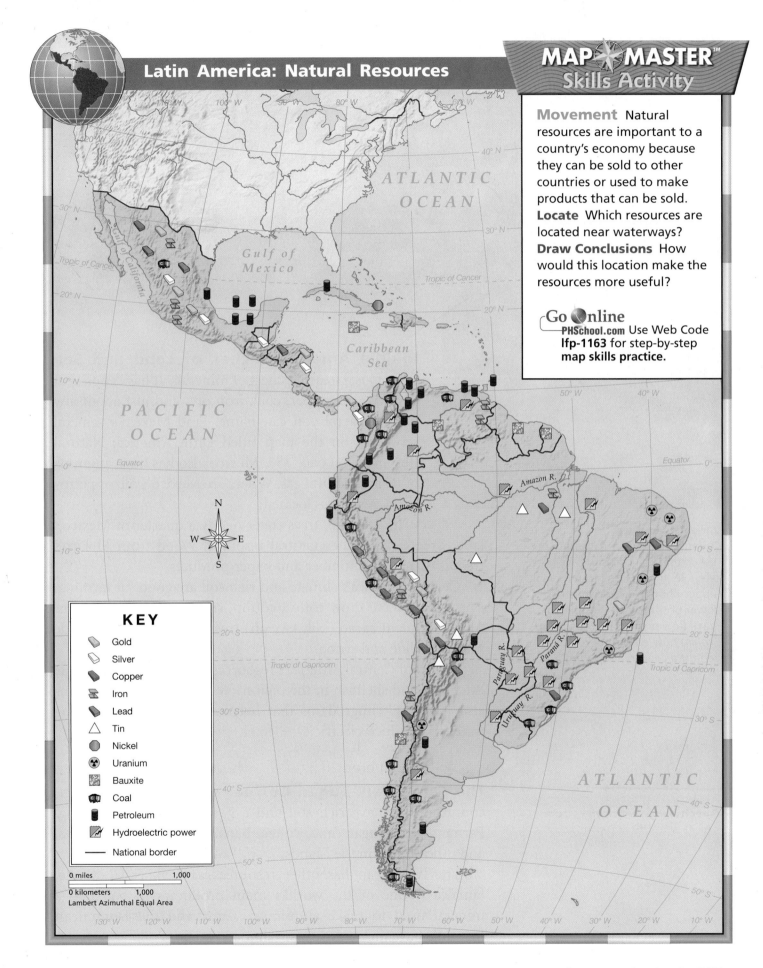

Latin America: Natural Resources

MAP★MASTER™
Skills Activity

Movement Natural resources are important to a country's economy because they can be sold to other countries or used to make products that can be sold. **Locate** Which resources are located near waterways? **Draw Conclusions** How would this location make the resources more useful?

Go Online
PHSchool.com Use Web Code **lfp-1163** for step-by-step map skills practice.

ATLANTIC OCEAN

Gulf of Mexico

Tropic of Cancer

Caribbean Sea

PACIFIC OCEAN

Equator

Amazon R.

Amazon R.

Paraguay R.

Paraná R.

Uruguay R.

Tropic of Capricorn

ATLANTIC OCEAN

KEY
- Gold
- Silver
- Copper
- Iron
- Lead
- Tin
- Nickel
- Uranium
- Bauxite
- Coal
- Petroleum
- Hydroelectric power
- — National border

0 miles 1,000
0 kilometers 1,000
Lambert Azimuthal Equal Area

Varied Resources
Countries depend on a variety of resources, from commercially grown cabbage in the Dominican Republic (upper photo) to hydroelectric power produced by this dam in Brazil (lower photo). **Generalize** *Explain how each resource could benefit a country's economy.*

Middle America: Riches of Land and Sea

Mexico is a treasure chest of minerals. It has deposits of silver, gold, copper, coal, iron ore, and just about any other mineral you can name. Find Mexico's mineral resources on the map titled Latin America: Natural Resources on page 353. Mexico also has huge amounts of oil and natural gas. Where are Mexico's oil, or petroleum, resources located?

In addition, trees cover nearly a quarter of Mexico's land. Trees are another natural resource. Wood from Mexico's trees is turned into lumber and paper products.

Central America's climate and rich soil are good for farming. The people there grow coffee, cotton, sugar cane, and bananas. They also plant cacao (kuh KAY oh) trees. Cacao seeds are made into chocolate and cocoa.

Not all of Central America's resources are on land. The people catch fish and shellfish in the region's waters. Central Americans also have built huge dams that harness the power of rushing water to produce electricity. Electric power created by rushing water is called **hydroelectricity.**

The Caribbean: Sugar, Coffee, and More

Caribbean countries also have rich soil and a good climate for farming. Farmers grow sugar cane, coffee, bananas, cacao, citrus fruits, and other crops on the islands.

The Caribbean has other resources as well. For example, Jamaica is one of the world's main producers of bauxite—a mineral used to make aluminum. Cuba and the Dominican Republic have nickel deposits. Trinidad is rich in oil.

Commercial Fishing
Workers unload their catch at a dock in Argentina. The fish shown below are tuna.
Compare and Contrast
How is this example of fishing different from that shown on page 342?

South America: A Wealth of Resources Like Mexico, South America is rich in minerals. It has gold, copper, tin, bauxite, and iron ore. Look again at the map titled Latin America: Natural Resources on page 353. Where are these resources located? South America also has oil. Much of South America's oil is found in Venezuela.

South America's plants and fish are natural resources, too. Forests cover about half the continent. Trees from these forests provide everything from wood for building to coconuts for eating. Mahogany and rosewood are used to make fine furniture. Some woods are used by local people for fuel. The rain forests of South America contain a wide variety of trees and other vegetation. Some of these plants are used to make medicines. Scientists are studying other plants to see if they, too, might have medical uses.

The people of South America harvest many kinds of fish. Tuna, anchovies, and other species of fish are plentiful in the waters off the Pacific coast. Shellfish, such as shrimp, are also important to the region's economy. Freshwater fish, those found in rivers, are an important food source in South America.

Like other parts of Latin America, South America has rich soil. Farmers grow many different crops there. For example, coffee is a key crop in Brazil and Colombia. Wheat is important in Argentina. Many South American economies rely on the production of sugar cane, cotton, and rice.

✓ **Reading Check** **What kinds of products are made from South America's forests?**

World Coffee Prices, 1965–2005

Prices adjusted for inflation, using U.S. dollars.
SOURCE: World Bank, International Coffee Association

▪ Graph Skills

World coffee prices affect not only the economies of many Latin American countries but also ordinary people, such as this Guatemalan coffee-picker. **Describe** What is the pattern of coffee prices over the 40 years shown in the graph above? **Analyze Information** What years were good years for coffee growers? What year might have been the worst? Explain your answer.

Resources and the Economy

Not every country shares equally in the wealth of Latin America's resources. Some Latin American countries have many resources, while others have few. Some countries do not have the money they need to develop all of their resources. Even when countries do develop their resources, not everyone in that country always enjoys the benefits. And sometimes countries rely too much on one resource or crop.

Problems of a One-Resource Economy Sometimes having a great deal of a valuable resource can lead to economic problems. That's because some countries then develop what is called a **one-resource economy,** an economy that depends largely on one resource or crop. Why is this a problem? Here is an example: When world copper prices are high, the copper mining industry is very successful. But suppose copper prices drop sharply. Then copper exports are not worth as much. When this happens, the mining industry loses money. Mining workers may lose their jobs. People and businesses—even a whole country—can go into debt. Chile is the leading producer of copper in the world. When prices plunge, Chile's whole economy suffers.

The World Economy Oil is one of Latin America's most valuable resources. But world oil prices go up and down, sometimes very suddenly. Mexico and Venezuela are major oil producers. In the mid-1980s, oil companies produced more oil than the world needed. As a result, prices dropped. Mexico earned much less income than it had expected.

Many people in Latin America make their living by farming. Some Latin American countries depend on only one or two crops, such as coffee, bananas, or sugar. Certain factors outside the country—such as increased production of coffee by other countries—may cause the price of the crop to drop. When the price of a crop goes down, exports of that crop bring less money into the country.

Weather Effects Weather brings challenges, too. Hurricanes, droughts, and plant diseases may damage crops. Weather can also hurt the fishing industry. Usually, the cold water of the Pacific supports a large number of small water plants on which fish feed. But when El Niño strikes, the warm water kills the plants and the fish die or move to other areas. The fishing industry of Peru has suffered great economic losses due to El Niño effects.

In each case described above, dependence on a particular resource—copper, oil, one particular crop, or fishing—has hurt the economy of the country that depended on it. That is because, if something unexpected happens to the major resource of a country with a one-resource economy, that country is left with few other sources of income.

Preview and Ask Questions
Ask a question that will help you learn something important from the paragraph at the left. Now read the paragraph and answer your question.

At the Mercy of the Weather
In 2001, a severe drought in Guatemala caused many crops to dry up. This man is sowing beans on top of his failed corn crop. **Predict** *What might be the result if this farmer depended only on corn?*

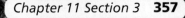

An automobile factory in Quito, Ecuador

Latin America Begins to Diversify

Because Latin American nations have learned the risks of depending on one resource or crop, they began to diversify their economies in the 1960s and 1970s. To **diversify** is to add variety. Many Latin American nations are building factories. Factories make products that can be sold to bring more money into the economy. Factories also provide jobs.

Rather than depending so much on oil, Venezuela has been promoting investment in its agriculture, steel, and tourism industries. The island nation Trinidad and Tobago also has large deposits of natural resources such as oil and natural gas. However, tourism and international business are also important parts of the economy.

El Salvador used to depend too heavily on its coffee crop. Now, cotton, sugar, corn, and other crops play an important role in the nation's economy. Brazil, too, has been building up its industries so that it does not have to depend so much on agriculture. In addition to farm products, Brazil now exports machinery, steel, and chemicals. The governments of Latin America continue to look for ways to protect their nations from the hazards of a one-resource economy.

✓ **Reading Check** How is Brazil diversifying its economy?

Section 3 Assessment

Key Terms
Review the key terms at the beginning of this section. Use each term in a sentence that explains its meaning.

Target Reading Skill
What questions helped you learn something important from this section? What are the answers to your questions?

Comprehension and Critical Thinking
1. (a) Identify Name the important natural resources of each region of Latin America.

(b) Compare How are the resources of South America similar to those of Middle America?
(c) Draw Conclusions How can rich soil and a mild climate benefit the economy of a region?
2. (a) Recall What resources have Venezuela and El Salvador depended on in the past?
(b) Synthesize Was depending on these resources good for the economies of these countries?
(c) Identify Cause and Effect Suppose a disease destroyed El Salvador's coffee crop. How would this loss affect coffee-plantation workers and the economy of El Salvador? Explain your answer.

Writing Activity
Suppose you are the president of a Latin American country. Your nation depends on sugar cane for nearly all of its income. Outline the arguments you would use in a speech to persuade your people of the need to diversify. Then write an introduction to your speech.

> **Writing Tip** A persuasive speech is like a persuasive essay. Be sure you have three reasons to support your main idea. Use persuasive language to introduce those ideas in your opening paragraph.

Review and Assessment

◆ Chapter Summary

Section 1: Land and Water

- Latin America is located south of the United States and is made up of three regions.
- Mountain ranges and rain forests dominate Latin America, but there are also islands, plains, plateaus, and deserts.
- Waterways such as the Amazon River provide transportation, food, and electric power to the people of Latin America.

Section 2: Climate and Vegetation

- Latin America has a wide range of climate regions.
- Climate is shaped by elevation, nearness to the Equator, and wind patterns.
- Latin America's diverse climate regions affect vegetation patterns and how people live.

Section 3: Resources and Land Use

- Latin America's resources include minerals, good farmland, forests, and fish.
- Depending on only a few resources, such as one crop or mineral, can lead to economic problems.
- Latin American countries are now diversifying their economies.

Argentina

Honduras

Brazil

◆ Key Terms

Each of the statements below contains a key term from the chapter. Decide whether each statement is true or false. If it is true, write *true*. If it is false, rewrite the sentence to make it true.

1. A plateau is a narrow strip of land that has water on both sides and joins two larger bodies of land.

2. A tributary is smaller than the river into which it flows.

3. Pampas are flat grasslands.

4. Rain forests thrive in hot, dry climates.

5. Elevation is the distance from the Equator.

6. The goods a country produces are its natural resources.

7. Hydroelectricity is electric power produced from rushing water.

8. To diversify an economy is to produce more of one resource.

Review and Assessment (continued)

◆ Comprehension and Critical Thinking

9. **(a) Recall** In what part of Mexico do most Mexicans live?
   (b) Describe What is this part of Mexico like?
   (c) Identify Causes What makes travel to and from this area difficult?

10. **(a) Identify** What is the major mountain range in South America?
    (b) Identify Effects Describe two effects this mountain range has on the climate, the vegetation, or the people.
    (c) Evaluate Do you think that the mountains help or hurt South America? Explain.

11. **(a) Define** What is El Niño?
    (b) Identify Effects What are some of El Niño's effects on land and sea?
    (c) Synthesize How can El Niño affect the economy of Latin America?

12. **(a) Recall** How does elevation affect climate?
    (b) Contrast How are the different vegetation regions in Latin America shaped by their climates?
    (c) Infer How do climate and vegetation affect how people live and work?

13. **(a) Identify** What are the major resources of Middle America?
    (b) Categorize Which of these resources helps produce power?
    (c) Analyze Explain what happens when too much of one resource is produced worldwide.

14. **(a) Define** What is a one-resource economy?
    (b) Summarize Describe how one Latin American country is diversifying its economy.
    (c) Generalize Why is it important for countries to diversify their economies?

◆ Skills Practice

Analyzing and Interpreting Climate Maps
In the Skills for Life activity in this chapter, you analyzed and interpreted a climate map. The skill you learned can be applied to other special-purpose maps.

Review the steps you followed to learn the skill. Then turn to the map titled Latin America: Vegetation Regions on page 348. Take the role of the travel agent again. This time respond to two people: one who wants to visit a rain forest and another who wants to visit grassy plains to observe Latin American cowboys.

◆ Writing Activity: Science

Suppose you are the television meteorologist for a small Caribbean island. As part of your weather report, you are doing an overview of the weather for the past three months. Explain to your broadcast audience why one side of your island has been rainy and the other side has been sunny. You can create a mental picture or a map of the geography of your island (including mountains and rivers) to aid in your explanation.

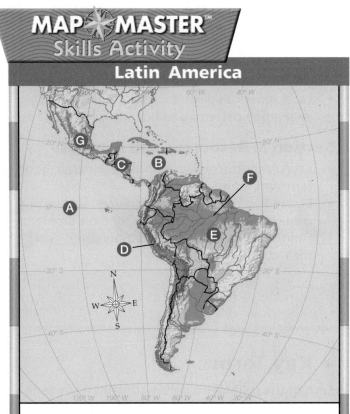

MAP★MASTER™
Skills Activity
Latin America

Place Location For each place listed below, write the letter from the map that shows its location.

1. South America
2. Caribbean Sea
3. Amazon River
4. Equator
5. Mexico
6. Central America
7. Andes Mountains

Go Online
PHSchool.com Use Web Code **lfp-1123** for an **interactive map**.

Standardized Test Prep

Test-Taking Tips

Some questions on standardized tests ask you to make mental maps. Read the passage below. Then follow the tips to answer the question.

TIP Try to picture the locations of the Southern Hemisphere and the Amazon River in your mind. Think of maps you have seen.

Pick the letter that best answers the question.

Zach's geography teacher asked his class to write clues for a game called What Country Is It? Zach wrote the following set of clues:

This country is mostly in the Southern Hemisphere. The Amazon River runs through it. It is larger than Argentina.

A Mexico.

B Brazil.

C Canada.

D Peru.

TIP First rule out answer choices that don't make sense. Pick the BEST answer from the remaining choices.

Think It Through Canada and Mexico are both in the Northern Hemisphere, so you can rule out answers A and C. The Amazon River runs across northern South America, including both Peru and Brazil. But Peru is smaller than Argentina. That leaves Brazil, answer B.

Practice Questions

Choose the letter of the best answer.

1. What two bodies of land does the isthmus of Central America connect?
   A the Caribbean and South America
   B Mexico and the United States
   C Mexico and the Caribbean
   D South America and North America

2. Which of the following factors does NOT affect a region's climate?
   A hurricanes
   B elevation
   C location
   D wind patterns

3. Throughout much of Latin America, people use rushing water to create
   A wells.
   B swimming pools.
   C water parks.
   D hydroelectricity.

4. The largest tropical rain forest in the world is located in
   A Mexico's central plateau.
   B the Amazon River Basin.
   C the isthmus of Central America.
   D the coral reefs of the Caribbean.

Read the following passage and answer the question that follows.

Yoshi is writing clues for a game called Name That Region. He wrote the following set of clues:
This region in Latin America is located in the Northern Hemisphere. It is made up of islands. Farming is especially good in this region.

5. What region do Yoshi's clues describe?
   A South America
   B the Caribbean
   C Mexico
   D North America

Go Online
PHSchool.com
Use Web Code lfa-1101
for a **Chapter 11 self-test.**

The Surveyor
By Alma Flor Ada

Prepare to Read

Background Information
Do people in your family tell you stories about their past? Are some of those stories repeated many times? What stories do you remember the best? What do you learn from these stories?

The stories that family members tell each other become a part of a family's history. They are important because they teach us about our cultural heritage. They connect us to events, to places, and to people. They show us the world from a particular, personal point of view.

Alma Flor Ada (AL muh flawr AY duh) grew up in Cuba. The following selection shows what Ada learned from one of the stories her father used to tell her.

Objectives
In this selection you will

1. Discover how a story from the past can shape the present.
2. Learn how geography can have an important effect on people's lives.

surveyor (sur VAY ur) *n.* a person who measures land and geographic features

Small farmers in Cuba live in villages like this one.

My father, named Modesto after my grandfather, was a surveyor. Some of the happiest times of my childhood were spent on horseback, on trips where he would allow me to accompany him as he plotted the boundaries of small farms in the Cuban countryside. Sometimes we slept out under the stars, stringing our hammocks between the trees, and drank fresh water from springs. We always stopped for a warm greeting at the simple huts of the neighboring peasants, and my eyes would drink in the lush green forest crowned by the swaying leaves of the palm trees.

Since many surveying jobs called for dividing up land that a family had inherited from a deceased parent or relative, my father's greatest concern was that justice be achieved. It was not enough just to divide the land into equal portions. He also had to ensure that all parties would have access to roads, to water sources, to the most fertile soil. While I was able to join him in some trips, other surveying work involved large areas of land. On these jobs, my father was part of a team, and I would stay home, eagerly awaiting to hear the stories from his trip on his return.

Surveyors use instruments like this one to help them take measurements.

Latin American families tend not to limit their family boundaries to those who are born or have married into it. Any good friend who spends time with the family and shares in its daily experiences is welcomed as a member. The following story from one of my father's surveying trips is not about a member of my blood family, but instead concerns a member of our extended family.

Félix Caballero, a man my father always liked to <u>recruit</u> whenever he needed a team, was rather different from the other surveyors. He was somewhat older, unmarried, and he kept his thoughts to himself. He came to visit our house daily. Once there, he would sit silently in one of the living room's four rocking chairs, listening to the lively conversations all around him. An occasional nod or a single word were his only contributions to those conversations. My mother and her sisters sometimes made fun of him behind his back. Even though they never said so, I had the impression that they questioned why my father held him in such high regard.

Then one day my father shared this story.

"We had been working on foot in mountainous country for most of the day. Night was approaching. We still had a long way to go to return to where we had left the horses, so we decided to cut across to the other side of the mountain, and soon found ourselves facing a deep <u>gorge</u>. The gorge was <u>spanned</u> by a railroad bridge, long and narrow, built for the sugarcane trains. There were no side rails or walkways, only a set of tracks resting on thick, heavy crossties suspended high in the air.

"We were all upset about having to climb down the steep gorge and up the other side, but the simpler solution, walking across the bridge, seemed too dangerous. What if a cane train should appear? There would be nowhere to go. So we all began the long descent . . . all except for Félix. He decided to risk

recruit (rih KROOT) *v.* to enlist or hire to join a group

gorge (gawrj) *n.* a narrow canyon with steep walls
span (span) *v.* to extend across a space

✓ **Reading Check**

What kind of work does Ada's father do?

dissuade (dis SWAYD) *v.* to persuade not to do something

ominous (AHM uh nus) *adj.* threatening

resilient (rih ZIL yunt) *adj.* able to withstand shock and bounce back from changes

walking across the railroad bridge. We all tried to <u>dissuade</u> him, but to no avail. Using an old method, he put one ear to the tracks to listen for vibrations. Since he heard none, he decided that no train was approaching. So he began to cross the long bridge, stepping from crosstie to crosstie between the rails, balancing his long red-and-white surveyor's poles on his shoulder.

"He was about halfway across the bridge when we heard the <u>ominous</u> sound of a steam engine. All eyes rose to Félix. Unquestionably he had heard it, too, because he had stopped in the middle of the bridge and was looking back.

"As the train drew closer, and thinking there was no other solution, we all shouted, 'Jump! Jump!', not even sure our voices would carry to where he stood, so high above us. Félix did look down at the rocky riverbed, which, as it was the dry season, held little water. We tried to encourage him with gestures and more shouts, but he had stopped looking down. We could not imagine what he was doing next, squatting down on the tracks, with the engine of the train already visible. And then, we understood. . . .

"Knowing that he could not manage to hold onto the thick wooden crossties, Félix laid his thin but <u>resilient</u> surveyor's poles across the ties, parallel to the rails. Then he let his body slip down between two of the ties, as he held onto the poles. And there he hung, below the bridge, suspended over the gorge but safely out of the train's path.

A train on a narrow railroad bridge travels high above the trees.

"The cane train was, as they frequently are, a very long train. To us, it seemed interminable. . . . One of the younger men said he counted two hundred and twenty cars. With the approaching darkness, and the smoke and shadows of the train, it was often difficult to see our friend. We had heard no human sounds, no screams, but could we have heard anything at all, with the racket of the train crossing overhead?

"When the last car began to curve around the mountain, we could just make out Félix's lonely figure still hanging beneath the bridge. We all watched in relief and amazement as he pulled himself up and at last finished walking, slowly and calmly, along the tracks to the other side of the gorge."

After I heard that story, I saw Félix Caballero in a whole new light. He still remained as quiet as ever, prompting a smile from my mother and her sisters as he sat silently in his rocking chair. But in my mind's eye, I saw him crossing that <u>treacherous</u> bridge, stopping to think calmly of what to do to save his life, emerging all covered with soot and smoke but triumphantly alive—a lonely man, hanging under a railroad bridge at dusk, suspended from his surveyor's poles over a rocky gorge.

If there was so much courage, such an ability to calmly confront danger in the quiet, aging man who sat rocking in our living room, what other wonders might lie hidden in every human soul?

treacherous (TRECH ur us) *adj.* dangerous

✓ **Reading Check**

What makes Félix think he will be safe?

Review and Assessment

Thinking About the Selection

1. (a) **Respond** What is your reaction to what Félix did?
(b) **Infer** What qualities did Ada's father see in Félix that shaped his opinion of the man?
2. (a) **Recall** How did Ada's mother and her sister treat Félix?
(b) **Analyze** Why did the women have such a response to Félix?
3. (a) **Recall** What parts of the story tell us about Ada and her father?

(b) **Evaluate Information** What has Ada learned and from whom did she learn it? What did you learn?

Writing Activity

Write a Short Story Choose a story you have heard from a friend or a family member, or a story that you have told about an event that was important or meaningful to you. Write the story. Include an introduction and a conclusion that explain why the story is important to you.

About the Author

Alma Flor Ada (b. 1938) was born in Camagüey (kah mah GWAY), Cuba. Her relatives were great storytellers. Their stories—part truth, part fiction—and her own childhood experiences are woven into her writing. Dr. Ada now lives in California where she is a professor at the University of San Francisco and an author and translator.

Chapter Preview

This chapter presents the history of Latin America and shows how that history affects the region to this day.

Section 1
Early Civilizations of Middle America

Section 2
The Incas: People of the Sun

Section 3
European Conquest

Section 4
Independence

Section 5
From Past to Present

Target Reading Skill

Clarifying Meaning In this chapter you will focus on skills you can use to clarify meaning as you read.

▶ Decorated wall of a Mayan building at Uxmal, Mexico

Latin America: Early Civilizations

Gulf of
Mexico

Tenochtitlán

Yucatán
Peninsula

Tikal

**CENTRAL
AMERICA**

Caribbean Sea

ATLANTIC
OCEAN

Tropic of Cancer

Equator

PACIFIC
OCEAN

ANDES

Amazon R.

Cuzco

**SOUTH
AMERICA**

Tropic of Capricorn

ANDES

ATLANTIC
OCEAN

KEY

Aztec Empire, 1325–1521

Mayan civilization, about 250–900

Incan Empire, early 1400s–1533

Other native peoples

0 miles 2,000

0 kilometers 2,000

Lambert Azimuthal Equal Area

Regions This map shows three civilizations that flourished in Latin America before Europeans arrived in the region. **Identify** Name the civilizations shown on the map. Which is the oldest? **Draw Conclusions** Which one is likely to have been influenced by another civilization shown on the map? Explain why.

Go Online
PHSchool.com Use Web Code **lfp-1221** for step-by-step **map skills practice.**

Early Civilizations of Middle America

Prepare to Read

Objectives

In this section you will
1. Find out what Mayan civilization was like.
2. Learn how the Aztecs built their empire and understand what kind of society they created.

Taking Notes

As you read this section, look for similarities and differences in the Mayan and Aztec civilizations. Copy the diagram below and record your findings in it.

Ancient Civilizations

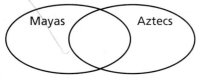

Mayas   Aztecs

Target Reading Skill

Reread Rereading can help you understand words and ideas in the text. If you do not understand a sentence or a paragraph, read it again to look for connections among the words and sentences. For example, rereading the first paragraph below can make it clear that the game being described took place long ago. Now you can better understand the surprising comparison of pok-ta-tok to basketball.

Key Terms

• **hieroglyphics** (hy ur oh GLIF iks) *n.* a system of writing using signs and symbols
• **maize** (mayz) *n.* corn
• **Tenochtitlán** (teh nawch tee TLAHN) *n.* capital city of the Aztec empire, located where Mexico City now stands

Fans cheered as the players brought the ball down the court. Suddenly, the ball flew into the air and sailed through the hoop. Fans and players shouted and screamed. Although this may sound like a championship basketball game, it is actually a moment in a game played more than 1,000 years ago. The game was called pok-ta-tok.

Pok-ta-tok was a game played by the ancient Mayas. Using only their leather-padded hips and elbows, players tried to hit a four-pound (1.9 kilogram), six-inch (15.2 centimeter) rubber ball through a stone hoop mounted 30 feet (9.1 meters) above the ground.

The Mayas

How do we know about this ancient game? Crumbling ruins of pok-ta-tok courts and ancient clay statues of players have been found at sites in Central America and southern Mexico. In these areas, Mayan civilization thrived from about A.D. 250 to A.D. 900. By studying ruins, scientists have learned much about Mayan civilization.

Mayan Civilization The Mayas built great cities, such as Copán (koh PAHN) in the present-day country of Honduras, and Tikal (tee KAHL) in present-day Guatemala. Mayan cities were economic, political, and religious centers. Large pyramid-shaped temples often stood in the middle of Mayan cities. Rival Mayan cities also engaged in frequent warfare with one another.

Mayan priests studied the stars and planets. They developed two calendars. They used one to schedule religious celebrations and the other, as we do today, to follow the seasons. The Mayas also developed a system of writing using signs and symbols called **hieroglyphics** (hy ur oh GLIF iks). Hieroglyphics found in books and in carvings have helped scientists understand Mayan culture.

Farmers worked in fields surrounding the cities. Their most important crop was maize, or corn, the main food of the Mayas. They also grew beans, squash, peppers, avocados, and papayas.

The Great Mystery of the Mayas About A.D. 900, the Mayan cities began to decline. No one knows why. Crop failures, war, disease, drought, or famine may have killed many Mayas. Or perhaps people rebelled against the control of the priests and nobles. The Mayas stayed in the region, however. Millions of Mayas still live in Mexico, Belize, and Guatemala.

✓ **Reading Check** What is the "great mystery of the Mayas"?

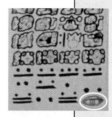

The Concept of Zero
The Mayas created a number system that included zero. Zero is important in math because it is a symbol that shows that there is none of something. For example, to write the number 308, you need a symbol to show that there are no tens. The idea of zero, which also developed in Asia, is considered to be one of the greatest inventions in mathematics. In the Mayan book above, the zero looks like a shell (circled above). Other numbers are made up of bars and dots.

Mayan Ruins
The Mayan city of Chichén Itzá had a pok-ta-tok court as well as this huge temple. **Infer** *What does this great temple suggest about Mayan culture and technology?*

The Aztec Empire

In the 1400s, another great civilization arose in Middle America. It was created by the Aztecs, who had arrived in the Valley of Mexico in the 1100s.

The Aztecs settled on an island in Lake Texcoco in 1325. They changed the swampy lake into a magnificent city. **Tenochtitlán** (teh nawch tee TLAHN), the Aztec capital, stood on the site of present-day Mexico City. When Europeans explored the area in the 1500s, they found the Aztecs ruling a rich empire from the city of Tenochtitlán.

Building an Empire In the 1400s, Aztec warriors began conquering the other people in the region. They forced the conquered people to pay tribute, or taxes. Tribute could be paid in food, cotton, gold, or slaves. The Aztecs grew rich from the tribute.

The Aztec emperor ruled over all Aztec lands. Nobles helped the emperor to govern. Soldiers fought in wars to expand the empire. They also protected the empire's trade routes. Priests were not only religious leaders, but were also important in society. People of the upper classes wore feathered garments and carried feathered fans as symbols of their status.

Farming Most of the people in the Aztec empire were farmers. The Aztecs used irrigation, or artificial systems for watering crops. As you can see in Eyewitness Technology: Aztec Farming on the next page, they also created new farmland by constructing artificial floating gardens called chinampas. Aztec farmers grew corn, squash, and beans on these chinampas.

Culture and Religion Tenochtitlán was a magnificent capital city. It had huge temples, busy markets, wide streets and canals, and floating gardens. It even had a zoo. The markets were filled with food, gold and silver jewelry, feathers, and fine crafts. The emperor and nobles lived in splendid palaces and had many slaves to serve them.

In the temples, priests performed rituals, including human sacrifice, or the offering of human lives, to please their gods. Aztec priests also used an advanced calendar based on the Maya calendar. Aztec astronomers also predicted eclipses and the movements of planets. They kept records using hieroglyphics similar to those used by the Mayas.

Aztec calendar
The face of the Aztec sun god is shown in the center of this stone calendar. The symbols surrounding the face represent the twenty days in each Aztec month. **Draw Conclusions** *Why would the Aztec sun god be associated with the calander?*

Target Skill **Reread**
Read the paragraph at the right again to find out two things Aztec astronomers did.

Aztec Farming

The Aztec city of Tenochtitlán, in central Mexico, grew quickly. The Aztecs soon used up all the farmland that was available on the island. To grow more crops, they learned how to create new farmland. At the outskirts of town, Aztec farmers dug canals through the marshy land to make small plots called *chinampas,* or "floating beds." People could paddle canoes through the many canals running among the chinampas.

The Floating City: Tenochtitlán
This painting shows what Tenochtitlán looked like. Built on a small island in the middle of a lake, it grew to a city of 200,000 people.

2 Mud and vegetation are piled onto mats that rest on the water's surface.

1 Wooden posts are set up to hold the sides of each plot in place.

3 Willow trees are planted to keep the mud in place. Over time, their roots will anchor the chinampas to the bottom of the lake.

4 Woven reeds are placed along the sides of the mud and vegetation to hold them in.

5 More layers of mud and fertile manure are added until the land is ready to plant.

6 Maize grows tall on a fully developed chinampa.

Modern-Day Living
Today, most of the lakes used by the Aztecs have been drained and covered by city growth. However, some chinampas are still used as farmland. The photo at the left shows Mexicans farming chinampas today.

ANALYZING IMAGES
How did the planting of willow trees make the Aztecs' chinampas more stable?

Past Meets Present
This girl is sketching an Aztec statue at the site of the Great Temple of the Aztecs in Mexico City. **Generalize** *Why do you think people still flock to see and study Aztec ruins?*

Aztec Medicine Aztec doctors were able to make more than 1,000 medicines from plants. They used the medicines to lower fevers, cure stomachaches, and heal wounds. Aztec doctors also set broken bones and practiced dentistry.

Trade Because of the power of the Aztec army, traders could travel long distances in safety. Crops from distant parts of the empire were brought to the capital and to other cities. Crafts, weapons, and tools were also carried throughout the empire and beyond. Luxury goods such as jaguar skins, cacao beans, and fine jewelry were also traded. These goods were carried by people called porters, because the Aztecs did not have pack animals to carry loads. Trade was usually done by barter, or the exchange of goods without the use of money.

The End of the Aztec Empire The Aztecs did not abandon their fine cities as the Mayas had done. Instead, they were conquered by newcomers from a faraway land. You will read about how the Aztec empire fell later in this chapter.

✔ **Reading Check** **How was trade carried out in the Aztec empire?**

Section 1 Assessment

Key Terms
Review the key terms at the beginning of this section. Use each term in a sentence that explains its meaning.

Target Reading Skill
What word or idea were you able to clarify by rereading? Explain how rereading helped.

Comprehension and Critical Thinking
1. (a) **Identify** Describe the main features of Mayan civilization.

(b) **Conclude** What do the facts that Mayas created accurate calendars and great cities tell about their civilization?
(c) **Infer** What can you infer about the mathematical skills of the Mayas?
2. (a) **Describe** How was Aztec society organized?
(b) **Sequence** Tell how the Aztecs created their large and powerful empire.
(c) **Infer** How do you think the conquered peoples felt about being ruled by the Aztecs? Explain your answer.

Writing Activity
If you could interview an ancient Maya or Aztec about his or her life, what would you ask? Write some questions that would help you understand one of these civilizations. Organize your questions into at least three different topics.

Writing Tip First decide which civilization to focus on. Then use the blue headings in the section to help you decide on topics. Reread the text under the headings to get ideas for your questions.

The Incas: People of the Sun

Prepare to Read

Objectives

In this section you will

1. Find out how the Incas created their empire.
2. Understand what Incan civilization was like.
3. Learn how the descendants of the Incas live today.

Taking Notes

As you read this section, look for details of Incan civilization. Copy the web below and fill in the ovals with information about the Incas.

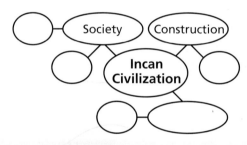

Target Reading Skill

Read Ahead Reading ahead can help you understand something you are not sure of in the text. If you do not understand a certain word or passage, keep reading. The word or idea may be clarified further on. For example, at first you may not understand why a second runner begins running beside the first one in the first paragraph below. Read the second paragraph to find the term *relay runners*. That will help you understand the idea in paragraph one.

Key Terms

- **Cuzco** (KOOS koh) *n.* capital of the Incan empire
- **Topa Inca** (TOH puh ING kuh) *n.* emperor of the Incas, who expanded their empire
- **census** (SEN sus) *n.* an official count of all the people in an area
- **quipu** (KEE poo) *n.* knotted strings on which the Incas recorded information
- **aqueduct** (AK wuh dukt) *n.* a pipe or channel that carries water from a distant source

The runner sped along the mountain road. He lifted a horn made from a shell to his lips and blew. A second runner appeared and began running beside him. Without stopping, the first runner gave the second runner the message he carried. The second runner was gone like the wind. He would not stop until he reached the next runner.

The Incas used relay runners to spread news from one place in their empire to another. Incan messengers carried news at a rate of 250 miles (402 kilometers) a day. Without these runners, controlling the vast empire would have been very difficult.

An Incan runner blowing a conch shell and carrying a quipu

Read Ahead
The paragraph at the right says that the Incan empire was "large and powerful." Read ahead to find out how big it was. Where did you find the answer?

Timeline Skills

Three great civilizations are shown on the timeline. Vertical lines indicate specific events. Horizontal brackets show periods of time. **Identify** Which civilization lasted the longest? Which empire lasted the shortest time? **Analyze Information** Why does the timeline show two dates for the Aztecs before the beginning of their empire?

The Rise of the Incas

The large and powerful empire of the Incas had small beginnings. In about 1200, the Incas settled in **Cuzco** (KOOS koh), a village in the Andes that became the Incan capital city. It is now a city in the country of Peru. Most Incas were farmers. They grew maize and other crops. Through wars and conquest, the Incas won control of the entire Cuzco Valley, one of many valleys that dot the Andes Mountains.

In 1438, Pachacuti (pahch ah KOO tee) became ruler of the Incas. The name Pachacuti means "he who shakes the earth." Pachacuti conquered the people of the Andes and the Pacific coast, from Lake Titicaca north to the city of Quito in present-day Ecuador. Pachacuti demanded loyalty from the people he conquered. If they were disloyal, he forced them off their land. He replaced them with people loyal to the Incas.

Later, Pachacuti's son, **Topa Inca,** became emperor of the Incas. He expanded the empire. In time, it stretched some 2,500 miles (4,023 kilometers) from what is now Ecuador south along the Pacific coast through Peru, Bolivia, Chile, and Argentina. The 12 million people ruled by the Incas lived mostly in small villages.

✓ **Reading Check** How did Pachacuti make sure conquered peoples were loyal to the Incas?

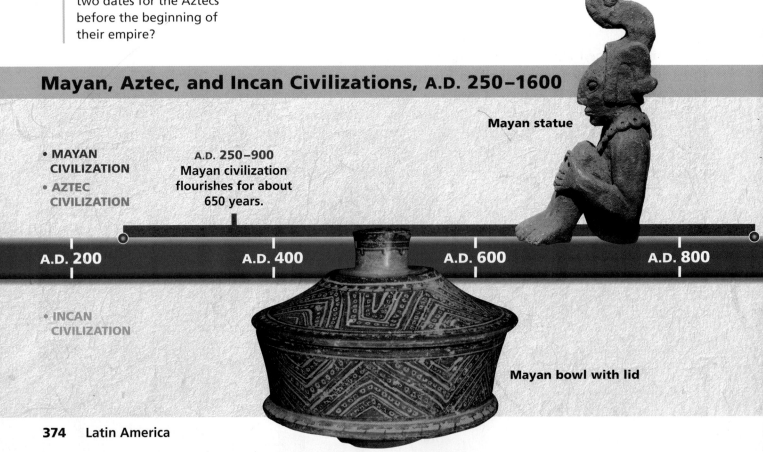

Mayan, Aztec, and Incan Civilizations, A.D. 250–1600

Mayan statue

- **MAYAN CIVILIZATION**
- **AZTEC CIVILIZATION**

A.D. 250–900
Mayan civilization flourishes for about 650 years.

A.D. 200   A.D. 400   A.D. 600   A.D. 800

- **INCAN CIVILIZATION**

Mayan bowl with lid

Incan Civilization

The Incas were excellent farmers, builders, and managers. The Incan capital, Cuzco, was the center of government, trade, learning, and religion. In the 1500s, one of the first Spaniards to visit Cuzco described it as "large enough and handsome enough to compare to any Spanish city."

The emperor, along with the nobles who helped him run the empire, lived in the city near the central plaza. Nobles wore special headbands and earrings that showed their high rank. Most of the farmers and workers outside Cuzco lived in mud-brick huts.

Government and Records The government of the Incan empire was carefully organized. The emperor chose nobles to govern each province. Each noble conducted a census so that people could be taxed. A **census** is an official count of all the people in an area. Local officials collected some of each village's crops as a tax. The villagers also had to work on government building projects. However, the government took care of the poor, the sick, and the elderly.

The Incas did not have a written language. Incan government officials and traders used **quipus** (KEE pooz), knotted strings on which they recorded information. Each quipu had a main cord with several colored strings attached to it. Each color represented a different item, and knots of different sizes at certain distances stood for numbers.

Keeping Count
Incan quipus like this one recorded information about births, deaths, trade, and taxes. **Generalize** *What would be some advantages and disadvantages of this system of record keeping?*

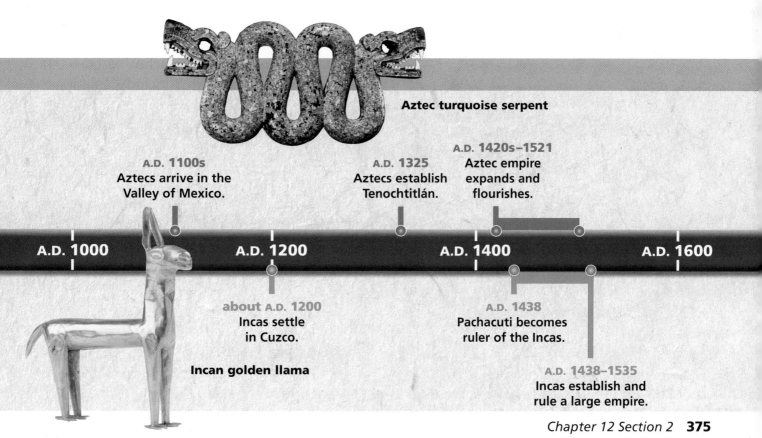

Aztec turquoise serpent

A.D. 1100s
Aztecs arrive in the Valley of Mexico.

A.D. 1325
Aztecs establish Tenochtitlán.

A.D. 1420s–1521
Aztec empire expands and flourishes.

A.D. 1000   A.D. 1200   A.D. 1400   A.D. 1600

about A.D. 1200
Incas settle in Cuzco.

A.D. 1438
Pachacuti becomes ruler of the Incas.

Incan golden llama

A.D. 1438–1535
Incas establish and rule a large empire.

Roads, Bridges, and Aqueducts The Incas built more than 14,000 miles (22,530 kilometers) of roads. The roads went over some of the most mountainous land in the world. The road system helped the Incas to govern their vast empire. Not only did runners use the roads to deliver messages, but Incan armies and trade caravans also used the roads for speedy travel.

In addition to roads, the Incas needed bridges to span the deep gorges of the Andes Mountains. Gorges are narrow passes or valleys between steep cliffs. In the Andes, swift-moving rivers often flow through gorges. The Incas developed rope bridges to carry people safely over these dangerous spaces. The bridges were made of braided vines and reeds. Similar bridges are still in use today in the Andes.

The Incas also built canals and aqueducts to carry water to dry areas. An **aqueduct** is a pipe or channel that carries water from a distant source. One stone aqueduct carried water from a mountain lake almost 500 miles (805 kilometers) to its destination. The system of canals and aqueducts allowed the Incas to irrigate land that was otherwise too dry to grow crops.

Incan Buildings The Incas were masters of building with stone. They constructed cities, palaces, temples, and fortresses without the use of modern tools. Using only hammers and chisels, Incan stoneworkers cut large stones so precisely that they fit together without mortar or cement. The stones fit together so tightly that even today a piece of paper cannot be slipped between them. Many Incan structures can still be seen in Peru. The most famous Incan ruin is Machu Picchu (MAH choo PEEK choo), a city that includes buildings, stairs carved into the side of the mountain, and roads cut into bare rock.

Religion Like the Mayas and the Aztecs, the Incas worshipped many gods and practiced human sacrifice. The sun god, Inti, was one of their most important gods. The Incas believed that Inti was their parent, and they referred to themselves as "children of the sun." Another important Incan god was Viracocha (vee ruh KOH chuh), the creator of all the people of the Andes.

✓ **Reading Check** Describe Incan stone buildings.

The Quechua: Descendants of the Incas

The Spanish conquered the Incan empire in the 1500s. However, descendants of the Incas still live in present-day Peru, Ecuador, Bolivia, Chile, and Colombia. They speak Quechua (KECH wuh), the Incan language.

Today, many of the Quechua live high in the Andes. Although they are isolated from many aspects of modern life, they have been influenced by it. For example, their religion combines elements of Roman Catholic and traditional practices.

Most Quechua who live in the mountains grow only enough food to feed their families. They continue to use farming methods similar to those of the ancient Incas. They also continue the weaving traditions of the Incas. They spin wool and weave fabric much as their ancestors did. They use this brightly colored cloth with complex patterns for their own clothing and also sell it to outsiders. Their clothing styles, such as the distinctive poncho, also reflect their Incan heritage.

Terrace Farming
The Incas built terraces into the sides of steep slopes to increase their farmland and to keep soil from washing down the mountains. **Infer** *Why do you think terrace farming is still used in the Andes Mountains today?*

✓ **Reading Check** How do the Quechua preserve Incan culture?

Section 2 Assessment

Key Terms
Review the key terms at the beginning of this section. Use each term in a sentence that explains its meaning.

Target Reading Skill
What word or idea were you able to clarify by reading ahead? Where did you find this clarification?

Comprehension and Critical Thinking
1. (a) Recall Where and when did the Incas create their empire?

(b) Sequence List the major events in the creation of the Incan empire in order.

2. (a) Identify What were the major achievements of Incan civilization?

(b) Draw Conclusions Why were a good network of roads and record keeping important to the Incan empire?

3. (a) Describe How do the descendants of the Incas live now?

(b) Infer Why do you think the Quechua still do many things the way their ancestors did?

Writing Activity
Which of the Incan achievements do you think was most important in creating their large and rich empire? Explain your choice in a paragraph. Give at least two reasons for your choice.

Go **O**nline
PHSchool.com

For: An activity on the Incas
Visit: PHSchool.com
Web Code: lfd-1202

Prepare to Read

Objectives

In this section you will

1. Learn why Europeans sailed to the Americas.
2. Find out how the conquistadors conquered the Aztecs and the Incas.
3. Understand how the Spanish empire was organized and how colonization affected the Americas.

Taking Notes

As you read this section, look for the major events in the European conquest of Latin America. Copy the timeline below, and record the events in the proper places on it.

Columbus arrives
in the Americas.

```
├──┼────┼──────────┼──────────┤
1490 1492
```

Target Reading Skill

Paraphrase When you paraphrase, you restate what you have read in your own words. This process can help you understand and remember what you read.

Key Terms

- **Moctezuma** (mahk tih ZOO muh) *n.* ruler of the Aztec empire at the time the Spanish arrived there
- **Christopher Columbus** (KRIS tuh fur kuh LUM bus) *n.* Italian explorer sponsored by Spain who landed in the West Indies in 1492

- **conquistador** (kahn KEES tuh dawr) *n.* one of the conquerors who claimed and ruled land in the Americas for the Spanish government in the 1500s
- **Hernán Cortés** (hur NAHN kohr TEZ) *n.* conquistador who conquered the Aztec empire
- **Francisco Pizarro** (frahn SEES koh pea SAHR oh) *n.* conquistador who conquered the Incas
- **mestizo** (meh STEE zoh) *n.* in Latin America, a person of mixed Spanish and Native American ancestry
- **hacienda** (hah see EN dah) *n.* a large farm or plantation

Cortés meets Moctezuma, in a 1976 mural by Roberto Cueva del Rio.

One day in 1519, the Aztec ruler **Moctezuma** (mahk tih ZOO muh) received startling news. Something strange had appeared offshore. He sent spies to find out about it. The spies reported back to Moctezuma:

> ❝We must tell you that we saw a house in the water, out of which came white men, with white hands and faces, and very long, bushy beards, and clothes of every color: white, yellow, red, green, blue, and purple, and on their heads they wore round hats.❞
>
> —An Aztec spy

The white men with round hats were a Spanish military force. They had sailed to the coast of Mexico in search of treasure. They would bring great changes to the land of the Aztecs.

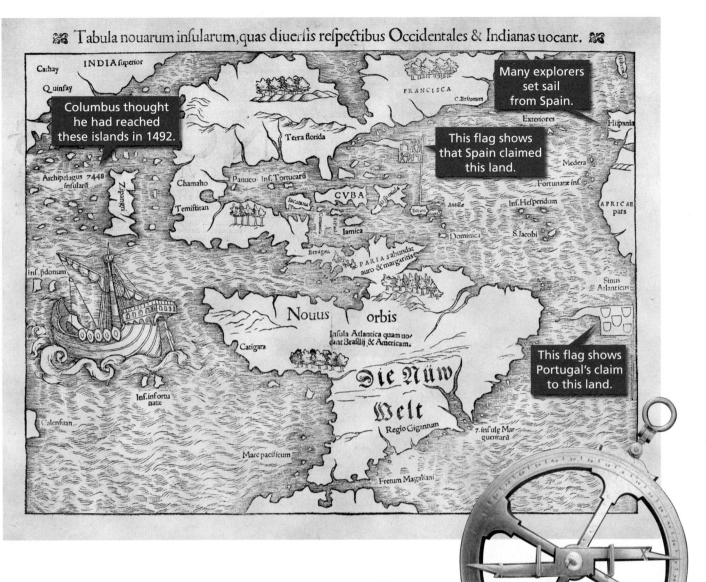

Tabula nouarum infularum, quas diuerfis refpectibus Occidentales & Indianas uocant.

Columbus thought he had reached these islands in 1492.

Many explorers set sail from Spain.

This flag shows that Spain claimed this land.

This flag shows Portugal's claim to this land.

Europeans Arrive in the Americas

In the 1400s, the European nations of Spain and Portugal were searching for new trade routes to Asia. They knew that in Asia they would find goods such as spices and silks. These goods could be traded for huge profits in Europe.

Columbus Reaches America Christopher Columbus, an Italian explorer, thought he could reach Asia by sailing west across the Atlantic Ocean. Columbus knew the world was round, as did most educated Europeans. But Columbus believed the distance around the world was shorter than it is. First Columbus asked Portugal to sponsor his voyage. Portugal refused. Then he asked Spain. Queen Isabella of Spain finally agreed.

Columbus set sail in early August, 1492. Some 10 weeks later, on October 12, he spotted land. Columbus thought he had reached the East Indies in Asia, so he called the people he met Indians.

Mapping the Americas
This 1540 map is based on information supplied by Columbus and other explorers. Also shown is an astrolabe, a navigational instrument from the 1500s. **Infer** *Find the islands Columbus was looking for, and the Caribbean islands he found instead. Why do you think he thought they were the same?*

Dividing a Continent Spain and Portugal each sent explorers to the Americas and tried to stop the other country from claiming land there. In 1494, the two nations signed an important treaty. (A treaty is an agreement in writing made between two or more countries.) The Treaty of Tordesillas (tawr day SEE yahs) set an imaginary line from the North Pole to the South Pole at about 50°W longitude, called the Line of Demarcation. It gave Spain the right to settle and trade west of the line. Portugal could do the same east of the line. The only part of South America that is east of the line is roughly the eastern half of present-day Brazil. Because of the Treaty of Tordesillas, the language and background of Brazil are Portuguese.

✓ **Reading Check** Why did Spain and Portugal become rivals?

The Success of the Conquistadors

Spanish explorers heard stories of wealthy kingdoms in the Americas. They hoped to find gold and other treasures there. Spanish rulers did not pay for the expeditions of the explorers. Instead, they gave the **conquistadors** (kahn KEES tuh dawrs), or conquerors, the right to hunt for treasure and to settle in the Americas. In exchange, conquistadors agreed to give Spain one fifth of any treasures they found.

Sculpture of the Aztec god Quetzalcoatl

Cortés Conquers the Aztecs Aztec rulers demanded heavy tribute from the peoples they had conquered. When the conquistador **Hernán Cortés** arrived in Mexico in 1519, he found many of these groups willing to help him against the Aztecs.

Cortés headed for Tenochtitlán with 500 soldiers and 16 horses. Aztec spies saw them coming. They had never seen horses before. Moctezuma's spies described the Spanish as "supernatural creatures riding on hornless deer, armed in iron, fearless as gods."

Moctezuma thought Cortés might be the god Quetzalcoatl (ket sahl koh AHT el). Quetzalcoatl had promised to return and rule the Aztecs. With a heavy heart, Moctezuma welcomed Cortés and his soldiers. Cortés tried to convince Moctezuma to surrender to Spain and then seized him as a hostage. After a brief period of peace, Spanish soldiers killed some Aztecs. Then the Aztecs rebelled against the Spanish. By the end of the fighting, Moctezuma was dead, and Cortés and his army barely escaped.

With the help of the Aztecs' enemies, Cortés defeated the Aztecs in 1521. By then, about 240,000 Aztecs had been killed and so had 30,000 of Cortés's allies. Tenochtitlán and the Aztec empire lay in ruins, but the region had been claimed for Spain.

Pizarro Conquers the Incas Francisco Pizarro (frahn SEES koh pea SAHR oh) was also a Spanish conquistador. He heard stories about the rich Incan empire. In 1531, Pizarro sailed to the Pacific coast of South America with a force of 180 Spanish soldiers. The Spanish captured and killed the Incan emperor and many other Incan leaders. By 1535, Pizarro had conquered most of the Incan empire, including the capital, Cuzco.

In only 15 years, the conquistadors had defeated the two most powerful empires in the Americas. How did they do it? The Spanish had guns and cannons and horses, all of which the Native Americans had never seen. Native American weapons were far less powerful. The Europeans also carried diseases such as smallpox, measles, and chicken pox. The Native Americans had never been exposed to these diseases, and entire villages got sick and died. Also, because of local rivalries, some Native Americans were eager to help the Spanish conquistadors.

✔ **Reading Check** What are two reasons the conquistadors were able to conquer the Aztecs and the Incas?

Advantages of the Conquistadors
This illustration shows conquistadors using guns ❶ to fight Aztec soldiers armed with spears ❷ . For protection, the Spanish have metal helmets, ❸ while the Aztecs use feather and animal skin shields ❹ .
Contrast *What other items in the picture might have contributed to the Spanish victory?*

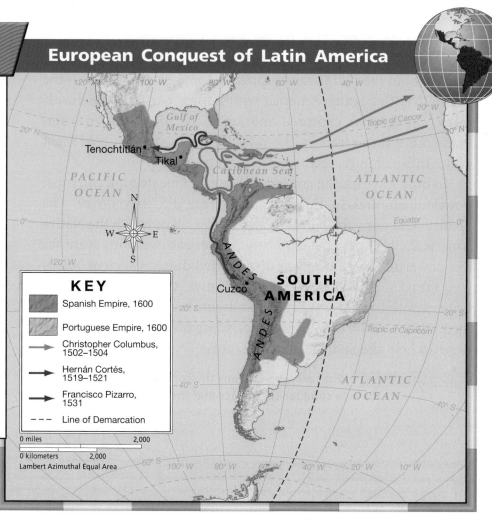

Movement The map shows Columbus's last voyage from Spain and the voyages of the conquistadors who conquered the Aztecs and the Incas. **Locate** Cortés and Pizarro were already in Latin America when they began their conquests. Find their starting points. **Identify Causes** Why were much of the Portuguese and Spanish empires located along the coasts? Why might the Spanish Empire have extended inland in certain areas?

Go Online
PHSchool.com Use Web Code **lfp-1213** for **an interactive map.**

KEY

Spanish Empire, 1600

Portuguese Empire, 1600

Christopher Columbus, 1502–1504

Hernán Cortés, 1519–1521

Francisco Pizarro, 1531

Line of Demarcation

0 miles 2,000
0 kilometers 2,000
Lambert Azimuthal Equal Area

Colonization

By the 1600s, Spain claimed land throughout much of the Americas. Spain's lands stretched from southern South America all the way north into the present-day United States, and included some islands in the Caribbean Sea. Later, the French and English also claimed some Caribbean islands. Portugal claimed Brazil.

European Settlers Arrive Settlers from Spain, Portugal, and other European nations began arriving in what came to be called Latin America. Some of them were missionaries, sent by the Catholic Church to spread Christianity to the peoples of the Americas. Others came to look for gold and other mineral riches. Still others wanted to settle and farm the land. If the Native American people resisted, the newcomers used their superior force to suppress them. The Europeans created the kinds of colonies that would benefit them and the countries from which they had come.

Paraphrase
Read the paragraph at the right carefully and then paraphrase it, or restate it in your own words. In your paraphrase, you might number the reasons people came to the Americas.

Spain Organizes Its Empire Spain controlled the largest portion of the Americas south of what is now the United States. The king of Spain wanted to keep strict control over his empire, so the territory was divided into provinces. The king appointed viceroys, or representatives who ruled the provinces in the king's name. Other settlers who had been born in Spain helped the viceroys rule. Meanwhile, a council in Spain supervised the colonial officials to make sure they did not become too powerful.

The two most important provinces in Spain's American empire were New Spain and Peru. The capital of New Spain was Mexico City. Lima became the capital of Peru.

Spanish social classes determined where people lived in Lima. The most powerful citizens lived in the center of the city. They either came from Spain or had Spanish parents. **Mestizos,** people of mixed Spanish and Native American ancestry, lived on the outskirts of Lima. Many mestizos were poor, but some were middle class or even quite wealthy. Native Americans were the least powerful class. Most Native Americans continued to live in the countryside. The Spanish forced them to work on haciendas. A **hacienda** (hah see EN dah) was a plantation owned by Spaniards or the Catholic Church.

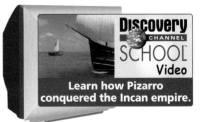

Discovery CHANNEL SCHOOL Video

Learn how Pizarro conquered the Incan empire.

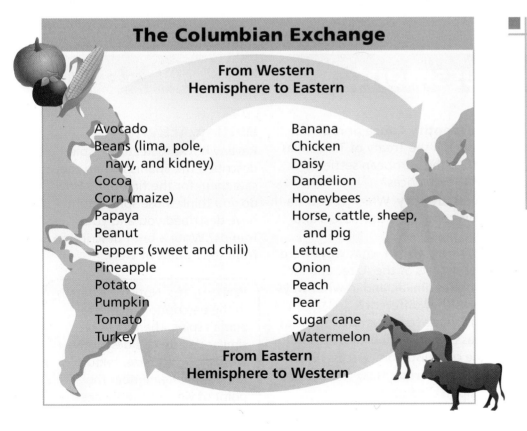

The Columbian Exchange

From Western Hemisphere to Eastern

Avocado	Banana
Beans (lima, pole, navy, and kidney)	Chicken
	Daisy
Cocoa	Dandelion
Corn (maize)	Honeybees
Papaya	Horse, cattle, sheep, and pig
Peanut	
Peppers (sweet and chili)	Lettuce
Pineapple	Onion
Potato	Peach
Pumpkin	Pear
Tomato	Sugar cane
Turkey	Watermelon

From Eastern Hemisphere to Western

Diagram Skills

Goods, as well as people, crossed the Atlantic Ocean in the years after Columbus's voyages. **Identify** Which animals were part of the exchange? **Infer** Which animal had the potential for making the greatest change in its new home? Explain your answer.

Devastating Diseases
This 1500s illustration shows a medicine man treating an Aztec for smallpox. Native Americans had never been exposed to European diseases. **Explain** *How did these diseases contribute to the success of Spanish rule?*

The Effect of European Rule Spain gave its settlers encomiendas (en koh mee EN dahs), which were rights to demand taxes or labor from Native Americans. At first, the Native Americans were forced to work only on the haciendas. But when silver was discovered in Mexico and Peru, the Spanish forced them to work in the mines as well. Many Native Americans died from overwork, malnutrition, and European diseases. Others rebelled unsuccessfully against the Spanish.

In the first 50 years of Spanish rule, the Native American population of New Spain declined from an estimated 25 million to 3 million. The Spanish now needed more workers for their haciendas and mines. They began importing enslaved Africans in large numbers. In Europe, the demand for products from the Americas continued to grow. Even more workers were needed. Millions more slaves were brought from Africa.

Brazil The situation was somewhat different in Brazil, which was a colony of Portugal. Most settlers remained near the coast. They took land from the Native Americans for sugar plantations and cattle ranches. Brazil also came to depend on the forced labor of Native Americans and enslaved Africans.

✓ **Reading Check** **Why did the Native American population decline?**

Section 3 Assessment

Key Terms
Review the key terms at the beginning of this section. Use each term in a sentence that explains its meaning.

Target Reading Skill
Paraphrase the second paragraph on this page. Present ideas in the order they appear in the paragraph.

Comprehension and Critical Thinking
1. (a) Recall Explain why Europeans came to the Americas in the 1500s.

(b) Identify Cause and Effect How did the Treaty of Tordesillas affect the European settlement of the Americas?

2. (a) Identify Which conquistadors conquered the Aztecs and the Incas?

(b) Compare In what ways were the defeats of the Aztec and Incan empires similar, and in what ways were they different?

(c) Evaluate Information What was the most important reason for the conquistadors' success? Explain.

3. (a) Describe How was Spain's empire organized?

(b) Draw Conclusions How did the Spanish conquest affect Native Americans and Africans?

Writing Activity
Review how Moctezuma's spies described the Spanish when they saw them for the first time. How do you think those spies might have described you and your friends? Write a brief description from their point of view.

Writing Tip Notice the details in the description by Moctezuma's spies. Then focus on similar details. Use descriptive words for color, size, texture, and sound. Remember the point of view of the speaker: a Native American of the 1500s.

Objectives

In this section you will
1. Learn what events inspired revolutions in Latin America.
2. Find out how Mexico gained its independence.
3. Discover how Bolívar and San Martín helped bring independence to South America.

Taking Notes

As you read the section, look for the ways revolutionary leaders helped bring independence to Latin America. Copy the table below and use it to record the name and accomplishments of each person.

Leader	Country	Accomplishment

Target Reading Skill

Summarize When you summarize, you restate the main points you have read in the correct order. Because you leave out less important details, a summary is shorter than the original text. Summarizing is a good technique to help you comprehend and study. As you read, pause to summarize occasionally.

Key Terms

- **Toussaint L'Ouverture** (too SAN loo vehr TOOR) *n.* leader of Haiti's fight for independence
- **revolution** (rev uh LOO shun) *n.* overthrow of a government, with another taking its place
- **criollo** (kree OH yoh) *n.* a person with Spanish parents who was born in Latin America
- **Simón Bolívar** (see MOHN boh LEE vahr) *n.* a South American revolutionary leader
- **José de San Martín** (hoh SAY deh sahn mahr TEEN) *n.* a South American revolutionary leader
- **caudillo** (kaw DEE yoh) *n.* a military officer who rules a country very strictly

On August 24, 1791, the night sky over Saint-Domingue (san duh MAYNG) glowed red and gold. The French Caribbean colony was on fire. The slaves were sick of being mistreated by their white masters. They finally had rebelled. Now they were burning every piece of white-owned property they could find. This Night of Fire was the beginning of the first great fight for freedom in Latin America. **Toussaint L'Ouverture** (too SAN loo vehr TOOR), a former slave, led the people of Saint-Domingue in this fight for independence for more than 10 years. Eventually they won, and they founded the independent country of Haiti (HAY tee) in 1804.

The Seeds of Revolution

The flame of liberty lit in Haiti soon spread across Latin America. By 1825, most of the region was independent. Latin Americans would no longer be ruled by Europe.

Toussaint L'Ouverture

People across Latin America were also inspired by two other revolutions. A **revolution** is the overthrow of a government, with another taking its place. During the 1770s and early 1780s, the British colonies in North America freed themselves from Britain's rule. In 1789, the people of France staged a violent uprising against their royal rulers.

Criollos (kree OH yohz) paid particular attention to these events. A **criollo** had Spanish parents, but had been born in Latin America. Criollos often were the best-educated and wealthiest people in the Spanish colonies, but they had little political power. Only people born in Spain could hold government office. Many criollos attended school in Europe. There, they learned about the ideas that inspired revolution in France and the United States.

The criollos especially liked the idea that people had the right to govern themselves. However, they were frightened by the slave revolt in Haiti. The criollos wanted independence from Spain but power for themselves.

✓ **Reading Check** **Which revolutions inspired ideas of independence in Latin America?**

Independence in Mexico

Mexico began its struggle for self-government in 1810. That's when Miguel Hidalgo (mee GEL hee DAHL goh), a criollo priest, began planning the Mexican revolution. He appealed to local mestizos and Native Americans.

The "Cry of Dolores" In September 1810, the Spanish government discovered Hidalgo's plot. But before the authorities could arrest him, Hidalgo took action. He wildly rang the church bells in the town of Dolores. A huge crowd gathered. "Recover from the hated Spaniards the land stolen from your forefathers," he shouted.

Hidalgo's call for revolution became known as the "Cry of Dolores." It attracted some 80,000 fighters, mostly mestizos and Native Americans. The rebels won some victories, but their luck soon changed. By the beginning of 1811, they were in full retreat. Hidalgo tried to flee the country, but government soldiers soon captured him. He was convicted of treason and then executed by firing squad in July 1811.

Cry of Dolores
This section of a mural by Juan O'Gorman shows Hidalgo and his followers. **Analyze Images** *Look carefully at the people behind Hidalgo. What does the painter suggest about the Mexican Revolution by showing these people?*

South American Independence

KEY

	1819 border of Gran Colombia
	Other border as of 1831
⊛	National capital
(1822)	Date of independence

0 miles 1,500
0 kilometers 1,500
Lambert Azimuthal Equal Area

Regions After freeing themselves from Spain, several former colonies formed Gran Colombia, modeled after the United States. **Identify** Which modern nations were part of Gran Colombia? **Compare** Look at the map of South America on page 331. Compare Peru's modern borders to those of 1831.

Go Online
PHSchool.com Use Web Code **lfp-1214** for step-by-step **map skills practice**.

Mexico Becomes Independent The Spanish could execute the revolution's leaders, but they could not kill its spirit. Small rebel groups kept fighting. Then a high-ranking officer in the Spanish army, Agustín de Iturbide (aw guh STEEN deh ee toor BEE day), joined the rebels. Many wealthy people who had viewed Hidalgo as a dangerous hothead trusted Iturbide to protect their interests. He was a criollo and an army officer. They decided to support the rebellion. In 1821, Iturbide declared Mexico independent.

✓ **Reading Check** What groups made up most of Hidalgo's army?

South American Independence

Simón Bolívar (see MOHN boh LEE vahr), one of South America's most important revolutionary leaders, was born in Venezuela in 1783. His family was one of the richest and most important families in Latin America. When Bolívar was at school in Spain, he met Prince Ferdinand, the heir to the Spanish throne. He played a game similar to present-day badminton with the prince. Custom required that Bolívar show respect for the prince by losing. Instead, Bolívar played hard and tried to win. He even knocked the prince's hat off with his racquet! The angry prince demanded an apology. Bolívar refused. He claimed it was an accident.

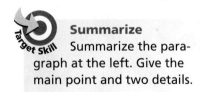

Summarize
Summarize the paragraph at the left. Give the main point and two details.

To Be a Leader: José Martí

José Martí grew up in Cuba when it was still a Spanish colony. At the age of 16, he started a newspaper dedicated to Cuban independence. After he supported an 1868 uprising, Martí was sent to prison. He spent many years in exile, working for Cuban freedom by writing and publishing, and by helping to form a revolutionary party. In 1895, Martí led an invasion of Cuba to free the island from Spanish rule. He was killed on the battlefield a month later—seven years before Cuba achieved independence. This statue of Martí is in New York City's Central Park.

Bolívar, The Liberator Many years later, Bolívar and Ferdinand faced off again. This time, Bolívar knocked Spanish America right out from under Ferdinand's feet. Bolívar joined the fight for Venezuelan independence in 1807. Six years later he became its leader. His confidence, courage, and daring inspired his soldiers. They enjoyed victory after victory. By 1822, Bolívar's troops had freed a large area from Spanish rule (the future countries of Colombia, Venezuela, Ecuador, and Panama).

This newly liberated region formed Gran Colombia. Bolívar became its president. Even though his country was free, Bolívar did not give up the cause of independence. "The Liberator," as he was now known, turned south toward Peru.

San Martín Fights for Freedom Another important revolutionary leader was **José de San Martín** (hoh SAY deh sahn mahr TEEN). He was an Argentine who had lived in Spain and served in the Spanish army. When Argentina began its fight for freedom, he quickly offered to help. San Martín took good care of his troops. He shared each hardship they had to suffer, and they loved him for it. Many said they would follow San Martín anywhere—even over the snow-capped Andes Mountains.

In 1817, his soldiers had to do just that. San Martín led them through high passes in the Andes into Chile. This bold action took the Spanish completely by surprise. In a matter of months, Spain was defeated. San Martín declared Chile's independence. Then he, too, turned his attention to Peru.

Again, San Martín planned a surprise. This time, he attacked from the sea. The Spanish were not prepared, and their defenses quickly collapsed. In July 1821, San Martín pushed inland and seized Lima, the capital of Peru.

An Important Meeting A year later, San Martín met with Bolívar to discuss the fight for independence. Historians do not know what happened in that meeting. But afterward, San Martín suddenly gave up his command. He left Bolívar to continue the fight alone. Eventually, Bolívar drove the remaining Spanish forces out of South America altogether. By 1825, only Cuba and Puerto Rico were still ruled by Spain.

Brazil Takes a Different Route Portugal's colony, Brazil, became independent without fighting a war. In the early 1800s, during a war in Europe, French armies invaded Spain and Portugal. Portugal's royal family fled to Brazil for safety. The king returned to Portugal in 1821. However, he left his son, Dom Pedro, to rule the colony. Dom Pedro took more power than the king expected. He declared Brazil independent in 1822. Three years later, Portugal quietly admitted that Brazil was independent.

Independence Brings Challenges Simón Bolívar dreamed of uniting South America as one country, a "United States of South America." Gran Colombia was the first step. But Bolívar found that his dream was impossible. Latin America was a huge area, divided by the Andes and dense rain forests. Also, the leaders of the countries in Gran Colombia wanted little to do with Bolívar. In poor health, he retired from politics.

Even though he did not remain in office, Bolívar set the standard for Latin American leaders. Most were **caudillos** (kaw DEE yohz), military officers who ruled very strictly. Bolívar cared about the people he governed. However, many caudillos did not. These later caudillos only wanted to stay in power and get rich. You will read about how these caudillos affected the nations they governed in the next section.

This July 2000 parade in Bogotá celebrates 181 years of Colombian independence.

✓ **Reading Check** What are two reasons that South America was not united into one country?

Section 4 Assessment

Key Terms
Review the key terms at the beginning of this section. Use each term in a sentence that explains its meaning.

Target Reading Skill
Write a summary of the last two paragraphs on this page. Include a main point and several details from each paragraph.

Comprehension and Critical Thinking
1. (a) Identify What events inspired independence movements in Latin America?

(b) Identify Cause and Effect Why were many criollos in favor of independence?

2. (a) Describe How did Hidalgo begin the Mexican Revolution?
(b) Analyze Information Explain why Iturbide was successful and Hidalgo was not.

3. (a) Recall What were the achievements of Bolívar, San Martín, and Dom Pedro?
(b) Infer What do you think Bolívar had in mind when he wanted to create the "United States of South America"?

Writing Activity
Suppose you are a soldier in Bolívar's or San Martín's army. Describe what you are doing, why you are doing it, and how you feel about your commander.

Writing Tip Remember to write your description in the first person, using the pronouns *I* or *we*. Use vivid words, such as *terrified*, *exhausted*, or *thrilled*, to describe your feelings.

If you want to show where cities and towns are located along a certain route, you can draw a road map. But how do you show when events occurred? In that case, you can draw a timeline.

You might say that a timeline is a map of time. It has a beginning date and an ending date. It shows when events occurred during that time period, and in what order. Look at pages 374 and 375 for an example of a historical timeline. Use a timeline whenever you need to organize a series of dates.

Golden bird made by the Incas

Learn the Skill

Use these steps to make a timeline.

1 **Create a title for your timeline.** Decide what your timeline will show. It might be "History of the Incas" or "The Life of Simón Bolívar."

2 **Put events in order.** On sticky notes or index cards, write down four or five important events. They will be the entries for your timeline. Put one entry on each sticky or card. Write the date and a short description of the event. Now arrange the entries in chronological order—that is, from the earliest to the latest date.

3 **Select a time span.** Choose a starting date that is earlier than your first entry. Choose an ending date that is later than your last entry.

4 **Build your timeline.** On a sheet of paper, draw a straight line across the page. Make a large dot on the line at each end, and label those dots with the starting and ending dates of your timeline.

5 **Mark the divisions of time periods.** Divide your timeline into equal time periods. Label each one.

6 **Put your entries on the timeline.** Put a dot at the appropriate place on the timeline for each entry. From each dot, draw a straight line upward or downward. Write the text of the entry next to the straight line.

Portrait of Simón Bolívar

Practice the Skill

Now make a timeline of your own life, the life of someone you know, or the life of someone famous. Create the timeline by following the steps below.

1 Your timeline can cover an entire life or some portion of it. Choose a title that reflects the topic and the time span.

2 Decide which important events you want to include. Write the events with their dates on sticky notes or index cards, and arrange them chronologically, that is, from the earliest to the latest date.

3 Choose starting and ending dates that include all your entries.

4 Draw your timeline and mark the starting and ending dates.

5 Add the time periods to your drawing. For instance, if you used 1995 as your starting date, your next date might be 1998 or 2000. Make sure the dates are equally spaced along the line.

6 Add your entries to the appropriate places on your timeline.

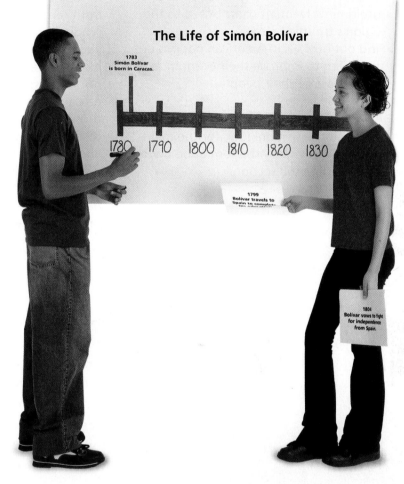

Apply the Skill

Identify what you think are the most important events in Section 4, Independence. Then create a timeline of the major events in the section, using no more than five entries.

From Past to Present

Prepare to Read

Objectives

In this section you will

1. Learn how Latin American caudillos and foreign involvement contributed to the region's troubled past.
2. Find out how Latin American nations are struggling to improve their economies and the welfare of their people.

Taking Notes

As you read the section, look for the main ideas and details. Copy the format below, and use it to outline the section.

> I. A troubled past
>   A. Colonial legacy
>   1.
>   2.
>   3.
>   B. Foreign involvement

Target Reading Skill

Reread or Read Ahead Both rereading and reading ahead can help you understand words and ideas in the text. If you do not understand a word or passage, use one or both of these techniques. In some cases, you may wish to read ahead first to see if the word or idea is clarified later on. If not, try going back and rereading the original passage.

Key Terms

- **dictator** (DIK tay tur) *n.* a ruler with complete power
- **export** (eks PAWRT) *v.* to send products from one country to be sold in another
- **import** (im PAWRT) *v.* to bring products into one country from another
- **foreign debt** (FAWR in det) *n.* money owed by one country to other countries
- **regime** (ruh ZHEEM) *n.* a particular administration or government

Slaves building a street in Rio de Janeiro, from an 1824 lithograph

Before independence, when Latin America was ruled by European nations, many of the ordinary people of the region were very poor. In the Spanish colonies, people born in Spain held government office. Criollos were often wealthy and owned large haciendas, or plantations. However, most mestizos and Native Americans owned little land. African Americans were slaves.

A Troubled Past

Latin America has changed a great deal since the nations of the region became independent. On the other hand, many problems with their roots in the colonial past still remain today.

Colonial Legacy After Spain's Latin American colonies became independent, the criollos gained political power. However, most mestizos and Native Americans remained poor. Many continued to work on the haciendas as they had before. Even after slavery was ended, former slaves had little opportunity for a better life.

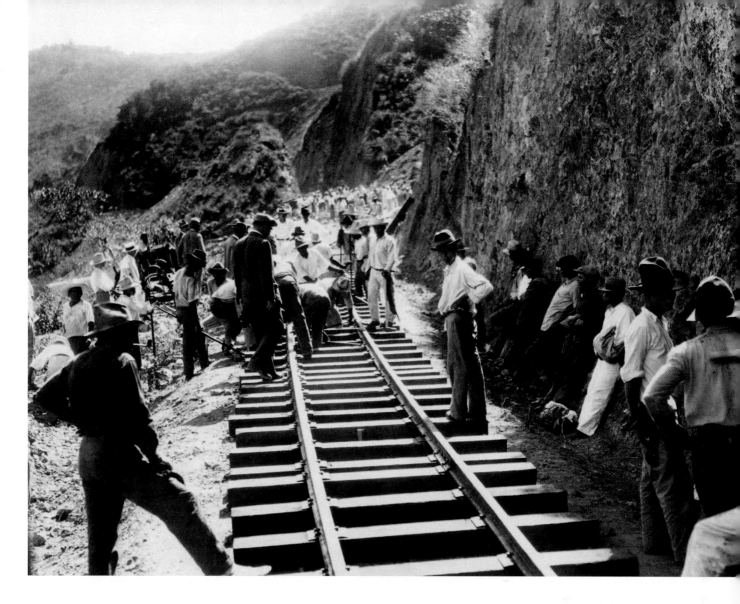

Many of the new Latin American countries were ruled by caudillos. These "strongmen" ignored the democratic constitutions that had been established by their new nations. They became **dictators**, or rulers with complete power. There were revolts, and some dictators were overthrown. Often they were replaced by other caudillos. Life changed little for the ordinary people.

Before independence, Latin American colonies exported farm products, minerals, and other resources to Spain and Portugal. To **export** is to send products from one country to be sold in another. The colonies bought manufactured products from the European countries that ruled them. After independence, the new nations of Latin America were free to trade with other countries. The United States became an important trading partner for Latin America. But Latin American countries still relied on exporting farm products and minerals. And they still imported manufactured goods. To **import** is to bring products into one country from another.

Working on the Railroad
This railroad linking El Salvador to Guatemala was built in the 1920s by an American company, using local laborers. **Identify Causes** *Why do you think an American company was interested in building a railroad there?*

Target Skill

Reread or Read Ahead Reread or read ahead to see why the United States became involved in Latin America. Which technique helped you clarify what you reread?

Foreign Involvement Foreign companies began to buy large farms, mines, and other land in Latin America. They built seaports and railroads that made it easier to export their products. These companies were interested in taking resources out of Latin America. The United States and other foreign nations supported Latin American governments that helped these companies.

In 1903, the United States wanted to build a canal across the Isthmus of Panama, in the nation of Colombia. A canal would benefit American trade and the American navy. When Colombia refused permission to build a canal, U.S. President Theodore Roosevelt backed a revolt by the people of Panama against Colombia. Once Panama was independent, it allowed the United States to build the Panama Canal.

As owner of the Panama Canal, the United States had even more interest in Latin America. In 1904, President Roosevelt claimed that the United States had a right to keep law and order there. He also said the United States could force Latin American nations to pay their **foreign debt,** or money they owed to other countries. For the next 20 years, the United States used Roosevelt's policy to intervene in Latin America.

✓ **Reading Check** What role did President Roosevelt think the United States should have in Latin America?

Graph Skills

Many Latin American nations have gone into debt to foreign countries and to world organizations. **Identify** Which country in the graph has the highest foreign debt? Which has the lowest? **Identify Cause and Effect** Brazil, Mexico, and Argentina are among the most industrialized Latin American countries. Why might building industries lead to debt?

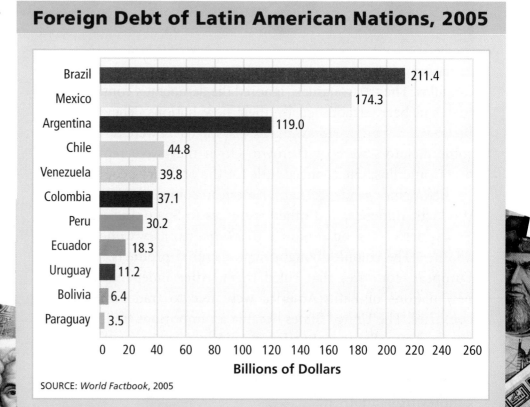

Foreign Debt of Latin American Nations, 2005

Nation	Billions of Dollars
Brazil	211.4
Mexico	174.3
Argentina	119.0
Chile	44.8
Venezuela	39.8
Colombia	37.1
Peru	30.2
Ecuador	18.3
Uruguay	11.2
Bolivia	6.4
Paraguay	3.5

SOURCE: *World Factbook*, 2005

The Struggle Continues

In the mid-1900s, there were still big gaps between the few who were rich and the many who were poor. Most of Latin America's land was owned by a small percentage of the people. Many businesses were owned by foreign companies.

The Beginnings of Reform At the same time, some groups wanted to improve conditions for the poor. Reformers of the 1930s and 1940s wanted to divide the land more equally and to diversify the economies of their countries. Some Latin American countries did begin to make reforms.

As demands for reform continued in the 1960s and 1970s, military regimes seized power in many Latin American countries. A regime is a particular administration or government. These military regimes ruled harshly. They censored the press, outlawed political parties, and imprisoned—or even killed—those who opposed them.

By the 1980s, however, some of these harsh regimes were replaced by elected governments. But problems still remained. Some elected leaders abused their power. President Alberto Fujimori of Peru, for example, dissolved Peru's legislature and later dismissed the high court justices when they disagreed with him. And many Latin American nations still had huge economic problems. One of these problems was foreign debt.

Foreign Debt Latin American countries had borrowed money to improve their economies. In the 1980s, oil prices went up at the same time that prices of many Latin American products fell. Latin American countries had to spend more money, but they were making less and less. To make up the difference, they borrowed money from wealthy countries such as the United States. Then they had to borrow more money to pay off their debts.

Although Mexico was a major oil producer, it too suffered an economic crisis. In the 1970s, Mexico began to rely more and more on oil exports to fuel its economy. But in the 1980s, more oil was being produced than the world needed. In 1982, Mexico found that it could not repay its debt.

Protests in Buenos Aires
In Argentina, foreign debt contributed to an economic crisis. In this 2003 protest, unemployed Argentines lift shovels as they march to demand jobs. **Apply Information** *Use the text to help explain how foreign debt might lead to unemployment.*

Two international organizations stepped in. The World Bank and the International Monetary Fund lent Mexico money—but there were strict conditions. Mexico found that it had to cut back on programs that helped the poor. Other Latin American countries also borrowed under these strict conditions. They had to allow more foreign ownership of businesses and farms. In Argentina, debt, unemployment, and other economic problems caused riots in the streets. In 2000, the president of Argentina was forced to resign.

Plaza in Montevideo, Uruguay
Although Latin American countries are still working to improve their economies, they do have large, thriving modern cities.

Looking Toward the Future Recently, Latin American countries have tried to improve their economies by joining trade organizations. In 1994, another trade treaty came into effect—the North American Free Trade Agreement (NAFTA). It made trade easier among Mexico, the United States, and Canada.

Efforts to improve the economies and the welfare of people in Latin America continue. You will read more about these efforts in the Focus on Countries chapters later in this book.

✓ **Reading Check** What happened when Mexico could not pay its debt?

Section 5 Assessment

Key Terms
Review the key terms at the beginning of this section. Use each term in a sentence that explains its meaning.

Target Reading Skill
What words or ideas in this section were you able to clarify by rereading or reading ahead?

Comprehension and Critical Thinking
1. (a) **Describe** How did caudillos rule their countries?

(b) **Explain** Describe foreign involvement in Latin America.
(c) **Compare and Contrast** How did Latin America's economy change after independence? How did it remain the same?
2. (a) **Recall** How did Mexico end up with a large foreign debt?
(b) **Draw Conclusions** The powerful groups that own the most land also run the governments of some Latin American countries. Why do you think these groups resist reform?

Writing Activity
What do you think is the most important challenge facing Latin America today? Write a paragraph explaining your choice.

For: An activity on Venezuela
Visit: PHSchool.com
Web Code: lfd-1205

Review and Assessment

◆ Chapter Summary

Section 1: Early Civilizations of Middle America

- The Mayas built great cities, created an advanced number system and calendars, and then mysteriously abandoned their cities.
- The Aztecs of central Mexico ruled a rich empire from their capital at Tenochtitlán, which was a center of trade and learning.

Section 2: The Incas

- The Incas built a huge empire based in what is now Peru.
- The Incas built excellent roads and aqueducts, and used quipus rather than a written language to manage their empire.
- The descendants of the Incas still live in the Andes Mountains.

Section 3: European Conquest

- Europeans came to the Americas for riches and for land.
- The conquistadors conquered the Aztecs and Incas in 15 years.
- Spain ruled a large empire in the Americas, bringing disease and enslavement to the Native Americans and importing enslaved Africans.

Mexico

Section 4: Independence

- Revolutions in North America, France, and Haiti helped inspire Latin Americans to seek independence.
- Mexico's revolution began with Hidalgo's "Cry of Dolores" and was completed by Iturbide.
- Bolívar and San Martín were the liberators of South America.

Section 5: From Past to Present

- Many problems in Latin America are the result of the region's colonial past, foreign involvement, and undemocratic governments.
- Reform movements are working to help the poor, elected governments have replaced military ones, and nations are struggling with their foreign debt.

◆ Key Terms

Define each of the terms below.

1. hieroglyphics
2. maize
3. census
4. regime
5. conquistador
6. mestizo
7. hacienda
8. revolution
9. criollo
10. caudillo
11. import
12. foreign debt

◆ Comprehension and Critical Thinking

13. (a) Recall Describe Mayan civilization.
(b) Compare How were the Aztec and Incan civilizations similar and different?
(c) Generalize What lessons in empire-building can be learned from the Aztecs and the Incas?

14. (a) Name Which Europeans were the first to explore Central and South America?
(b) Identify Causes Why did the Spanish want to explore the Americas?
(c) Conclude Why did many Native Americans help Hernán Cortés defeat the Aztecs?

15. (a) Recall How did Spain organize its empire?
(b) Explain What were encomiendas and what effect did they have on Native Americans?
(c) Identify Causes Why did the Spanish start to import enslaved Africans to the Americas? Why did this practice increase over time?

16. (a) Identify Who led the Mexican Revolution?
(b) Compare Compare the ways Mexico, Haiti, and Peru gained their independence.
(c) Draw Conclusions How did independence affect criollos? Native Americans?

17. (a) Recall Describe how caudillos ruled their countries.
(b) Identify Causes Why did foreign nations build seaports and railroads in Latin America?
(c) Explain What is one way a nation can develop foreign debt?

◆ Writing Activity: Math

Look again at the photo of the quipu on page 375. Suppose you have five strings of different colors to record the number of people in your class: girls, boys, and the teacher. How would you show this information? Use string or make a drawing with colored pencils. Now write directions for using the mathematical system you just invented. Have another student read and follow your directions. Evaluate how well your partner used your mathematical system.

◆ Skills Practice

Making a Timeline In the Skills for Life activity in this chapter, you learned to create a timeline. Review the steps you followed to learn the skill.

Use an encyclopedia or other reliable source to research one of the people you read about in this chapter. Then make a timeline of the important events in that person's life.

MAP MASTER™
Skills Activity

Latin America

Place Location For each place listed below, write the letter from the map that shows its location.

1. Peru
2. Venezuela
3. Cuzco
4. Mexico City
5. Brazil
6. Panama
7. Mexico

Go Online
PHSchool.com Use Web Code **lfp-1215** for an **interactive map.**

Standardized Test Prep

Test-Taking Tips

Some questions on standardized tests ask you to analyze a point of view. Read the paragraph below. Then follow the tips to answer the sample question.

Pick the letter that best answers the question.

In 1519, the Spanish conquistador Hernán Cortés marched toward the great Aztec capital, Tenochtitlán, with 500 soldiers. Somebody watching the troops whispered: *This is a happy day! These white gods could mean the end to Moctezuma and his bloodthirsty followers. Let us help them on their way.*

Which onlooker might have made those comments?

- **A** a spy of Moctezuma
- **B** a soldier of Francisco Pizarro
- **C** a Native American neighbor of the Aztecs
- **D** a wife of Moctezuma

Think It Through Moctezuma's own spies would not want an end to him or call themselves bloodthirsty. The same would be true for his wife. Francisco Pizarro was a conqueror who didn't arrive in South America until years after Cortés. A neighbor of the Aztecs might have been happy to see Cortés, because Moctezuma was a powerful enemy who conquered many of his neighbors. So the best answer is C.

TIP Make sure you understand the question. Restate it in your own words: *The person who said those words was probably _____.*

TIP Use what you know about history along with common sense to choose the BEST answer.

Practice Questions

Choose the letter of the best answer.

1. Unlike the Incas and Aztecs, the Mayas did NOT have
   - **A** an emperor.
   - **B** a calendar.
   - **C** cities.
   - **D** a form of writing.

2. Brazil's language and culture—Portuguese—were established by
   - **A** the voyage of Columbus.
   - **B** Pizarro's conquest.
   - **C** the Treaty of Tordesillas.
   - **D** the encomienda system.

3. What is one way that Latin American countries have been trying to improve their economies?
   - **A** by cooperating with one another
   - **B** by increasing their foreign debt
   - **C** by giving more land to large companies
   - **D** by depending on one resource

Read the following passage and answer the question that follows.

The following is taken from a speech made by someone living in Latin America in the early 1800s: "I love my country, but I deserve to govern myself. I learned plenty about governing when I attended school in Europe!"

4. Who most likely made this speech?
   - **A** the king of Spain
   - **B** a criollo
   - **C** a poor mestizo
   - **D** a Native American

Go Online
PHSchool.com

Use Web Code lfa-1201
for a **Chapter 12 self-test.**

Chapter Preview

This chapter will introduce you to the cultures of the three regions of Latin America.

Section 1
The Cultures of Mexico and Central America

Section 2
The Cultures of the Caribbean

Section 3
The Cultures of South America

Target Reading Skill

Cause and Effect In this chapter you will focus on recognizing cause and effect in the text you are reading. Recognizing cause and effect will help you understand relationships among situations or events.

▶ A boy playing steel drums during a Carnival celebration in St. Thomas

MAP MASTER
Skills Activity

Regions Notice that many languages are spoken in Latin America and that language regions do not follow political boundaries. **Locate** Where in the region do people speak English? Spanish? Portuguese? **Conclude** Why are those languages spoken in those places?

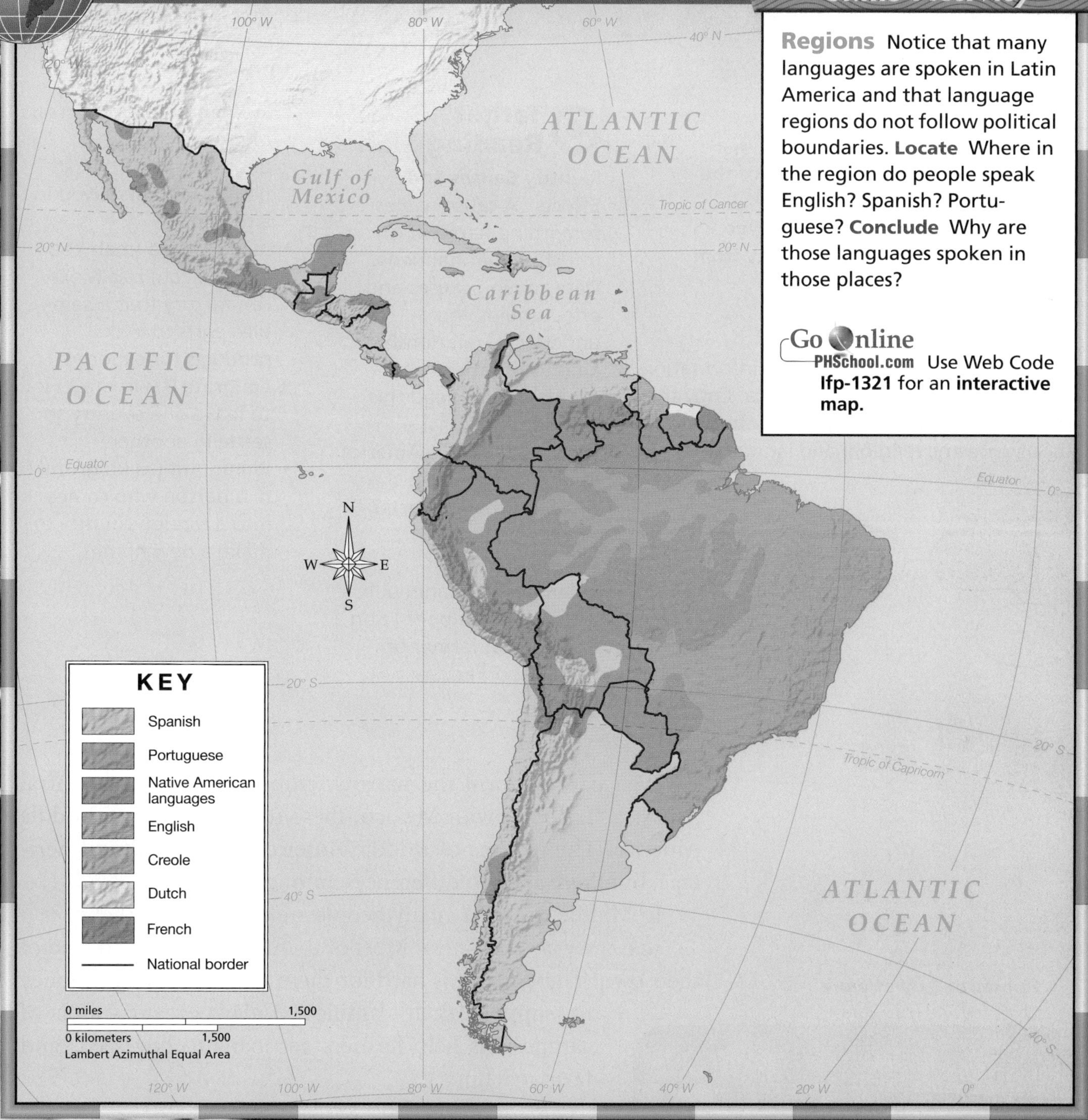

Go Online
PHSchool.com Use Web Code **lfp-1321** for an **interactive map.**

KEY

- Spanish
- Portuguese
- Native American languages
- English
- Creole
- Dutch
- French
- —— National border

0 miles 1,500
0 kilometers 1,500
Lambert Azimuthal Equal Area

Cultures of Mexico and Central America

Prepare to Read

Objectives

In this section you will
1. Discover the cultural heritage of the people of Middle America.
2. Find out why many people in this region have been moving away from the countryside.

Reading to Learn

As you read this section, look for information on the cultures of Middle America. Copy the web diagram below and record information about ancestry, religion, and language.

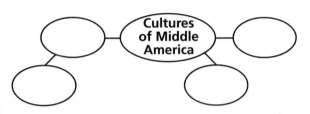

Cultures of Middle America

Target Reading Skill

Identify Causes and Effects A cause makes something happen. An effect is what happens. Determining causes and effects helps you understand relationships among situations and events. As you read this section, think of the cultures of Middle America as effects. What are the causes of these effects?

Key Terms

- **campesino** (kahm peh SEE noh) *n.* a poor Latin American farmer or farm worker
- **indigenous people** (in DIJ uh nus PEA pul) *n.* descendants of the people who first lived in a region
- **maquiladora** (mah kee luh DOHR ah) *n.* a Mexican factory that assembles parts to make products for export
- **emigrate** (EM ih grayt) *v.* to leave one country to settle in another
- **immigrant** (IM uh grunt) *n.* a person who comes into a foreign country to make a new home

Seven nations form the narrow, crooked isthmus of Central America. Together with Mexico, these nations make up Middle America. The nations of Middle America share a cultural heritage, but there are also differences among them.

In Middle America, many people are **campesinos** (kahm peh SEE nohz), or poor farmers. Most of them have little or no land of their own. Therefore, it is hard for them to make enough money to support their families. Today, organizations of campesinos help farmers get loans to buy seeds and farm machinery.

Cultural Heritage

There is much diversity, or variety, among the people of Middle America. Many people are mestizo. That means they have both Spanish and indigenous ancestors. **Indigenous people** are descendants of the people who first lived in a region. In Latin America, indigenous people are also called Native Americans or Indians.

A Honduran boy at work

One Region, Many Faces In Honduras, most of the people are mestizo. About one third of Guatemala's people are mestizo. Another 60 percent are indigenous. Many Costa Ricans are direct descendants of Spaniards. And more than 40 percent of the people of Belize are of African or mixed African and European descent.

The countries of Central America have many languages, too. Guatemala is home to more than 20 languages. Spanish is the language of government and business, but the indigenous people in Guatemala speak their own languages. So do indigenous people in Panama, El Salvador, and Nicaragua. Spanish is the main language in six of the seven countries. People in Belize speak English.

Mexico also blends Native American and Spanish influences. Spanish is the first language for most Mexicans, but some Mexicans speak Native American languages as well. About 30 percent of the people of Mexico are indigenous, and about 60 percent of the population are mestizos.

Art of Middle America Art made by Native Americans before the arrival of Europeans is called Pre-Columbian art. Archaeologists have found beautiful wall paintings and painted vases, sculptures, and metalwork in Mexico and Central America. Gold jewelry was a specialty of the Mixtec people, while the Olmecs created huge stone heads and lovely figures made of jade.

This 1930 self-portrait is by the Mexican artist Frida Kahlo.

Mexican History
This detail of *Sugar Cane* (1931) by Diego Rivera shows some people hard at work. Because the Aztecs and Mayas had painted murals, these more recent artworks revived a Native American art form. **Infer** *Which people are not hard at work? What do you learn about Mexican history from these details?*

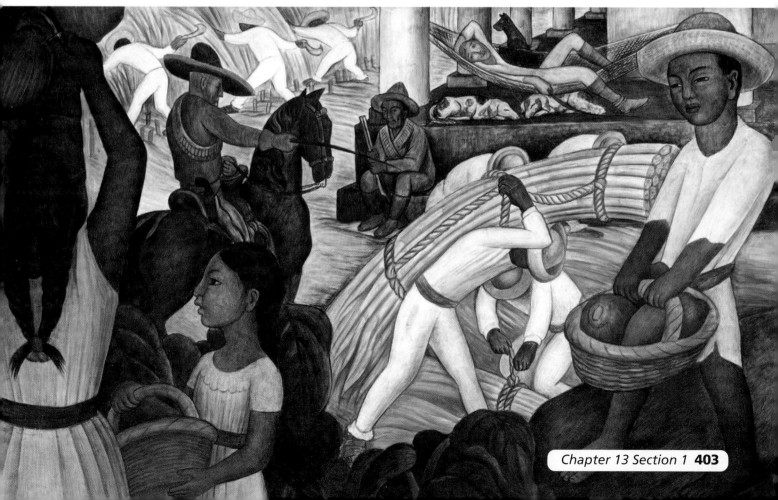

A Blend of Cultures
Indigenous people attend a church service in the Mexican state of Chiapas. **Infer** *What evidence is there in the photo that these people have blended Christianity with their traditional culture?*

The art of Mexico reflects both its Spanish and its Native American cultures. In the 1920s, the government invited Mexican artists to create murals on public buildings. Murals are large pictures painted directly on walls. The murals by such artists as Diego Rivera (dee AY goh rih VEHR uh) and José Clemente Orozco (ho SAY kleh MEN teh oh ROHS koh) show the history of Mexico, including the contributions of the indigenous people to the nation.

The Church Religion is important to the people of Mexico and Central America. The Spanish settlers who came to the region were Roman Catholic. In the 1500s and 1600s, Spanish missionaries converted many Native Americans to Christianity. The Catholic Church has been important to this region ever since. Most of the people are Catholic. Native Americans have blended many elements of their religions with Christianity.

Fighting Injustice In Middle America, priests and bishops have spoken out against injustice. Following the Church's lead, citizens have taken steps to end poverty and injustice. Ordinary people have started health clinics, farms, and organizations.

Elvia Alvarado (el VEE uh al vuh RAH doh) works for one of these organizations, and her work is not easy. "The communities we work in are hard to get to," she says. "Sometimes I don't eat all day, and in the summertime the streams dry up and there's often no water to drink." Sometimes Alvarado does not get paid. "But I couldn't be happy if my belly was full while my neighbors didn't have a plate of beans and tortillas to put on the table," she says.

✓ **Reading Check** **Name two ways people have worked to fight poverty and injustice.**

Leaving the Countryside

The population of Mexico and Central America is growing rapidly. This rapid population growth has made it hard for young people in rural areas to find jobs. Many have left their homes to look for work in the cities. Today, most people in Middle America live in cities.

In Mexico, some people move to towns and cities along the border with the United States. There, they can work in factories owned by American companies. These companies place their factories in Mexico because wages and other costs are lower there. Border factories that assemble imported parts to make products for export are called **maquiladoras** (mah key luh DOHR ahs).

Other urban areas in the region also offer jobs and other opportunities. Many rural people have moved to large cities such as Mexico City in Mexico, Panama City and Colón in Panama, and San José, the capital of Costa Rica. As a result, these cities have grown rapidly and often have trouble providing housing and services for new arrivals.

Identify Causes and Effects

What factor makes it difficult for young people in rural areas to find jobs? List that as a cause. What is the result of this unemployment? List that as an effect.

The World's Five Largest Urban Areas, 2003

Tokyo, Japan
Mexico City, Mexico
New York City, United States
São Paulo, Brazil
Mumbai (Bombay), India

0 5 10 15 20 25 30 35

Population (millions)

SOURCE: *UN Population Division*

▮ Graph Skills

The skyscrapers of São Paulo, Brazil, one of the five largest urban areas in the world, are shown in the photo. **Identify** Which of the cities in the population graph are in Latin America? **Draw Conclusions** What does the fact that Latin America has such large, modern cities tell you about the region?

A Market in Guatemala
Guatemalans shop at a traditional market in Totonicapán, one of the country's largest cities.
Analyze Images *What details in this photo reflect Guatemalan culture?*

Life in the City In many cities in the region, there are sharp contrasts between the lives of the wealthy and the lives of the poor. Wealthy people live in big houses on wide streets. They go to good schools and can afford to pay for medical care. Many of them have a lifestyle similar to that of wealthy people in the United States.

For the poor, however, life in the city can be hard. There is a shortage of housing. It is not easy to find work. Sometimes, the only way to make a living is selling fruit or soda on street corners. It is hard to feed a family on the income that can be earned this way.

Nevertheless, many people are willing to live with the hardships they find in the cities. Cecilia Cruz can explain why. She moved with her husband and their two sons to Mexico City from the southern state of Oaxaca (wah HAH kah). They live in a two-room house made of cinder blocks. It is on the outermost boundary of the city. "We came here for the schools," says Cruz. "There are more choices here. The level of education is much higher." Most newcomers to the city would agree.

Moving to the United States Most people in Mexico and Central America move somewhere else within their own country if they cannot find work. However, there are also thousands of people who emigrate. To **emigrate** is to leave one country and settle in another. Most leave to find jobs. Many of them emigrate to the United States.

Fermin Carrillo (fehr MEEN kah REE yoh) is one worker who did just that. He left his home town of Huaynamota (wy nah MOH tah), Mexico. There were no more jobs at home, and his parents needed food and medical care. Carrillo moved to a town in Oregon. Now he works in a fish processing plant. He sends most of the money he earns home to his parents. Carrillo hopes one day to become an American citizen.

Other immigrants are different. An **immigrant** is a person who has moved into one country from another. These immigrants want to return home after earning some money to help their families.

Building a Better Life Many Mexicans and Central Americans, like Fermin Carrillo, have left the region in search of a better life. Many more have followed Elvia Alvarado's example. You read about Alvarado's work with community groups in Honduras. She helps poor farmers get seeds, farm machinery, and more land. Like Alvarado, many Middle Americans have stayed at home and begun to build a better life for themselves and their neighbors.

A modern Tarahumara Indian of Mexico wearing traditional clothing

✔ **Reading Check** Why do many Mexicans move to the United States?

Section 1 Assessment

Key Terms
Review the key terms at the beginning of this section. Use each term in a sentence that explains its meaning.

Target Reading Skill
What are three effects of the Spanish colonization of Middle America?

Comprehension and Critical Thinking
1. (a) Identify What are the main languages and religions of the people of Middle America?

(b) Identify Cause and Effect How do the languages and religions of Middle America reflect the region's history?
(c) Predict How might this diversity lead to challenges for the region?
2. (a) Recall Describe life in the countryside and in the city.
(b) Identify Causes What is one reason that rural people in Mexico and Central America are moving to the cities?
(c) Predict What impact might the emigration of many Mexicans have on their country?

Writing Activity
Write a journal entry from the point of view of one of the people you read about in this section. Think about what life is like for that person. Include his or her hopes, dreams, and experiences.

Go Online
PHSchool.com

For: An activity on indigenous peoples
Visit: PHSchool.com
Web Code: lfd-1301

Kate was excited. She was going to Papantla, Mexico. Lila had just been there. "The bus ride is very long and boring," she told Kate. "The town is not interesting. You should skip that trip!"

Kate's guidebook said that Papantla is near the ruins of an ancient Indian city and that traditional dances are still performed there. The bus schedule said it was a three-hour ride. Her map showed that the bus traveled through the mountains.

Kate hurried off to buy a ticket. She relied on facts rather than opinions. That the bus ride is three hours long is a **fact.** Lila's statement that the bus ride "is very long and boring" is an **opinion.**

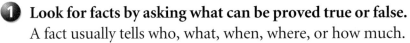

Distinguishing fact from opinion is something you need to do almost every day. You do it as you—like Kate—reach your own decisions.

Learn the Skill

To distinguish fact from opinion, use the following steps.

1 **Look for facts by asking what can be proved true or false.** A fact usually tells who, what, when, where, or how much.

2 **Ask how you could check whether each fact is true.** Could you do your own test by measuring or counting? Could you find information in an encyclopedia?

3 **Look for opinions by identifying personal beliefs or value judgments.** Look for words that signal personal feelings, such as *I think.* Look for words that judge, such as *beautiful* and *ugly* or *should* and *ought to.* An opinion cannot be proved true *or* false.

4 **Ask whether each opinion is supported by facts or good reasons.** A well-supported opinion can help you make up your own mind—as long as you recognize it as an opinion and not a fact.

Practice the Skill

Read the paragraph in the box at the right until you are sure that you understand its meaning. Then read for facts and opinions.

 Identify facts in the paragraph that tell how much, what, where, or when.

 Explain how each fact you identified could be proven true or false.

3 **(a)** Identify two words that judge. Could the statements containing these words be proved true or false? **(b)** Identify one example of words that signal personal feelings. Could this statement be proved true or false?

4 The second sentence of the paragraph expresses an opinion. Is the opinion well supported with facts and reasons?

> Urbanization takes place when people move from rural areas to urban areas. I believe that urbanization in Mexico is bad. First, the cities are already too crowded. There are thousands of homeless people in urban areas. Many people can't find jobs. Second, the city streets were not designed for so many cars. Traffic jams are a huge headache. Finally, the water and electrical systems do not have the capacity to serve more people. I think the time has come for the government to stop urbanization.

Relaxing Beaches

Exotic Animals

Beautiful Rain Forests

Amazing Volcanoes

Visit **Costa Rica!**

Costa Rica is the most beautiful country in Latin America! It has rain forests and beaches. It even has volcanoes! And the weather is perfect all year long.

Apply the Skill

Look at the travel brochure above. List three facts and two opinions from the brochure. Are the opinions well supported? How useful would this brochure be if you were planning a trip? Explain your answer.

The Cultures of the Caribbean

Prepare to Read

Objectives

In this section you will
1. Find out what ethnic groups make up the people of the Caribbean.
2. Learn how the different cultures of the region blended to create Caribbean food, music, and celebrations.

Taking Notes

As you read the section, look for the main ideas and details about Caribbean culture. Copy the format below and use it to outline the section.

> I. The people of the Caribbean
>   A. The first people of the Caribbean
>   1.
>   2.
>   3.
>   B. People in the Caribbean today

Target Reading Skill

Recognize Multiple Causes A cause makes something happen. An effect is what happens. Sometimes an effect can have more than one cause. For example, the distinctive quality of Caribbean food is an effect with several causes, including local fishing and farming as well as the cultural heritage of the West Indian people. As you read this section, identify multiple causes for other characteristics of Caribbean culture.

Key Terms

- **West Indies** (west IN deez) *n.* the Caribbean islands
- **ethnic group** (ETH nik groop) *n.* a group of people who share the same ancestry, language, religion, or cultural traditions
- **Carnival** (KAHR nuh vul) *n.* a lively annual celebration just before Lent in Latin America

The Caribbean islands are spread across more than 2,000 miles (3,219 kilometers), from Florida to the northeast coast of South America. There are more than a dozen different nations in the Caribbean region. As you might expect, a variety of peoples with many different cultures live within this large area.

This watercolor showing the Arawaks was painted in the 1800s.

The People of the Caribbean

The Caribbean islands are also called the **West Indies** because Christopher Columbus, when he first arrived there, thought he had reached the Indies in Asia. That's why he called the people of the islands *Indians.*

The First People of the Caribbean Long before Columbus arrived, the first people to live on these islands were a Native American group called the Ciboney (see buh NAY). The Ciboney lived in the region for thousands of years. In about 300 B.C., they were joined by another indigenous group, the Arawaks (AH rah wahks), who came from South America. In about 1000, the Caribs (KAR ibz), another South American group, arrived.

The Caribs gave the region its name. They lived in the Caribbean for more than 400 years before the first Europeans arrived. Christopher Columbus and other Spaniards enslaved the Native Americans. Almost all of the Caribs, Arawaks, and other indigenous groups died either of overwork or of diseases the Spanish brought with them. Today, there are just a few hundred Caribs. They live on the island of Dominica.

Other Europeans followed the Spanish. They hoped to make money from the region's wealth of natural resources. In the 1600s, Dutch, French, and English colonists began claiming territory. They built large sugar plantations and brought many enslaved Africans to work on them.

Most of the Caribbean people today are descended from these Africans. Immigrants from China, India, and the Middle East have also come to the region to work.

People in the Caribbean Today Because so many people came to the Caribbean as colonists, slaves, or immigrants, the area has a rich ethnic variety. An **ethnic group** is a group of people who share the same ancestry, language, religion, or cultural traditions. The ethnic groups of the Caribbean are Native American, African, European, Asian, and Middle Eastern.

Recognize Multiple Causes
There are very few Native Americans left on the Caribbean islands. What causes of this effect are given in the paragraph at the left?

Caribbean Diversity
These teenagers are students in the French West Indies. **Generalize** *How does this group reflect the population of the Caribbean?*

V. S. Naipaul: Trinidad and Beyond When V. S. Naipaul was born in Trinidad in 1932, more than one third of the island's population was from India. Like many other Indian immigrants, Naipaul's grandparents had come to Trinidad to work on sugar plantations owned by Europeans. Naipaul grew up knowing people from Africa, China, South America, and Europe. For him, the culture of Trinidad was a mix of languages, religions, and customs. When he was 18, Naipaul won a scholarship to study in England, where he still lives. Naipaul has written about life in Trinidad, about England, and about his worldwide travels. In 2001, he was awarded the Nobel Prize for Literature.

Depending on their island's history, the people of a Caribbean island may speak one of several European languages. Their language may also be a mixture of European and African languages. For example, two countries and two cultures exist on the island of Hispaniola. On the eastern half is one country, the Dominican Republic. Its population is Spanish-speaking and mostly mestizo. West of the Dominican Republic is the country of Haiti. Nearly all of Haiti's people are descended from Africans. They speak French and Haitian Creole, a French-based language with some African and Spanish words.

Most West Indians are Christians, but there are also small groups of Hindus, Muslims, and Jews. Some people practice traditional African religions.

Life on the Islands Most of the Caribbean islands have very fertile soil, and many people in the region make their living farming. Dorothy Samuels is a ten-year-old from Jamaica, one of the Caribbean islands. Her family are farmers. They plant yams and other vegetables and fruits. They also plant cacao beans. Every Saturday, Dorothy's mother and grandmother take their fruits and vegetables to the market to sell. All the traders at their market are women.

Dorothy is a good student. She hopes one day to go to college in Kingston, Jamaica's capital city. Jamaican laws require that women have as much opportunity for education as men have. Equality for women is important in Jamaican culture because many Jamaican women are independent farmers and business owners.

✓ **Reading Check** How are women's rights and opportunities protected in Jamaica?

A Blend of Cultures

The rich culture of the Caribbean has a variety of sources. West Indians enjoy many kinds of music and dance, celebrations, and food. They also play a variety of sports. Baseball, soccer, and track and field are popular. On some islands, people also play cricket, which is a British game similar to baseball. Dominoes—although not a sport—is a popular game throughout the region.

Carnival Many people in the Caribbean observe the Roman Catholic tradition of Lent, which is the period of 40 days before Easter Sunday. Because Lent is a very solemn time, these people have a lively public festival called **Carnival** just before Lent.

Different countries celebrate Carnival in different ways. In Trinidad and Tobago, for example, people spend all year making costumes and floats for the celebration. Lent always starts on a Wednesday. At 5 A.M. the Monday before, people go into the streets in their costumes. Calypso bands play. Thousands of fans follow the bands through the streets, dancing and celebrating. At the stroke of midnight on Tuesday, the party stops. Lent has begun.

Explore three types of Caribbean music.

Carnival Celebration
The dancers below are Carnival performers in Port of Spain, Trinidad, while the girl on the facing page has dressed up for the celebration.
Draw Inferences *What do the costumes and props indicate about how much time and effort goes into preparing for this celebration?*

This waiter in Grenada shows a variety of Caribbean dishes.

Food Caribbean food is a mixture that represents the different cultures of the islands. It also makes use of the rich natural resources of the region. Caribbean people can enjoy many types of seafood that are not found in United States waters. For instance, the people of Barbados love to eat flying fish and sea urchin eggs. Bammy—a bread made from the cassava plant—is still made the way the African slaves made it. West Indians also cook spicy curries from India, sausages from England, and Chinese dishes. Many tropical fruits grow on the islands. The fruits are used to make many juices and other drinks that are not readily available in the United States.

Music Caribbean music, which has both African and European sources, is famous around the world. Calypso is a form of song that uses humorous lyrics and has a distinctive beat. Reggae (REHG ay) music and ska come from Jamaica. Reggae songs have a strong rhythm with a "chunking" sound at the end of each measure. The lyrics of traditional reggae songs often have political messages.

Another distinctive Caribbean musical sound is that made by steel drums. These instruments are made from recycled oil drums. A steel drum can be tuned so that different parts of it play different notes. Players strike the instruments with rubberized drumsticks.

✓ **Reading Check** **Describe two types of Caribbean music.**

Section 2 Assessment

Key Terms
Review the key terms at the beginning of this section. Use each term in a sentence that explains its meaning.

Target Reading Skill
What are three reasons, or causes, for the diversity of ethnic groups and cultures in the Caribbean?

Comprehension and Critical Thinking
1. (a) Identify Who were the first inhabitants of the Caribbean islands?

(b) Explain What happened to those people? Why?
(c) Identify Causes Why do West Indians speak a variety of languages today?
2. (a) Recall What kinds of activities do Caribbean people enjoy?
(b) Categorize Which traditions have these activities come from?
(c) Draw Conclusions Why is there more of a cultural blend in the Caribbean than in Middle America?

Writing Activity
Select one aspect of Caribbean culture, such as food, music, or celebrations. Write a paragraph comparing and contrasting that aspect of Caribbean culture with the cultural practices where you live.

> **Writing Tip** Before you begin, decide how you will organize your paragraph. One way is to cover all the similarities first and then all the differences.

The Cultures of South America

Prepare to Read

Objectives

In this section you will
1. Find out what ethnic groups are represented in the different cultural regions of South America.
2. Learn what life is like in the countryside and the cities of South America.

Taking Notes

As you read this section, look for information about the cultural regions of South America. Copy the table below and record your findings in it.

Location of Region	Countries	Characteristics
Caribbean Coast		

Target Reading Skill

Understand Effects An effect is what happens as the result of a specific cause or factor. For example, you can see in the paragraph below that the geography of the Lake Titicaca region has had several effects on the way the Native Americans there live. This section discusses the effects of geography and colonization on different regions of South America. As you read, note the effects of each of these factors on the way South Americans live today.

Key Terms

- **gauchos** (GOW chohz) *n.* cowboys of the pampas of Argentina
- **subsistence farming** (sub SIS tuns FAHR ming) *n.* growing only enough food to meet the needs of the farmer's family
- **cash crop** (kash krahp) *n.* a crop grown mostly for sale rather than for the farmer's own use

Between Peru and Bolivia is the deep lake called Lake Titicaca. It lies high in the Andes Mountains. This area is cool and dry. There are few trees. Native Americans here make their living from totora reeds, a kind of thick, hollow grass that grows on the lakeshore. They use these reeds to make houses, mats, hats, ropes, sails, toys, roofs, and floors. They eat the reeds, feed them to livestock, and brew them into tea. Totora reeds can even be made into medicine.

Long ago, a number of Native American groups built floating islands with totora reeds. They used the islands to hide from the Incas. Today, some Native Americans still live on floating islands on Lake Titicaca.

Native Americans who live on Lake Titicaca make their boats out of totora reeds.

Understand Effects
What two effects of Spanish colonization are described in the paragraph at the right?

An Ancient Way of Life
Toco Indians in Peru wear traditional clothing and herd llamas much as their ancestors did. **Conclude** *Look at the setting of the photo. How do you think geography has contributed to these people keeping their traditional way of life?*

The People of South America

Most South Americans today are descended from Native Americans, Africans, or Europeans. In this way, they are like the people of Mexico and Central America. Like its neighbors to the north, South America, too, was colonized mainly by Spain. Today, many South Americans speak Spanish and are Catholic, yet different regions within South America have their own unique cultures.

Caribbean South America There are four cultural regions in South America. The first region includes Colombia, Venezuela, Guyana, Suriname, and French Guiana. These countries are in northern South America, on or near the Caribbean Sea. Their cultures are similar to those of the Caribbean islands.

Local history has also influenced the cultures of each nation. Colombia and Venezuela were Spanish colonies, and their people are mainly mestizo. Their official language is Spanish, and most of the people are Roman Catholic. On the other hand, Guyana, Suriname, and French Guiana were colonized by different European nations. Guyana was once an English colony, and its official language is English. Suriname was a Dutch colony until 1975, and the people there still speak Dutch. In both countries, many people are Muslim or Hindu. French Guiana is not an independent nation; it is an overseas department of France. While its official language is French, many of its people are of mixed African and European descent.

Cityscapes
This avenue in Buenos Aires, Argentina (left photo) is said to be the widest boulevard in the world. Signs in São Paulo, Brazil, (right photo) are in Portuguese and Japanese. **Draw Conclusions** *What can you conclude about South America's cities and culture from these two photos?*

The Andean Countries and the South   To the south and west, the culture is very different. Peru, Ecuador, and Bolivia are Andean countries. Many Native Americans live high in the Andes Mountains. In Bolivia, there are more indigenous people than mestizos. The Quechua and Aymara (eye muh RAH) peoples speak their own languages and follow the traditional ways of their ancestors.

The third cultural region consists of Chile, Argentina, Paraguay, and Uruguay. The long, narrow country of Chile has mountains, beaches, deserts, forests, and even glaciers. Although its geography is diverse, its people are not. Most people in Chile are mestizos. In Argentina and Uruguay, however, the big cities are very diverse. Many different ethnic groups live there.

Another culture exists on Argentina's pampas, or plains. The pampas are the traditional home of the **gauchos** (GOW chohz), the Argentinean cowboys. While cattle raising is still important, wheat fields are beginning to replace grazing lands on the pampas, and the day of the gaucho may be coming to an end.

Brazil   South America's largest country was once a colony of Portugal, and today its people speak Portuguese. However, Brazil is culturally diverse. Many Native Americans live in Brazil, as do people of African and European descent. Some Brazilians are of mixed descent. Many people have moved to Brazil from other countries. Brazil's largest city, São Paulo (sow PAW loh), is home to more Japanese than any other place in the world except Japan.

Mothers of the "Disappeared"

In 1976, a military government took control of Argentina and began arresting people who opposed their regime. Other opponents of the government simply "disappeared"—kidnapped by unidentified armed men. Fourteen mothers of these "disappeared" demanded information about their children. When the government did not respond, the women began to march in front of the presidential palace every Thursday at 3:30 P.M. They became know as the Mothers of Plaza de Mayo (PLAH zuh day MY oh). Their peaceful protests brought worldwide attention to their cause. As one observer put it, "These are women who moved from being housewives in Argentina to being global leaders for justice."

South American Literature South America has produced many famous writers. Gabriela Mistral (gah bree AY lah mees TRAHL), a poet from Chile, was the first Latin American to win the Nobel Prize for Literature. Her poetry reflects her love of children, and so does her second career as a teacher. When she was a school principal, she encouraged the young Chilean poet Pablo Neruda (PAH bloh neh ROO duh). He went on to win the Nobel Prize in 1971. When he was a young man, Neruda composed complex poems. Toward the end of his life, however, he wrote about simple, everyday objects, such as onions and socks.

Another South American winner of the Nobel Prize for Literature was the Colombian novelist Gabriel García Márquez (gah bree EL gahr SEE ah MAHR kes). He is best known for novels in the style of magic realism, which mixes fantasy with historical facts and realistic stories. Isabel Allende (EES uh bel ah YEN day), a novelist from Chile, also uses magic realism in many of her novels and stories. She is also known for her "letters" to members of her family, which were published as books.

The Role of Women In some ways, women do not yet play a role equal to that of men in South America. Women in South America are more likely than men to be poor. They also do not attend school for as many years as men do.

More and more women in South America today are fighting to make a living for themselves and their children. They are demanding equal rights. Women are struggling for the rights to go to school, to work in all types of jobs, to have good health care, and to have a voice in government. Some women are getting bank loans to start small businesses. These businesses are sometimes based on traditional skills such as sewing, weaving, or preparing food.

✓ **Reading Check** What rights are women fighting for?

Country and City Life

South America has cities with millions of people, but it also has vast areas with almost no people at all. Many South Americans still live in the countryside, but others are leaving farms and moving to cities.

Farming in South America Outside of Argentina, Chile, and Uruguay, most rural people with land of their own do **subsistence farming.** That means they grow only enough food to meet their families' needs. They have only small plots of land. These farmers plant corn, beans, potatoes, and rice.

Very large farms grow crops to export to other countries. The main export cash crops of South America are coffee, sugar, cacao, and bananas. **Cash crops** are crops grown mostly for sale rather than for the farmer's own use. Export farming uses so much land for cash crops that South America has to import food for its own people to eat.

South America's Cities The cities of South America illustrate the region's mix of cultures. Many major cities—Lima, Peru, and Buenos Aires, Argentina, for example—were founded by Spanish colonists more than 400 years ago. Much of their architecture is Spanish in style. Some buildings in even older cities follow Native American designs.

Two Ways to Farm
The top photo shows a banana processing plant on a plantation in Ecuador. Below is a small family-owned coffee farm in Colombia.
Infer *Why might plantation owners not be interested in farming the area in the lower photo? How easy do you think it is to make a living there?*

City of Contrasts
This view of Buenos Aires shows poor neighborhoods in the foreground while the modern downtown rises in the distance. **Infer** *What city services do the people in the foreground seem to lack?*

In contrast, modern office blocks and apartment buildings of concrete, steel, and glass tower above the downtown areas of many South American cities. One or two cities were built quite recently. Brasília, the Brazilian capital, was constructed in the 1950s. It was a completely planned city, designed to draw people to the country's interior.

On the other hand, the slums of many South American cities have certainly been unplanned. They are called *favelas* (fuh VEH lus) in Brazil and *ranchos* in Venezuela. The population of South America is booming. Like Mexicans and Central Americans, South Americans cannot find enough jobs in rural areas. Every day, thousands of rural people move to the cities looking for work. Usually they end up in poor neighborhoods. City governments try to provide electricity and running water to everyone. But people move into cities so quickly that it is hard for city governments to keep up.

✔ **Reading Check** What types of buildings are found in South American cities?

Section 3 Assessment

Key Terms
Review the key terms at the beginning of this section. Use each term in a sentence that explains its meaning.

Target Reading Skill
What are two effects of the fact that many Native Americans still live high in the Andes Mountains?

Comprehension and Critical Thinking
1. (a) Recall Describe two cultural regions of South America.

(b) Identify Cause and Effect Explain two ways in which the geography of South America has shaped how people live.
2. (a) Identify Describe two different kinds of farms in South America.
(b) Compare and Contrast How are city life and rural life similar and different?
(c) Analyze Information How does the movement of people from the countryside to urban areas put pressure on cities?

Writing Activity
Suppose you were a newspaper reporter visiting Argentina in 1976. Write a short article about the Mothers of Plaza de Mayo for your American readers.

Go Online
PHSchool.com
For: An activity on South America
Visit: PHSchool.com
Web Code: lfd-1303

Review and Assessment

◆ Chapter Summary

Section 1: The Cultures of Middle America

- Many different cultural groups live in Middle America, and the languages and arts of the region reflect this diversity.
- Population growth and lack of jobs have caused many rural Middle Americans to move to the cities or to emigrate to the United States.

Section 2: The Cultures of the Caribbean

- The people of the Caribbean are made up of many ethnic groups, including descendants of Africans and Europeans.
- West Indian sports, food, music, and celebrations reflect the blend of cultures in the Caribbean.

Section 3: The Cultures of South America

- Life in the different cultural regions of South America is influenced by geography and by the ethnic groups that settled there.
- South America has both large farms that export their crops and small subsistence farms.
- South American cities are overcrowded with poor rural people coming to look for work.

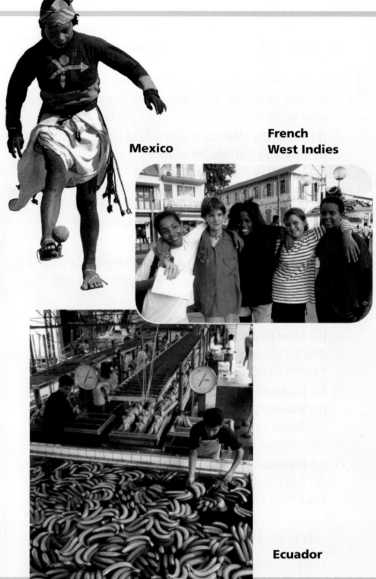

Mexico

French West Indies

Ecuador

◆ Key Terms

Match the definitions in Column I with the key terms in Column II.

Column I

1. a group of people who share ancestry, language, religion, or cultural traditions
2. descendants of the people who first lived in a region
3. growing only enough food to meet the needs of their families
4. a person who has moved from one country to settle in another
5. a poor farmer who owns little or no land

Column II

A indigenous people

B campesino

C immigrant

D ethnic group

E subsistence farming

◆ Comprehension and Critical Thinking

6. **(a) Recall** Describe population growth in Middle America.
   (b) Identify Effects How has population growth affected the movement of people in that region?

7. **(a) Identify** Who were the first people to inhabit the Caribbean islands?
   (b) Identify Cause and Effect What happened to those people, and why?
   (c) Draw Conclusions Why is there such cultural diversity in the Caribbean today?

8. **(a) Define** What is Carnival?
   (b) Identify Cause and Effect How does Carnival reflect both West Indian culture and Roman Catholic traditions?

9. **(a) Describe** What language is spoken in Brazil?
   (b) Identify Effects Why are Brazil's culture and language different from the rest of South America's?

10. **(a) Define** What are *ranchos* and *favelas*?
    (b) Identify Causes Why are they growing?
    (c) Draw Conclusions How do conditions in the countryside affect these city neighborhoods?

11. **(a) Define** What are cash crops?
    (b) Conclude Why does export farming cause problems for some South American countries?

◆ Skills Practice

Distinguishing Fact and Opinion In the Skills for Life activity in this chapter, you learned how to distinguish facts from opinions. You also learned how to use facts and well-supported opinions to help you make decisions.

Read the paragraph below. List the facts and the opinions. Explain how this paragraph could help you decide whether to try the Carib Heaven Restaurant.

Caribbean food is the best in the world. There is so much variety from the different cultures of the area. There are also lots of tropical fruits and juices. A lot of the food is quite spicy—just the way I like it! The Carib Heaven Restaurant will give you a chance to try this great cuisine.

◆ Writing Activity: Geography

Suppose you are a writer for a travel magazine. Write an article about one of the places you "visited" in this chapter. Include descriptions of the landforms, waterways, climate, and vegetation. Explain how geography has affected the way people live in that place.

Refer to the maps in the Regional Overview and in Chapter 11 as well as to the information in this chapter. You can also do additional research if you wish.

MAP MASTER™ Skills Activity

Latin America

Place Location For each place listed below, write the letter from the map that shows its location.

1. Trinidad and Tobago
2. Bolivia
3. Jamaica
4. Guatemala
5. Honduras
6. Hispaniola

Go Online
PHSchool.com Use Web Code lfp-1323 for an **interactive map**.

Standardized Test Prep

Test-Taking Tips

Some questions on standardized tests ask you to analyze graphs and charts. Look at the circle graph at the right. Then follow the tips to answer the sample question.

Think It Through Because only one percent of Mexicans are Protestant, you can eliminate answer D. You can also eliminate A easily, because England had little influence on Mexico. You know from the text that the Aztec influence was important, but you can see from the graph that the Aztec religion does not play a large role in Mexico today. That leaves the Roman Catholic country of Spain, which makes sense when you consider Mexico's history. Therefore, the correct answer is B.

> **TIP** Draw your own conclusions about the graph before you look at the answer choices.

Mexico Today: Religious Groups

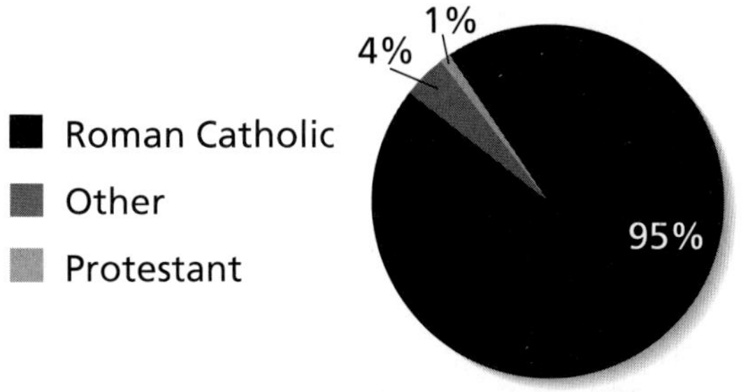

■ Roman Catholic
■ Other
■ Protestant

1%
4%
95%

Pick the letter that best answers the question.

The information in the graph could be used to show the influence of

- **A** England on the development of modern Mexico.
- **B** Spain on the development of modern Mexico.
- **C** Ancient Aztecs on the development of modern Mexico.
- **D** Protestantism on the development of modern Mexico.

> **TIP** Look for the BEST answer, as more than one answer choice may seem to fit.

Practice Questions

Choose the letter of the best answer.

1. Most of the people of Mexico and Central America are
   - **A** indigenous or of mixed ancestry.
   - **B** European or Spanish.
   - **C** indigenous or European.
   - **D** Spanish or of mixed ancestry.

2. Rapid population growth in Mexico and Central America has caused all of the following EXCEPT
   - **A** migration to cities.
   - **B** emigration to other countries.
   - **C** fewer jobs for everyone.
   - **D** better living conditions in the cities.

3. The Andean countries of South America include
   - **A** Bolivia, Peru, and Ecuador.
   - **B** Peru, Brazil, and Bolivia.
   - **C** Brazil, Argentina, and Chile.
   - **D** Bolivia, Ecuador, and Argentina.

Study the circle graphs and answer the question that follows.

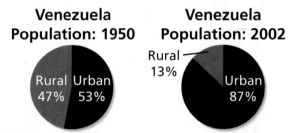

Venezuela Population: 1950
Rural 47% Urban 53%

Venezuela Population: 2002
Rural 13% Urban 87%

4. Which sentence best describes the population trend in Venezuela?
   - **A** The rural population has steadily increased.
   - **B** The urban and rural populations have remained the same.
   - **C** The urban population has steadily increased.
   - **D** The urban population has steadily decreased.

Go Online PHSchool.com

Use Web Code **lfa-1301** for a **Chapter 13 self-test**.

Chapter
14 Mexico and Central America

Chapter Preview

This chapter will introduce you to the northernmost region of Latin America: Mexico and Central America.

Country Databank
The Country Databank provides data and descriptions of each of the countries in the region: Belize, Costa Rica, El Salvador, Guatemala, Honduras, Mexico, Nicaragua, and Panama.

Section 1
Mexico
Moving to the City

Section 2
Guatemala
Descendants of an Ancient People

Section 3
Panama
An Important Crossroads

Target Reading Skill

Context In this chapter you will focus on using context to help you understand unfamiliar words. Context includes the words, phrases, and sentences surrounding the word.

▶ A Guatemalan woman walking home from a rural market

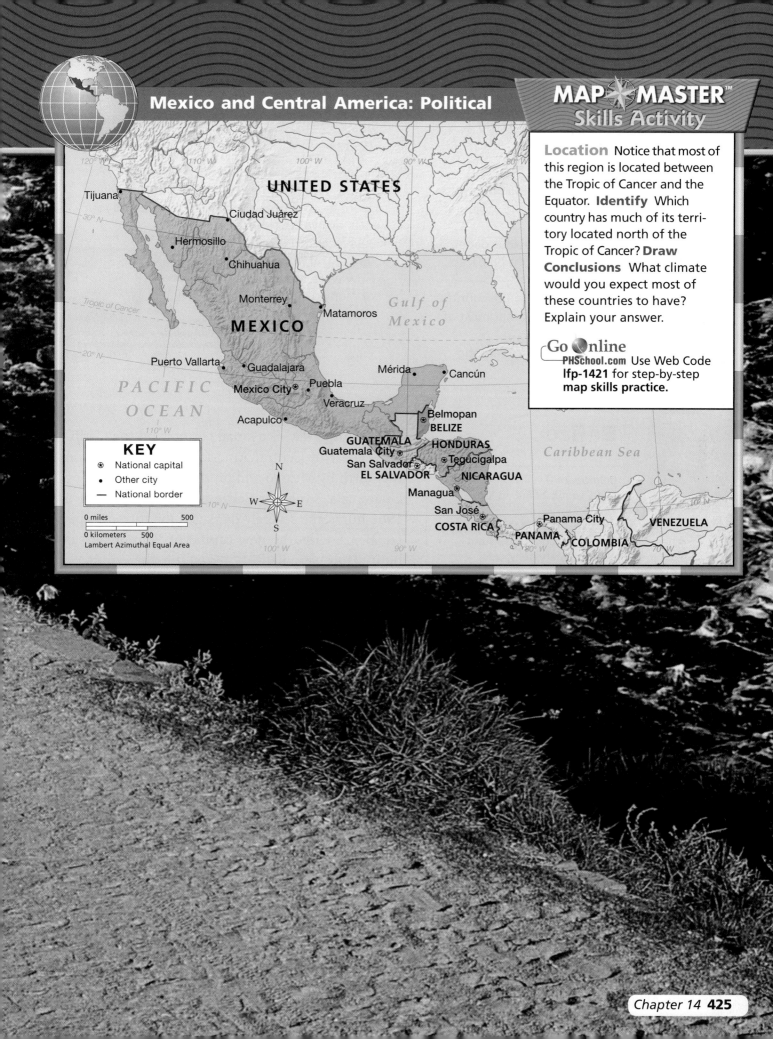

Mexico and Central America: Political

UNITED STATES

Tijuana

Ciudad Juárez

Hermosillo

Chihuahua

Monterrey

Matamoros

Gulf of Mexico

MEXICO

Tropic of Cancer

Puerto Vallarta

Guadalajara

Mérida

Cancún

PACIFIC OCEAN

Mexico City

Puebla

Veracruz

Acapulco

Belmopan

BELIZE

GUATEMALA

Guatemala City

HONDURAS

Tegucigalpa

San Salvador

EL SALVADOR

NICARAGUA

Caribbean Sea

Managua

San José

COSTA RICA

Panama City

PANAMA

COLOMBIA

VENEZUELA

KEY

⊛ National capital

• Other city

— National border

0 miles 500
0 kilometers 500
Lambert Azimuthal Equal Area

N
W E
S

Location Notice that most of this region is located between the Tropic of Cancer and the Equator. **Identify** Which country has much of its territory located north of the Tropic of Cancer? **Draw Conclusions** What climate would you expect most of these countries to have? Explain your answer.

Go Online
PHSchool.com Use Web Code
lfp-1421 for step-by-step map skills practice.

Guide for Reading

This section provides an introduction to the eight countries that make up the region of Mexico and Central America.

- Look at the map on the previous page and then read the paragraphs below to learn about each nation.
- Analyze the data to compare the countries.
- What are the characteristics that most of the countries share?
- What are some key differences among the countries?

Viewing the Video Overview

View the World Studies Video Program Overview to learn more about each of the countries. As you watch, answer this question:

- Seven countries make up Central America. How were the borders of many countries determined?

Discovery CHANNEL SCHOOL Video
Explore the geography of Mexico and Central America.

Belize

Capital	Belmopan
Land Area	8,805 sq mi; 22,806 sq km
Population	262,999
Ethnic Group(s)	mestizo, Creole, Maya, Garifuna
Religion(s)	Roman Catholic, Protestant
Government	parliamentary democracy
Currency	Belizean dollar
Leading Exports	sugar, bananas, citrus, clothing, fish products, molasses, wood
Language(s)	English (official), English Creole, Spanish, Mayan, Garifuna (Carib)

Belize (buh LEEZ) is a small country on the Caribbean coast of Central America. It is bordered on the north by Mexico and on the south and west by Guatemala. Much of Belize is rain forest. After a 1961 hurricane severely damaged the former capital, Belize City, the new capital of Belmopan was built. However, Belize City is still the country's largest and most important city. Formerly known as British Honduras, Belize was the last British colony in North America. It didn't become independent until 1981. Today, its government is based on the British model.

Jaguar in Belize

Costa Rica

Capital	San José
Land Area	19,560 sq mi; 50,660 sq km
Population	3.8 million
Ethnic Group(s)	white, mestizo, black, indigenous Indian, East Asian
Religion(s)	Roman Catholic, Protestant
Government	democratic republic
Currency	Costa Rican colón
Leading Exports	coffee, bananas, sugar, pineapples, textiles, electronics
Language(s)	Spanish (official), English Creole, Bribri, Cabecar

Costa Rica (KAHS tah REE kuh) is a narrow country located between the Pacific Ocean and the Caribbean Sea. It is bordered by Nicaragua and Panama. Even though its name means "rich coast," few riches were found there, and the Spanish colony grew slowly. Costa Rica gained its independence in 1838. Today it is known for its stable government, democratic traditions, and the fact that its army was abolished in 1948. Wealth is more evenly divided in Costa Rica than in other countries in the region, and more government resources go to education and public welfare.

El Salvador

Capital	San Salvador
Land Area	8,000 sq mi; 20,720 sq km
Population	6.4 million
Ethnic Group(s)	mestizo, indigenous Indian, white
Religion(s)	Roman Catholic, Protestant
Government	republic
Currency	Salvadoran colón, U.S. dollar
Leading Exports	offshore assembly exports, coffee, sugar, shrimp, textiles, chemicals, electricity
Language(s)	Spanish (official)

Small and densely populated, El Salvador (el SAL vuh dawr) is one of the poorest countries in the region. It is bordered by Guatemala, Honduras, and the Pacific Ocean. A row of volcanoes runs through El Salvador. In 2001, violent earthquakes killed many people and shattered the economy. El Salvador also suffered from political unrest and a bloody civil war from 1979 to 1992. For much of its history, El Salvador's economy depended on coffee, but manufacturing increased in the 1960s when El Salvador joined the Central American Common Market.

Guatemala

Capital	Guatemala City
Land Area	41,865 sq mi; 108,430 sq km
Population	13.3 million
Ethnic Group(s)	mestizo, indigenous Indian, white
Religion(s)	Roman Catholic, Protestant, traditional beliefs
Government	constitutional democratic republic
Currency	quetzal
Leading Exports	coffee, sugar, bananas, fruits and vegetables, cardamom, meat, apparel, petroleum, electricity
Language(s)	Spanish (official), Quiché, Cakchiquel, Kekchi

One third of the people in Central America live in Guatemala (gwaht uh MAH luh), and Guatemala City is the largest city in Central America. Guatemala is bordered by Mexico, Belize, Honduras, and El Salvador as well as the Caribbean Sea and the Pacific Ocean. Earthquakes, volcanic eruptions, and hurricanes have caused repeated disasters. Guatemala was once home to the ancient Mayan civilization. More recently, it has suffered from harsh military dictatorships, civil war, and discrimination against its large indigenous population.

Introducing **Mexico and Central America**

Honduras

Capital	Tegucigalpa
Land Area	43,201 sq mi; 111,890 sq km
Population	6.6 million
Ethnic Group(s)	mestizo, indigenous Indian, black, white
Religion(s)	Roman Catholic, Protestant
Government	democratic constitutional republic
Currency	Lempira
Leading Exports	coffee, bananas, shrimp, lobster, meat, zinc, lumber
Language(s)	Spanish (official), Black Carib, English Creole

Honduras (hahn DOOR us) stretches from the Caribbean Sea to the Pacific Ocean. It is also bordered by Guatemala, El Salvador, and Nicaragua. Much of the country is mountainous, and the Mosquito Coast on the Caribbean has few people. Most of the population lives in the central highlands. During the early 1900s, foreign-owned banana plantations dominated the economy, and Honduras was ruled by a series of military governments. There was a return to democracy in 1984, and diversification of the economy began. In 2005, the country was devastated by Hurricane Stan, and it is still recovering from this disaster.

Mayan statue at Copán in Honduras

The Flower Carrier **(1935) by Mexican artist Diego Rivera**

Mexico

Capital	Mexico City
Land Area	742,486 sq mi; 1,923,040 sq km
Population	103.4 million
Ethnic Group(s)	mestizo, Amerindian, European
Religion(s)	Roman Catholic, Protestant
Government	federal republic
Currency	Mexican peso
Leading Exports	manufactured goods, oil and oil products, silver, fruits, vegetables, coffee, cotton
Language(s)	Spanish (official), Nahuatl, Mayan, Zapotec, Mixtec

Mexico (MEK sih koh) is located south of the United States and northwest of Central America. It stretches from the Pacific Ocean to the Gulf of Mexico and the Caribbean Sea. Like the United States, Mexico is a federal republic. It has 31 states. The election of President Vicente Fox in 2000 and subsequent elections reflected a move toward greater democracy and the growth of a multiparty system. Mexico is a major oil producer, but also has considerable foreign debt.

Nicaragua

Capital	Managua
Land Area	46,430 sq mi; 120,254 sq km
Population	5.2 million
Ethnic Group(s)	mestizo, white, black, indigenous Indian
Religion(s)	Roman Catholic, Protestant
Government	republic
Currency	Córdoba oro
Leading Exports	coffee, shrimp and lobster, cotton, tobacco, beef, sugar, bananas, gold
Language(s)	Spanish (official), English Creole, Miskito

Nicaragua (nik uh RAH gwuh) stretches across Central America from the Caribbean Sea to the Pacific Ocean. It is bordered on the north by Honduras and on the south by Costa Rica. Like its neighbors, Nicaragua has a row of volcanoes and has experienced many eruptions and earthquakes. After the overthrow of a 40-year dictatorship in 1979, Nicaragua was plunged into civil war, which ended in 1990. In 2005, the country was devastated by Hurricane Stan and is still recovering from the aftermath of the hurricane and the years of civil war.

Panama

Capital	Panama City
Land Area	29,340 sq mi; 75,990 sq km
Population	2.9 million
Ethnic Group(s)	mestizo, mixed black and indigenous Indian, white, indigenous Indian
Religion(s)	Roman Catholic, Protestant
Government	constitutional democracy
Currency	Balboa
Leading Exports	bananas, shrimp, sugar, coffee, clothing
Language(s)	Spanish (official), English Creole, indigenous Indian languages

The narrow country of Panama (PAN uh mah) has been both a barrier and a bridge between the Atlantic and Pacific oceans. It is bordered on the west by Costa Rica and on the east by the South American nation of Colombia. At first, Panama's rough terrain and rain forests hindered travel across the isthmus. The Panama Canal, which opened in 1914, made Panama a main shipping route and led to its economic growth. Most Panamanians live near the canal. Panama City is located at the canal's Pacific entrance. Another major city, Colón, is found near the Caribbean entrance to the canal.

SOURCES: DK World Desk Reference Online; *CIA World Factbook*; *The World Almanac*, 2003

Assessment

Comprehension and Critical Thinking

1. Compare and Contrast Compare the physical size and the population size of Honduras and Guatemala.

2. Draw Conclusions What are the characteristics that most of the countries share?

3. Compare and Contrast What are some key differences among the countries?

4. Categorize What kinds of products are the major exports of this region?

5. Infer What can you infer about a country if many of its exports are made in factories?

6. Make a Bar Graph Create a bar graph showing the population of the countries in the region.

Keeping Current

Access the **DK World Desk Reference Online at PHSchool.com** for up-to-date information about all eight countries in this chapter.

Web Code: lfe-1410

Prepare to Read

Objectives

In this section you will

1. Learn what life is like for people in rural Mexico.
2. Find out why many Mexicans have been moving from the countryside to the cities.
3. Understand why the growth of Mexico City presents challenges for people and the environment.

Taking Notes

As you read this section, look for ways that life is similar and different in rural and in urban Mexico. Copy the Venn diagram below and record your findings in it.

Life in Mexico

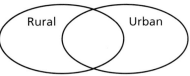

Rural   Urban

Target Reading Skill

Use Context Clues When you come across an unfamiliar word, you can often figure out its meaning from clues in the context. The context refers to the surrounding words, phrases, and sentences. Sometimes the context will define the word. In this example, the phrase in italics explains what smog is: "Smog, *a low-lying layer of polluted air,* hung over the city."

Key Terms

- **migrant worker** (MY grunt WUR kur) *n.* a laborer who travels from one area to another, picking crops that are in season
- **plaza** (PLAH zuh) *n.* a public square at the center of a village, a town, or a city
- **squatter** (SKWAHT ur) *n.* a person who settles on someone else's land without permission

Using oxen to plow a field

Most farm families in Mexico are poor. Many are campesinos. Some work their own small farms. They often plow the land and harvest their crops by hand because they cannot afford expensive farm machinery. Other campesinos do not own land. They work on large farms owned by rich landowners. These **migrant workers** travel from one area to another, picking the crops that are in season.

Mexico's population has risen dramatically over the last 30 years. The country's population is growing at one of the highest rates in the world. There is not enough farm work for so many people. A large family cannot support itself on a small farm. And there are not enough jobs for all the migrant workers.

Many rural Mexicans are moving from the countryside to Mexico City. Why are they making this move? How does moving to the city change their lives? How is this trend changing the country of Mexico?

Life in Rural Mexico

Find the Plateau of Mexico on the map titled Physical Latin America on page 332. The southern part of the plateau has Mexico's best farmland. Throughout much of this region, life has changed little over many years.

Rural Villages Nearly every village in the Mexican countryside has a church and a market. At the center of most villages is a public square called a **plaza.** Farm families grow their own food. If they have extra food, they sell it at the market in the plaza. Rural people buy nearly everything they need—clothing, food, toys, and housewares—at the market rather than in stores.

Farm Work Ramiro Avila (rah MEE roh ah VEE luh) grew up in the state of Guanajuato (gwah nah HWAH toh), in central Mexico. In his small village, Ramiro knew everyone and everyone knew him.

Ramiro's family were campesinos who owned no land. Even as a young child, Ramiro had to work to help support his family. He and his father had jobs as farm laborers. They worked on someone else's farm. They made less than a dollar a day. When Ramiro was 13, his parents decided to move to Mexico City. They joined many other Mexicans who were making this move.

✔ **Reading Check** What is life like in rural Mexican villages?

A Village Market in Mexico
Like many Mexican markets, this one sells a wide variety of goods. **Infer** *Why do you think markets like this one become the center of village life?*

Mexico

As Mexico's population has expanded, large numbers of Mexicans have been moving to the cities to find jobs. Some of the jobs available in the cities are industrial, or jobs in which people produce manufactured goods. Most of Mexico's industry takes place in Mexico City and other large cities. Mexico exports most of the manufactured goods it produces. Study the map and graphs to learn about Mexico's exports and trade partners. Think about how the country's economy shapes the lives of ordinary Mexicans.

Mexico: Resources and Manufacturing

KEY

— National border
⊛ National capital
• Other city
🚗 Car manufacture
⚗ Chemicals
⚡ Electronics
👕 Textiles
　 Oil deposits
　 Gas deposits
　 Industrial area

0 miles 600
0 kilometers 600
Lambert Azimuthal Equal Area

Mexico's Exports

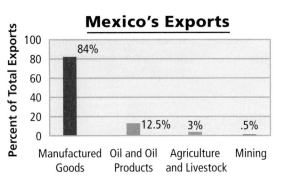

84%

12.5% 3% .5%

Manufactured Goods | Oil and Oil Products | Agriculture and Livestock | Mining

Percent of Total Exports

SOURCE: National Institute of Statistics; *Geography and Informatics 2005*

Mexico's Trading Partners

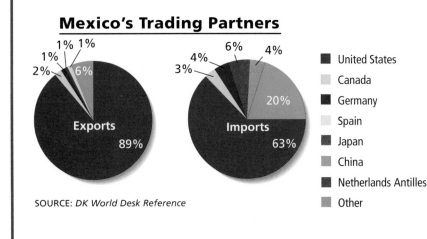

1% 1%
1%
2% 6%

Exports
89%

4% 6% 4%
3%

20%

Imports
63%

■ United States
□ Canada
■ Germany
□ Spain
■ Japan
■ China
■ Netherlands Antilles
■ Other

SOURCE: *DK World Desk Reference*

Map and Chart Skills

1. **Identify** Where are most of Mexico's manufacturing jobs located?

2. **Infer** To what country does Mexico export the most goods? What role might geography play in this trade partnership?

3. **Synthesize** How can a country's economy and trade partners affect where its people live?

Go Online
PHSchool.com

Use Web Code **Ife-1411** for **DK World Desk Reference Online.**

Moving to Mexico City

Many rural people move to the cities because they cannot find work in the countryside. They hope they can make a better living in urban areas such as Mexico City. They also hope that their children will get a better education in city schools. Although city life will be very different from life in the countryside, these families leave their familiar villages behind to make a new start in the city.

Housing in the City Like thousands of other campesino families coming to the city, Ramiro's family did not have much money. When they arrived in Mexico City, they could not afford a house. They went to live in Colonia Zapata, one of many neighborhoods where poor people become squatters. A **squatter** is a person who settles on someone else's land without permission.

Many small houses built by squatters cling to the sides of a steep hill in the Colonia. The older houses near the bottom of the hill are built of concrete. However, most people cannot afford to make sturdy houses when they first arrive. Therefore many of the newer houses higher up the hill are constructed of scrap metal. Most squatter families hope that they will soon be able to buy land from the government. Then they can build their own permanent houses and even have a garden and a patio.

Work and School Once they settle in Mexico City, many families discover that it is still difficult to find work. Sometimes the men of the family look for jobs across the border, in the United States. They often work as farm laborers in states near the Mexican border, such as Texas and California. These men leave their families behind in Mexico, but many of them send money home every month.

Children in these families not only have to get used to city life. They must also adjust to being without their fathers for months at a time. The older children have many new responsibilities. Sometimes they care for the younger children. Or they may work at low-paying jobs in the daytime to help support their families and then go to school at night.

✔ **Reading Check** What new responsibilities might older children face when they move to Mexico City?

Opportunities and Challenges

Large cities in Mexico—and around the world—share many problems as well as many advantages. Even so, each city is unique. Take a closer look at Mexico City.

Mexico's Capital City Mexico City was built on the site of the Aztec capital, Tenochtitlán. During colonial times, it was the capital of New Spain. Today, it is the capital of the modern nation of Mexico.

Much of Mexico's urban population lives in Mexico City. If you count the people in outlying areas, Mexico City has nearly 20 million people. It is one of the largest cities in the world.

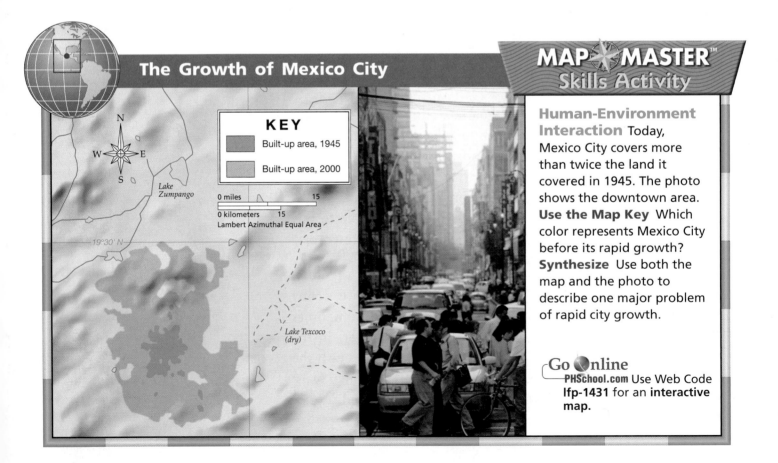

The Growth of Mexico City

MAP MASTER Skills Activity

KEY
- Built-up area, 1945
- Built-up area, 2000

0 miles 15
0 kilometers 15
Lambert Azimuthal Equal Area

Lake Zumpango
19°30' N
Lake Texcoco (dry)

Human-Environment Interaction Today, Mexico City covers more than twice the land it covered in 1945. The photo shows the downtown area. **Use the Map Key** Which color represents Mexico City before its rapid growth? **Synthesize** Use both the map and the photo to describe one major problem of rapid city growth.

Go Online
PHSchool.com Use Web Code lfp-1431 for an interactive map.

Smog in Mexico City

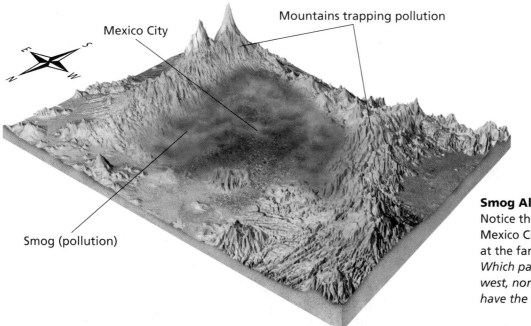

Mexico City

Mountains trapping pollution

Smog (pollution)

Smog Alert
Notice the mountains surrounding Mexico City, and study the compass at the far left. **Analyze Images** *Which part of Mexico City—east, west, north, or south—seems to have the least smog? Explain why.*

Old and New, Rich and Poor Mexico City has both modern skyscrapers and older, historic areas with two- and three-story buildings. Wide avenues and highways along with narrower side streets can barely handle the traffic of this sprawling city. The subway, the underground railroad system, carries more than four million people each day.

Small neighborhoods of very wealthy people are tucked away from the rest of the city. But most of Mexico City's residents are not wealthy. The poorest live on the outskirts of the city. Some of them must travel several hours a day just to get to their jobs.

Pollution and Geography Because of their rapid population growth, many of Mexico's large cities face problems of traffic, pollution, and water shortages. In Mexico City, millions of cars and trucks jam the streets. They compete with taxis, trolleys, and buses. The exhaust fumes from these vehicles pollute the air. Mexico City has also outgrown its fresh water supply. The city must now pump in water from sources as far as 100 miles away.

Mexico City's geography makes its pollution problem worse. The city spreads across a bowl-shaped valley. The surrounding mountains trap automobile exhaust, factory smoke, and other kinds of pollution near the city. The resulting smog cannot blow away, and it hangs over Mexico City as a brown cloud.

Target Skill

Use Context Clues If you do not know what a subway is, look in the surrounding words for a context clue. Here, the phrase following *subway* is a definition of the term. What is a subway?

Making a Living In spite of all their problems, large cities offer many ways to make a living. Millions of people work in factories and offices. Thousands more sell goods from stalls in the street. These street vendors are an important part of city life. For example, some vendors sell juice or bottled water.

Looking to the Future Two events have recently brought changes to Mexico. One of these was the signing of the North American Free Trade Agreement (NAFTA) in 1994. As you read in Chapter 12, the purpose of NAFTA was to improve trade among Canada, the United States, and Mexico.

In Mexico, manufacturing and exports did increase. So did foreign investment. But some say that poor Mexican farmers and factory workers did not benefit from NAFTA. Their incomes actually went down. What's more, new industrial development has increased pollution in Mexico's cities.

In 2000, Mexicans elected Vicente Fox president. Until Fox's election, one political party, the Institutional Revolutionary Party (PRI), had ruled Mexico for 71 years. During his six years as president, Fox focused on improving the economy and strengthening Mexico's relationship with the United States. Elections in 2006 revealed a deep divide within the country, and for months, the results of the close presidential election remained contested.

✓ **Reading Check** What changes has Mexico recently gone through?

The 2000 election of President Vicente Fox, of the National Action Party, was a historic change in Mexico.

Section 1 Assessment

Key Terms
Review the key terms at the beginning of this section. Use each term in a sentence that explains its meaning.

Target Reading Skill
Find the word *sprawling* on page 435. Use context to figure out its meaning. What clue helped you figure out its meaning?

Comprehension and Critical Thinking
1. (a) Recall Describe life in a Mexican village.

(b) Identify Causes Why do so many rural Mexicans move to the cities?
2. (a) Describe How do poor people live in Mexico City?
(b) Synthesize What new problems do rural Mexicans face when they move to the city?
3. (a) Describe What is Mexico City like?
(b) Identify Causes What factors cause pollution in Mexico City?
(c) Evaluate Information Identify the benefits and drawbacks of moving to Mexico City.

Writing Activity
Write an entry in your journal comparing Mexico City with your hometown. How are the two places similar and how are they different? How would your life be different if you lived in a place like Mexico City?

Go Online
PHSchool.com

For: An activity on Mexico City
Visit: PHSchool.com
Web Code: lfd-1401

Guatemala
Descendants of an Ancient People

Prepare to Read

Objectives

In this section you will
1. Learn why there is a struggle for land in Guatemala.
2. Find out how the Mayas lost their land.
3. Discover how groups are working to improve the lives of Guatemala's indigenous people.

Taking Notes

As you read this section, look for details about the Mayas' struggle for their rights. Copy the chart below, and record your findings in it.

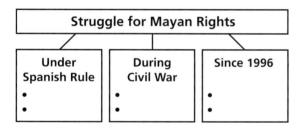

Struggle for Mayan Rights

Under Spanish Rule	During Civil War	Since 1996
•	•	•
•	•	•

Target Reading Skill

Use Context Clues
Context, the words and phrases surrounding a word, can help you understand a new word. One context clue is contrast, a word or words that have the opposite meaning of the unfamiliar word. In this example, the contrast with the newly arrived Spanish helps explain the word *indigenous:* "The struggle of the indigenous people of Guatemala to keep their land began when the Spanish first arrived."

Key Terms

- **ladino** (luh DEE noh) *n.* a mestizo, or person of mixed Spanish and Native American ancestry in Guatemala
- **land reform** (land ree FAWRM) *n.* the effort to distribute land more equally and fairly
- **political movement** (puh LIT ih kul MOOV munt) *n.* a large group of people who work together for political change
- **strike** (stryk) *n.* a refusal to work until certain demands of workers are met

In Guatemala, Native Americans make up the majority of the population. They form 23 ethnic groups. Even though the indigenous groups of Guatemala are related to one another, each group is different. Each one has its own language and customs. The largest group is the Quiché Maya.

Mayan families are often poor. They raise corn on tiny plots of land, but can barely earn enough money to survive. Children often work to help support their families. Mayan girls do weaving to bring in extra money. One Mayan girl described her childhood as similar to the childhoods of "all Indian girls, at the side of my mother, making tortillas and learning to weave and embroider."

Like many other indigenous people, the Mayas have found it difficult to get an education and escape poverty. They have also struggled to preserve their traditional culture as they become part of modern Guatemala.

Modern Mayan women weave much as their ancestors did.

Farming in the Mountains
This small Mayan farm clings to a Guatemalan hillside. **Analyze Images** *Look carefully at the buildings and the fields. What do these details tell you about making a living on this farm?*

Target Skill **Use Context Clues** If you do not remember what *hacienda* means, consider these context clues. A hacienda is "where crops are grown to sell abroad." Haciendas are also contrasted with small farms. Therefore a hacienda is _____.

The Struggle for Land

Land is a valuable resource in Guatemala, as it is in all of Latin America. Fair distribution of the land is a serious problem throughout the region.

The People and the Land Much of the land in Guatemala belongs to a few rich families. The rich landowners of Guatemala are **ladinos** (luh DEE nohz), mestizos who are descended from Native Americans and Spaniards. Native Americans who follow European ways are also considered to be ladinos.

For many years, most Mayas have lived in the mountains because it was the only land available to Native Americans. Although Mayan families work hard on their farms, they often fail to produce good crops. The soil of the Guatemalan highlands is not very good. Soil erosion makes farming even more difficult.

Land Distribution In many Latin American countries, the best land is used for haciendas where crops are grown to sell abroad. Guatemalan haciendas produce coffee, cotton, sugar cane, and bananas. In contrast, campesinos grow maize, beans, and squash on small farms in the highlands. These crops are often sold in village markets and provide food for the local population.

Since the 1930s, **land reform**, the effort to distribute land more equally, has been a major goal of many reform and political groups. The wealthy landowners, who have the greatest political power in many Latin American countries, have often resisted these reforms. Clashes between those in favor of reform and those against it have even led to violence and civil war. You will read about the Guatemalan civil war later in this section.

✓ **Reading Check** How is land distributed in many Latin American countries?

The Mayas Lose Their Land

In order to get enough land to make a living—or even to keep the land they have—the Mayas of Guatemala have faced many challenges. One challenge relates to their culture. Indigenous people do not always think of themselves as citizens of the country in which they live. A Mayan woman is more likely to think of herself as a Maya than as a Guatemalan.

Discovery CHANNEL SCHOOL Video
Learn about growing coffee in Guatemala.

COUNTRY PROFILE
Focus on Culture

Guatemala

Guatemala today has two distinct cultures: indigenous and ladino. Ladinos speak Spanish, the country's official language, and live mainly in the cities. The majority of Guatemala's population, however, are Mayas. Most Mayas live in villages and towns in the country's highlands. From town to town, Mayan groups speak slightly different languages and create unique art. Their art includes distinctive fabric patterns woven by each group. Study the map and charts to learn more about Guatemalan culture.

Guatemala: Languages
KEY
- Spanish
- Native American
- ⊛ National capital
- • Other city

Ethnic Groups

Other 10%
Mestizo 30%
Indian 60%

SOURCE: *DK World Desk Reference*

Mayan Towns

Town Name	Language	Sample Fabric
Patzún	Cakchiquel	
Cobán	Kekchí	
Chichicastenango	Quiché	
San Juan Cotzal	Ixil	
Rabinal	Pokomchi	

Map and Chart Skills

1. **Identify** In what parts of the country is Spanish spoken? What language would you expect the people in Rabinal to speak?
2. **Infer** What advantages and disadvantages result from having so many languages in one country?

Go Online PHSchool.com Use Web Code lfe-1412 for **DK World Desk Reference Online.**

**Justina Tzoc:
A Voice for Change**

For many years, Justina Tzoc (hoo STEE nah tsohk) has worked to help Mayan women in remote areas of Guatemala. She calls her effort "the kind of work that has no beginning and no end." During the Guatemalan civil war, Tzoc faced many dangers as she helped these women organize to fight for their rights. Although the civil war is over, Tzoc's work goes on. According to Tzoc, the indigenous women of Guatemala will continue to work "so that we are recognized—have a voice and a vote."

In addition, the majority of Native Americans in Guatemala cannot read or write. For these two reasons, most Mayas have not filed any papers with the government showing that they own land. Even after they have worked hard for many years to grow crops on a piece of land, a Mayan family often has no way to prove that their land belongs to them.

A 500-Year-Old Struggle The indigenous people of Guatemala have fought to keep both their land and their culture for more than 500 years. This struggle began when the Spanish first arrived in the Americas.

The Spanish conquistadors conquered the Native Americans by force. Many were killed. Others died of hunger or the hardships of slavery. Still others died from European diseases. In many Latin American countries, there are few indigenous people left. In contrast, Guatemala is largely Native American. However, the Native Americans have little political power or land.

Civil War Beginning around 1960, a civil war raged in Guatemala for more than 30 years. First, an elected leader who favored land reform was overthrown by the military. Then government military forces fought rebel groups that were living in the highlands. Armed fighters were not the only ones killed in the fighting. Thousands of civilians were also killed, and many others fled the country. Those who fought for human rights or opposed the government were treated harshly by a series of military rulers.

The Mayas suffered during the civil war. In hundreds of villages throughout Guatemala, soldiers came to claim the Mayas' land. Many Mayas lost all of their belongings and were forced out of their villages. Some had to move to other countries to live.

✓ **Reading Check** **What happened to the Mayas during the civil war?**

Working for a Better Life

Some Mayas remained in Guatemala during the civil war. They started **political movements,** which are large groups of people who work together for political change. One such movement, called Nukuj Akpop (nooh KOO ahk POHP), still works to fight poverty and bring human rights to Mayas.

A political demonstration in Guatemala City

Defending Campesino Rights Today, Mayan political movements seek to defend campesino rights. They help villages plan ways to protect themselves. They teach people the history of their land and how to read. They also help organize meetings, protests, and strikes. A **strike** is a refusal to work until certain demands of workers are met. Above all, these political movements defend Native American land rights.

Changes Come to Guatemala These efforts brought change in Guatemala. For the first time, Mayas gained a voice in their government. Mayan priests were appointed to advise government officials about Mayan culture. Radio programs were broadcast in Mayan languages, and Mayan-language books and newspapers also appeared.

In 1996, agreements were signed ending the civil war. Among these was a promise that indigenous communities would be rebuilt. However, not all of these agreements have been carried out. Violations of human rights by the government increased again in 2000, and many Guatemalans protested in the streets. The fight for the rights of the Mayas—and for all the ordinary people of Guatemala—continues.

Some political movements in Guatemala are geared toward helping indigenous people, such as the man above.

✓ **Reading Check** How do political movements try to help the Mayas?

Section 2 Assessment

Key Terms
Review the key terms at the beginning of this section. Use each term in a sentence that explains its meaning.

Target Reading Skill
Find the word *civilians* on page 440. Look for a contrast near the word. How does this contrast help you define *civilians*?

Comprehension and Critical Thinking
1. (a) Describe How is land used in Guatemala?
(b) Identify Causes Why do the Mayas often fail to earn a living from their land?

2. (a) Recall What are two reasons the Mayas lost their land?
(b) Synthesize Explain how the Mayas have been at a disadvantage in their struggle against their rulers.
3. (a) Identify What are two ways that political movements work to help the Mayas?
(b) Summarize What kinds of changes have these groups brought about?
(c) Predict Do you think life will improve for the Mayas in the decades ahead? Explain.

Writing Activity
Suppose you are a reporter for a radio news program. Write a report on the situation of the Mayas in Guatemala. Present background information about Mayan culture and history. Then tell your listeners about current conditions. Be sure that your report can be read in two to three minutes.

Writing Tip Introduce your report with a "hook," an interesting event or observation that will make your listeners stay tuned.

When Mr. Macintosh walked into the classroom, Tina watched him carefully.

"Uh-oh," she said quietly. "Looks like a pop quiz." Tina started flipping through the pages of last night's homework assignment.

Miguel heard Tina. "Why do you think there's going to be a quiz?" he whispered to Tina.

"For starters, it's Friday. He tends to give quizzes at the end of the week. And do you see that blue notebook he's got in his hand?" Miguel saw it. "He always writes test questions in it. Whenever he pulls it out, we have a test."

Just then Mr. Macintosh said, "Good morning, class. Please close your books for a pop quiz."

Tina was correct that the class would have a pop quiz. You can understand why. She drew good inferences and a strong conclusion.

An inference is an educated guess based on facts or evidence. A conclusion is a judgment. Conclusions are often based on several inferences.

Learn the Skill

Use the steps below to draw logical inferences and a strong conclusion.

1. **Identify what you know or assume to be true.** Tina stated these facts: First, it was Friday. Mr. Macintosh tends to give quizzes at the end of the week. Second, he was carrying his blue notebook in which he writes test questions.

2. **Use the facts to draw inferences.** Inferences can usually be stated as an "if . . . then" sentence. The "if" part is the facts you know. The "then" part is an educated guess that follows logically from the facts.

3. **Use two or more inferences to draw a reasoned judgment or conclusion.** From her two inferences, Tina was able to draw this conclusion: The class was about to have a pop quiz.

A protest by Mayas in Guatemala City

Practice the Skill

Read the passage titled Working for a Better Life on pages 440 and 441. Then use the steps below to draw inferences and a conclusion about the situation of the Mayas in Guatemala.

Smog in Mexico City

1 Answer these questions in order to help you find facts: What have political movements done to improve life for Guatemalans? What changes have occurred in Guatemala?

2 Use the facts to create at least two inferences, or educated guesses. State your inferences as "if . . . then" sentences. For example: If Mayas learn to read, then they will be more successful at defending their rights.

3 Using the inferences you have written, what conclusion can you draw about the Mayas in Guatemala?

Apply the Skill

Turn to Section 1 of Chapter 14 and reread the passage titled Opportunities and Challenges on pages 434 and 435. Use the steps of this skill to draw inferences and a conclusion about some aspect of life in Mexico City, such as traffic or pollution.

Panama
An Important Crossroads

Prepare to Read

Objectives

In this section you will

1. Find out why people wanted to build a canal across the Isthmus of Panama.
2. Learn how the Panama Canal was built.
3. Understand how the canal has affected the nation of Panama.

Taking Notes

As you read this section, look for the problems the builders of the Panama Canal faced and how they solved those problems. Copy the table below, and record your findings in it.

Building the Panama Canal

Problem	Solution

Target Reading Skill

Use Context Clues
Sometimes you come across a word you know that is being used in an unfamiliar way. You can use context clues and your own general knowledge to understand the new use of the word. For example, you may know that *vessel* often means "ship," and that a cargo ship carries cargo. Therefore, a water vessel is probably a container that holds, or carries, water.

Key Terms

- **Panama Canal** (PAN uh mah kuh NAL) *n.* a shipping canal across the Isthmus of Panama, linking the Atlantic Ocean to the Pacific Ocean
- **lock** (lahk) *n.* a section of waterway in which ships are raised or lowered by adjusting the water level
- **Canal Zone** (kuh NAL zohn) *n.* a 10-mile strip of land along the Panama Canal, once governed by the United States
- **ecotourism** (ek oh TOOR iz um) *n.* travel to unspoiled areas in order to learn about the environment

Statue of Vasco Nuñez de Balboa in Panama City, Panama

Ever since Christopher Columbus first explored the Isthmus of Panama, the Spanish had been looking for a water route through it. They wanted to be able to sail west from Spain all the way to Asia. The Spanish were also looking for gold. In 1513, the conquistador Vasco Nuñez de Balboa heard of "a mighty sea beyond the mountains" of what is now Panama. He also heard that the streams flowing into that sea were filled with gold.

Balboa organized an expedition of Spaniards and Indians. They struggled across the isthmus, through very difficult country, for over a month. Finally Balboa waded into the Pacific Ocean, which he claimed for Spain. Balboa went on to explore the Pacific coast and found gold and other treasure there.

Balboa still hoped that a water route could be found through the isthmus. But if not, he said, "it might not be impossible to make one." The effort to create this waterway has shaped the history of the isthmus and led to the creation of the nation of Panama. Even today, geography has a major effect on Panama.

Why Build a Canal?

The **Panama Canal,** a manmade waterway across the Isthmus of Panama, is a shortcut through the Western Hemisphere. It is the only way to get from the Pacific Ocean to the Atlantic Ocean by ship without going all the way around South America. Sailors had dreamed of a canal through Central America since the 1500s. A canal could shorten the trip from the Atlantic to the Pacific by 7,800 miles (12,553 kilometers), saving both time and money. But it was not until the 1900s that engineers had the technology to make such a canal.

Crossing the Isthmus By 1534, the Spanish had built a seven-foot-wide stone road across the isthmus. It was used to carry treasure to the Atlantic coast for shipment to Spain. More than 300 years later, during the California Gold Rush, prospectors wanted to get from the east coast of the United States to California as quickly as possible. However, there was not yet a transcontinental railroad in the United States, and travel by horse and wagon was slow and difficult. Instead, many prospectors traveled by boat to Panama, trekked across the isthmus, and took another boat to California.

Passing Through the Canal
Special Panama Canal pilots steer ships through the canal. Here, the captain and first mate of a ship consult with a pilot. **Infer** *Why do you think the passage of ships through the canal is controlled so carefully?*

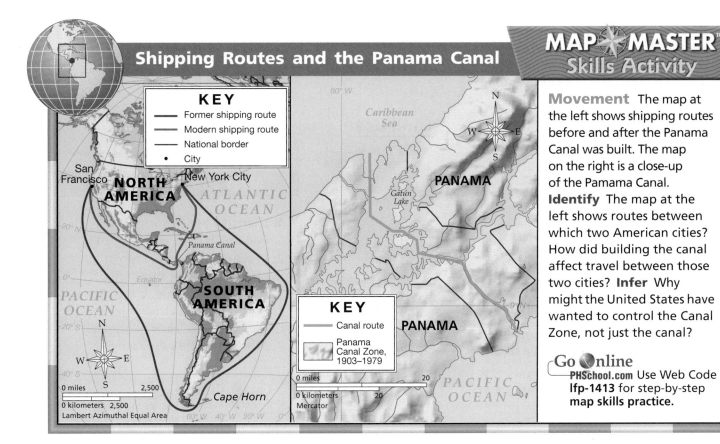

Shipping Routes and the Panama Canal

KEY
— Former shipping route
— Modern shipping route
— National border
• City

San Francisco
New York City
NORTH AMERICA
ATLANTIC OCEAN
Panama Canal
Equator
PACIFIC OCEAN
SOUTH AMERICA
Cape Horn

0 miles 2,500
0 kilometers 2,500
Lambert Azimuthal Equal Area

80° W
Caribbean Sea
PANAMA
Gatún Lake

KEY
— Canal route
☐ Panama Canal Zone, 1903–1979

PANAMA

0 miles 20
0 kilometers 20
Mercator

PACIFIC OCEAN

MAP MASTER™
Skills Activity

Movement The map at the left shows shipping routes before and after the Panama Canal was built. The map on the right is a close-up of the Pamama Canal.
Identify The map at the left shows routes between which two American cities? How did building the canal affect travel between those two cities? **Infer** Why might the United States have wanted to control the Canal Zone, not just the canal?

Go Online
PHSchool.com Use Web Code **lfp-1413** for step-by-step **map skills practice.**

The French Begin a Canal In 1881, when Panama was part of Colombia, a French company gained the rights to build a canal through Panama. However, the builders had to struggle with mud slides, a mountain range, and a dense tropical forest. Tropical diseases killed many workers. After several years of digging and blasting, the French company went bankrupt. Work on the canal stopped.

In 1902, the United States government bought the French company's equipment. Then, the United States began negotiating with Colombia for the rights to continue building a canal.

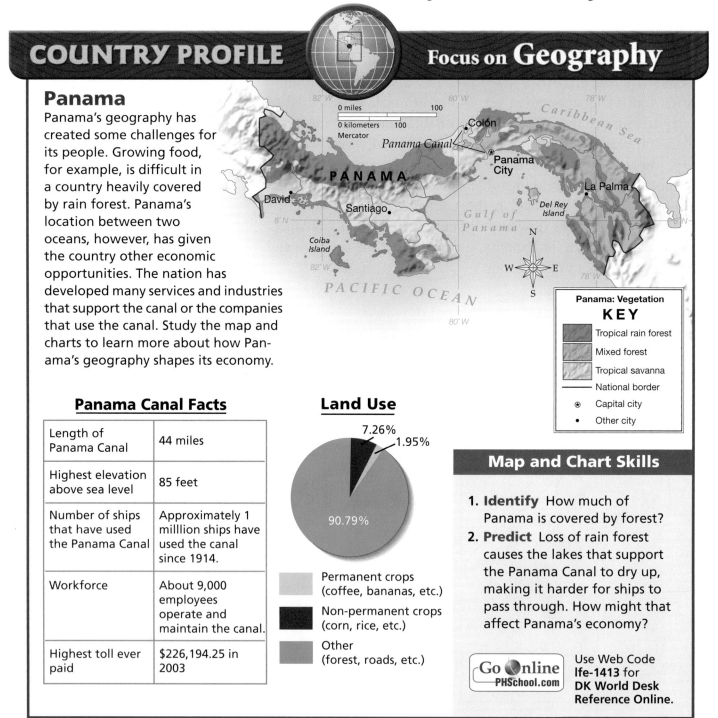

COUNTRY PROFILE

Focus on Geography

Panama

Panama's geography has created some challenges for its people. Growing food, for example, is difficult in a country heavily covered by rain forest. Panama's location between two oceans, however, has given the country other economic opportunities. The nation has developed many services and industries that support the canal or the companies that use the canal. Study the map and charts to learn more about how Panama's geography shapes its economy.

Panama: Vegetation
KEY
- Tropical rain forest
- Mixed forest
- Tropical savanna
- National border
- ⊛ Capital city
- • Other city

Panama Canal Facts

Length of Panama Canal	44 miles
Highest elevation above sea level	85 feet
Number of ships that have used the Panama Canal	Approximately 1 milllion ships have used the canal since 1914.
Workforce	About 9,000 employees operate and maintain the canal.
Highest toll ever paid	$226,194.25 in 2003

Land Use

7.26%
1.95%
90.79%

- Permanent crops (coffee, bananas, etc.)
- Non-permanent crops (corn, rice, etc.)
- Other (forest, roads, etc.)

Map and Chart Skills

1. **Identify** How much of Panama is covered by forest?
2. **Predict** Loss of rain forest causes the lakes that support the Panama Canal to dry up, making it harder for ships to pass through. How might that affect Panama's economy?

Go Online
PHSchool.com
Use Web Code Ife-1413 for DK World Desk Reference Online.

The New Nation of Panama Colombia refused to grant the United States rights to build a canal. But business people in Panama thought a canal would benefit the local economy. Also, many Panamanians wanted to be free of Colombia's rule. They saw the canal as an opportunity to win independence.

At the same time, President Theodore Roosevelt felt that the canal was important for the United States. It would speed trade between the Atlantic and Pacific coasts. It would also allow the American navy to move back and forth in case of war. Roosevelt did not wait for events to unfold. He took action. In November 1903, the United States helped Panama revolt against Colombia. Two weeks after Panama declared its independence, the United States received the rights to build the canal.

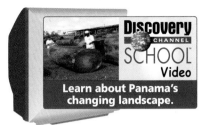

Learn about Panama's changing landscape.

✓ **Reading Check** Why did Panamanians want a canal?

Building the Canal: A Heroic Effort

The Americans faced the same challenges of moving earth and rock that the French had faced. In addition, the project called for a dam to be built to form a lake. There were locks to design and build. A **lock** is a section of waterway in which ships are raised or lowered by adjusting the water level.

While the work on the canal was difficult and slow, by far the biggest problem was disease. Some 20,000 workers had died of malaria and yellow fever while the French worked on the canal. Scientists did not know what caused these diseases, so they could do little to prevent them.

Digging the Canal
Canal workers wore the badges shown above. In the photo at the left, they use steam shovels and trains to build the Panama Canal.
Draw Conclusions *From what you see in the photo, how were trains used in the construction?*

In the early 1900s, doctors discovered that malaria and yellow fever were both carried by mosquitoes. The mosquitoes bred in standing water. In 1904, the Panama Canal Company hired a doctor and a large crew to deal with the mosquito problem. It took more than a year to complete the job. Workers burned sulfur in every house to kill mosquitoes. They covered every water vessel with mesh to keep mosquitoes out. They filled in swampy breeding grounds with dirt. Without these efforts, the Panama Canal probably could not have been built.

It took eight years and more than 70,000 workers, mostly Caribbean islanders, to build the Panama Canal. It remains one of the greatest engineering feats of modern times.

✓ **Reading Check** **How did workers fight the mosquitoes?**

Panama and Its Canal

When the United States gained the rights to build a canal, it signed a treaty with Panama. The treaty gave the United States the right to build the Panama Canal and to control it forever.

The Canal Zone The United States also controlled an area called the Canal Zone. The **Canal Zone** was an area containing the canal, the land on either side of the canal, the ports, the port cities, and the railroad. The treaty allowed the United States to govern the Canal Zone according to its laws and gave the United States the right to invade Panama to protect the canal. The United States built 14 military bases in the Canal Zone and stationed thousands of soldiers there.

Many Panamanians felt the United States had too much power in Panama. For years, Panama held talks with the United States about transferring control of the canal to Panama. In the 1960s and 1970s, angry Panamanians rioted to protest American control.

A Change of Ownership In 1977, after years of talks, President Jimmy Carter signed two new treaties with Panama's government. These treaties gave Panama more control over the canal. In 1999, Panama finally gained full control of the Panama Canal.

Panama Today The Panama Canal dominated life in Panama for much of the 1900s, and it continues to be extremely important today. Because of the canal, Panama has become an international crossroads for trade. The ships that pass through the Panama Canal each day pay tolls according to their weight. International trade is very important to Panama's economy. The canal has made Panama a leading banking and finance center.

Panama City at night

The Panama Canal

Every day, an average of 33 ships pass through the Panama Canal. It takes each ship around nine hours to cross from one ocean to the other. The Panama Canal is like a water elevator with lakes. Ships are raised and lowered in the locks as they travel from one ocean to the other.

Gatún Locks
The construction of the canal's locks was a massive task involving a total workforce of more than 70,000 people. As shown above, the railroad was used to haul earth and other materials through the central channel of the canal.

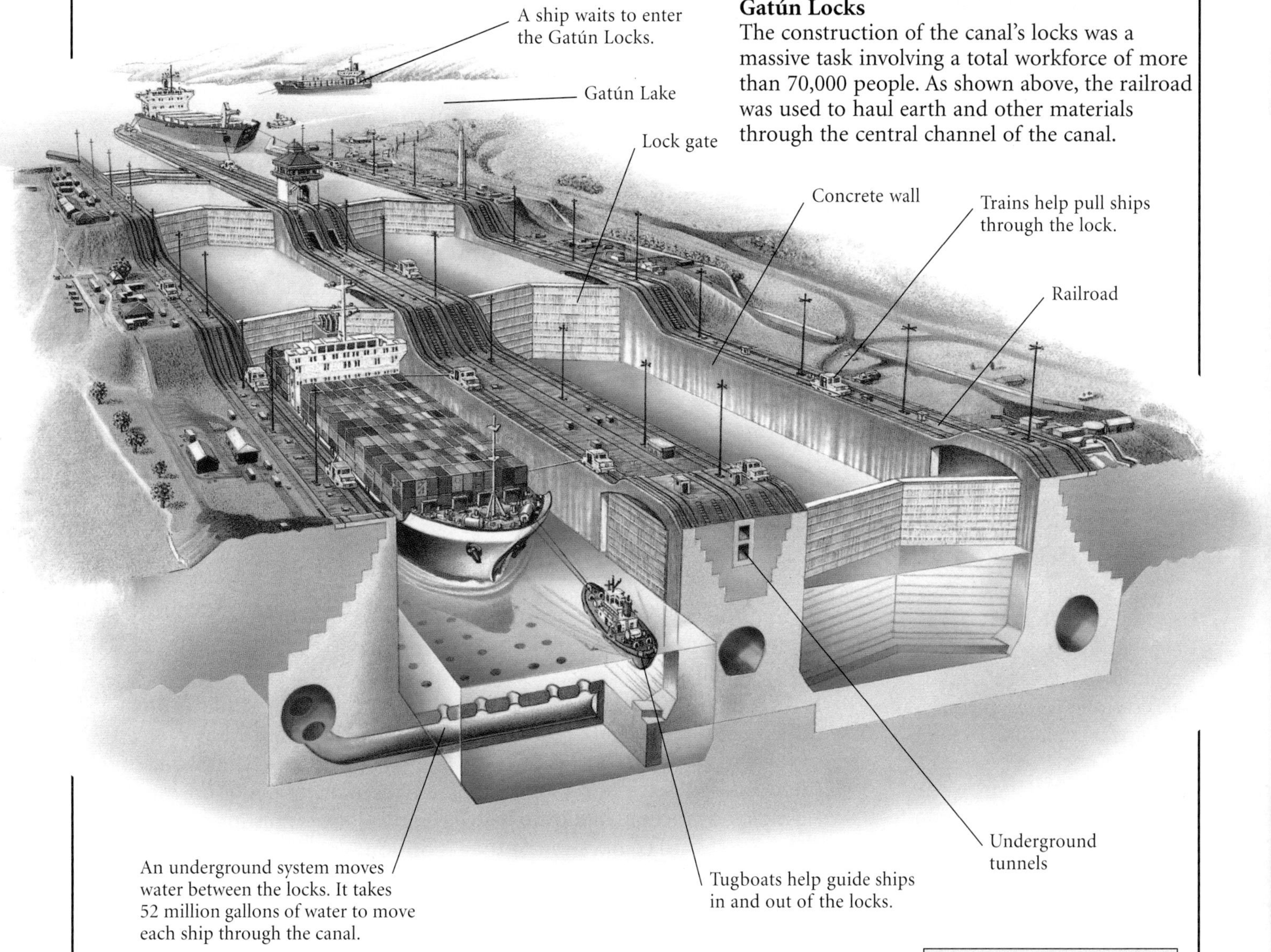

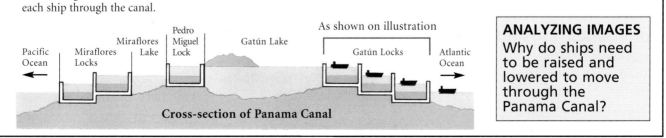

A ship waits to enter the Gatún Locks.

Gatún Lake

Lock gate

Concrete wall

Trains help pull ships through the lock.

Railroad

An underground system moves water between the locks. It takes 52 million gallons of water to move each ship through the canal.

Tugboats help guide ships in and out of the locks.

Underground tunnels

Cross-section of Panama Canal

Pacific Ocean — Miraflores Locks — Miraflores Lake — Pedro Miguel Lock — Gatún Lake — As shown on illustration: Gatún Locks — Atlantic Ocean

ANALYZING IMAGES
Why do ships need to be raised and lowered to move through the Panama Canal?

An ecotourist riding through Panama's rain forest

New Industries Traffic through the canal has also encouraged warehousing and manufacturing. Many factories in Panama are similar to the maquiladoras in Mexico. They assemble parts imported from abroad and then export the finished products. Materials for these factories come from Hong Kong, the United States, and Japan as well as other countries. Most finished products are shipped to Latin American nations or are sold within Panama itself.

Panama is also a communications hub. International fiber-optic networks cross through Panama. Fiber-optic networks are used for long-distance telephone lines and computer networks.

Tourism Another important industry in Panama is tourism. Many tourists come to travel through the canal. They also visit Panama's rain forests. Look at the map in the Country Profile on page 446 to see how much of Panama is covered by rain forests. Tourism in unspoiled areas to observe wildlife and learn about the environment is called **ecotourism.** Ecotourists come to see the wide variety of plants and animals in the rain forest. These include howler monkeys, sloths, harpy eagles, and capybaras—huge rodents that look like guinea pigs. Panama's government has recently invested millions of dollars to promote ecotourism in its rain forests.

✓ **Reading Check** Why is the canal important to Panama today?

Section 3 Assessment

Key Terms
Review the key terms at the beginning of this section. Use each term in a sentence that explains its meaning.

Target Reading Skill
Find the word *unfold* on page 447. Use your own knowledge and the surrounding words and phrases to explain what *unfold* means in this context.

Comprehension and Critical Thinking
1. (a) Recall What are the benefits of a canal across the Isthmus of Panama?

(b) Sequence List three events, in order, that led to the building of the canal.
2. (a) Describe What kinds of difficulties did the builders of the canal face?
(b) Identify Cause and Effect How did advances in medicine lead to the successful completion of the Panama Canal?
3. (a) Define What was the Canal Zone?
(b) Explain How was the Canal Zone governed?
(c) Draw Conclusions Why was it so important to Panamanians to gain control of the canal?

Writing Activity
Suppose you are an American newspaper editor in the 1970s. Write an editorial either for or against giving control of the Panama Canal and the Canal Zone to Panama. State your position clearly. Be sure to support your position with reasons and facts.

Go Online
PHSchool.com

For: An activity on Panama
Visit: PHSchool.com
Web Code: lfd-1403

Review and Assessment

◆ Chapter Summary

Section 1: Mexico

- Many farmers in Mexico are poor, and jobs in the countryside are scarce.
- Many rural Mexicans move to the cities to look for work, but they find that city life is hard and very different from life in the countryside.
- Mexico City is a huge city that is facing overcrowding and pollution problems.

Section 2: Guatemala

- Most of the land in Guatemala is owned by only a few wealthy ladino families who grow crops for export.
- The Mayas lost much of their land to their Spanish conquerors and later they lost more land during the civil war.
- Today, political movements are working to improve life for the Mayas.

Section 3: Panama

- The Panama Canal shortens sea travel between the Atlantic Ocean and the Pacific Ocean.
- After the French could not complete the canal, the United States overcame engineering challenges and disease to build it.
- The Panama Canal is a key water route today and is important to Panama's economy.

Mexico

Guatemala

Panama

◆ Key Terms

Each of the statements below contains a key term from the chapter. If the statement is true, write *true*. If it is false, rewrite the statement to make it true.

1. A migrant worker is a person who settles on someone else's land without permission.

2. A plaza is an open field in the countryside.

3. A canal uses a series of locks to raise and lower ships by adjusting the water level.

4. Land reform is a new and better way of farming the land.

5. When people strike, they stop working in order to achieve a goal.

6. Ecotourism can involve visiting the rain forest to learn about its environment.

7. A ladino is any person from Latin America.

8. The Panama Canal shortens the route ships must travel between the Atlantic Ocean and the Pacific Ocean.

◆ Comprehension and Critical Thinking

9. (a) Identify Name two places many rural Mexicans go when they leave the countryside.
(b) Generalize Why do so many people make these moves?

10. (a) Recall Describe population growth in Mexico.
(b) Identify Effects How does population growth affect Mexico's cities?

11. (a) Summarize What happened to the Mayas during the Guatemalan civil war?
(b) Synthesize Why have so many Mayas been forced from their land?

12. (a) Identify What groups are working to improve life for the Mayas?
(b) Identify Cause and Effect What are two methods these groups use, and how might these methods bring about change?

13. (a) Identify What country first tried to build a canal across Panama?
(b) Identify Causes Why did that country fail to complete the canal?
(c) Draw Conclusions How does the whole world benefit from the Panama Canal?

14. (a) Summarize How did Panama become an independent nation?
(b) Identify Causes Why did Panama want the United States to build the Panama Canal?
(c) Identify Effects What benefits has the Panama Canal brought to Panama?

◆ Skills Practice

Drawing Inferences and Conclusions In the Skills for Life activity in this chapter, you learned how to draw inferences. You also learned how to draw a conclusion, or make a reasoned judgment, using two or more inferences.

Review the steps you followed to learn this skill. Then reread The New Nation of Panama on page 447. List several inferences you can draw about the events described there. Finally, use your inferences to draw a conclusion about those events.

◆ Writing Activity: Science

Suppose you were the science reporter for a newspaper covering the building of the Panama Canal. Write a brief report about how advances in science contributed to the successful completion of the Panama Canal.

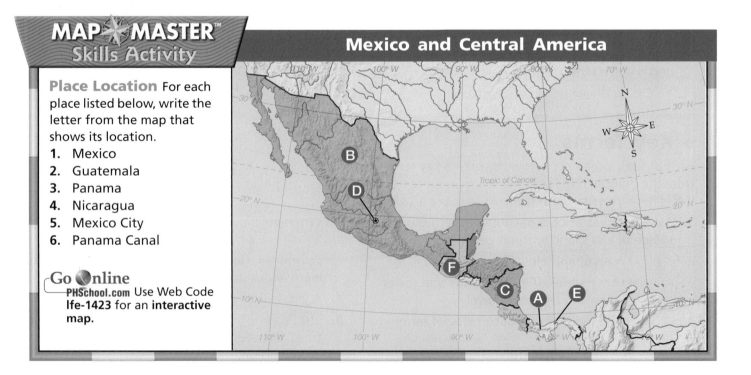

MAP★MASTER™ Skills Activity

Mexico and Central America

Place Location For each place listed below, write the letter from the map that shows its location.
1. Mexico
2. Guatemala
3. Panama
4. Nicaragua
5. Mexico City
6. Panama Canal

Go Online
PHSchool.com Use Web Code lfe-1423 for an interactive map.

Standardized Test Prep

Test-Taking Tips

Some questions on standardized tests ask you to analyze a reading selection. Study the passage below. Then follow the tips to help you answer the sample question.

> Many people have moved to Mexico City to find jobs in factories. Cars and buses clog the city streets. In addition, the city is located in a valley surrounded by mountains, and pollution gets trapped there. <u>Because</u> of its geography and heavy traffic, Mexico City has one of the worst cases of air pollution in the world.

TIP Look for words that signal causes or reasons, such as the word *because* in the last sentence.

Pick the letter that best completes the statement.

Mexico City's air pollution problem is made worse by

A ~~smog from South America~~.

B its location.

C its textile factories.

D ~~its lack of rain~~.

TIP First cross out answers that you know are wrong. Then consider each remaining choice before selecting the best answer.

Think It Through Look at the remaining answer choices. Answer C might be correct, but the passage does not mention textile factories. Remember the signal word *because*. The sentence beginning with *because* gives geography as one reason for Mexico City's pollution. Geography includes location, so B is the correct answer.

Practice Questions

Use the tips above and other tips in this book to help you answer the following questions.

1. Which of the following was not a problem for the builders of the Panama Canal?

   A disease carried by mosquitoes

   B mudslides

   C blizzards

   D a mountain range blocking the route

2. In Guatemala, most of the land is owned by

   A Native Americans.

   B Spanish conquerors.

   C a few wealthy ladino families.

   D the Mayas.

3. What is one result of rapid population growth in Mexico?

   A Farms are getting overcrowded.

   B The economy is improving because there are more people to buy things.

   C Rural people are moving to the cities to find work.

   D Factories are shutting down.

Use the circle graph below to answer Question 4. Choose the letter of the best answer to the question.

Population of Guatemala

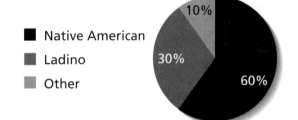

- Native American
- Ladino
- Other

10%
30%
60%

4. According to the circle graph, which of the following statements is true?

   A Most people in Guatemala are descended from Europeans and Native Americans.

   B Half of Guatemala's population is ladino.

   C Most Guatemalans are Native American.

   D There are more Spaniards than ladinos in Guatemala.

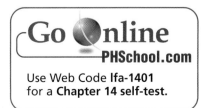

Go Online
PHSchool.com
Use Web Code lfa-1401
for a **Chapter 14 self-test**.

Chapter

15 The Caribbean

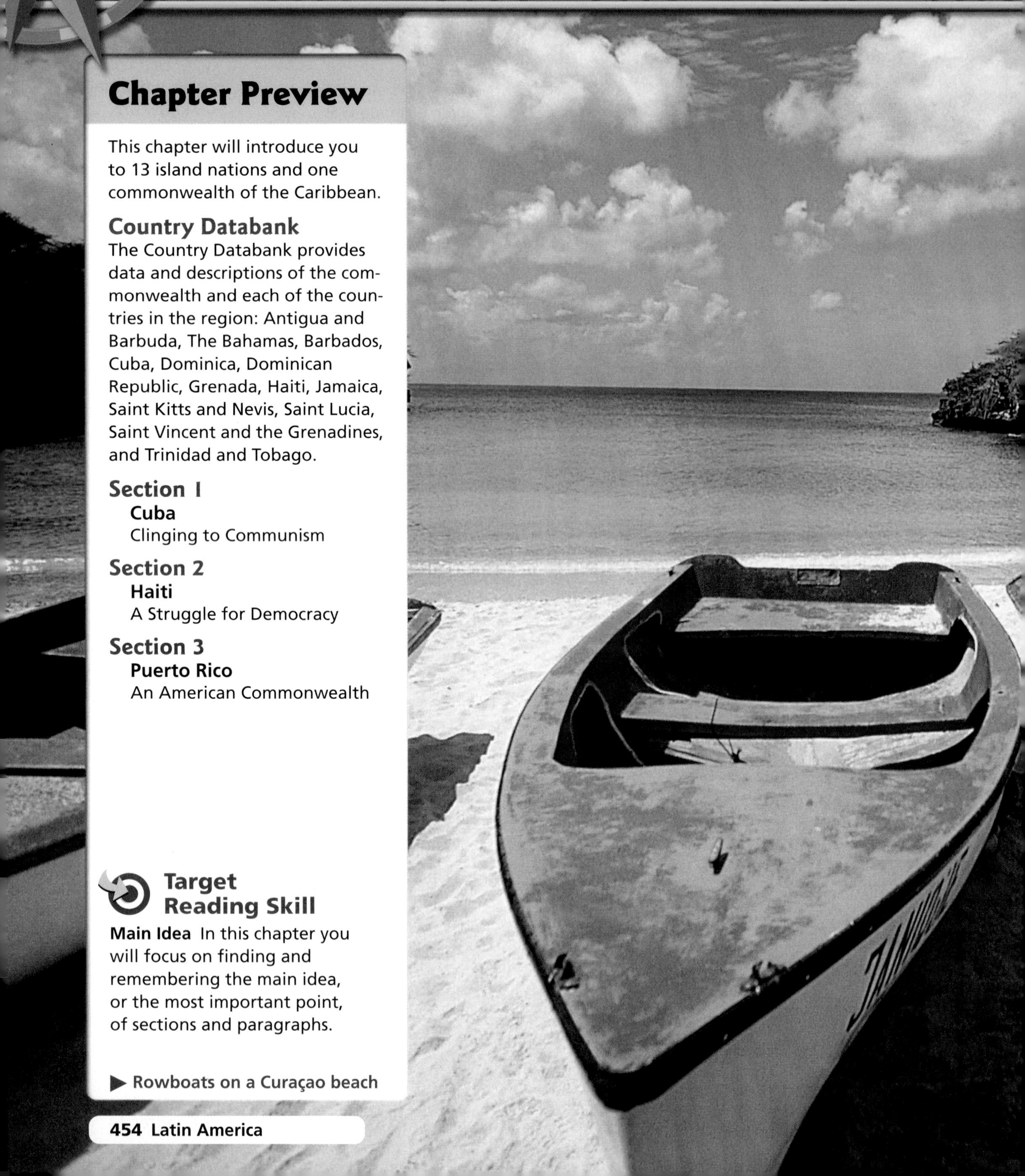

Chapter Preview

This chapter will introduce you to 13 island nations and one commonwealth of the Caribbean.

Country Databank

The Country Databank provides data and descriptions of the commonwealth and each of the countries in the region: Antigua and Barbuda, The Bahamas, Barbados, Cuba, Dominica, Dominican Republic, Grenada, Haiti, Jamaica, Saint Kitts and Nevis, Saint Lucia, Saint Vincent and the Grenadines, and Trinidad and Tobago.

Section 1

Cuba
Clinging to Communism

Section 2

Haiti
A Struggle for Democracy

Section 3

Puerto Rico
An American Commonwealth

Target Reading Skill

Main Idea In this chapter you will focus on finding and remembering the main idea, or the most important point, of sections and paragraphs.

▶ Rowboats on a Curaçao beach

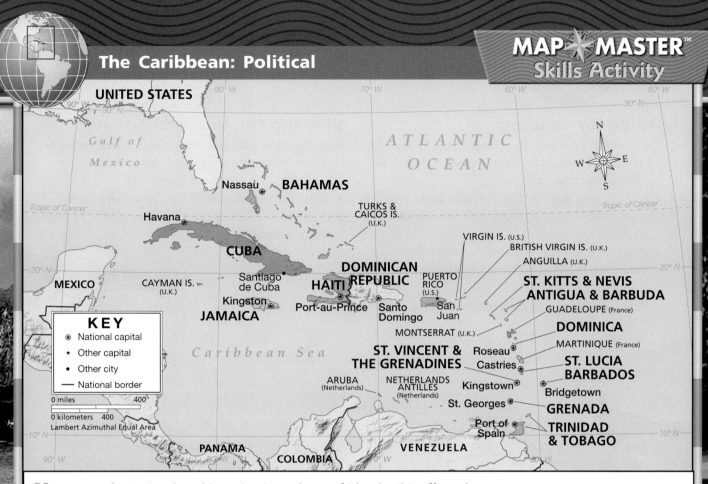

UNITED STATES

Gulf of Mexico

ATLANTIC OCEAN

Nassau

BAHAMAS

Tropic of Cancer

Havana

CUBA

TURKS & CAICOS IS. (U.K.)

VIRGIN IS. (U.S.)
BRITISH VIRGIN IS. (U.K.)
ANGUILLA (U.K.)

MEXICO

CAYMAN IS. (U.K.)

Santiago de Cuba

DOMINICAN REPUBLIC

HAITI

PUERTO RICO (U.S.)

San Juan

ST. KITTS & NEVIS
ANTIGUA & BARBUDA

GUADELOUPE (France)

Kingston

Port-au-Prince

Santo Domingo

MONTSERRAT (U.K.)

DOMINICA

MARTINIQUE (France)

JAMAICA

KEY
⊛ National capital
★ Other capital
• Other city
— National border

0 miles 400
0 kilometers 400
Lambert Azimuthal Equal Area

Caribbean Sea

ST. VINCENT & THE GRENADINES

Roseau

Castries

ST. LUCIA
BARBADOS

ARUBA (Netherlands)

NETHERLANDS ANTILLES (Netherlands)

Kingstown

Bridgetown

St. Georges

GRENADA

Port of Spain

TRINIDAD & TOBAGO

PANAMA

COLOMBIA

VENEZUELA

Movement Notice that this region is made up of islands. This affected how people and ideas moved from one place to another. **Infer** Before the invention of radio and airplanes, how do you think people in Jamaica communicated with people in Puerto Rico? **Conclude** How might the sea have affected the economies of the Caribbean islands?

Go Online
PHSchool.com Use Web Code
lfp-1521 for an **interactive map.**

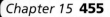

Introducing
The Caribbean

Guide for Reading

This section provides an introduction to the 13 countries and one commonwealth that make up the Caribbean region.

- Look at the map on the previous page and then read the paragraphs to learn about each nation.
- Analyze the data to compare countries.
- What are the characteristics that most of these countries share?
- What are some key differences among the countries?

Viewing the Video Overview

View the World Studies Video Program Overview to learn more about each of the countries. As you watch, answer these questions:

- How did the islands of the Caribbean form?
- What factors influence the cultural diversity of these islands?

Explore the lands and cultures of the Caribbean.

Antigua and Barbuda

Capital	Saint John's
Land Area	171 sq mi; 442 sq km
Population	67,448
Ethnic Group(s)	black, white, Southwest Asian
Religion(s)	Protestant, Roman Catholic, traditional beliefs
Government	constitutional monarchy
Currency	East Caribbean dollar
Leading Exports	petroleum products, manufactured goods, machinery and transport equipment, food and live animals
Language(s)	English (official), English Creole

The tiny nation of Antigua and Barbuda (an TIG wuh and bahr BOO dah) is made up of three islands located in the eastern Caribbean Sea. Christopher Columbus landed on the main island, Antigua, in 1493. English settlers began arriving there in the 1630s. They raised tobacco and then sugar cane. Enslaved Africans were imported to work on the plantations. However, slavery was abolished in the British colony in 1834. In 1981, Antigua joined with neighboring Barbuda and with Redonda, a nearby uninhabited island, to become an independent nation. Today, tourism is the nation's main source of income.

English Harbor, Antigua

The Bahamas

Capital	Nassau
Land Area	3,888 sq mi; 10,070 sq km
Population	308,529
Ethnic Group(s)	black, white, Asian, Hispanic
Religion(s)	Anglican, Baptist, Roman Catholic, Methodist, Church of God
Government	constitutional parliamentary democracy
Currency	Bahamian dollar
Leading Exports	fish and crawfish, rum, salt, chemicals, fruits and vegetables
Language(s)	English (official), English Creole, French Creole

More than 700 islands make up the nation called The Bahamas (buh HAH muz), but fewer than 30 of them are inhabited. The island chain stretches southward off the east coast of Florida to within 50 miles (80.5 kilometers) of Cuba. It is thought that Christopher Columbus first landed in the Americas on the Bahamian island of San Salvador. The Bahamas are generally flat, with a mild climate and beautiful beaches, so it is not surprising that tourism is a major industry. Banking has also become important. Once a British colony, The Bahamas now has a government based on the British parliamentary model.

Barbados

Capital	Bridgetown
Land Area	166 sq mi; 431 sq km
Population	276,607
Ethnic Group(s)	black, white, mixed white and black
Religion(s)	Protestant, Roman Catholic
Government	parliamentary democracy
Currency	Barbados dollar
Leading Exports	sugar and molasses, rum, other foods and beverages, chemicals, electrical components, clothing
Language(s)	English (official), Bajan

Barbados (bahr BAY dohs) is a triangular-shaped island in the eastern Caribbean Sea. It was settled by the British in the 1600s and gained its independence in 1966. Today, both the culture and the government of Barbados reflect its British colonial heritage. In the past, much of Barbados was used for sugar plantations. Today, the government promotes smaller farms that grow food for the local population. The government spends approximately 20 percent of its budget on education, and 98 percent of the people can read and write.

Cuba

Capital	Havana
Land Area	42,803 sq mi; 110,860 sq km
Population	11.2 million
Ethnic Group(s)	mixed white and black, white, black, East Asian
Religion(s)	Roman Catholic, Protestant
Government	communist state
Currency	Cuban peso
Leading Exports	sugar, nickel, tobacco, fish, medical products, citrus, coffee
Language(s)	Spanish

Cuba (KYOO buh) is the largest country in the Caribbean region. Its main island lies south of Florida in the Caribbean Sea near the Gulf of Mexico. The island has many beaches, bays, and harbors. In 1903, the United States leased Guantánamo Bay from Cuba for use as a naval base, and it is still under American control today. The rest of the island is a communist state headed by Fidel Castro, who has governed Cuba since the revolution of 1959. Cuban culture reflects its Spanish colonial past and African influences.

Introducing **The Caribbean**

Dominica

Capital	Roseau
Land Area	291 sq mi; 754 sq km
Population	73,000
Ethnic Group(s)	black, mixed white and black, white, Southwest Asian, Carib
Religion(s)	Roman Catholic, Protestant
Government	parliamentary democracy
Currency	East Caribbean dollar
Leading Exports	bananas, soap, bay oil, vegetables, grapefruit, oranges
Language(s)	English (official), French Creole

Dominica (dahm uh NEE kuh) lies between Guadeloupe and Martinique in the Caribbean Sea. The island was formed by volcanic activity. Hot springs, such as those that feed Boiling Lake, are still active. In spite of its rich soil and pleasant climate, Dominica is very poor. Hurricanes often destroy crops. Tourism is hampered by poor transportation and lack of hotels. Dominica is one of the few Caribbean islands on which Carib Indians still live and continue to practice the cultural traditions of their ancestors.

Dominican Republic

Capital	Santo Domingo
Land Area	18,679 sq mi; 48,380 sq km
Population	8.7 million
Ethnic Group(s)	mixed white and black, white, black
Religion(s)	Roman Catholic
Government	representative democracy
Currency	Dominican Republic peso
Leading Exports	ferronickel, sugar, gold, silver, coffee, cocoa, tobacco, meats, consumer goods
Language(s)	Spanish (official), French Creole

The Dominican Republic (doh MIN ih kun rih PUB lik) occupies the eastern two thirds of Hispaniola. The island was first colonized by Spain. In 1697, France acquired the western third of Hispaniola. That part of the island became the independent country of Haiti in 1804. The remaining portion—which later became the Dominican Republic—was controlled by France, Spain, and Haiti at various times. It also suffered many revolutions and dictatorships. Today, its government is stable. Agriculture and tourism are important to the economy of the Dominican Republic.

Grenada

Capital	Saint George's
Land Area	133 sq mi; 344 sq km
Population	89,211
Ethnic Group(s)	black, mixed white and black, white, South Asian, Carib
Religion(s)	Roman Catholic, Protestant
Government	constitutional monarchy
Currency	East Caribbean dollar
Leading Exports	bananas, cocoa, nutmeg, fruits and vegetables, clothing, mace
Language(s)	English (official), English Creole

Nutmeg, Grenada

Grenada (gruh NAY duh) is an oval-shaped island in the eastern Caribbean Sea. It has forested mountains as well as highlands with many rivers and streams. Bays, natural harbors, and beaches dot the southern coast. Grenada is sometimes called the Isle of Spice because of its production of nutmeg, cinnamon, cloves, ginger, and vanilla. Agricultural exports and tourism support the economy. Once governed by France and later by Great Britain, Grenada is now an independent nation.

Haiti

Capital	Port-au-Prince
Land Area	10,641 sq mi; 27,560 sq km
Population	7.1 million
Ethnic Group(s)	black, mixed white and black, white
Religion(s)	Roman Catholic, Protestant, traditional beliefs
Government	elected government
Currency	gourde
Leading Exports	manufactured goods, coffee, oils, cocoa
Language(s)	French (official), French Creole (official)

Occupying the western third of the island of Hispaniola, Haiti (HAY tee) was once heavily forested. Today, there are few woodlands left, and much of the land is no longer able to support farming due to soil erosion. Even so, most of Haiti's people are farmers, although they have little modern machinery or fertilizers. Haiti is one of the most densely populated nations in the world and the poorest in the Western Hemisphere. Numerous revolutions and dictatorships have plagued Haiti since its hopeful beginning as the first independent nation in Latin America.

Jamaica

Capital	Kingston
Land Area	4,182 sq mi; 10,831 sq km
Population	2.7 million
Ethnic Group(s)	black, mixed white and black, South Asian, white, East Asian
Religion(s)	Protestant, Roman Catholic, traditional beliefs
Government	constitutional parliamentary democracy
Currency	Jamaican dollar
Leading Exports	alumina, bauxite, sugar, bananas, rum
Language(s)	English (official), English Creole

Jamaica (juh MAY kuh) is a mountainous island located 90 miles (145 kilometers) south of Cuba in the Caribbean Sea. Tourism is vital to the economy of this beautiful island. Most of the population lives on the coastal plains, and more than half of Jamaicans live in cities. The island was first colonized by the Spanish and then by the British. Enslaved Africans were brought to Jamaica to work on the sugar and coffee plantations. Today, Jamaica's population is diverse, including Asian and Arab immigrants as well as people of European and African descent.

Puerto Rico

Capital	San Juan
Land Area	3,459 sq mi; 8,959 sq km
Population	4.0 million
Ethnic Group(s)	white, black, indigenous Indian, Asian, mixed white and black
Religion(s)	Roman Catholic, Protestant
Government	commonwealth
Currency	U.S. dollar
Leading Exports	pharmaceuticals, electronics, apparel, canned tuna, beverage concentrates, medical equipment
Language(s)	Spanish and English (official)

The self-governing commonwealth of Puerto Rico (PWEHR tuh REE koh) lies approximately 50 miles (80 kilometers) east of the Dominican Republic in the Caribbean Sea. The northern shore of the main island faces the Atlantic Ocean. Several smaller islands are also part of the commonwealth. The island's economy originally depended on sugar. In the mid-1900s, however, industry and trade became more important. Today, Puerto Rico has a more diverse economy than any of the other Caribbean islands.

Introducing The Caribbean

St. Kitts and Nevis

Capital	Basseterre
Land Area	101 sq mi; 261 sq km
Population	38,736
Ethnic Group(s)	black, white, Southwest Asian
Religion(s)	Roman Catholic, Protestant
Government	constitutional monarchy
Currency	East Caribbean dollar
Leading Exports	machinery, food, electronics, beverages, tobacco
Language(s)	English (official), English Creole

Two small islands located in the eastern Caribbean Sea make up the Federation of St. Kitts and Nevis (saynt kits and NEE vis). They gained their independence from Great Britain in 1983, and are now part of the British Commonwealth. The islands are of volcanic origin, and a dormant volcano is the highest point on St. Kitts. The beaches of that island have black, volcanic sands. Nevis is known for its hot and cold springs, and is surrounded by coral reefs. St. Kitts and Nevis have become popular tourist destinations.

St. Lucia

Capital	Castries
Land Area	234 sq mi; 606 sq km
Population	160,145
Ethnic Group(s)	black, mixed white and black, South Asian, white
Religion(s)	Roman Catholic, Protestant
Government	parliamentary democracy
Currency	East Caribbean dollar
Leading Exports	bananas, clothing, cocoa, vegetables, fruits, coconut oil
Language(s)	English (official), French Creole

The island nation of St. Lucia (saynt LOO shuh) is located in the eastern Caribbean Sea. Its geography is marked by wooded mountains and fertile valleys as well as by two huge pyramids of rock, called the Twin Pitons, which rise more than 2,400 feet (731.5 kilometers) from the sea. In the crater of a dormant volcano are boiling sulphur springs, which attract many tourists. St. Lucia's rain forests are also a major tourist attraction. Sugar cane was the most important crop on the island until 1964, when most of the land was converted to raising bananas.

St. Vincent and the Grenadines

Capital	Kingstown
Land Area	150 sq mi; 389 sq km
Population	116,394
Ethnic Group(s)	black, mixed white and black, South Asian, Carib
Religion(s)	Protestant, Roman Catholic, Hindu
Government	parliamentary democracy
Currency	East Caribbean dollar
Leading Exports	bananas, eddoes and dasheen, arrowroot starch, tennis racquets
Language(s)	English (official), English Creole

The nation of St. Vincent and the Grenadines (saynt VIN sunt and thuh GREN uh deenz) is made up of the island of St. Vincent and a string of islands called the Grenadines. They are located in the eastern Caribbean Sea, between St. Lucia and Grenada. St. Vincent has forested volcanic mountains. Its tallest volcano, Soufrière, last erupted in 1979, causing extensive damage. However, the volcanic ash has also made the soil fertile. The Grenadines are made up of coral reefs and have fine beaches. Therefore, it is not surprising that agriculture and tourism play important roles in the nation's economy.

Trinidad and Tobago

Capital	Port-of-Spain
Land Area	1,980 sq mi; 5,128 sq km
Population	1.2 million
Ethnic Group(s)	black, South Asian, mixed white and black, white, East Asian
Religion(s)	Roman Catholic, Hindu, Muslim, Protestant
Government	parliamentary democracy
Currency	Trinidad and Tobago dollar
Leading Exports	petroleum and petroleum products, chemicals, steel products, fertilizer, sugar, cocoa, coffee, citrus, flowers
Language(s)	English (official), English Creole, Hindi, French, Spanish

SOURCES: DK World Desk Reference Online; *CIA World Factbook*, 2002; *World Almanac*, 2003

Trinidad and Tobago (TRIN ih dad and toh BAY goh) are located close to the South American coast, northeast of Venezuela. Trinidad, the larger island, has mountains with spectacular waterfalls as well as swampy areas. Tobago is surrounded by coral reefs. The reefs have rich marine life, and are popular tourist attractions. The bird sanctuary at Caroni Swamp also attracts tourists. Trinidad has a very diverse population, with Spanish, French, African, English, East Indian, and Chinese influences, and many languages are spoken there. Trinidad is known for its calypso and steel-drum music.

Green honeycreeper, Trinidad and Tobago

Assessment

Comprehension and Critical Thinking

1. Compare and Contrast Compare the physical size and population of Cuba to those of the Dominican Republic.

2. Draw Conclusions What are the characteristics that most Caribbean countries share?

3. Compare and Contrast What are some key differences among the countries?

4. Categorize Which countries rely on agricultural products as their major exports? Which rely on other products?

5. Infer How has geography influenced the economies of the Caribbean countries?

6. Make a Bar Graph Use your answer to Question 1 to make a bar graph. What does the graph reveal about the population densities of Cuba and the Dominican Republic?

Keeping Current

Access the **DK World Desk Reference Online** at **PHSchool.com** for up-to-date information about all the countries in this chapter.

Go Online
PHSchool.com

Web Code: lfe-1510

Prepare to Read

Objectives

In this section you will
1. Find out how Cuba's history led to thousands of Cubans leaving their homeland.
2. Discover how Cuban exiles feel about their lives in the United States and about their homeland.
3. Learn about recent changes in Cuba.

Taking Notes

As you read this section, look for details about life in communist Cuba. Copy the web diagram below, and record your findings in it.

Life in Communist Cuba

Target Reading Skill

Identify Main Ideas It is impossible to remember every detail that you read. Good readers identify the main idea in every section or paragraph. The main idea is the most important point—the one that includes all the other points. For example, the first sentence under the red heading Cuban Exiles, on page 465, states the main idea of that portion of text.

Key Terms

- **Fidel Castro** (fih DEL KAS troh) *n.* the leader of Cuba's government
- **communism** (KAHM yoo niz um) *n.* an economic system in which the government owns all large businesses and most of the country's land
- **illiterate** (ih LIT ur ut) *adj.* unable to read and write
- **ally** (AL eye) *n.* a country joined to another country for a special purpose
- **exile** (EK syl) *n.* a person who leaves his or her homeland for another country, often for political reasons

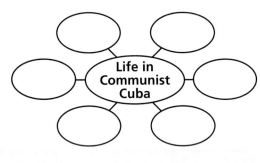

Cubans in a makeshift raft set out for the United States.

In the summer of 1994, more than 20,000 Cubans took to the sea. They sailed on anything that would float—rubber tires, old boats, and homemade rafts. One hope kept them going. It was the thought of making it to the United States. They wanted desperately to live in the United States as immigrants.

These Cubans left their homeland for two main reasons. One reason was Cuba's struggling economy. People often did not have enough to eat. Clothing, medicine, and other basic necessities were also hard to get. A desire for freedom was even more important to many Cubans. Cuba's leader, **Fidel Castro** (fih DEL KAS troh), was a dictator. He did not allow Cubans to speak out against government policies they disagreed with.

Political and economic changes in Cuba caused many of its citizens to leave their country. How and why did these changes occur? How has Cuba changed since then?

Cuba's History

Cuba's government and economy had once been very different than they were in 1994. Although it is a small country, Cuba has many advantages. It has fertile farmland. It is located at the entrance to the Gulf of Mexico, and has excellent harbors. The map titled The Caribbean: Political, at the beginning of this chapter, shows why Cuba's location makes it a good place for trade with the United States and other parts of the Caribbean.

Cuban Independence When the United States won the Spanish-American War in 1898, Cuba gained its independence from Spain. In the years that followed, Cuba became the richest country in the Caribbean. Sugar planters made money selling to people in the United States. Hotels were built, and tourists came to Cuba to enjoy its beautiful beaches and wonderful climate. Many Cubans became businesspeople, teachers, doctors, and lawyers.

Not all Cubans shared in the country's wealth, however. Most farm and factory workers earned low wages. Cuba also had many harsh leaders who ruled as dictators. In the 1950s, Fulgencio Batista (fool HEN see oh bah TEE stah) ruled Cuba. Rebel groups began forming. They wanted to remove the corrupt Batista regime and change the country.

Communism in Cuba A young lawyer named Fidel Castro led one of these small rebel groups. After two attempts to overthrow the government, he was finally successful in 1959.

Fidel Castro still holds power in Cuba today. Castro's government is communist. Under **communism,** the government owns all large businesses and most of the country's land. After Castro took power, the Cuban government nationalized, or took over, private businesses and land. Further, Castro said that newspapers and books could print only information supporting his government. Anyone who disagreed with government policy was put in jail. Huge numbers of Cubans fled the island. Many settled in Miami, Florida, in a neighborhood that came to be called Little Havana, named after the capital of Cuba.

An Important Vote
Fulgencio Batista, "strong man" of Cuba, casts his vote in the 1940 presidential election. **Infer** *Why do you think dictators hold "elections"?*

Learn about baseball in Cuba.

The Cold War Heats Up
The photograph above shows Fidel Castro (left) and Nikita Khrushchev (right), the Soviet premier. At the right, an American patrol plane flies over a Soviet freighter during the Cuban Missile Crisis. **Infer** *What kind of relationship did Cuba and the Soviet Union have in the 1960s?*

Identify Main Ideas
What sentence states the main idea of the text headed Cold War Crisis?

At the same time, Castro's government brought some improvements to Cuba. In the 1960s and 1970s, many Cubans were **illiterate,** or unable to read and write. Castro sent teachers into the countryside, and literacy improved dramatically. Today, about 97 percent of Cubans can read and write. The government also provides basic health care for all.

As a communist country, Cuba became an ally of the Soviet Union. An **ally** is a country joined with another country for a special purpose. The Soviet Union was the most powerful communist nation in the world. It wanted to spread communism worldwide. The Soviets sent money and supplies to Cuba. Relations between Cuba and the United States grew worse when the United States openly welcomed the people who fled from Cuba.

Cold War Crisis The United States viewed communist Cuba as a threat to American interests in the region. This was a period of tension between the United States and the Soviet Union and their allies. It was called the Cold War as the conflict did not involve "hot," or military, action. It lasted from 1945 to 1991.

In the 1960s, the Soviets began sending military support to Cuba. Then, in 1962, photographs taken by American aircraft revealed the construction of Soviet atomic-missile sites in Cuba. Those missiles, if fired, would be able to reach the United States.

U.S. President John F. Kennedy demanded the missiles be removed, and sent the American navy to prevent Soviet ships from going to Cuba. He said that an attack from Cuba would be viewed as an attack by the Soviet Union. After a week of tension called the Cuban Missile Crisis, Soviet Premier Nikita Khrushchev agreed to remove the missiles if the United States promised not to invade Cuba. A "hot" war was prevented, but the Cold War continued.

✓ **Reading Check** **What was the Cuban Missile Crisis?**

Cuban Exiles

Cubans have been leaving their country ever since Castro took power. They have become exiles. An **exile** is a person who leaves his or her homeland for another country, usually for political reasons. A large number of Cuban exiles have come to the United States to live.

COUNTRY PROFILE

Focus on Government

Cuba

Fidel Castro came to power in 1959 and set up a one-party communist system in Cuba. He has led the Communist Party and the country ever since. Due to economic distress after Soviet support to Cuba ended in 1991, Castro had to modify communist economic principles to allow for some private ownership of businesses and land. The data below can help you understand how the economic and political situations in Cuba have changed over time and how they have remained the same.

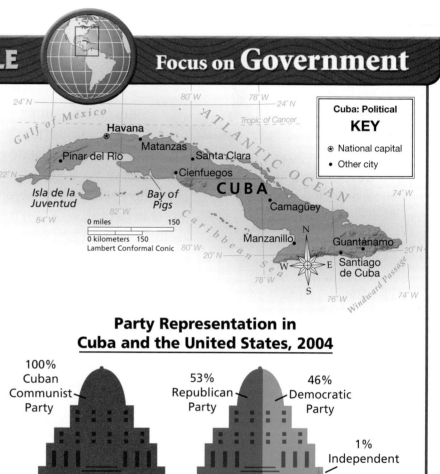

Party Representation in Cuba and the United States, 2004

100% Cuban Communist Party

53% Republican Party

46% Democratic Party

1% Independent

SOURCE: *DK World Desk Reference*

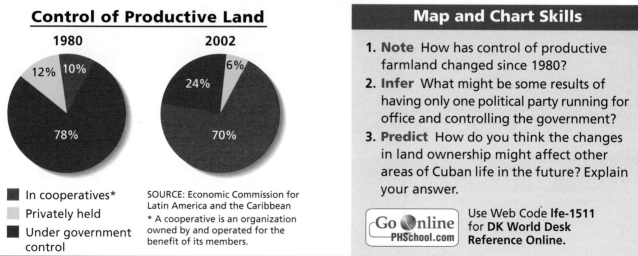

Control of Productive Land

1980

12%   10%

78%

2002

6%

24%

70%

- ■ In cooperatives*
- ■ Privately held
- ■ Under government control

SOURCE: Economic Commission for Latin America and the Caribbean

* A cooperative is an organization owned by and operated for the benefit of its members.

Map and Chart Skills

1. **Note** How has control of productive farmland changed since 1980?
2. **Infer** What might be some results of having only one political party running for office and controlling the government?
3. **Predict** How do you think the changes in land ownership might affect other areas of Cuban life in the future? Explain your answer.

Go Online
PHSchool.com

Use Web Code lfe-1511 for **DK World Desk Reference Online.**

The Baseball Connection

You've probably heard that baseball is "America's pastime," but did you know that it is also the national pastime of Cuba? Baseball has been played on the island since the 1860s, and major league teams used Cuba for spring training until Castro took power. Cubans also played in the major leagues. Today, however, the Cuban government regards baseball stars who leave the country as traitors. Nevertheless, many Cuban players have defected, or come to the United States. Orlando Hernandez, called El Duque (el DOO kay), or "The Duke," fled Cuba by boat in 1997. He became a starring pitcher for the New York Yankees as shown above.

A New Life Lydia Martin left Cuba in 1970 when she was only six years old. Her mother had grown tired of the limits on freedom and lack of opportunity in communist Cuba. She wanted to take Lydia to the United States. Lydia's father begged them to stay. He asked them, "Have you stopped to think you may never see me again?"

Like Lydia, many Cuban exiles left family members behind. They dream of returning to Cuba—once it is no longer a communist country. Meanwhile, many Cubans have made successful new lives in the United States. A large number have settled in Miami, Florida. In the Cuban neighborhood of Little Havana, they keep their language and their culture alive. At the same time, they have become important in the economic, cultural, and political life of Miami and the state of Florida. They own successful businesses, serve as elected officials, and influence government policy.

When relations between the United States and Cuba grew worse in the 1970s, Cuban exiles suffered. They could not even write to the families they had left behind. Castro's government might punish people who got a letter from the United States. What's more, the United States did not allow Americans to visit Cuba.

Cuban exiles playing dominoes in Little Havana, Miami, Florida

Another Wave of Exiles In 1991, the government of the Soviet Union collapsed and could no longer help Cuba. Food, medicine, tools, and other necessities became even more scarce in Cuba. Many families had little more than rice to eat.

As the situation in Cuba worsened, more people wanted to leave the island. Vanesa Alonso (vah NES uh ah LOHN soh) was one of them. In 1994, Vanesa and her family left Cuba on a rickety raft. Today, Vanesa lives in Miami, just a few miles from the ocean, but she hardly ever goes to the beach. The blue waves and roaring surf remind her of her terrifying trip from Cuba to the United States. That memory still gives her bad dreams.

✓ **Reading Check** What caused another wave of exiles?

Changes Come to Cuba

In the 1990s, when Cuba's economy was near collapse, Castro began allowing private ownership of some businesses. In addition, the Cuban government began encouraging tourism. The United States also loosened some restrictions on travel to Cuba. American businesspeople and farmers have begun to visit Cuba, hoping to sell their products there. The Cuban economy is improving. Castro has ruled Cuba for more than 40 years. Many Cuban exiles hope that the regime that follows Castro's will encourage better relations with the United States. They hope that they will be able to return home or to visit there in freedom.

✓ **Reading Check** What changes did Castro make in the 1990s?

New Visitors
Tourism increased in Cuba during the 1990s. **Analyze Images** *Judging from this photo of Havana, why might tourists want to visit Cuba?*

Section 1 Assessment

Key Terms
Review the key terms at the beginning of this section. Use each term in a sentence that explains its meaning.

Target Reading Skills
One important main idea of this section is stated on the first page. What is it?

Comprehension and Critical Thinking
1. (a) Describe How did Castro come to power in Cuba?

(b) Identify Effects How did life for Cubans change—for better and for worse—under Castro's rule?
(c) Synthesize What role did the Soviet Union play in Cuba?
2. (a) Define What is Little Havana?
(b) Find Main Ideas How have many Cubans adapted to life in the United States?
3. (a) Recall What do Cuban exiles hope will happen in Cuba in the near future?
(b) Predict What changes do you think are in store for Cuba? Explain your answer.

Writing Activity
Write a letter to a relative in Cuba from the point of view of a Cuban exile in the United States. Have another student write a response from the point of view of the Cuban relative. The relatives should exchange information about their daily lives and their hopes for the future.

> **Writing Tip** Before you begin, decide on the age, gender, and personality of the person writing the letter.

"Come to the Caribbean," say the TV ads. But which Caribbean will you choose: an island with a Spanish culture or one with Native American, African, British, or French heritage? Do you want a luxury resort or a small village?

To plan your trip, you'd have to think about what you want to see and do and about which islands have these characteristics.

Then you would use the skill of comparing and contrasting to decide which country to visit.

To compare and contrast means to look for similarities and differences. It is a skill you use often, but you can learn to use it even more effectively by following the steps below.

Learn the Skill

Follow the steps below to learn the skill of comparing and contrasting.

1 **Identify a topic and purpose.** What do you want to compare, and why? Some examples of a purpose are to make a choice, to understand a topic, and to discover patterns.

2 **Select some categories for comparison.** For example, if you wanted to choose between two cars, your categories might be model, cost, and power seats.

3 **Make notes or a chart about the categories you're comparing.** A category such as power seats calls for a *yes* or a *no*. For other categories, such as model or cost, you need to note specific details.

4 **Identify the similarities and differences.** For each category, are the things you are comparing the same or different? What are the differences? Which differences are most important for your purpose?

5 **Draw conclusions.** Use the similarities and differences you found to answer an important question about your topic or to make a choice.

Practice the Skill

Suppose you are planning a January vacation. Use the postcards above to help you decide between two possible vacation spots: one in the Caribbean and one in the northern United States. Follow the steps on the previous page to compare and contrast the two choices.

 In this example, the purpose is provided for you: to make a choice. What is the topic?

 Ask yourself, "What aspects of these two places could I compare based on the postcards?" Jot down ideas. These ideas will be your categories.

❸ Use your categories to jot down notes about each place.

❹ For each category, decide whether the two vacation spots are similar or different. In what ways are they different?

❺ Draw a conclusion. Are the two vacation spots basically similar or different? Which differences are important to your decision? Write a conclusion stating where you want to spend your vacation and why.

A Jamaican family

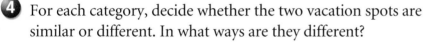

Apply the Skill

Turn to the Country Databank at the beginning of Chapter 14 or 15. Choose two countries, each from a different region. Compare and contrast the two countries and draw a conclusion about them.

Haiti
A Struggle for Democracy

Prepare to Read

Objectives

In this section you will
1. Find out how democracy has been threatened in Haiti.
2. Learn what life is like for the people of Haiti, both in the countryside and in the cities.

Taking Notes

As you read this section, look for the events in Haiti's struggle for democracy. Copy the timeline below, and record the events in the appropriate places on it.

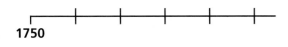

1750

Target Reading Skill

Identify Supporting Details The main idea of a paragraph or section is supported by details that give further information about it. These details may explain the main idea or give examples or reasons. The main idea of the portion of text titled The Boat People is "The Haitians who fled by sea became known as the Haitian boat people." As you read, notice how the example that follows helps explain who the boat people were and why they fled.

Key Terms

- **Jean-Bertrand Aristide** (zhan behr TRAHN ah rees TEED) *n.* former president of Haiti
- **refugee** (ref yoo JEE) *n.* someone who leaves his or her homeland to protect personal safety and escape persecution
- **Creole** (KREE ohl) *n.* a person of mixed African and European descent; in Haiti, a language that mixes French and African languages

In 2004, armed rebels (left) forced Haitian president Jean-Bertrand Aristide to leave office.

Over the years, Haiti's military and its wealthy elite have used violence to block the country's attempts at democracy and economic improvement. One percent of Haiti's population controls nearly 50 percent of the country's wealth. This small, wealthy group is prepared to use violence when its control is challenged.

In 2006, though, with the support of the country's poor majority, René Préval was elected Haiti's president. Préval was already an important Haitian leader. In the 1970s, he had helped get rid of Haiti's military dictator. In the 1990s, he also worked closely with Jean-Bertrand Aristide (zhan behr TRAHN ah rees TEED), who ruled at various times. They both wanted to fight poverty in Haiti. However, in 2004, armed groups overthrew Aristide and took control. The year 2006 marked the first presidential election since that time.

Democracy in Danger

Haiti's problems in 2004 were not unusual. The country has a long history of tensions between rich and poor, political instability, and violence. For example, Aristide was first elected president in 1990 but was forced out after only seven months in office.

The Boat People Thousands of Aristide's supporters had to flee Haiti's capital, Port-au-Prince (pawrt oh PRANS). Many of them fled by sea. They became known as the Haitian boat people. Because they left their homeland to protect their own personal safety and escape persecution, they are called **refugees.** Many Haitian boat people headed for the United States.

The Beaubrun (boh BRUN) family was among those refugees. Bazelais (bah zuh LAY) Beaubrun had spoken out against the military government in Haiti. After soldiers threatened him, he knew his life was in danger if he stayed. First Bazelais went into hiding. Then he took his family onto a crowded boat that was headed for the United States.

The U. S. Coast Guard stopped the boat and took the Haitians to an American military base. If Bazelais was really in danger for his political beliefs, he and his family could immigrate to the United States. After three months, the Beaubruns were allowed to enter the United States. Some families were not so lucky. U. S. officials sent them back to Haiti.

Refugees
The Beaubrun family escaped from Haiti and now live in Brooklyn, New York. **Infer** *Why would it be particularly difficult for a family like the Beaubruns, with young children, to make the journey described here?*

The Birth of Haiti The overthrow of the elected government in 2004 does not mean that most Haitians did not want democracy. Their country was born out of a desperate struggle for freedom. Haiti is the only nation in the Americas formed from a successful revolt of enslaved Africans.

As you can see on the map of Haiti on the next page, Haiti lies on the western third of the island of Hispaniola. It was once a colony of France. Europeans brought enslaved Africans to Haiti to work on sugar cane and coffee plantations. In the 1790s, slave revolts began. The Haitian leader Toussaint L'Ouverture helped banish slavery from Haiti in 1801. He also offered Haitians a new way of life, based on the idea that all people could live as equals.

Discovery CHANNEL
SCHOOL Video
Learn about everyday life in Haiti.

Haiti

Haiti has a stormy history of colonization, revolution, and dictatorships. The nation's European and African roots can still be seen in its vibrant Creole language and heritage. Yet Haiti's history has shaped the country in other ways as well. Today, Haiti is the poorest country in Latin America. Years of political and economic unrest have caused many Haitians to leave the country. Study the map, time-line, and charts. Think about how Haiti's history affects the life of an ordinary Haitian.

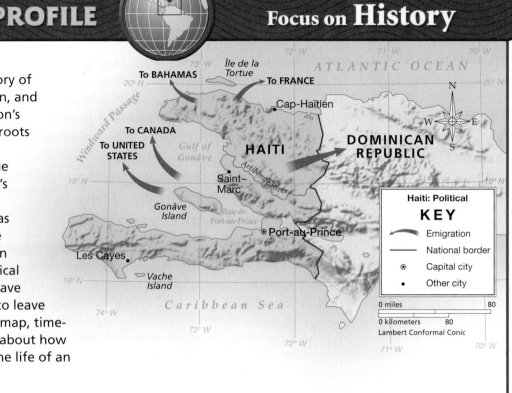

Foreign Influence in Haiti Since Independence

1915 United States occupies Haiti.

1990 Aristide is elected president.

2004 Aristide leaves the country.

1800 — **1900** — **2000**

1804 Haiti expels the French and gains independence.

1957 A series of brutal dictatorships begins.

1994 International pressure allows Aristide to return.

About One in Seven Haitians Has Emigrated

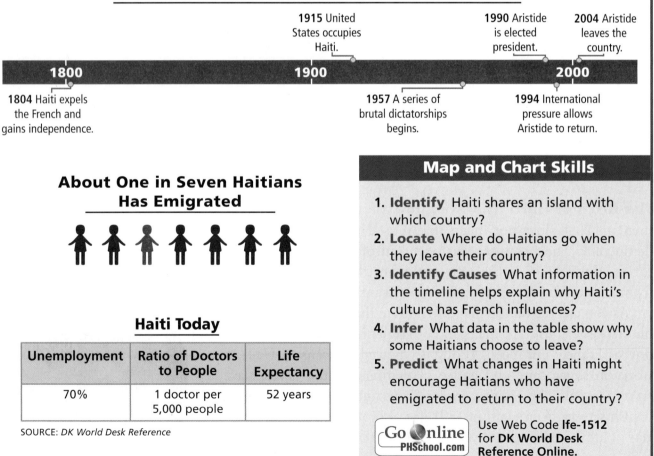

Haiti Today

Unemployment	Ratio of Doctors to People	Life Expectancy
70%	1 doctor per 5,000 people	52 years

SOURCE: *DK World Desk Reference*

Map and Chart Skills

1. **Identify** Haiti shares an island with which country?
2. **Locate** Where do Haitians go when they leave their country?
3. **Identify Causes** What information in the timeline helps explain why Haiti's culture has French influences?
4. **Infer** What data in the table show why some Haitians choose to leave?
5. **Predict** What changes in Haiti might encourage Haitians who have emigrated to return to their country?

Go Online PHSchool.com
Use Web Code lfe-1512 for **DK World Desk Reference Online.**

Years of Dictatorship In the years that followed, Toussaint L'Ouverture's goal of freedom and equality was never fully realized. Most of Haiti's presidents became dictators once they got into power. One of the worst was François Duvalier (frahn SWAH doo vahl YAY), who took power in 1957. Because Duvalier had been a country doctor, Haitians called him "Papa Doc." Papa Doc was followed by his son, Jean-Claude Duvalier (zhan KLAWD doo vahl YAY), or "Baby Doc." Both were cruel leaders who stole government funds and used violence to keep power.

In 1986, rebels forced Baby Doc to leave the country. Many Haitians thought a period of freedom and prosperity was about to begin. Instead, Haiti was ruled by one military dictator after another.

A Brief Period of Hope Aristide's election in 1990 briefly brought hope to Haitians. However, these hopes were dashed when yet another military uprising forced Aristide to flee the country. The United States and other nations pressured the military to give power back to Aristide. In 1994, Aristide returned to Haiti, restoring democratic government. Haitians rejoiced, believing that peace and progress would follow.

In national elections held in 2000, it seemed that Aristide's supporters had won control of the legislature, and Aristide again assumed the presidency. But the election results were challenged. Armed rebels began to attack government offices. In early 2004, after rebel groups gained control of much of Haiti, Aristide left the country. Democracy in Haiti was threatened again. It took two years to organize new elections. Finally in 2006, René Préval was elected president.

✓ **Reading Check** What were the results of the 2000 elections?

Citizen Heroes

Loune Viaud: Winner of Human Rights Award

Loune Viaud (loon vee OH) has been fighting injustice for a long time. During "Baby Doc's" regime, she courageously spoke out for human rights. Today she fights for all Haitians to have the right to healthcare—no matter how poor or sick they are. Viaud runs a clinic and works to ensure safe drinking water. When she received the 2002 Robert F. Kennedy Human Rights Award, Viaud called herself "a humble foot soldier in the struggle for health and human rights."

The dictator Jean-Claude "Baby Doc" Duvalier ruled Haiti from 1971 to 1986.

Identify Supporting Details

What details in the paragraph at the right are examples that support this idea: Haitian culture blends African, French, and West Indian traditions?

The People of Haiti

The Haitian people have suffered a great deal. Nevertheless, Haitian refugees remember many good things about their homeland: the warm weather, children playing soccer with their friends, dressing up for church, and many festivals. Haitian culture blends African, French, and West Indian traditions. Nearly all of Haiti's people are descended from the enslaved Africans who were brought to Haiti during colonial times. Haitians of mixed African and European ancestry are referred to as **Creole.** They are a minority in Haiti, but they have much of the wealth and power. Creole also refers to the language spoken in Haiti, which is based on both French and African languages.

Rural Life   Today, Haiti is the poorest country in the Western Hemisphere. About two thirds of the people struggle to make a living farming small plots of land. But the land has been overused. Most trees have been cut. Rains wash the topsoil into the sea. When farmer Pierre Joseph stands on his small farm, he can see the calm waters of the Caribbean. When he looks down, he sees the dry, cracked earth of his one-acre field. Joseph is thin because he rarely gets enough to eat. "The land just doesn't yield enough," he says. He points to the few rows of corn and beans that he can grow on his one acre.

Fishing and Farming
A rural fisherman casts his net (above). The homes in the photo at the right have adobe walls and thatched roofs.
Synthesize *What can you learn about rural life in Haiti from these photos?*

City Life Because of rural poverty, many people have left the countryside for the cities. They come to Port-au-Prince looking for work. Most poor people from the country cannot afford decent housing. They live in the poorest neighborhoods. These areas are dirty and crowded. The streets are not paved, so the rain turns them to mud. Many of the tiny homes are made of crumbling concrete. At the same time, the wealthy live in large wooden houses on the hills overlooking the city. There is also a small middle class of doctors, lawyers, teachers, and owners of small businesses. These people live fairly well. But the overwhelming majority of Haitians—in the city as well as in the countryside—are poor.

What Lies Ahead Recent election disputes and political violence have put Haitian democracy at risk once again. And these conditions have hurt the economy as well. Most people in Haiti are still poor. Many live in cities where violence is common. And many still try to leave their homeland, in search of a better life.

✓ **Reading Check** Describe the poor neighborhoods of Port-au-Prince.

Colorful Culture
Haitians often decorate buses and trucks in bright colors. **Analyze Images** *What can you learn about city life in Haiti from this photo of Port-au-Prince?*

Section 2 Assessment

Key Terms
Review the key terms at the beginning of this section. Use each term in a sentence that explains its meaning.

Target Reading Skills
State the details that support the main idea on page 473: *Toussaint L'Ouverture's goal of freedom and equality was never fully realized.*

Comprehension and Critical Thinking
1. (a) Define Who are the Haitian boat people?

(b) Sequence List the major events of Haiti's history in the order they occurred.
(c) Identify Cause and Effect How did the events of Haiti's history lead to the migration of the boat people?
2. (a) Describe What is rural life like for many Haitians?
(b) Compare and Contrast How is life in the city similar to and different from life on a farm?
(c) Find Main Ideas What are the major problems facing Haiti today?

Writing Activity
Suppose you were an American newspaper reporter in Haiti in 2004. Write an article about conditions in Haiti immediately after President Aristide was forced from power. Include the experiences of individual Haitians.

For: An activity on Haiti
Visit: PHSchool.com
Web Code: lfd-1502

Puerto Rico
An American Commonwealth

Prepare to Read

Objectives

In this section you will
1. Understand why the people of Puerto Rico are both American and Puerto Rican.
2. Find out what life is like on the island of Puerto Rico.
3. Learn about the three kinds of political status Puerto Ricans are considering for their future.

Taking Notes

As you read this section, look for ways that life is similar and different in Puerto Rico and on the mainland United States. Copy the Venn diagram below, and record your findings in it.

Puerto Rican Life

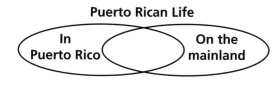

In Puerto Rico | On the mainland

🎯 Target Reading Skill

Identify Implied Main Ideas Identifying main ideas can help you remember the most important points you read. Sometimes the main idea is not stated directly. All the details in that portion of text add up to a main idea, but you must state the main idea yourself. For example, you could state the main idea of the text headed A Mix of Cultures this way: *Puerto Rico shows influences of Spanish, African, Caribbean, and United States mainland culture.*

Key Terms

- **constitution** (kahn stuh TOO shun) *n.* a statement of a country's basic laws and values
- **citizen** (SIT uh zun) *n.* a person with certain rights and responsibilities under a particular government
- **commonwealth** (KAHM un welth) *n.* a self-governing political unit that has strong ties to a particular country

A government building in Puerto Rico

Puerto Rico was once a Spanish colony. When the United States defeated Spain in the Spanish-American War, Spain ceded, or gave, Puerto Rico to the United States. The United States slowly granted Puerto Rico more control of its own government and affairs. In 1951, Puerto Ricans voted to adopt their own constitution. A **constitution** is a statement of a country's basic laws and values. This gave Puerto Rico its own lawmakers. But it was still connected to the United States.

What is the nature of Puerto Rico's connection to the United States? How does that relationship affect life in Puerto Rico? And why do some Puerto Ricans want to change the nature of their island's relationship to the United States?

Puerto Ricans in the Mainland United States, 2000

Population	
Total	3,406,178
Northeast	2,074,574
South	759,305
Midwest	325,363
West	246,936

Distribution by Region

- 7.2%
- 9.6%
- 22.3%
- 60.9%

■ Northeast
■ South
■ Midwest
■ West

SOURCE: United States Census Bureau

Puerto Rican and American

People move from Puerto Rico to the United States mainland and back again very easily because Puerto Rico is part of the United States. Puerto Ricans are American citizens. **Citizens** are individuals with certain rights and responsibilities under a particular government. But Puerto Rico is not a state of the Union. It has a different status.

The Commonwealth of Puerto Rico   Today, Puerto Rico is a commonwealth of the United States. A **commonwealth** is a self-governing political unit that has strong ties to a particular country. Although Puerto Ricans are American citizens, they cannot vote in presidential elections. They do not pay United States taxes. And they have only a nonvoting representative in the United States Congress. However, Puerto Ricans do serve in the armed forces of the United States.

Puerto Ricans on the Mainland   Many Puerto Ricans have moved to the mainland United States. Most settle in cities in the Northeast. Life is very different there. While Puerto Rico has a warm Caribbean climate, winters in Northern cities can be cold and harsh. And cities like New York are much bigger than any city in Puerto Rico. The language of the mainland is English, while people speak Spanish in Puerto Rico. There is a lot to get used to.

■ Chart Skills

This market is in an area of New York City called Spanish Harlem, where many Puerto Ricans have settled. **Identify** According to the graph, which region has the largest Puerto Rican population? The smallest? **Infer** Why do you think that people tend to settle in areas where there are already many people from their former homes?

Esmeralda Santiago

Coming to New York City Esmeralda Santiago (ez mehr AHL dah sahn tee AH goh) moved from Puerto Rico to New York City when she was 13 years old. At first, she found life on the mainland strange and confusing. One problem was that to succeed in school, she had to improve her English. She also found that Puerto Ricans living in New York were different from her friends on the island. Instead of the salsa and merengue music she loved, they preferred rock music. Most of the time they spoke neither pure Spanish nor English, but a mixture of the two that they called "Spanglish." Although they were Puerto Rican, Esmeralda felt different from them. Eventually, she learned their ways. She became more like them and thought less about her old life on the island.

✓ **Reading Check** **When Puerto Ricans move to New York City, what kinds of differences do they find?**

Life on the Island

Many people travel back and forth between the mainland and Puerto Rico. They live for a while in each place. Many Puerto Ricans moved to the mainland during the 1950s. However, since 1965, just as many Puerto Ricans have been moving back to their island as are leaving it.

Returning Home Julia de Jesus Chaparro (HOO lee ah day HAY soos chah PAH roh) moved back to a small mountain village in Puerto Rico after spending more than 14 years in Boston, Massachusetts. To explain why, she takes visitors to her back porch. From there, she can see a row of steep mountains. Peeking between them is the bright blue of the Caribbean Sea. The mountain slopes steeply down from Julia's back porch, but she has managed to clear some land. Her garden of mangoes, coconuts, grapefruit, and lemons thrives in the sun. Behind a nearby tree, a hen and six chickens are pecking in the dirt.

Puerto Rican Hillside
This hilly region is in the Central Mountains of Puerto Rico. **Draw Conclusions** *What can you learn about the geography, climate, and land use of this region from the photograph?*

Much of Puerto Rico is made up of hills and mountains—the kind of landscape you would see from Julia's back porch. In the hills, Puerto Rican cowhands, called *jíbaros* (HEE bahr ohs), raise cattle. They also hunt, fish, and raise chickens and pigs. On other parts of the island, farmers ride horses through fields of tall sugar cane. To the southwest, where the land is lower, fishing villages dot the coast.

Learn about Puerto Rico, past and present.

COUNTRY PROFILE

Focus on Government

Puerto Rico

Since becoming a United States Territory in 1898, Puerto Rico has been slowly gaining self-government. In 1917, the people of Puerto Rico were given American citizenship. In 1948, they elected their own governor, and in 1951, they adopted their own constitution. Today, Puerto Rico is a commonwealth of the United States with one nonvoting commissioner in the House of Representatives. As you study the charts below, think about how Puerto Rico's commonwealth status affects the lives of its people.

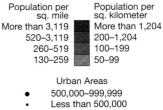

Puerto Rico: Population Density

KEY

Population per sq. mile	Population per sq. kilometer
More than 3,119	More than 1,204
520–3,119	200–1,204
260–519	100–199
130–259	50–99

Urban Areas
- 500,000–999,999
- Less than 500,000

Citizen Status in Iowa versus Puerto Rico

	If Born in Iowa	If Born in Puerto Rico
Citizen of United States	Yes	Yes
Vote for U.S. president	Yes	No
Pay income taxes	Yes	No
Serve in military	Yes	Yes
Representatives in U.S. Congress	Five	One (with no vote)
Senators in U.S. Congress	Two	None

2004 Puerto Rico Election Results

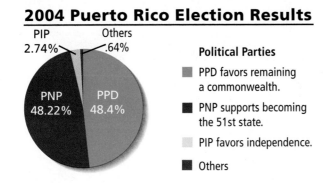

PIP 2.74%
Others .64%
PNP 48.22%
PPD 48.4%

Political Parties
- PPD favors remaining a commonwealth.
- PNP supports becoming the 51st state.
- PIP favors independence.
- Others

SOURCE: Elections Around the World Online

Map and Chart Skills

1. **Identify** What two rights and responsibilities do people born in Iowa have that someone born in Puerto Rico does not have?
2. **Analyze** What do the results of the 2004 elections tell you about how Puerto Ricans feel about their relationship with the United States?
3. **Draw Conclusions** Why do you think political opinion is divided the way it is?

Go Online
PHSchool.com
Use Web Code **Ife-1513** for DK World Desk Reference Online.

A Mix of Cultures As people travel back and forth, they bring customs and products with them. If you visited Puerto Rico, you would see many influences from the United States mainland. You would also see that in Puerto Rico, there is a strong cultural connection to the Caribbean. Most people are a mix of Spanish and African ancestry.

Puerto Rican cities show influences of Spanish, Caribbean, and United States mainland culture. About 75 percent of Puerto Ricans live in cities. Many city people work in factories. Others work in the hotels and restaurants that draw many tourists. Puerto Rico's capital, San Juan (san HWAHN), has a large waterfront area known as the Condado (kohn DAH do). It is packed with luxury hotels. Not far away, modern skyscrapers pierce the brilliant sky.

In the old section of San Juan, Spanish-style buildings are everywhere. A 450-year-old Catholic church built by the Spanish has been carefully restored. Not far from the church sit ancient houses graced with iron balconies in lacy Spanish style.

This guitar maker is playing a cuatro, Puerto Rico's national instrument.

✓ **Reading Check** **Compare old and new San Juan.**

Old and New
The San Geronimo Fortress, built in the 1500s by the Spanish, stands in sharp contrast to the modern hotels of San Juan. **Infer** *How do you think the fortress might contribute to the current economy of San Juan?*

Statehood Now!
These people are rallying for Puerto Rican statehood in a 1996 demonstration. **Transfer Information** *What arguments in favor of statehood might these demonstrators give?*

Seeking a New Direction

Puerto Rico is bound by many United States laws, and Puerto Ricans have many questions about this situation. Is it good for Puerto Rico? Should Puerto Rico become independent? Or should it become a state of the United States?

Commonwealth or Statehood?   Puerto Ricans have many disagreements over what the status of their island should be. Many feel that having "one foot" in Puerto Rico and "one foot" in the United States can lead to problems. Others point out how the relationship with the United States has helped Puerto Rico. American businesses on the island have raised the standard of living. Each year, the United States government sends millions of dollars to the island to help people in need.

Some people still feel that Puerto Rico is at a disadvantage because Puerto Ricans cannot vote in United States elections. They say Puerto Rico should try to become a state. But if it does, it will become the poorest state in the union. Puerto Ricans earn more money than people in other Caribbean countries. However, they earn less than people on the United States mainland. Also, if Puerto Rico becomes a state, Puerto Ricans will have to pay United States taxes. This could lower the earnings of many people who have little to spare. For these reasons, in 1993 and again in 1998, Puerto Ricans voted not to become the 51st state of the United States.

Identify Implied Main Ideas
In one sentence, state what all the details in the paragraph at the left are about.

Rally for Independence
This rally of the Independenista Party was held in 1980. **Predict** *Do you think these demonstrators or those on the previous page will ever get their wish for Puerto Rico? Explain your answer.*

The Question of Independence Some people who voted against statehood have even bigger dreams for Puerto Rico. They want it to become a separate nation. If it does not, they fear that Puerto Ricans will become confused about their identity. They stress Puerto Rico's connection to other Caribbean nations. They want to make sure that Puerto Ricans always identify with the Spanish language and Spanish culture. But for now, Puerto Rico will keep its links to the mainland. Many Puerto Ricans hope that their relationship with the United States will lead to a profitable and peaceful future.

✓ **Reading Check** **Why do some people favor Puerto Rican independence?**

Section 3 Assessment

Key Terms
Review the key terms at the beginning of this section. Use each term in a sentence that explains its meaning.

Target Reading Skills
State two main ideas of Section 3.

Comprehension and Critical Thinking
1. (a) Explain What is Puerto Rico's relationship to the United States?
(b) Sequence How did Puerto Rico gain more control over its own affairs?

2. (a) Describe List three different regions of Puerto Rico, and tell how people earn a living in each one.
(b) Synthesize How does Puerto Rican culture show Spanish, Caribbean, and mainland influences?
3. (a) List What are the three options Puerto Ricans consider for the future of their relationship with the United States?
(b) Analyze What are the benefits and drawbacks of each option?

Writing Activity
Write a journal entry from the point of view of either Julia or Esmeralda. Discuss your feelings about life on the mainland and in Puerto Rico. Explain where you would prefer to live and why.

Go Online
PHSchool.com

For: An activity on San Juan
Visit: PHSchool.com
Web Code: lfd-1503

Review and Assessment

◆ Chapter Summary

Section 1: Cuba

- Cuba became a communist country under Fidel Castro and then became an ally of the Soviet Union.
- During the Cold War, relations between Cuba and the United States worsened.
- Many Cubans have fled Cuba for the United States, where they have made successful new lives, but some dream of returning to a free and democratic Cuba.
- Recently Castro has allowed some private ownership of businesses and is encouraging tourism and trade.

Cuba

Section 2: Haiti

- Haiti has struggled for democracy since independence, but has enjoyed only short periods of elected government.
- The election of President Aristide brought a brief period of hope, but then a military take-over caused many Haitians to flee their country.
- The people of Haiti are poor. Farmers struggle on land that has been overused, crowded city slums do not have basic services, and political violence is a fact of life.

Section 3: Puerto Rico

- Puerto Rico is a commonwealth of the United States. Puerto Ricans are American citizens, and many of them move to the United States mainland.
- Life in Puerto Rico blends Caribbean and mainland influences.
- Puerto Ricans disagree over whether they should become a state, become independent, or remain a commonwealth.

◆ Key Terms

Match the definitions in Column I with the key terms in Column II.

Column I

1. a statement of a country's basic laws and values
2. a country joined to another country for a special purpose
3. a place that has its own government but also has strong ties to another country
4. those who leave their homeland for their own personal safety and to escape persecution
5. individuals with certain rights and responsibilities under a particular government

Column II

A citizens

B ally

C commonwealth

D constitution

E refugees

Review and Assessment (continued)

◆ Comprehension and Critical Thinking

6. (a) Name What are two advantages Cuba has because of its geography?
(b) Identify Cause and Effect How did these advantages lead to Cuba's prosperity?
(c) Synthesize Information How did Cuba change from a prosperous country to a poor one?

7. (a) Recall Why did revolutionary leaders like Fidel Castro gain support in Cuba?
(b) Describe What is life like under Castro's communist government of Cuba?
(c) Identify Effects What happened in Cuba when the communist regime of the Soviet Union collapsed? Explain why.

8. (a) Name Haiti was a colony of which European country?
(b) Synthesize Describe Toussaint L'Ouverture's ideals for Haiti, and explain whether or not the rule of the Duvaliers fulfilled those ideals.

9. (a) Identify Who is Jean-Bertrand Aristide?
(b) Sequence What are the main events of Aristide's struggle for power?
(c) Draw Conclusions How did what happened to Aristide affect ordinary people who supported him? Explain why.

10. (a) List What rights and responsibilities of United States citizenship do Puerto Ricans have?
(b) Find Main Ideas Explain why so many Puerto Ricans move back and forth between their island and the mainland.
(c) Compare What are the advantages and disadvantages of commonwealth status for Puerto Rico?

◆ Skills Practice

Comparing and Contrasting In the Skills for Life activity in this chapter, you learned how to compare and contrast. Review the steps of this skill.

Now look again at the first two sections of this chapter. As you recall, people from both Cuba and Haiti have fled their countries to come to the United States. What kinds of countries did they leave behind? How are Cuba and Haiti similar and different? Use a chart to compare the two countries. Then write a conclusion sentence on the topic.

◆ Writing Activity: Math

Review the charts in Country Profile: Haiti on page 472. Also consider the current population of Haiti, which is approximately 8 million. Use this information and your math skills to write a paragraph about Haiti's loss of population. You may wish to convert numbers into percentages or explain ratios in your paragraph.

MAP★MASTER™
Skills Activity

Place Location For each place listed below, write the letter from the map that shows its location.
1. Havana
2. Cuba
3. San Juan
4. Haiti
5. Puerto Rico
6. Port-au-Prince

Go Online
PHSchool.com Use Web Code **lfp-1523** for an **interactive map.**

The Caribbean

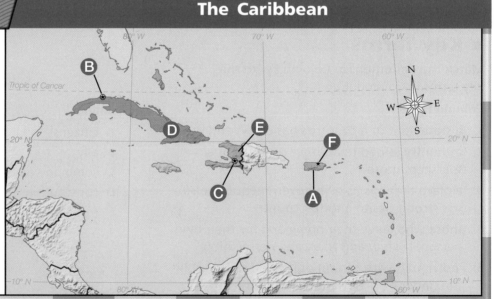

Standardized Test Prep

Test-Taking Tips

Some questions on standardized tests ask you to sequence information. Study the timeline below. Then follow the tips to answer the sample question.

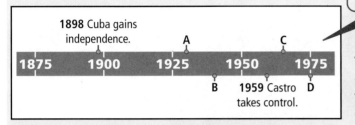

TIP Notice that the leader lines connect events to their dates on the timeline. See which dates are closest to each answer choice.

Pick the letter that best answers the question.

At which point on the timeline did large numbers of Cuban exiles <u>begin</u> going to the United States?

A point A

B point B

C point C

D point D

TIP Preview the question first. Look for information relating to the question as you examine the timeline.

Think It Through Notice the key word *begin* in the question. You know that many Cubans left Cuba for the United States because they opposed Castro's government. Therefore, they must have *started* leaving after Castro came to power. So you can rule out choices A and B. Although exiles may still have been leaving Cuba in 1975, the exile movement most likely *began* shortly after Castro's new government was formed. So the correct answer is C.

Practice Questions

Choose the letter of the best answer.

1. Before Cuba gained independence, it was a colony of
   A France.
   B Spain.
   C the United States.
   D Portugal.

2. Which of the following nations was formed from a revolt of enslaved Africans?
   A Haiti
   B Cuba
   C Puerto Rico
   D Hispaniola

3. Which of the following statements best describes Puerto Rico's relationship with the United States?
   A It is a colony of the United States.
   B It is a state of the United States.
   C It is a country with special ties to the United States.
   D It is a commonwealth of the United States.

Study the timeline below and answer the question that follows.

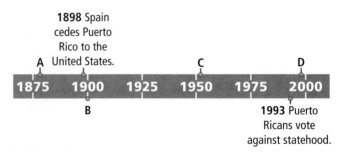

4. At which point on the timeline did Puerto Rico become a commonwealth?
   A point A
   B point B
   C point C
   D point D

Go Online
PHSchool.com

Use Web Code lfa-1501
for a **Chapter 15 self-test.**

Chapter 16 South America

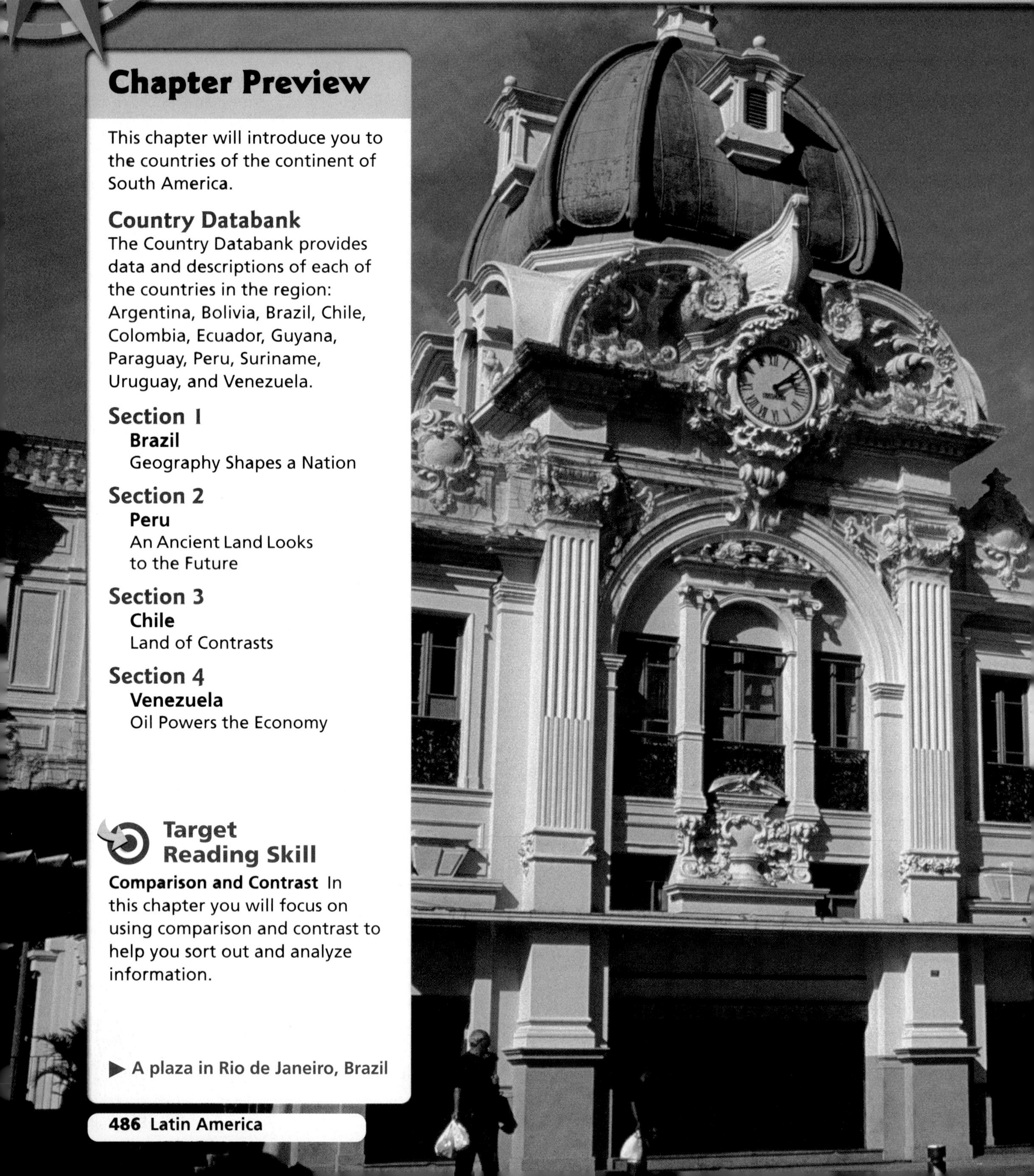

Chapter Preview

This chapter will introduce you to the countries of the continent of South America.

Country Databank

The Country Databank provides data and descriptions of each of the countries in the region: Argentina, Bolivia, Brazil, Chile, Colombia, Ecuador, Guyana, Paraguay, Peru, Suriname, Uruguay, and Venezuela.

Section 1
Brazil
Geography Shapes a Nation

Section 2
Peru
An Ancient Land Looks to the Future

Section 3
Chile
Land of Contrasts

Section 4
Venezuela
Oil Powers the Economy

Target Reading Skill

Comparison and Contrast In this chapter you will focus on using comparison and contrast to help you sort out and analyze information.

▶ A plaza in Rio de Janeiro, Brazil

South America: Political

MAP MASTER™
Skills Activity

Caribbean Sea

ATLANTIC OCEAN

Barranquilla
Maracaibo
⊛ Caracas
GUYANA
VENEZUELA
SURINAME
Medellín
Georgetown
Paramaribo
★ Cayenne
Bogotá
FRENCH GUIANA (France)
GALÁPAGOS ISLANDS (Ecuador)
Cali
Equator
COLOMBIA
Equator
0°
ECUADOR ⊛ Quito
Belém
Guayaquil
Manaus
Amazon River
Fortaleza

PACIFIC OCEAN
B R A Z I L
Recife

PERU
Lima ⊛
Cuzco
Salvador

Arequipa
La Paz
BOLIVIA
Brasília
20° S
⊛ Sucre
Belo Horizonte
20° S
Tropic of Capricorn
PARAGUAY
Rio de Janeiro
Tropic of Capricorn
São Paulo
CHILE
Asunción
Curitiba
Córdoba
Porto Alegre
Santiago ⊛
Rosario
URUGUAY
⊛ Montevideo
ATLANTIC OCEAN
Buenos Aires
ARGENTINA
40° S
40° S

N
W ✦ E
S

KEY
⊛ National capital
★ Other capital
• Other city
— National border

0 miles 1,000
0 kilometers 1,000
Lambert Azimuthal Equal Area

FALKLAND ISLANDS (U.K.)
Tierra del Fuego
SOUTH GEORGIA (U.K.)

Regions Notice that the Equator runs through South America. **Locate** Which countries are completely north of the Equator? Which ones have land both north and south of the Equator? **Identify Effects** If you were to start at the Equator and travel south, how do you think the climate would change? Explain why.

Go Online
PHSchool.com Use Web Code **lfp-1621** for an **interactive map.**

Introducing
South America

Guide for Reading

This section provides an introduction to the 12 countries of South America.

- Look at the map on the previous page and then read the paragraphs to learn about each nation.
- Analyze the data to compare the countries.
- What characteristics do most of these countries share?
- What are some key differences among the countries?

Viewing the Video Overview

View the World Studies Video Overview to learn more about each of the countries. As you watch, answer these questions:

- What topographical feature has a major influence on the climate of South America?
- What topographical features influence the climate where you live?

Explore the varied landscape of South America.

Argentina

Capital	Buenos Aires
Land Area	1,056,636 sq mi; 2,736,690 sq km
Population	37.8 million
Ethnic Group(s)	white, mestizo, indigenous Indian
Religion(s)	Roman Catholic, Protestant, Jewish
Government	republic
Currency	Argentine peso
Leading Exports	edible oils, fuels and energy, cereals, feed, motor vehicles
Language(s)	Spanish (official), Italian, indigenous Indian languages

The second-largest country in South America, Argentina (ahr jun TEE nuh) covers more than 1 million square miles (2.7 million square kilometers). It is located in the southern part of the continent, between the Andes Mountains and the Atlantic Ocean, and extends to the southern tip of South America. The Andes slope down to a fertile plain called the pampas, where raising livestock and wheat dominates the culture and the economy. Argentina has suffered from a series of harsh military regimes. In 1983, however, the nation established a democratic government.

Albatross chicks, Diego Ramirez Islands, Chile

Bolivia

Capitals	La Paz and Sucre
Land Area	418,683 sq mi; 1,084,390 sq km
Population	8.5 million
Ethnic Group(s)	Quechua, mestizo, Aymara, white
Religion(s)	Roman Catholic, Protestant
Government	republic
Currency	boliviano
Leading Exports	soybeans, natural gas, zinc, gold, wood
Language(s)	Spanish (official), Quechua (official), Aymara (official)

Bolivia (buh LIV ee uh) is a landlocked country in central South America. Much of its population lives in the Altiplano, or high plateau region, which Bolivia shares with Peru. This plain lies between two ranges of the Andes Mountains. Mountains and rain forests isolate the Altiplano from the sea and from the rest of South America. Although Bolivia has rich mineral resources, mining is difficult at high altitudes. It is also difficult to transport the minerals to market. So, in spite of its resources, Bolivia has remained poor. More than half of Bolivians are indigenous people.

Brazil

Capital	Brasília
Land Area	3,265,059 sq mi; 8,456,510 sq km
Population	176 million
Ethnic Group(s)	white, mixed white and black, black, Asian, Arab, indigenous Indian
Religion(s)	Roman Catholic
Government	federal republic
Currency	real
Leading Exports	manufactured goods, iron ore, soybeans, footwear, coffee, autos
Language(s)	Portuguese (official), German, Italian, Spanish, Polish, Japanese, indigenous Indian languages

Brazil (bruh ZIL) is the largest country in South America. It occupies the eastern-central region of the continent, bordering the Atlantic Ocean. Brazil is known as the home of the huge Amazon rain forest and for its vibrant culture. The influence of its Portuguese colonial past can still be seen in Brazil's language, culture, and architecture. However, other groups have also made contributions to a distinctive Brazilian culture. These groups include the native Indians, Africans originally brought to Brazil as slaves, and immigrants from northern Europe and Japan.

Chile

Capital	Santiago
Land Area	289,112 sq mi; 748,800 sq km
Population	15.5 million
Ethnic Group(s)	white, mestizo, indigenous Indian
Religion(s)	Roman Catholic, Protestant
Government	republic
Currency	Chilean peso
Leading Exports	copper, fish, fruits, paper and pulp, chemicals
Language(s)	Spanish (official), indigenous Indian languages

Chile (CHIL ee) is a long, narrow country. It lies along the western coast of South America, from its northern border with Peru to the southern tip of the continent. Chile has varied landforms and climates, from deserts in the north and central fertile plains, to its rainy, stormy southern tip. Mountains, lakes, and glaciers complete the picture. Most Chileans live in the fertile valley of central Chile. About one third of Chile's people live in the vibrant capital of Santiago.

Introducing South America

Colombia

Capital	Bogotá
Land Area	401,042 sq mi; 1,038,700 sq km
Population	41 million
Ethnic Group(s)	mestizo, white, mixed white and black, mixed black and indigenous Indian, indigenous Indian
Religion(s)	Roman Catholic
Government	republic
Currency	Colombian peso
Leading Exports	petroleum, coffee, coal, apparel, bananas, cut flowers
Language(s)	Spanish (official), indigenous Indian languages

Located on the northwest corner of South America, Colombia (kuh LUM bee uh) has coastlines on both the Pacific Ocean and the Caribbean Sea. To the northwest, it is bordered by Panama, which was once part of its territory. Colombia is located at the intersection of Central and South America and near the Panama Canal. This location makes it important to transportation and communication between the regions. Three ranges of the Andes Mountains divide the country. Most of Colombia's people live in the central valley or the hot, wet western region.

Ecuador

Capital	Quito
Land Area	106,888 sq mi; 276,840 sq km
Population	13.5 million
Ethnic Group(s)	mestizo, indigenous Indian, white, black
Religion(s)	Roman Catholic
Government	republic
Currency	U.S. dollar
Leading Exports	petroleum, bananas, shrimp, coffee, cocoa, cut flowers, fish
Language(s)	Spanish (official), Quechua, other indigenous Indian languages

Once part of the Incan empire, Ecuador (EK wuh dawr) was colonized by Spain in 1533 and became independent in 1830. A small country on the Pacific Coast, Ecuador has three regions. The lowland coastal region is the industrial center as well as the farm belt of Ecuador. Subsistence farming is the main economic activity in the highlands of the Andes Mountains. This is the region where the descendants of the Incas live and struggle to maintain their languages and traditional ways of life. The inland region benefits from large deposits of oil.

Giant tortoise, Ecuador

Guyana

Capital	Georgetown
Land Area	76,004 sq mi; 196,850 sq km
Population	698,209
Ethnic Group(s)	South Asian, black, indigenous Indian, white, East Asian, mixed white and black
Religion(s)	Christian, Hindu, Muslim
Government	republic
Currency	Guyanese dollar
Leading Exports	sugar, gold, bauxite/alumina, rice, shrimp, molasses, rum, timber
Language(s)	English (official), English Creole, Hindi, Tamil, indigenous Indian languages

Guyana (gy AN uh) lies on the northeast coast of South America. It is similar to its Caribbean island neighbors. Guyana was originally colonized by the Dutch, who imported enslaved Africans to work on their plantations. It became a British colony in 1814. After slavery ended in 1838, the British brought workers from India to do farm work. The descendants of these Africans and Indians form the largest ethnic groups in Guyana today. Most of the population lives on the narrow, wet coastal plain. The interior of the country is covered with dense rain forests.

Paraguay

Capital	Asunción
Land Area	153,398 sq mi; 397,300 sq km
Population	5.9 million
Ethnic Group(s)	mestizo
Religion(s)	Roman Catholic, Protestant
Government	constitutional republic
Currency	guaraní
Leading Exports	soybeans, feed, cotton, meat, edible oils, electricity
Language(s)	Spanish (official), Guaraní (official)

A small landlocked country, Paraguay (PA ruh gway) is bordered by Brazil, Argentina, and Bolivia. The Paraguay River divides the country into two sections. Much of the population is clustered in the fertile plains and hills of the eastern region. The west is sparsely populated. Most of the people of Paraguay are descended from the Spanish and the Guaraní, an indigenous group. In the cities, both Spanish and Guaraní are spoken, but in the countryside most people speak Guaraní.

Peru

Capital	Lima
Land Area	494,208 sq mi; 1,280,000 sq km
Population	28 million
Ethnic Group(s)	indigenous Indian, mestizo, white, black, East Asian
Religion(s)	Roman Catholic
Government	constitutional republic
Currency	nuevo sol
Leading Exports	fish and fish products, gold, copper, zinc, crude petroleum and byproducts, lead, coffee, sugar, cotton
Language(s)	Spanish (official), Quechua (official), Aymara

Peru (puh ROO) lies along the Pacific coast of South America, south of Colombia and Ecuador, and north of Chile. The Andes Mountains run the length of the country. A high plateau called the Altiplano is home to descendants of the Incas and other indigenous groups. Many of them live much as their ancestors did and speak Indian languages. The economic center of Peru is Lima, on the coast. Peru has been slow to modernize and industrialize. It has also suffered from military dictatorships and government corruption, but today it has an elected democratic government.

Introducing **South America**

Suriname

Capital	Paramaribo
Land Area	62,344 sq mi; 161,470 sq km
Population	436,494
Ethnic Group(s)	South Asian, Creole, Javanese, Maroon, indigenous Indian, East Asian, white
Religion(s)	Christian, Hindu, Muslim, traditional beliefs
Government	constitutional democracy
Currency	Suriname guilder or florin
Leading Exports	alumina, crude oil, lumber, shrimp and fish, rice, bananas
Language(s)	Dutch (official), Sranan, Javanese, Sarnami Hindi, Saramaccan, Chinese, Carib

Suriname (soor ih NAHM) is a small country on the northern coast of South America. Mountains and rain forest dominate its geography. Most of the people live on a narrow coastal plain. Suriname was settled by the Dutch, who imported enslaved Africans to work their coffee and sugar cane plantations. After slavery ended, workers from India, Java, and China were brought to work in the fields. The result is an ethnically mixed population. Suriname became independent in 1975. A series of military regimes followed, but democratic rule was established in 1987.

A gaucho in Uruguay

Uruguay

Capital	Montevideo
Land Area	67,108 sq mi; 173,620 sq km
Population	3.4 million
Ethnic Group(s)	white, mestizo, black
Religion(s)	Roman Catholic, Protestant, Jewish
Government	constitutional republic
Currency	Uruguayan peso
Leading Exports	meat, rice, leather products, wool, vehicles, dairy products
Language(s)	Spanish (official)

Uruguay (YOOR uh gway) is a small country located between two large ones: Brazil to the north and Argentina to the west. The capital, Montevideo, is situated where the River Platte empties into the Atlantic Ocean, making the city an important port for international trade. Most of Uruguay is made up of grassy plains and low hills. Raising cattle and sheep are the main occupations of that region. Tourism has become important along the country's sandy coastal beaches. Banking and other service industries also contribute to the economy.

Venezuela

Capital	Caracas
Land Area	340,560 sq mi; 882,050 sq km
Population	24.3 million
Ethnic Group(s)	white, Southwest Asian, black, indigenous Indian
Religion(s)	Roman Catholic, Protestant
Government	federal republic
Currency	bolívar
Leading Exports	petroleum, bauxite and aluminum, steel, chemicals, agricultural products, basic manufactured goods
Language(s)	Spanish (official), indigenous Indian languages

SOURCES: DK World Desk Reference Online; *CIA World Factbook,* 2002 and 2006; *World Almanac,* 2003

Venezuela (ven uh ZWAY luh) is located on the northern coast of South America, along the Caribbean Sea. The government has encouraged both agriculture and industry in an effort to diversify the economy. However, Venezuela still depends largely on its huge deposits of oil. Most of Venezuela's people live in cities, primarily in the northern part of the country. Some of the country's indigenous population lives in isolated areas of rain forest. Once a Spanish colony, Venezuela freed itself from Spain in 1821 and then became part of Gran Colombia. Venezuela became an independent republic in 1830.

Caraballeda, Venezuela

Assessment

Comprehension and Critical Thinking

1. Compare and Contrast Which is the largest country in South America? Which is the smallest? What do these two countries have in common, in spite of their difference in size?

2. Categorize What characteristics do the countries south of the Equator share?

3. Contrast How have such contrasting geographic features as rolling, grassy plains and high altitudes affected the cultures and economies of the countries in which they are found?

4. Draw Conclusions Which countries have the most diverse populations? Explain how you reached that conclusion.

5. Make a Bar Graph Create a population graph of the five most populous countries of South America.

Keeping Current

Access the **DK World Desk Reference Online** at **PHSchool.com** for up-to-date information about all the countries in this chapter.

Go Online
PHSchool.com

Web Code: lfe-1433

Brazil
Geography Shapes a Nation

Prepare to Read

Objectives

In this section you will
1. Learn about the geography of Brazil.
2. Discover why the rain forests are important to Brazil and to the whole world.
3. Find out what groups make up the people of Brazil and how they live.

Taking Notes

As you read this section, look for information about the rain forest. Copy the flowchart below and record your findings in it.

```
┌─────────────────────────────────────┐
│         Amazon Rain Forest          │
└─────────────────────────────────────┘
┌──────────┐  ┌──────────┐  ┌──────────┐
│Importance│  │ Dangers  │  │ Efforts to│
│          │  │          │  │ Protect It│
│   •      │  │    •     │  │    •     │
│   •      │  │    •     │  │    •     │
└──────────┘  └──────────┘  └──────────┘
```

🎯 Target Reading Skill

Compare and Contrast When you compare, you examine the similarities between things. When you contrast, you look at the differences. Comparing and contrasting can help you sort out and analyze information. As you read this section, look for similarities and differences in the geographic regions, cultures, and cities of Brazil.

Key Terms

- **canopy** (KAN uh pea) *n.* the dense mass of leaves and branches that form the top layer of a rain forest
- **Amazon rain forest** (AM uh zahn rayn FAWR ist) *n.* a large tropical rain forest occupying the Amazon Basin in northern South America
- **Rio de Janeiro** (REE oh day zhuh NEHR oh) *n.* a large city in Brazil
- **Brasília** (bruh ZIL yuh) *n.* Brazil's new capital city
- **savanna** (suh VAN uh) *n.* a flat, grassy region, or plain

A toucan from Brazil's rain forest

Deep in Brazil's rain forest, the light barely penetrates. At the top of the trees, the leaves form a dense mass called a **canopy.** Sun and rain beat down upon the canopy. But on the ground, it is almost chilly. The cool, moist air is filled with sounds, such as the calls of birds, monkeys, and insects.

The **Amazon rain forest** is a large area of abundant rainfall and dense vegetation in northern Brazil. It occupies the Amazon Basin, the land drained by the Amazon River and its tributaries. Find the Amazon River and the Amazon Basin on the map titled Physical Latin America on page 332. The Amazon rain forest gets more than 80 inches (200 centimeters) of rain each year and has an average temperature of 80°F (27°C). It has millions of species of plants and animals, including orchids, jaguars, and toucans.

The dense foliage makes travel through the rain forest difficult, and few people live there. Even so, the Amazon rain forest is very important to the people of Brazil. It is also important to the rest of the world. Find out what Brazil is doing to protect and develop its rain forest resources.

The Geography of Brazil

Brazil, the largest country in South America, is nearly as big as the United States. It is also one of the richest countries in the world in land and resources. Until recently, its immense rain forests remained undisturbed. Only the few indigenous groups that had lived in them for centuries ever explored them.

Rain Forest and More Brazil's rain forests take up more than a third of the country. Look at the map titled Latin America: Vegetation Regions on page 348. In the southeast, the forests give way to a large plateau divided by mountain ranges and river valleys. The plateau reaches Brazil's long coast. Many harbors lie along the coast. **Rio de Janeiro** (REE oh day zhuh NEHR oh), Brazil's former capital, is one of many Brazilian cities that grew up around these coastal harbors. Most of Brazil's people live near the coast, far from the rain forests.

Brazil's New Capital: Brasília In the 1950s, the government of Brazil wanted to develop Brazil's interior region using the resources of the rain forest. But few Brazilians wanted to move to the interior of the country. How could the government tempt Brazilians to move?

The government's solution was to build a new capital city called **Brasília** in the interior, near the rain forest. They chose a site on the vast interior plain, or **savanna,** called the Cerrado (suh RAH doh). Work started in 1957, and the government began to move to the partly-completed capital in 1960. Today, Brasília has a population of nearly 2 million people, and many of Brazil's companies and organizations have their headquarters there.

✓ **Reading Check** Why was Brasília built?

Links to Science

The Photosynthesis "Factory" What is the source of the oxygen we breathe? The food we eat? The fuels we burn? They all begin with photosynthesis. This process is carried out by green plants. They transform water, sunlight, carbon dioxide, and other minerals into energy-rich substances. Plants store these substances for their own nourishment. But animals eat the plants as food. And people eat those animals, as well as eating plants directly. At the same time, the process of photosynthesis releases oxygen into the air. The Amazon rain forest, with its wealth of green plants, is such an important source of oxygen that it is sometimes called "the lungs of Earth."

And there's more. Fuels such as coal and oil are the remains of ancient plants. So photosynthesis, in a way, powers the world.

The Importance of the Rain Forest

The rain forest is very important to life all over the world. Scientists estimate that rain forests produce about one third of the world's oxygen. They also calculate that the Amazon rain forest has several million different species of plants, animals, and insects—some that have not even been discovered yet. That is more species than any other region in the world.

Using Rain Forest Resources Many modern medicines have been made from rain forest plants, and scientists hope to discover even more species that have practical uses. The rain forest also holds about one fifth of the world's fresh water. But many scientists think that when people begin to use the resources of the rain forest, they upset the delicate balance of nature.

For example, in the past, Brazil made efforts at land reform by moving poor farmers to the Amazon rain forest and giving them land there. The farmers burned down trees to clear the land for their crops. After a few years, the soil in the rain forest became unfit for farming.

■ Graph Skills

Differences in temperature and rainfall create different environments for plants, animals, and people. **Transfer Information** Which city shown in the graphs gets more rainfall? Which has the higher temperatures? **Contrast** Use these climate differences to infer how life might be different in Brasília and Manaus.

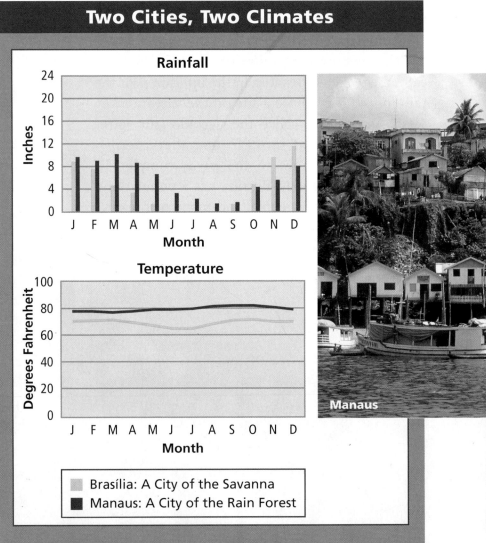

Two Cities, Two Climates

Rainfall

Inches / Month

Temperature

Degrees Fahrenheit / Month

Brasília: A City of the Savanna
Manaus: A City of the Rain Forest

Brasília

Manaus

Threats to the Amazon Rain Forest

Today, Brazil's leaders are trying to control development of the rain forest. They want to find ways to help the economy and the farmers while protecting this important resource. They are working to protect the rain forest from the following dangers:

First, if too much timber is cut down, there will not be enough trees to absorb the carbon dioxide in the atmosphere. The buildup of carbon dioxide may trap heat near Earth's surface, altering the world's climate. When part of the forest is destroyed, the animals and plants that live there may not survive. Plants that might produce important medicines could be destroyed before they are even discovered.

Smuggling is another problem. Approximately 12 million animals are smuggled out of Brazil each year. Many are endangered, and it is illegal to capture or kill them. There are also laws to slow down the logging of mahogany, a wood used to make furniture. But these laws are being broken. Illegal logging continues to threaten the rain forest.

Pollution caused by mining is a third problem. In the late 1980s, the mercury used in gold mining polluted streams in the forest. It made people in several Native American villages sick. The government of Brazil passed strict laws about mining in the rain forest. Sometimes the government insisted that the miners leave. At times, military police had to be called in to make sure they did.

Illegal Logging
The small boat is towing a long raft of illegally cut logs down the Amazon River. **Analyze Images** *Which details in the photo suggest why logging might be difficult in the rain forest? Which details suggest why it might be easy?*

Threats to Traditional Ways of Life

Threats to the Amazon rain forest are also threats to the people who have traditionally lived there. The difficulty of traveling in the rain forest had kept many indigenous peoples isolated. They continued their ancient ways of life. Once the rain forest was opened to development, however, miners, farmers, and land speculators arrived. These newcomers brought diseases the Indians had not been exposed to before, and many died. Conflicts between the developers and the Indians were sometimes violent, and Indians were killed. And the isolated culture of the indigenous people began to change as it was brought into contact with modern ways.

Compare and Contrast What are some differences between the way the indigenous people lived before the development of the rain forest and the way they live now?

✓ **Reading Check** **Describe three dangers threatening the rain forest.**

Brazil

Brazil's culture is vibrant and diverse. Portuguese and African influences are evident in Brazilian architecture, religion, music, and food. They also shape the culture of Brazil's cities, where 82 percent of the people live. The indigenous Indian culture, however, has remained largely separate from the rest of Brazil, isolated in the interior of the Amazon rain forest. As you study the map and charts, consider how geography and settlement patterns shape a nation's culture.

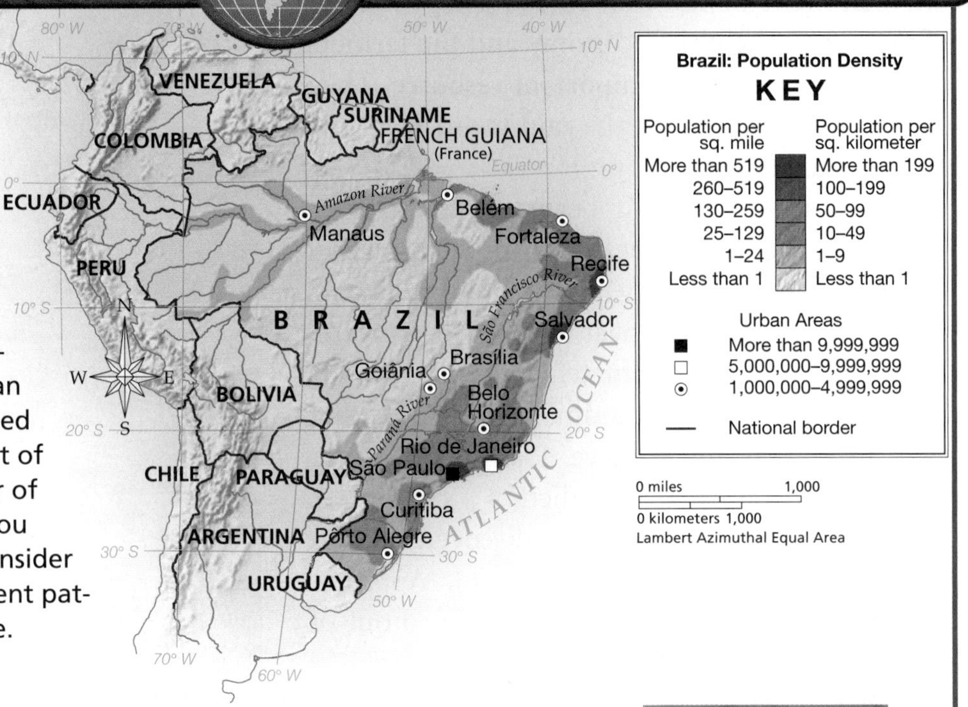

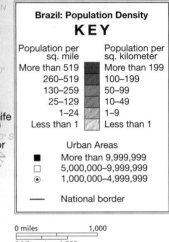

Brazil: Population Density
KEY

Population per sq. mile	Population per sq. kilometer
More than 519	More than 199
260–519	100–199
130–259	50–99
25–129	10–49
1–24	1–9
Less than 1	Less than 1

Urban Areas
■ More than 9,999,999
□ 5,000,000–9,999,999
◉ 1,000,000–4,999,999

— National border

0 miles 1,000
0 kilometers 1,000
Lambert Azimuthal Equal Area

Cultural Regions of Brazil

The Northeast
Sugar plantations shaped the culture of the northeast. Enslaved Africans imported to work on the plantations brought their culture with them. Today, the area is rich in art and music. The dance called the samba (shown above) was born here.

SOURCE: *Encyclopedia Britannica*

The South
European immigrants shaped the culture of the south. People mainly of Portuguese descent brought cattle ranching, wheat farming, and coffee production to the region. A distinct diet based on meat products developed here.

The Rain Forests
European immigrants had little contact with Brazil's indigenous peoples. These peoples continued to lead traditional lives, isolated in Brazil's rain forests. Some 230 groups live here today. Among them are the Yanomami, who are hunter-gatherers.

The Cities
In urban centers such as Rio de Janeiro (above) and São Paulo, African and European cultures blended together. For example, the Brazilian celebration called Carnival mixes Catholic and African traditions.

Brazil's Ethnic Groups

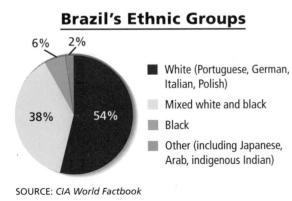

6% 2%
38% 54%

■ White (Portuguese, German, Italian, Polish)
Mixed white and black
■ Black
■ Other (including Japanese, Arab, indigenous Indian)

SOURCE: *CIA World Factbook*

Map and Chart Skills

1. **Identify** Where do most Brazilians live?
2. **Identify Causes** What are some of the reasons why Brazilians live where they do?
3. **Draw Conclusions** Why do you think Brazil's cities are more culturally diverse than the interior rain forest?

Go Online
PHSchool.com

Use Web Code **lfe-1611** for **DK World Desk Reference Online.**

The People of Brazil

The Native Americans living in the rain forest were some of the first people to live in Brazil. Today, many Brazilians are a mix of Native American, African, and European heritages. The Yanomami (yah noh MAH mee) are one of the larger Native American groups. They still live in traditional communities in the rain forest. As the rain forest is threatened, however, so too is the Yanomami way of life. Some Native Americans have left the rain forest for the cities.

The Different Cultures of Brazil Daniel Monteiro Costa is a writer and teacher who lives in São Paulo, Brazil. He is also known as Daniel Munduruku (mun duh ROO koo). Daniel is a Munduruku Indian. Many Munduruku still live in small villages in the rain forest. Daniel was born in the city of Belém (buh LEM), but he often visited his relatives in a nearby village. There, he heard stories the Munduruku people told about their history and culture. When he was growing up, Daniel saw that Indians were often treated with disrespect. He began studying the indigenous peoples of Brazil and became proud of his heritage. Now, Daniel works to keep Munduruku stories alive and to end discrimination against Indians in Brazil.

Native Americans are not the only cultural groups in Brazil. Many features of African culture also flourish there. The most African of Brazilian cities, Salvador, lies on the coastal plain. Most of the people who live here are descendants of the millions of Africans brought to Brazil as slaves.

Many Brazilians also have a European heritage. Some are descended from the Portuguese who colonized the area. Other more recent immigrants come from countries such as Italy. There are also Asian immigrants from Japan.

Working on Farms and in Factories In Brazil, most of the land that is suitable for growing crops is owned by only a few people. Sometimes they choose not to farm their land. About one third of Brazil's farmland, approximately 300 million acres (122 million hectares), is unused.

In the 1990s, Brazil's government gave some of this unused land to poor farmers. People began starting small farms just north of Rio de Janeiro. The farms allow them to support themselves.

Modern and Traditional
In the top photo, Brazilian soccer star Sissi participates in the 1999 Women's World Cup competition. The photo above shows a Kaiapo Indian from the rain forest.
Synthesize *Use the text to help you describe the two very different Brazilian ways of life represented by the photos.*

The plantations, or large farms, of Brazil produce crops for export. Brazil is the largest coffee producer in the world. But Brazilians know that they cannot depend on only one or two crops. The government has discouraged coffee production and tried to diversify the economy by building more factories. Today, Brazil produces iron and steel, cars, and electrical equipment. Since 1960, about 30 million people have left farms and plantations and moved into the cities to get jobs in these new industries.

A Brazilian City: Rio de Janeiro Brazilian cities are home to both the rich and the very poor. Rio de Janeiro is a good example of these contrasts. It lies on the Atlantic coast, surrounded by huge mountains that dip to the sea. If you climbed to the top of one, you could see the whole city. To the south, you would see expensive hotels and shops for tourists. In the downtown area, you would see old palaces and government buildings. Rio de Janeiro was Brazil's capital from 1822 to 1960.

But to the north, you would see clusters of small houses where factory workers live. On the slopes of the mountains are neighborhoods crowded with homes that have no electricity or running water. About 20 percent of Rio's more than 10 million people live in these *favelas*, or slums. However, most of Rio's people live in well-built houses with electricity and running water.

✓ **Reading Check** What is Rio de Janeiro like?

Rio de Janeiro

Section 1 Assessment

Key Terms
Review the key terms at the beginning of this section. Use each term in a sentence that explains its meaning.

Target Reading Skills
What are two ways Brasília and Rio de Janeiro are similar? What are two ways they are different?

Comprehension and Critical Thinking
1. (a) Name What are the main features of Brazil's geography?
(b) Infer Why do you think many people moved to Brasília?
2. (a) Identify Effects Why are Brazil's rain forests important to the whole world?
(b) Analyze Explain why it is difficult for Brazil to protect its rain forest and improve its economy at the same time.
3. (a) Identify What is the cultural heritage of Brazilians?
(b) Draw Conclusions How does unequal land distribution affect the economy and people of Brazil?

Writing Activity
Suppose you lived in a Brazilian city, such as Rio de Janeiro or Salvador, in 1960. Would you have moved to the new city of Brasília if you had been given the chance? Write a letter to a friend explaining why you are planning to move to Brasília or why you are not moving there.

> **Writing Tip** State your choice clearly. Then give three reasons to support your choice.

Prepare to Read

Objectives

In this section you will

1. Learn how geography has affected the way people live in the three regions of Peru.
2. Discover what life is like in the cities and towns of the Altiplano.

Taking Notes

As you read this section, look for the ways that people live in the three regions of Peru. Copy the table below and record your findings in it.

Region	Geography	How People Live
	• •	• •

🎯 Target Reading Skill

Identify Contrasts When you contrast two regions, you examine how they are different. In this section you will read about the three geographic regions of Peru and about the ways people have adapted to them. As you read, list the differences between the regions and the ways people live there.

Key Terms

- **Altiplano** (al tih PLAH noh) *n.* a high plateau in the Andes Mountains
- **sierra** (see EHR uh) *n.* the mountain region of Peru
- **oasis** (oh AY sis) *n.* a fertile area in a desert that has a source of water

When people on Tribuna, an island in Lake Titicaca, play soccer, they are very careful. That's because the island is made of straw. The ground is uneven, and when they walk on it they can feel the water shifting below. "It seems crazy to play soccer on water," says Luis Colo, who lives on Tribuna. "We don't jump on each other after a goal, or we'd probably fall through the field."

Tribuna is one of about 70 islands made by the Uros (oo ROHS). The Uros have adapted to the geography of Lake Titicaca. As you read in Chapter 13, they make their islands out of totora reeds. They join the floating roots together and then lay cut reeds on top. This process creates an island that is firm enough to support small communities of people with huts and livestock. When the Uros need more land, they simply build another island.

From the time of the Incas, the people of Peru—like people everywhere—have adapted to their geography. The Uros are only one example. You will read about other examples of how geography has affected culture in this section.

Reed boats moored by a totora-reed island

Peru

Peru is a country of geographic extremes. In the high mountains of the sierra, the air is almost too thin to breathe. The coast is largely desert except for scattered oases where rivers flow down from the mountains to the Pacific. Rain forest covers much of the eastern half of the country, or selva. As you study the map and charts below, think about how geography and climate affect the lives of Peruvians.

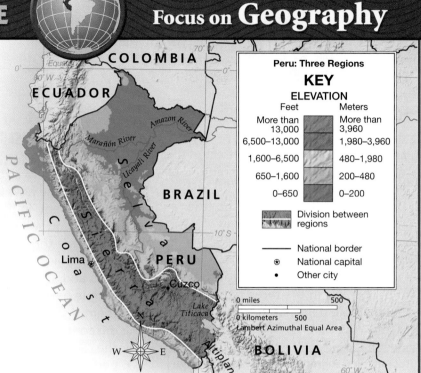

Characteristics of Three Regions

Characteristic	Coastal Region	Sierra	Selva
Land area	11%	26%	63%
Dominant feature	Desert and oases	Mountains	Rain forest
Yearly precipitation	2 inches	Varies	75–125 inches
Main language	Spanish	Quechua	Varied indigenous languages
Major occupations	Professional; manufacturing and refining; agriculture	Farming and herding; tourism	Fishing; hunting and gathering

SOURCES: *Peru, Country Study, Department of the Army Handbook,* 1981; *Encyclopaedia Britannica; The World Today Series, Latin America 2002;* Library of Congress online

Peru's Population

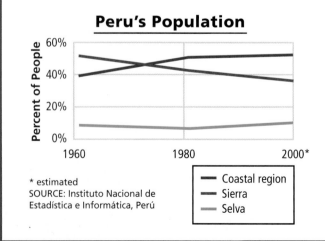

* estimated
SOURCE: Instituto Nacional de Estadística e Informática, Perú

Map and Chart Skills

1. **Identify** How do people earn a living in different parts of Peru?
2. **Analyze** What region of Peru has the most people? What region has lost population?
3. **Infer** What information in the map and charts indicates why these changes in population might have occurred?

Go Online PHSchool.com
Use Web Code lfe-1612 for **DK World Desk Reference Online.**

The Regions and People of Peru

The Uros live on Lake Titicaca. Find Lake Titicaca on the map of Peru in the Country Profile. Lake Titicaca is in Peru's **Altiplano** (al tih PLAH noh), a high plateau in the Andes Mountains. The Altiplano is about 12,000 feet (3,658 meters) above sea level. It is located in southern Peru near the Bolivian border.

Peru's Three Geographic Regions The Andes Mountains, which run from northwest to southeast Peru, divide the country into three geographic regions. The mountain region, including the Andes and the Altiplano, is known as the **sierra.** Much of this region is so high that lower layers of the soil remain frozen all year. This kind of treeless plain, which supports only low-growing vegetation, is called tundra. Even so, people have lived in this region for centuries. The Incas built their empire in the Altiplano, with Cuzco as its capital. Today, some descendants of the Incas live much as their ancestors did. In addition to farming, these Native Americans herd sheep, cattle, llamas, and alpacas. Wool is one of the major products of the region.

The coastal region of Peru is very different from the sierra. This dry area is dotted with oases. An **oasis** is a fertile area in a desert that has a source of water. Before Europeans arrived, indigenous groups settled by these oases. Later, the Spanish also built cities along the coast. Today, this area is the economic center of Peru. In Lima (LEE muh), Peru's capital, historic Spanish buildings from the 1600s and 1700s stand next to modern skyscrapers. More than 6 million people—more than a quarter of Peru's population—live in Lima.

The third region of Peru is the large forested area that stretches from the lower slopes of the mountains to the lowlands of northeast Peru. Here, the weather is hot and humid all year. This isolated region is called the selva. It has few roads connecting it to the sierra and the coast. Little modern development has occurred here. Some Native American groups live in this rain forest much as their ancestors did.

A modern skyscraper stands beside a Spanish-style home in Lima.

A Peruvian Oasis
This small fertile area is surrounded by desert. **Draw Inferences** *Why do you think people settled by oases in this area of Peru?*

Explore how people make a living in Peru.

Peru's People Native Americans make up almost half of Peru's population. Most Native Americans living in Peru are Quechua. Another third of Peru's people are mestizo. The remaining Peruvians are of European, African, and Asian descent. Even though Native Americans are such a large part of the population of Peru, until recently many of them have remained isolated from the modern world.

✓ **Reading Check** **Which two groups make up the majority of Peruvians?**

Life in the Altiplano

Many Quechuas, Uros, and other Native Americans living on the Altiplano follow traditions that are hundreds of years old. Their communities, however, are slowly changing. Thousands of Native Americans have left for jobs in the city. And life is changing even for those who stay in their villages.

Lost City of the Incas
The ruins of Machu Picchu were "discovered" in 1911 when a local guide led American scholars to the site. It has stone buildings, walkways, and staircases, as well as agricultural terraces that were once watered by an aqueduct. **Conclude** *How did the Incan builders adapt their city to the mountain site?*

Old and New The past is constantly present in the Altiplano. The ruins of Incan cities, such as Machu Picchu, are found in the countryside. Even in modern cities, the old mixes with the new. Most city dwellers in the Altiplano have electricity. The streets are paved, and there are telephones. But there are also remnants of the past. In Cuzco, for example, parts of the old Incan wall that once surrounded the city are still standing. Modern houses are made of adobe and have red tile roofs, but their foundations are the remains of Incan stonework. There are also buildings constructed by the Spanish colonists.

A Day in a Quechua Village

Village life is very different from city life. In the isolated towns of the Altiplano, there are no telephones. Few buses drive through the villages. Most people are Quechua or Aymara.

Like their Incan ancestors, many Quechua rely on raising animals for their wool. The Incas tamed wild llamas and alpacas, and then they raised them to use as pack animals and as a source of wool. Today, many Quechua families keep sheep instead. Sheep are not native to the region but were brought to the Americas by European settlers.

Modesto Mamani (moh DES toh MUH mahn ee) is a 13-year-old Quechua boy. He wakes before dawn to the freezing mountain air and eats breakfast as soon as the sun comes up. Breakfast is always the same: a few rolls, coffee with sugar, and whole wheat kernels that can be eaten like popcorn. His only other meal may be lunch. It is usually potato and barley soup with *chunos*—freeze-dried potato skins.

On some days, Modesto spends much of his time working in the field with his father and brothers. On other days, he looks after the sheep or goes with his mother to the market. Even with school and chores, Modesto finds time to play soccer on the tundra in back of his house.

Like many other children who live in Altiplano villages, Modesto's life mixes the modern and the traditional. He wants to study to become an engineer so he can bring technology to the Altiplano. Meanwhile, much of his time revolves around the sheep his family raises. Not only does Modesto tend the sheep, he also uses their wool to knit sweaters.

School, Work, and Play
Modesto attends school—with his soccer ball! (left), and shows off one of his family's sheep (right). **Infer** *Why do you think people raise sheep in the region seen in the photo?*

Identify Contrasts
Target Skill What are two ways that life in a Quechua village differs from life in Cuzco?

Modern Suspension Bridge
Tourists stand on a modern suspension bridge that is based on a design developed by the Incas. **Analyze** *How does this type of bridge suit its environment?*

Geography and Culture You have seen how the Uros adapted to their environment by living on islands they create themselves, much as their ancestors did. But they are also modern people who play soccer. In another part of the Altiplano, Quechua families raise sheep, animals that are suited to the tundra. But their children learn about technology in school.

Long ago, the Incas solved a problem of their mountain environment: how to cross the deep gorges between mountain peaks. They invented suspension bridges. Modern versions of these bridges are still used in the Andes today. They are one more example of how geography and the past influence the present in Peru.

✓ **Reading Check** Explain how one group of Peruvians has adapted to their environment.

Section 2 Assessment

Key Terms
Review the key terms at the beginning of this section. Use each term in a sentence that explains its meaning.

Target Reading Skills
How are the three geographic regions of Peru different?

Comprehension and Critical Thinking
1. (a) Describe What are the three regions of Peru, and what are they like?

(b) Identify Cause and Effect Why is the coastal plain the economic center of Peru?
2. (a) Describe How does Cuzco represent both old and new?
(b) Compare How is life for the Quechua similar to and different from life for the Uros?
(c) Predict Do you think the Uros and Quechua will preserve their traditional ways of life in this century? Explain.

Writing Activity
Write a letter that Modesto might send to a friend in Cuzco, inviting the friend to visit him in his village. Have Modesto describe what his friend might see and do on his visit.

Go Online
PHSchool.com

For: An activity on Peru
Visit: PHSchool.com
Web Code: lfd-1602

Chile
Land of Contrasts

Prepare to Read

Objectives

In this section you will
1. Find out how the geography of Chile creates regions where people live very differently.
2. Learn how Chile's people live and what products they produce.
3. Find out how Chile restored democracy.

Taking Notes

As you read this section, look for the main ideas and details and how they relate to each other. Use the format below to create an outline of the section.

```
I. The geography of Chile
   A. The longest, narrowest country
      1. Only 100 miles wide
      2.
```

Target Reading Skill

Compare and Contrast One way to understand regions is to compare and contrast them, or identify similarities and differences. When you compare, you look at similarities between things. When you contrast, you look at differences. As you read this section, compare and contrast the geographic regions and lifestyles of Chile.

Key Terms

- **Ferdinand Magellan** (FUR duh nand muh JEL un) *n.* Portuguese explorer sailing for Spain, whose expedition first circumnavigated the globe
- **circumnavigate** (sur kum NAV ih gayt) *v.* to sail or fly all the way around something, such as Earth
- **glacier** (GLAY shur) *n.* a large, slow-moving mass of ice and snow
- **Augusto Pinochet Ugarte** (ah GOO stoh pea noh SHAY oo gahr TAY) *n.* military dictator of Chile from 1973 to 1988

When Ferdinand Magellan first saw the Pacific Ocean in 1520, tears ran down his cheeks. **Ferdinand Magellan was a Portuguese explorer sailing for Spain.** He was searching for a way around or through the Americas. Ever since Christopher Columbus had failed to find a westward sea route all the way to Asia, explorers had been looking for one. But the continents of North and South America were in the way.

Magellan sailed from Spain in 1519 and worked his way south along the coast of South America. Bad weather forced him to spend the winter on the stormy southern coast. His crew threatened to rebel, but Magellan kept exploring. Finally, he found a way through the islands at the "bottom" of South America. His ships sailed through this narrow, dangerous passage to the Pacific Ocean. Magellan wept when he realized his great accomplishment. He knew that now he could sail to Asia—and all the way around the world.

The passage that Magellan discovered is in present-day Chile. It allowed European sailors to explore the western coast of South America.

Magellan's ship nears the strait that bears his name.

Chile

Chile produces more copper than any other country in the world. To avoid relying too much on one resource, however, the government of Chile has encouraged agriculture and new industry. The United States is Chile's largest trade partner. About 18 percent of Chile's exports are sold to the United States. Today, Chile's economy is seen as strong and stable. Study the map and charts. Think about how Chile's location and resources have affected its economy.

Chile: Products and Resources

KEY

	Copper
	Petroleum
	Manufacturing
	Fruits
	Fish
———	National border
⊛	National capital
•	Other city

0 miles 800
0 kilometers 800
Lambert Azimuthal Equal Area

Average Annual Income per Citizen

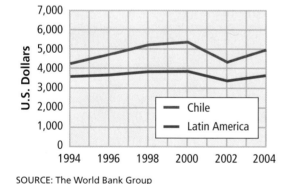

SOURCE: The World Bank Group

Chile's Exports

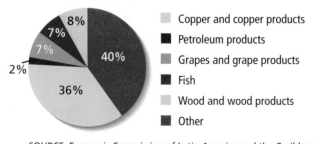

- Copper and copper products
- Petroleum products
- Grapes and grape products
- Fish
- Wood and wood products
- Other

SOURCE: Economic Commission of Latin America and the Caribbean

Map and Chart Skills

1. **Locate** Where are Chile's mineral resources found?
2. **Identify** Which economic resources are found in most parts of the country?
3. **Compare** How do Chile's agricultural and seafood exports compare to its copper exports?
4. **Analyze Information** What do you learn about Chile's economy from the line graph?
5. **Draw Conclusions** Do you think Chile has been successful in using its resources to create a diversified economy? Explain your answer.

Go Online
PHSchool.com

Use Web Code **lfe-1613** for **DK World Desk Reference Online.**

The Geography of Chile

The passage that Magellan discovered is now named after him. Find the Strait of Magellan on the map of Chile in the Country Profile. It is a major sea lane to this day. Although it is dangerous to sail through, the Strait of Magellan is safer than going all the way around Cape Horn to the south. Many ships have been lost in the Strait's stormy waters. While Magellan was lucky to get through the Strait, he was not lucky enough to return to Spain. He died during the voyage. Of the five ships that started Magellan's expedition, only one returned all the way to Spain. But it was the first ship to **circumnavigate,** or go all the way around, the globe.

The Longest, Narrowest Country Look at the map titled Physical Latin America on page 332. Find the Andes Mountains. They run down the whole length of Chile like a giant spine. Chile is narrow and shaped like a string bean. On average, it is only about 100 miles (161 kilometers) wide, but it is extremely long. It runs 2,650 miles (4,265 kilometers) down the Pacific Coast all the way to the tip of South America. It is the longest, narrowest country in the world.

The Driest Place in the World Chile contains an amazing variety of landforms and climates. In the north is the Atacama Desert, the driest region in the world. Not many plants or animals can survive there. But the desert is rich in copper, so the region is dotted with mines. Chile exports more copper than any country in the world.

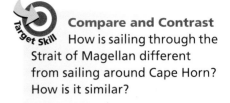

Compare and Contrast How is sailing through the Strait of Magellan different from sailing around Cape Horn? How is it similar?

A man examines salt formations in the Atacama Desert (above). Magellanic penguins (left) sometimes come ashore near the Strait of Magellan.

Varied Landscapes Chile's long central valley has rolling hills, high grasses, and dense forests. This is the region where most of the people live and where the capital of Chile, Santiago, is located. Both farming and mining are important here. In the southern part of central Chile is the beautiful Lakes Region, with forests, waterfalls, and mountains topped by glaciers. A glacier is a huge mass of slowly moving ice and snow. Many of the mountains of this region are volcanoes, and volcanic eruptions and earthquakes occur often in Chile.

The southern third of Chile is cold and wet and often stormy. Far to the south, the Strait of Magellan separates the mainland of Chile from the islands of Tierra del Fuego (tee EHR uh del FWAY goh), which are divided between Chile and Argentina. Tierra del Fuego is Spanish for "Land of Fire." When Magellan sailed past these islands, he saw smoke from the fires of the indigenous people who lived there. Because of the smoke, he called the large island Tierra del Fuego. This region is only about 600 miles (970 kilometers) from Antarctica. Icebergs dot the sea, and penguins come ashore.

✓ **Reading Check** Describe the central region of Chile.

Land of Contrasts
Icebergs float away from a glacier off Chile's southern coast (small photo). Below, a waterfall cascades in the central forest region. **Draw Conclusions** *What accounts for this difference in Chile's waterways?*

Chile's People and Products

The lifestyles of Chileans vary from region to region. In the far south, sheep herders in heavy wool sweaters brave the strong winds. Farther north in the central valley, farmers grow wheat, potatoes, sugar beets, corn, tomatoes, and many fruits. In the cities, people in business suits hurry in and out of tall skyscrapers. Few people live in the Atacama Desert of the far north. While mining continues today, there are also ghost towns, or abandoned mining settlements, in the Atacama.

The People of Chile Chile's early Spanish settlers married Native Americans already living there. Today, mestizos make up more than 90 percent of the population. Only about 10 percent of Chileans are Native Americans.

Tonino Fuentes (toh NEE noh FWEN tays) lives in the countryside near Santiago. His family is mestizo. They work on a farm owned by a wealthy man of Spanish descent. Tonino's father trains horses that will appear in rodeos. He is teaching Tonino to be a rodeo rider. But Tonino has other things he must do. Every morning at sunrise, he and his mother milk their two cows. Then Tonino does his homework. That's because his school is in the afternoon, from 2:00 P.M. until 6:00 P.M. In the evening, Tonino often plays soccer with his friends.

Chile's Cities Today, more than 80 percent of Chile's people live in cities. Many rural Chileans have come to Santiago. In this capital city, old Spanish buildings stand near gleaming skyscrapers. The city is in the valley of the central plain, so the altitude is low enough to allow mild weather. The sea makes the air humid. Palm trees grow in the public parks. The snowcapped Andes lie to the east.

Unfortunately, the beautiful sights of Santiago are sometimes blocked by a thick layer of smog. The city is surrounded by mountains on three sides. The mountains trap exhaust from vehicles and smoke from factories in the valley. This is especially true in the winter, when there is not much wind. Pollution has become so bad that it makes many small children and elderly people sick. On a bad day, people wear surgical masks in order to breathe, or they press scarves to their faces.

The Spanish designed many of Chile's cities around a central square. Their buildings could not withstand Chile's earthquakes, however. Few colonial structures remain in Valparaiso, an important port. Chile's second-largest city, Concepción, was moved several miles inland in 1754 to protect it from tsunamis.

Explore Chile's capital, Santiago.

Chile's Agricultural Revolution When copper prices fell in the 1980s, Chile realized that it must diversify its economy. One way was to sell more crops. By the late 1980s, agriculture had become a billion-dollar industry, providing jobs for about 900,000 Chileans. Chile shipped wheat, potatoes, and other vegetables and fruits around the world.

The United States, Japan, and Europe are especially good markets for Chilean produce. From October through May, it is cold in the Northern Hemisphere but warm in the Southern Hemisphere. Chile provides fruits and vegetables to the United States during the months when American farmers cannot.

Another reason that Chilean produce is welcome in other countries is that Chile's fruits and vegetables are free of many common plant pests. Chile's farming regions are protected by the Andes Mountains, so some of the insect pests and animal diseases that plague other countries never reach Chile. The government wants to make sure that Chilean produce remains this way. Customs inspectors at Chile's airports search baggage carefully. They are checking that no plant or animal matter from foreign places is allowed into the country because it might bring disease to Chile's crops.

✓ **Reading Check** Why is Chilean produce free of many plant pests?

Farming Fuels the Economy
Grapes are harvested (below) and then shipped around the world from ports like this one in Valparaiso (bottom photo). **Identify Effects** *How does farming create jobs for people other than farm workers?*

Restoring Democracy

Today, Chile has a democratic government. But a dark cloud from its past still hangs over the country. In 1973, the armed forces took control of the government. They were led by General **Augusto Pinochet Ugarte** (ah GOO stoh pea noh SHAY oo gahr TAY), who became a brutal dictator. The Chilean congress could not meet during his rule. Opposition political parties were banned. People who spoke out against the military regime were killed, imprisoned, or "disappeared."

Nevertheless, there were national days of protest. The Catholic Church spoke out against the human rights abuses of the government. In the 1988 elections—even though Pinochet's name was the only one on the ballot—the people of Chile rejected him by voting "no." Democratic government was restored. Pinochet, however, remained an army general.

In 1998, at the age of 82, Pinochet went to London, England, for medical treatment. The government of Spain issued a warrant for his arrest for crimes against humanity. This caused an international crisis. Eventually, Pinochet was declared unfit for trial, and he returned to Chile. Some Chileans wanted him prosecuted; others did not. There is still controversy over bringing to trial those responsible for the abuses of the Pinochet regime.

Anti-Pinochet demonstrators gathered in London when the former dictator was there for medical treatment.

✓ **Reading Check** How did Pinochet's rule end?

Section 3 Assessment

Key Terms

Review the key terms at the beginning of this section. Use each term in a sentence that explains its meaning.

Target Reading Skills

What are two ways that Tonino's life in the countryside is different from life in Santiago?

Comprehension and Critical Thinking

1. (a) Identify Describe Chile's geographic regions.

(b) Identify Cause and Effect How does Chile's geography contribute to its variety of climates and vegetation?

2. (a) Name What kinds of crops are grown in Chile?

(b) Identify Causes Why is Chilean produce so popular in foreign countries?

3. (a) Recall Describe life in Chile when Pinochet was in power.

(b) Evaluate Information Do you think Pinochet should be brought to trial? Explain.

Writing Activity

How do you think Magellan's crew must have felt during their exploration of Tierra del Fuego? Write a journal entry that one of the crew might have written about the experience.

Go Online
PHSchool.com

For: An activity on Chile
Visit: PHSchool.com
Web Code: lfd-1603

When Madelyn returned from Chile, she entertained the class with a wonderful presentation—a map of the route she had taken, a slide show of the Andes Mountains, and a videotape she had made of life in a small village. She had even managed to ask the villagers a couple of questions in Spanish.

When she finished, the class applauded. Her teacher beamed.

"Madelyn, the amount of information you have gathered is stunning," Mr. Rishell said. "Now perhaps you could synthesize all this material for us."

"Sure!" Madelyn replied. Then she paused. "Um . . . how do you synthesize something?"

When you synthesize information, you find the main ideas of several different sources and use them to draw a conclusion. This skill is particularly useful when you are doing research for a report.

Learn the Skill

To synthesize information, follow these steps.

1 **Identify the main idea of each of your sources.** Main ideas are broad, major ideas that are supported by details.

2 **Identify details that support each main idea.** Look in each source for supporting details. Jot them down or create a chart.

3 **Look for connections between pieces of information.** These connections may be similarities, differences, causes, effects, or examples.

4 **Draw conclusions based on the connections you found.** Be sure to use all of your sources.

Peru	
Main Ideas	**Supporting Details**
1. Peru has three distinct geographic regions:	• Coastal Region—Desert and oases
	• Sierra—Mountains
	• Selva—Rain forest
2. Peruvians speak different languages:	•
	•
	•

Practice the Skill

Use the steps on page 514 to synthesize information about Peru. Use these sources: the text under the heading The Regions and People of Peru and the Country Profile of Peru on page 502. Make a table like the one started above.

1. Study the information about Peru in the text as well as in the map and charts in the Country Profile. Add at least two main ideas to the first column of the table.

2. Now write details that support each main idea. You may find details that support one idea in several different sources.

3. Do the main ideas show contrasts or similarities within Peru's geographic regions? Jot down connections.

4. Your main ideas should help you write a one- or two-sentence conclusion that answers a question such as, "What have I learned about the regions of Peru?"

Apply the Skill

Use the steps you have just practiced to synthesize information about Brazil. Select information from text, maps, photographs, captions, and other sources beginning on page 494. Do not try to summarize everything you read about Brazil, but choose a major topic, such as city life.

Brasília, Brazil

Section 4

Venezuela
Oil Powers the Economy

Prepare to Read

Objectives

In this section you will

1. Find out how Venezuela was made wealthy by oil.
2. Learn how the ups and downs of oil prices affected the economy and people of Venezuela.
3. Understand how Venezuela is changing.

Taking Notes

As you read this section, look for ways that oil prices affect Venezuela. Copy the cause-and-effect chain below and record your findings in it. Add boxes as needed.

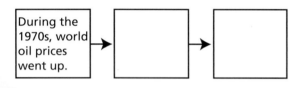

Target Reading Skill

Make Comparisons Comparing two or more situations enables you to see how they are alike. As you read this section, compare life in Venezuela before and after the oil boom. Consider the economy, the government, and the lives of ordinary people.

Key Terms

- **Caracas** (kuh RAH kus) *n.* the capital of Venezuela
- **boom** (boom) *n.* a period of business growth and prosperity
- **privatization** (pry vuh tih ZAY shun) *n.* the government's sale of land or industries it owns to private businesses or individuals
- **coup** (koo) *n.* the overthrow of a ruler or government by an organized group, which then takes power

Caracas, Venezuela

Welcome to **Caracas** (kuh RAH kus), the capital and largest city of Venezuela. The view from a high-rise apartment building can be breathtaking. At night, thousands of lights dot the surrounding hills. Steep mountains rise in the distance. Now look down at street level. During the day, well-dressed people walk to their jobs in modern office buildings. Others may be going to a museum or to one of the city's public gardens. Later, they may stroll by on their way to dinner or the theater or a concert.

Outside, the air is balmy. It is also clean. Caracas is in a valley that runs from east to west. Winds blow through it. They sweep the exhaust of the city's many cars, buses, and taxis out of Caracas. The subway system also helps by transporting many people who would otherwise have to drive.

Of course, not everyone in Caracas is wealthy and well dressed. The city—and the whole nation of Venezuela—went through a period of rapid growth and prosperity. However, much of the country's population lives in poverty. The contrast between rich and poor has led to political tensions in Venezuela.

A Land Made Wealthy by Oil

Except for the Persian Gulf region, Venezuela has the largest oil reserves in the world. The map of Venezuela in the Country Profile on page 518 shows where Venezuela's vast supplies of oil are located. Venezuela's oil has earned millions of dollars on the world market. In the 1970s, many Venezuelans migrated from the countryside to work for the oil companies. They helped maintain the giant oil rigs in Lake Maracaibo (mar uh KY boh). They also worked in oil refineries.

Both the government and private corporations own oil companies in Venezuela. They have grown rich pumping, processing, and selling oil. In the early 1980s, Venezuela was the richest country in Latin America. Much of the money went to Caracas, the economic center of Venezuela. At that time, there seemed to be no end to the money that could be made in the oil industry.

Ups and Downs of Oil Prices During the 1970s, the price of oil went up. An oil **boom** began. A **boom** is a period of business growth and prosperity. The government spent huge sums of money and hired people to run government agencies and build roads and subways. Many people moved from the countryside to the cities to take these jobs. But from the mid-1980s through the 1990s, oil exporting countries produced more oil than the world needed. The price of oil fell, and many Venezuelans lost their jobs.

This economic downturn continued through the early twenty-first century. In 2002 and 2003, thousands of Venezuelan oil workers went on strike. Oil production and exports came to a standstill. The crisis kept about 200 million barrels of oil and gasoline from the world market. Soon after, oil prices began to rise. By 2004, oil prices were at their highest point in 20 years. They continued to soar into 2006.

Graph Skills

Oil pumped in Venezuela is important not only to that country but also to the United States. **Describe** According to the graph, what is the overall pattern of American imports of Venezuelan oil? **Predict** What do you think might happen to both countries if oil production were interrupted?

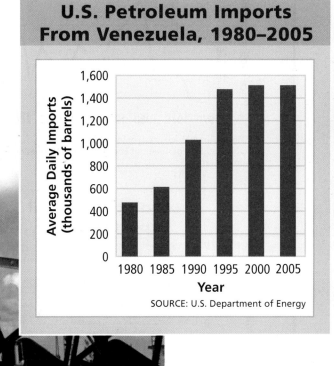

U.S. Petroleum Imports From Venezuela, 1980–2005

SOURCE: U.S. Department of Energy

Venezuela

Venezuela's economy is dominated by oil. Much of this oil lies under Lake Maracaibo, but there are also large deposits in the northeastern part of the country and near the Orinoco River. Venezuela also has large amounts of coal, iron ore, and minerals. In addition, Venezuela has large areas of rain forest that have less economic value. As you examine the map and graphs, notice where Venezuela's resources are located. Think about how resources and their location can shape a nation's economy and culture.

Venezuela: Products and Resources

KEY

- Oil field
- Gold
- Petroleum
- Coffee
- Cocoa
- Fruit
- Tropical rain forest
- Tropical savanna
- Desert scrub
- National border
- ⊛ National capital
- • Other city

Venezuela: Earnings from Exports, 2005

Other 20%
Oil 80%

SOURCE: *CIA World Factbook*

World Crude Oil Prices, 1970–2005

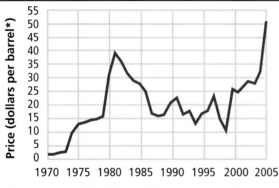

Price (dollars per barrel*)

* Figures are not adjusted for inflation.
SOURCE: U.S. Department of Energy, Energy Information Administration

Leading World Oil Exporters, 2004

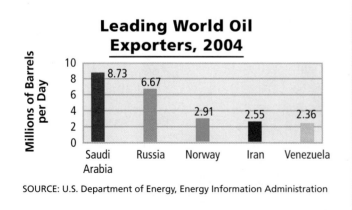

Millions of Barrels per Day

Saudi Arabia	Russia	Norway	Iran	Venezuela
8.73	6.67	2.91	2.55	2.36

SOURCE: U.S. Department of Energy, Energy Information Administration

Map and Chart Skills

1. **Describe** What is the pattern of the world price of oil from 1990 to 2005?
2. **Synthesize Information** How do two of the graphs show the importance of oil to Venezuela?
3. **Predict** In what ways could changes in the world price of oil affect Venezuela?
4. **Draw Conclusions** More than 80 percent of Venezuela's people live in cities. Use the information on the map and graphs to explain why Venezuela's cities are located in the north of the country.

Go Online PHSchool.com

Use Web Code lfe-1614 for **DK World Desk Reference Online.**

The New Poverty Despite growing prosperity from high oil prices, poverty remains a major problem in Venezuela. People who came from conditions of poverty in the countryside often moved to areas in the cities that lacked basic services, such as roads, hospitals, and permanent housing. Although the poverty rate began to decline in the early 2000s, it remained well above 30 percent in 2006.

✓ **Reading Check** **Why did many people lose their jobs in the 1980s and 1990s?**

Make Comparisons Many people moved to the cities to change their situation. How was their situation in the countryside similar to their situation after they moved to the cities?

The Economy and the People

During the oil boom, Venezuela changed from a traditional culture based on agriculture to a modern urban country. Now more than 80 percent of the population lives in cities.

Venezuelans and the Oil Economy This change can be seen in the story of Juan Varderi's family. Juan's grandfather raised sheep on a ranch east of Lake Maracaibo. He made a fairly good living selling wool and meat to people in Caracas. But Juan's father left the countryside and went to work on an oil rig that was owned by the government. By the time Juan was born, the family was living in Caracas in a small apartment. His father was making enough money for the family to have a television.

Juan loved living in the city, playing baseball in the street, and watching American television programs. "In the early 1980s, we thought we could live just like rich Americans seemed to live. We didn't understand it was only taking place on TV," Juan says. "We didn't know what was going to happen to us in just a few years."

Play Ball!
Boys enjoying a baseball game in Caracas **Infer** *Why do you think these boys are playing in this empty lot rather than on a baseball field?*

When Juan turned 15, oil prices suddenly fell. Juan's father was one of the many who lost their jobs. And like many other Venezuelan families, Juan's family was in danger of losing their apartment. Things looked bleak for those who had depended on the oil industry for their living.

Government Businesses Go Public In the late 1980s and the 1990s, the government sold some of its businesses to private corporations. **Privatization** (pry vuh tih ZAY shun) occurs when the government sells its industries to individuals or private companies. Under this policy, the government hoped the private companies would make big profits and hire more workers. The companies were able to hire many workers, but employees received less pay than they did when they worked for the government. This is what happened to Juan's father.

The Role of Weather The economic crisis grew in 1999 when Venezuela was hit by massive floods and mudslides. In some areas, unstable shacks were swept away or buried in mud, and many people were killed or made homeless. The destruction was so great that reconstruction and resettling of the homeless went on for years.

✓ **Reading Check** How did salaries compare before and after privatization?

Disaster!
In 1999, flooding and landslides caused devastation around Caracas (left), and destroyed much of the town of Macuto (right). **Draw Conclusions** *Explain how a major disaster like this would probably affect a country's economy.*

A Change in Government

In 1998, Hugo Chavez was elected president of Venezuela on a platform to help the poor. Many of his new programs caused deep political divisions between the rich and poor, and Chavez survived many challenges to his presidency. In April 2002, he was forced out of office for two days during a failed coup attempt. A coup (koo) is the overthrow of a ruler or government by an organized group, which then takes power. In 2002 and 2003, Chavez dealt with protests to his administration and the strike that halted oil production. In August 2004, a referendum, or vote, was called to remove him from office. The referendum failed when 59 percent of voters supported Chavez.

Learn about Simón Bolívar, the liberator of Venezuela.

Supporters and Opponents Many of Chavez's supporters defended the programs that were designed to help people living in poverty. Under the programs, oil revenues began to be used to provide health care, clean water, low cost food, electricity, and other basic services to the country's poor. The government also built new schools and created literacy programs.

Chavez's critics did not agree with many of his government policies, though. They denounced the government's increased military spending and interference in business. People in the international community condemned Chavez's strict control over the media. Many of Chavez's policies damaged the relationship between Venezuela and the United States.

Some Venezuelans support Hugo Chavez (left), while others oppose his government (right).

Recent improvements Chavez faces another presidential election in December 2006. The slow upturn in the economy may help Chavez's chances in the election. Since 2003, the number of people living in poverty has gradually declined. The unemployment rate decreased from 17% in 2004 to 14% in 2005.

Because of the recent spike in oil prices, Venezuela earned $36 billion from its oil industry in 2005-triple the amount received in 1998. Today oil accounts for 80% of Venezuelan exports. Oil prices will probably continue to control Venezuela's economy for some time. Whatever the country's future is, one thing is certain. The oil boom brought Venezuela into the modern world.

✓ **Reading Check** What are some recent signs that Venezuela's economy is improving?

Section 4 Assessment

Key Terms
Review the key terms at the beginning of this section. Use each term in a sentence that explains its meaning.

Target Reading Skills
How were the effects of the fall of oil prices in the 1980s similar to the effects of the torrential rainstorms of 1999?

Comprehension and Critical Thinking
1. (a) Describe How did the government of Venezuela react to the oil boom?

(b) Draw Conclusions Why did the drop in oil prices affect Venezuela so much?

2. (a) Recall What brought many people from the countryside to the cities in the 1970s?

(b) Identify Effects How did the oil boom and then privatization affect oil workers?

3. (a) Sequence How did Hugo Chavez gain power?

(b) Infer Why do you think that most Venezuelans supported Chavez in the 2004 referendum?

Writing Activity
Juan Varderi learned about American families from television programs. Write the first scene of a television script about a Venezuelan family. First choose a time and place for your program, such as the 1970s in Caracas or today in the countryside. Then think about how a family would live in that setting.

> **Writing Tip** List the setting and characters first. Then use the correct form to write dialogue and stage directions.

Review and Assessment

◆ Chapter Summary

Section 1: Brazil

- The geography of Brazil includes rain forests, plateaus, and savannas.
- Rain forests are important to Brazil and affect the whole world, but they face many dangers.
- Most Brazilians live in cities along the coast, but some live on farms and in the rain forest.

Section 2: Peru

- Most Peruvians live in the modern cities of the coastal plain.
- Many Native Americans still lead traditional lives in the mountain and forest regions.
- Old and new ways of life exist side by side in the Altiplano, the high plateau in the Andes Mountains.

Section 3: Chile

- The regions of Chile have distinct types of climate and geography, and people live very differently in each region.
- Although most of Chile's people live in cities, agriculture is very important to Chile's economy.
- Chileans voted out a dictator and replaced his brutal regime with a democratic government.

Section 4: Venezuela

- Oil production made Venezuela rich.
- A decrease in oil prices caused problems for Venezuela's economy and for ordinary people.
- Venezuela's president, Hugo Chavez, has worked against poverty and supported many controversial policies.

Brazil

◆ Key Terms

Define each of the following terms.

1. Altiplano
2. sierra
3. oasis
4. boom
5. savanna
6. coup
7. canopy
8. Brasília
9. circumnavigate
10. privatization
11. Caracas
12. glacier
13. Rio de Janeiro
14. Amazon rain forest

Review and Assessment (continued)

◆ Comprehension and Critical Thinking

15. (a) Describe What are the characteristics of a rain forest?
(b) Apply Information Why is the Amazon rain forest important even to countries far from Brazil?

16. (a) Identify Where do most of Brazil's people live?
(b) Identify Causes Why did the Brazilian government want people to move to the interior of the country?
(c) Analyze Why do you think Brazil's population is distributed the way it is?

17. (a) Identify Describe the three geographical regions of Peru.
(b) Predict How do you think the coming of modern conveniences such as electricity will change life for the indigenous people of Peru? Explain.

18. (a) Summarize Describe Magellan's discovery of the strait that bears his name.
(b) Identify Effects How does Chile's geography contribute to both its pollution problem and its agricultural boom?
(c) Infer How might the fact that Chile is so long and narrow affect Chilean society?

19. (a) Describe How did Venezuela grow rich from oil?
(b) Contrast In what ways have Chile's and Venezuela's economic histories been different?

◆ Skills Practice

Synthesizing Information In the Skills for Life activity in this chapter, you learned how to synthesize information from many sources. You also learned how to use what you found out to draw a conclusion about a particular topic.

Review the steps you followed to learn the skill. Then use those steps to synthesize information about Venezuela's economy from different sources within Section 4. Finally, draw a conclusion that pulls together what you learned.

◆ Writing Activity: Science

Suppose you are a science reporter for a local television station in Santiago, Chile. Santiago has been experiencing a week of very bad smog. Write a report explaining why the smog is so bad this week and suggesting how people might protect themselves from the pollution. Make sure your report can be read in two to three minutes.

MAP✦MASTER™
Skills Activity

South America

Place Location For each place listed below, write the letter from the map that shows its location.

1. Peru
2. Brasília
3. Chile
4. Lake Titicaca
5. Tierra del Fuego
6. Venezuela
7. Rio de Janeiro

Go Online
PHSchool.com Use Web Code **lfp-1301** for an **interactive map**.

Standardized Test Prep

Test-Taking Tips

Some questions on standardized tests ask you to analyze a reading selection to find the main ideas. Read the passage below. Then follow the tips to answer the sample question.

> Brazil is a major world coffee grower. Brazil's farms and plantations also grow soybeans, wheat, rice, corn, sugar cane, cacao, oranges, and lemons. The country's factories make many goods. Cars, iron, steel, shoes, textiles, and electrical equipment are all important industries.

This paragraph concerns which basic economic question?

- **A** What goods does Brazil produce?
- **B** What services does Brazil produce?
- **C** How are goods and services produced in Brazil?
- **D** Who will buy these goods and services?

TIP Read the whole passage to understand the main idea. Notice that it lists two kinds of goods from Brazil, those that grow and those made in factories.

Think It Through Notice that three of the answers contain the word *produce* or *produced*. You know that the main idea of the paragraph is that Brazil produces two kinds of goods—crops grown on farms and goods made in factories. The passage does not describe how the goods are produced (answer C) or who buys them (answer D). There is nothing in the paragraph about services (answer B). Therefore the answer is A.

TIP Look for key words in the passage and in the answer choices to help you answer the question. *Grow* and *make* both mean "produce."

Practice Questions

Choose the letter of the best answer.

1. Chilean produce has a large market in the United States from October through May because
   - **A** Americans eat more produce over the winter.
   - **B** less produce is grown in the United States during the winter than in the summer.
   - **C** Chileans do not consume as much of their own produce during those months.
   - **D** it is easiest to transport goods during those months.

2. What caused Venezuela's oil industry to decline in the mid-1980s?
   - **A** The oil fields began to dry up.
   - **B** People weren't driving cars as much.
   - **C** The country began to focus on steel production.
   - **D** World oil prices fell.

Read the passage below and answer the question that follows.

Peru has three distinct geographic regions: the cold, mountainous sierra; the dry coastal plain; and the warm, forested selva. The ways people live in these regions are very different. For example, many people on the coastal plain live in cities, while most people in the sierra live in small villages.

3. Which statement best expresses the main idea of the passage?
   - **A** Peru's geography is varied.
   - **B** Peru's sierra is mountainous and cold.
   - **C** Peru's geography affects the lives of its people.
   - **D** There are no cities in Peru's sierra region.

Go Online
PHSchool.com
Use Web Code **lfa-1601**
for a **Chapter 16 self-test.**

Projects

Create your own projects to learn more about Latin America. At the beginning of this section, you were introduced to the **Guiding Questions** for studying the chapters and special features. But you can also find answers to these questions by doing projects on your own or with a group. Use the questions to find topics you want to explore further. Then try the projects described on this page or create your own.

1 **Geography** What are the main physical features of Latin America?

2 **History** How has Latin America been shaped by its history?

3 **Culture** What factors have affected cultures in Latin America?

4 **Government** What types of government have existed in Latin America?

5 **Economics** How has geography influenced the ways in which Latin Americans make a living?

Project

CREATE A CLASS BULLETIN BOARD

Latin America in the News
As you read about Latin America, keep a class bulletin board display called Latin America in the News. Look in magazines and newspapers for articles about Latin American culture and current events. Print out articles from reliable online news sources. Choose a time, such as once a week, for the class to review and discuss the articles. You might have several students present the information to the class as a radio or television news report.

Project

RESEARCH LATIN AMERICAN MUSIC

A Latin American Concert
As you study Latin America, find out about the music of each region. Research the kinds of instruments people play and what they are made of. Learn how history and geography influenced the development of different kinds of music. Did you know, for example, that people in the Andes make a kind of rattle out of the hooves of llamas? That reggae developed as political protest? Find some examples of recorded Latin American music in the library, play them for your class, and report on what you learned about the music.

Reference

Table of Contents

Atlas **530**

The World: Political 530

The World: Physical 532

North and South America: Political 534

North and South America: Physical 535

United States: Political 536

Europe: Political 538

Europe: Physical 539

Africa: Political 540

Africa: Physical 541

Asia: Political 542

Asia: Physical 543

Oceania 544

The Arctic 545

Antarctica 545

Country Databank **546**

Glossary of Geographic Terms **554**

Gazetteer **556**

Glossary **562**

Index **576**

Acknowledgments **605**

The World: Political

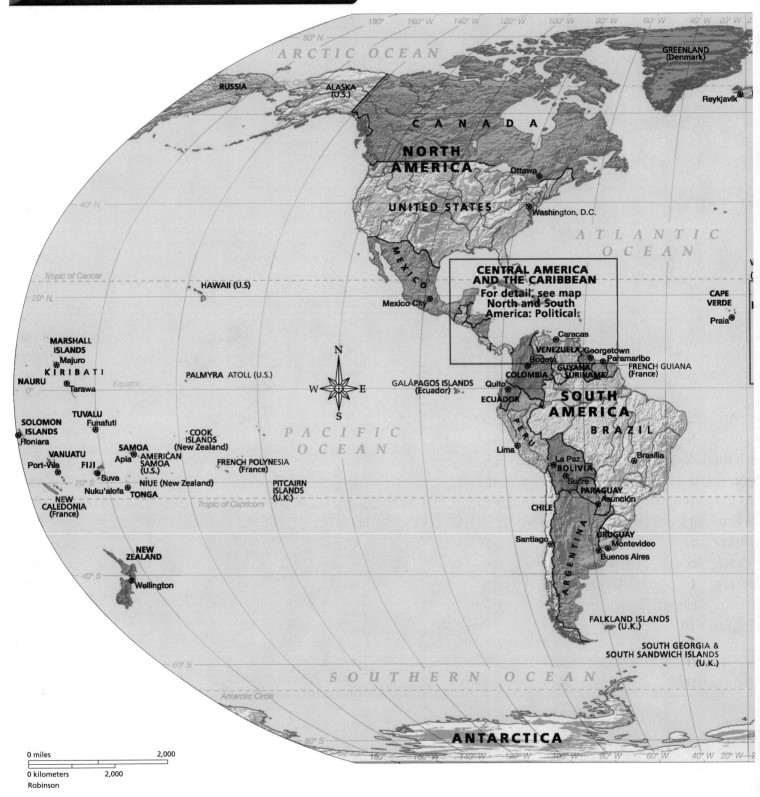

ARCTIC OCEAN

RUSSIA

ALASKA (U.S.)

GREENLAND (Denmark)

Reykjavík

C A N A D A

NORTH AMERICA

UNITED STATES

Ottawa

Washington, D.C.

ATLANTIC OCEAN

Tropic of Cancer

HAWAII (U.S)

M E X I C O

Mexico City

CENTRAL AMERICA AND THE CARIBBEAN

For detail, see map North and South America: Political.

CAPE VERDE

Praia

MARSHALL ISLANDS

Majuro

K I R I B A T I

Caracas

VENEZUELA Georgetown

Bogotá Paramaribo

COLOMBIA GUYANA SURINAME FRENCH GUIANA (France)

NAURU

Tarawa

Equator

PALMYRA ATOLL (U.S.)

GALÁPAGOS ISLANDS (Ecuador)

Quito

ECUADOR

SOUTH AMERICA

BRAZIL

TUVALU

SOLOMON ISLANDS

Honiara

Funafuti

COOK ISLANDS (New Zealand)

PACIFIC OCEAN

PERU

Lima

La Paz

BOLIVIA

Brasília

VANUATU

Port-Vila FIJI

Suva

SAMOA

Apia AMERICAN SAMOA (U.S.)

NIUE (New Zealand)

Nuku'alofa TONGA

FRENCH POLYNESIA (France)

PITCAIRN ISLANDS (U.K.)

Tropic of Capricorn

Sucre

PARAGUAY

Asunción

CHILE

NEW CALEDONIA (France)

NEW ZEALAND

Wellington

Santiago

URUGUAY

Montevideo

Buenos Aires

A R G E N T I N A

FALKLAND ISLANDS (U.K.)

SOUTH GEORGIA & SOUTH SANDWICH ISLANDS (U.K.)

S O U T H E R N   O C E A N

Antarctic Circle

ANTARCTICA

0 miles 2,000

0 kilometers 2,000

Robinson

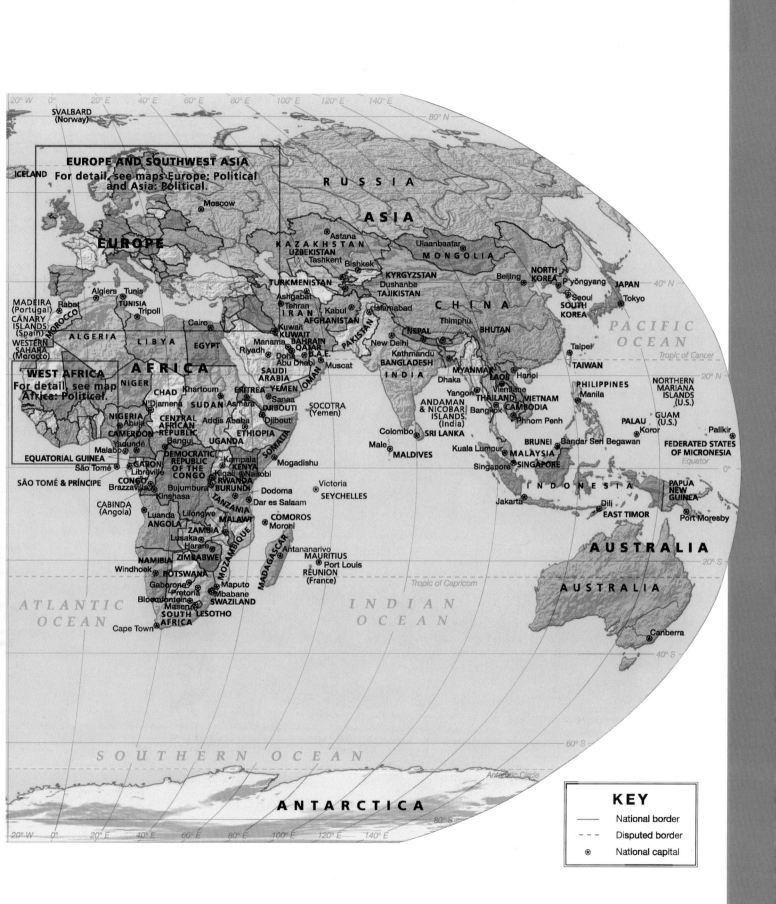

SVALBARD
(Norway)

ICELAND

EUROPE AND SOUTHWEST ASIA
For detail, see maps Europe: Political
and Asia: Political.

Moscow

EUROPE

RUSSIA

ASIA

Astana
KAZAKHSTAN
UZBEKISTAN
Tashkent   Bishkek

MONGOLIA

Ulaanbaatar

Beijing

NORTH
KOREA
P'yŏngyang   JAPAN

PACIFIC
OCEAN

Tropic of Cancer

Algiers Tunis
MADEIRA
(Portugal) Rabat
CANARY
ISLANDS
(Spain)
WESTERN
SAHARA
(Morocco)

TUNISIA
Tripoli

MOROCCO

ALGERIA

LIBYA

EGYPT

TURKMENISTAN
Ashgabat
IRAN
Tehran

KYRGYZSTAN
Dushanbe
TAJIKISTAN
Kabul
AFGHANISTAN
Islamabad

CHINA

Thimphu   BHUTAN

Seoul
SOUTH
KOREA
Tokyo

40° N

Cairo

Kuwait
KUWAIT
Manama BAHRAIN
Riyadh   QATAR
Doha   U.A.E.
Abu Dhabi   Muscat

NEPAL
New Delhi
Kathmandu
BANGLADESH
INDIA
Dhaka

MYANMAR
Yangon
THAILAND
Bangkok

Hanoi
LAOS
Vientiane
VIETNAM
CAMBODIA

Taipei

TAIWAN

Manila
PHILIPPINES

NORTHERN
MARIANA
ISLANDS
(U.S.)

20° N

WEST AFRICA
For detail, see map
Africa: Political.

NIGER

AFRICA

CHAD
N'Djamena

Khartoum
SUDAN
Ashara

ERITREA
YEMEN
Sanaa

Addis Ababa
DJIBOUTI
Djibouti

OMAN
SAUDI
ARABIA

SOCOTRA
(Yemen)

Phnom Penh

PALAU

GUAM
(U.S.)
Koror

Palikir

Colombo
SRI LANKA

ANDAMAN
& NICOBAR
ISLANDS
(India)

BRUNEI   Bandar Seri Begawan

FEDERATED STATES
OF MICRONESIA

NIGERIA
Abuja
CAMEROON
Yaoundé

CENTRAL
AFRICAN
REPUBLIC
Bangui

UGANDA

ETHIOPIA

SOMALIA

Male
MALDIVES

Kuala Lumpur
MALAYSIA
Singapore   SINGAPORE

Equator

EQUATORIAL GUINEA
Malabo
São Tomé
SÃO TOMÉ & PRÍNCIPE

GABON
Libreville
CONGO
Brazzaville
Kinshasa

DEMOCRATIC
REPUBLIC
OF THE
CONGO

Kampala   KENYA
Kigali   Nairobi
RWANDA
Bujumbura   BURUNDI
Dodoma

Mogadishu

Victoria
SEYCHELLES

Jakarta

INDONESIA

Dili
EAST TIMOR

PAPUA
NEW
GUINEA
Port Moresby

0°

CABINDA
(Angola)

TANZANIA
Dar es Salaam

AUSTRALIA

Luanda
ANGOLA

Lilongwe
MALAWI
ZAMBIA
Lusaka

COMOROS
Moroni

AUSTRALIA

20° S

NAMIBIA
Windhoek
BOTSWANA

Harare
ZIMBABWE

MOZAMBIQUE

MADAGASCAR

Antananarivo
MAURITIUS
Port Louis
RÉUNION
(France)

Tropic of Capricorn

INDIAN
OCEAN

ATLANTIC
OCEAN

Gaborone
Pretoria
Bloemfontein   Mbabane
Maseru   SWAZILAND
SOUTH   LESOTHO
AFRICA
Cape Town

Maputo

Canberra

40° S

SOUTHERN   OCEAN

Antarctic Circle

ANTARCTICA

20° W   0°   20° E   40° E   60° E   80° E   100° E   120° E   140° E

80° S

KEY

─────   National border
- - - -   Disputed border
⊛   National capital

The World: Physical

0 miles 2,000
0 kilometers 2,000
Robinson

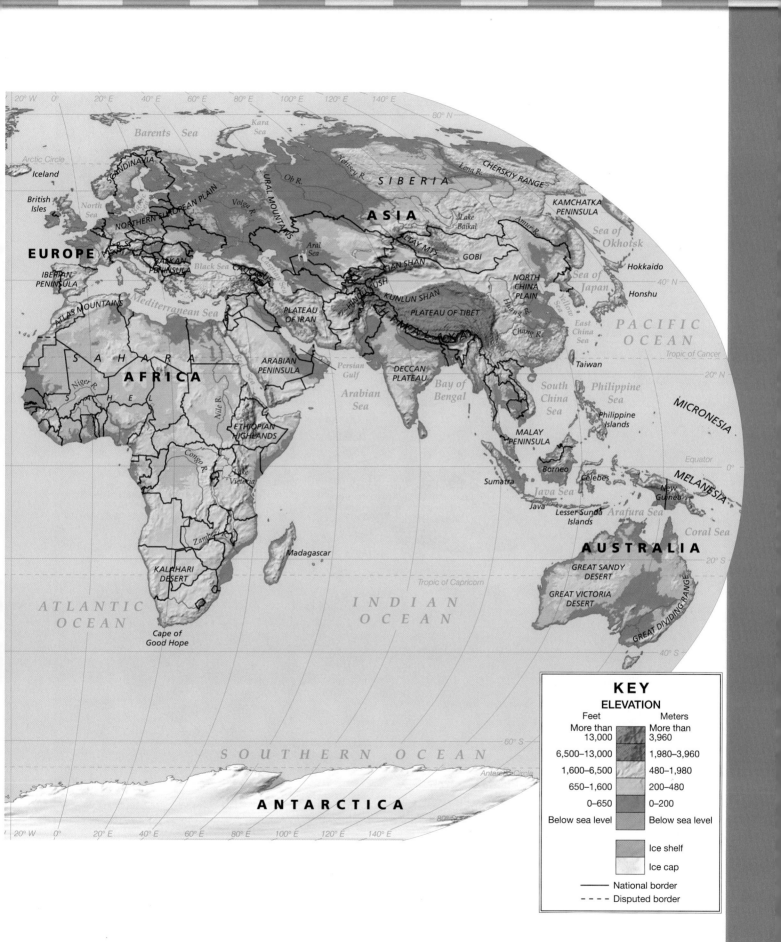

Barents Sea

Kara Sea

Arctic Circle

Iceland

British Isles

North Sea

SCANDINAVIA

NORTHERN EUROPEAN PLAIN

URAL MOUNTAINS

Volga R.

Ob R.

Yenisey R.

SIBERIA

Lena R.

CHERSKIY RANGE

KAMCHATKA PENINSULA

80° N

EUROPE

ASIA

ALTAY MTS

Lake Baikal

Amur R.

Sea of Okhotsk

Hokkaido

40° N

IBERIAN PENINSULA

BALKAN PENINSULA

Black Sea

CAUCASUS MTS

Caspian Sea

Aral Sea

TIAN SHAN

GOBI

NORTH CHINA PLAIN

Sea of Japan

Honshu

ATLAS MOUNTAINS

Mediterranean Sea

PLATEAU OF IRAN

HINDU KUSH

KUNLUN SHAN

PLATEAU OF TIBET

Huang R.

Yellow Sea

East China Sea

PACIFIC OCEAN

SAHARA

Red Sea

ARABIAN PENINSULA

Persian Gulf

HIMALAYA

Chang R.

Tropic of Cancer

AFRICA

Niger R.

SAHEL

Nile R.

DECCAN PLATEAU

Arabian Sea

Bay of Bengal

Taiwan

20° N

South China Sea

Philippine Sea

MICRONESIA

ETHIOPIAN HIGHLANDS

Philippine Islands

Congo R.

Lake Victoria

MALAY PENINSULA

Sumatra

Borneo

Celebes

Equator

MELANESIA

Java Sea

New Guinea

Zambezi

Java

Lesser Sunda Islands

Arafura Sea

Coral Sea

Madagascar

AUSTRALIA

KALAHARI DESERT

GREAT SANDY DESERT

20° S

ATLANTIC OCEAN

INDIAN OCEAN

Tropic of Capricorn

GREAT VICTORIA DESERT

GREAT DIVIDING RANGE

Cape of Good Hope

40° S

60° S

SOUTHERN OCEAN

Antarctic Circle

ANTARCTICA

80° S

20° W   0°   20° E   40° E   60° E   80° E   100° E   120° E   140° E

KEY

ELEVATION

Feet		Meters
More than 13,000		More than 3,960
6,500–13,000		1,980–3,960
1,600–6,500		480–1,980
650–1,600		200–480
0–650		0–200
Below sea level		Below sea level

Ice shelf

Ice cap

——— National border

– – – Disputed border

North and South America: Political

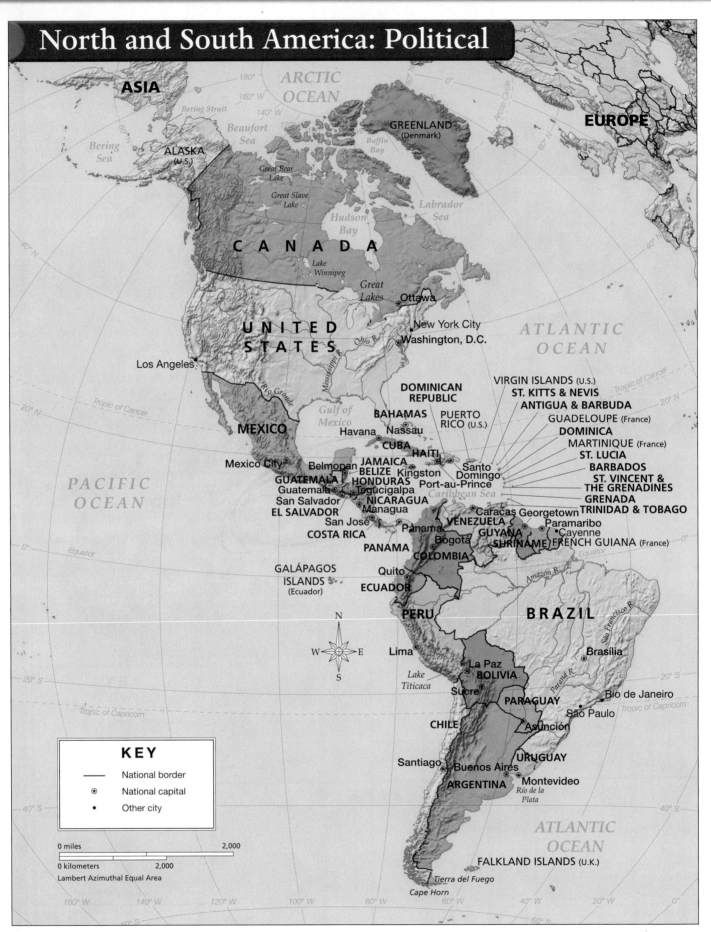

ASIA

ARCTIC OCEAN

EUROPE

Bering Strait

Bering Sea

GREENLAND (Denmark)

ALASKA (U.S.)

Beaufort Sea

Baffin Bay

Great Bear Lake

Great Slave Lake

Labrador Sea

Hudson Bay

C A N A D A

Lake Winnipeg

Great Lakes

Ottawa

U N I T E D S T A T E S

Ohio R.

New York City

Washington, D.C.

ATLANTIC OCEAN

Los Angeles

Rio Grande

Mississippi R.

Tropic of Cancer

VIRGIN ISLANDS (U.S.)

ST. KITTS & NEVIS

ANTIGUA & BARBUDA

DOMINICAN REPUBLIC

GUADELOUPE (France)

BAHAMAS

PUERTO RICO (U.S.)

DOMINICA

MEXICO

Gulf of Mexico

Havana   Nassau

MARTINIQUE (France)

ST. LUCIA

CUBA

HAITI

Mexico City

Belmopan

JAMAICA

Kingston

BARBADOS

ST. VINCENT & THE GRENADINES

GRENADA

PACIFIC OCEAN

GUATEMALA

BELIZE

HONDURAS

Santo Domingo

Guatemala

Tegucigalpa

Port-au-Prince

Caribbean Sea

San Salvador

NICARAGUA

TRINIDAD & TOBAGO

EL SALVADOR

Managua

San José

Panama

VENEZUELA

GUYANA

Georgetown

Paramaribo

COSTA RICA

Bogotá

SURINAME

Cayenne

FRENCH GUIANA (France)

PANAMA

COLOMBIA

Equator

GALÁPAGOS ISLANDS (Ecuador)

Quito

ECUADOR

Amazon R.

Equator

B R A Z I L

São Francisco R.

PERU

Lima

Brasília

N

W   E

S

Lake Titicaca

La Paz

BOLIVIA

Sucre

Paraná R.

Rio de Janeiro

São Paulo

Tropic of Capricorn

PARAGUAY

CHILE

Asunción

URUGUAY

Santiago

Buenos Aires

Montevideo

ARGENTINA

Río de la Plata

KEY

——— National border

⊛ National capital

• Other city

0 miles   2,000

0 kilometers   2,000

Lambert Azimuthal Equal Area

ATLANTIC OCEAN

FALKLAND ISLANDS (U.K.)

Tierra del Fuego

Cape Horn

North and South America: Physical

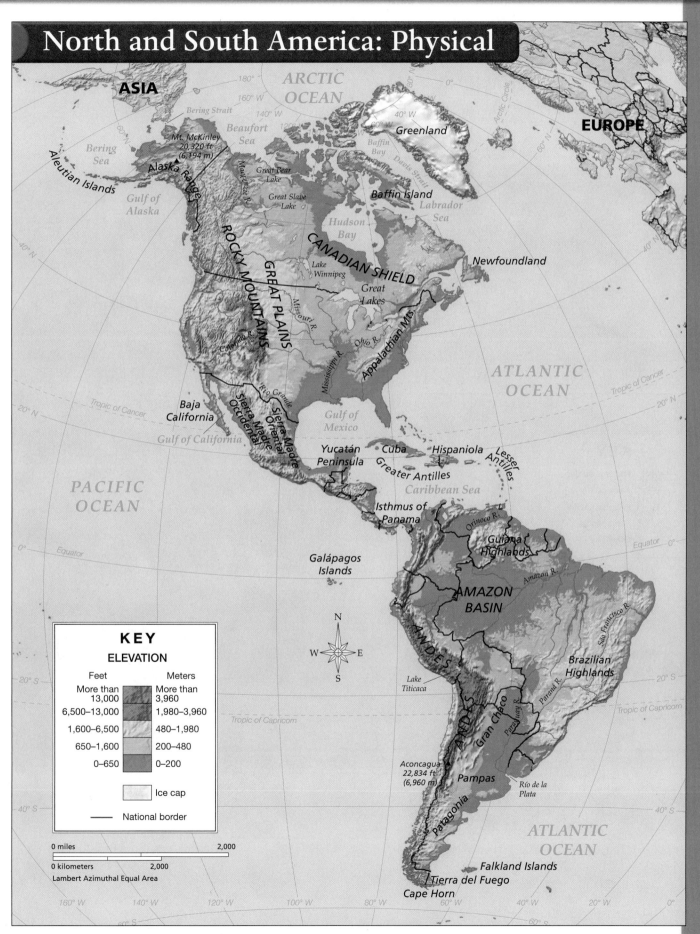

ASIA

ARCTIC OCEAN

EUROPE

Bering Strait

Beaufort Sea

Bering Sea

Mt. McKinley
20,320 ft
(6,194 m)

Alaska Range

Greenland

Aleutian Islands

Gulf of Alaska

Great Bear Lake

Great Slave Lake

Mackenzie R.

Baffin Bay

Davis Strait

Baffin Island

Labrador Sea

ROCKY MOUNTAINS

Hudson Bay

CANADIAN SHIELD

Lake Winnipeg

Great Lakes

Newfoundland

GREAT PLAINS

Missouri R.

Colorado R.

Mississippi R.

Ohio R.

Appalachian Mts.

ATLANTIC OCEAN

Tropic of Cancer

Baja California

Rio Grande

Sierra Madre Occidental

Sierra Madre Oriental

Gulf of California

Gulf of Mexico

Yucatán Peninsula

Cuba

Hispaniola

Greater Antilles

Lesser Antilles

Tropic of Cancer

20° N

PACIFIC OCEAN

Caribbean Sea

Isthmus of Panama

Orinoco R.

Galápagos Islands

Equator

Guiana Highlands

AMAZON BASIN

Amazon R.

ANDES

São Francisco R.

Equator

N
W E
S

Brazilian Highlands

Lake Titicaca

20° S

Tropic of Capricorn

Paraná R.

Gran Chaco

Paraguay R.

Aconcagua
22,834 ft
(6,960 m)

Pampas

Río de la Plata

Tropic of Capricorn

20° S

KEY

ELEVATION

Feet	Meters
More than 13,000	More than 3,960
6,500–13,000	1,980–3,960
1,600–6,500	480–1,980
650–1,600	200–480
0–650	0–200

Ice cap

National border

0 miles 2,000

0 kilometers 2,000

Lambert Azimuthal Equal Area

Patagonia

ATLANTIC OCEAN

Falkland Islands

Tierra del Fuego

Cape Horn

United States: Political

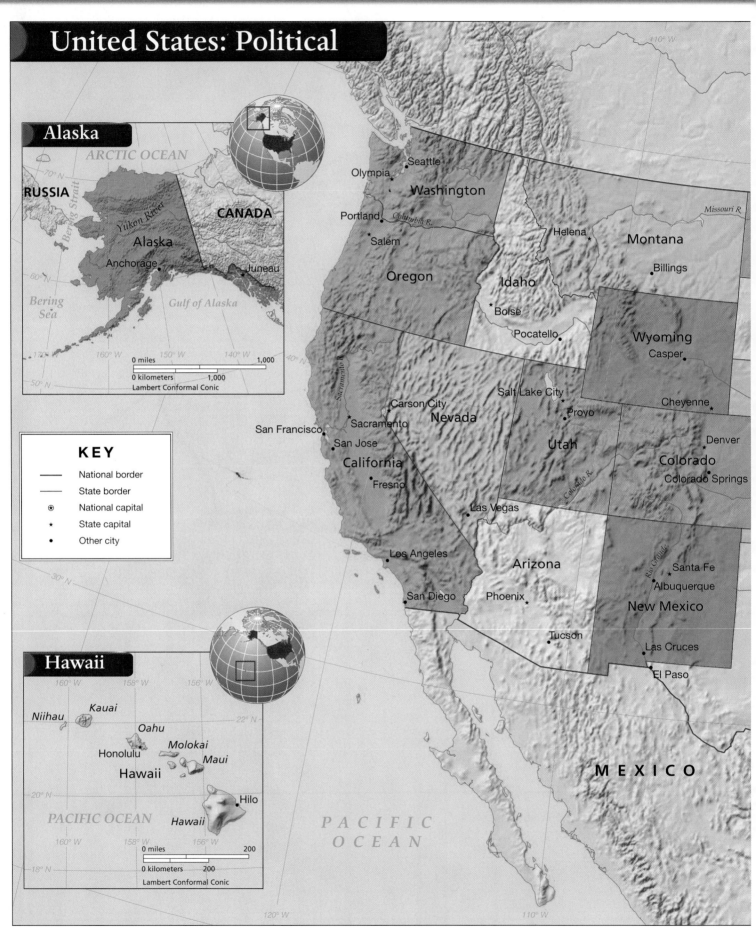

Alaska

ARCTIC OCEAN

RUSSIA

CANADA

Yukon River

Alaska

Anchorage

Juneau

Bering Sea

Gulf of Alaska

70° N

60° N

50° N

170° W   160° W   150° W   140° W

0 miles   1,000
0 kilometers   1,000
Lambert Conformal Conic

KEY

——— National border

——— State border

⊛ National capital

★ State capital

• Other city

Hawaii

Niihau   Kauai

Oahu   Molokai   Maui

Honolulu   Hawaii

22° N

20° N

18° N

PACIFIC OCEAN   Hawaii   Hilo

160° W   158° W   156° W

0 miles   200
0 kilometers   200
Lambert Conformal Conic

Seattle
Olympia
Washington
Portland   Columbia R.
Salem
Oregon
Idaho
Boise
Pocatello
Helena
Montana
Billings
Missouri R.
Wyoming
Casper
Cheyenne
Salt Lake City
Provo
Utah
Denver
Colorado
Colorado Springs
Carson City
Sacramento   Nevada
San Francisco
San Jose
California
Fresno
Las Vegas
Colorado R.
Los Angeles
Arizona
Santa Fe
Albuquerque
New Mexico
San Diego
Phoenix
Tucson
Las Cruces
El Paso
Rio Grande
Sacramento R.

PACIFIC OCEAN

MEXICO

40° N

30° N

120° W   110° W

CANADA

North Dakota
Bismarck ★
● Fargo

Minnesota

South Dakota
Pierre ★
● Sioux Falls

St. Paul ★
Minneapolis ●

Wisconsin

Lake Superior

Michigan

Lake Huron

Lake Ontario

Maine
Augusta ★
Montpelier ★ Portland ●
Vermont
New Hampshire
Concord ★

Albany ●
New York
Buffalo ●

Massachusetts
Boston ●
Providence ● Rhode Island
Hartford ★
Connecticut

Nebraska
Omaha ●
Lincoln ★

Iowa
Des Moines ★
Cedar Rapids ●

Milwaukee ●
Madison ★

Grand Rapids ●
Lansing ★

Detroit ●

Lake Michigan

Chicago ●

Fort Wayne ●

Illinois

Indiana
Indianapolis ★

Ohio
Columbus ★

Cleveland ●
Pittsburgh ●

Pennsylvania
Harrisburg ●

New York City

New Jersey
Trenton ★
Philadelphia ●

Baltimore ●
Washington, D.C. ●
Delaware
Dover ★
Annapolis ●
Maryland

Mississippi R.
Missouri R.

Kansas
Topeka ★
Wichita ●
Arkansas R.

Kansas City ●
Jefferson City ★
St. Louis ●

Missouri

Springfield ●

Louisville ●

Cincinnati ●
Ohio R.

Frankfort ★
Kentucky

Charleston ●
West
Virginia

Richmond ●
District of Columbia

Virginia

Norfolk ●

Oklahoma
Tulsa ●
Oklahoma City ★
Red R.

Arkansas
Fort Smith ●
Little Rock ★
Mississippi R.

Memphis ●

Nashville ●
Tennessee

Tennessee R.

Knoxville ●

North Carolina
Raleigh ★
Charlotte ●

South Carolina
Columbia ★
Charleston ●

ATLANTIC
OCEAN

Texas
Fort Worth ●
Dallas ●
Austin ★
San Antonio ●

Shreveport ●
Louisiana

Mississippi
Jackson ★

Baton Rouge ★
Gulfport ●
New Orleans ●

Birmingham ●
Alabama
Montgomery ★
Mobile ●

Atlanta ★
Georgia
Columbus ●

Savannah ●
Jacksonville ●

Tallahassee ★

Florida
Orlando ●
Tampa ●
Miami ●

Gulf of Mexico

N
W ● E
S

0 miles 250
0 kilometers 250
Lambert Azimuthal Equal Area

100° W   90° W   80° W   70° W
50° N
40° N
30° N

Europe: Political

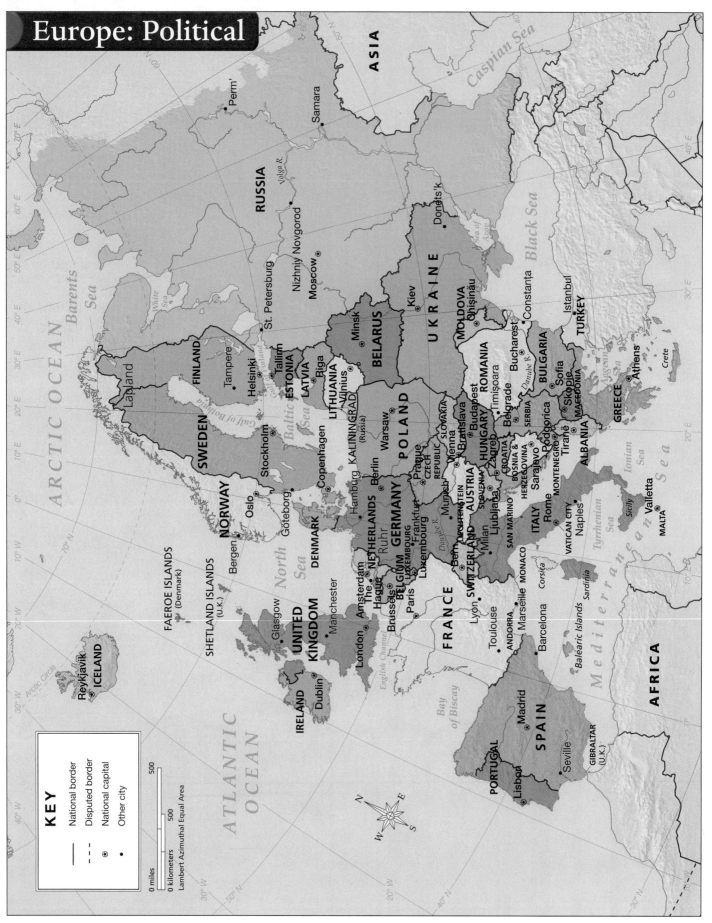

ASIA

Caspian Sea

Perm'

Samara

RUSSIA

Volga R.

Nizhniy Novgorod

Moscow ⊛

Barents Sea

White Sea

St. Petersburg ⊛

Donets'k

Sea of Azov

Black Sea

U K R A I N E

Kiev ⊛

MOLDOVA
Chişinău ⊛

Constanţa

Istanbul

TURKEY

ARCTIC OCEAN

Minsk ⊛

BELARUS

ROMANIA
Bucharest ⊛

Danube R.

Timişoara

BULGARIA
Sofia ⊛

Tampere

Helsinki ⊛
Tallinn ⊛

ESTONIA

Riga ⊛

LATVIA

Vilnius ⊛

LITHUANIA

KALININGRAD
(Russia)

Warsaw ⊛

POLAND

Belgrade ⊛

SERBIA

Skopje ⊛

MACEDONIA

Tiranë ⊛

ALBANIA

GREECE
Athens ⊛

Aegean Sea

Crete

FINLAND

Lapland

Gulf of Finland

Baltic Sea

SWEDEN

Stockholm ⊛

Copenhagen ⊛

Hamburg

Berlin ⊛

GERMANY

Prague ⊛
CZECH REPUBLIC

Vienna ⊛
SLOVAKIA
Bratislava ⊛

Budapest ⊛
HUNGARY

AUSTRIA

Zagreb ⊛
CROATIA

SLOVENIA
Ljubljana ⊛

Sarajevo ⊛
BOSNIA & HERZEGOVINA

Podgorica ⊛
MONTENEGRO

ITALY
Rome ⊛

VATICAN CITY

Naples

Tyrrhenian Sea

Valletta ⊛
MALTA

Gulf of Bothnia

NORWAY

Oslo ⊛

Göteborg

Bergen

North Sea

DENMARK

Amsterdam ⊛
The Hague ⊛
NETHERLANDS

Brussels ⊛
BELGIUM
LUXEMBOURG
Luxembourg ⊛

Frankfurt

Ruhr

Munich

LIECHTENSTEIN
Bern ⊛
SWITZERLAND

Milan

SAN MARINO

MONACO

Sardinia

Corsica

Sicily

Mediterranean Sea

FAEROE ISLANDS
(Denmark)

SHETLAND ISLANDS
(U.K.)

Glasgow

Manchester

UNITED KINGDOM

London ⊛

English Channel

Paris ⊛

FRANCE

Lyon

Danube R.

Marseille

Toulouse

ANDORRA

Barcelona

Balearic Islands

AFRICA

ATLANTIC OCEAN

Reykjavik ⊛
ICELAND

Arctic Circle

IRELAND
Dublin ⊛

Bay of Biscay

Madrid ⊛

SPAIN

Seville

PORTUGAL
Lisbon ⊛

GIBRALTAR
(U.K.)

KEY

— National border
- - - Disputed border
⊛ National capital
• Other city

0 miles   500
0 kilometers   500
Lambert Azimuthal Equal Area

N E S W

Europe: Physical

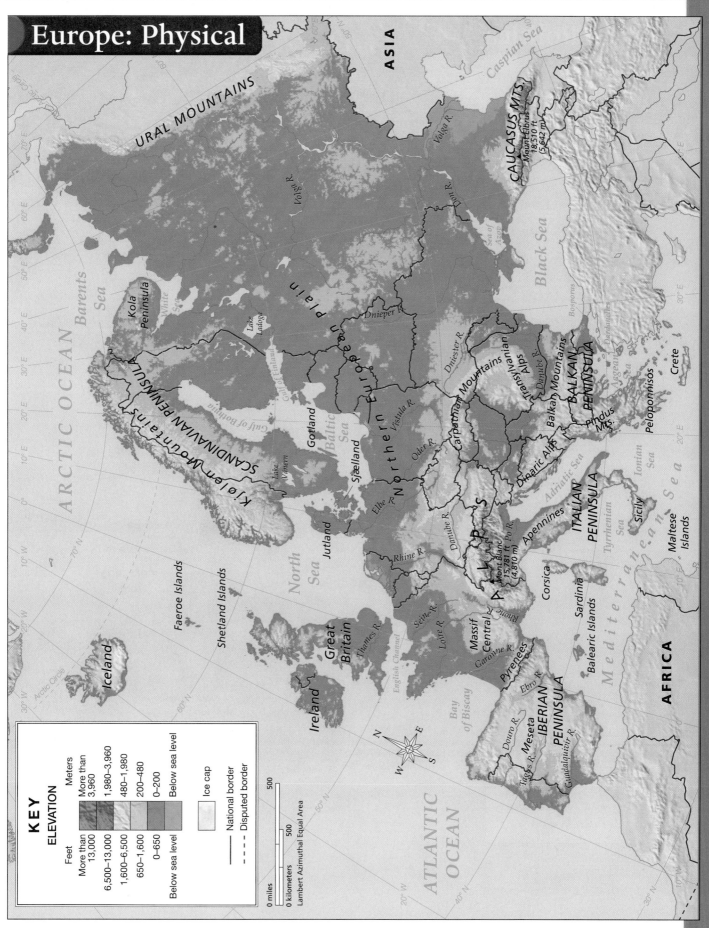

ASIA

URAL MOUNTAINS

Caspian Sea

CAUCASUS MTS.
Mount Elbrus
18,510 ft
(5,642 m)

ARCTIC OCEAN

Barents Sea

Kola Peninsula

White Sea

Lake Ladoga

Volga R.

Don R.

Sea of Azov

Black Sea

Bosporus

Northern European Plain

Dnieper R.

Dniester R.

Carpathian Mountains

Transylvanian Alps

Danube R.

Balkan Mountains

BALKAN PENINSULA

Dardanelles

Gulf of Finland

Gulf of Bothnia

Lake Vänern

Lake Vättern

Vistula R.

Oder R.

Pindus Mts.

Aegean Sea

Crete

Peloponnisos

Kjölen Mountains

SCANDINAVIAN PENINSULA

Gotland

Baltic Sea

Sjælland

Elbe R.

Dinaric Alps

Adriatic Sea

Ionian Sea

North Sea

Jutland

Rhine R.

Danube R.

A L P S

Mont Blanc
15,781 ft
(4,810 m)

Apennines

ITALIAN PENINSULA

Tyrrhenian Sea

Sicily

Maltese Islands

Mediterranean Sea

Faeroe Islands

Shetland Islands

Iceland

Arctic Circle

Ireland

Great Britain

English Channel

Thames R.

Seine R.

Loire R.

Bay of Biscay

Massif Central

Garonne R.

Pyrenees

Rhône R.

Corsica

Sardinia

Balearic Islands

Ebro R.

IBERIAN PENINSULA

Douro R.

Meseta

Tagus R.

Guadalquivir R.

ATLANTIC OCEAN

AFRICA

KEY

ELEVATION

Feet	Meters
More than 13,000	More than 3,960
6,500–13,000	1,980–3,960
1,600–6,500	480–1,980
650–1,600	200–480
0–650	0–200
Below sea level	Below sea level

Ice cap

—— National border

--- Disputed border

0 miles 500
0 kilometers 500
Lambert Azimuthal Equal Area

Africa: Political

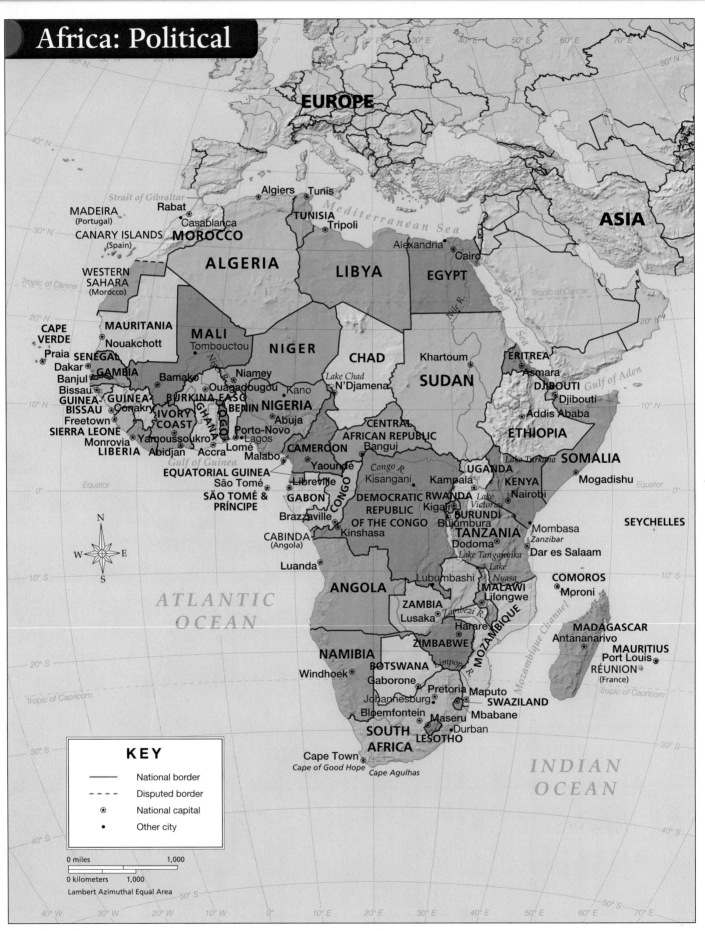

EUROPE

ASIA

Strait of Gibraltar

Mediterranean Sea

MADEIRA (Portugal)

Algiers • Tunis
Rabat •
Casablanca •
TUNISIA
Tripoli •
Alexandria •
Cairo ⊛

CANARY ISLANDS (Spain)

MOROCCO

ALGERIA

LIBYA

EGYPT

WESTERN SAHARA (Morocco)

Tropic of Cancer

Nile R.

Red Sea

Tropic of Cancer

CAPE VERDE

MAURITANIA

MALI

NIGER

CHAD

Khartoum •

ERITREA

Nouakchott ⊛
Tombouctou •
Asmara ⊛
Praia ⊛
SENEGAL
Dakar ⊛
Niamey ⊛
Lake Chad
DJIBOUTI
Gulf of Aden
GAMBIA
Bamako ⊛
N'Djamena ⊛
SUDAN
Djibouti ⊛
Banjul ⊛
Ouagadougou ⊛
Kano •
Bissau ⊛
BURKINA FASO
Addis Ababa ⊛
GUINEA-BISSAU
GUINEA
BENIN
NIGERIA
Conakry ⊛
IVORY COAST
GHANA
TOGO
Abuja ⊛
CENTRAL AFRICAN REPUBLIC
ETHIOPIA
Freetown ⊛
SIERRA LEONE
Yamoussoukro ⊛
Porto-Novo ⊛
Lagos •
Bangui ⊛
Monrovia ⊛
Lomé ⊛
LIBERIA
Abidjan •
Accra ⊛
Malabo ⊛
CAMEROON
UGANDA
SOMALIA
EQUATORIAL GUINEA
Yaoundé ⊛
Congo R.
Kisangani •
Kampala ⊛
KENYA
Mogadishu ⊛
São Tomé ⊛
Libreville ⊛
DEMOCRATIC REPUBLIC OF THE CONGO
RWANDA
Lake Victoria
Nairobi ⊛
SÃO TOMÉ & PRÍNCIPE
GABON
CONGO
Kigali ⊛
BURUNDI
SEYCHELLES
Brazzaville ⊛
Bujumbura ⊛
Mombasa •
CABINDA (Angola)
Kinshasa ⊛
TANZANIA
Zanzibar •
Dodoma ⊛
Dar es Salaam •
Luanda ⊛
Lake Tanganyika
Lake Nyasa
COMOROS
Lubumbashi •
MALAWI
Moroni ⊛
ANGOLA
Lilongwe ⊛
ZAMBIA
Zambezi R.
MOZAMBIQUE
Mozambique Channel
MADAGASCAR
Lusaka ⊛
Harare ⊛
Antananarivo ⊛
MAURITIUS
ZIMBABWE
Port Louis ⊛
NAMIBIA
BOTSWANA
Limpopo R.
RÉUNION (France)
Windhoek ⊛
Gaborone ⊛
Pretoria ⊛
Maputo ⊛
Tropic of Capricorn
Johannesburg •
SWAZILAND
Bloemfontein ⊛
Mbabane ⊛
Maseru ⊛
Durban •
SOUTH AFRICA
LESOTHO
Cape Town •
Cape of Good Hope
Cape Agulhas

Equator

Equator

ATLANTIC OCEAN

INDIAN OCEAN

N
W   E
S

KEY

——— National border

- - - Disputed border

⊛ National capital

• Other city

0 miles   1,000
0 kilometers   1,000
Lambert Azimuthal Equal Area

Africa: Physical

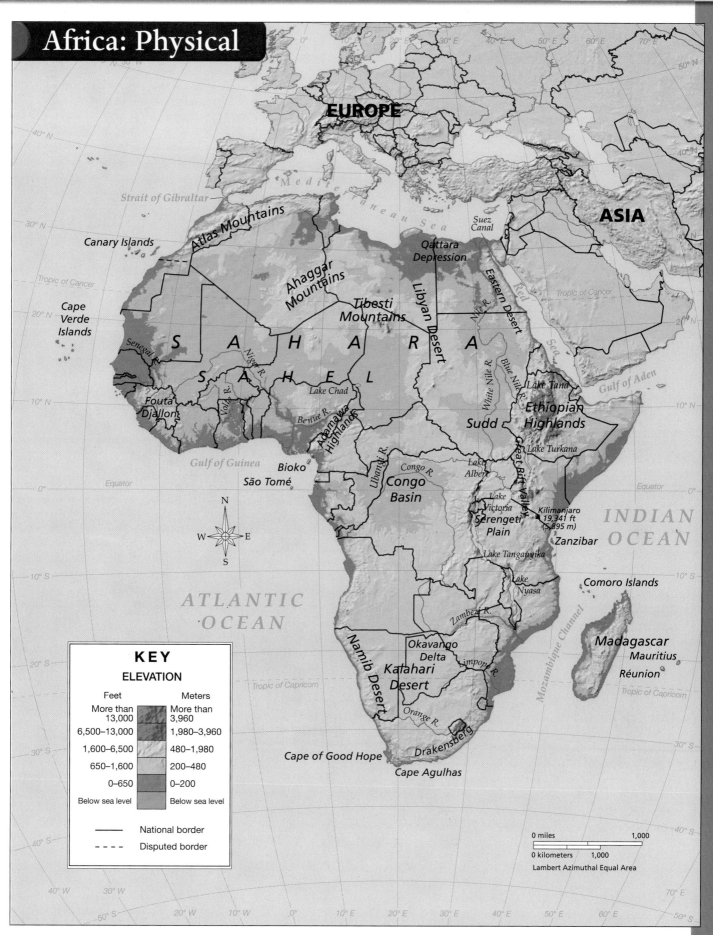

EUROPE

ASIA

Strait of Gibraltar

Mediterranean Sea

Suez Canal

Canary Islands

Atlas Mountains

Tropic of Cancer

Cape Verde Islands

Ahaggar Mountains

Qattara Depression

Tibesti Mountains

Libyan Desert

S A H A R A

Eastern Desert

Red Sea

Tropic of Cancer

Senegal R.

S A H E L

Niger R.

Lake Chad

Nile R.

Blue Nile R.

White Nile R.

Lake Tana

Gulf of Aden

Fouta Djallon

Volta R.

Benue R.

Adamawa Highlands

Ethiopian Highlands

Sudd

Gulf of Guinea

Bioko

São Tomé

Ubangi R.

Congo R.

Congo Basin

Lake Albert

Lake Turkana

Equator

Great Rift Valley

Lake Victoria

Kilimanjaro 19,341 ft (5,895 m)

Equator

Serengeti Plain

Zanzibar

INDIAN OCEAN

Lake Tanganyika

Lake Nyasa

Comoro Islands

ATLANTIC OCEAN

Zambezi R.

Namib Desert

Okavango Delta

Kalahari Desert

Limpopo R.

Madagascar

Mauritius

Réunion

Mozambique Channel

Tropic of Capricorn

Tropic of Capricorn

Orange R.

Cape of Good Hope

Drakensberg

Cape Agulhas

KEY
ELEVATION

Feet	Meters
More than 13,000	More than 3,960
6,500–13,000	1,980–3,960
1,600–6,500	480–1,980
650–1,600	200–480
0–650	0–200
Below sea level	Below sea level

——— National border

- - - - Disputed border

0 miles 1,000

0 kilometers 1,000

Lambert Azimuthal Equal Area

N W E S

Asia: Political

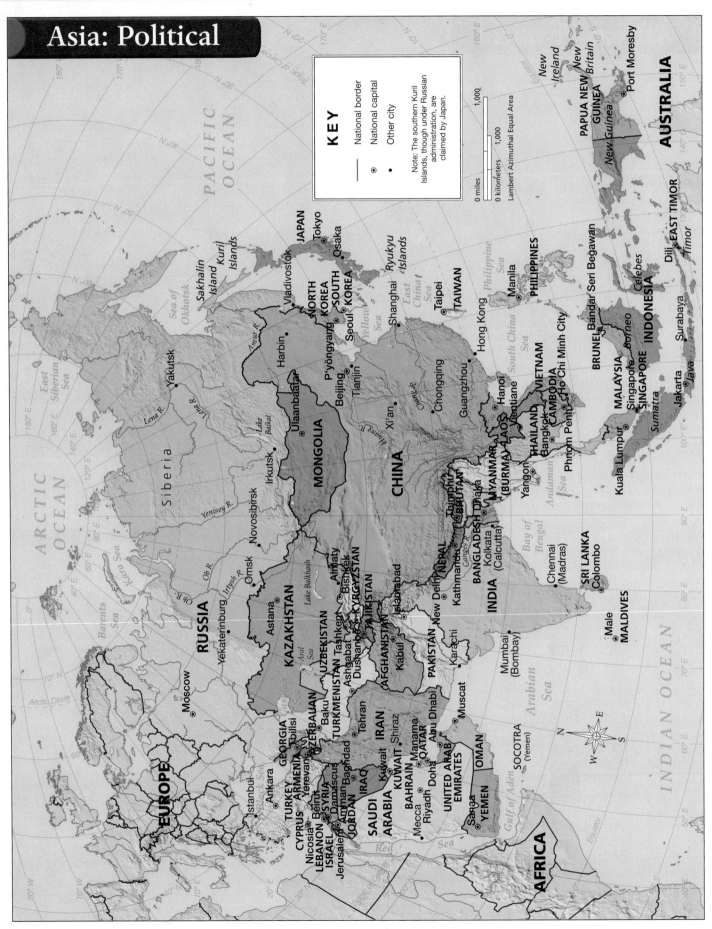

KEY

— National border
⊛ National capital
• Other city

Note: The southern Kuril Islands, though under Russian administration, are claimed by Japan.

0 miles 1,000
0 kilometers 1,000
Lambert Azimuthal Equal Area

ARCTIC OCEAN

PACIFIC OCEAN

Tropic of Cancer

East Siberian Sea

Yakutsk

Sea of Okhotsk

Sakhalin Island

Kuril Islands

JAPAN
Tokyo
Osaka

Vladivostok

NORTH KOREA
P'yŏngyang
SOUTH KOREA
Seoul

Ryukyu Islands

Shanghai

Yellow Sea

East China Sea

TAIWAN
Taipei

Hong Kong

Guangzhou

Philippine Sea

Manila

PHILIPPINES

New Ireland
New Britain
PAPUA NEW GUINEA
Port Moresby
New Guinea

AUSTRALIA

Equator

Siberia

Harbin

Amur R.

MONGOLIA
Ulaanbaatar

Lena R.

Lake Baikal

Irkutsk

Novosibirsk

Omsk

RUSSIA
Moscow

Yekaterinburg

Yenisey R.

Ob R.
Irtysh R.

Kara Sea

Barents Sea

Arctic Circle

EUROPE

Caspian Sea

Istanbul

Ankara
TURKEY
Nicosia
CYPRUS
LEBANON Beirut
ISRAEL Damascus
Jerusalem
JORDAN Amman Baghdad
IRAQ
SYRIA
GEORGIA Tbilisi
ARMENIA
Yerevan AZERBAIJAN
Baku

Tehran
IRAN
Shiraz

Kuwait
KUWAIT
BAHRAIN Manama
Riyadh Doha QATAR
Mecca
SAUDI ARABIA
Sana YEMEN
SOCOTRA (Yemen)
Abu Dhabi
UNITED ARAB EMIRATES
Muscat
OMAN

Gulf of Aden

Red Sea

Tropic of Cancer

AFRICA

CHINA

Beijing
Tiananjin

Xi'an

Chongqing

Chang R.
Huang R.

KAZAKHSTAN
Astana

Aral Sea
Lake Balkhash

Almaty
Bishkek
KYRGYZSTAN
Tashkent
UZBEKISTAN
TAJIKISTAN
Dushanbe
TURKMENISTAN
Ashgabat
AFGHANISTAN
Kabul

Islamabad

PAKISTAN

Karachi

NEPAL
Kathmandu

New Delhi

INDIA

Mumbai (Bombay)

Arabian Sea

Male
MALDIVES

BHUTAN
Thimphu
BANGLADESH
Dhaka

Kolkata (Calcutta)

Ganges R.

Bay of Bengal

Chennai (Madras)

SRI LANKA
Colombo

MYANMAR (BURMA)
Yangon

LAOS
Vientiane
THAILAND
Bangkok
CAMBODIA
Phnom Penh

VIETNAM
Hanoi
Ho Chi Minh City

South China Sea

Andaman Sea

MALAYSIA
Kuala Lumpur
Singapore
SINGAPORE
Sumatra
Borneo
BRUNEI
Bandar Seri Begawan

INDONESIA
Celebes
Java
Jakarta
Surabaya

EAST TIMOR
Dili *Timor*

INDIAN OCEAN

N
W E
S

Asia: Physical

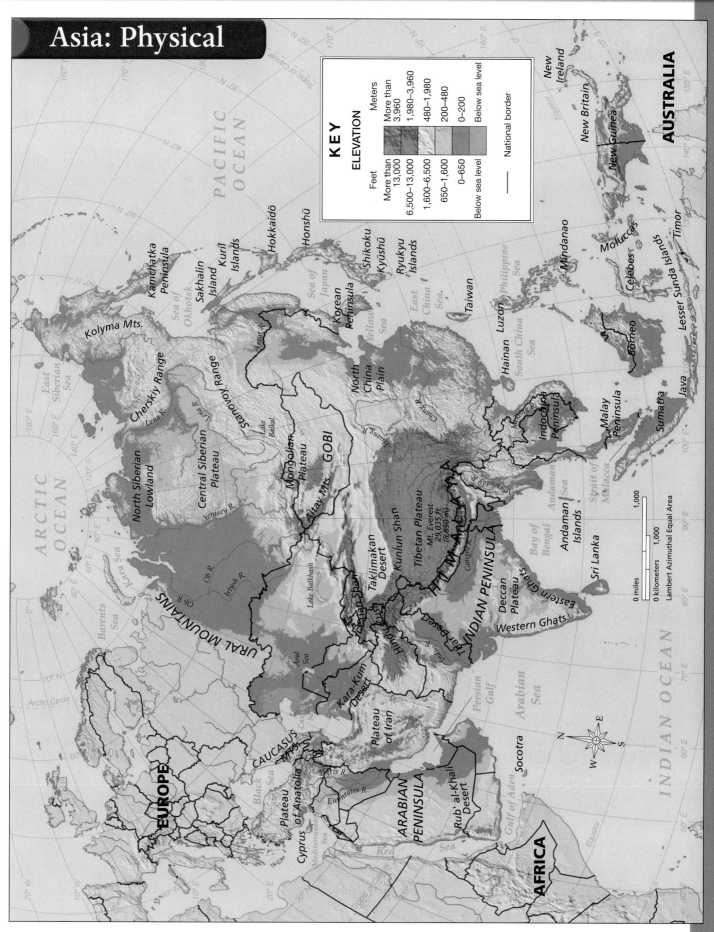

KEY

ELEVATION

Feet	Meters
More than 13,000	More than 3,960
6,500–13,000	1,980–3,960
1,600–6,500	480–1,980
650–1,600	200–480
0–650	0–200
Below sea level	Below sea level

——— National border

PACIFIC OCEAN

ARCTIC OCEAN

INDIAN OCEAN

AUSTRALIA

EUROPE

AFRICA

Kamchatka Peninsula
Sea of Okhotsk
Sakhalin Island
Kuril Islands
Hokkaidō
Honshū
Shikoku
Kyūshū
Ryukyu Islands
Sea of Japan
Korean Peninsula
Yellow Sea
East China Sea
Taiwan
Hainan
Luzon
Mindanao
Philippine Sea
South China Sea
Moluccas
Celebes
Borneo
Lesser Sunda Islands
Timor
New Ireland
New Britain
New Guinea
Java
Sumatra
Malay Peninsula
Strait of Malacca
Andaman Islands
Andaman Sea
Bay of Bengal
Sri Lanka
Eastern Ghats
Deccan Plateau
Western Ghats
INDIAN PENINSULA
HIMALAYA
Ganges R.
Thar Desert
Mt. Everest 29,035 ft (8,850 m)
Tibetan Plateau
Kunlun Shan
Taklimakan Desert
GOBI
Mongolian Plateau
Altay Mts.
Sayanskiy Range
Lake Baikal
Central Siberian Plateau
North Siberian Lowland
Kolyma Mts.
Cherskiy Range
Lena R.
Amur R.
North China Plain
Chang R.
Huang R.
Indochina Peninsula
Mekong R.
Irrawaddy R.
Tian Shan
Hindu Kush
Indus R.
Kara-Kum Desert
Aral Sea
Lake Balkhash
Ob R.
Irtysh R.
Yenisey R.
URAL MOUNTAINS
Caspian Sea
CAUCASUS MTS.
Plateau of Iran
Plateau of Anatolia
Black Sea
Cyprus
Mediterranean Sea
Tigris R.
Euphrates R.
ARABIAN PENINSULA
Rub' al-Khali Desert
Persian Gulf
Arabian Sea
Gulf of Aden
Socotra
Red Sea
Barents Sea
Kara Sea
East Siberian Sea
New Siberian Islands

0 miles 1,000
0 kilometers 1,000
Lambert Azimuthal Equal Area

N E S W

Oceania

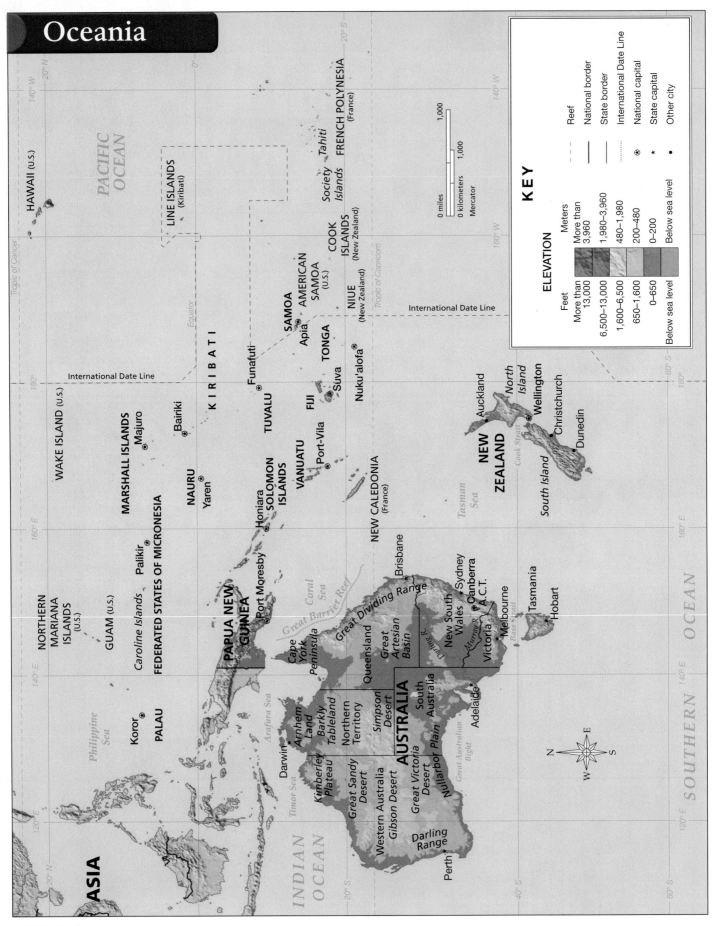

PACIFIC OCEAN

HAWAII (U.S.)

Tropic of Cancer

LINE ISLANDS (Kiribati)

WAKE ISLAND (U.S.)

MARSHALL ISLANDS
Majuro

NORTHERN MARIANA ISLANDS (U.S.)

GUAM (U.S.)

Caroline Islands   Palikir

FEDERATED STATES OF MICRONESIA

Koror
PALAU

Philippine Sea

Equator

K I R I B A T I

Bairiki

NAURU
Yaren

Funafuti
TUVALU

SAMOA
Apia   AMERICAN SAMOA (U.S.)

TONGA
Nuku'alofa

Society Islands   *Tahiti*
FRENCH POLYNESIA (France)

COOK ISLANDS (New Zealand)

NIUE (New Zealand)

Tropic of Capricorn

International Date Line

FIJI
Suva

VANUATU
Port-Vila

SOLOMON ISLANDS
Honiara

NEW CALEDONIA (France)

PAPUA NEW GUINEA
Port Moresby

Arafura Sea

Coral Sea

Great Barrier Reef

Cape York Peninsula

Darwin
Arnhem Land

Kimberley Plateau

Great Sandy Desert

Barkly Tableland

Northern Territory

Simpson Desert

Queensland

Great Artesian Basin

Great Dividing Range

Brisbane

New South Wales
Sydney
Canberra
A.C.T.

Murray R.   *Darling R.*

Melbourne
Victoria

Bass Strait

Tasmania
Hobart

Tasman Sea

NEW ZEALAND
North Island
Auckland
Wellington
Christchurch
Cook Strait
South Island
Dunedin

Western Australia
Gibson Desert

Great Victoria Desert

Nullarbor Plain

South Australia

Adelaide

Great Australian Bight

Darling Range

Perth

AUSTRALIA

INDIAN OCEAN

SOUTHERN OCEAN

International Date Line

N W E S

KEY

ELEVATION

Feet	Meters	
More than 13,000	More than 3,960	
6,500–13,000	1,980–3,960	
1,600–6,500	480–1,980	
650–1,600	200–480	
0–650	0–200	
Below sea level	Below sea level	

Reef
National border
State border
International Date Line
⊛ National capital
★ State capital
• Other city

0 miles   1,000
0 kilometers   1,000
Mercator

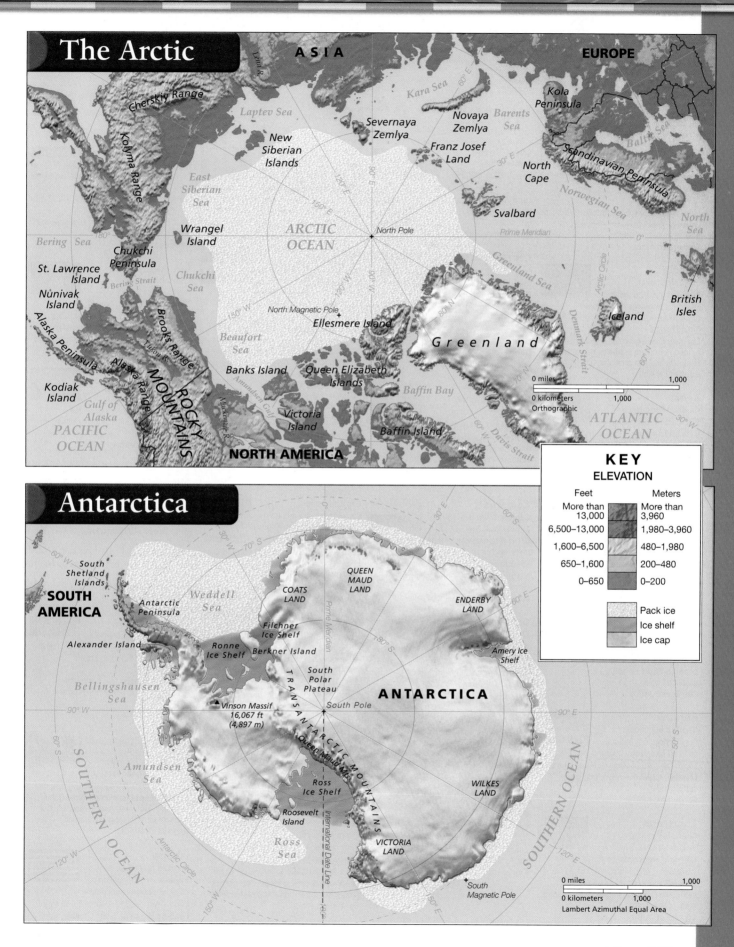

The Arctic

ASIA **EUROPE**

Cherskiy Range

Kolyma Range

Laptev Sea

Kara Sea

New Siberian Islands

Severnaya Zemlya

Novaya Zemlya

Franz Josef Land

Barents Sea

Kola Peninsula

Scandinavian Peninsula

Baltic Sea

North Cape

East Siberian Sea

ARCTIC OCEAN

North Pole

Svalbard

Norwegian Sea

Prime Meridian

Bering Sea

Wrangel Island

Chukchi Peninsula

Chukchi Sea

Greenland Sea

North Sea

St. Lawrence Island

Bering Strait

North Magnetic Pole

Arctic Circle

Iceland

British Isles

Nunivak Island

Beaufort Sea

Ellesmere Island

Denmark Strait

Alaska Peninsula

Brooks Range

Yukon R.

Greenland

Banks Island

Queen Elizabeth Islands

Baffin Bay

0 miles 1,000

Kodiak Island

ROCKY MOUNTAINS

Alaska Range

Mackenzie R.

Amundsen Gulf

Victoria Island

Baffin Island

0 kilometers 1,000

Orthographic

ATLANTIC OCEAN

Gulf of Alaska

PACIFIC OCEAN

NORTH AMERICA

Davis Strait

Antarctica

South Shetland Islands

SOUTH AMERICA

Antarctic Peninsula

Weddell Sea

COATS LAND

QUEEN MAUD LAND

ENDERBY LAND

Alexander Island

Filchner Ice Shelf

Ronne Ice Shelf

Berkner Island

Prime Meridian

Amery Ice Shelf

Bellingshausen Sea

Vinson Massif 16,067 ft (4,897 m)

TRANSANTARCTIC MOUNTAINS

South Polar Plateau

South Pole

ANTARCTICA

Queen Maud Mts.

SOUTHERN OCEAN

Amundsen Sea

Ross Ice Shelf

WILKES LAND

Roosevelt Island

International Date Line

VICTORIA LAND

Ross Sea

South Magnetic Pole

Antarctic Circle

0 miles 1,000

0 kilometers 1,000

Lambert Azimuthal Equal Area

KEY
ELEVATION

Feet		Meters
More than 13,000		More than 3,960
6,500–13,000		1,980–3,960
1,600–6,500		480–1,980
650–1,600		200–480
0–650		0–200

Pack ice

Ice shelf

Ice cap

Country Databank

Africa

Algeria

Capital: Algiers
Population: 32.3 million
Official Languages: Arabic and Tamazight
Land Area: 2,381,740 sq km; 919,590 sq mi
Leading Exports: petroleum, natural gas, petroleum products
Continent: Africa

Angola

Capital: Luanda
Population: 10.6 million
Official Language: Portuguese
Land Area: 1,246,700 sq km; 481,551 sq mi
Leading Exports: crude oil, diamonds, refined petroleum products, gas, coffee, sisal, fish and fish products, timber, cotton
Continent: Africa

Benin

Capital: Porto-Novo
Population: 6.9 million
Official Language: French
Land Area: 110,620 sq km; 42,710 sq mi
Leading Exports: cotton, crude oil, palm products, cocoa
Continent: Africa

Botswana

Capital: Gaborone
Population: 1.6 million
Official Language: English
Land Area: 585,370 sq km; 226,011 sq mi
Leading Exports: diamonds, copper, nickel, soda ash, meat, textiles
Continent: Africa

Burkina Faso

Capital: Ouagadougou
Population: 12.6 million
Official Language: French
Land Area: 273,800 sq km; 105,714 sq mi
Leading Exports: cotton, animal products, gold
Continent: Africa

Burundi

Capital: Bujumbura
Population: 6.4 million
Official Languages: Kirundi and French
Land Area: 25,650 sq km; 9,903 sq mi
Leading Exports: coffee, tea, sugar, cotton, hides
Continent: Africa

Cameroon

Capital: Yaoundé
Population: 16.1 million
Official Languages: English and French
Land Area: 469,440 sq km; 181,251 sqmi
Leading Exports: crude oil and petroleum products, lumber, cocoa, aluminum, coffee, cotton
Continent: Africa

Cape Verde

Capital: Praia
Population: 408,760
Official Language: Portuguese
Land Area: 4,033 sq km; 1,557 sq mi
Leading Exports: fuel, shoes, garments, fish, hides
Location: Atlantic Ocean

Central African Republic

Capital: Bangui
Population: 3.6 million
Official Language: French
Land Area: 622,984 sq km; 240,534 sq mi
Leading Exports: diamonds, timber, cotton, coffee, tobacco
Continent: Africa

Chad

Capital: N'Djamena
Population: 9 million
Official Languages: Arabic and French
Land Area: 1,259,200 sq km; 486,177 sq mi
Leading Exports: cotton, cattle, gum arabic
Continent: Africa

Comoros

Capital: Moroni
Population: 614,382
Official Languages: Arabic, Comoran, and French
Land Area: 2,170 sq km; 838 sq mi
Leading Exports: vanilla, ylang-ylang, cloves, perfume oil, copra
Location: Indian Ocean

Congo, Democratic Republic of the

Capital: Kinshasa
Population: 55.2 million
Official Language: French
Land Area: 2,267,600 sq km; 875,520 sq mi
Leading Exports: diamonds, copper, coffee, cobalt, crude oil
Continent: Africa

Congo, Republic of the
Capital: Brazzaville
Population: 3.3 million
Official Language: French
Land Area: 341,500 sq km; 131,853 sq mi
Leading Exports: petroleum, lumber, sugar, cocoa, coffee, diamonds
Continent: Africa

Djibouti

Capital: Djibouti
Population: 472,810
Official Languages: Arabic and French
Land Area: 22,980 sq km; 8,873 sq mi
Leading Exports: reexports, hides and skins, coffee (in transit)
Continent: Africa

Egypt
Capital: Cairo
Population: 70.7 million
Official Language: Arabic
Land Area: 995,450 sq km; 384,343 sq mi
Leading Exports: crude oil and petroleum products, cotton, textiles, metal products, chemicals
Continent: Africa

Equatorial Guinea

Capital: Malabo
Population: 498,144
Official Languages: Spanish and French
Land Area: 28,050 sq km; 10,830 sq mi
Leading Exports: petroleum, timber, cocoa
Continent: Africa

Eritrea

Capital: Asmara
Population: 4.5 million
Official Language: Tigrinya
Land Area: 121,320 sq km; 46,842 sq mi
Leading Exports: livestock, sorghum, textiles, food, small manufactured goods
Continent: Africa

Ethiopia

Capital: Addis Ababa
Population: 67.7 million
Official Language: Amharic
Land Area: 1,119,683 sq km; 432,310 sq mi
Leading Exports: coffee, qat, gold, leather products, oilseeds
Continent: Africa

Gabon
Capital: Libreville
Population: 1.2 million
Official Language: French
Land Area: 257,667 sq km; 99,489 sq mi
Leading Exports: crude oil, timber, manganese, uranium
Continent: Africa

Gambia
Capital: Banjul
Population: 1.5 million
Official Language: English
Land Area: 10,000 sq km; 3,861 sq mi
Leading Exports: peanuts and peanut products, fish, cotton lint, palm kernels
Continent: Africa

Ghana

Capital: Accra
Population: 20.2 million
Official Language: English
Land Area: 230,940 sq km; 89,166 sq mi
Leading Exports: gold, cocoa, timber, tuna, bauxite, aluminum, manganese ore, diamonds
Continent: Africa

Guinea
Capital: Conakry
Population: 7.8 million
Official Language: French
Land Area: 245,857 sq km; 94,925 sq mi
Leading Exports: bauxite, alumina, gold, diamonds, coffee, fish, agricultural products
Continent: Africa

Guinea-Bissau

Capital: Bissau
Population: 1.4 million
Official Language: Portuguese
Land Area: 28,000 sq km; 10,811 sq mi
Leading Exports: cashew nuts, shrimp, peanuts, palm kernels, lumber
Continent: Africa

Ivory Coast

Capital: Yamoussoukro
Population: 16.8 million
Official Language: French
Land Area: 318,000 sq km; 122,780 sq mi
Leading Exports: cocoa, coffee, timber, petroleum, cotton, bananas, pineapples, palm oil, cotton, fish
Continent: Africa

Kenya
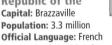
Capital: Nairobi
Population: 31.3 million
Official Languages: Swahili and English
Land Area: 569,250 sq km; 219,787 sq mi
Leading Exports: tea, horticultural products, coffee, petroleum products, fish, cement
Continent: Africa

Lesotho
Capital: Maseru
Population: 2.2 million
Official Languages: Sesotho and English
Land Area: 30,355 sq km; 11,720 sq mi
Leading Exports: manufactured goods (clothing, footwear, road vehicles), wool and mohair, food and live animals
Continent: Africa

Liberia

Capital: Monrovia
Population: 3.3 million
Official Language: English
Land Area: 96,320 sq km; 37,189 sq mi
Leading Exports: rubber, timber, iron, diamonds, cocoa, coffee
Continent: Africa

Libya

Capital: Tripoli
Population: 5.4 million
Official Language: Arabic
Land Area: 1,759,540 sq km; 679,358 sq mi
Leading Exports: crude oil, refined petroleum products
Location: Indian

Madagascar

Capital: Antananarivo
Population: 16.5 million
Official Languages: French and Malagasy
Land Area: 581,540 sq km; 224,533 sq mi
Leading Exports: coffee, vanilla, shellfish, sugar, cotton cloth, chromite, petroleum products
Location: Indian Ocean

Malawi

Capital: Lilongwe
Population: 10.7 million
Official Languages: English and Chichewa
Land Area: 94,080 sq km; 36,324 sq mi
Leading Exports: tobacco, tea, sugar, cotton, coffee, peanuts, wood products, apparel
Continent: Africa

Mali

Capital: Bamako
Population: 11.3 million
Official Language: French
Land Area: 1,220,000 sq km; 471,042 sq mi
Leading Exports: cotton, gold, livestock
Continent: Africa

Mauritania

Capital: Nouakchott
Population: 2.8 million
Official Language: Arabic
Land Area: 1,030,400 sq km; 397,837 sq mi
Leading Exports: iron ore, fish and fish products, gold
Continent: Africa

Mauritius

Capital: Port Louis
Population: 1.2 million
Official Language: English
Land Area: 2,030 sq km; 784 sq mi
Leading Exports: clothing and textiles, sugar, cut flowers, molasses
Location: Indian Ocean

Morocco

Capital: Rabat
Population: 31.2 million
Official Language: Arabic
Land Area: 446,300 sq km; 172,316 sq mi
Leading Exports: phosphates and fertilizers, food and beverages, minerals
Continent: Africa

Mozambique

Capital: Maputo
Population: 19.6 million
Official Language: Portuguese
Land Area: 784,090 sq km; 302,737 sq mi
Leading Exports: prawns, cashews, cotton, sugar, citrus, timber, bulk electricity
Continent: Africa

Namibia

Capital: Windhoek
Population: 1.8 million
Official Language: English
Land Area: 825,418 sq km; 318,694 sq mi
Leading Exports: diamonds, copper, gold, zinc, lead, uranium, cattle, processed fish, karakul skins
Continent: Africa

Niger

Capital: Niamey
Population: 11.3 million
Official Language: French
Land Area: 1,226,700 sq km; 489,073 sq mi
Leading Exports: uranium ore, livestock products, cowpeas, onions
Continent: Africa

Nigeria

Capital: Abuja
Population: 129.9 million
Official Language: English
Land Area: 910,768 sq km; 351,648 sq mi
Leading Exports: petroleum and petroleum products, cocoa, rubber
Continent: Africa

Rwanda

Capital: Kigali
Population: 7.4 million
Official Languages: Kinyarwanda, French, and English
Land Area: 24,948 sq km; 9,632 sq mi
Leading Exports: coffee, tea, hides, tin ore
Continent: Africa

São Tomé and Príncipe

Capital: São Tomé
Population: 170,372
Official Language: Portuguese
Land Area: 1,001 sq km; 386 sq mi
Leading Exports: cocoa, copra, coffee, palm oil
Location: Atlantic Ocean

Senegal

Capital: Dakar
Population: 10.6 million
Official Language: French
Land Area: 192,000 sq km; 74,131 sq mi
Leading Exports: fish, groundnuts (peanuts), petroleum products, phosphates, cotton
Continent: Africa

Seychelles

Capital: Victoria
Population: 80,098
Official Languages: English and French
Land Area: 455 sq km; 176 sq mi
Leading Exports: canned tuna, cinnamon bark, copra, petroleum products (reexports)
Location: Indian Ocean

Sierra Leone

Capital: Freetown
Population: 5.6 million
Official Language: English
Land Area: 71,620 sq km; 27,652 sq mi
Leading Exports: diamonds, rutile, cocoa, coffee, fish
Continent: Africa

Somalia

Capital: Mogadishu
Population: 7.8 million
Official Languages: Somali and Arabic
Land Area: 627,337 sq km; 242,215 sq mi
Leading Exports: livestock, bananas, hides, fish, charcoal, scrap metal
Continent: Africa

South Africa

Capital: Cape Town, Pretoria, and Bloemfontein
Population: 43.6 million
Official Languages: Eleven official languages: Afrikaans, English, Ndebele, Pedi, Sotho, Swazi, Tsonga, Tswana, Venda, Xhosa, and Zulu
Land Area: 1,219,912 sq km; 471,008 sq mi
Leading Exports: gold, diamonds, platinum, other metals and minerals, machinery and equipment
Continent: Africa

Sudan

Capital: Khartoum
Population: 37.1 million
Official Language: Arabic
Land Area: 2,376,000 sq km; 917,374 sq mi
Leading Exports: oil and petroleum products, cotton, sesame, livestock, groundnuts, gum arabic, sugar
Continent: Africa

Swaziland

Capital: Mbabane
Population: 1.1 million
Official Languages: English and siSwati
Land Area: 17,20 sq km; 6,642 sq mi
Leading Exports: soft drink concentrates, sugar, wood pulp, cotton yarn, refrigerators, citrus and canned fruit
Continent: Africa

Tanzania

Capital: Dar es Salaam and Dodoma
Population: 37.2 million
Official Languages: Swahili and English
Land Area: 886,037 sq km; 342,099 sq mi
Leading Exports: gold, coffee, cashew nuts, manufactured goods, cotton
Continent: Africa

Togo

Capital: Lomé
Population: 5.2 million
Official Language: French
Land Area: 54,385 sq km; 20,998 sq mi
Leading Exports: cotton, phosphates, coffee, cocoa
Continent: Africa

Tunisia

Capital: Tunis
Population: 9.8 million
Official Language: Arabic
Land Area: 155,360 sq km; 59,984 sq mi
Leading Exports: textiles, mechanical goods, phosphates and chemicals, agricultural products, hydrocarbons
Continent: Africa

Uganda

Capital: Kampala
Population: 24.7 million
Official Language: English
Land Area: 199,710 sq km; 77,108 sq mi
Leading Exports: coffee, fish and fish products, tea, gold, cotton, flowers, horticultural products
Continent: Africa

Zambia

Capital: Lusaka
Population: 10.1 million
Official Language: English
Land Area: 740,724 sq km; 285,994 sq mi
Leading Exports: copper, cobalt, electricity, tobacco, flowers, cotton
Continent: Africa

Zimbabwe

Capital: Harare
Population: 11.3 million
Official Language: English
Land Area: 386,670 sq km; 149,293 sq mi
Leading Exports: tobacco, gold, iron alloys, textiles and clothing
Continent: Africa

Asia and the Pacific

Afghanistan
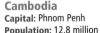
Capital: Kabul
Population: 27.8 million
Official Languages: Pashtu and Dari
Land Area: 647,500 sq km; 250,000 sq mi
Leading Exports: agricultural products, hand-woven carpets, wool, cotton, hides and pelts, precious and semiprecious gems
Continent: Asia

Armenia

Capital: Yerevan
Population: 3.3 million
Official Language: Armenian
Land Area: 29,400 sq km; 10,965 sq mi
Leading Exports: diamonds, scrap metal, machinery and equipment, brandy, copper ore
Continent: Asia

Australia

Capital: Canberra
Population: 19.6 million
Official Language: English
Land Area: 7,617,930 sq km; 2,941,283 sq mi
Leading Exports: coal, gold, meat, wool, alumina, iron ore, wheat, machinery and transport equipment
Continent: Australia

Azerbaijan

Capital: Baku
Population: 7.8 million
Official Language: Azerbaijani
Land Area: 86,100 sq km; 33,243 sq mi
Leading Exports: oil and gas, machinery, cotton, foodstuffs
Continent: Asia

Bahrain

Capital: Manama
Population: 656,397
Official Language: Arabic
Land Area: 665 sq km; 257 sq mi
Leading Exports: petroleum and petroleum products, aluminum, textiles
Continent: Asia

Bangladesh

Capital: Dhaka
Population: 133.4 million
Official Language: Bengali
Land Area: 133,910 sq km; 51,705 sq mi
Leading Exports: garments, jute and jute goods, leather, frozen fish and seafood
Continent: Asia

Bhutan

Capital: Thimphu
Population: 2.1 million
Official Language: Dzongkha
Land Area: 47,000 sq km; 18,147 sq mi
Leading Exports: electricity, cardamom, gypsum, timber, handicrafts, cement, fruit, precious stones, spices
Continent: Asia

Brunei

Capital: Bandar Seri Begawan
Population: 350,898
Official Language: Malay
Land Area: 5,270 sq km; 2,035 sq mi
Leading Exports: crude oil, natural gas, refined products
Continent: Asia

Cambodia

Capital: Phnom Penh
Population: 12.8 million
Official Language: Khmer
Land Area: 176,520 sq km; 68,154 sq mi
Leading Exports: timber, garments, rubber, rice, fish
Continent: Asia

China

Capital: Beijing
Population: 1.29 billion
Official Languages: Mandarin and Chinese
Land Area: 9,326,410 sq km; 3,600,927 sq mi
Leading Exports: machinery and equipment, textiles and clothing, footwear, toys and sports goods, mineral fuels
Continent: Asia

Cyprus

Capital: Nicosia
Population: 767,314
Official Languages: Greek and Turkish
Land Area: 9,240 sq km; 3,568 sq mi
Leading Exports: citrus, potatoes, grapes, wine, cement, clothing and shoes
Location: Mediterranean Sea

East Timor

Capital: Dili
Population: 952,618
Official Languages: Tetum and Portuguese
Land Area: 15,007 sq km; 5,794 sq mi
Leading Exports: coffee, sandalwood, marble
Continent: Asia

Fiji

Capital: Suva
Population: 856,346
Official Language: English
Land Area: 18,270 sq km; 7,054 sq mi
Leading Exports: sugar, garments, gold, timber, fish, molasses, coconut oil
Location: Pacific Ocean

Georgia
Capital: Tbilisi
Population: 5 million
Official Languages: Georgian and Abkhazian
Land Area: 69,700 sq km; 26,911 sq mi
Leading Exports: scrap metal, machinery, chemicals, fuel reexports, citrus fruits, tea, wine, other agricultural products
Continent: Asia

India

Capital: New Delhi
Population: 1.05 billion
Official Languages: Hindi and English
Land Area: 2,973,190 sq km; 1,147,949 sq mi
Leading Exports: textile goods, gems and jewelry, engineering goods, chemicals, leather manufactured goods
Continent: Asia

Indonesia

Capital: Jakarta
Population: 231.3 million
Official Language: Bahasa Indonesia
Land Area: 1,826,440 sq km; 705,188 sq mi
Leading Exports: oil and gas, electrical appliances, plywood, textiles, rubber
Continent: Asia

Iran
Capital: Tehran
Population: 66.6 million
Official Language: Farsi
Land Area: 1,636,000 sq km; 631,660 sq mi
Leading Exports: petroleum, carpets, fruits and nuts, iron and steel, chemicals
Continent: Asia

Iraq

Capital: Baghdad
Population: 24.7 million
Official Language: Arabic
Land Area: 432,162 sq km; 166,858 sq mi
Leading Exports: crude oil
Continent: Asia

Israel
Capital: Jerusalem
Population: 6.0 million
Official Language: Hebrew, Arabic
Land Area: 20,330 sq km; 7,849 sq mi
Leading Exports: machinery and equipment, software, cut diamonds, agricultural products, chemicals, textiles and apparel
Continent: Asia

Japan
Capital: Tokyo
Population: 127 million
Official Language: Japanese
Land Area: 374,744 sq km; 144,689 sq mi
Leading Exports: motor vehicles, semiconductors, office machinery, chemicals
Continent: Asia

Jordan
Capital: Amman
Population: 5.3 million
Official Language: Arabic
Land Area: 91,971 sq km; 35,510 sq mi
Leading Exports: phosphates, fertilizers, potash, agricultural products, manufactured goods, pharmaceuticals
Continent: Asia

Kazakhstan

Capital: Astana
Population: 16.7 million
Official Language: Kazakh
Land Area: 2,669,800 sq km; 1,030,810 sq mi
Leading Exports: oil and oil products, ferrous metals, machinery, chemicals, grain, wool, meat, coal
Continent: Asia

Kiribati

Capital: Bairiki (Tarawa Atoll)
Population: 96,335
Official Language: English
Land Area: 811 sq km; 313 sq mi
Leading Exports: copra, coconuts, seaweed, fish
Location: Pacific Ocean

Korea, North

Capital: Pyongyang
Population: 22.3 million
Official Language: Korean
Land Area: 120,410 sq km; 46,490 sq mi
Leading Exports: minerals, metallurgical products, manufactured goods (including armaments), agricultural and fishery products
Continent: Asia

Korea, South

Capital: Seoul
Population: 48.3 million
Official Language: Korean
Land Area: 98,190 sq km; 37,911 sq mi
Leading Exports: electronic products, machinery and equipment, motor vehicles, steel, ships, textiles, clothing, footwear, fish
Continent: Asia

Kuwait

Capital: Kuwait City
Population: 2.1 million
Official Language: Arabic
Land Area: 17,820 sq km; 6,880 sq mi
Leading Exports: oil and refined products, fertilizers
Continent: Asia

Kyrgyzstan

Capital: Bishkek
Population: 4.8 million
Official Languages: Kyrgyz and Russian
Land Area: 191,300 sq km; 73,861 sq mi
Leading Exports: cotton, wool, meat, tobacco, gold, mercury, uranium, hydropower, machinery, shoes
Continent: Asia

Laos

Capital: Vientiane
Population: 5.8 million
Official Language: Lao
Land Area: 230,800 sq km; 89,112 sq mi
Leading Exports: wood products, garments, electricity, coffee, tin
Continent: Asia

Lebanon

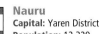

Capital: Beirut
Population: 3.7 million
Official Language: Arabic
Land Area: 10,230 sq km; 3,950 sq mi
Leading Exports: foodstuffs and tobacco, textile, chemicals, precious stones, metal and metal products, electrical equipment and products, jewelry, paper and paper products
Continent: Asia

Malaysia

Capital: Kuala Lumpur and Putrajaya
Population: 22.7 million
Official Language: Bahasa Malaysia
Land Area: 328,550 sq km; 126,853 sq mi
Leading Exports: electronic equipment, petroleum and liquefied natural gas, wood and wood products, palm oil, rubber, textiles, chemicals
Continent: Asia

Maldives

Capital: Malé
Population: 320,165
Official Language: Dhivehi (Maldivian)
Land Area: 300 sq km; 116 sq mi
Leading Exports: fish, clothing
Location: Indian Ocean

Marshall Islands

Capital: Majuro
Population: 73,360
Official Languages: Marshallese and English
Land Area: 181.3 sq km; 70 sq mi
Leading Exports: copra cake, coconut oil, handicrafts
Location: Pacific Ocean

Micronesia, Federated States of

Capital: Palikir (Pohnpei Island)
Population: 135,869
Official Language: English
Land Area: 702 sq km; 271 sq mi
Leading Exports: fish, garments, bananas, black pepper
Location: Pacific Ocean

Mongolia

Capital: Ulaanbaatar
Population: 2.6 million
Official Language: Khalkha Mongolian
Land Area: 1,555,400 sq km; 600,540 sq mi
Leading Exports: copper, livestock, animal products, cashmere, wool, hides, fluorspar, other nonferrous metals
Continent: Asia

Myanmar (Burma)

Capital: Rangoon (Yangon)
Population: 42.2 million
Official Language: Burmese (Myanmar)
Land Area: 657,740 sq km; 253,953 sq mi
Leading Exports: apparel, foodstuffs, wood products, precious stones
Continent: Asia

Nauru

Capital: Yaren District
Population: 12,329
Official Language: Nauruan
Land Area: 21 sq km; 8 sq mi
Leading Exports: phosphates
Location: Pacific Ocean

Nepal

Capital: Kathmandu
Population: 25.9 million
Official Language: Nepali
Land Area: 136,800 sq km; 52,818 sq mi
Leading Exports: carpets, clothing, leather goods, jute goods, grain
Continent: Asia

New Zealand

Capital: Wellington
Population: 3.8 million
Official Languages: English and Maori
Land Area: 268,680 sq km; 103,737 sq mi
Leading Exports: dairy products, meat, wood and wood products, fish, machinery
Location: Pacific Ocean

Oman

Capital: Muscat
Population: 2.7 million
Official Language: Arabic
Land Area: 212,460 sq km; 82,030 sq mi
Leading Exports: petroleum, reexports, fish, metals, textiles
Continent: Asia

Pakistan

Capital: Islamabad
Population: 147.7 million
Official Languages: Urdu and English
Land Area: 778,720 sq km; 300,664 sq mi
Leading Exports: textiles (garments, cotton cloth, and yarn), rice, other agricultural products
Continent: Asia

Palau

Capital: Koror
Population: 19,409
Official Languages: English and Palauan
Land Area: 458 sq km; 177 sq mi
Leading Exports: shellfish, tuna, copra, garments
Location: Pacific Ocean

Papua New Guinea

Capital: Port Moresby
Population: 5.2 million
Official Language: English
Land Area: 452,860 sq km; 174,849 sq mi
Leading Exports: oil, gold, copper ore, logs, palm oil, coffee, cocoa, crayfish, prawns
Location: Pacific Ocean

Philippines

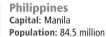

Capital: Manila
Population: 84.5 million
Official Languages: Filipino and English
Land Area: 298,170 sq km; 115,123 sq mi
Leading Exports: electronic equipment, machinery and transport equipment, garments, coconut products
Continent: Asia

Qatar

Capital: Doha
Population: 793,341
Official Language: Arabic
Land Area: 11,437 sq km; 4,416 sq mi
Leading Exports: petroleum products, fertilizers, steel
Continent: Asia

Samoa

Capital: Apia
Population: 178,631
Official Languages: Samoan and English
Land Area: 2,934 sq km; 1,133 sq mi
Leading Exports: fish, coconut oil cream, copra, taro, garments, beer
Location: Pacific Ocean

Saudi Arabia

Capital: Riyadh and Jiddah
Population: 23.5 million
Official Language: Arabic
Land Area: 1,960,582 sq km; 756,981 sq mi
Leading Exports: petroleum and petroleum products
Continent: Asia

Singapore

Capital: Singapore
Population: 4.5 million
Official Languages: Malay, English, Mandarin, Chinese, and Tamil
Land Area: 683 sq km; 264 sq mi
Leading Exports: machinery and equipment (including electronics), consumer goods, chemicals, mineral fuels
Continent: Asia

Solomon Islands

Capital: Honiara
Population: 494,786
Official Language: English
Land Area: 27,540 sq km; 10,633 sq mi
Leading Exports: timber, fish, copra, palm oil, cocoa
Location: Pacific Ocean

Sri Lanka

Capital: Colombo
Population: 19.6 million
Official Language: Sinhala, Tamil, and English
Land Area: 64,740 sq km; 24,996 sq mi
Leading Exports: textiles and apparel, tea, diamonds, coconut products, petroleum products
Continent: Asia

Syria

Capital: Damascus
Population: 17.2 million
Official Language: Arabic
Land Area: 184,050 sq km; 71,062 sq mi
Leading Exports: crude oil, textiles, fruits and vegetables, raw cotton
Continent: Asia

Taiwan

Capital: Taipei
Population: 22.5 million
Official Language: Mandarin Chinese
Land Area: 32,260 sq km; 12,456 sq mi
Leading Exports: machinery and electrical equipment, metals, textiles, plastics, chemicals
Continent: Asia

Tajikistan

Capital: Dushanbe
Population: 6.7 million
Official Language: Tajik
Land Area: 142,700 sq km; 55,096 sq mi
Leading Exports: aluminum, electricity, cotton, fruits, vegetables, oil, textiles
Continent: Asia

Thailand

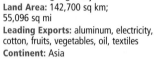

Capital: Bangkok
Population: 62.5 million
Official Language: Thai
Land Area: 511,770 sq km; 197,564 sq mi
Leading Exports: computers, transistors, seafood, clothing, rice
Continent: Asia

Tonga

Capital: Nuku'alofa
Population: 106,137
Official Languages: Tongan and English
Land Area: 718 sq km; 277 sq mi
Leading Exports: squash, fish, vanilla beans, root crops
Location: Pacific Ocean

Turkey

Capital: Ankara
Population: 67.3 million
Official Language: Turkish
Land Area: 770,760 sq km; 297,590 sq mi
Leading Exports: apparel, foodstuffs, textiles, metal manufactured goods, transport equipment
Continent: Asia

Turkmenistan

Capital: Ashgabat
Population: 4.7 million
Official Language: Turkmen
Land Area: 488,100 sq km; 188,455 sq mi
Leading Exports: gas, oil, cotton fiber, textiles
Continent: Asia

Asia and the Pacific (continued)

Tuvalu

Capital: Fongafale
Population: 10,800
Official Language: English
Land Area: 26 sq km; 10 sq mi
Leading Exports: copra, fish
Location: Pacific Ocean

United Arab Emirates

Capital: Abu Dhabi
Population: 2.4 million
Official Language: Arabic
Land Area: 82,880 sq km; 32,000 sq mi
Leading Exports: crude oil, natural gas, reexports, dried fish, dates
Continent: Asia

Uzbekistan

Capital: Tashkent
Population: 25.5 million
Official Language: Uzbek
Land Area: 425,400 sq km; 164,247 sq mi
Leading Exports: cotton, gold, energy products, mineral fertilizers, ferrous metals, textiles, food products, automobiles
Continent: Asia

Vanuatu
Capital: Port-Vila
Population: 196,178
Official Languages: English, French, and Bislama
Land Area: 12,200 sq km; 4,710 sq mi
Leading Exports: copra, kava, beef, cocoa, timber, coffee
Location: Pacific Ocean

Vietnam
Capital: Hanoi
Population: 81.1 million
Official Language: Vietnamese
Land Area: 325,320 sq km; 125,621 sq mi
Leading Exports: crude oil, marine products, rice, coffee, rubber, tea, garments, shoes
Continent: Asia

Yemen
Capital: Sanaa
Population: 18.7 million
Official Language: Arabic
Land Area: 527,970 sq km; 203,849 sq mi
Leading Exports: crude oil, coffee, dried and salted fish
Continent: Asia

Europe and Russia

Albania

Capital: Tiranë
Population: 3.5 million
Official Language: Albanian
Land Area: 27,398 sq km; 10,578 sq mi
Leading Exports: textiles and footwear, asphalt, metals and metallic ores, crude oil, vegetables, fruits, tobacco
Continent: Europe

Andorra
Capital: Andorra la Vella
Population: 68,403
Official Language: Catalan
Land Area: 468 sq km; 181 sq mi
Leading Exports: tobacco products, furniture
Continent: Europe

Austria
Capital: Vienna
Population: 8.2 million
Official Language: German
Land Area: 82,738 sq km; 31,945 sq mi
Leading Exports: machinery and equipment, motor vehicles and parts, paper and paperboard, metal goods, chemicals, iron and steel, textiles, foodstuffs
Continent: Europe

Belarus
Capital: Minsk
Population: 10.3 million
Official Languages: Belarussian and Russian
Land Area: 207,600 sq km; 80,154 sq mi
Leading Exports: machinery and equipment, mineral products, chemicals, textiles, food stuffs, metals
Continent: Europe

Belgium
Capital: Brussels
Population: 10.3 million
Official Languages: Dutch and French
Land Area: 30,230 sq km; 11,172 sq mi
Leading Exports: machinery and equipment, chemicals, metals and metal products
Continent: Europe

Bosnia and Herzegovina

Capital: Sarajevo
Population: 4.0 million
Official Language: Serbo-Croat
Land Area: 51,129 sq km; 19,741 sq mi
Leading Exports: miscellaneous manufactured goods, crude materials
Continent: Europe

Bulgaria

Capital: Sofia
Population: 7.6 million
Official Language: Bulgarian
Land Area: 110,550 sq km; 42,683 sq mi
Leading Exports: clothing, footwear, iron and steel, machinery and equipment, fuels
Continent: Europe

Croatia

Capital: Zagreb
Population: 4.4 million
Official Language: Croatian
Land Area: 56,414 km; 21,781 sq mi
Leading Exports: transport equipment, textiles, chemicals, foodstuffs, fuels
Continent: Europe

Czech Republic

Capital: Prague
Population: 10.3 million
Official Language: Czech
Land Area: 78,276 sq km; 29,836 sq mi
Leading Exports: machinery and transport equipment, intermediate manufactured goods, chemicals, raw materials and fuel
Continent: Europe

Denmark

Capital: Copenhagen
Population: 5.4 million
Official Language: Danish
Land Area: 42,394 sq km; 16,368 sq mi
Leading Exports: machinery and instruments, meat and meat products, dairy products, fish, chemicals, furniture, ships, windmills
Continent: Europe

Estonia

Capital: Tallinn
Population: 1.4 million
Official Language: Estonian
Land Area: 43,211 sq km; 16,684 sq mi
Leading Exports: machinery and equipment, wood products, textiles, food products, metals, chemical products
Continent: Europe

Finland

Capital: Helsinki
Population: 5.2 million
Official Languages: Finnish and Swedish
Land Area: 305,470 sq km; 117,942 sq mi
Leading Exports: machinery and equipment, chemicals, metals, timber, paper, pulp
Continent: Europe

France

Capital: Paris
Population: 59.8 million
Official Language: French
Land Area: 545,630 sq km; 310,668 sq mi
Leading Exports: machinery and transportation equipment, aircraft, plastics, chemicals, pharmaceutical products, iron and steel, beverages
Continent: Europe

Germany

Capital: Berlin
Population: 83 million
Official Language: German
Land Area: 349,223 sq km; 134,835 sq mi
Leading Exports: machinery, vehicles, chemicals, metals and manufactured goods, foodstuffs, textiles
Continent: Europe

Greece

Capital: Athens
Population: 10.6 million
Official Language: Greek
Land Area: 130,800 sq km; 50,502 sq mi
Leading Exports: food and beverages, manufactured goods, petroleum products, chemicals, textiles
Continent: Europe

Holy See (Vatican City)
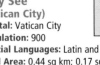
Capital: Vatican City
Population: 900
Official Languages: Latin and Italian
Land Area: 0.44 sq km; 0.17 sq mi
Leading Exports: no information available
Continent: Europe

Hungary

Capital: Budapest
Population: 10.1 million
Official Language: Hungarian
Land Area: 92,340 sq km; 35,652 sq mi
Leading Exports: machinery and equipment, other manufactured goods, food products, raw materials, fuels and electricity
Continent: Europe

Iceland

Capital: Reykjavík
Population: 279,384
Official Language: Icelandic
Land Area: 100,250 sq km; 38,707 sq mi
Leading Exports: fish and fish products, animal products, aluminum, diatomite, ferrosilicon
Location: Atlantic Ocean

Ireland

Capital: Dublin
Population: 3.9 million
Official Languages: Irish Gaelic and English
Land Area: 68,890 sq km; 26,598 sq mi
Leading Exports: machinery and equipment, computers, chemicals, pharmaceuticals, live animals, animal products
Continent: Europe

Italy

Capital: Rome
Population: 57.7 million
Official Language: Italian
Land Area: 294,020 sq km; 113,521 sq mi
Leading Exports: fruits, vegetables, grapes, potatoes, sugar beets, soybeans, grain, olives, beef, diary products, fish
Continent: Europe

Latvia

Capital: Riga
Population: 2.4 million
Official Language: Latvian
Land Area: 63,589 sq km; 24,552 sq mi
Leading Exports: wood and wood products, machinery and equipment, metals, textiles, foodstuffs
Continent: Europe

Liechtenstein

Capital: Vaduz
Population: 32,842
Official Language: German
Land Area: 160 sq km; 62 sq mi
Leading Exports: small specialty machinery, dental products, stamps, hardware, pottery
Continent: Europe

Lithuania

Capital: Vilnius
Population: 3.6 million
Official Language: Lithuanian
Land Area: 65,200 sq km; 25,174 sq mi
Leading Exports: mineral products, textiles and clothing, machinery and equipment, chemicals, wood and wood products, foodstuffs
Continent: Europe

Luxembourg
Capital: Luxembourg
Population: 448,569
Official Languages: Luxembourgish, French, and German
Land Area: 2,586 sq km; 998 sq mi
Leading Exports: machinery and equipment, steel products, chemicals, rubber products, glass
Continent: Europe

Macedonia, The Former Yugoslav Republic of

Capital: Skopje
Population: 2.1 million
Official Languages: Macedonian and Albanian
Land Area: 24,856 sq km; 9,597 sq mi
Leading Exports: food, beverages, tobacco, miscellaneous manufactured goods, iron and steel
Continent: Europe

Malta
Capital: Valletta
Population: 397,499
Official Languages: Maltese and English
Land Area: 316 sq km; 122 sq mi
Leading Exports: machinery and transport equipment, manufactured goods
Location: Mediterranean Sea

Moldova

Capital: Chişinău
Population: 4.4 million
Official Language: Moldovan
Land Area: 33,371 sq km; 12,885 sq mi
Leading Exports: foodstuffs, textiles and footwear, machinery
Continent: Europe

Monaco
Capital: Monaco
Population: 31,987
Official Language: French
Land Area: 1.95 sq km; 0.75 sq mi
Leading Exports: no information available
Continent: Europe

Montenegro
Capital: Podgorica
Population: 620,145
Official Language: Serbian
Land Area: 13,812 sq km; 5,333 sq mi
Leading Exports: food products
Continent: Europe

Netherlands

Capital: Amsterdam and The Hague
Population: 16.1 million
Official Language: Dutch
Land Area: 33,883 sq km; 13,082 sq mi
Leading Exports: machinery and equipment, chemicals, fuels, foodstuffs
Continent: Europe

Norway
Capital: Oslo
Population: 4.5 million
Official Language: Norwegian
Land Area: 307,860 sq km; 118,865 sq mi
Leading Exports: petroleum and petroleum products, machinery and equipment, metals, chemicals, ships, fish
Continent: Europe

Poland
Capital: Warsaw
Population: 38.6 million
Official Language: Polish
Land Area: 304,465 sq km; 117,554 sq mi
Leading Exports: machinery and transport equipment, intermediate manufactured goods, miscellaneous manufactured goods, food and live animals
Continent: Europe

Portugal

Capital: Lisbon
Population: 10.1 million
Official Language: Portuguese
Land Area: 91,951 sq km; 35,502 sq mi
Leading Exports: clothing and footwear, machinery, chemicals, cork and paper products, hides
Continent: Europe

Romania
Capital: Bucharest
Population: 22.3 million
Official Language: Romanian
Land Area: 230,340 sq km; 88,934 sq mi
Leading Exports: textiles and footwear, metals and metal products, machinery and equipment, minerals and fuels
Continent: Europe

Russia

Capital: Moscow
Population: 145 million
Official Language: Russian
Land Area: 16,995,800 sq km; 6,592,100 sq mi
Leading Exports: petroleum and petroleum products, natural gas, wood and wood products, metals, chemicals, and a wide variety of civilian and military manufactured goods
Continents: Europe and Asia

San Marino

Capital: San Marino
Population: 27,730
Official Language: Italian
Land Area: 61 sq km; 24 sq mi
Leading Exports: building stone, lime, wood, chestnuts, wheat, wine, baked goods, hides, ceramics
Continent: Europe

Serbia
Capital: Belgrade
Population: 9.4 million
Official Language: Serbian
Land Area: 88,361 sq km; 34,116 sq mi
Leading Exports: food and live animals, manufactured goods, raw materials
Continent: Europe

Slovakia

Capital: Bratislava
Population: 5.4 million
Official Language: Slovak
Land Area: 48,800 sq km; 18,842 sq mi
Leading Exports: machinery and transport equipment, intermediate manufactured goods, miscellaneous manufactured goods, chemicals
Continent: Europe

Slovenia

Capital: Ljubljana
Population: 1.9 million
Official Language: Slovene
Land Area: 20,151 sq km; 7,780 sq mi
Leading Exports: manufactured goods, machinery and transport equipment, chemicals, food
Continent: Europe

Spain

Capital: Madrid
Population: 40.1 million
Official Languages: Spanish, Galician, Basque, and Catalan
Land Area: 499,542 sq km; 192,873 sq mi
Leading Exports: machinery, motor vehicles, foodstuffs, other consumer goods
Continent: Europe

Europe and Russia (continued)

Sweden

Capital: Stockholm
Population: 8.9 million
Official Language: Swedish
Land Area: 410,934 sq km;
158,662 sq mi
Leading Exports: machinery, motor vehicles, paper products, pulp and wood, iron and steel products, chemicals
Continent: Europe

Switzerland
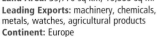
Capital: Bern
Population: 7.3 million
Official Languages: German, French, and Italian
Land Area: 39,770 sq km; 15,355 sq mi
Leading Exports: machinery, chemicals, metals, watches, agricultural products
Continent: Europe

Ukraine

Capital: Kiev
Population: 48.4 million
Official Language: Ukrainian
Land Area: 603,700 sq km;
233,090 sq mi
Leading Exports: ferrous and nonferrous metals, fuel and petroleum products, machinery and transport equipment, food products
Continent: Europe

United Kingdom

Capital: London
Population: 59.8 million
Official Languages: English and Welsh
Land Area: 241,590 sq km; 93,278 sq mi
Leading Exports: manufactured goods, fuels, chemicals, food, beverages, tobacco
Continent: Europe

Latin America

Antigua and Barbuda

Capital: Saint John's
Population: 67,448
Official Language: English
Land Area: 442 sq km; 171 sq mi
Leading Exports: petroleum products, manufactured goods, machinery and transport equipment, food and live animals
Location: Caribbean Sea

Argentina

Capital: Buenos Aires
Population: 37.8 million
Official Language: Spanish
Land Area: 2,736,690 sq km;
1,056,636 sq mi
Leading Exports: edible oils, fuels and energy, cereals, feed, motor vehicles
Continent: South America

Bahamas
Capital: Nassau
Population: 300,529
Official Language: English
Land Area: 10,070 sq km; 3,888 sq mi
Leading Exports: fish and crawfish, rum, salt, chemicals, fruit and vegetables
Location: Caribbean Sea

Barbados

Capital: Bridgetown
Population: 276,607
Official Language: English
Land Area: 431 sq km; 166 sq mi
Leading Exports: sugar and molasses, rum, other foods and beverages, chemicals, electrical components, clothing
Location: Caribbean Sea

Belize

Capital: Belmopan
Population: 262,999
Official Language: English
Land Area: 22,806 sq km; 8,805 sq mi
Leading Exports: sugar, bananas, citrus, clothing, fish products, molasses, wood
Continent: North America

Bolivia
Capital: La Paz and Sucre
Population: 8.5 million
Official Language: Spanish, Quechua, and Aymara
Land Area: 1,084,390 sq km;
418,683 sq mi
Leading Exports: soybeans, natural gas, zinc, gold, wood
Continent: South America

Brazil

Capital: Brasília
Population: 176 million
Official Language: Portuguese
Land Area: 8,456,510 sq km;
3,265,059 sq mi
Leading Exports: manufactured goods, iron ore, soybeans, footwear, coffee, autos
Continent: South America

Chile

Capital: Santiago
Population: 15.5 million
Official Language: Spanish
Land Area: 748,800 sq km;
289,112 sq mi
Leading Exports: copper, fish, fruits, paper and pulp, chemicals
Continent: South America

Colombia
Capital: Bogotá
Population: 41 million
Official Language: Spanish
Land Area: 1,038,700 sq km;
401,042 sq mi
Leading Exports: petroleum, coffee, coal, apparel, bananas, cut flowers
Continent: South America

Costa Rica

Capital: San José
Population: 3.8 million
Official Language: Spanish
Land Area: 51,660 sq km; 19,560 sq mi
Leading Exports: coffee, bananas, sugar, pineapples, textiles, electronic components, medical equipment
Continent: North America

Cuba

Capital: Havana
Population: 11.2 million
Official Language: Spanish
Land Area: 110,860 sq km; 42,803 sq mi
Leading Exports: sugar, nickel, tobacco, fish, medical products, citrus, coffee
Location: Caribbean Sea

Dominica
Capital: Roseau
Population: 73,000
Official Language: English
Land Area: 754 sq km; 291 sq mi
Leading Exports: bananas, soap, bay oil, vegetables, grapefruit, oranges
Location: Caribbean Sea

Dominican Republic
Capital: Santo Domingo
Population: 8.7 million
Official Language: Spanish
Land Area: 48,380 sq km; 18,679 sq mi
Leading Exports: ferronickel, sugar, gold, silver, coffee, cocoa, tobacco, meats, consumer goods
Location: Caribbean Sea

Ecuador

Capital: Quito
Population: 13.5 million
Official Language: Spanish
Land Area: 276,840 sq km;
106,888 sq mi
Leading Exports: petroleum, bananas, shrimp, coffee, cocoa, cut flowers, fish
Continent: South America

El Salvador

Capital: San Salvador
Population: 6.4 million
Official Language: Spanish
Land Area: 20,720 sq km; 8,000 sq mi
Leading Exports: offshore assembly exports, coffee, sugar, shrimp, textiles, chemicals, electricity
Continent: North America

Grenada
Capital: Saint George's
Population: 89,211
Official Language: English
Land Area: 344 sq km; 133 sq mi
Leading Exports: bananas, cocoa, nutmeg, fruit and vegetables, clothing, mace
Location: Caribbean Sea

Guatemala

Capital: Guatemala City
Population: 13.3 million
Official Language: Spanish
Land Area: 108,430 sq km;
41,865 sq mi
Leading Exports: coffee, sugar, bananas, fruits and vegetables, cardamom, meat, apparel, petroleum, electricity
Continent: North America

Guyana

Capital: Georgetown
Population: 698,209
Official Language: English
Land Area: 196,850 sq km;
76,004 sq mi
Leading Exports: sugar, gold, bauxite/alumina, rice, shrimp, molasses, rum, timber
Continent: South America

Haiti

Capital: Port-au-Prince
Population: 7.1 million
Official Language: French and French Creole
Land Area: 27,560 sq km; 10,641 sq mi
Leading Exports: manufactured goods, coffee, oils, cocoa
Location: Caribbean Sea

Honduras
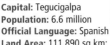
Capital: Tegucigalpa
Population: 6.6 million
Official Language: Spanish
Land Area: 111,890 sq km;
43,201 sq mi
Leading Exports: coffee, bananas, shrimp, lobster, meat, zinc, lumber
Continent: North America

Jamaica

Capital: Kingston
Population: 2.7 million
Official Language: English
Land Area: 10,831 sq km; 4,182 sq mi
Leading Exports: alumina, bauxite, sugar, bananas, rum
Location: Caribbean Sea

Mexico

Capital: Mexico City
Population: 103.4 million
Official Language: Spanish
Land Area: 1,923,040 sq km; 742,486 sq mi
Leading Exports: manufactured goods, oil and oil products, silver, fruits, vegetables, coffee, cotton
Continent: North America

Nicaragua

Capital: Managua
Population: 5 million
Official Language: Spanish
Land Area: 120,254 sq km; 46,430 sq mi
Leading Exports: coffee, shrimp and lobster, cotton, tobacco, beef, sugar, bananas, gold
Continent: North America

Panama

Capital: Panama City
Population: 2.9 million
Official Language: Spanish
Land Area: 75,990 sq km; 29,340 sq mi
Leading Exports: bananas, shrimp, sugar, coffee, clothing
Continent: North America

Paraguay

Capital: Asunción
Population: 5.9 million
Official Language: Spanish
Land Area: 397,300 sq km; 153,398 sq mi
Leading Exports: electricity, soybeans, feed, cotton, meat, edible oils
Continent: South America

Peru

Capital: Lima
Population: 28 million
Official Languages: Spanish and Quechua
Land Area: 1,280,000 sq km; 494,208 sq mi
Leading Exports: fish and fish products, gold, copper, zinc, crude petroleum and byproducts, lead, coffee, sugar, cotton
Continent: South America

Saint Kitts and Nevis

Capital: Basseterre
Population: 38,736
Official Language: English
Land Area: 261 sq km; 101 sq mi
Leading Exports: machinery, food, electronics, beverages, tobacco
Location: Caribbean Sea

Saint Lucia

Capital: Castries
Population: 160,145
Official Language: English
Land Area: 606 sq km; 234 sq mi
Leading Exports: bananas, clothing, cocoa, vegetables, fruits, coconut oil
Location: Caribbean Sea

Saint Vincent and the Grenadines

Capital: Kingstown
Population: 116,394
Official Language: English
Land Area: 389 sq km; 150 sq mi
Leading Exports: bananas, eddoes and dasheen, arrowroot starch, tennis racquets
Location: Caribbean Sea

Suriname

Capital: Paramaribo
Population: 436,494
Official Language: Dutch
Land Area: 161,470 sq km; 62,344 sq mi
Leading Exports: alumina, crude oil, lumber, shrimp and fish, rice, bananas
Continent: South America

Trinidad and Tobago

Capital: Port-of-Spain
Population: 1.2 million
Official Language: English
Land Area: 5,128 sq km; 1,980 sq mi
Leading Exports: petroleum and petroleum products, chemicals, steel products, fertilizer, sugar, cocoa, coffee, citrus, flowers
Location: Caribbean Sea

Uruguay

Capital: Montevideo
Population: 3.4 million
Official Language: Spanish
Land Area: 173,620 sq km; 67,100 sq mi
Leading Exports: meat, rice, leather products, wool, vehicles, dairy products
Continent: South America

Venezuela

Capital: Caracas
Population: 24.3 million
Official Language: Spanish
Land Area: 882,050 sq km; 340,560 sq mi
Leading Exports: petroleum, bauxite and aluminum, steel, chemicals, agricultural products, basic manufactured goods
Continent: South America

United States and Canada

Canada

Capital: Ottawa
Population: 31.9 million
Official Languages: English and French
Land Area: 9,220,970 sq km; 3,560,217 sq mi
Leading Exports: motor vehicles and parts, industrial machinery, aircraft, telecommunications equipment, chemicals, plastics, fertilizers, wood pulp, timber, crude petroleum, natural gas, electricity, aluminum
Continent: North America

United States

Capital: Washington, D.C.
Population: 281.4 million
Official Language: English
Land Area: 9,158,960 sq km; 3,536,274 sq mi
Leading Exports: capital goods, automobiles, industrial supplies and raw materials, consumer goods, agricultural products
Continent: North America

SOURCE: CIA World Factbook Online, 2002 and 2006

Glossary of Geographic Terms

basin
an area that is lower than surrounding land areas; some basins are filled with water

bay
a body of water that is partly surrounded by land and that is connected to a larger body of water

butte
a small, high, flat-topped landform with cliff-like sides

▲ **butte**

canyon
a deep, narrow valley with steep sides; often with a stream flowing through it

cataract
a large waterfall or steep rapids

◀ **cataract**

delta
a plain at the mouth of a river, often triangular in shape, formed where sediment is deposited by flowing water

flood plain
a broad plain on either side of a river, formed where sediment settles during floods

glacier
a huge, slow-moving mass of snow and ice

hill
an area that rises above surrounding land and has a rounded top; lower and usually less steep than a mountain

island
an area of land completely surrounded by water

isthmus
a narrow strip of land that connects two larger areas of land

mesa
a high, flat-topped landform with cliff-like sides; larger than a butte

mountain
a landform that rises steeply at least 2,000 feet (610 meters) above surrounding land; usually wide at the bottom and rising to a narrow peak or ridge

▶ **glacier**

◀ **delta**

mountain pass
a gap between mountains

peninsula
an area of land almost completely surrounded by water but connected to the mainland

plain
a large area of flat or gently rolling land

plateau
a large, flat area that rises above the surrounding land; at least one side has a steep slope

river mouth
the point where a river enters a lake or sea

strait
a narrow stretch of water that connects two larger bodies of water

tributary
a river or stream that flows into a larger river

valley
a low stretch of land between mountains or hills; land that is drained by a river

volcano
an opening in Earth's surface through which molten rock, ashes, and gases escape from the interior

▶ **volcano**

Glossary of Geographic Terms **555**

Gazetteer

A

Acadia (51° N, 110° W) the first permanent French settlement in North America, p. 314

Africa (10° N, 22° E) the world's second-largest continent, surrounded by the Mediterranean Sea, the Atlantic Ocean, the Indian Ocean, and the Red Sea, p. 15

Amazon rain forest (0° S, 49° W) a large tropical rain forest in the drainage basin of the Amazon River in northern South America, p. 494

Amazon River (0° S, 49° W) the longest river in South America, flowing across Brazil into the Atlantic Ocean, p. 342

Andes Mountains (20° S, 67° W) a mountain system extending along the western coast of South America, p. 341

Antarctic Circle (66°30′ S) a line of latitude around Earth near the South Pole, p. 32

Antarctica (87° S, 60° E) the continent that contains the South Pole; almost completely covered by an ice sheet, p. 35

Antofagasta (23°39′ S, 70°24′ W) a coastal city in Chile, p. 43

Appalachian Mountains (41° N, 77° W) a mountain system in eastern North America, p. 39

Arctic Circle (66°30′ N) a line of latitude around Earth near the North Pole, p. 30

Arctic a region located around the North Pole, p. 31

Argentina (34° S, 64° W) a country in South America, p. 488

Asia (50° N, 100° E) the world's largest continent, the main part of the Eurasian landmass, surrounded by the Arctic Ocean, the Pacific Ocean, the Indian Ocean, the Mediterranean Sea, and Europe, p. 54

Atacama Desert (25° S, 69° W) a desert in Chile, South America, p. 345

Atlanta (33°44′ N, 84°23′ W) the capital of the state of Georgia, p. 259

Australia (25° S, 135° E) a continent in the Southern Hemisphere, the world's smallest continent; also a country including the continent and Tasmania, p. 68

B

Bangladesh (24° N, 90° E) a country located in South Asia, p. 66

Bolivia (17° S, 65° W) a country in South America, p. 489

Boston (42°21′ N, 71°3′ W) the capital of the state of Massachusetts, p. 251

Brasília (15°47′ S, 47°55′ W) the capital city of Brazil, p. 495

Brazil (10° S, 55° W) the largest country in South America, p. 71

C

Calgary (51° N, 114° W) a city in southern Alberta, Canada, p. 303

Canada (60° N, 95° W) a large country in North America, p. 63

Canadian Shield a region of rocky, rugged land that covers about half of Canada, p. 151

Canal Zone (9° N, 80° W) a 10-mile strip of land along the Panama Canal, stretching from the Atlantic Ocean to the Pacific Ocean, once governed by the United States, p. 448

Caracas (10°30′ N, 66°56′ W) the capital city of Venezuela, p. 516

Caribbean Sea (15° N, 73° W) a sea bounded by the West Indies, Central America, and South America. It is part of the Atlantic Ocean. p. 340

Cariboo Mountains (59° N, 116° W) a mountain range in eastern British Columbia, Canada; a place where prospectors discovered gold in the 1800s, p. 307

Central America (11° N, 80° W) the part of Latin America south of Mexico and north of South America. It includes the seven republics of Guatemala,

Honduras, El Salvador, Nicaragua, Costa Rica, Panama, and Belize. p. 103

Chicago (41°51′ N, 87°39′ W) a major city in the state of Illinois, on Lake Michigan, p. 268

Chile (30° S, 71° W) a country in South America, p. 507

China (35° N, 105° E) a large country in East Asia, officially the People's Republic of China, p. 20

Coast Ranges (55° N, 129° W) a series of mountain ranges along the Pacific coast of North America, p. 150

Colombia (4° N, 72° W) a country in South America, p. 490

Cuba (22° N, 80° W) the largest island country in the Caribbean Sea, p. 68

Cuyahoga River (41° N, 82° W) a river in northeastern Ohio, p. 203

Cuzco (13°31′ S, 71°59′ W) a city in Peru; capital of the Incan empire, p. 374

D

Dawson (64°4′ N, 139°25′ W) a city located in western Yukon Territory, Canada, p. 321

Death Valley (36° N, 116° W) the hottest, driest region of North America, located in southeastern California, p. 150

Denmark (56° N, 10° E) a country in northern Europe, p. 118

Detroit (42°20′ N, 83°3′ W) a city in the state of Michigan, p. 269

E

Egypt (27° N, 30° E) a country in North Africa, p. 60

El Salvador (13° N, 88° W) a country in Central America, p. 427

Equator (0°) a line of latitude that circles Earth at the center of the tropics, midway between the North and South poles, along which days and nights are always equal in length, p. 11

Europe (50° N, 28° E) the world's second-smallest continent, a peninsula of the Eurasian landmass bounded by the Arctic Ocean, the Atlantic Ocean, the Mediterranean Sea, and Asia, p. 43

F

Florida (28° N, 82° W) a state in the southeastern United States that is largely a peninsula, p. 12

Fraser River (49° N, 123° W) a major river of western North America, mainly in British Columbia, p. 152

G

Genoa (44°25′ N, 8°57′ E) a seaport city of Italy, p. 104

Georgia (33° N, 83° W) a state in the southeastern United States, p. 12

Germany (51° N, 10° E) a country in Western Europe, p. 97

Great Lakes a group of five large lakes in central North America: lakes Superior, Michigan, Huron, Erie, and Ontario, p. 151

Great Plains (42° N, 100° W) a semiarid plain located in North America, stretching from the Rio Grande at the U. S.-Mexico border in the south to the Mackenzie River Delta in the north, and from the Canadian Shield in the east to the Rocky Mountains in the west, p. 128

Greece (39° N, 22° E) a country in southeastern Europe, p. 93

Greenland (70° N, 40° W) a self-governing island in the northern Atlantic Ocean; Earth's largest island, a possession of Denmark, p. 18

Greenwich (51°28′ N, 0°) a borough of London, England, and location of the Royal Greenwich Observatory, whose site serves as the basis for longitude and for setting standard time, p. 12

Guatemala (15° N, 90° W) a country in Central America, p. 437

Gulf Stream a warm ocean current in the North Atlantic, flowing northeastward off the North American coast, p. 43

H

Haiti (19° N, 72° W) a country in the Caribbean Sea, on the island of Hispaniola, p. 470

Hispaniola (19° N, 71° W) an island in the Caribbean Sea, divided between Haiti in the west and the Dominican Republic in the east, p. 412

I

India (20° N, 77° E) a large country occupying most of the Indian subcontinent in South Asia, p. 13

Indonesia (5° S, 120° E) a country in Southeast Asia consisting of many islands, p. 93

Iqaluit (63°44′ N, 68°28′ W) the capital of Nunavut, Canada, p. 322

Iran (32° N, 53° W) a country in Southwest Asia, p. 118

Isthmus of Panama (9° N, 79° W) the narrow strip of land in Panama that separates the Atlantic Ocean and the Pacific Ocean, p. 444

Italy (43° N, 13° E) a boot-shaped country in southern Europe, p. 104

J

Jakarta (6°10′ S, 106°48′ E) the capital and largest city of Indonesia, p. 71

Jamaica (18° N, 77° W) an island country in the Caribbean Sea, p. 459

Jamestown (37°30′ N, 75°55′ W) the first permanent English settlement in North America, located in Virginia; now a site of historic preservation, p. 178

Japan (36° N, 138° E) an island country in the Pacific Ocean off the east coast of Asia, consisting of four main islands, p. 63

L

L'Anse aux Meadows (51°36′ N, 55°32′ W) the earliest known North American Viking settlement, located on Newfoundland, p. 311

Lake Titicaca (16° S, 69° W) the world's highest lake on which vessels can travel, located in the Andes Mountains in South America, p. 415

Libya (27° N, 17° E) a country in North Africa, p. 82

Lima (12°3′ S, 77°3′ W) the capital city of Peru, p. 503

London (51°30′ N, 0°10′ W) the capital and largest city of the United Kingdom, p. 22

Los Angeles (34°3′ N, 118°14′ W) a major city on the southwest coast of the state of California, p. 276

M

Mackenzie River (69° N, 134° W) a large river in the Northwest Territories of Canada, flowing northwest from the Great Slave Lake into the Beaufort Sea, p. 152

Mexico (23° N, 102° W) a country in North America, south of the United States, p. 67

Mexico City (19°24′ N, 99°9′ W) the capital of and largest city in Mexico; one of the largest urban areas in the world, p. 433

Miami (25°46′ N, 80°11′ W) a city on the southeast coast of Florida, p. 12

Middle America (11° N, 80° W) another term for Mexico and Central America, p. 339

Milky Way a galaxy consisting of several billions of stars, including the sun, p. 28

Minneapolis and St. Paul (44°58′ N, 93°15′ W) two cities in Minnesota; also called the Twin Cities, p. 270

Mississippi River (29° N, 89° W) a large river in the central United States flowing south from Minnesota to the Gulf of Mexico, p. 152

Missouri River (39° N, 90° W) a large river in the west central United States flowing southeast from Montana into the Mississippi River, p. 152

Montreal (45°31′ N, 73°34′ W) the largest city in the province of Quebec, Canada, p. 294

Mount Everest (27°59′ N, 86°56′ E) the highest point on Earth, located in the Himalayas on the border between Nepal and China, p. 54

Myanmar (22° N, 98° E) a country in Southeast Asia, also known as Burma, p. 82

N

Nepal (28° N, 83° E) a country in South Asia, p. 54

New York (43° N, 75° W) a state in the northeastern United States, p. 132

New York City (40°43′ N, 74°1′ W) a large city and port at the mouth of the Hudson River in the state of New York, the largest city in the United States, p. 84

New Zealand (41° S, 174° E) an island country in the Pacific Ocean, p. 122

Niagara Falls (43°5′ N, 79°4′ W) a waterfall on the Niagara River between Ontario, Canada, and New York state, p. 206

Nile Valley the fertile land located on both sides of the Nile River in northeastern Africa; site of one of the earliest civilizations, p. 63

North America (45° N, 100° W) the world's third-largest continent, consisting of Canada, the United States, Mexico, Central America, and many islands, p. 17

North Atlantic Current a warm ocean current in the North Atlantic, flowing eastward toward western and northern Europe, p. 43

North Korea (40° N, 127° E) a country in East Asia, officially the Democratic People's Republic of Korea, p. 82

North Pole (90° N) the northernmost end of Earth's axis, located in the Arctic Ocean, p. 11

Northwest Territories (65° N, 120° W) a region of northern Canada, p. 319

Norway (62° N, 10° E) a country in northern Europe, p. 118

Nunavut (70° N, 95° W) a Canadian territory in the northern part of Canada; home to a large Inuit population, p. 319

O

Ontario (50° N, 88° W) the second-largest province in Canada, p. 291

Ottawa (45°25′ N, 75°42′ W) the capital city of Canada, located in Ontario, p. 291

P

Pacific Northwest the region in the northwestern United States that includes Oregon, Washington, and northern California, p. 273

Panama (9° N, 80° W) a country in Central America, p. 444

Panama Canal (9° N, 79° W) an important shipping canal across the Isthmus of Panama, linking the Caribbean Sea (and the Atlantic Ocean) to the Pacific Ocean, p. 445

Pangaea according to scientific theory, a single landmass that broke apart to form today's separate continents; thought to have existed about 180 million years ago, p. 38

Paraguay (23° S, 58° W) a country in South America, p. 491

Pennsylvania Colony a colony in America founded in 1682 by William Penn, p. 178

Peru (10° S, 76° W) a country in South America, p. 501

Peru Current a cold-water current of the southeast Pacific Ocean; flows northward between 40° S and 4° S, p. 43

Philadelphia (39°57′ N, 75°9′ W) a city and port in Pennsylvania, on the Delaware River, p. 251

Philippines (13° N, 122° E) an island country located near Southeast Asia, p. 67

Port-au-Prince (18°32′ N, 72°20′ W) the capital city and chief port of Haiti, p. 471

Portland (45°31′ N, 122°40′ W) the largest city in the state of Oregon, p. 274

Puerto Rico (18° N, 64° W) an island commonwealth of the United States in the Caribbean Sea, p. 476

Q

Quebec (52° N, 72° W) a province in eastern Canada, p. 295

R

Ring of Fire a circle of volcanic mountains that surrounds the Pacific Ocean, including those on the islands of Japan and Indonesia, in the Cascades of North America, and in the Andes of South America, p. 33

Rio de Janeiro (22°55′ S, 43°30′ W) a major city in Brazil, p. 495

Rocky Mountains (48° N, 116° W) the major mountain range in western North America, extending from central New Mexico to northeastern British Columbia, p. 12

Rotterdam (51°55′ N, 4°28′ E) a seaport city in the Netherlands, p. 131

Russia (60° N, 80° E) a country stretching across eastern Europe and northern Asia, the largest country in the world, p. 3

S

Sahara the largest desert in the world, covering almost all of North Africa, p. 53

St. Lawrence River (49° N, 67° W) a river in eastern North America; the second-longest river in Canada, p. 153

St. Lawrence Seaway (46° N, 73° W) a navigable seaway from the Atlantic Ocean to the western end of the Great Lakes, p. 206

St. Louis (38°37′ N, 90°11′ W) a major city in Missouri, on the Mississippi River, p. 45

San Francisco (37°46′ N, 122°25′ W) a coastal city in California, p. 45

San Jose (37°20′ N, 121°53′ W) a city in western California, p. 275

San Juan (18°28′ N, 66°7′ W) the capital and largest city in Puerto Rico, p. 480

Santiago (33°27′ S, 70°40′ W) the capital city of Chile, p. 511

São Paulo (23°32′ S, 46°37′ W) the largest city in Brazil, p. 48

Saudi Arabia (25° N, 45° E) a country in Southwest Asia, p. 101

Seattle (47°36′ N, 122°19′ W) a city in the state of Washington on Puget Sound, p. 275

Sierra Nevada a mountain range in California in the western United States, p. 150

South Africa (30° S, 26° E) a country in Southern Africa, p. 70

South America (15° S, 60° W) the world's fourth-largest continent, bounded by the Caribbean Sea, the Atlantic Ocean, and the Pacific Ocean, and linked to North America by the Isthmus of Panama, p. 17

South Korea (37° N, 128° E) a country in East Asia, p. 67

South Pole (90° S) the southernmost end of Earth's axis, located in Antarctica, p. 12

Strait of Magellan (54° S, 71° W) a waterway separating mainland South America from the islands of Tierra del Fuego, at the southernmost tip of South America, p. 507

Switzerland (47° N, 8° E) a country in central Europe, p. 78

T

Tenochtitlán (19°24′ N, 99°9′ W) the capital of the Aztec Empire, located on the site of present-day Mexico City, p. 370

Texas (32° N, 99° W) a state in the south-central United States, p. 68

Tierra del Fuego (54° S, 67° W) an archipelago, or chain of islands, at the southernmost tip of South America, separated from the mainland by the Strait of Magellan, p. 508

Tokyo (35°42′ N, 139°46′ E) the capital and largest city of Japan, also the largest city in the world, p. 63

Toronto (43°39′ N, 79°23′ W) the largest and most populous city in Canada; the capital of the province of Ontario, p. 293

Trinidad and Tobago (11° N, 61° W) a republic of the West Indies, on the two islands called Trinidad and Tobago, p. 461

Tropic of Cancer (23°30′ N) the northern boundary of the tropics, or the band of Earth that receives the most direct light and heat energy from the sun. Such a region lies on both sides of the Equator, p. 30

Tropic of Capricorn (23°30′ S) the southern boundary of the tropics, p. 31. *See also* Tropic of Cancer.

U

United States (38° N, 97° W) a large country in North America, p. 12

V

Valley of Mexico (19° N, 99° W) the area in central Mexico where Mexico City is located and where most of the population lives, p. 370

Vancouver (49°16′ N, 123°7′ W) a city in southwestern British Columbia, Canada, p. 304

Vatican City (41°54′ N, 12°27′ E) a nation-state of southern Europe, the smallest nation-state in the world, completely surrounded by the city of Rome, Italy, p. 81

Venezuela (8° N, 66° W) a country in northern South America, p. 516

Victoria (48°25′ N, 123°22′ W) the capital of British Columbia, Canada, p. 307

Vietnam (16° N, 108° E) a country located in Southeast Asia, p. 67

W

Washington, D.C. (38°53′ N, 77°2′ W) the capital city of the United States, located between Maryland and Virginia on the Potomac River, p. 261

West Indies (19° N, 70° W) the islands of the Caribbean, p. 410

Y

Yukon (64° N, 135° W) a territory in northwestern Canada, p. 319

Glossary

A

abolitionist (ab uh LISH un ist) *n.* a person who believed that enslaving people was wrong and who wanted to end the practice, p. 185

absolute location (AB suh loot loh KAY shun) *n.* the exact position of a place on Earth, p. 12

absolute monarchy (AB suh loot MAHN ur kee) *n.* a system of complete control by a king or queen who inherits the throne by birth, p. 82

acculturation (uh kul chur AY shun) *n.* the process of accepting new ideas from one culture and fitting them into another culture, p. 106

acid rain (AS id rayn) *n.* a rain, containing acid, that is harmful to plants and trees, often formed when pollutants from cars and factories combine with moisture in the air, p. 204

aerial photograph (EHR ee ul FOHT uh graf) *n.* a photographic image of Earth's surface taken from the air, p. 17

agribusiness (AG ruh biz niz) *n.* a large company that runs huge farms to produce, process, and distribute agricultural products, p. 164

agriculture (AG rih kul chur) *n.* farming, including growing crops and raising livestock, p. 94

alliance (uh LY uns) *n.* a formal agreement to pursue common interests formed between governments, often for military purposes, p. 180

alluvial soil (uh LOO vee ul soyl) *n.* soil deposited by water; fertile topsoil left by rivers after a flood, p. 164

ally (AL eye) *n.* a country joined with another for a special purpose, p. 464

Altiplano (al tih PLAH noh) *n.* a high plateau in the Andes, p. 503

Amazon rain forest (AM uh zahn rayn FAWR ist) *n.* a large tropical rain forest occupying the Amazon basin in northern South America, p. 494

Amazon River (AM uh zahn RIV ur) *n.* a long river in northern South America, p. 342

Andes (AN deez) *n.* a mountain system extending along the western coast of South America, p. 341

aquaculture (AHK wuh kul chur) *n.* the cultivation of fish and water plants, p. 315

aqueduct (AK wuh dukt) *n.* a pipe or channel used to carry water from a distant source, p. 376

arid (A rid) *adj.* dry, p. 44

Aristide, Jean-Bertrand (ah rees TEED, zhan behr TRAHN) *n.* former president of Haiti, p. 470

atmosphere (AT muh sfeer) *n.* a layer of gases surrounding a planet, p. 35

aurora borealis (aw RAWR uh bawr ee AL us) *n.* colorful bands of light that can be seen in northern skies, p. 318

axis (AK sis) *n.* an imaginary line around which a planet turns. Earth's axis runs through its center from the North Pole to the South Pole, p. 29

B

barometer (buh RAHM uh tur) *n.* an instrument for forecasting changes in the weather; anything that indicates a change, p. 89

bilingual (by LIN gwul) *adj.* speaking two languages; having two official languages, p. 197

biodiversity (by oh duh VUR suh tee) *n.* a large variety of living things in a region, p. 129

birthrate (BURTH rayt) *n.* the number of live births each year per 1,000 people, p. 64

bison (BY sun) *n.* the American buffalo, p. 175

blizzard (BLIZ urd) *n.* a heavy snowstorm with strong winds, p. 47

Bolívar, Simón (boh LEE vahr, see MOHN) *n.* a leader in the fight to free South America from Spanish rule, p. 387

boom (boom) *n.* a period of business growth and prosperity, p. 517

boomtown (boom town) *n.* a settlement that springs up quickly, often to serve the needs of miners, p. 307

boycott (BOY kaht) *n.* a refusal to buy or use goods and services, p. 179

Brasília (bruh ZIL yuh) *n.* capital of Brazil, founded in the 1950s to encourage people to move to the interior of the country, p. 495

C

campesino (kahm peh SEE noh) *n.* a poor Latin American farmer or farm worker, p. 402

Canal Zone (kuh NAL zohn) *n.* a ten-mile-wide strip of land along the Panama Canal, once governed by the United States, p. 448

canopy (KAN uh pea) *n.* the dense mass of leaves and branches forming the top layer of a forest, p. 52

capitalism (KAP ut ul iz um) *n.* an economic system in which private individuals or private groups of people own most businesses, p. 75

Caracas (kuh RAH kus) *n.* the capital of Venezuela, p. 516

cardinal directions (KAHR duh nul duh REK shunz) *n.* north, east, south, and west, p. 11

Carnival (KAHR nuh vul) *n.* a lively annual celebration just before Lent in Latin America, similar to Mardi Gras in the United States, p. 413

cash crop (kash krahp) *n.* a crop grown mostly for sale rather than for the needs of the farmer's family, p. 419

Castro, Fidel (KAS troh, fih DEL) *n.* the leader of Cuba's government, p. 462

caudillo (kaw DEE yoh) *n.* a military officer who rules a country very strictly, p. 389

census (SEN sus) *n.* an official count of all the people in an area, p. 375

circumnavigate (sur kum NAV ih gayt) *v.* to sail or fly all the way around something, such as Earth, p. 509

citizen (SIT uh zun) *n.* a person with certain rights and responsibilities under a particular government, p. 477

city-state (SIH tee stayt) *n.* a small, city-centered state, p. 81

civil engineering (SIV ul en juh NIHR ing) *n.* technology for building structures that alter the landscape, such as dams, roads, and bridges, p. 131

civilization (sih vuh luh ZAY shun) *n.* an advanced culture with cities and the use of writing, p. 94

civil rights (SIV ul ryts) *n.* the basic rights due to all citizens, p. 191

Civil War (SIV ul wawr) *n.* the war between the northern and southern states in the United States, which began in 1861 and ended in 1865, p. 185

African American soldiers fighting in the Civil War

climate (KLY mut) *n.* the average weather of a place over many years, p. 40

Cold War (kohld wawr) *n.* a period of great tension between the United States and the Soviet Union, which lasted for more than 40 years after World War II, p. 191

colonization (kahl uh nih ZAY shun) *n.* the movement of settlers and their culture to a new country, p. 125

Columbus, Christopher (kuh LUM bus, KRIS tuh fur) *n.* Italian explorer sponsored by Spain, who landed in the West Indies in 1492, p. 379

commercial farmer (kuh MUR shul FAHR mur) *n.* a farmer who grows most of his or her food for sale rather than for the needs of his or her family, p. 76

commonwealth (KAHM un welth) *n.* a self-governing political unit with strong ties to a particular country, p. 477

San Juan, the capital of the commonwealth of Puerto Rico

communism (KAHM yoo niz um) *n.* an economic system in which the government owns all large businesses and most of a country's land; a political system in which the central government controls all aspects of citizens' lives, p. 75

commute (kuh MYOOT) *v.* to travel regularly to and from a place, particularly to and from a job, p. 248

compass rose (KUM pus rohz) *n.* a diagram of a compass showing direction on a map, p. 21

conformal map (kun FAWR mul map) *n.* a flat map of the entire Earth, which shows correct shapes but not true distances or sizes; also known as a Merca-

tor projection after geographer Gerardus Mercator, p. 18

coniferous tree (koh NIF ur us tree) *n.* a tree that produces cones that carry seeds, p. 52

conquistador (kahn KEES tuh dawr) *n.* one of a group of conquerors who claimed and ruled land in the Americas for the Spanish king in the 1500s, p. 380

constitution (kahn stuh TOO shun) *n.* a set of laws that defines and limits a government's power, p. 83

constitutional monarchy (kahn stuh TOO shun ul MAHN ur kee) *n.* a government in which the power of the king or queen is limited by law, p. 83

consumer (kun SOOM ur) *n.* a person who buys and uses goods and services, p. 74

Continental Divide (kahn tuh NEN tul duh VYD) *n.* the boundary that separates rivers flowing toward opposite sides of North America, located in the Rocky Mountains, p. 152

copse (kahps) *n.* a thicket of small trees or shrubs, p. 89

core (kawr) *n.* the ball of hot metal at the center of Earth, p. 34

corporate farm (KAWR puh rit fahrm) *n.* a large farm run by a corporation, often consisting of many smaller farms, p. 267

Cortés, Hernán (kohr TEZ, hur NAHN) *n.* conquistador who conquered the Aztecs, p. 380

coup (koo) *n.* short for *coup d'état* (koo day TAH), a French term meaning the overthrow of a ruler or government by an organized group that takes power, p. 521

Creole (KREE ohl) *n.* a person of mixed European and African descent; in Haiti, a language that mixes French and African languages, p. 474

criollo (kree OH yoh) *n.* a person with Spanish parents who was born in the Spanish colonies in Latin America, p. 386

crust (krust) *n.* the thin layer of rocks and minerals that surrounds Earth's mantle, p. 34

cultural diffusion (KUL chur ul dih FYOO zhun) *n.* the movement of customs and ideas from one culture to another, p. 106

cultural diversity (KUL chur ul duh VUR suh tee) *n.* a wide variety of cultures, p. 214

cultural exchange (KUL chur ul eks CHAYNJ) *n.* a process in which different cultures share ideas and ways of doing things, p. 215

cultural landscape (KUL chur ul LAND skayp) *n.* the parts of a people's environment that they have shaped and that reflect their culture, p. 93

cultural trait (KUL chur ul trayt) *n.* a skill, custom, idea, or way of doing things that forms part of a culture, p. 92

culture (KUL chur) *n.* the way of life of a people, including their language, beliefs, customs, and practices, p. 92

Cuzco (KOOS koh) *n.* the capital of the Incan Empire; a city in modern Peru, p. 374

D

death rate (deth rayt) *n.* the number of deaths each year per 1,000 people, p. 64

deciduous tree (dee SIJ oo us tree) *n.* a tree that loses its leaves in the fall, p. 52

deforestation (dee fawr uh STAY shun) *n.* a loss of forest cover in a region, p. 129

degrees (dih GREEZ) *n.* units that measure angles; units that measure temperature, p. 11

demography (dih MAH gruh fee) *n.* the scientific study of population change and population distribution, p. 60

dependency (dee PEN dun see) *n.* a region that belongs to another state, p. 81

descendant (dee SEN dunt) *n.* a child, grandchild, great-grandchild (and so on) of an ancestor, p. 294

descent (dee SENT) *n.* ancestry, p. 299

desert (DEZ urt) *n.* a hot, dry region with little vegetation, p. 52

desert scrub (DEZ urt skrub) *n.* desert vegetation that needs little water, p. 52

developed nation (dih VEL upt NAY shun) *n.* a nation with many industries and advanced technology, p. 76

developing nation (dih VEL up ing NAY shun) *n.* a nation with few industries and simple technology, p. 76

dictator (DIK tay tur) *n.* a ruler of a country with complete power, p. 82

direct democracy (duh REKT dih MAHK ruh see) *n.* a form of government in which all adults take part in decisions, p. 82

discrimination (dih skrim ih NAY shun) *n.* the practice of treating certain groups of people unfairly, p. 191

distortion (dih STAWR shun) *n.* loss of accuracy. Every map projection causes some distortion of shape or size, p. 17

diversify (duh VUR suh fy) *v.* to add variety, p. 358

diversity (duh VUR suh tee) *n.* variety, p. 402

dominion (duh MIN yun) *n.* a self-governing area subject to Great Britain; for example, Canada prior to 1939, p. 196

E

economy (ih KAHN uh mee) *n.* a system for producing, distributing, consuming, and owning goods, services, and wealth, p. 74

ecotourism (ek oh TOOR iz um) *n.* travel to unspoiled areas in order to observe wildlife and learn about the environment, p. 450

elevation (el uh VAY shun) *n.* the height of land above sea level, p. 346

El Niño (el NEEN yoh) *n.* a warming of the ocean water along the western coast of South America; a current that influences global weather patterns, p. 343

emigrate (EM ih grayt) *v.* to leave one country to settle in another, p. 407

empire (EM pyr) *n.* a state containing several countries, p. 81

encomienda (en koh mee EN dah) *n.* the right of Spanish colonists to demand taxes or labor from Native Americans, granted by the Spanish government, p. 384

energy (EN ur jee) *n.* usable heat or power; capacity for doing work, p. 115

enslave (en SLAYV) *v.* to force someone to become a slave, p. 177

environment (en VY run munt) *n.* natural surroundings, p. 120

equal-area map (EEK wul EHR ee uh map) *n.* a map showing landmasses with the correct sizes, but with altered shapes, p. 19

Equator (ee KWAYT ur) *n.* the line of latitude around the middle of the globe, p. 11

equinox (EE kwih nahks) *n.* one of two days in the year when the sun is directly over the Equator and the days are almost exactly as long as the nights; known as spring and fall equinoxes, p. 30

erosion (ee ROH zhun) *n.* a process in which water, ice, or wind removes pieces of rock, p. 39

ethics (ETH iks) *n.* the standards or code of moral behavior distinguishing between right and wrong, p. 101

ethnic group (ETH nik groop) *n.* a group of people who share the same ancestry, language, religion, or cultural traditions, p. 216

exile (EK syl) *n.* a person who leaves or is forced to leave his or her homeland for another country, often for political reasons, p. 465; *v.* to force to leave an area, p. 314

export (eks PAWRT) *v.* to send products from one country to be sold in another country, p. 393; (EKS pawrt) *n.* a product that is sold in another country, p. 207

A barge on the St. Lawrence Seaway carries goods for export.

extended family (ek STEN did FAM uh lee) *n.* a family that includes several generations, p. 97

F

fault (fawlt) *n.* a crack in Earth's crust, p. 37

federation (fed ur AY shun) *n.* a union of states, groups, provinces, or nations, p. 291

foreign debt (FAWR in det) *n.* money owed by one country to another country or a foreign financial institution, p. 394

forty-niner (FAWRT ee NY nur) *n.* a miner of the California Gold Rush of 1849, p. 273

fossil fuel (FAHS ul FYOO ul) *n.* a fuel formed over millions of years, from animal and plant remains, including coal, petroleum, and natural gas, p. 117

Francophone (FRANG koh fohn) *n.* a person who speaks French as his or her first language, p. 294

free trade (free trayd) *n.* trade with no tariffs, or taxes, on imported goods, p. 208

fugitive (FYOO jih tiv) *n.* a runaway; someone who runs from danger, p. 184

G

gaucho (GOW choh) *n.* a cowboy of the pampas of South America, p. 417

geographic information systems (jee uh GRAF ik in fur MAY shun SIS tumz) *n.* computer-based systems that store and use information linked to geographic locations, p. 17

geography (jee AHG ruh fee) *n.* the study of Earth, p. 10

glacier (GLAY shur) *n.* a large, slow-moving mass of ice and snow, p. 150

globe (glohb) *n.* a model of Earth with the same round shape as Earth itself, p. 16

goods (gudz) *n.* physical products, p. 75

government (GUV urn munt) *n.* a system that creates and enforces laws in a region, p. 80

grassland (GRAS land) *n.* a region of flat or rolling land covered with grasses, p. 159

Great Lakes (grayt layks) *n.* the world's largest group of freshwater lakes, located between the United States and Canada; the five lakes Erie, Huron, Michigan, Ontario, and Superior, p. 151

Green Revolution (green rev uh LOO shun) *n.* the increased use of chemicals, machinery, and new crop varieties in agriculture since the 1950s that has greatly increased the world's food supply. It has also created environmental challenges. p. 65

H

hacienda (hah see EN dah) *n.* a large farm or plantation, often growing cash crops for export, p. 383

haze (hayz) *n.* dust, smoke, or other materials dispersed in air, which reduce visibility; often caused by pollution, p. 204

hemisphere (HEM ih sfeer) *n.* one half of Earth, p. 11

hemlock (HEM lahk) *n.* an evergreen tree with drooping branches and short, flat needles, p. 89

hieroglyphics (hy ur oh GLIF iks) *n.* a system of writing made up of signs and symbols, used by the Maya, the ancient Egyptians, and other cultures, p. 369

high latitudes (hy LAT uh toodz) *n.* the areas north of the Arctic Circle and south of the Antarctic Circle, p. 32

hill (hil) *n.* a landform with a rounded top that rises above the surrounding land but is lower and less steep than a mountain, p. 35

Holocaust (HAHL uh kawst) *n.* the killing of millions of Jews and others by the Nazis in World War II, p. 190

Homestead Act (HOHM sted akt) *n.* a law passed by the U. S. Congress in 1862 giving 160 acres (65 hectares) of land on the Midwestern plains to any adult willing to live on and farm it for five years, p. 188

human-environment interaction (HYOO mun en vy run munt in tur AK shun) *n.* how people affect the environment and the physical characteristics of their surroundings and how the environment affects them, p. 13

humid continental climate (HYOO mid kahn tuh NENT ul KLY mut) *n.* a climate with moderate to hot summers but very cold winters, supporting grasslands and forests, p. 51

hurricane (HUR ih kayn) *n.* a violent tropical storm, or cyclone, that forms over the Atlantic Ocean, p. 47

hydroelectricity (hy droh ee lek TRIH suh tee) *n.* electric power produced by rushing water, p. 165

I

illiterate (ih LIT ur ut) *adj.* unable to read or write, p. 464

immigrant (IM uh grunt) *n.* a person who moves to a new country in order to settle there, p. 67

immunity (ih MYOO nuh tee) *n.* a natural resistance to disease, p. 301

import (im PAWRT) *v.* to bring products into one country from another, p. 393; (IM pawrt) *n.* a product brought to one country from another for sale, p. 207

indentured servant (in DEN churd SUR vunt) *n.* a person who, in exchange for benefits received, must work for a period of years to gain freedom, p. 178

indigenous (in DIJ uh nus) *adj.* belonging to a certain place, p. 175

indigenous people (in DIJ uh nus PEA pul) *n.* people who are descended from the people who first lived in a region, p. 402

industrialization (in dus tree ul ih ZAY shun) *n.* the development of manufacturing in an economy, p. 125

Industrial Revolution (in DUS tree ul rev uh LOO shun) *n.* the change from making goods by hand to making them by machine, p. 183

institution (in stuh TOO shun) *n.* a custom or organization with social, educational, or religious purposes, p. 95

interdependent (in tur dee PEN dunt) *adj.* dependent on one another, p. 79

international (in tur NASH uh nul) *adj.* involving more than one nation, p. 84

Inuktitut (ih NOOK tih toot) *n.* the native language of the Inuit, p. 322

irrigation (ihr uh GAY shun) *n.* supplying dry land with water, p. 94

isthmus (IS mus) *n.* a narrow strip of land that has water on both sides and joins two larger bodies of land, p. 340

K

key (kee) *n.* the section of a map that explains the symbols and shading on the map, p. 21

L

labor force (LAY bur fawrs) *n.* the workers in a country or region, p. 188

Ladino (luh DEE noh) *n.* a mestizo, or person of mixed Spanish and Native American ancestry in Guatemala, p. 438

land bridge (land brij) *n.* a bridge formed by a narrow strip of land connecting one landmass to another, p. 175

landform (LAND fawrm) *n.* a shape or type of land, p. 35

landmass (LAND mas) *n.* a large area of land, p. 19

land reform (land ree FAWRM) *n.* the effort to distribute land more equally and fairly, p. 438

latitude (LAT uh tood) *n.* the distance north or south of the Equator, measured in units called degrees, p. 11

lichen (LY kun) *n.* a plant that is a combination of a fungus and an alga that grows and spreads over rocks and tree trunks, p. 39

life expectancy (lyf ek SPEK tun see) *n.* the average number of years that people live, p. 65

literacy (LIT ur uh see) *n.* the ability to read and write, p. 218

lock (lahk) *n.* an enclosed section of a canal used to raise or lower a ship to another level, p. 153

longitude (LAHN juh tood) *n.* the distance east or west of the Prime Meridian, measured in degrees, p. 11

Louisiana Purchase (loo ee zee AN uh PUR chus) *n.* the sale of land in 1803 by France to the United States; all the land between the Mississippi River and the eastern slope of the Rocky Mountains, p. 181

L'Ouverture, Toussaint (loo vehr TOOR, too SAN) *n.* a former slave who led the people of Haiti in their fight for independence, p. 385

lowland (LOH land) *n.* a land that is lower than the surrounding land, p. 151

low latitudes (loh LAT uh toodz) *n.* the area between the Tropic of Cancer and the Tropic of Capricorn, p. 32

M

Magellan, Ferdinand (muh JEL un, FUR duh nand) *n.* a Portuguese explorer sailing for Spain whose expedition was the first to circumnavigate the globe, p. 507

magma (MAG muh) *n.* soft, hot, molten rock, p. 36

maize (mayz) *n.* corn, p. 369

Manifest Destiny (MAN uh fest DES tuh nee) *n.* a belief that the United States had a right to own all the land from the Atlantic Ocean to the Pacific Ocean, p. 183

mantle (MAN tul) *n.* the thick, rocky layer around Earth's core, p. 34

manufacturing (man yoo FAK chur ing) *n.* processing raw materials to make a finished product, p. 123

maquiladora (mah kee luh DOHR ah) *n.* a factory that assembles imported parts to make products for export, often located in Mexico near the United States border, p. 405

marine west coast climate (muh REEN west kohst KLY mut) *n.* moderate climate occurring in areas cooled by ocean currents, supporting forests more often than grasses, p. 51

maritime (MA rih tym) *adj.* having to do with navigation or shipping on the sea, p. 315

mass transit (mas TRAN sit) *n.* a system of subways, buses, and commuter trains used to transport large numbers of people, p. 275

Mediterranean climate (med uh tuh RAY nee un KLY mut) *n.* moderate climate that receives most of its rain in winter and has hot and dry summers, supporting plants with leathery leaves that hold water, p. 51

megalopolis (meg uh LAHP uh lis) *n.* a number of cities and suburbs that blend into one very large urban area, p. 249

melting pot (MELT ing paht) *n.* a country in which all cultures blend together to form a single culture, p. 227

meridian (muh RID ee un) *n.* a line of longitude, p. 12

mestizo (meh STEE zoh) *n.* in Latin America, a person of mixed Spanish and Native American ancestry, p. 383

Mexico City (MEK sih koh SIT ee) *n.* the capital and largest city of Mexico, p. 433

Middle America (MID ul uh MEHR ih kuh) *n.* Mexico and Central America, p. 339

middle latitudes (MID ul LAT uh toodz) *n.* the areas between the high latitudes and the low latitudes, p. 32

migrant worker (MY grunt WUR kur) *n.* a laborer who travels from one area to another, picking crops that are in season, p. 430

Migrant workers in Mexico

migration (my GRAY shun) *n.* the movement of people from one country or region to another in order to make a new home, p. 67

mineral (MIN ur ul) *n.* a natural resource that is obtained by mining, such as gold, iron, or copper, p. 114

missionary (MISH un ehr ee) *n.* a person who tries to convert others to his or her religion, p. 177

mixed-crop farm (mikst krahp fahrm) *n.* a farm that grows several different kinds of crops, p. 266

Moctezuma (mahk tih ZOO muh) *n.* ruler of the Aztec empire at the time the Spanish arrived there, p. 378

mountain (MOWN tun) *n.* a steep landform that rises usually more than 2,000 feet (610 m) above sea level or the surrounding flatlands, p. 35

N

NAFTA (NAF tuh) *n.* North American Free Trade Agreement, signed in 1994 by Canada, the United States, and Mexico to establish mutual free trade, p. 208

nation-state (NAY shun stayt) *n.* a state that is independent of other states, p. 81

natural resource (NACH ur ul REE sawrs) *n.* a material found in nature that people use to meet their needs, p. 114

navigate (NAV uh gayt) *v.* to plot or direct the course of a ship or aircraft, p. 153

nomadic (noh MAD ik) *adj.* frequently moving from one place to another in search of food or pastureland, p. 229

nonrenewable resource (nahn rih NOO uh bul REE sawrs) *n.* a resource that cannot be replaced, p. 116

nuclear family (NOO klee ur FAM uh lee) *n.* a mother, a father, and their children, p. 97

An oasis in the Sahara

O

oasis (oh AY sis) *n.* a fertile area, in a desert, that has a source of water, p. 503

ocean current (OH shun KUR unt) *n.* a moving stream of water in the ocean created by uneven heating of Earth's surface, p. 42

oligarchy (AHL ih gahr kee) *n.* a government controlled by a small group of people, p. 82

one-resource economy (wun REE sawrs ih KAHN uh mee) *n.* a country's dependence largely on one resource or crop for income, p. 356

orbit (AWR bit) *n.* the path one body makes as it circles around another body, p. 28

P

Pacific Rim (puh SIF ik rim) *n.* the group of countries bordering on the Pacific Ocean, p. 309

pampas (PAM puz) *n.* the flat grasslands in the southern part of South America; a region similar to the Great Plains in the United States, p. 341

Panama Canal (PAN uh mah kuh NAL) *n.* a shipping canal across the Isthmus of Panama, linking the Caribbean Sea (and the Atlantic Ocean) to the Pacific Ocean, p. 445

parallel (PA ruh lel) *n.* in geography, a line of latitude, p. 12

permafrost (PUR muh frawst) *n.* a permanently frozen layer of ground below the top layer of soil, p. 159

petrochemical (pet roh KEM ih kul) *n.* a substance, such as a plastic, paint, or asphalt, that is made from petroleum, p. 258

petroleum (puh TROH lee um) *n.* an oily substance found under Earth's crust; the source of gasoline and other fuels; an energy resource, p. 116

Pinochet Ugarte, Augusto (pea noh SHAY oo gahr TAY, ah GOO stoh) *n.* military dictator of Chile from 1973 to 1988, p. 513

Pizarro, Francisco (pea SAHR oh, frahn SEES koh) *n.* conquistador who conquered the Incas, p. 381

plain (playn) *n.* a large area of flat or gently rolling land, p. 35

plantation (plan TAY shun) *n.* a large, one-crop farm with many workers, common in the southern United States before the Civil War, p. 178

plate (playt) *n.* in geography, a huge section of Earth's crust, p. 36

plateau (pla TOH) *n.* a large, mostly flat area that rises above the surrounding land, p. 35

plaza (PLAH zuh) *n.* a public square at the center of a village, a town, or a city, p. 431

polar climate (POH lur KLY mut) *n.* a climate of the high latitudes that is cold all year and has short summers, p. 50

political movement (puh LIT ih kul MOOV munt) *n.* a large group of people who work together for political change, p. 440

pollution (puh LOO shun) *n.* waste, usually made by people, which makes a place's air, water, or soil less clean, p. 132

population (pahp yuh LAY shun) *n.* total number of people in an area, p. 60

population density (pahp yuh LAY shun DEN suh tee) *n.* the average number of people per square mile or square kilometer, p. 62

population distribution (pahp yuh LAY shun dis trih BYOO shun) *n.* the way the population is spread out over an area, p. 60

prairie (PREHR ee) *n.* a region of flat or rolling land covered with tall grasses, p. 159

precipitation (pree sip uh TAY shun) *n.* water that falls to the ground as rain, sleet, hail, or snow, p. 40

Prime Meridian (prym muh RID ee un) *n.* the meridian that runs through Greenwich, England; 0° longitude, p. 11

prime minister (prym MIN is tur) *n.* the chief official in a government with a parliament, p. 291

privatization (pry vuh tih ZAY shun) *n.* a government's sale of land or industries it owns, to individuals or private companies, p. 520

producer (pruh DOOS ur) *n.* a person who makes products that are used by other people, p. 74

projection (proh JEK shun) *n.* method of mapping Earth on a flat surface, p. 18

province (PRAH vins) *n.* a political division of land in Canada, similar to a state in the United States, p. 159

push-pull theory (push pul THEE uh ree) *n.* a theory of migration claiming that difficulties "push" people to leave their old homes, while a hope for better living conditions "pulls" them to a new country, p. 68

Q

Quiet Revolution (KWY ut rev uh LOO shun) *n.* a peaceful change in the government of Quebec, Canada, in which the Parti Québécois won control of the legislature and made French the official language, p. 295

quipu (KEE poo) *n.* knotted strings on which the Incas recorded information, p. 375

R

rain forest (rayn FAWR ist) *n.* a dense evergreen forest that has abundant rainfall throughout the year, p. 341

rain shadow (rayn SHAD oh) *n.* an area on the side of a mountain away from the wind, which receives little rainfall, p. 157

raw materials (raw muh TIHR ee ulz) *n.* natural resources that must be processed to be useful, p. 114

recession (rih SESH un) *n.* a downturn in business activity and economic prosperity, not as severe as a depression, p. 266

Reconstruction (ree kun STRUK shun) *n.* the United States plan for rebuilding the nation after the Civil War, including a period when the South was governed by the United States Army, p. 186

referendum (ref uh REN dum) *n.* a ballot or vote in which voters decide for or against a particular issue, p. 295

refugee (ref yoo JEE) *n.* a person who leaves his or her homeland for personal safety or to escape persecution, p. 471

regime (ruh ZHEEM) *n.* a particular administration or government, p. 395

region (REE jun) *n.* an area with a unifying characteristic such as climate, land, population, or history, p. 12

relative location (REL uh tiv loh KAY shun) *n.* the location of a place described in relation to places near it, p. 12

renewable resource (rih NOO uh bul REE sawrs) *n.* a natural resource that can be replaced, p. 115

representative democracy (rep ruh ZEN tuh tiv dih MAHK ruh see) *n.* a government run by representatives that the people choose, p. 83

reservation (rez ur VAY shun) *n.* land set aside for a specific purpose, as by the United States government for Native Americans, p. 223

reserve (rih ZURV) *n.* land set aside for a specific purpose, as by the Canadian government for indigenous peoples, p. 228

responsible development (rih SPAHN suh bul dih VEL up munt) *n.* balancing the needs of the environment, community, and economy against one another, p. 274

revolution (rev uh LOO shun) *n.* a circular journey, p. 1; the overthrow of an existing government, with another government taking its place, p. 28

Revolutionary War (rev uh LOO shun ehr ee wawr) *n.* the war in which 13 American colonies won their independence from Britain, fought from 1775 to 1781, p. 179

Rio de Janeiro (REE oh day zhuh NEHR oh) *n.* a large city in Brazil, p. 495

Protesting a regime's policies in Argentina

Rocky Mountains (RAHK ee MOWN tunz) *n.* the major mountain range in western North America, extending south from Alberta, Canada, through the western United States to Mexico, p. 149

rotation (roh TAY shun) *n.* a complete turn, p. 29

rural (ROOR ul) *adj.* having to do with the countryside, p. 71

S

sanitation (san uh TAY shun) *n.* disposal of sewage and waste, p. 65

San Martín, José de (sahn mahr TEEN, hoh SAY deh) *n.* a leader in the fight to free South America from Spanish rule, p. 388

satellite image (SAT uh lyt IM ij) *n.* an image of Earth's surface taken from a satellite in orbit, p. 17

savanna (suh VAN uh) *n.* a flat, grassy region, or open plain with scattered trees and thorny bushes, p. 52

scale (skayl) *n.* relative size, p. 16

segregate (SEG ruh gayt) *v.* to set apart and force to use separate schools, housing, parks, and so on because of race or religion, p. 186

semiarid climate (sem ee A rid KLY mut) *n.* a hot, dry climate with little rain, supporting only shrubs and grasses, p. 44

separatist (SEP ur uh tist) *n.* someone who wants the province of Quebec to break away from the rest of Canada, p. 295

services (SUR vih siz) *n.* work done for other people that does not produce goods, p. 123

sierra (see EHR uh) *n.* a range of mountains, such as the one that runs from northwest to southeast Peru, p. 503

slum (slum) *n.* a usually crowded area of a city, often with poverty and poor housing, p. 187

social class (SOH shul klas) *n.* a grouping of people based on rank or status, p. 97

social structure (SOH shul STRUK chur) *n.* a pattern of organized relationships among groups of people within a society, p. 96

society (suh SY uh tee) *n.* a group of people sharing a culture and social structure, p. 96

sod (sahd) *n.* the top layer of soil containing grass plants and their roots, p. 298

solstice (SAHL stis) *n.* one of two days in the year when the sun is directly overhead at its farthest point from the Equator. Summer solstice, in the hemisphere where the sun is overhead, is the longest day and shortest night of the year. Winter solstice, on the same day in the opposite hemisphere, is the shortest day and longest night of the year. p. 30

squatter (SKWAHT ur) *n.* a person who settles on someone else's land without permission, p. 433

standard of living (STAN durd uv LIV ing) *n.* the level at which a person or nation lives, as measured by the availability of food, clothing, shelter, and so forth, p. 219

state (stayt) *n.* a region that shares a government, p. 80

strike (stryk) *n.* a refusal to work until certain demands of workers are met, p. 441

subarctic climate (sub AHRK tik KLY mut) *n.* a continental dry climate with cool summers and cold winters, p. 51

subsistence farmer (sub SIS tuns FAHR mur) *n.* a farmer who raises his or her food and animals mainly to feed his or her own family, p. 77

subsistence farming (sub SIS tuns FAHR ming) *n.* growing only enough food to meet the needs of the farmer's family, p. 419

Sun Belt (sun belt) *n.* the area of the United States stretching from the southern Atlantic Coast to the coast of California, known for its warm weather, p. 260

T

tariff (TAR if) *n.* a tax charged on imported goods, p. 208

technology (tek NAHL uh jee) *n.* a way of putting knowledge to practical use, p. 76

temperature (TEM pur uh chur) *n.* the hotness or coldness of the air or some other substance, p. 40

tenement (TEN uh munt) *n.* an apartment house that is crowded and poorly built, p. 187

Tenochtitlán (teh nawch tee TLAHN) *n.* the capital of the Aztec Empire, located on the site of present-day Mexico City, p. 370

terrorist (TEHR ur ist) *n.* a person who uses violence and fear to achieve goals, p. 192

textile (TEKS tyl) *n.* cloth, p. 183

Topa Inca (TOH puh ING kuh) *n.* an emperor of the Incas, who expanded their empire, p. 374

tornado (tawr NAY doh) *n.* a storm in the form of a swirling funnel of wind, moving as fast as 200 miles (320 kilometers) per hour, p. 47

totem pole (TOHT um pohl) *n.* a tall, carved wooden pole containing symbols, found among Native Americans of the Pacific Northwest, p. 305

A totem pole in Alaska

treaty (TREE tee) *n.* an agreement in writing made between two or more countries, p. 84

tributary (TRIB yoo tehr ee) *n.* a river or stream that flows into a larger river, p. 152

tropical cyclone (TRAHP ih kul SY klohn) *n.* an intense wind and rain storm that forms over oceans in the tropics, p. 47

tundra (TUN druh) *n.* an area of cold climate and low-lying vegetation, p. 51

U

urban (UR bun) *adj.* located in cities and nearby towns, p. 71

urbanization (ur ban ih ZAY shun) *n.* the movement of people to cities, p. 70

V

vegetation (vej uh TAY shun) *n.* plants that grow in a region, p. 50

vertical climate (VUR tih kul KLY mut) *n.* the overall weather patterns of a region, as influenced by elevation; the higher the elevation, the colder the climate, p. 54

W

weather (WETH ur) *n.* the condition of the air and sky from day to day, p. 40

weathering (WETH ur ing) *n.* a process that breaks rocks down into tiny pieces, p. 39

West Indies (west IN deez) *n.* the Caribbean islands, p. 410

Index

The *m, g,* or *p* following some page numbers refers to maps (*m*), charts, tables, graphs, timelines or diagrams (*g*), or pictures (*p*).

A

abolitionists, 185, 562
Aborigines, 108*p*
absolute location, M1, 12, 562
absolute monarchy, 82, 562
Acadia, 194, 314, 556
acculturation, 104, 106, 562
acid rain, 204, 204*m,* 204*p,* 562
Acoma Pueblo, New Mexico, 176, 176*p*
Ada, Alma Flor, 362–365
Addams, Jane, 188
adobe, 176, 176*p*
aerial photographs, 17, 562
Afghanistan, 191*g,* 192, 199, 542*m*
Africa, M10*m,* M11*m,* 3*m,* 5*m,* 7*m,* 531*m,* 533*m,* 540*m,* 541*m,* 556
  developing nations, 77
  plate movements, 38*m*
  population, 63*m,* 66
  slave trade, 68, 178, 384
  urbanization, 71
African Americans
  civil rights of, 191
  Jim Crow laws and, 186
  literature of, 225, 225*p*
  migration of, 256, 256*g*
  music of, 225–226, 225*p*
  rights of, 182
  slavery and, 392
  soldiers, 185*p*
agribusiness, 164, 562
Agricultural Revolution, 94
agriculture, 562
  in Canada, 286–289
  in the Caribbean, 458
  colonization, 125
  cultural change and, 106
  cultural development, 94, 94*p*
  cultural landscape, 93, 93*p,* 565

  defined, 562
  developed nations, 76
  developing nations, 77
  early farming and industrialization, 61*m*
  economic activity, 122, 122*p*
  effects on environment, 128, 129
  irrigation, 121, 121*p*
  land use, 121
  population distribution, 61, 61*m*
  population growth, 65
  renewable resources, 116
  in the South, 257, 257*p*
  subsistence farmers, M16, 77, 377, 419, 490*p,* 573
  in the United States, 236–247
  See also farming
air circulation, 42*g*
air pollution, 132, 204, 204*m,* 204*p*
air pressure, tornadoes, 47
air temperature, 40
Alabama, 141*m,* 235*m,* 537*m*
  data about, 236
  farming in, 257
  land use in, 256*m*
  mining in, 258
  in Sun Belt, 260*m*
Alaska, 4*p,* 148, 148*p,* 149, 158, 181*m,* 271, 530*m,* 536*m*
  data about, 141*m,* 235*m,* 236
  glaciers in, 150
  land bridge to, 175
  natural resources of, 165, 166
  purchase of, 188
Albania, 550
Albany, New York, 243
Alberta, 167, 196*m,* 298, 300*m*
  data about, 141*m,* 285*m,* 286
  indigenous people of, 299
  population of, 301
Alexander Island, 35*p,* 545*m*
Algeria, 546
Allende, Isabel, 418
alliances, 562
  nations, 84
  trade, 79
Allied Powers, 189

alluvial soil, 164, 562
ally, 464, 562
Alonso, Vanesa, 467
Altiplano, 489, 491, 503, 504, 562
Alvarado, Elvia, 404
Amazon Basin, 4*m,* 332, 332*m,* 494, 532*m,* 535*m*
Amazon rain forest, 489, 494, 556, 562
  importance of, 496–497, 496*g,* 497*p*
  photosynthesis and, 495
  threats to the, 497
Amazon River, 342, 494, 556, 562
American Indian Movement (AIM), 223, 223*p*
American Revolution. *See* Revolutionary War
Americas, migration to, M14, M14*m,* M15*m*
America's Breadbasket, 145*p*
Amritsar, India, 101*p*
Amsterdam, Netherlands, 72*p*
Anasazi people, 103
Andes Mountains, 341, 417, 488, 491, 509, 512, 535*m,* 556, 562
Angola, 546
animals, 129
Annapolis, Maryland, 240
Antarctic Circle, 32, 556
Antarctic Peninsula, 4*m*
Antarctica, 530*m*–531*m,* 532–533*m,* 545*m,* 556
  ice floes, 35*p*
  ocean currents, 42
antibiotics, 65
Antigua and Barbuda, 456, 456*p*
Antofagasta, 43, 556
Appalachian Mountains, 4*m,* 39, 149, 556
aquaculture, 313*g,* 315, 562
aqueducts, 376, 562
Arawaks, 411
archaeological dig, 311, 311*p*
Arches National Park, Utah, 26–27*p*
architecture, 419–420, 420*p*
  Incan, 376, 376*p*

See also housing

Arctic, 31*p*, 120, 545*m*, 556

Arctic Circle, 30*g*, 31*g*, 32, 51, 556

Arctic Ocean, 2*m*, 3*m*, 4*m*, 5*m*, 6*m*, 7*m*, 56, 142*m*, 149, 152, 545*m*

areas of influence, 173*m*

Argentina, 487*m*, 488, 534*m*, 556
  climate of, 345
  culture of, 417
  farming in, 419
  foreign debt of, 394*g*, 395
  gauchos in, 341*p*
  government of, 418, 418*p*, 488
  independence in, 387*m*
  landforms of, 341
  Mothers of Plaza de Mayo, 418, 418*p*
  natural resources in, 355, 355*p*
  vegetation of, 347, 348*m*
  waterways in, 342

arid, 44, 562

arid climates, 44*p*, 51

Aristide, Jean Bertrand, 470, 473, 562

Arizona, 158, 536*m*
  climate in, 272*m*
  data about, 141*m*, 235*m*, 237
  hydroelectricity in, 272*g*
  in Sun Belt, 260*m*

Arkansas, 537*m*
  data about, 141*m*, 235*m*, 237
  farming in, 257
  land use in, 256*m*
  in Sun Belt, 260*m*

Armenia, 548

Armstrong, Louis, 225*p*, 226

art
  Aztec, 403
  Mayan, 428*p*
  of Middle America, 403–404, 403*p*
  of Native Americans, 404
  Pre-Columbian, 403

Articles of Confederation, 179

Aruba, 455*m*

Asantehene, 3*p*

Ashanti people, 3*p*

Asia, 3*m*, 5*m*, 7*m*, 531*m*, 533*m*, 556
  cultural change, 104
  developing nations, 77
  maps of, 542*m*, 543*m*
  population, 63*m*, 66
  religions, 100
  Silk Road, 78
  urbanization, 71

Asian Americans, 276

Assiniboine people, 299

astrolabe, 379*p*

Atacama Desert, 337*m*, 345, 347, 348*m*, 509, 509*p*, 511, 556

Atlanta, Georgia, 239, 259, 556

Atlantic Ocean, 2*m*, 4*m*, 6*m*, 56, 142*m*, 149, 152, 203, 206*g*, 207
  currents, 42
  hurricanes, 47
  slave trade, 68

Atlantic Provinces, 145*m*, 145*p*, 311–315
  economy of, 313, 313*g*, 313*m*
  fishing in, 313*g*, 313*m*, 315
  natural resources of, 313*m*
  profile of, 313, 313*g*, 313*m*

atmosphere, 34*g*, 35, 562

atomic bomb, 190

atomic energy, 118

Atwood, Margaret, 230

Augusta, Maine, 240

aurora borealis, 318, 318*p*

Austin, Texas, 245, 259

Australia, 3*m*, 5*m*, 7*m*, 531*m*, 533*m*, 544*m*, 556
  colonization, 125, 125*p*
  cultural change, 107, 108*p*
  families, 97
  immigrants, 68

Austria-Hungary, 189

automobile industry, 269
  See also cars

Avila, Ramiro, 431

axis, Earth's, 28, 29, 30, 30*p*, 562

Aymara people, 417, 505, 505*p*

Aztecs, 370–372, 370*p*, 371*p*, 372*p*, 374, 375*p*
  art of, 403

Cortés and, 378*p*, 380–381
farming and the, 371
Spain and, 378*p*, 380–381
See also Native Americans

B

Baffin Bay, 545*m*

Bahamas, 455*m*, 457, 534*m*

Bahrain, 548

Baja California, 535*m*

Balboa, Vasco Nuñez de, 444, 444*p*

Bali, 93, 93*p*

balloons, weather, 46

bammy, 414

bananas, 349, 353*m*, 354, 460

Bangladesh, 66*p*, 542*m*, 556

banks, 75

Banks, Dennis, 223, 223*p*

Barbados, 414, 455*m*, 457

barometers, 89, 562

Barton, Clara, 186*p*

baseball, 106, 218*p*, 226, 465, 466

basins, 150, 554

basketball, 226, 226*p*

Basseterre, 460

Batista, Fulgencio, 463, 463*p*

Baton Rouge, Louisiana, 240

bauxite, 353*m*, 354, 355

bay, 554

Bay of Bengal, 5*m*

Bay of Fundy, 314

Beatrix, Queen of the Netherlands, 83*p*

Beaubrun, Bazelais, 471, 471*p*

Beaufort Sea, 4*m*

Bedspread Alley, 255

Belgium, 550

Belize, 425*m*, 426, 534*m*
  cultural heritage of, 403
  languages of, 403
  Mayas in, 369

Belize City, 426

Belmopan, Belize, 426

Benin, 546

Bering Sea, 4m
Bhutan, 548
bilingual, 197, 562
biodiversity, 128, 129, 562
biomass energy, 118
birthrate, 60, 64–65, 64g, 562
Bismarck, North Dakota, 244
bison, 299, 562
Black Sea, 5m
Blackfoot people, 299
blizzards, 47, 562
Boiling Lake, 458
Boise, Idaho, 239
Bolívar, Simón, 387–388, 389,
  390p, 521, 562
Bolivia, 332m, 489, 534m, 556
  culture of, 417
  economy of, 352, 352p, 394g
  independence in, 387m
boll weevil, 257, 257p
Bonneville Dam, 117p
boom, 517, 563
boomtown, 307, 563
borders, 2, 2p
Bosnia and Herzegovina, 550
Boston, Massachusetts, 124m,
  124p, 240, 249m, 251, 251p, 254,
  556
boycott, 179, 563
Brasília, 420, 495, 496g, 566, 563
Brazil, 52p, 71, 487m, 489, 534m,
  556
  Carnival in, 496, 498
  cities of, 420, 420p
  climate of, 345, 494
  culture of, 417, 498, 498g
  economy of, 358, 394g, 525
  ethnic groups of, 489, 498g, 499,
   499p
  exports of, 489, 500
  farming in, 499–500
  geography of, 495–498, 495p,
   496g, 497p, 498g, 498m
  government of, 489
  hydroelectricity in, 333, 333g, 333p
  immigrants in, 499
  independence in, 387m, 389

  indigenous people in, 497, 498
  landforms of, 341
  languages of, 331m, 331p, 417, 489
  mining in, 497
  Native Americans in, 499, 499p
  natural resources in, 353m, 354p,
   355
  population of, 489, 495, 498m
  Portugal and, 380
  rain forest in, 335, 335m, 335p,
   494, 494p, 495, 495p
  religion in, 489
  rivers in, 342p
  slavery in, 384, 489, 498, 499
Brazilian Highlands, 4m, 532m,
  535m
bridges, 376
Bridgetown, 457
Britain. *See* England; Great Britain;
  United Kingdom
British Columbia, 144p, 168,
  196m, 205, 205p, 217p, 218,
  304–310
  data about, 141m, 285m, 286
  economy of, 309–310, 309m
  gold rush in, 307, 307p
  Haida people, 193, 193p
  indigenous people in, 305, 305p,
   307–308, 308p
  mining in, 306, 306g, 306m
  natural resources in, 306, 306g,
   306m
  Pacific Rim and, 309–310, 309m
  profile of, 306, 306g, 306m
British Honduras. *See* Belize
**British North America Act
  (1867),** 196
Brunei, 548
Buddhism, 100, 100p
Buenos Aires, Argentina, 417,
  417p, 419, 420p
buffalo, 299, 562
buildings. *See* architecture
bulletin boards, 526
Burkina Faso, 546
Burma, *See* Myanmar
buttes, 142p, 554, 554p

C

Cabot, John, 312
cacao, 353m, 354
Cajuns, 314
calendars, 369, 370, 370p
Calgary, Alberta, 303, 303p, 556
California, 53p, 133p, 149, 158,
  216, 236–237p, 536m
  admitted to the Union, 184
  climate in, 272m
  data about, 141m, 235m, 237
  forests, 163, 163p
  Gold Rush, 161, 224, 273
  hydroelectricity in, 272g
  natural resources of, 273, 274
  in Sun Belt, 260m
  water resources in, 272g
calypso music, 414, 461
Cambodia, 548
campesinos, 402, 430, 441, 563
Canada, 141m, 285m, 530m, 534m,
  556
  agriculture in, 286–289
  climates of, 157, 157g
  Commonwealth of Nations, 199
  cultural diversity and, 215
  cultural patterns of, 216–219, 217p,
   218p, 219p
  culture of, 230, 230p
  economic issues, 76, 206–208, 206g
  energy resources, 118
  environmental issues of, 203–205,
   203p, 204m, 204p, 205p
  ethnic groups in, 293
  First Nations, 193, 193p, 228–229,
   229p
  flag of, 162
  France and, 194, 194p, 195–196,
   294, 314, 314m
  French Canadians in, 228
  geographic features of, 151
  government of, 83, 198, 291, 291g,
   292, 292g, 319
  Great Britain and, 194, 194p, 195–
   196, 198, 291, 291g, 292, 292g,
   294, 314, 314m

immigration to, 197, 214, 216–219, 216*p*, 227, 228*g*, 229–230, 293, 299

imports and exports of, 207

industry in, 286–289

lakes, 151, 151*p*

landforms of, 149–151

languages of, 99, 197, 286–289

literature of, 230

location of, 149

mining in, 196

music of, 230

NAFTA and, 79, 208, 395, 436

natural resources of, 164*m*, 167–168, 167*p*, 168*p*

parliamentary democracy, 198, 198*p*

peaceful revolution in, 196

physical map, 147*m*

population density, 62*p*, 63

population of, 218, 228, 229, 286–289

railroads in, 308

regions of, 144–145, 144–145*m*, 144*p*, 145*p*

religion in, 218

rivers of, 152–153

Spain and, 314, 314*m*

sports in, 230, 230*p*

standard of living in, 219

territories of, 141*m*

trade, 79, 207–208

United States and, 199, 202–208, 214, 218–219, 218*p*, 230

vegetation zones, 159–162, 159*p*, 160*m*, 161*p*, 162*p*

World War I and, 196

See also North America; individual provinces

Canada Day, 227*p*

Canada's Breadbasket, 302

Canadian National Tower, 293, 293*p*

Canadian Pacific Railway, 195*p*, 308

Canadian Shield, 151, 167, 291, 532*m*, 535*m*, 556

Canal Zone, 448, 556, 563

canals, 153, 371, 371*p*, 376. *See also* Panama Canal

canopy, rain forest, 50, 52, 494, 563

canyon, 554

Cape Canaveral, Florida, 259

Cape Horn, 337*m*, 508*m*, 509

Cape Town, South Africa, 70*p*

capitalism, 74, 75, 563

Caracas, 516, 516*p*, 517, 521, 556, 563

carbon cycle, 115

carbon dioxide, 35, 497

cardinal directions, 10, 11, 563

Carib Indians, 458

Caribbean Islands, 455*m*, 530*m*

Carnival in, 413, 413*p*

climate of, 345, 346

cultures of, 410–414, 410*p*, 411*p*, 412*p*, 413–414, 413*p*, 414*p*

ethnic groups of, 411–412, 411*p*, 456–461

exports of, 456–461

farming in, 412

food of, 414, 414*p*

government in, 456–461

immigrants from, 67

immigrants in, 411

landforms of, 340

languages of, 412, 456–461

location of, 339, 339*m*, 484*m*

music of, 413, 414, 461

natural resources of, 353*m*, 354, 354*p*

population of, 456–461

religion in, 412, 456–461

Spain and, 175

See also individual islands

Caribbean Sea, 4*m*, 56, 340, 556

Cariboo Mountains, 307, 556

Carib people, 411

Carnival, 413, 413*p*, 496, 498, 563

Caroni Swamp, 461

Carrillo, Fermin, 407

cars, 269

air pollution, 132

cultural change and, 105

energy consumption, 119

hybrid, 119, 130, 130*g*, 132

suburbanization and, 70

traffic jams, 130*p*

Carson City, Nevada, 242

Carter, Jimmy, 448

Cartier, Jacques, 294

Cascade Mountains, 150

cash crops, 419, 563

Castries, 460

Castro, Fidel, 457, 462, 463–464, 464*p*, 465, 467, 563

cataract, 554, 554*p*

Cather, Willa, 264

Catholic Church, 382, 404, 413, 413*p*

caudillos, 389, 563

cells, air circulation, 42*p*

census, 375, 563

Central America, 425*m*, 530*m*, 557

early civilizations of, 367*m*, 368–372, 369*p*, 370*p*, 371*p*, 372*p*

ethnic groups in, 426–429

exports of, 426–429

immigrants from, 67, 68

landforms of, 340

languages of, 403, 426–429

location of, 339, 339*m*, 452*m*

Mayas, 103

natural resources of, 353*m*, 354

population of, 405, 426–429

religion in, 404, 404*p*, 426–429

vegetation of, 348*m*, 349

See also Middle America; individual countries

Central American Common Market, 427

Central Plains, 149, 152

Cerrado, 495

Chad, 546

Chaparro, Julia de Jesus, 478–479

Charleston, West Virginia, 247

Charlottetown, Prince Edward Island, 288

Chavez, Hugo, 521, 522

Cherokee people, 182*m*, 215*m*, 232*m*

Cherrapunji, India, 41*p*

Chesapeake Bay, 258

Cheyenne, Wyoming, 247

Cheyenne people, 215*m*, 232*m*

Chicago, Illinois, 204*m*, 265*g*, 265*m*, 268, 268*p*, 269*m*, 557

Chichén Itzá, 369*p*

Chickasaw, 182*m*

children, families, 96, 97

Childtimes **(Greenfield and Little),** 280–283

Chile, 42, 335, 335*m*, 335*p*, 487*m*, 334*m*, 557

  climate of, 345, 509

  culture of, 417

  data about, 489

  economy of, 356, 394*g*, 508, 508*g*

  exports, 489, 508, 508*g*, 509, 512

  farming in, 419, 511–512, 512*p*

  geography of, 509–510, 509*p*, 510*p*

  government, 489, 513, 513*p*

  human rights in, 513

  independence in, 387*m*, 388

  landforms of, 489, 509

  literature of, 418

  Native Americans in, 511

  natural resources in, 356

  vegetation of, 347, 348*m*

China, 135, 542*m*, 557

  economy, 77

  emigrants, 67, 68

  government, 82

  language, 98*p*, 99

  population, 6*p*

  rice harvest, 58–59*p*, 85*p*

  Silk Road, 78

chinampas, 370, 371, 371*p*

Chinook effect, 157

Chipewyan people, 299

Chippewa people, 232*m*

Choctaw people, 182*m*

Christianity, 98, 100, 101, 382, 404

Chrysler Building, 252, 252*p*

Chukchi people, 216

Churchill, Manitoba, 51

Ciboney, 411

circumnavigate, 509, 563

Cisneros, Sandra, 225*p*

cities

  development of culture, 94

  growth of, 61

  industrialization and, 125

  of the Midwest, 268–270, 268*p*, 269*m*, 270*p*

  of the Northeast, 248–254

  population of, 405*g*, 406

  of the South, 259–261, 261*p*

  of South America, 419–420, 420*p*

  suburbs, 70, 105, 125

  urbanization, 67, 70–71, 70*g*

  of the West, 274–276, 275*p*, 276*p*

citizenship, 83, 477, 563

citrus fruits, 257

city-states, 80, 81, 563

civil engineering, 128, 131, 563

civil rights, 191, 191*g*, 563

Civil War, 184*m*, 563, 563*p*

  causes of, 184

  Lincoln and, 185

  Reconstruction and, 186

  slavery and, 184–186

civil war, 429, 440–441

civilization, 92, 94, 563

  early, 367*m*, 368–372, 369*p*, 370*p*, 371*p*, 372*p*, 374

Clark, William, 180, 180*p*, 181, 272

Clayoquot Sound, 205, 205*p*

Clermont **(steamboat),** 183*p*

Cleveland, Ohio, 203

climate, M1, 40–55, 150, 157, 343–349, 343*p*, 344*m*, 346*g*, 348*m*, 360, 360*m*, 563

  air pollution and, 132

  arid and semiarid, 44*p*, 51

  of Brazil, 494, 496*g*

  of Canada, 143, 143*m*, 157, 157*g*

  of Chile, 509

  climate change, 132

  defined, 40

  differences from weather, 40

  dry, 43*g*, 50, 51

  effect on vegetation, 50–54, 53*m*

  factors affecting, 346

  graphs, 48–49, 48*g*, 56

  land use and, 121

  latitude and, 32, 41

  of Peru, 502*g*

  polar, 43*g*, 50, 51

  regions, 44*m*–45*m*, 50

  of the South, 255–256

  temperate continental, 50, 51

  temperate marine, 50, 51

  tropical, 50

  of United States, 143, 143*m*

  vertical, 54

  of the West, 272*m*

  See also weather

climate maps, M12*m*, 350–351, 350*m*, 351*m*, 360

climate regions, M1, 44–45*m*, 50, 343*p*, 344*m*, 345–349, 346*g*, 348*m*, 351*m*

climate zones, 157–158, 157*g*, 158*p*

clothes, 104

clouds, water cycle, 41

coal, 117, 117*p*, 164*m*, 165, 333, 333*g*

Coast Mountains, 151

Coast Ranges, 150, 557

coffee, 349, 353*m*, 354, 355, 356*g*, 439, 500

cold climates, 41

Cold War, 191, 191*g*, 464, 563

Colombia, 487*m*, 490, 534*m*, 557

  culture of, 416

  foreign debt of, 394*g*

  independence in, 387*m*, 388

  literature of, 418

  natural resources in, 353*m*, 355

  Panama Canal and, 394, 447

Colón, 405, 429

colonization, 120, 125, 382–384, 382*m*, 383*g*, 564

Colorado, 271*p*, 536*m*

  climate in, 272*m*

  data about, 141*m*, 235*m*, 237

  natural resources of, 273

  in Sun Belt, 260*m*

Colorado River, 44, 152

Columbia, South Carolina, 245

Columbia River, 152

Columbian exchange, 383*g*

Columbus, Christopher, M14, 175, 379, 382*m,* 564

Columbus, Ohio, 244

Comanche people, 215*m,* 232*m*

commercial farmers, 76, 564

commonwealth, 564, 564*p*

Commonwealth of Nations, 199

communications, 450
cultural change and, 107
language, 98

communism, 74, 75, 82, 463, 564

communities
political systems, 80, 82–83
social structure, 96

commute, 248, 564

compass, M5

compass rose, M8, 16, 20*m,* 21, 564

computers, 275
cultural change, 106, 107
geographic information systems (GIS), 16, 17
trade, 78, 79

Concord, New Hampshire, 242

Condado, 480

Confederate States of America, 184*m,* 185

conformal maps, 18, 564

Congaree Swamp National Monument, 245*p*

Congo, Democratic Republic of the, 546

Congo, Republic of the, 546

coniferous trees and forests, 50, 51, 52, 53*p,* 54, 162, 564

Connecticut, 537*m*
data about, 141*m,* 235*m,* 238

conquistadors, 380–381, 564

constitution, 80, 83, 476, 564

Constitution, Canadian, 198

Constitution, U.S., 179

constitutional monarchy, 83, 564

consumers, 74, 79, 564

container ships, 79

continental climate, 51, 158

Continental Divide, 152, 564

continents, 2–3*m,* 3

compare, 7
location of, 86
movement of, 36, 36*g,* 38

Cook, James, 305

Copán, Honduras, 369

copper, 164*m,* 166, 167, 353*m,* 355, 508, 508*g,* 509

copses, 89, 564

coral islands, 340

coral reefs, 460, 461

core, Earth's, 33, 34, 34*g,* 564

corporate farm, 267, 564

Cortés, Hernán, 378*p,* 380–381, 382*m,* 399, 564

Costa, Daniel Monteiro, 499

Costa Rica, 405, 425*m,* 427, 534*m*
cultural heritage of, 403

Côte d'Ivoire (Ivory Coast), 546

cotton, 117, 257, 257*p,* 353*m,* 354

cotton gin, 184

coup, 521, 564

cowboys, 341*p*

Cree people, 299

Creek people, 182*m*

Creoles, 474, 564

criollos, 386, 387, 392–393, 564

critical thinking
analyze, 32, 47, 54, 56, 79, 132, 134, 186, 219, 232, 297, 310, 315, 324, 360, 365, 389, 482, 500, 524
analyze cause and effect, 506
analyze images, 194*p,* 203*p,* 205*p,* 217*p,* 229*p,* 294, 295, 299*p,* 305*p,* 341, 371, 386, 406, 435, 438, 449, 467, 475
analyze information, 226, 266*g,* 275*g,* 307*p,* 342, 356, 374, 389, 420
apply information, 22, 24, 56, 110, 119, 170, 349, 524
bar graphs, 493
categorize, 24, 84, 119, 125, 132, 247, 289, 360, 414, 429, 461, 493
compare, 89, 168, 210, 254, 302*p,* 358, 384, 398, 484, 506, 519
compare and contrast, 39, 54, 71, 79, 84, 86, 108, 110, 125, 134, 170, 228*g,* 232, 247, 278, 289,

322, 324, 355, 396, 420, 429, 461, 475, 493, 497, 509, 524
conclude, 218*p,* 273*p,* 372, 398, 422, 504
contrast, 13, 47, 56, 66, 86, 170, 289, 291*g,* 297, 360, 493
define, 13, 22, 32, 54, 66, 84, 86, 95, 170, 210, 360, 422, 450, 467, 475
describe, 24, 32, 56, 79, 89, 108, 110, 125, 134, 153, 206*g,* 210, 266*g,* 275*g,* 356, 372, 377, 384, 422, 436, 441, 450, 467, 475, 482, 484, 506, 522, 524
draw conclusions, 24, 101, 110, 119, 153, 170, 183*p,* 185*p,* 188*p,* 195*p,* 197*p,* 198*p,* 210, 219, 224*g,* 230, 232, 247, 261, 278, 289, 303, 346, 358, 377, 384, 396, 398, 405, 414, 416, 417, 422, 429, 447, 450, 452, 461, 478, 484, 493, 500, 510, 520, 522
draw inferences, 189*p,* 210, 226, 270, 413, 503
evaluate, 22, 32, 54, 56, 89
evaluate information, 360, 365, 384, 436
explain, 13, 39, 47, 54, 56, 66, 71, 79, 86, 95, 101, 108, 110, 134, 153, 168, 170, 179, 192, 199, 208, 210, 226, 230, 232, 261, 270, 276, 278, 303, 315, 324, 398, 450, 482
explore main idea, 170, 186, 219, 270
find main idea, 467, 475, 484
generalize, 86, 162, 208, 230, 247, 297, 354, 360, 375, 398, 411, 452
identify, 22, 24, 32, 39, 47, 56, 71, 79, 84, 86, 89, 95, 101, 119, 170, 186, 190, 210, 224*g,* 228*g,* 278, 291*g,* 297, 342, 346, 349, 358, 360, 372, 374, 377, 383, 384, 388, 389, 398, 405, 407, 414, 420, 422, 441, 452, 477, 484, 500, 513, 524
identify cause, 125, 186, 192, 216, 226, 232, 360, 393, 398, 407, 414, 422, 436, 441, 452, 513, 524
identify cause and effect, 32, 66, 71, 86, 95, 101, 132, 170, 179, 192, 210, 254, 261, 276, 342, 358, 384, 394, 407, 420, 422, 450, 452, 475, 484, 513

identify effect, 153, 162, 186, 190, 206*g*, 208, 253, 270, 303, 310, 322, 324, 360, 422, 452, 467, 484, 500, 512, 522, 524

identify frame of reference, 210, 232

identify main idea, 208, 230, 254

identify point of view, 179, 232, 322

infer, 24, 86, 110, 125, 134, 162, 168, 276, 289, 342, 349, 360, 365, 369, 372, 377, 383, 389, 403, 404, 419, 420, 429, 431, 433, 445, 461, 463, 464, 471, 473, 477, 480, 500, 505, 519, 522, 524

interpret, 89

link past and present, 110, 199, 310

list, 24, 39, 54, 79, 84, 86, 108, 110, 119, 132, 134, 168, 186, 192, 199, 219, 230, 261, 278, 303, 310, 315, 322, 324, 482, 484

locate, 153, 162, 278, 324, 379

make a bar graph, 289

make a reasonable judgment, 513

make a timeline, 247

name, 179, 210, 278, 342, 349, 398, 484, 500, 513

note, 168, 208, 226

predict, 13, 22, 39, 47, 56, 79, 101, 108, 134, 153, 175*p*, 219, 232, 270, 276, 278, 315, 324, 357, 407, 441, 467, 482, 506, 524

recall, 13, 14, 21, 22, 24, 30, 32, 37, 39, 47, 49, 54, 56, 61, 66, 68, 70, 71, 79, 86, 89, 92, 94, 101, 108, 110, 113, 122, 124, 125, 132, 134, 139, 153, 156, 162, 170, 179, 192, 199, 219, 232, 254, 261, 270, 276, 278, 297, 303, 310, 315, 322, 324, 342, 349, 358, 360, 365, 377, 384, 389, 396, 398, 407, 414, 420, 422, 436, 441, 450, 452, 467, 484, 513, 522

respond, 365

sequence, 95, 179, 192, 199, 372, 377, 450, 475, 482, 484, 522

summarize, 162, 168, 179, 199, 208, 261, 276, 278, 297, 315, 324, 360, 441, 452, 524

synthesize, 22, 24, 32, 39, 56, 226, 342, 349, 360, 436, 441, 452, 467, 474, 482, 499

transfer information, 54, 66, 481

Croatia, 538*m*

***Crown of Columbus* (Erdrich),** 174

crust, Earth's, 33, 34, 34*g*, 36–37, 36–37*p*, 565

Cruz, Cecilia, 406

Cry of Dolores, 386

cuatro, 480*p*

Cuba, 340, 455*m*, 457, 534*m*, 557
  baseball and, 465
  dictatorship, 82
  immigrants from, 68, 68*p*, 462, 462*p*
  exiles from, 465–467, 466*p*
  government of, 462, 463–464, 465, 465*g*, 465*m*
  independence in, 388, 463
  literature of, 362–365, 362*p*, 363*p*, 364*p*
  natural resources of, 353*m*, 354
  Spain and, 388
  timeline of, 485

Cuban Missile Crisis, 464

cultural diffusion, 104, 106, 565

cultural diversity, 214–215, 215, 225, 565

cultural exchange, 215–216, 565

cultural landscape, 92, 93, 93*p*, 565

cultural patterns, 216–219, 217*p*, 218*p*, 219*p*

cultural trait, 92, 565

culture, M1, 1, 90–111, 136, 565
  Aztec, 370
  of Brazil, 498
  cultural change, 104–108
  cultural diffusion, 104, 106, 565
  cultural landscape, 92, 93, 93*p*, 565
  cultural traits, 92, 565
  defined, 92–93
  development of, 94–95
  environment and, 93
  geography and, 506
  of Guatemala, 439
  land use and, 120–121
  language and, 92, 98–99, 98–99*m*
  of Middle America, 402–404, 402*p*, 403*p*, 404*p*

migration and, M14–M15
  of Peru, 506
  of Prairie Provinces, 303, 303*p*
  projects, 136, 526
  of Quebec, 294–297, 296, 296*g*, 297, 297*p*
  religions, 100*m*, 101
  social structure and, 96–97
  of the South, 256, 256*g*, 256*m*

culture regions, M1

currents
  air, 42*g*
  ocean, 43

customs, 218*p*

Cuyahoga River, 203, 203*p*, 557

Cuzco, 374, 375, 381, 503, 504, 557, 565

Czech Republic, 550

D

Dakar, Senegal, M10

Dakota people, 299

dams, 165, 274
  civil engineering, 131
  hydroelectric power, 117, 117*p*
  water supply, 127

Dawson, Canada, 321, 557

day and night, 29

death rates, 60, 64–65, 64*g*, 565

Death Valley, 150, 158, 160, 557

Deccan Plateau, 5*m*, 543*m*

deciduous trees and forests, 50, 51, 52, 162, 565

Declaration of Independence, 179

Defoe, Daniel, 511

deforestation, 121, 128, 129, 129*p*, 447, 565

degrees, latitude and longitude, 11, 565

Delaware, 537*m*
  data about, 141*m*, 235*m*, 238
  land use in, 256*m*

Delaware River, 249*m*, 251

Delhi, M12

Delicate Arch, Utah, 55*p*

delta, 554, 555*p*

democracy, 82, 83, 513
demography, 60, 565
Dene people, 215*m*, 319
Denmark, 2*p*, 18, 557
Denver, Colorado, 237, 273
dependency, government, 80, 81, 565
Des Moines, Iowa, 239
descendant, 294, 565
descent, 299, 565
desert scrub, 50, 51, 52, 160–161, 160*m*, 565
deserts, 52, 565
  air circulation and, 43*g*
  Sahara, 53*p*
Detroit, Michigan, 241*p*, 269, 269*m*, 557
developed nations, 565
  economies, 74, 75
  land use, 122, 123
  levels of development, 77*m*
  trade, 78, 79
developing nations, 565
  economies, 74, 76, 77
  levels of development, 77*m*
  trade, 78, 79
dictatorships, 82, 393, 565
Dion, Celine, 230
direct democracy, 82, 565
directions
  cardinal, 11
  intermediate, 11
Discovery (space shuttle), 8–9*p*
discrimination, 191, 565
diseases, 381, 384, 447–448, 497
  migration and, 68
  Native Americans and, 177, 301
  population growth and, 64, 65
distance, 21
distortion, maps, 16, 17, 18–19, 565
District of Columbia, 537*m*
diversify, 500, 511–512, 512*p*, 521, 565
diversity, 128, 129, 358, 428, 461, 565
Dom Pedro, 389

Dominica, 411, 458
Dominican Republic, 455*m*, 458, 534*m*
  culture of, 412
  natural resources of, 353*m*, 354
dominion, 196, 565
Dominion of Canada, 291
Dover, Delaware, 239
drilling, 258, 258*p*
drought, 357*p*
dry climates, 43*g*, 50, 51
Dubai, United Arab Emirates, 79*p*
Durham, Earl of, 195
Dutch colonies, 411, 416, 491, 492
Duvalier, François, 473
Duvalier, Jean-Claude, 473

E

Earth
  atmosphere, 34*g*, 35
  axis, 28, 29, 30, 30*g*
  core of, 33, 34, 34*g*
  crust of, 33, 34, 34*g*, 36–37, 36–37*g*
  day and night, 29
  distance from sun, 28
  forces inside, 36–38, 36–37*g*, 38*m*
  forces on surface, 39
  forces shaping, 33–39
  hemispheres, M5, 10, 11*g*, 11*p*, 567
  mantle, 33, 34, 34*g*, 36*g*
  maps and globes, M4–M5, 16–22
  movements of, M2–M3
  orbit of, 28, 30
  rotation of, 29
  seasons and latitude, 30–32, 30–31*g*
  structure, 34–35, 34*g*
  time zones, 29, 29*m*
  viewed from space, 8–9*p*, 23*p*
earthquakes, 33, 37, 37*p*, 340, 376, 427, 429
east, 11

East Timor, 3*p*, 542*m*
Eastern Hemisphere, M5, 11*g*
Eastern Orthodox Church, 100*p*
economies and economic systems, 74–79
  of Atlantic Provinces, 313, 313*g*, 313*m*
  of Brazil, 525
  of British Columbia, 309–310, 309*m*
  of Canada, 219
  of Chile, 508, 508*g*
  climate and, 349
  diversifying, 358, 428, 500, 511–512, 512*p*, 521
  economic downturns, 192
  foreign debt, 394, 394*g*, 395–396
  Great Depression, 189, 190*g*
  of Guatemala, 439
  of Honduras, 428
  international alliances, 84
  kinds of, 74–75
  land use and, 122–123
  levels of economic development, 76–77
  of Mexico, 432*g*, 432*m*
  of the Midwest, 265, 265*g*, 265*m*
  migration and, 68
  natural resources and, 356–358, 356*g*, 357*p*, 358*p*
  of Northeast, 250, 250*g*, 250*m*
  one resource, 356, 357
  of Prairie Provinces, 300, 300*g*, 300*m*
  projects, 136, 526
  of Puerto Rico, 459
  recession, 266
  stages of economic activity, 122–123
  standard of living, 219
  of the United States, 206–208, 206*g*, 219
  of Venezuela, 518, 518*g*, 518*m*, 519–520
  world, 357
  world trade patterns, 78–79, 78*g*
economy, 74, 565
ecotourism, 450, 450*p*, 565

Ecuador, 487*m*, 490, 490*p*, 534*m*
culture of, 417
factories in, 358*p*
farming in, M16*m*, M16*p*, 419*p*
foreign debt of, 394*g*
independence in, 387*m*, 388
editorial pages, RW1
Edmonton, Alberta, 286, 303
education, 251
Egypt, 60*p*, 540*m*, 557
El Niño, 343, 343*p*, 357, 566
El Salvador, 425*m*, 427, 534*m*, 557
economy of, 358
languages of, 403
elections, 83
electricity, 115
hybrid cars, 119, 130, 130*g*, 132
elevation, M11, 332, 332*m*, 346, 349, 565
Elizabeth II, Queen of England, 199, 199*p*
Ellington, Duke, 225*p*, 226
Ellis Island, New York, 67*p*, 222, 254, 254*p*
Emancipation Proclamation, 185
Emerson, Ralph Waldo, 225, 225*p*
emigration, 406*p*, 407, 566
from Cuba, 462, 462*p*
Empire of Gold, 383*p*
Empire State Building, 252
empires, 80, 81, 566
employment
developed nations, 76
land use and, 131
in Mexico City, 433–434, 436
encomiendas, 384, 566
endangered species, 301
energy, 333, 566
fossil fuels, 117, 118, 119
geothermal, 115, 118, 119*p*
resources, 115, 117–119, 132, 164*m*, 165, 167, 333, 333*g*
engineering, civil, 131
England
colonies of, 382, 411, 416, 426, 457, 458, 460
See also Great Britain; United Kingdom

English language, 98, 99
enslave, 177, 566
entertainment industry, 276, 276*p*, 310
environment, 13, 112–135, 566
climate and, 343–349
cultural landscape, 92, 93, 93*p*, 565
culture and, 93
defined, 120
earthquakes and, 340, 376, 427, 429
human-environment interaction, M1, 128–132
importance of the rain forest to, 496–497, 496*g*, 497*p*
issues regarding, 203–205, 203*p*, 204*m*, 204*p*, 205*p*
land use, 120–125
modification of, 131
natural resources, 114–119
photosynthesis and, 495
population growth and, 66
smog and the, 511
See also pollution
equal-area maps, M7, 19, 19*p*, 566
Equator, M2, M3, M4, M7, 11, 11*g*, 157, 330, 344*m*, 346, 557, 566
air circulation and, 43*g*
global grid, 12*g*
Mercator projection, 18
ocean currents, 42
seasons, 30*g*, 31*g*
equinoxes, 30*g*, 566
Erdrich, Louise, 174
Ericsson, Leif, 311, 311*p*
Eritrea, 80*p*, 540*m*
erosion, 33, 39, 39*p*, 566
Eskimos, 159
ethics, 101, 566
Ethiopia, 546
Ethiopian Highlands, 5*m*, 541*m*
ethnic groups, 216, 224*g*, 228, 411–412, 411*p*, 566
of Argentina, 488
of Bolivia, 489
of Brazil, 489, 498*g*, 499, 499*p*
of British Columbia, 304, 304*p*, 305, 309–310

of Canada, 293
of the Caribbean, 456–461
of Central America, 426–429
of Chile, 489
of Colombia, 490
of Ecuador, 490
of Guatemala, 437, 438, 439, 439*g*, 439*m*
of Guyana, 491
of Haiti, 474
of Mexico, 428
of Panama, 446*g*
of Paraguay, 491
of Peru, 491
of South America, 488–493
of Suriname, 492
of the United States, 236–247, 263*g*
of Uruguay, 492
of Venezuela, 493
Europe, 3*m*, 5*m*, 7*m*, 135, 531*m*, 533*m*, 557
climate, 43
colonization, 125
cultural change, 104
economy, 76
emigration, 67
land use, 121
nation-states, 81
physical map, 539*m*
political map, 538*m*
suburbanization, 70
See also individual countries
European Union, 79, 84
Evans Manufacturing Company, 255
Everglades National Park, 238*p*
exiles, 314, 465–467, 466*p*, 566
exports, 207, 393, 405, 419, 566
of Argentina, 488
of Bolivia, 489
of Brazil, 489
of the Caribbean, 456–461
of Central America, 426–429
of Chile, 489, 508, 508*g*, 509, 512
of Colombia, 490
of Ecuador, 490
of Guyana, 491

of Mexico, 428, 432g, 432m
of Paraguay, 491
of Peru, 491
of South America, 488–493
of Suriname, 492
of Uruguay, 492
of Venezuela, 493, 518, 518g, 518m
expository essays, RW4
extended families, 96, 97, 103p, 566

F

factories, 183, 197p, 358, 358p, 450, 499–500. *See also* industrialization
Falkland Islands, 337m, 487m, 534m
fall, 31, 31g, 32
fallout shelters, 191p
families, 96, 96p, 97, 97p, 103p, 566, 570
farming, 164, 164m, 167, 279g, 357
  Aztec, 370–371, 371p
  in Brazil, 499–500
  in Canada, 216p
  in Caribbean Islands, 353m, 354, 412
  in Chile, 510, 511–512, 512p
  in Ecuador, M16m, M16p
  in Guatemala, 438, 438p
  in Mexico, 431
  in the Midwest, 264–265, 264p, 266–267, 266g
  on the plains, 149
  in Prairie Provinces, 300g, 302, 302p
  in the South, 257, 257p
  in South America, 355, 419
  subsistence, 377, 419, 490p, M16
  technology and, 264p, 266–267, 300
  in the United States, M16m, M16p
  in Vietnam, M17p
  See also agriculture

faults, 37, 566
favelas, 420, 420p, 500
federation, 291, 566
Ferdinand, Prince of Spain, 387, 388
fertilizers, 129
festivals, 90–91p, 99
fiber-optic networks, 450
fire, 94, 106
First Nations, 228–229, 229p. *See also* Native Americans
fishing, 202, 202p, 258, 353m, 354, 355, 355p, 357
  in Atlantic Provinces, 313g, 313m, 315
  effect on environment, 129
flags, 162, 234p
floating beds, 371, 371p
flood plain, 554
flooding, 47, 66, 131, 152, 520p, 521, 521p
Florida, 156, 158, 181m, 217p, 218, 238p, 537m, 557
  data about, 141m, 235m, 238
  farming in, 257
  fishing in, 258
  Hurricane Katrina, 47p
  land use in, 256m
  Spain and, 175
  in Sun Belt, 260m
food, 349, 353m, 354, 414, 414p, 460
  and development of culture, 94
  natural resources, 114
  and population growth, 66
  See also agriculture; farming
Food and Agriculture Organization, 84
football, 226
foreign aid, 84
foreign debt, 394, 394g, 395–396, 566
foreign trade, 207–208
forests and forestry, 160m, 162, 162p, 163, 163p, 164m, 165, 168, 168p, 205, 205p, 258
  in Canada, 306, 306g, 306m, 315
  coniferous, 51, 52, 53p, 54
  deciduous, 51, 52

deforestation, 121, 128, 129, 129p, 447
  effect on environment, 129
  mixed, 52, 53p
  population growth and, 66
  rain forest, 50, 52, 52p
  See also trees
Fort Garry, 214p
forty-niner, 273, 273p, 566
fossil fuels, 117, 118, 119, 164m, 165, 166, 204, 566
fossils, 51p
Fox, Vicente, 428, 436, 436p
France, 104, 538m
  areas of influence, 173m, 177m
  Canada and, 194, 194p, 195–196, 294, 314, 314m
  colonization by, 382, 411, 416, 471
  French and Indian War, 178
  Louisiana Territory, 181, 181m
  Native Americans and, 177, 177m
  Panama Canal and, 446
  revolution in, 386
Francophone, 294–295, 566
Frankfort, Kentucky, 240
Fraser River, 152, 305, 307, 557
Fredericton, New Brunswick, 287
free-market economy, 75
free trade, 567
Free Trade Agreement (FTA), 208
French and Indian War, 178, 194
French Canadians, 194, 197, 228
French Guiana, 416
French language, 99
fresh water, 35
fruit trees, 349
FTA. *See* Free Trade Agreement (FTA)
fuels
  fossil, 117, 118, 119, 164m, 165, 166, 204
  natural resources, 116, 117
  See also energy
fugitive, 184, 566
Fugitive Slave Act, 184
Fujimori, Alberto, 395

Fulton, Robert, 183*p*
fur trade, 177, 193, 194, 214*p*, 305

G

Gabon, 540*m*
Gabrielino, 216
Gadsden Purchase, 181*m*
Galápagos Islands, 337*m*, 535*m*
galaxies, 28, 28*p*
games, 368, 413. *See also* sports
gas
  atmospheric, 34*g*, 35
  natural resources, 116, 117
gasoline engines, 119, 130, 130*g*,
  132
Gatún Locks, 449, 449*p*
gauchos, 341*p*, 347, 417, 492*p*, 567
Genoa, Italy, 104, 557
**geographic information systems
  (GIS),** 16, 17, 567
geographic signature, M1
geography, 567
  of Brazil, 495–498, 495*p*, 496*g*,
    497*p*, 498*g*, 498*m*
  of British Columbia, 306, 306*g*,
    306*m*
  of Chile, 509–510, 509*p*, 510*p*
  culture and, 506
  defined, 10
  five themes of, 10–13, 23
  Guiding Questions, 1, 139, 329
  of Latin America, 339*m*
  maps and globes, 16–22, 23
  of Mexico City, 435, 435*p*
  of Panama, 444–448, 446, 446*g*,
    446*m*
  of Peru, 501, 501*p*, 502, 502*g*,
    502*m*, 503–506
  physical geography, 26–57
  projects, 136, 526
  themes of, M1–M2, 10–13, 23
  of the West, 272, 272*g*, 272*m*
  writing skills, 24
  See also physical geography
George, Jean Craighead, 88–89,
  89*p*

Georgia, Republic of, 548
Georgia, (United States), 120,
  120*p*, 121, 537*m*, 542*m*, 557
  data about, 141*m*, 235*m*, 238
  farming in, 257
  industry in, 255, 257
  land use in, 256*m*
  in Sun Belt, 260*m*
  textile industry, 259
geothermal energy, 115, 118,
  119*p*
Germany, 97, 98, 116*p*, 118, 189,
  190, 538*m*, 557
geyser, 274*p*
Ghana, M15, 3*p*, 540*m*
GIS. *See* geographic information
  systems
Glacier National Park, 274
glaciers, 4*p*, 150, 151, 554, 554*p*,
  567
global grid, M5, 12, 12*g*
globes, M4–M5, M6, 16, 567. *See
  also* maps
**GOES (Geostationary
  Operational Environmental
  Satellites),** 46*p*
gold, 164*m*, 166, 167, 196, 353*m*,
  355
  in British Columbia, 307, 307*p*
  in Yukon Territory, 321
Gold Rush, 161, 224, 273
Gondwanaland, 38*m*
goods, 75, 567
gores, M6, M7
gorges, 376
government, 567
  of Argentina, 418, 418*p*, 488
  of Bolivia, 489
  of Brazil, 489
  of Canada, 198, 291, 291*g*, 292,
    292*g*, 319
  of the Caribbean, 456–461
  of Chile, 489, 513, 513*p*
  of Colombia, 490
  of Cuba, 462, 463–464, 465, 465*g*,
    465*m*
  development of culture and, 94
  of Ecuador, 490

  government ownership, 75
  of Guyana, 491
  of Haiti, 470, 470*p*, 473
  Incan, 375
  of Mexico, 428
  of Northern Territories, 320, 320*g*,
    320*m*
  oil boom and, 517, 520
  of Paraguay, 491
  of Peru, 491
  projects, 136, 526
  of Puerto Rico, 476, 479, 479*g*,
    479*m*
  in South America, 488–493
  of Suriname, 492
  types of, 80–81, 82–83
  of United States, 292*g*
  of Uruguay, 492
  of Venezuela, 493, 521, 522, 522*p*
governor-general, 198
Gran Colombia, 387*m*, 389, 493
Grand Banks, 312
Grand Canyon, 44*p*, 219*p*
Grand Coulee Dam, 165
graphs, climate, 48–49, 48*g*, 56
grasslands, 51, 52, 54, 159, 159*p*,
  160*m*, 567
Grasslands National Park, 301
Great Basin, 150, 160–161, 160*m*
Great Britain, 539*m*
  areas of influence, 173*m*, 177*m*
  Canada and, 194, 194*p*, 195–196,
    198, 291, 291*g*, 292, 292*g*, 294,
    314, 314*m*
  colonies of, 177*m*, 178, 178*p*
  Commonwealth of Nations, 199
  French and Indian War, 178
  Native Americans and, 177*m*, 178,
    178*p*
  parliamentary system of, 198
  Revolutionary War, 179, 179*p*
  See also England; United Kingdom
Great Depression, 189, 190, 190*g*,
  190*p*
Great Lakes, 142*m*, 142*p*, 151, 151*p*,
  202, 203, 204*m*, 537*m*, 557, 567
  transportation on, 206–207, 206*g*
Great Lakes Fishery Commission,
  202

Great Plains, 4*m,* 128, 149, 158, 160, 532*m,* 535*m,* 557

Great Salt Lake, 150

Greece, 93, 100*p,* 538*m,* 557

Green Revolution, 65, 567

Greenfield, Eloise, 280–283

Greenland, 18, 62*m,* 530*m,* 532*m,* 545*m,* 557

Greenwich, England, M5, 12*p,* 557

Grenada, 414*p,* 455*m,* 458

Guam, 188, 544*m*

Guantánamo Bay, 457

Guaraní, 491

Guatemala, 425*m,* 427, 534*m,* 557

  civil war in, 440–441

  coffee from, 439

  culture of, 403, 439

  economy of, 439

  ethnic groups in, 437, 438, 439, 439*g,* 439*m*

  farming in, 438, 438*p*

  indigenous people in, 440

  land reform in, 438, 438*p*

  languages of, 403, 439*m*

  Mayas in, 369, 427, 439, 439*g,* 439*m*

  Native Americans in, 437, 438, 439, 439*g,* 439*m,* 440

  political movements in, 440–441, 440*p*

  population of, 453*g*

  weather in, 357*p*

  women in, 424*p,* 440

Guatemala City, 427

Guinea, 546

Guinea-Bissau, 546

Gulf-Atlantic Coastal Plains, 150

Gulf of Mexico, 142*m,* 149, 152

Gulf Stream, 42, 558

Guyana, 487*m,* 491, 534*m*

  culture of, 416

  data about, 491

  landforms of, 341

Guyana Highlands, 4*m*

H

haciendas, 383, 384, 392, 567

Haida people, 193, 193*p*

hail, 40

Hainan, 50*p*

Haiti, 385, 455*m,* 458, 459, 534*m,* 558

  culture of, 412

  data about, 474

  government of, 470, 470*p,* 473

  history of, 472, 472*g,* 472*m*

  housing in, 474*p*

  human rights in, 473

  poverty in, 474–475

  refugees, 471, 471*p*

  slaves in, 334, 334*p,* 471

  United States and, 471, 473

Halifax, Nova Scotia, 287

Harrisburg, Pennsylvania, 244

Hartford, Connecticut, 239

Harvard University, 251

Havana, 457

Hawaii, M1, 33*p,* 37, 37*p,* 74*p,* 149, 158, 181*m,* 188, 271, 536*m*

  data about, 141*m,* 235*m,* 239

  volcanoes in, 150

  in World War II, 190

haze, 204, 567

health, 64, 65, 68

heat, inside Earth, 36

Helena, Montana, 242

Helsinki, Finland, 56*g*

hemispheres, M5, 10, 11*g,* 11*p,* 567

hemlock, 89, 567

herding, M17*p,* 229, 347

Hernandez, Orlando, 466

Hidalgo, Miguel, 386–387, 386*p*

hieroglyphics, 369, 370, 567

high latitudes, 32, 32*m,* 41, 567

highland vegetation, 52

highlands, 341

highways, 21*m,* 265*g,* 265*m*

hills, 35, 554, 567

Hindi language, M13*m*

Hinduism, 69*m,* 100, 412

Hispanic Americans, 256, 256*g,* 276

Hispaniola, 340, 412, 458, 459, 471, 558

history

  of Haiti, 472, 472*g,* 472*m*

  interdisciplinary links, 78

  projects, 136, 326, 526

Hitler, Adolf, 190

hockey, 230, 230*p*

Hohokam people, 103

Holocaust, 190, 567

Holy See. *See* Vatican City

Homestead Act (1862), 188, 567

Honduras, 425*m,* 428, 534*m*

  cultural heritage of, 402*p,* 403

  economy of, 428

  Mayas in, 369

  vegetation of, 348*m,* 349

Hong Kong, China, 45*p*

Honolulu, Hawaii, 74*p,* 239

horses, 215–216, 215*p*

hot climates, 41

House of Commons, 198, 319

housing

  cultural change and, 105

  in Haiti, 474*p*

  in Mexico, 433–436, 433*p,* 434*m,* 435*p*

  natural resources, 114

  in Peru, 503, 503*p*

  and population growth, 66

  See also architecture

Houston, Texas, 259

How the Other Half Lives (Riis), 187, 187*p*

Hudson Bay, 142*m,* 194, 298, 298*p*

Hudson River, 253

human-environment interaction, M1, 13, 123, 124, 128– 132, 567

  economic activity, 122–123

  Boston, Massachusetts, 124

  land use, 131*p*

  landforms as barriers, 5, 5*p*

  population density, 72*p*

  railroads, 269*m*

human geography, 58–89
  economic systems, 74–79
  migration, 67–71
  political systems, 80–84
  population, 60–66
human rights, 473, 513
humid continental climate, 51, 567
humid subtropical climate, 51, 345
Hungary, 550
Huntsville, Alabama, 259, 259p
Huron, 215m, 232m
Hurricane Katrina, 47p
hurricanes, 46, 46p, 47, 47p, 158, 191g, 345, 345p, 428, 429, 567
Hurston, Zora Neale, 225, 225p
hybrid cars, 119, 130, 130g, 132
hydroelectricity, 117, 117p, 165, 167, 272g, 333, 333m, 353m, 354, 567

I

ice
  ice caps, 51, 52
  ice floes, 35p
  ice packs, 52
  ice sheets, 35
  on mountains, 54
  weathering and erosion, 39
ice age, 175
Iceland, 119p, 538m
Idaho, 536m
  climate in, 272m
  data about, 141m, 235m, 239
  hydroelectricity in, 272g
  natural resources of, 273
ideas, cultural change and, 106, 107
Illinois, 537m
  data about, 141m, 235m, 239
illiterate, 464, 567
immigrants, 367, 567
immigration, 67, 67p, 213m, 407, 411, 568
  to Brazil, 489, 499
  to Canada, 197, 214, 216–219, 216p, 227, 228g, 229–230, 293

Ellis Island, 254, 254p
  Industrial Revolution and, 183, 188
  to the United States, 216–219, 222–226, 222p, 223p, 224g, 225p, 301
immunity, 301, 568
imports, 207, 393, 568
Incas, 373–376, 373p, 374, 374p, 375p, 376p
  in Ecuador, 490p
  Machu Picchu, 504, 504p
  in Peru, 503, 506, 506p
  Pizarro and, 381
indentured servants, 178, 568
India, 558
  agriculture, 13p
  climate of, M12m
  cultural landscape, 93
  government, 83
  languages of, M13m, 99
  migration, 67, 69m
  religions, 100, 101p
  traditional dress, 90p–91p, 109p
  weather, 40
Indian Ocean, 3m, 5m, 7m, 56
Indian Removal Act (1830), 182, 182m
Indiana, 537m, 542m
  data about, 141m, 235m, 239
Indianapolis, Indiana, 239
Indians. See First Nations; indigenous people; Native Americans
indigenous people, 175, 402, 417, 491, 568
  aurora borealis and, 318
  in Brazil, 497, 498
  in British Columbia, 305, 305p, 307–308, 308p
  diseases and, 301
  in Guatemala, 440
  in Northern Territories, 319, 319p, 320g, 320m
  of Prairie Provinces, 298, 299, 301
  in rain forest, 497, 498
  of Venezuela, 493
  See also Native Americans
Indonesia, 71, 93, 93p, 542m, 558
Industrial Revolution, 76, 95, 183, 188, 568

industrialization, 259, 358, 358p, 450, 568
  cultural change and, 105
  defined, 120
  developing nations, 77
  early farming and, 61m
  economic development and, 76
  land use, 125, 131–132, 131p
  urbanization and, 70
industry, 236–247
  in Canada, 286–289
  ownership, 74–75
  in the South, 259–261
informational texts, RW1
Ingstad, Helge, 311
injustice, 404
institutions, 92, 95, 568
interaction, M1
interdependence, 79, 568
Interdisciplinary
  history, 78
  language arts, 412, 511
  math, 11, 29, 129, 216, 369
  music, 107
  science, 51, 150, 301, 314, 345, 345p, 360, 376, 495
  technology, 107
  time, 191p, 340
  world, 268, 466
interest payments, 75
Interior Plains, 149
intermediate directions, 11
international, 84, 568
International Monetary Fund, 395
international organizations, 84
Internet, 107g, 192, 275g
Inti (sun god), 376
Inuit, 40p, 120, 121, 155, 155p, 215m, 229, 319, 319p, 320, 322, 322p
Inuktitut, 322, 568
investment, 75
involuntary migration, 68
Iowa, 537m
  data about, 141m, 235m, 239
Iqaluit, Nunavut, 31p, 288, 321p, 322, 558

Iran, 82, 542*m*, 558
Iraq, 135, 191*p*, 191*g*, 192, 542*m*
Ireland, 68, 538*m*, 539*m*
iron ore, 164*m*, 166, 353*m*, 355
Iroquois people, 202*p*, 215*m*, 232*m*, 294
irrigation, 94, 121, 121*p*, 568
Isabella, Queen of Spain, 379
Islam, 69*m*, 100, 101, 103*p*
island, 554
Isle of Spice, 458
Israel, 548
isthmus, 340, 554, 568
Isthmus of Panama, 337*m*, 535*m*, 558
Itaipú Dam, 333, 333*p*
Italy, 104, 538*m*, 558
Iturbide, Agustín de, 387

J

jackfruit, 50*p*
Jackson, Mississippi, 241
Jakarta, Indonesia, 71, 558
Jamaica, 340, 455*m*, 459, 558
  farming in, 412
  music of, 414
  natural resources of, 353*m*, 354
Jamestown, Virginia, 178, 558
Japan, 5*p*, 135, 542*m*, 558
  bullet trains, 105*p*
  cultural change, 104, 106
  culture, 92*p*, 93
  economy, 76
  energy resources, 118
  land use, 120, 121
  population density, 63
  in World War II, 190
jeans, 104
Jefferson, Thomas, 179, 180
Jefferson City, Missouri, 241
Jews, 98, 190. *See also* Judaism
jíbaros, 479
Jim Crow laws, 186
Johnson, Andrew, 186
Jordan, 39*p*, 542*m*

Judaism, 100, 101, 412. *See also* Jews
Juneau, Alaska, 236

K

Kahlo, Frida, 403*p*
Kalahari Desert, 5*m*, 541*m*
Kamchatka Peninsula, 5*m*
Kansas, 537*m*
  data about, 141*m*, 235*m*, 240
  farming in, 267
Kazakhstan, 548
Kennedy, John F., 206, 464
Kentucky, 537*m*
  data about, 141*m*, 235*m*, 240
  land use in, 256*m*
  mining in, 258
  natural resources of, 164*m*, 166
  population density, 249
Kenya, M17*p*, 114*p*, 540*m*
keys, maps, M8, M9, 16, 20*m*, 21, 57
Khrushchev, Nikita, 464, 464*p*
Kim Jong Il, 82
King, Martin Luther, Jr., 191
kings and queens, 82, 83
Kingston, Jamaica, 459
Kingstown, St. Vincent and the Grenadines, 460
Klondike River, 321
Kocour, Ruth, 148
Korea, North, 82, 548
Korea, South, 67, 548
Korean War, 191, 191*g*
Kuwait, 83, 542*m*

L

La Paz, Bolivia, 338, 338*p*, 489
labor force, 188, 568
Labrador, 196*m*
Labrador Sea, 4*m*
lacrosse, 226
ladinos, 438, 439, 439*g*, 439*m*, 568

Lake Erie, 151, 203, 203*p*, 210*m*, 537*m*
Lake Huron, 151, 537*m*
Lake Maracaibo, 342, 517
Lake Michigan, 151, 537*m*
Lake Ontario, 151, 537*m*
Lake Superior, 142*m*, 142*p*, 151, 206*g*, 207, 537*m*
Lake Texcoco, 370
Lake Titicaca, 333, 333*p*, 342, 415, 415*p*, 501, 503, 558
Lake Washington, 275
lakes, 35, 44, 151–152, 151*p*
Lakes Region, 510
land bridge, 175, 568
land reform, 438, 438*p*, 568
land use, M16–M17, 120–125, 438, 438*p*
  changes in, 125
  culture and, 120–121
  economics and, 122–123
  in Prairie Provinces, 300*g*
  in the South, 256*m*
  See also farming
landforms, M1, 35, 149–151, 149*p*, 151*p*, 340–341, 340*p*, 341*p*, 568
  as barriers, 5, 5*p*
  of Chile, 489, 509
  of Latin America, 332, 332*m*
landmasses, 19, 568
landscape. *See* environment
landslides, 520*p*, 521, 521*p*
language arts, 134, 210, 324, 412, 511
languages, M1, 401*m*
  of Argentina, 488
  of Bolivia, 489
  of Brazil, 331*m*, 331*p*, 417, 489
  of Canada, 197, 286–289
  of Caribbean Islands, 412, 456–461
  of Central America, 403, 426–429
  of Chile, 489
  of Colombia, 490
  culture and, 92, 98–99, 106
  of Ecuador, 490
  of El Salvador, 403

English, 98, 99
of First Nations, 228
French, 99, 194, 197
of Guatemala, 403, 439*m*
of Guyana, 491
of Haiti, 472, 474
Incan, 377
of the Inuit, 322, 322*p*
Latin, 340
of Latin America, 340, 377, 401*m*, 403, 412, 416, 417, 426–429
major groups of, 98–99*m*
maps of, M13*m*
of Mexico, 428
movement and, 331
of Native Americans, 377
of Panama, 403
of Paraguay, 491
of Peru, 491, 502*g*
of Puerto Rico, 477
of Quebec, 295, 296*g*
Russian, 99*p*
of South America, 416, 488–493
Spanglish, 478
Spanish, 99
of Suriname, 492
of Uruguay, 492
of Venezuela, 493
L'Anse aux Meadows, 311, 311*p*, 558
Lansing, Michigan, 241
Laos, 548
Latin America, 330*m*, 331*m*, 332*m*, 334*m*
climate of, 343–349, 343*p*, 344*m*, 346*g*, 348*m*
developing nations, 77
foreign debt of, 394, 394*g*
geographic features of, 339
landforms of, 340–341, 340*p*, 341*p*
languages of, 331, 340, 377, 401*m*, 403, 412, 416, 417, 426–429
location of, 330*m*, 339, 339*m*, 360*m*, 398*m*, 422*m*
migration to, M15*m*
natural resources of, 352–358, 352*p*, 353*m*, 354*p*, 355*p*, 356*g*, 357*p*, 358*p*

physical geography, 337*m*
regions of, 339*m*
United States and, 330
urbanization, 71
waterways in, 342, 342*p*
See also Middle America; South America
latitude, M4, 11–12, 11*p*, 157, 568
climate and, 41
defined, 10
global grid, 12, 12*g*
high, 32, 32*m*, 41
low, 32, 32*m*, 41
middle, 32, 32*m*
seasons and, 30–32, 30–31*g*
winds and, 42*g*
zones of, 32*m*
Laurentian Highlands, 149
lava, 36, 142*p*, 150
laws, 80, 81, 94
lead, 164*m*, 166
Lebanon, 549
legend, maps, 21
Lent, 413, 413*p*
Lesage, Jean, 295
Lewis, Meriwether, 180, 180*p*, 181, 272
Liberia, 546
Libya, 82, 540*m*, 558
lichen, 34, 568
life expectancy, 64, 65, 568
Lima, Peru, 383, 419, 491, 503, 503*p*, 558
Lincoln, Abraham, 185–186
Lincoln, Nebraska, 242
Line of Demarcation, 380
literacy, 457, 464, 568
literature, 225, 225*p*
of Canada, 230
Childtimes (Greenfield and Little), 280–283
of Chile, 418
of Colombia, 418
of Cuba, 362–365, 362*p*, 363*p*, 364*p*
My Side of the Mountain (George), 88–89
Surveyor (Ada), 362–365

of Trinidad, 412
Uncle Tom's Cabin (Stowe), 185
Lithuania, 538*m*
Little, Lessie Jones, 280–283
Little Havana, 463, 466*p*
Little Rock, Arkansas, 237
living resources, 116
llamas, 334, 334*p*, 347, 416*p*
location, M1, 11–12, 330
borders, 2, 2*p*
Canada, 140*m*
climate and, 41
hydroelectricity, 333, 333*g*
United States, 140*m*
See also place location
locator globe, M8
locks, 153, 568
locomotive, 201*p*
logging, 205, 205*p*, 497, 497*p*
Loihi (volcano), 150
London, England, M9, 22, 22*m*, 558
Lone Star Republic, 183
longitude, M5, 11–12, 11*p*, 568
defined, 10
global grid, 12, 12*g*
Mercator projection, 18
time zones and, 29
Los Angeles, California, 276, 276*p*, 558
Louisiana, M5, 177*m*, 537*m*
Cajuns in, 314
data about, 141*m*, 235*m*, 240
drilling in, 258
farming in, 257
land use in, 256*m*
music of, 225
natural resources of, 164*m*, 166
in Sun Belt, 260*m*
Louisiana Purchase, 181–182, 181*m*, 569
Louisiana Territory, 181, 181*m*, 272
L'Ouverture, Toussaint, 385, 385*p*, 471, 473, 568
low latitudes, 32, 32*m*, 41, 569
Lower Canada, 194, 195, 291

lowlands, 151, 569. *See also* plains
Loyalists, 194
lumber, 164*m,* 165, 205, 205*p*

M

Macdonald-Cartier Bridge, 290, 290*p*
Machapuchare, Nepal, 54*p*
machines, 76. *See also* industrialization
Machu Picchu, 376, 504, 504*p*
Mackenzie, William, 195
Mackenzie River, 152, 167, 558
Madeira, 46*p*
Madison, Wisconsin, 247
magazines, 107
Magellan, Ferdinand, 507, 507*p,* 509, 510, 569
magma, 33, 36, 36–37*g,* 150, 569
Maine, 30*p,* 537*m*
  data about, 141*m,* 235*m,* 240
maize, 369, 569
malaria, 447–448
Malay Peninsula, 5*m*
Malaysia, 103*p,* 542*m*
Malcolm, Andrew H., 227
Mali, 547
Managua, Nicaragua, 429
Manifest Destiny, 183, 569
Manitoba, Canada, 196*m,* 216*p,* 298, 300*m*
  data about, 141*m,* 285*m,* 287
  indigenous people of, 299
mantle, Earth's, 33, 34, 34*p,* 36*p,* 569
manufacturing, 120, 123, 569. *See also* industrialization
map key, M8, M9, 568
map skills
  analyze, 22, 173*m,* 502, 508
  apply information, 455*m*
  compare, 63, 249*m*
  compare and contrast, 45, 53, 124, 337*m,* 348*m,* 508
  contrast, 69, 235*m*

draw conclusions, 177*m,* 184*m,* 204*m,* 215*m,* 260*m,* 269*m,* 285*m,* 309*m,* 314*m,* 344*m,* 353*m,* 367*m,* 508, 518
draw inferences, 77, 100
human-environment interaction, 124, 269*m,* 434*m*
identify, 63, 69, 77, 124, 173*m,* 177*m,* 181*m,* 309*m,* 502, 508
identify effects, 181*m,* 487
infer, 4, 115, 339*m,* 502
interaction, 115, 204*m*
link past and present, 99
list, 184*m,* 215*m,* 249*m,* 269*m*
locate, 173*m,* 204*m,* 213*m,* 260*m,* 285*m*
location, 53, 330*m,* 344*m,* 348*m,* 360*m,* 398*m,* 422*m,* 425*m,* 508, 524*m*
make generalizations, 182*m*
movement, 69, 182*m,* 213*m,* 249*m,* 260*m,* 309*m,* 353*m,* 382*m,* 445*m*
name, 182*m,* 196*m*
natural resources, 164*m*
physical map, 147*m*
place, 99, 100, 177*m,* 196*m,* 337*m*
place location, 210*m,* 232*m*
predict, 213*m*
read a map key, 235*m,* 314*m*
regions, 45, 63, 77, 181*m,* 184*m,* 215*m,* 235*m,* 285*m,* 314*m,* 337*m,* 351*m,* 367*m,* 387*m,* 401*m*
tornadoes, 158*m,* 158*p*
vegetation, 160*m*
maple leaf, 162
maps, 16–22
  colors of, 21
  conformal, 18
  of different scales, M9
  distortion, 16, 17, 18–19
  equal-area, M7, 19, 19*p,* 566
  highway, 21*m*
  how to use, M8–M9
  keys, M8, M9, 16, 20*m,* 21, 57, 235*m,* 314*m,* 568
  latitude and longitude in, 11–12, 11*g,* 12*g*
  legend, 21
  locator globes, 20*m*

mental maps, 25
Mercator projection, M6, 18, 18*g*
parts of, 21
physical, M11, M339, 20, 20*m,* 136, 332, 332*m,* 532–533*m,* 535*m,* 539*m,* 541*m,* 543*m,* 544*m,* 545*m*
political, M10, 331*m,* 487*m,* 530–531*m,* 534*m,* 536–537*m,* 538*m,* 540*m,* 542*m*
population density, 6–7*m,* 72–73, 73*m,* 86
projections, M6–M7, 16, 18–19, 18*g,* 19*g*
reading, 20–22
Robinson projection, M7, 19, 19*g*
same-shape, M6
scale, 16, 21, 22*m*
scale bars, 20*m,* 21, 573
special purpose, M12*m,* M13*m*
symbols, 21
titles, M8
weather forecasting, 46*p*
See also globes
maquiladoras, 405, 569
Marconi, Guglielmo, 312
Mardi Gras, 144*p*
marine west coast climate, 51, 157, 569
maritime, 315, 569
Maritime Provinces, 315
markets, 74*p*
Márquez, Gabriel García, 418
Marshall Islands, 544*m,* 549
Martí, José de San, 388
Martin, Lydia, 466
Martinique, 455*m*
Maryland, 537*m*
  data about, 141*m,* 235*m,* 240
  fishing in, 258
mass transit, 275, 569
Massachusetts, 537*m*
  data about, 141*m,* 235*m,* 240
  Pilgrims in, 178
Massachusetts Institute of Technology, 251
Massif Central, 539*m*
materials. *See* resources
math, 86, 110, 216, 232, 369

interdisciplinary links, 11, 29, 129, 216, 369

population bar graphs, 86

predictions, 110

writing activities, 86, 110

Mayas, M14, 103, 368–369, 368*p*, 369*p*, 374, 374*p*, 427, 439, 439*g*, 439*m*

art of, 403, 428*p*

civil war and, 440–441

women, 437, 440

See also Native Americans

Mayflower, 178*p*

measles, 177

medicine

Aztec, 372

population growth and, 65

from the rain forest, 496, 497

Mediterranean climate, 51, 569

Mediterranean Sea, 5*m*, 56

Mediterranean vegetation, 51, 52

megalopolis, 249, 249*m*, 569

Meining, D. W., 214

Melanesia, 5*m*, 532*m*

melting pot, 227, 569

mental maps, 25

Mercator, Gerardus, 18

Mercator projection, M6, 18, 18*g*

meridians, 10, 12, 569

mesa, 554

mestizos, 383, 392, 417, 504, 511, 569

in Middle America, 402

revolts led by, 386

metals, 116

Métis people, 195, 319

Mexican Americans, 191

Mexican Territory, 183

Mexico, 135, 149, 181*m*, 334, 334*p*, 425*m*, 426, 428, 530*m*, 534*m*, 536*m*, 558

art of, 403–404, 403*p*, 428*p*

climate of, 345

data about, 428

early civilizations of, 367*m*, 368–372, 369*p*, 370*p*, 371*p*, 372*p*

economy of, 394*g*, 395, 432*g*, 432*m*

energy resources, 118

exports of, 428, 432*g*, 432*m*

farming in, 431

immigrants, 67

independence in, 386–387, 386*p*

landforms of, 340

languages of, 403, 428

location of, 330, 330*p*, 339, 339*m*, 452*m*

Mayas in, M14, 103, 369

NAFTA and, 79, 208, 395, 436

Native Americans in, 407*p*, 428

natural hazards in, 434

natural resources of, 353*m*, 354, 357

population of, 405, 428, 430, 434

religion in, 404, 404*p*, 423*g*, 428

trade, 79

vegetation of, 348*m*, 349

volcanoes in, 332, 332*p*

Mexico City, 334, 334*p*, 383, 405, 434*m*, 558, 569

employment in, 433–434, 436

geography of, 435, 435*p*

housing in, 433–436, 433*p*, 434*m*, 435*p*

pollution in, 435, 435*p*

Miami, Florida, 42, 43*p*, 217*p*, 218, 260, 463, 466*p*, 558

Miami Indians, 182*m*

Michigan, 537*m*

data about, 141*m*, 235*m*, 241

Micronesia, 5*m*, 532*m*

Middle America, 339, 558, 569

art of, 403–404, 403*p*

Aztecs in, 370–372, 370*p*, 371*p*, 372*p*

cultures of, 402–404, 402*p*, 403*p*, 404*p*

early civilizations of, 367*m*, 368–372, 369*p*, 370*p*, 371*p*, 372*p*

natural resources of, 353*m*, 354

See also Central America

middle class, 188

Middle East, 121, 121*p*

middle latitudes, 32, 32*m*, 569

Midwest (United States), 145*m*, 145*p*, 188, 235*m*, 264–270, 264*p*, 266*g*, 267*p*, 268*p*, 269*m*, 270*p*

cities in, 268–270, 268*p*, 269*m*, 270*p*

economy of, 265, 265*g*, 265*m*

farming in, 264–265, 264*p*, 266–267, 266*g*

profile of, 265, 265*g*, 265*m*

railroads in, 268, 269*m*

migrant workers, 430, 569, 569*p*

migration, M1, M14–M15, M14*m*, M15*m*, 67–71, 405, 407, 411, 570

of African Americans, 256, 256*g*

of Native Americans, 174–175, 182*m*

to North America, 213*m*

in South Asia, 69*m*

urbanization, 67, 70–71, 70*g*

voluntary, 68

warfare and, 68

Milky Way Galaxy, 28, 28*p*, 558

mineral resources, 116, 164*m*, 165, 166, 166*p*, 167, 353*m*, 354, 489, 570

mines and mining, 258, 273, 273*p*, 384, 497, 510

in Canada, 196, 306, 306*g*, 306*m*

Minneapolis-St. Paul, Minnesota, 270, 558

Minnesota, 207, 537*m*

data about, 141*m*, 235*m*, 241

Minutemen, 179*p*

missionaries, 177, 382, 570

Mississippi, 537*m*

data about, 141*m*, 235*m*, 241

farming in, 257

land use in, 256*m*

in Sun Belt, 260*m*

Mississippi River, 152, 165, 177, 177*m*, 181, 181*m*, 269, 269*m*, 558

Mississippi Valley, 68

Missouri, 152, 537*m*

data about, 141*m*, 235*m*, 241

Missouri River, 152, 165, 180, 559

Mistral, Gabriela, 418

mixed-crop farm, 266, 570

mixed forests, 52, 53*p*

mixed ownership, 75

Mixtec people, 403

Moctezuma, 378, 378*p*, 380–381, 399, 570

Mojave Desert, 12
monarchy, 82, 83, 198
money, 75
Mongolia, 549
Montana, 536*m*
　climate in, 272*m*
　data about, 141*m*, 235*m*, 242, 242*p*
　hydroelectricity in, 272*g*
　natural resources of, 273, 274
Montenegro, 551
Montevideo, 492
Montgomery, Alabama, 236
Montgomery, Lucy Maud, 230
Montpelier, Vermont, 246
Montreal, Canada, 289*p*, 294, 296*g*, 559
Morocco, 547
mosquitoes, 448, 448*p*
Mother Jones, 188
Mothers of Plaza de Mayo, 418, 418*p*
Mount Everest, 54, 559
Mount Fuji, 5*p*
Mount Logan, 151
Mount McKinley, 148, 148*p*
Mount St. Helens, 150
mountain effects, 157–158
mountain pass, 555
mountain sickness, 338
mountains, 35, 88–89*g*, 148*p*, 149, 554, 555*p*, 570
　Appalachian, 39
　climate and, 41
　formation, 36*g*
　Rocky, 12, 39
　vertical climate zones, 54
　water cycle, 41*g*
movement, M1, 13
　continents, 7
　languages and, 331
Munduruku Indian, 499
Munro, Alice, 230
music, 107, 225–226, 225*p*, 230, 526
　of the Caribbean, 413, 414, 461
　of Puerto Rico, 480*p*
Muslims, 69*m*, 100, 101, 103*p*, 412

My Side of the Mountain (George), 88–89
Myanmar (Burma), 82, 542*m*, 559

N

NAFTA. *See* North American Free Trade Agreement
Naipaul, V. S., 412
narrative essays, RW2
NASA. *See* National Aeronautics and Space Administration
Nashville, Tennessee, 245
Nassau, 457
Natchez, 215*m*
nation-states, 80, 81, 84, 570
National Aeronautics and Space Administration (NASA), 259
national parks, 274, 274*p*
Native Americans, 173*m*, 410
　American Indian Movement and, 223, 233*p*
　in Andean countries, 417
　art of, 403, 404
　artifacts, 174*p*
　in Bolivia, 352, 352*p*
　in Brazil, 499, 499*p*
　in Chile, 511
　Columbus and, 379, 411
　diseases and, 177, 381, 384, 497
　encomiendas, 384
　Europeans and, 215*m*
　fishing, 202, 202*p*
　France and, 177, 177*m*
　French and Indian War, 178
　Great Britain and, 177*m*, 178, 178*p*
　in Guatemala, 437, 438, 439, 439*g*, 439*m*, 440
　horses and, 215–216, 215*p*
　housing, 176, 176*p*
　Indian Removal Act (1830), 182, 182*m*
　lacrosse and, 226
　languages of, 99, 377

　Lewis and Clark and, 180, 180*p*
　literature of, 225
　llamas and, 347
　in Mexico, 407*p*, 428
　migration of, 174–175, 182*m*
　number systems and, 216
　in Peru, 383, 503–504
　population, 223
　poverty and, 392
　rain forest and, 335, 335*m*, 335*p*
　religion of, 404
　reservations and, 223
　revolts led by, 386
　rights of, 182
　Spain and, 175, 175*p*, 177, 177*m*
　totora reeds and, 415, 415*p*
　treaties and, 223
　See also First Nations; indigenous people; individual cultures
NATO. *See* North Atlantic Treaty Organization
natural gas, 164*m*, 165, 166, 333, 333*g*, 353*m*, 354
natural resources, 570
　in Atlantic Provinces, 313*m*
　in British Columbia, 306, 306*g*, 306*m*
　in Canada, 167–168, 167*p*, 168*p*
　defined, 114–119, 115*m*, 134*m*
　economy and, 356–358, 356*g*, 357*p*, 358*p*
　in Latin America, 352–358, 352*p*, 353*m*, 354*p*, 355*p*, 356*g*, 357*p*, 358*p*
　in the United States, 164–166, 164*m*, 165*p*, 166*p*
　in the West, 272–274, 273*p*, 274*p*
navigate, 18, 570
Nebraska, 537*m*
　data about, 141*m*, 235*m*, 242
Nepal, 54, 54*p*, 542*m*, 559
Neruda, Pablo, 418
Netherlands, the, 72, 83, 83*p*, 538*m*
Nevada, 160, 536*m*
　climate in, 272*m*
　data about, 141*m*, 235*m*, 242
　natural resources of, 273

in Sun Belt, 260*m*
New Brunswick, 195, 196*m*, 291, 314
data about, 141*m*, 285*m*, 287
New Deal, 189
New England, 82
New Hampshire, 537*m*
data about, 141*m*, 235*m*, 242
New Jersey, 537*m*
data about, 141*m*, 235*m*, 243
population density, 249, 249*m*
New Mexico, 175*p*, 176, 176*p*, 536*m*
climate in, 272*m*
data about, 141*m*, 235*m*, 243
in Sun Belt, 260*m*
New Orleans, M5, 225, 260, 261
New Spain, 383, 384, 434
New York, 153, 537*m*, 559
data about, 141*m*, 235*m*, 243
hydroelectricity in, 272*g*
New York City, 67*p*, 248, 248*p*, 249*m*, 252, 252*p*, 253, 253*p*, 254, 559
population, 253
September 11th attacks, 191*g*, 192, 192*p*, 253
New York Stock Exchange, 75*p*, 253
New Zealand, 7*p*, 122–123*p*, 530*m*, 544*m*, 559
Newfoundland, 167, 194, 195, 196*m*
Newfoundland and Labrador, 312*p*, 313, 313*g*, 313*m*, 315
data about, 141*m*, 285*m*, 287
newspapers, RW1
Niagara Falls, 2*p*, 141*p*, 206, 559
Nicaragua, 403, 425*m*, 429, 534*m*
Niger, 547
Nigeria, 547
night and day, 29
Night of Fire, 385
Nile River, 60*p*, 541*m*
Nile River Valley, 63, 63*m*, 559
nitrogen cycle, 115
nomadic herding, M17*p*, 229, 570

nonrenewable resources, 114, 116, 570
Nootka people, 305
north, 11
North America, 2*m*, 4*m*, 6*m*, 379*m*, 530*m*, 532*m*, 534*m*, 535*m*, 559
colonization, 125
human-environment interaction, 128
migration to, 213*m*
physical maps, 535*m*
political maps, 534*m*
population density, 62*m*
revolution in, 386
satellite image, 17*p*
slave trade, 68
storms, 47
suburbanization, 70
See also Canada; United States
North American Free Trade Agreement (NAFTA), 79, 208, 395, 436, 570
North Atlantic Current, 42, 559
North Atlantic Treaty Organization (NATO), 84
North Carolina, 537*m*
data about, 141*m*, 235*m*, 243
forestry in, 258
land use in, 256*m*
in Sun Belt, 260*m*
textile industry, 259
North China Plain, 5*m*, 543*m*
North Dakota, 537*m*
data about, 141*m*, 235*m*, 244
North Korea, 82, 82*p*, 542*m*, 559
North Pole, M2, M4, M5, M7, 11*p*, 12, 12*g*, 29, 35, 346, 545*m*, 559
Northeast (United States), 235*m*, 248*p*, 249*m*, 251*p*, 253*p*, 254*p*
cities of, 248–254
population density, 249, 249*m*, 250*g*, 250*m*
profile of, 250, 250*g*, 250*m*
Northern Hemisphere, M3, M4, 11*g*, 512
seasons, 30–31, 30–31*g*
northern lights, 318, 318*p*
Northern Territories, 140*p*, 318–322

government in, 319, 320*g*
indigenous people in, 319, 319*p*, 320*g*, 320*m*
population of, 319, 320*g*, 320*m*
Northwest Territories, 196*m*, 319, 320, 320*g*, 320*m*, 321, 559
data about, 141*m*, 285*m*, 287
Norway, 118, 538*m*, 559
Nova Scotia, 195, 196*m*, 284*p*, 291, 314, 315*p*
data about, 141*m*, 285*m*, 287
nuclear energy, 333, 333*g*
nuclear families, 96, 96*p*, 97, 570
nuclear radiation, 191, 191*p*
Nukuj Akpop, 440
number systems, 216, 369
Nunavut, 155, 199, 199*p*, 319, 320, 320*g*, 320*m*, 321*p*, 322, 325, 559
data about, 141*m*, 285*m*, 288
Nunivak Island, 545*m*

O

***O Pioneers!* (Cather),** 264
OAS. *See* Organization of American States (OAS)
oasis, 53*p*, 503, 570, 570*p*
ocean effects, 157
oceans, 35
climate and, 41, 42, 44–45
currents, 42, 570
ocean floor, 36, 37
tidal energy, 118
tropical cyclones, 47
See also individual oceans
Ohio, 537*m*
data about, 141*m*, 235*m*, 244
environmental issues in, 203, 203*p*
Ohio River, 152, 165
oil, 127, 353*m*, 354, 355, 357
natural resources, 116, 117, 118
oil fields, 118*p*
production and consumption, 118*g*
trade, 78, 79
in Venezuela, 517, 517*g*, 517*p*, 518*g*, 519–520
Oklahoma, 537*m*

data about, 141*m*, 235*m*, 244
drilling in, 258
land use in, 256*m*
in Sun Belt, 260*m*
Oklahoma City, Oklahoma, 244
Oklahoma Territory, 188*p*
oligarchies, 82, 570
Olmecs, 403
Olympia, Washington, 246
Oman, 549
one-resource economy, 356, 570
O'Neill, Eugene, 225
Ontario, 145*m*, 145*p*, 153, 168,
194, 196*m*, 204*p*, 210*m*, 291–293,
559
data about, 141*m*, 285*m*, 288
profile of, 292, 292*g*, 292*m*
Quebec and, 290
orbit, Earth's, M2, 28, 30, 570
Oregon, M16*p*, 536*m*
climate in, 272*m*
data about, 141*m*, 235*m*, 244
hydroelectricity in, 272*g*
natural resources of, 273
Oregon Country, 181*m*
**Organization of American
States (OAS),** 208, 208*p*
Orinoco River, 342, 518, 518*m*
Orozco, José Clemente, 403
Ottawa, 291, 292*m*, 559
Ottawa River, 290, 290*p*
Oxford University, 95*p*
oxygen, 34*g*, 35
oxygen starvation, 338

P

Pachacuti, 374
Pacific Northwest, 273, 559
Pacific Ocean, 2*m*, 3*m*, 4*m*, 5*m*,
6*m*, 7*m*, 56, 142*m*, 149, 152, 203,
444, 507
climate and, 45, 157, 158
Ring of Fire, 33, 37
volcanoes in, 150
Pacific Rim, 309–310, 309*m*, 570
Pakistan, 69*m*, 118*p*, 542*m*

palm trees, 349
pampas, 4*m*, 341, 347, 417, 532*m*,
535*m*, 570
Panama, 394, 425*m*, 429, 534*m*,
559
Canal Zone, 448
deforestation, 447
factories in, 450
geography of, 444–448, 446,
446*g*, 446*m*
independence in, 388
languages of, 403
population of, 6*g*
rain forest, 450, 450*p*
vegetation of, 446*m*
Panama Canal, 394, 429, 559, 570
building, 445, 447–448, 447*p*
shipping in, 445, 445*p*, 449, 449*p*
Panama City, 405, 429
Pangaea, 38, 38*m*, 559
paper, 114, 132
Papineau, Louis, 195
Papua New Guinea, 549
Paraguay, 487*m*, 491, 534*m*, 559
climate of, 345
culture of, 417
foreign debt of, 394*g*
hydroelectricity in, 333, 333*g*,
333*p*
independence in, 387*m*
Paraguay River, 342, 491
parallels, 10, 12, 571
Paraná River, 342
parliament, 198, 198*p*, 291, 291*g*,
292*g*, 319
parliamentary democracy, 198
Patagonia, 341*p*, 345
peanuts, 120, 120*p*
Pearl Harbor, 190
peninsula, 555
Penn, William, 178, 178*p*
Pennsylvania, 537*m*, 559
data about, 141*m*, 235*m*, 244
natural resources of, 164*m*, 166
Pennsylvania Colony, 178
Pentagon, U.S., 192
permafrost, 159, 571

Peru, 4*p*, 333, 333*p*, 373–376,
373*p*, 374*p*, 375*p*, 376*p*, 383,
487*m*, 491, 534*m*, 559
climate of, 502*g*
culture of, 417
economy of, 394*g*, 504
geography of, 501, 501*p*, 502*g*,
502*m*, 503–506
Incas in, 506, 506*p*
independence in, 387*m*, 388
languages of, 491, 502*g*
llamas in, 334, 334*p*
Native Americans in, 416*p*, 503–
504
population of, 491, 502*g*, 504
reforms in, 395
weather in, 357
Peru Current, 42, 559
petrochemicals, 258, 571
petroleum, 116, 117, 164*m*, 165,
333, 333*g*, 353*m*, 354, 571
in Venezuela, 517, 517*g*, 517*p*,
518*g*, 519–520
Pettygrove, Francis W., 274
Philadelphia, Pennsylvania,
249*m*, 251, 254, 559
Philippines, 67, 121, 188, 542*m*,
560
Phoenix, Arizona, 237
photosynthesis, 495
physical geography, 26–57,
337*m*
Earth and sun, 28–29
forces shaping Earth, 33–39
seasons and latitude, 30–32,
30–31*g*
See also geography
physical maps, M11, 532–533*m*,
535*m*, 539*m*, 541*m*, 543*m*, 544*m*,
545*m*
Pierre, South Dakota, 245
Pilgrims, 178, 178*p*
Pinochet Ugarte, Augusto, 513,
571
Pizarro, Francisco, 381, 382*m*,
383, 383*p*, 571
place, M1, 13
landforms of Latin America, 332,
332*m*

provinces, 141*m*

territories, 141*m*

place location

continents, 86*m*

the globe, 24*m*

natural resources, 134*m*

oceans, 56*m*

religions, 110*m*

plains, 35, 39, 149, 340, 347, 417, 555, 571

planets, 28

plantations, 178, 498, 500, 571

plants, M1

biodiversity, 129

biomass energy, 118

effect of climate, 50–54

fossils, 51*p*

See also agriculture

Plateau of Iran, 5*m*, 543*m*

Plateau of Tibet, 5*m*

plateaus, 35, 150, 340, 555, 571

plates, 33, 36–38, 36–37*g*, 38*m*, 571

Platte River, 152

plaza, 406*p*, 431, 431*p*, 571

Plymouth, Massachusetts, 178

pok-ta-tok, 368, 369*p*

Poland, 551

polar bears, 51*p*

polar climate, 571

polar zones, 32*m*

climate, 32, 41, 43*g*, 50, 51

population density, 62*m*

political maps, M10, 530–531*m*, 534*m*, 536–537*m*, 538*m*, 540*m*, 542*m*

political movement, 571

political regions, M1

political systems, 80–84, 440–441, 440*p*

institutions, 95

and migration, 68

pollution, 132, 203, 203*p*, 204, 204*m*, 204*p*, 435, 435*p*, 497, 511, 571

from agriculture, 129

atomic energy and, 118

defined, 128

developed nations and, 76

hybrid cars, 119, 130, 130*g*, 132

suburbanization and, 70

traffic jams, 130*p*

See also environment

Polynesia, 5*m*, 532*m*

poncho, 377

Popocatépetl Volcano, 332, 332*p*

population, 60–66, 571

of Alberta, 301

of Argentina, 488

of Bolivia, 489

of Brazil, 489, 495, 498*m*

of Canada, 218, 228, 229, 286–289

of Caribbean Islands, 456–461

of Central America, 426–429

of Chile, 489

of cities, 405*g*, 406

of Colombia, 490

defined, 60

of Ecuador, 490

growth, 64–66, 65*g*

of Guatemala, 453*g*

of Guyana, 491

of Mexico, 428, 430, 434

migration, 67–71

Native American, 223

of New York City, 253

of Northern Territories, 319, 320*g*, 320*m*

of Paraguay, 491

of Peru, 491, 502*g*, 504

of Puerto Rico, 479*m*

of South America, 488–493

of Suriname, 492

of United States, 218, 222, 236–247

urbanization, 67, 70–71

of Uruguay, 492

of Venezuela, 423*g*, 493

world, 6, 6*g*

population density, 62–63, 571

defined, 60

maps, 6–7*m*, 62–63*m*, 72–73, 73*m*, 86

of the Northeast, 249, 249*m*, 250*g*, 250*m*

of Ontario, 292*m*

of Quebec, 296*m*

of the world, 6–7

population distribution, 60–61, 62, 571

Port-au-Prince, Haiti, 459, 471, 475, 560

Port-of-Spain, 461

Portland, Oregon, 274, 560

Portugal, 538*m*

Brazil and, 331*m*, 331*p*, 380, 389, 489

colonization by, 382–384, 507

settlers from, 340

Potawatomi, 182*m*

Potomac River, 261, 261*p*

poverty, 187, 187*p*, 392, 427, 489, 500

in Haiti, 459, 474–475

in South America, 420, 420*p*

in Venezuela, 519

Prairie Provinces, 160, 167, 216, 298–303

culture of, 303, 303*p*

economics of, 300, 300*g*, 300*m*

farming in, 300*g*, 302, 302*p*

immigration to, 301

indigenous people of, 298, 299, 301

prairies, 52, 571

Pre-Columbian art, 403

precipitation, 40, 41*g*, 42*m*, 43*g*, 57, 571. *See also* rain; snow

Préval, René, 470, 473

Prime Meridian, M5, 11, 11*p*, 12*g*, 571

prime minister, 198, 291, 291*g*, 292*g*, 571

Prince Edward Island, 195, 196*m*, 288*p*, 314

data about, 141*m*, 285*m*, 288

private ownership, 75

privatization, 520, 571

producers, 74, 571

projects, 136, 326, 526

projection maps, 16, 18–19, 571

Providence, Rhode Island, 244

Province of Canada, 195, 291

provinces, 141*m*, 571

Pueblo Indians, 176, 176*p*, 215*m*, 232*m*

Puerto Rico, 188, 340, 455*m*, 459, 534*m*, 560, 564*p*

commonwealth of, 477

culture of, 480, 480p

government of, 476, 479, 479g, 479m

independence question, 482, 482p

languages of, 477

music of, 480p

population of, 479m

Spain and, 388

statehood question, 481, 481p

timeline of, 485

United States and, 476–478, 477g, 477p, 479, 479g, 481–482, 481p, 482p

push-pull theory, M15, 68, 571

Q

qanats, 121, 121p

Qatar, 549

Quebec, 145m, 145p, 162p, 167, 168, 194, 196m, 197, 210m, 228, 560

data about, 141m, 285m, 289

French culture in, 294–297, 296, 296g, 297, 297p

history of, 296

language in, 295, 296g

Ontario and, 290

population density, 296m

Quiet Revolution in, 295, 295p

Separatists in, 295, 295p

timeline, 296

Quebec, Battle of, 194, 194p

Quebec Act, 194

Quebec City, 219p

Quechua, 377, 417, 504, 505, 505p, 506

Queen Elizabeth Islands, 545m

Quetzalcoatl, 381, 381p

Quiché Maya, 437

Quiet Revolution, 295, 295p, 571

quipu, 373p, 375, 571

R

radar, 46

radio, 106, 107

radioactivity, atomic energy, 118

railroads, 105p, 183, 188, 188p, 190g, 195p, 393p

in Canada, 308

in the Midwest, 268, 269m

rain, 40, 41, 42m, 158

climate graphs, 48–49, 48g, 56

dry climates, 51

storms, 47

temperate marine climates, 51

tropical climate, 50

tropical cyclones, 47

water cycle, 35, 41g, 115

rain forest, 4p, 50, 52, 52p, 341, 347, 348m, 450, 450p, 460, 572

in Brazil, 335, 335m, 335p, 494, 494p, 495, 495p

deforestation, 129p

importance of, 496–497, 496g, 497p

indigenous people in, 498

medicine from, 496, 497

of Peru, 502

threats to, 497

rain shadow, 161, 572

Raleigh, North Carolina, 243, 243p, 259

rancho, 420

raw materials, 114, 128, 572

reading skills

analyze author's purpose, RW1

asking questions, 163, 352

cause and effect, 400, 402

clarifying meaning, 8, 172, 366

compare and contrast, 54, 58, 60, 234, 248, 486, 494, 507

context clues, 26, 28, 30, 32, 33, 35, 39, 40, 50, 52, 284, 290, 304, 311, 318, 424, 430, 437, 444

contrast signal words, 80

distinguish between facts and opinions, RW1

evaluate credibility, RW1

identify contrasts, 67, 264, 501

identify evidence, RW1

identify main ideas, 87, 112, 114, 128, 135, 212, 214, 227, 454, 462, 476

identify supporting details, 120, 222, 470

informational texts, RW1

interpret nonliteral meanings, 298

make comparisons, 74, 271, 516

paraphrasing, 16, 22, 187, 378, 382

predicting, 156, 343

prereading strategies, 42

previewing, 163, 338, 343, 352

reading ahead, 10, 180, 202, 373, 392

reading process, 146, 336

recognizing multiple causes, 410

recognizing words that signal sequence, 104

rereading, 10, 174, 202, 392

setting a purpose, 148, 151, 338

signal words, 80, 255

summarize, 193, 385

understanding effects, 415

understanding sequence, 90, 92, 96

See also writing skills

recession, 266, 572

Reconstruction, 186, 190g, 572

recycling, 116, 132, 132p

Red Cross, 186p

Red River Basin, 181m

Redonda, 456

redwood forests, 163, 163p

referendum, 295, 572

reforms, 295, 395

refugees, 471, 572

reggae music, 414, 526

regime, 395, 572

Regina, Saskatchewan, 289, 299

regions, M1, 12, 330, 572

Atlantic Provinces, 311–315

British Columbia, 304–310

of Canada, 140, 140m, 144–145, 144–145m, 144p, 145p

Midwest, 264–270

Northeast, 248–254
Northern Territories, 318–322
Ontario and Quebec, 290–297
Prairie Provinces, 298–303
South, 255–261
of United States, 140, 140*m*, 144–145, 144–145*m*, 144*p*, 145*p*, 235*m*
West, 271–276
relative location, M1, 12, 572
relief, M11
religion, 95, 98, 100*m*, 101, 110*m*
in Argentina, 488
Aztec, 370
in Bolivia, 489
in Brazil, 489
in Canada, 218, 263*g*
in Caribbean Islands, 412, 456–461
in Central America, 404, 404*p*, 426–429
in Chile, 489
in Colombia, 490
in Ecuador, 490
in Guyana, 491
Incan, 376
Mayan, 369, 369*p*
in Mexico, 404, 404*p*, 423*g*, 428
missionaries and, 177
Native American, 404
in Paraguay, 491
in Peru, 491
in South America, 488–493
in Suriname, 492
in United States, 218, 263*g*
in Uruguay, 492
in Venezuela, 493
renewable resources, 114, 115–116, 118, 132, 572
representative democracy, 83, 572
research papers, RW4–RW5
reservations, 223, 572
reserves, 228, 572
reservoirs, 131
resources
industry and, 131
living, 116
natural, 114–119, 115*m*, 134*m*
nonrenewable, 114, 116

recycling, 116
renewable, 114, 115–116, 118, 132
responsible development, 274, 572
Revere, Paul, 251
revolution, 28, 385–386, 572
Revolutionary War, 179, 179*p*, 214, 251, 572
Rhode Island, 537*m*
data about, 141*m*, 235*m*, 244
rice, M17*p*, 58–59*p*, 76*p*, 85*p*, 93*p*, 120, 121, 257
Richmond, Virginia, 246
ridges, underwater, 37*g*
Riel, Louis, 195
Riis, Jacob, 187, 187*p*, 188
Ring of Fire, 33, 37, 560
Rio de Janeiro, Brazil, 331*m*, 331*p*, 392*p*, 495, 500, 500*p*, 560, 572
Río de la Plata, 342
river mouth, 555
River Platte, 492
Rivera, Diego, 403*p*, 404, 428*p*
rivers, 35, 152, 152*p*, 342, 342*p*
erosion, 39
water energy, 118
water supply, 127
roads, 131, 376
Robinson Crusoe (Defoe), 511
Robinson projection, M7, 19, 19*g*
rocks
Earth's crust, 34, 34*g*
magma, 36, 36–37*g*
plant fossils, 51*p*
weathering and erosion, 39, 39*p*
Rocky Mountains, 4*m*, 12, 39, 149, 152, 181, 181*m*, 203, 271*p*, 532*m*, 535*m*, 545*m*, 560, 573
Rome, Italy, 81
Roosevelt, Franklin D., 189, 190
Roosevelt, Theodore, 394, 447
Roseau, Dominica, 458
rotation, M2, 28, 29, 43*g*, 573
Rotterdam, the Netherlands, 131*p*, 560
rural areas, 67, 71, 573
Russia, 3*p*, 135, 188, 538*m*, 542*m*, 560

Russian language, 99*p*
Ruth, Babe, 226
Rwanda, 547

S

Sacajawea, 180, 180*p*
Sacramento, California, 237
Sahara, 5*m*, 53*p*, 541*m*, 560
Sahel, 5*m*, 541*m*
Saint-Domingue, 385
Saint George's, 458
St. Jean-Baptiste, 297
St. John's, Newfoundland, 287, 456, 456*p*
St. Kitts and Nevis, 460
St. Lawrence Lowlands, 151, 167
St. Lawrence River, 151, 153, 167, 177, 194, 206, 560
St. Lawrence Seaway, 206–207, 206*g*, 210*m*, 560
St. Louis, Missouri, 45, 269, 269*m*, 560
St. Lucia, 455*m*, 460
St. Paul, Minnesota, 241, 270
St. Vincent and the Grenadines, 455*m*, 460
Salamon, Lazarus, 222
Salem, Oregon, 244
Salt Lake City, 161, 246
salt water, 35
same-shape maps, M6
Samoa, 544*m*, 549
Samuels, Dorothy, 412
San Andreas Fault, 36*p*
San Francisco, California, 45, 560
San Geronimo Fortress, 480*p*
San Jose, California, 275, 560
San José, Costa Rica, 405, 427
San Juan, 459, 480, 480*p*, 560
San Martín, José de, 573
San Salvador, 427, 457
sanitation, 65, 66, 573
Santa Fe, New Mexico, 243
Santiago, Chile, 489, 510, 511, 560
Santiago, Esmeralda, 478, 478*p*
Santo Domingo, 458

São Paulo, Brazil, 71, 71*p*, 335, 335*m*, 417, 417*p*, 560
São Tomé and Príncipe, 540*m*
Saskatchewan, 196*m*, 298, 300*m*
  data about, 141*m*, 285*m*, 289
  farming in, 302, 302*p*
  Grasslands National Park, 301
  indigenous people of, 299
satellite images, 17, 573
satellites, 8–9*p*, 17, 17*p*, 46, 46*p*
Saudi Arabia, 77, 78, 82, 101, 118, 135, 542*m*, 560
Sault Sainte Marie, 202
Saulteaux people, 298, 299
savanna, 50, 52, 495, 573
scale bar, M8, 20*m*, 21, 573
scale, maps, 16, 21, 22*m*
schools, 66
science, 345, 345*p*, 360, 376, 452, 495
  aurora borealis, 318, 318*p*
  Bay of Fundy, 314
  interdisciplinary links, 51, 150, 301, 314, 345, 345*p*, 360, 376, 495
  prairies, 301
  volcanoes, 150
  writing skills, 56, 278
  See also technology
Sears Tower, 268
seas, 35
seasons, 30–32, 30–31*g*
Seattle, Washington, 275, 560
Sechelt Indians, 308
segregation, 186, 191, 573
Selkirk, Alexander, 511
selva, 502*g*, 503
semiarid climate, 44*p*, 51, 573
Seminole people, 182*m*
Senate, Canadian, 198
Senegal, 547
Separatists, 295, 573
September 11th attacks, 191*g*, 192, 192*p*, 253
Serbia, 551
services, 123, 131, 573
Seven Years' War, 194, 194*p*
Shawnee people, 182*m*

sheep, 122, 122*p*
shipbuilding, 315
shipping, 445, 445*p*, 449, 449*p*
  on the Great Lakes, 151
  on the Mackenzie River, 152–153
  on the Mississippi River, 152
  trade, 79*p*
shopping malls, 131
Siberia, 5*m*, 175, 542*m*
sierra, 502, 503, 573
Sierra Leone, 135, 540*m*
Sierra Nevada, 150, 560
sign language, 98*p*
Sikhism, 100, 101*p*
Silicon Valley, 275
Silk Road, 78
silver, 167
Singapore, 549
Sioux people, 299
Sisi, 499*p*
ska music, 414
skyscrapers, 252, 252*p*, 253, 268, 293, 293*p*
Slave Coast, M15
slave trade, 68
slavery, 178, 384, 385, 392, 392*p*
  African Americans and, 392
  in Brazil, 489, 498, 499
  in the Caribbean, 456
  Civil War and, 184–186
  Emancipation Proclamation, 185
  Haiti and, 334, 334*p*, 471
  in Suriname, 492
sleet, 40
slums, 187, 187*p*, 573
smallpox, 177
smog, 435, 435*p*, 511
smuggling, 497
snow, 40, 41, 47
soccer, 499*p*
social classes, 96, 97, 383, 573
Social Security, 189
social structure, 96, 573
Social Studies Skills
  analyzing climate maps, 350–351, 350*m*, 351*m*, 360, 360*p*
  comparing and contrasting, 468–469, 468*p*, 469*p*, 484

  distinguishing fact and opinion, 408–409, 409*p*, 422
  drawing inferences, 442–443, 442*p*, 443*p*, 452
  identifying frame of reference, 154–155, 170
  interpreting diagrams, 200–201, 200*p*, 201*p*, 210
  making predictions, 110, 126–127, 134
  making timelines, 390–391, 390*p*, 398
  making valid generalizations, 102–103, 110
  synthesizing information, 514–515, 514*p*, 515*p*, 524
  understanding circle graphs, 262–263, 263*g*, 278
  using climate graphs, 48–49
  using graphic organizers, 220–221, 232
  using population density maps, 72–73, 86
  using reliable information, 14–15, 24
  using special geography graphs, 56
  writing a summary, 316–317, 324
  writing and, RW2–RW5
society, 96–97, 573
sod, 298, 573
soddies, 298
soil, 39, 66
solar energy, 115, 116*p*, 117, 118, 132
solar system, M2, 28
solstices, 30, 30*g*, 31, 31*g*, 573
Somalia, 547
Sonoran Desert, 345
Soufrière, 460
South (United States), 144*p*, 235*m*, 257*p*, 258*p*, 259*p*, 260*m*, 261*p*
  agriculture in, 257, 257*p*
  cities of, 259–261, 261*p*
  climate of, 255–256
  culture of, 256, 256*g*, 256*m*
  land use, 256*m*
  profile of, 256, 256*g*, 256*m*

tourism in, 261
transportation in, 260
south, 11
South Africa, 77, 540*m*, 560
South America, 2*m*, 4*m*, 6*m*, 379*m*, 487*m*, 530*m*, 532*m*, 560
cities of, 419–420, 420*p*
climate, 42
colonization, 125
cultural regions of, 416
early civilizations of, 367*m*
ethnic groups of, 488–493
exports of, 488–493
farming in, 419
geography of, 488
government in, 488–493
independence in, 387–389, 387*m*, 388*p*
landforms of, 341
languages of, 416, 488–493
literature of, 418
location of, 339, 339*m*, 524*m*
Mercator projection, 18
natural resources in, 353*m*, 355
plate movements, 38*m*
political map, 487*m*, 534*m*
population of, 488–493
religions in, 488–493
satellite image, 17*p*
slave trade, 68
women in, 418
See also Latin America
South Asia
migration, 69*m*
population density, 73*m*
See also Asia
South Carolina, 537*m*
data about, 141*m*, 235*m*, 245, 245*p*
land use in, 256*m*
in Sun Belt, 260*m*
textile industry, 259
South Dakota, 537*m*
data about, 141*m*, 235*m*, 245
South Korea, 67, 542*m*, 560
South Pole, M2, M4, M5, M7, 12, 12*g*, 29, 35, 346, 545*m*, 560
Southern Hemisphere, M3, M4, 11*g*, 512, 544*m*

seasons, 31
Southern Ocean, 56
Southwest, U.S., 176, 176*p*
Southwest Asia
population growth, 66
religions, 100
states, 81
water supply, 127
See also Asia
Soviet Union, 191, 464, 467
space shuttle, 8–9*p*
Spain, 538*m*
areas of influence, 173*m*, 175, 177*m*
Aztecs and, 378*p*, 380–381
Canada and, 314, 314*m*
colonization by, 382–384, 416, 458, 476, 490, 493, 511
conquistadors and, 380–381
exploration by, 379–380
Incas and, 377
Louisiana Territory, 181, 181*m*
Native Americans and, 175, 175*p*, 177, 177*m*
revolts against, 386–387, 386*p*
settlers from, 340
Spanglish, 478
Spanish American War, 188, 190*g*, 463, 476
Spanish language, 99
sports, 218*p*, 226, 226*p*, 230, 230*p*, 413. *See also* games
spring, 30*g*, 31, 32
Springfield, Illinois, 239
squatter, 433, 573
Sri Lanka, 549
Stadacona, 294
standard of living, 219, 573
Standardized Test Prep
analyze a reading selection, 325, 453
analyze graphs and charts, 279*g*, 423
analyze point of view, 399
analyze primary sources, 211
analyzing main ideas, 87, 135
find the main idea, 87, 135, 233, 525
make mental maps, 25, 171, 361

sequence, 485
use map keys, 57
use prior knowledge, 111
stars, 28
states, 80–83, 95, 573
Statue of Liberty, 222*p*
steam engine, 183, 183*p*
steel drums, 414, 461
stock exchange, 75*p*
storms, 17*p*, 47, 158
Stowe, Harriet Beecher, 185
strait, 555
Strait of Magellan, 508*m*, 509, 510, 560
Strauss, Levi, 104
strike, 441, 573
stumptown, 307
subarctic climate, 51, 573
subsistence farming, M16, 77, 377, 419, 490*p*, 573
suburbs, 70, 105, 125
Sudan, 547
sugar cane, 349, 353*m*, 354, 460
sulphur springs, 460
summer, 30, 30*g*, 32, 51
sun
air circulation and, 43*g*
climate and, 41
day and night, 29
Earth's distance from, 28
renewable resources, 115
seasons, 30–31, 30–31*g*
Sun Belt, 260–261, 260*m*, 573
Suriname, 416, 487*m*, 492, 534*m*
Surveyor **(Ada),** 362–365
surveys, mapmaking, 17
suspension bridge, 506, 506*p*
Sweden, 551
Switzerland, 78, 561
Syria, 549

T

Taiwan, 549
Tallahassee, Florida, 239
Tanzania, 64*p*, 540*m*
Taos, New Mexico, 175*p*, 176, 176*p*

tariff, 208, 574

taxes, 179

technology, 574

  Aztec farming, 371, 371p

  culture and, 93, 94–95, 105–106, 107

  dams, 165

  economic development and, 76

  energy consumption and, 119

  environmental issues and, 203

  farming and, 264p, 266–267, 300

  hybrid cars, 119, 130, 130g, 132

  hydroelectricity, 165, 167

  Inuits and, 319, 319p

  Panama Canal, 449, 449p

  Pueblo village, 176, 176p

  skyscrapers, 252, 252p

  in the South, 259

  suspension bridge, 506, 506p

  trade, 79

  weather forecasting, 46, 46p

  See also science

telegraph, 312

telephones, 107, 131

television, 106, 107

temperate continental climate, 43g, 50, 51

temperate grasslands, 52

temperate marine climate, 43g, 50, 51

temperate zones, 32

temperature, 40, 574

  climate graphs, 48–49, 48g

  Earth's structure, 34g

  oceans and, 42, 44–45

tenement, 187, 574

Tennessee, 537m

  data about, 141m, 235m, 245

  land use in, 256m

  mining in, 258

  in Sun Belt, 260m

Tenochtitlán, 370, 371, 371p, 380–381, 434, 561, 574

territories, 141m, 184m, 574

terrorists, 192, 574

Texas, 68, 537m, 561

  annexation of, 181m

  data about, 141m, 235m, 245

  drilling in, 258

  farming in, 257

  fishing in, 258

  land use in, 256m

  Mexico and, 183

  natural resources of, 164m, 166

  in Sun Belt, 260m

Texas, Republic of, 181m

textile industry, 183, 184, 259, 574

Thailand, 76p, 100p, 542m

thunderstorms, 47

tidal energy, 118

Tierra del Fuego, 487m, 510, 561

Tigre River, 4p

Tikal, Guatemala, 369

time, 191p, 340

time zones, 29, 29m

timelines, 190–191g, 326, 390–391, 390p

  of Cuba, 485

  of early civilizations, 374, 374p

  of Haiti, 472

  making, 390–391, 398

  of Puerto Rico, 485

  of Quebec, 296

tin, 352, 352p, 353m, 355

Tobago. *See* Trinidad and Tobago

Toco Indians, 416p

Togo, 540m

Tokyo, Japan, 63, 63p, 561

tools, 94, 94p

Topa Inca, 374, 574

Topeka, Kansas, 240

tornadoes, 47, 158m, 158p, 574

Toronto, 156, 157g, 204p, 229, 288, 293, 293p, 561

totem pole, 305, 305p, 574, 574p

totora reeds, 415, 415p, 501, 501p

tourism, 450, 450p

  in the Caribbean, 456, 457, 458, 459, 460

  in Cuba, 467, 467p

  in the South, 261

  in Uruguay, 492

trade, 198–208, 383g

  Aztec, 372

  development of culture and, 94

  exports and imports, 393

  fur, 177, 193, 194, 214p, 305

  NAFTA, 79, 208, 395, 436

  Pacific Rim, 309–310, 309m

  world trade patterns, 78–79, 78g

traditions, 108, 218p

traffic jams, 130p

transportation, 376

  cultural change and, 106, 107

  Great Lakes, 206–207, 206g

  river, 152

  in the South, 260

  See also cars; railroads

treaties, 84, 223, 380, 575

Treaty of Paris (1763), 194

Treaty of Paris (1783), 177m, 179, 181m

Treaty of Tordesillas, 380

Treaty of Versailles (1918), 189

trees, 50, 52, 114, 115, 353m, 355. *See also* forests and forestry

Trenton, New Jersey, 243

tribal rule, 82

Tribuna, 501

tributaries, 152, 342, 555, 575

tribute, 370

Trinidad and Tobago, 455m, 461, 461p, 561

  Carnival in, 413, 413p

  literature of, 412

  natural resources of, 353m, 354

Tropic of Cancer, M2, 30g, 32, 54, 561

Tropic of Capricorn, M3, 31g, 32, 561

tropical climate region, M1

tropical cyclones, 40, 47, 575

tropical rain forest, 347, 348m

tropical storms, 158

tropical wet and dry climate, M12, 345

tropical wet climate, M12, 345

tropics, 32, 32m

  air circulation, 43g

  climate, 41, 50

  rain forest, 50, 52, 52p

  savanna, 52

Truman, Harry S, 190

tufa, 236–237p

tundra, 50, 51, 51*p*, 52, 54, 159, 159*p*, 160*m*, 503, 575
Tunisia, 547
Turkey, 127, 189, 538*m*, 542*m*
Twain, Shania, 230
Twin Cities, 270
Twin Pitons, 460
Tzoc, Justina, 440

U

Uganda, 547
Ukraine, 552
Uncle Tom's Cabin **(Stowe),** 185
unemployment, 76
Union states (Civil War), 184*m*
United Arab Emirates, 79*p*, 542*m*
United Kingdom, 6*g*, 68, 83, 538*m*. *See also* England; Great Britain
United Nations, 84, 84*p*
United Nations Children's Fund (UNICEF), 84
United States, 135, 141*m*, 147*m*, 530*m*, 534*m*, 536–537*m*, 561
agriculture in, 236–247
Canada and, 199, 202–208, 214, 218–219, 218*p*, 230
Chile and, 508, 508*g*
climate of, 158, 158*m*, 158*p*
Cuba and, 457, 463, 464, 465–467, 466*p*
cultural change, 104–105, 106
cultural diversity and, 215
cultural patterns of, 216–219, 217*p*, 218*p*, 219*p*
culture of, 225–226, 225*p*, 226*p*
economic issues, 75, 76, 206–208, 206*g*
employment, 131
energy resources, 118
environmental issues of, 132, 132*p*, 203–205, 203*p*, 204*m*, 204*p*, 205*p*
ethnic groups in, 236–247
families, 97
farming in, M16*m*, M16*p*
geographic features of, 150
government, 83
Haiti and, 471, 473

immigration to, 67, 67*p*, 68, 216–219, 222–226, 222*p*, 223*p*, 224*g*, 225*p*, 407
imports and exports, 207
industry in, 236–247
international alliances, 84
irrigation, 121, 121*p*
lakes, 151–152, 151*p*
land use, 120
landforms of, 149–151
languages, 99
Latin America and, 330, 394, 394*g*
life expectancy, 65
literature of, 225, 225*p*
location of, 149
music of, 225–226, 225*p*
NAFTA and, 395
Native American treaties and, 223
natural resources of, 164–166, 164*m*, 165*p*, 166*p*
oil imports, 517*g*
Panama Canal and, 394, 446–448
physical maps, 147*m*
political maps, 536*m*–537*m*
population of, 218, 222, 236–247
Puerto Rico and, 476–478, 477*g*, 477*p*, 479, 479*g*, 481–482, 481*p*, 482*p*
regions of, 144–145, 144*m*–145*m*, 144*p*, 145*p*, 235*m*
religion in, 101, 218
rivers, 152, 152*p*
sports in, 226, 226*p*
standard of living in, 219
states, 80, 81
suburbanization, 70, 125
Sun Belt, 260, 260*m*
trade, 78, 79, 207–208
trade agreements, 208, 395
vegetation zones, 159–162, 159*p*, 160*m*, 161*p*, 162*p*
See also North America; individual states
Upper Canada, 194, 195, 291
Upper Mississippi Valley, 152
uranium, 167
urban, 71, 575

urbanization, 67, 70–71, 70*g*, 405, 405*g*, 406, 409, 419–420, 420*p*, 575
Uros, 501, 503, 506
Uruguay, 487*m*, 492, 492*p*, 534*m*
climate of, 345
culture of, 417
farming in, 419
foreign debt of, 394*g*
independence in, 387*m*
landforms of, 341
vegetation of, 347, 348*m*
waterways in, 342
Uruguay River, 342
Utah, 142*p*, 160, 536*m*
climate in, 272*m*
data about, 141*m*, 235*m*, 246
in Sun Belt, 260*m*
Uzbekistan, 550

V

vaccines, 64*p*, 65
valley, 555
Valley of Mexico, 370, 561
Vancouver, British Columbia, 205, 205*p*, 217*p*, 218, 229, 304, 304*p*, 561
Vancouver Island, 305, 307
Vatican City, 81, 81*p*, 561
vegetation, 446*m*, 575
climate and, 50–54, 347–349, 347*p*, 348*m*, 349*p*
defined, 50
regions, 50, 51–53, 53*m*
vertical climate zones, 54
See also agriculture
vegetation zones, 159–162, 159*p*, 160*m*, 161*p*, 162*p*
Venezuela, 135, 387, 487*m*, 493, 493*p*, 534*m*, 516
culture of, 416
economy of, 358, 498, 498*m*, 518, 518*g*, 518*m*, 519–520
exports of, 493, 518, 518*g*, 518*m*
foreign debt of, 394*g*
government of, 493, 521, 522, 522*p*

independence in, 387*m*, 388

landforms of, 341

natural disasters in, 520, 520*p*, 521*p*

natural resources of, 353*m*, 355, 357

oil and, 517, 517*g*, 517*p*, 518*g*, 519–520

population of, 423*g*, 493

waterways in, 342

Vermont, 537*m*

data about, 141*m*, 235*m*, 246

vertical climate zones, 54, 346, 346*g*, 349, 575

Viaud, Louane, 473

Victoria, British Columbia, 286, 307, 561

Vietnam, 6*g*, 67, 68, 542*m*, 561

Vietnam War, 191, 191*g*

Vikings, 311, 311*p*

villages, 61*p*

vineyards, 125*p*

Vinland, 311

Viracocha, 376

Virginia, 178, 537*m*

data about, 141*m*, 235*m*, 246

fishing in, 258

land use in, 256*m*

textile industry, 259

volcanoes, 35, 36, 150, 332, 332*p*, 340, 427, 429, 460, 555, 555*p*

Hawaiian Islands, 33*p*, 37, 37*p*

plate boundaries and, 37, 37*g*

Ring of Fire, 33, 37

voluntary migration, 68

vote, right to, 189

W

wagon trains, 183, 188*p*

Waldman, Louis, 254

Wales, 117*p*

Wall Street, 253

War in Iraq, 191*p*, 191*g*

War of 1812, 195

Ware, Otumfuo Opoku, 3*p*

warfare, migration and, 68

Washington, 536*m*

climate in, 272*m*

data about, 141*m*, 235*m*, 246

hydroelectricity in, 272*g*

natural resources of, 165, 273

Washington, D.C., 192, 261, 261*p*, 561

Washington, George, 179

waste recycling, 132, 132*p*

water, 35, 164*m*, 165, 167

bodies of, 142*m*, 142*p*

in California, 272, 272*g*

hydroelectric power, 117, 117*p*

irrigation, 94, 121, 121*p*

natural resources, 114, 115

oases, 53*p*

pollution, 129, 203, 203*p*

reservoirs, 131

water cycle, 41*g*, 115

water supply, 35, 65, 66, 127

weathering and erosion, 39

See also lakes; oceans; rain; rivers; seas

Watt, James, 183*p*

weather, 88–89*g*, 326, 357, 575

balloons, 46

defined, 40

differences from climate, 40

forecasting, 46, 46*p*

storms, 47

See also climate

weathering, 33, 39, 39*p*, 575

weaving, 377

Weddell Sea, 4*m*, 545*m*

West (United States), 144*p*, 235*m*, 271–276, 271*p*, 273*p*, 274*p*, 275*g*, 275*p*, 276*p*

boundaries of, 271

cities of, 274–276, 275*p*, 276*p*

climate of, 272*m*

natural resources of, 272–274, 273*p*, 274*p*

profile of, 272, 272*g*, 272*m*

west, 11

West Indies, 561, 575. *See* Caribbean Islands

West Virginia, 537*m*

data about, 141*m*, 235*m*, 247

land use in, 256*m*

mining in, 258

natural resources of, 164*m*, 166

Western Europe, M8*m*

Western Hemisphere, 11*g*, M5

Weyburn, Saskatchewan, 303

wheat, 300, 300*g*, 300*m*, 301, 301*p*, 302, 302*p*

White House, 126*p*

Whitehorse, Yukon Territory, 289

Whitener, Catherine Evans, 255, 255*p*

Whitney, Eli, 184

Wilson, Woodrow, 189

wind, 157, 204*m*

ocean currents and, 42

patterns, 43*g*, 346

tornadoes, 47

tropical cyclones, 47

wind energy, 112–113*p*, 115, 117, 132, 133*p*

Winnipeg, Manitoba, 157, 287, 303

winter, 31, 31*g*, 32, 51

Winter Carnival, 297, 297*p*

Wisconsin, 537*m*

data about, 141*m*, 235*m*, 247, 247*p*

women

in Brazil, 499*p*

in the Civil War, 186*p*

in Guatemala, 424*p*, 440

Mayan, 437, 440

mountain climbers, 148, 148*p*

rights of, 182, 191

in South America, 418

voting rights, 189

wood, deforestation and, 129

wool, 122, 122*p*

workplaces, 74

world, 268, 466

physical maps, 532*m*–533*m*

political maps, 530*m*–531*m*

population, 6, 6*g*

World Bank, 395
World Trade Center, 192, 192p, 253
World War I, 189, 189p, 190g, 196
World War II, 190, 191g, 196
writing activities
five themes of geography, 24
language arts, 134
math, 86, 110
science, 56
writing skills, 342, 349, 377, 396
advertisement, 261, 303
compare and contrast, 54, 199, 210, 414, 436, RW4
descriptive, 22, 54, 66, 153, 162, 276, 322, 349, 384
diary entries, 186
editorial, 450
encyclopedia article, 125
essays, RW2, RW3, RW4, 89, 358
ethnic groups, 232
evaluating your writing, RW5
explain a process, RW4
explain cause and effect, RW4
expository essays, RW4
first person, 389
geography, 24, 422
interviewing, 372
journal entry, 101, 119, 132, 226, 310, 436, 482, 513
language arts, 134, 210, 324, 398

letter writing, 79, 139, 270, 467, 500, 506
list, 108
math, 86, 110, 232, 398, 484
narrative essays, RW2
newspaper, 420, 450, 475
paragraphs, 13, 39, 47, 71, 84, 95, 168, 179, 192, 208, 230, 254, 297, 315, 377, 396
passages, 32
persuasive essays, RW3, 358
poetry, 219
point of view, 384, 407, 467, 482
radio, 441
reporting, 441, 475
reports, 278
research papers, RW4–RW5
science, 56, 170, 278, 360, 452, 524
short story, 365, 398
social studies, RW2–RW5
songs, 398
storyboard, 324
television script, 522
See also reading skills
writing systems, 94, 369
Wyoming, 51p, 536m
climate in, 272m
data about, 141m, 235m, 247
natural resources of, 164m, 166, 274p

Y

Yanomami, 498, 499
year (Earth's orbit), 28
yellow fever, 447–448
Yellowknife, Northwest Territories, 287
Yellowstone National Park, 274p
Yemen, 121p, 542m
Yosemite National Park, 274
Yucatán Peninsula, 535m
Yukon Territory, 151, 196, 196m, 210m, 319, 320, 320g, 320m, 561
data about, 141m, 285m, 289
gold in, 321

Z

zero, concept of, 369
Zimbabwe, 547
zinc, 167

Acknowledgments

Cover Design

Pronk&Associates

Staff Credits

The people who made up *World Studies* team—representing design services, editorial, editorial services, educational technology, marketing, market research, photo research and art development, production services, project office, publishing processes, and rights & permissions—are listed below. Bold type denotes core team members.

Greg Abrom, Ernie Albanese, Rob Aleman, Susan Andariese, **Rachel Avenia-Prol,** Leann Davis Alspaugh, Penny Baker, Barbara Bertell, **Peter Brooks,** Rui Camarinha, John Carle, **Lisa Del Gatto,** Paul Delsignore, Kathy Dempsey, Anne Drowns, Deborah Dukeshire, Marlies Dwyer, **Frederick Fellows,** Paula C. Foye, Lara Fox, Julia Gecha, **Mary Hanisco,** Salena Hastings, Lance Hatch, Kerri Hoar, **Beth Hyslip,** Katharine Ingram, Nancy Jones, John Kingston, Deborah Levheim, Constance J. McCarty, **Kathleen Mercandetti,** Art Mkrtchyan, Ken Myett, **Mark O'Malley,** Jen Paley, Ray Parenteau, **Gabriela Pérez Fiato,** Linda Punskovsky, Kirsten Richert, **Lynn Robbins,** Nancy Rogier, Bruce Rolff, Robin Samper, Mildred Schulte, Siri Schwartzman, **Malti Sharma,** Lisa Smith-Ruvalcaba, Roberta Warshaw, Sarah Yezzi

Additional Credits

Jonathan Ambar, Tom Benfatti, Lisa D. Ferrari, Paul Foster, Florrie Gadson, Phil Gagler, Ella Hanna, Jeffrey LaFountain, Karen Mancinelli, Michael McLaughlin, Lesley Pierson, Debi Taffet

The DK Designs team who contributed to *World Studies* were as follows: Hilary Bird, Samantha Borland, Marian Broderick, Richard Czapnik, Nigel Duffield, Heather Dunleavy, Cynthia Frazer, James A. Hall, Lucy Heaver, Rose Horridge, Paul Jackson, Heather Jones, Ian Midson, Marie Ortu, Marie Osborn, Leyla Ostovar, Ralph Pitchford, Ilana Sallick, Pamela Shiels, Andrew Szudek, Amber Tokeley.

Maps

Maps and globes were created by **DK Cartography.** The team consisted of Tony Chambers, Damien Demaj, Julia Lunn, Ed Merritt, David Roberts, Ann Stephenson, Gail Townsley, and Iorwerth Watkins.

Illustrations

DK images: 31, 34, 36, 41, 43; Kevin Jones Associates: 140; Kenneth Batelman: 291, 320, 383, 469 t; Geosystems: 206; Morgan Cain & Associates: 435; Jill Ort: 221, 263; Jen Paley: 148, 156, 157, 163, 167, 174, 180, 187, 190–191, 193, 202, 214, 222, 224, 227, 228, 248, 250, 255, 256, 264, 265, 266, 271, 272, 275, 279, 290, 292, 296, 298, 300, 304, 306, 311, 313, 318, 320, 338, 343, 352, 356, 368, 373, 374–375, 378, 385, 392, 394, 402, 405, 408, 409, 410, 415, 423, 430, 432, 437, 439, 444, 446, 453, 459 b, 459 t, 462, 465, 468, 469, 470, 472, 476, 477, 479, 485, 489, 494, 496, 498, 501, 502, 507, 508, 514, 515, 516, 517, 518

Photos

Cover

tl, Steve Dunwell/Getty Images, Inc.; **tm,** David Muir/Masterfile Corporation; **tr,** Dann Tardif/Corbis/Magmaphoto, **b,** Karl Kummels/SuperStock, Inc.

Title Page

Karl Kummels/SuperStock, Inc.

Table of Contents

iv–v b, Philip Blenkinsop/Dorling Kindersley; **v t,** Steve Gorton/Dorling Kindersley; **vi–vii t,** Royalty-Free/Corbis; **vii b,** Brenda Tharp/Corbis; **viii t,** Kevin Fleming/Corbis; **viii b,** Michio Hoshino/Minden Pictures; **ix t,** Joe Caveretta/LatinFocus.com; **ix b,** Allen Prier/Panoramic Images; **x t,** Michel Zab/Dorling Kindersley; **x b,** Robert Frerck/Odyssey Productions, Inc.; **xi,** Wayne Lynch/DRK Photo; **xiii,** Rudi von Briel/PhotoEdit; **xv,** David Zimmerman/Corbis; **xvii,** Bob Kristi/Corbis; **xviii–xix,** Andre Jenny/Visuals Unlimited

Learning With Technology

xiii, Discovery Channel School

Reading and Writing Handbook

RW, Michael Newman/PhotoEdit; **RW1,** Walter Hodges/Getty Images, Inc.; **RW2,** Digital Vision/Getty Images, Inc.; **RW3,** Will Hart/PhotoEdit; **RW5,** Jose Luis Pelaez, Inc./Corbis

MapMaster Skills Handbook

M, James Hall/DK Images; **M1,** Mertin Harvey/Gallo Images/Corbis; **M2–3 m,** NASA; **M2–3,** (globes) Planetary Visions: **M5 br,** Barnabas Kindersley/DK Images; **M6 tr,** Mike Dunning/DK Images; **M10 b,** Bernard and Catherine Desjeux/Corbis; **M11,** Hutchinson Library; **M12 b,** Pa Photos; **M13 r,** Panos Pictures; **M14 l,** Macduff Everton/Corbis; **M14 t,** MSCF/NASA; **M15 b,** Ariadne Van Zandbergen/Lonely Planet Images; **M16 l,** Bill Stormont/Corbis; **M16 b,** Pablo Corral/Corbis; **M17 t,** Stone Les/Sygma/Corbis; **M17 b,** W. Perry Conway/Corbis

Guiding Questions

1, Christine Osborne/World Religions Photo Library

World Overview

2 l, 2 t, DK Images; **3 l,** Daniel Laine/Corbis; **3 tr,** DK Images; **3 br,** Sipa/Rex Features; **4 bl,** Layne Kennedy/Corbis; **4 tr,** DK Images; **5 t,** Royalty Free Images/Corbis; **6 t,** Roger Ressmeyer/Corbis; **7 br,** Amet Jean Pierre/Sygma/Corbis; **7tr,** DK Images

Chapter One

8–9, Johnson Space Center/NASA; **10,** Steve Gorton/DK Images; **13,** M. Balan/DK Images; **14,** Will & Deni McIntyre/Corbis; **15 b,** Richard Powers/Corbis; **15 t,** DK Images; **16,** Peter Wilson/DK Images; **17,** MSFC/NASA; **23,** Johnson Space Center/NASA

Chapter Two

26–27, George H. Huey/Corbis; **28,** Daniel Pyne/DK Images; **30 bl,** Alan Briere/DK Images; **30–31,** sun, DK Images; globes, Planetary Visions; **31 tr,** Barnabas Kindersley/DK Images; **33,** Brenda Tharp/Corbis; **35,** C. M. Leask/Eye Ubiquitous; **36 bl,** James Balog/Getty Images; **37 tr,** James A. Sugar/Corbis; **39,** Alan Hills/DK Images; **40,** Galen Rowell/Corbis; **41 tr,** Hutchison Library; **43 tr,** Royalty Free Images/Corbis; **44 b,** Demetrio Carrasco/DK Images; **45 bl,** Chris Stowers/DK Images; **46 m,** DK Images; **46 bl,** NASA; **46 tr,** N.H.P.A.; **46 mr,** Lelan Statom, meteorologist; Mark Martin, photojournalist/network operations manager, WTVF-Newschannel 5 Network, Nashville, Tenn.; **47,** Chris Graythen/Getty Images; **48 t,** Michael S. Yamashita/Corbis; **50,** Liu Liqun/Corbis; **51 br,** Terry W. Eggers/Corbis; **51 tr,** Denver Museum of Nature and Science; **52,** Alan Watson/DK Images; **53 t,** Photowood Inc./Corbis; **53 bl,** Neil Lukas; **53 br,** Stephen Hayward/DK Images; **54,** Galen Rowell/Corbis; **55,** George H. Huey/Corbis

Chapter Three

58–59, Keren Su/Corbis; **60,** James Strachan/Getty Images; **61 t,** Royalty Free Images/Corbis; **62 bl,** Wolfgang Kaehler/Corbis; **63 br,** Peter Wilson/DK Images; **64 t,** Howard Davies/Corbis; **65 b,** Patricia Aithie/Ffotograff; **66,** Dirk R. Frans/Hutchison Library; **67,** Bettmann Corbis; **68,** Dave King/DK Images; **69 bl,** Bettmann/Corbis; **70 bl,** Hulton-Deutsch Collection/Corbis; **70 br,** Paul Almasy/Corbis; **71,** Stephanie Maze/Corbis; **72,** Bill Ross/Corbis; **74,** Rob Reichenfeld/DK Images; **75 t,** Corbis; **76,** Philip Blenkinsop/DK Images; **77 b,** Tom Wagner/Corbis; **78 l,** Mark E. Gibson/Corbis; **78 b,** Annebicque Bernard/Sygma/Corbis; **78 r,** Mary Ann McDonald/Corbis; **79,** Peter Blakely/SABA/Corbis; **80,** Patrick Durand/ Sygma/Corbis; **81,** Franz-Marc Frei/Corbis; **82,** Tom Haskell/ Sygma/Corbis; **83 t,** Pa Photos; **83 b,** Ron Sachs/Rex Features; **84,** Joseph Sohm/Chromosohm Inc./Corbis; **85,** Keren Su/Corbis; **88,** Peter Finger/Corbis

School; **308,** Vince Streano/Corbis; **310,** Barry Rowland/Getty Images, Inc.; **311** Patrick J. Wall/Danita Delimont; **312 t,** Discovery Channel School; **312–313 b,** Michael S. Lewis/Corbis; **315,** Patrick J. Wall/Danita Delimont; **316 t,** Antonio Mo/Getty Images, Inc.; **316 b,** Amos Morgan/Getty Images, Inc.; **317,** Mark Antman/Image Works; **318,** Michio Hoshino/Minden Pictures; **319,** Jim Brandenburg/Minden Pictures; **321 t,** Discovery Channel School; **321 b,** AFP/Corbis/Magma; **322,** Wolfgang Kaehler/Corbis; **323,** Harvey Lloyd/Getty Images, Inc.

Projects

326 t, Bob Winsett/Index Stock Imagery, Inc.; **326 b,** National Archives and Records Administration/Presidential Library

Guiding Questions

329 t, Michel Zab/Dorling Kindersley; **329 b,** Travel Pix/Getty Images, Inc.

Regional Overview

330 l, Linda Whitwam/DK Images; **331 tr,** Art Directors & TRIP; **332 tr,** Charles and Josette Lenars/Corbis; **333 b,** Hubert Stadler/Corbis; **333 tr,** Getty Images; **334 b,** Galen Rowell/Corbis; **334 l,** Nik Wheeler/Corbis; **334 r,** Carol Halebian Photography; **335 t,** Owen Franken/Corbis: **335 br,** T. Bognar/Art Directors & TRIP

Chapter Eleven

336–337, Darell Gulin/Getty Images, Inc.; **338,** Jimmy Dorantes/ LatinFocus.com; **339,** Discovery Channel School; **340,** Jeff Hunter/Getty Images, Inc.; **341,** Corbis; **342,** Herve Collart/Corbis; **343,** R. B. Husar/ NASA/SPL/Photo Researchers, Inc.; **345,** Prenas Nicaragua/Corbis Sygma; **346 t,** Bobby Model/Getty Images, Inc.; **346 b,** Ed Simpson/Getty Images, Inc.; **347,** Jonathan Blair/Corbis; **349,** Miguel Reyes/LatinFocus.com; **350,** Richard Haynes; **351,** Warren Morgan/Corbis; **352,** Fenno Jacobs/SuperStock, Inc.; **354 t,** Richard Bickel/Corbis; **354 b,** Jacques Jangoux/Peter Arnold, Inc.; **355 l,** Jonathan Smith; Cordaiy Photo/Corbis; **355 r,** Carlos Goldin/DDB Stock Photo; **356,** Sean Sprague/Stock Boston; **357,** AP/Wide World Photos/Jaime Puebla; **358,** Pablo Corral Vega/Corbis; **359 t,** Corbis; **359 m,** Miguel Reyes/LatinFocus.com; **359 b,** Jacques Jangoux/Peter Arnold, Inc.; **362,** Bryan Knox/Corbis; **363,** EyeWire Collection/Getty Images, Inc.; **364,** David Zimmerman/Corbis; **365,** Courtesy of Alma Flor Ada

Chapter Twelve

366–367, Macduff Everton/Corbis; **368-369 b,** Allen Prier/Panoramic Images; **369 t,** Private Collection/Bridgeman Art Library; **370,** Chip and Rosa Maria de la Cueva Peterson; **371 m,** DK Images, **371 t,** Mary Evans Picture Library; **371 b,** South American Pictures; **372,** David Hiser/ PictureQuest; **373,** Werner Forman/Art Resource, New York; **374 t,** Chris Sharp/DDB Stock Photo; **374 b,** Bowers Museum of Cultural Art/Corbis; **375 t,** Charles & Josette Lenars/Corbis; **375 m,** Lee Boltin/Boltin Picture Library; **375 b,** Dorling Kindersley; **376,** Katie Attenborough/Bridgeman Art Library; **377,** Larry Luxner/Luxner News; **378,** Bridgeman Art Library; **379 t,** Sebastian Munster/The New York Public Library/Art Resource, New York; **379 b,** The Granger Collection, New York; **380,** Gianni Dagli Orti/Corbis; **381,** Biblioteca Nacional Madrid, Spain/Bridgeman Art Library; **381 inset l,** Dave King/Dorling Kindersley; **381 inset m,** Michel Zab/Dorling Kindersley; **381 inset r,** Michel Zab/Dorling Kindersley; **381 inset b,** Dorling Kindersley; **383,** Discovery Channel School; **384,** The Granger Collection, New York; **385,** North Wind Picture Archives; **386,** Robert Frerck/Odyssey Productions; **388,** Rudi von Briel/PhotoEdit; **389,** AFP/Corbis; **390 t,** Werner Forman/Art Resource, New York; **390 b,** Bettmann/Corbis; **391,** Richard Haynes; **392,** Bibliothèque Nationale, Paris, France/Bridgeman Art Library; **393,** Underwood & Underwood/Corbis; **394,** Brand X Pictures/Getty Images, Inc.; **395,** AP/Wide World Photos/ Natacha Pisarenko; **396,** D. Donne Bryant/DDB Stock Photo; **397,** Lee Boltin/Boltin Picture Library

Chapter Thirteen

400–401, Steve Simonsen/Lonely Planet Images; **402,** Sheryl Bjorkgren/ LatinFocus.com; **403 t,** CNAC/MNAM/Dist. Réunion des Musées Nationaux/ Art Resource, New York; **403 b,** Philadelphia Museum of Art/Corbis; **404,** AP/Wide World Photos/Victor M. Camacho; **405,** Tibor Bognar/Corbis; **406,** Lonely Planet Images; **407,** Joe Caveretta/LatinFocus.com; **410,** Michael Graham-Stewart/Bridgeman Art Library; **411,** Robert Fried Photography; **412 t,** MC Pherson Colin/Corbis Sygma; **412 b,** Doug Armand/Getty Images, Inc.; **413 t,** Discovery Channel School; **413 b,** Craig Duncan/DDB Stock Photo; **414,** Bob Krist/Corbis; **415,** Alex Irvin Photography; **416,** A. Ramey/Woodfin Camp & Associates; **417,** D. Donne Bryant/DDB Stock Photo; **417 inset,** Larry Luxner/Luxner News; **418,** Pelletier Micheline/Corbis Sygma; **419 t,** Owen Franken/Corbis; **419 b,** Bo Zaunders/Corbis; **420,** Michael Brennan/Corbis; **421 t,** Joe Caveretta/ LatinFocus.com; **421 m,** Robert Fried Photography; **421 b,** Owen Franken/Corbis

Chapter Fourteen

424–425, Sandy Ostroff/Index Stock Imagery, Inc.; **426 t,** Discovery Channel School; **426 b,** Frans Lanting/Minden Pictures; **428 t,** National Geographic Image Collection; **428 b,** Ben Blackwell/San Francisco Museum of Modern Art; **430,** Jimmy Dorantes/LatinFocus.com; **431,** Bob Krist/Corbis; **433 l,** Mark Edwards/Peter Arnold, Inc.; **433 r,** National Geographic Image Collection; **434 t,** Discovery Channel School; **434 b,** Keith Dannemiller/Corbis; **436,** Cuartoscuro/Corbis Sygma; **437 t,** Keith Gunnar/Bruce Coleman Inc.; **437 b,** Michel Zab/Dorling Kindersley; **438,** Suzanne Murphy-Larronde; **439,** Discovery Channel School; **440,** AP/Wide World Photos/Jaime Puebla; **441,** Stone/Allstock/Getty Images Inc.; **442,** GoodShoot/SuperStock, Inc.; **443 t,** AP/Wide World Photos/Rodrigo Abd; **443 b,** Wesley Bocxe/Photo Researchers, Inc.; **444,** Jimmy Dorantes/LatinFocus.com; **445,** Alex Farnsworth/The Image Works; **447 t,** Discovery Channel School; **447 m,** Panama Canal Museum; **447 b,** Getty Images, Inc./Hulton Archive Photos; **448 t,** C. W. Brown/Photo Researchers, Inc.; **448 b,** J. Raga/Masterfile Corporation; **449 t,** Corbis; **449 b,** DK Images; **450,** Danny Lehmann/Corbis; **451 t,** Keith Dannemiller/Corbis; **451 m,** Michel Zab/Dorling Kindersley; **451 b,** Alex Farnsworth/The Image Works

Chapter Fifteen

454–455, Philip Coblentz/Digital Vision/Getty Images, Inc.; **456 t,** Discovery Channel School; **456 b,** Bob Krist/Corbis; **458,** Reinhard Eisele/Corbis; **459 t,** Jimmy Dorantes/LatinFocus.com; **459 b,** Jimmy Dorantes/LatinFocus.com; **461,** Konrad Wothe/Minden Pictures; **462,** Najlah Feanny/Corbis; **463,** Bettmann/Corbis; **464 l,** AP/Wide World Photos; **464 r,** 2002 Getty Images Inc.; **465,** Discovery Channel School; **466 t,** Peter Muhly/AFP/Corbis; **466 b,** Robert Holmes/Corbis; **467,** Angelo Cavalli/SuperStock Inc.; **468** Paul Thompson/Eye Ubiquitous/Corbis; **469,** Jan Butchofsky-Houser/Corbis; **470,** AP Wide World Photos; **471 t,** Carol Halebian Photography; **471 b,** Discovery Channel School; **473,** Bettmann/Corbis; **474 t,** Wesley Bocxe/Photo Researchers, Inc.; **474 b,** Bettmann/Corbis; **475,** Owen Franken/Corbis; **476,** Robert Fried Photography; **477,** Rudy Von Briel/PhotoEdit; **478 t,** Benno Friedman; **478 b,** Tom Bean/Corbis; **479,** Discovery Channel School; **480 t,** Stephanie Maze/Corbis; **480 b,** Robert Frerck/Odyssey Productions Inc.; **481,** AP/Wide World Photos; **482,** Stephanie Maze/Corbis; **483,** Angelo Cavalli/SuperStock Inc.

Chapter Sixteen

486–487, Barbara Haynor/Index Stock Imagery, Inc.; **488 t,** Discovery Channel School; **488 b,** Paul A. Souders/Corbis; **490,** Art Wolfe/Getty Images, Inc.; **492,** Carlos Goldin/Focus/DDB Stock Photo; **493,** Ulrike Welsch/PhotoEdit; **494,** Wayne Lynch/DRK Photo; **495,** Fabio Colombini/Animals Animals/Earth Scenes; **496 t,** Discovery Channel School; **496 m,** David Frazier/Image Works; **496 bl,** Larry Luxner/Luxner News; **497,** Domingo Rodrigues/UNEP/Peter Arnold, Inc.; **498 l,** AFP/Vanderlei Almeida/Corbis; **498 r,** Joel W. Rogers/Corbis; **499 t,** Greg Fiume/Corbis; **499 b,** Cynthia Brito/DDB Stock Photo; **500,** PhotoDisc/Getty Images, Inc.; **501,** Roman Soumar/Corbis; **503 t,** Inga Spence/DDB Stock Photo; **503 b,** Alejandro Balaguer/Getty Images, Inc.; **504 t,** Discovery Channel School; **504 b,** Philippe Colombi/Getty Images, Inc.; **505 l,** David Mangurian/Intern-American Development Bank; **505 r,** David Mangurian/Intern-American Development Bank; **506,** Stuart Westmorland/Corbis; **507,** Gebbie & Co./Library of Congress; **509 l,** Joseph Van Os/Getty Images, Inc.; **509 r,** Charles O'Rear/Corbis; **510 t,** Zezmer Amos/Omni-Photo Communications, Inc.; **510 b,** Ludovic Maisant/Corbis; **511,** The

Wilmington Library; **512 t,** Discovery Channel School; **512 m,** Jaime Villaseca/Getty Images, Inc.; **512 b,** HIRB/Index Stock Imagery, Inc.; **513,** AP/Wide World Photos/Alistair Grant; **514 lt,** Hubert Stadler/Corbis; **514 lb,** Hubert Stadler/Corbis; **514 rt,** Jeremy Horner/Corbis; **514 rb,** Frank Perkins/Index Stock Imagery, Inc.; **515,** Yann Arthus-Bertrand/Corbis; **516,** Larry Lee/Corbis; **517,** AP/Wide World Photos/Jose Caruci; **519,** Pablo Corral V/Corbis; **520,** Kike Arnal/Corbis; **521 t,** Discovery Channel School; **521 b,** AFP/Corbis; **522 l,** Reuters NewMedia Inc./Corbis; **522 r,** AFP/Corbis; **523,** Greg Fiume/Corbis

Projects

526 t, Travel Pix/Getty Images, Inc.; **526 m,** C Squared Studios/Getty Images, Inc.; **526 b,** Steve Cole/Getty Images, Inc.

Reference

528, Johnson Space Center/NASA

Glossary of Geographic Terms

554 t, A & L Sinibaldi/Getty Images, Inc.; **554 b,** John Beatty/Getty Images, Inc.; **554–555 b,** Spencer Swanger/Tom Stack & Associates; **555 t,** Hans Strand/Getty Images, Inc.; **555 m,** Paul Chesley/Getty Images, Inc.

Glossary

563, Magma Photo News/Corbis; **564,** Robert Fried Photography; **566,** Nik Wheeler/Nik Wheeler Photography; **569,** Jimmy Dorantes/LatinFocus.com; **570,** Photowood, Inc./Corbis; **572,** AP/Wide World Photos/Natacha Pisarenko; **574,** Harvey Lloyd/Getty Images, Inc.

Text

Chapter Three

88, Excerpt from *My Side of the Mountain* by Jean Craighead George. Copyright © 1959 by Jean Craighead George.

Chapter Six

345, Excerpt from "Facts About Canada: Nunavut Communities, 1999" by Natural Resources Canada. Copyright © 2003 by Natural Resources Canada. Used by permission. **364,** From *The Crown of Columbus* by Louise Erdrich and Michael Dorris.

Copyright © 1991 by Michael Dorris and Louise Erdrich. Published by HarperCollins Publishers.

Chapter Seven

377, Excerpt from *How the Other Half Lives* by Jacob A. Riis. Copyright by Jacob A. Riis. Copyright © 1971 by Dover Publications, Inc.

Chapter Eight

404, Excerpt from *The Shaping of America: A Geographical Perspective on 500 Years of History,* Volume 2, by D. W. Meinig. Copyright © 1993 by D. W. Meinig. Published by Yale University. **407,** Excerpt from *Remix: Conversations with Immigrant Teenagers,* by Marina Budhos. Copyright © 1999 by Marina Budhos. Published by Henry Holt and Company. **407,** Excerpt from *Memories and Dreams,* Volume 1, Edited by M. W. Buckley. Published by Saskatchewan Literacy Network in 1991. **412,** Excerpt from *I Was Dreaming to Come to America: Memories from the Ellis Island Oral History Project* by Veronica Lawlor. Copyright © 1995 by Veronica Lawlor. Published by Viking. **417,** Excerpt from *The Land and People of Canada* by Andrew H. Malcolm. Copyright © 1991 by Andrew H. Malcolm. Published by HarperCollins Publishers.

Chapter Nine

444, Excerpt from *The Jewish American Family Album,* by Dorothy and Thomas Hoobler. Copyright © 1995 by Dorothy and Thomas Hoobler. Published by Oxford University Press, Inc. **470–471,** Excerpt from *Childtimes: A Three-Generation Memoir* by Eloise Greenfield and Lessie Jones Little. Copyright © 1979 by Eloise Greenfield and Lessie Jones Little.

Chapter Eleven

362, Exerpt from "The Surveyor," from *Where the Flame Trees Bloom* by Alma Flor Ada. Copyright © 1994 by Alma Flor Ada.

Note: Every effort has been made to locate the copyright owner of material used in this textbook. Omissions brought to our attention will be corrected in subsequent editions.